Fodor's 93
California

Fodor's Travel Publications, Inc.
New York • Toronto • London • Sydney • Auckland

Fodor's California

Editor: Larry Peterson
Editorial Contributors: Kevin Brass, Toni Chapman, Bruce David Colen, Laura Del Rosso, Vicky Elliott, Pamela Faust, Marie Felde, Rosemary Freskos, Sheila Gadsden, Sharon K. Gillenwater, Pamela Hegarty, Mary Jane Horton, Dan Janeck, Marael Johnson, Edie Jarolim, Jacqueline Killeen, Mimi Kmet, Jane Lasky, Maria Lenhart, Jillian Magalaner, Ellen Melinkoff, Maribeth Mellin, David Nelson, Denise Nolty, Carolyn Price, Marcy Pritchard, Linda K. Schmidt, Peter Segal, Aaron Shurin, Dan Spitzer, Aaron Sugarman, Robert Taylor, Casey Tefertiller, Julie Tomasz, Bobbi Zane
Creative Director: Fabrizio La Rocca
Cartographer: David Lindroth
Illustrator: Karl Tanner
Cover Photograph: Ayako Parks/TSW

Design: Vignelli Associates

Special Sales

Contents

Maps

Foreword

From sea lions barking, off Monterey Peninsula, and John Muir's "Range of Light," to the temperate and foggy north coast and the extremes of snow and heat found in the southern deserts, California is diverse enough and vast enough to satisfy nearly every visitor.

This edition of *Fodor's California* covers more California sights than ever before. There are separate chapters on the Wine Country, Lake Tahoe, and the Far North and much expanded treatment of Santa Barbara, Sacramento, and Monterey. There are extended chapters on San Francisco, Los Angeles, and San Diego, with plenty of information for a week's stay, but this book has been written primarily for those travelers who plan to visit several regions of the state. All the writers are local, and they share their best advice on what to see and do up and down the state.

While every care has been taken to ensure the accuracy of the information in this guide, the passage of time will always bring change, and consequently, the publisher cannot accept responsibility for errors that may occur.

All prices and opening times quoted here are based on information supplied to us at press time. Hours and admission fees may change, however, and the prudent traveler will avoid inconvenience by calling ahead.

Fodor's wants to hear about your travel experiences, both pleasant and unpleasant. When a hotel or restaurant fails to live up to its billing, let us know and we will investigate the complaint and revise our entries where the facts warrant it.

Send your letters to the editors of Fodor's Travel Publications, 201 E. 50th Street, New York, NY 10022.

Highlights'93 and Fodor's Choice

Highlights '93

San Francisco For more than a decade, since San Francisco's Moscone Convention Center was completed, there have been on-again, off-again plans for a grand outdoor plaza and arts complex to draw more than conventioneers to this vast downtown redevelopment area south of Market Street. In the summer of 1993 the first phase of this **Yerba Buena Gardens** project should open in the block between the Marriott Hotel and the newly expanded and landscaped convention center. According to the schedule the Yerba Buena Gardens Esplanade will open during the summer, offering a downtown meadow, waterfall, terraced gardens with plants from San Francisco's sister cities abroad, and a memorial to Martin Luther King, Jr., featuring excerpts from the civil-rights leader's writings etched on tall glass panels. Expected to open in fall is the Yerba Buena Gardens Center for the Arts, including a 752-seat theater for multicultural performances and a gallery for contemporary art. The entire Yerba Buena project is a magnet for the city's museums and galleries. The **Ansel Adams Center**'s photography gallery is already open nearby on 4th Street, the new **Museum of Modern Art** is under construction on 3rd Street (due to open in 1995), and the **Mexican Museum** and **California Historical Society** will follow.

In other museum news, the California Palace of the Legion of Honor, in Lincoln Park, is closed until 1994 for expansion and structural upgrading to meet earthquake-safety standards. A portion of its collection of European art is on display at the M. H. de Young Memorial Museum in Golden Gate Park. The de Young, the adjacent Asian Art Museum, and the nearby California Academy of Sciences, Conservatory of Flowers, and Japanese Tea Garden can all be visited for a single-day admission price of $10. The **Golden Gate Culture Pass,** which saves 30% over separate admissions, is available at each attraction and at the visitor-information center at Powell and Market streets. The first independent museum focusing on the city's history, the **Museum of the City of San Francisco,** has opened in The Cannery shopping complex (2801 Leavenworth St., tel. 415/928–0289). One of the museum's major benefactors is Del Monte Foods, which owned the redbrick waterfront building when it really was a cannery.

The results of the 1989 earthquake continue to change the face of the city. The damaged Embarcadero Freeway has been demolished, opening the vista between downtown and San Francisco Bay. There are plans for a **waterfront boulevard** lined with palm trees and a plaza in front of the Ferry Building at the foot of Market Street. Street-level and underground construction will continue in the area, however, on a route for historic streetcars to Fisherman's Wharf and an extension of the Muni Metro subway. Farther west, the 1992 demolition of the portion of the Central Freeway that has long shadowed the neighborhood behind City Hall should bring an expansion to the stretch of cafés and shops along Hayes Street.

Los Angeles Long known for its sights—palm trees, the Pacific, celebrities—Los Angeles is increasingly recognizable by certain sounds, as well: the roar of bulldozers, the pounding of steel girders, and all the auditory trademarks of rampant real-estate development. Much of the hammering and concrete-pouring comes courtesy of the travel industry, with a slew of new hotels and tourist attractions in the works.

West L.A. awaits the arrival of the **J. Paul Getty Center,** set to occupy some 110 acres atop a hill that allows panoramic views of the Pacific and the Los Angeles basin. All this is scheduled to happen sometime in the mid-1990s. Elsewhere on the west side, the posh Beverly Hills Hotel is scheduled to shut down for extensive renovations throughout much of 1993.

In Downtown L.A., construction continues on the **Walt Disney Concert Hall,** the future home of the Los Angeles Philharmonic. Scheduled for completion in time for the 1995 music season, the hall is being designed by local hero Frank Gehry, although the word is that this structure will be simpler and somewhat more conservative than typical Gehry creations.

Fans of the **Farmer's Market** eagerly await the mid-1990s expansion of this landmark. A movie theater, restaurants, and hotel will be enhanced by landscaping, fountains, plazas, and walkways. All of this will make the market an even more attractive place to spend time (although the ongoing construction hasn't deterred determined shoppers).

After the Disney Company announced it would not renew its lease on the *Queen Mary/Spruce Goose* complex in Long Beach, rumors about the fate of these attractions were the talk of the town. At press time (fall 1992) the *Spruce Goose* had been sold and was being moved to Oregon, and the future of the *Queen Mary* was still undecided. Of course, what may or may not happen to the *Queen Mary* isn't all that's going on in Long Beach. The city's revitalized downtown area has a dozen-or-so restaurants popular with trendy Angelenos as well as food critics; and the town's location, size, proximity to downtown L.A. and Orange County, and its status as the southern terminus of the Metro Rail Blue Line have tourists and Southern Californians giving the place a closer, long-overdue look.

Sadly, though, much of the news from Southern California in 1992 wasn't good. Winter rains early in the year caused flooding and much damage. The ground was so hard (much of it devoid of vegetation after five years of drought) that it simply couldn't absorb the sudden, heavy downpour. The riots in South Central L.A. in spring brought to the surface many long-simmering social, economic, and racial tensions—few of them unique to the city of Los Angeles. What changes this unrest brings about remain to be seen. Reforms of local government are already under way, but, of course, many of the underlying causes run deeper than any problems specific to this region. Having been at the forefront of so much innovative thinking, perhaps Los Angeles can provide solutions that serve as a model for other cities.

San Diego The downtown San Diego skyline continues to change in subtle and startling ways. Along the waterfront, landmark buildings are finally opening after years of development and construction. **One Harbor Drive,** the most prestigious address in town these days, is now selling million-dollar, drop-dead condos in two sleek black-glass towers across from the convention center on Harbor Drive. The **Hyatt Regency,** whose slender 504-foot-tall tower is the tallest structure on the waterfront in the mainland United States and Canada, was scheduled to open in late 1992, also on Harbor Drive. Both buildings reflect and complement the futuristic **San Diego Convention Center,** whose opening in 1990 served as catalyst and reward for those who have invested heavily in the downtown area through decades of redevelopment.

Seaport Village is undergoing a $40 million expansion (scheduled for completion in 1993) that will include the redevelopment of the abandoned Spanish-Colonial police headquarters and a "Night Court" area with clubs, restaurants, and bars. Designed to link the waterfront's many new developments, the landscaped **King Promenade,** a 12½-acre linear park, will stretch along Harbor Drive from Seaport Village to the convention center and north to the Gaslamp Quarter. A section of the park near the convention center was completed in 1992; the rest is expected to be finished by 1995.

The waterfront **Embarcadero** area has become an exciting place to stay, thanks to the new hotels, restaurants, and nightclubs that have opened by the harbor. Major cruise lines now dock at the B Street Pier, and a seafaring taxi service sails from one waterfront hotel to another. The San Diego Trolley's Bayfront Line now connects the convention center and waterfront hotels with the center of downtown. **One America Plaza,** a transportation hub linking the trolley's ever-increasing number of lines running east and north into the surrounding county and south to the Mexican border, has opened on Broadway and Kettner Boulevard by the Santa Fe Depot.

Sea World debuted a new "Shark Encounter" exhibit in 1992, with a 680,000-gallon tank housing the world's largest collection of sharks, as well as a fascinating bird show called "Wings of the World" in the popular "City Streets" exhibit. In addition, the show featuring ever-popular killer whale Shamu has a new feature, called Shamu Vision, with diamond-vision video screens affording a view of the whales through underwater cameras.

The building boom has spread south to Baja California, where the Mexican government and private investors are banking on prosperity. Rosarito Beach now offers exclusive condos and time-share resorts, and new hotels and restaurants are springing up continually. Ensenada is changing just as quickly, becoming much more than a weekend getaway. U.S. tour buses are allowed across the Mexican border now, and a new crop of tour companies specializing in Baja make the trek south hassle-free.

Fodor's Choice

No two people will agree on what makes a perfect vacation, but it's fun—and it can be helpful—to know what others think. Here, then, is a very personal list of Fodor's Choices. We hope you'll have a chance to experience some of them yourself while visiting California. We have tried to offer something for everyone and from every price category. For detailed information about each entry, refer to the appropriate chapters within this guidebook.

Lodging

Claremont Hotel, Oakland *(Very Expensive)*

Four Seasons Biltmore Hotel, Santa Barbara *(Very Expensive)*

Four Seasons Cleft Hotel, San Francisco *(Very Expensive)*

Hotel Bel-Air, Los Angeles *(Very Expensive)*

St. James' Club, Los Angeles *(Very Expensive)*

Ventana Inn, Big Sur *(Very Expensive)*

Casa Del Zorro, Anza-Borrego *(Moderate)*

Scenic Drives

17-mile Drive, Carmel

Highway 49, the Gold Country

I–80, San Francisco to Truckee (for a cross section of the state)

Kings Canyon Highway (Highway 180)

Mulholland Drive, Los Angeles

Historic Buildings

Coit Tower, San Francisco

General Vallejo's House, Sonoma

Hotel del Coronado, San Diego

Larkin House, Monterey

Mann's Chinese Theater, Hollywood

Mission San Carlos Borromeo, Carmel

State Capitol, Sacramento

Romantic Sites

Buena Vista Winery, Sonoma

Carnelian Room, Bank of America, San Francisco

Emerald Bay, Lake Tahoe

Griffith Observatory, Los Angeles

Highlands Inn, Carmel

Taste Treats

California wines, tasted at the wineries

Chorrizo burrito, burrito stands, Los Angeles

French-fried artichoke hearts, roadside stands, Monterey Peninsula

Fresh salmon steaks, restaurants along the north coast

Garlic ice cream, Garlic Festival, Gilroy

Orange freeze, Merlino's, Fulton Avenue, Sacramento

Ripe peaches, especially in the Central Valley

Sourdough bread and sweet butter, San Francisco

State Parks

Anza-Borrego Desert State Park, Borrego Springs

California State Railroad Museum, Sacramento

Columbia State Historic Park, Columbia

Del Norte Coast Redwoods State Park, Crescent City

Empire Mine State Historic Park, Grass Valley

Marshall Gold Discovery State Historic Park, Coloma

Point Lobos State Reserve, Carmel

San Juan Bautista State Historic Park, San Juan Bautista

Restaurants with Fabulous Atmosphere

Château Souverain Restaurant at the Winery, Geyserville

George's at the Cove, La Jolla

Green's at Fort Mason, San Francisco

Spago, Los Angeles

St. Orres, Gualala

Ventana Inn, Big Sur

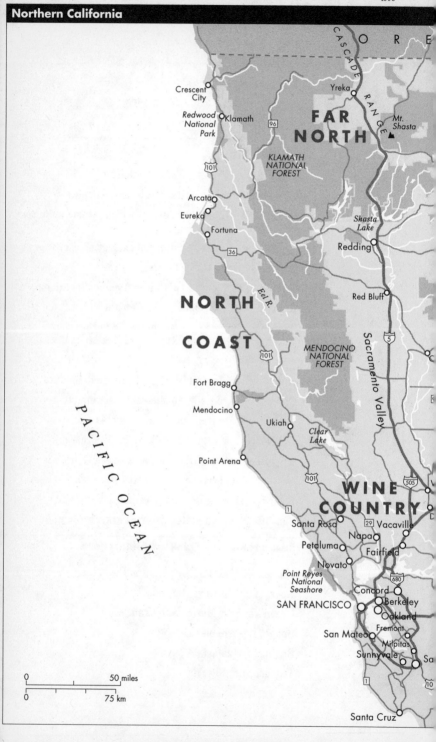

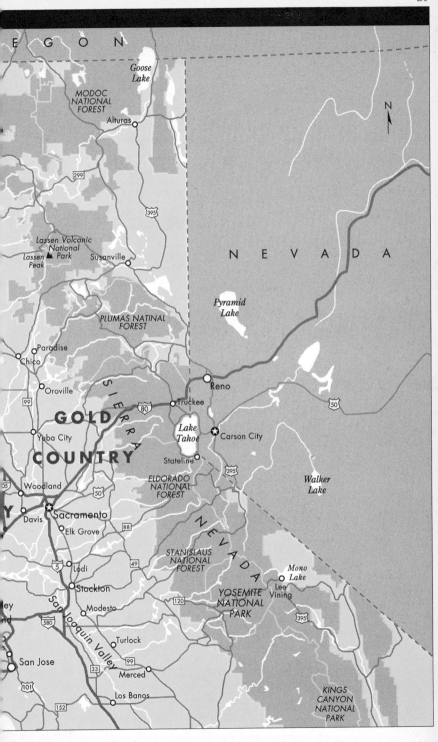

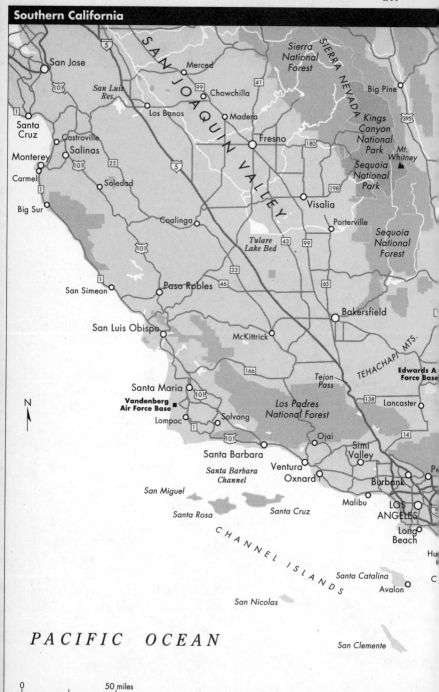

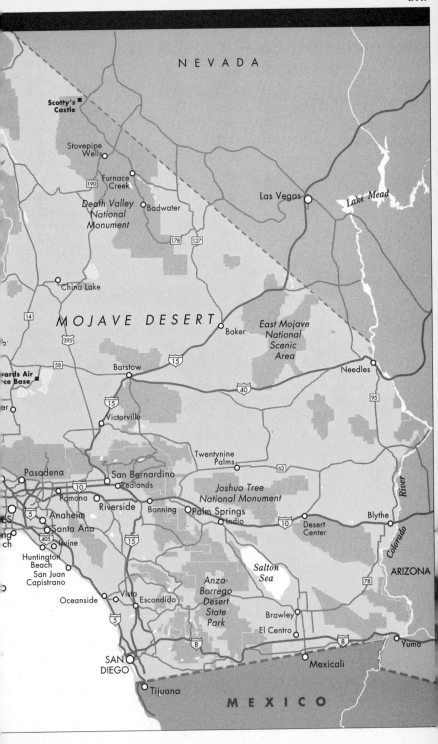

The United States

CANADA

Vancouver

BRITISH COLUMBIA
Calgary
ALBERTA
SASKATCHEWAN
Regina
MANITOBA

Trans-Canada Hwy.

Winnipeg

Seattle
Olympia
WASHINGTON
Spokane
Columbia R.

Portland
Salem
OREGON

Great Falls
Missouri R.
MONTANA
Helena
Billings
NORTH DAKOTA
Fargo
Bismarck

IDAHO
Boise
Snake R.

SOUTH DAKOTA
Pierre
Missouri R.

WYOMING

Carson City
Sacramento
NEVADA
Salt Lake City
UTAH

Cheyenne
NEBRASKA
Lincoln

San Francisco
Fresno

Denver
COLORADO
Colorado Springs

Top
Ka
KANSAS

CALIFORNIA
Las Vegas
Colorado R.

Santa Barbara
Los Angeles
San Diego
PACIFIC OCEAN

Flagstaff
ARIZONA
Phoenix
Tucson
Albuquerque
Santa Fe
NEW MEXICO
Amarillo
OKLAHOMA
Oklahoma City

BAJA CALIFORNIA
SONORA

El Paso
CHIHUAHUA
Rio Grande

TEXAS
Austin
San Antonio
De
H

RUSSIA
ARCTIC OCEAN

Bering Strait
Bering Sea
Nome
ALASKA
Fairbanks
CANADA
Anchorage

MEXICO
COAHUILA

ALEUTIAN ISLANDS

Juneau

NUEVO LEON

PACIFIC OCEAN

0   400 miles
0   400 km

N

Honolulu
Oahu
Maui
HAWAII
Hawaii
PACIFIC OCEAN

TAM-AULIPAS

CANADA

ONTARIO

QUÉBEC

NEW BRUNSWICK

Québec

Fredericton

MAINE

MINNESOTA

Duluth

Montréal

Ottawa

Montpelier

N.H.

Augusta

Concord

Boston

WISCONSIN

Lake Superior

Lake Huron

MICHIGAN

NEW YORK

VT.

St. Paul

Green Bay

Toronto

Lake Ontario

Albany

Providence

Minneapolis

Milwaukee

Lansing

Buffalo

Lake Erie

Hartford

CONN.

R.I.

MASS.

Madison

Detroit

Cleveland

New York

IOWA

Chicago

PENNSYLVANIA

Trenton

Pittsburgh

Harrisburg

Philadelphia

N.J.

Omaha

Des Moines

ILLINOIS

INDIANA

OHIO

Columbus

Baltimore

Dover

DEL.

MD.

Washington, D.C.

Lincoln

Springfield

Indianapolis

WEST VIRGINIA

Annapolis

Topeka

Kansas City

Jefferson City

St. Louis

Cincinnati

Mississippi R.

Ohio R.

Frankfort

Charleston

Richmond

VIRGINIA

Norfolk

MISSOURI

KENTUCKY

Nashville

Raleigh

NORTH CAROLINA

Tulsa

ARKANSAS

Memphis

TENNESSEE

Tennessee R.

Columbia

SOUTH CAROLINA

Little Rock

Savannah R.

ATLANTIC OCEAN

Birmingham

Atlanta

GEORGIA

Mississippi R.

MISSISSIPPI

Montgomery

Savannah

Dallas

ALABAMA

Jackson

Mobile

Baton Rouge

New Orleans

LOUISIANA

Tallahassee

Jacksonville

FLORIDA

Orlando

Houston

Gulf of Mexico

Bahama Islands

Miami

Nassau

TAM-IPAS

N

0   200 miles

0   300 km

World Time Zones

Numbers below vertical bands relate each zone to Greenwich Mean Time (0 hrs.).
Local times frequently differ from these general indications,
as indicated by light-face numbers on map.

Algiers, **29**	Berlin, **34**	Delhi, **48**	Istanbul, **40**
Anchorage, **3**	Bogotá, **19**	Denver, **8**	Jerusalem, **42**
Athens, **41**	Budapest, **37**	Djakarta, **53**	Johannesburg, **44**
Auckland, **1**	Buenos Aires, **24**	Dublin, **26**	Lima, **20**
Baghdad, **46**	Caracas, **22**	Edmonton, **7**	Lisbon, **28**
Bangkok, **50**	Chicago, **9**	Hong Kong, **56**	London (Greenwich), **27**
Beijing, **54**	Copenhagen, **33**	Honolulu, **2**	Los Angeles, **6**
	Dallas, **10**		Madrid, **38**
			Manila, **57**

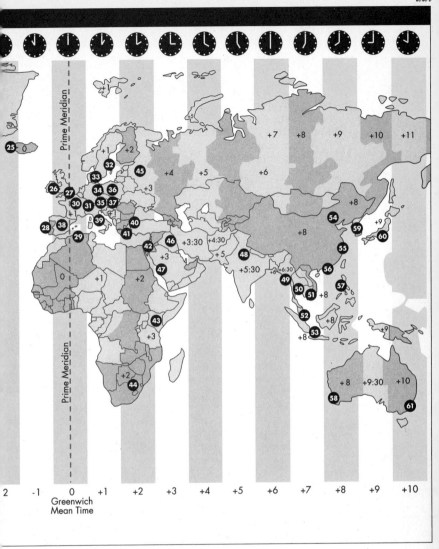

Mecca, **47**
Mexico City, **12**
Miami, **18**
Montréal, **15**
Moscow, **45**
Nairobi, **43**
New Orleans, **11**
New York City, **16**

Ottawa, **14**
Paris, **30**
Perth, **58**
Reykjavík, **25**
Rio de Janeiro, **23**
Rome, **39**
Saigon (Ho Chi Minh City), **51**

San Francisco, **5**
Santiago, **21**
Seoul, **59**
Shanghai, **55**
Singapore, **52**
Stockholm, **32**
Sydney, **61**
Tokyo, **60**

Toronto, **13**
Vancouver, **4**
Vienna, **35**
Warsaw, **36**
Washington, D.C., **17**
Yangon, **49**
Zürich, **31**

Introduction

Coastal California began its migration from some-where far to the south millions of years ago. It's still moving north along the San Andreas fault, but you have plenty of time for a visit before Santa Monica hits the Arctic Circle. If you've heard predictions that some of the state may fall into the Pacific, take the long view and con-sider that much of the state has been in and out of the ocean all through its history. The forces that raised the mountains and formed the Central Valley are still at work.

For a good introduction to the natural history and geology of the state, there is no better place to start than at the Oakland Museum. An impressive light-and-audio show pro-jected over a large model of the state explains the geogra-phy. Exhibits illustrate the state's ecosystems; walking through the exhibit hall is like walking across the state, from the ocean, across the Coast Ranges, the Central Val-ley, and the Sierra Nevada. On another floor there is a fine collection of artifacts and remains of the state's human his-tory; especially interesting are the Native American bas-kets, tools, and ceremonial clothing.

Those of you who can't start at the museum but who do travel through a few of California's tourist regions will see a wide variety of geography and nature. The state's history often is not as evident as its physical makeup. None of the cities is much more than 200 years old (Junípero Serra didn't come to San Diego until 1769), and the immediate im-pression is of a 20th-century culture. Still you will find rel-ics of early days in San Diego, San Francisco, and Los Angeles.

The chapters of this book are arranged in a generally north-to- south order. When planning your trip, keep in mind the very long distances. If you drive between San Francisco and Los Angeles on Highway 1, remember that it is not only more than 400 miles but is a difficult road to drive. Scenic routes, such as Highway 1 along the coast, Highway 49 in the Gold Country, and Highways 50 and 120 across the Sier-ra Nevada, require attention to driving and enough time for frequent stops.

California's north coast is a dramatically beautiful region whose main industries are tourism, fishing, and logging. There are no large cities, no large amusement parks, few luxury resorts. There isn't even much swimming, because of a cold current that runs down the coast for most of the state (turning out to sea before it reaches Southern Califor-nia beaches). And, although the ocean keeps the weather temperate, that doesn't mean there aren't winter storms. August is often the coldest month of the year here (as it can be in San Francisco, too). What you will find along the north coast are a wonderful scenic drive (Highway 1 and U.S. 101), many small inns (some of them quite luxurious), interesting restaurants serving locally produced fare, some good galleries, and a number of wineries. This is a region for leisurely exploring. It shouldn't be on the itinerary of anyone not interested in the beauties of nature, because the main attractions are tide pools under coastal cliffs, redwood trees, rhododendron, and banana slugs (a large yellow-and-black local oddity) in the lush coastal mountains. The Russians settled this region briefly in the 19th century, and you will find reminders of their presence.

The two main attractions in the Far North are Mt. Shasta, a large volcano that dominates the scenery of the northern part of the state, and Lassen Volcanic National Park. The park is at the southern end of the Cascade Range and is particularly interesting because of the record of past volcanic activity and evidence of current geothermal activity (such as the Sulphur Works). This region also suits those interested in nature, even more than the north coast, because lodging and dining opportunities are much more limited. Keep in mind also that much of this region can be very hot in summer.

The Wine Country is one of California's most popular tourist regions. There are narrow crowded highways dotted with wineries among the vineyards and valleys of the Coast Ranges north of San Francisco. Many of the wineries are beautiful sites for meals, picnics, or tastings, and there are fine bed-and-breakfasts and restaurants in the area.

San Francisco is a sophisticated city offering world-class hotels and the greatest concentration of excellent restaurants in the state. Because the city is so compact, a visitor can do very well without a car, but this is also a fine base for tours up the coast and to the Wine Country. If you want to drive down to Los Angeles from here, you can do it in a day (7–8 hours) if you take I–5 down the Central Valley, but you should budget at least two days if you want to take the coastal route. A long day's drive down U.S. 101 will get you to Santa Barbara, but you'll bypass Monterey and Big Sur.

The Gold Country, also known as the Mother Lode, is the gold-mining region of the Sierra Nevada foothills. There are many historic sites and small towns to explore, many of them of interest to children. Most impressive are the Empire Mine in Grass Valley, the gold-discovery site at Coloma, and Columbia State Historic Park, a town restored to its Gold Rush condition. As in the Wine Country, there are many B&Bs and small inns, but this is a less expensive, if also less sophisticated, region to visit. In spring there are wildflowers, and in fall the hills are colored by bright-red berries and changing leaves. In summer the hills are golden—and hot. Visitors in that season should probably check weather reports: There are many fine days, but exploring in 90° or hotter weather is not much fun. We've included Sacramento in the Gold Country chapter because it is adjacent and because its history is one with that of the Gold Rush.

Lake Tahoe is famous for its deep blue water and as the largest alpine lake on the continent. It stands up well to its reputation, despite crowded areas around the Nevada casinos. Lake Tahoe is a four-hour drive from San Francisco along I–80; the traffic to the lake on Friday afternoon and to San Francisco on Sunday is horrendous. If you plan to visit in winter, remember to carry chains in your car; they are sometimes required even on the interstate. In summer it's generally cooler here than in the foothills, but still sometimes pretty hot. Luckily, there are lots of beaches where you can swim.

The highlight for many travelers to California is a visit to one of the Sierra Nevada's national parks. Yosemite is the state's most famous park and every bit as sublime as promised. Its Yosemite-type or U-shape valleys were formed by the action of glaciers on the Sierra Nevada during recent ice ages. Other examples are found in Kings Canyon and Sequoia National Parks (which are adjacent to each other and usually visited together). At all three parks, but especially at the latter two, there are fine groves of Big Trees (*Sequoiadendron gigantea*), some of the largest living things in the world. The parks are open year-round, but large portions of the higher backcountry are closed in winter. Yosemite Valley is only 4,000 feet high, so winter weather is mild, and the waterfalls are beautiful when hung with ice.

The Monterey Peninsula, a two- or three-hour drive south of San Francisco, offers some of the state's most luxurious resorts and golf courses, interesting historic sites (Monterey was the capital during Spanish and Mexican rule, the state constitution was written here, and Junípero Serra is buried at the Carmel Mission), beautiful coastal scenery (Point Lobos would receive many votes for most treasured state park), and perhaps the most famous scenic drive (the 17-Mile Drive). There are also good restaurants in Monterey and Carmel and, for those interested, plenty of places to shop. The weather is usually mild, but any visitor should be prepared for fog and cool temperatures.

Between Carmel and Santa Barbara is another spectacular stretch of Highway 1, requiring concentration and nerve to drive. This is where you'll find those bridges spanning the cliffs along the Pacific—and Big Sur. Don't expect much in the way of dining, lodging, shopping, or even history until you get to Hearst Castle. Santa Barbara flaunts its Spanish/Mexican heritage. There's a well-restored mission, and almost all of downtown (including some pleasant shopping areas) is done in Spanish-style architecture. The centerpiece is the courthouse, built in the 1920s and displaying some beautiful tile work and murals.

In certain lights Los Angeles displays its own Spanish heritage, but much more evident is its cultural vibrancy as a 20th-century center on the Pacific Rim. Hollywood, the beaches, and Disneyland are all within an hour's drive. Also here are Beverly Hills, noted for its shops and mansions; important examples of 20th-century domestic architecture; and freeways. Dining options are improving, if still not up to the range of San Francisco's choices. Despite the city's reputation for a laid-back lifestyle, a visit here can be fairly overwhelming because of the size and variety of the region. Careful planning will help.

San Diego, at the southwestern edge of the state and the country, is usually the first stop. Junípero Serra founded his first mission in Alta California (as opposed to Baja California, which is still part of Mexico) here in 1769. There are historical sites from Mexican and Victorian times, one of the best zoos in the country, and fine beaches. The weather is agreeable, so this is a year-round destination.

The California deserts are extensive and varied and usually divided into two general areas: the Mojave, or High, Desert and the Colorado, or Low, Desert. Palm Springs and the new cities nearby (including Rancho Mirage) are filling up with expansive new resorts offering elaborate gardens, waterfalls, serpentine sidewalks, and—of course—golf courses. That area doesn't offer much of a desert experience, but it has great weather in winter, and you can use it as an elegant base for exploration. Joshua Tree National Monument is a good day trip (or two trips) from Palm Springs; the northern part is High Desert and the southern part Low Desert, so you can see the difference. Death Valley (*see* Chapter 16) and Anza-Borrego Desert Park (*see* Excursions from San Diego in Chapter 14) are of interest to those who want to explore the beauties of the desert landscape. Anza-Borrego is far less developed than Palm Springs but has a resort and a fancy golf course.

Running 400 miles down the center of the state from below Mt. Shasta to the Tehachapi Mountains, lying between the Coast Ranges and the Sierra Nevada, is the Central Valley. We haven't written much about the area (*see* Red Bluff and Redding in Chapter 4 and Sacramento in Chapter 7) because this is not much of a tourist region. You may drive across some of it on I–80 or down it on I–5, but there isn't much to stop and see, except in the state capital. This is, however, the most important agricultural region in the state and the fastest growing in terms of population.

California is as varied as any state and larger than most and could be the subject of many visits. Don't expect to visit everything the first time. As you travel through the state's regions you will get a sense of its great diversity of cultures, the ongoing pull between preservation and development, and the state's unique place in the landscapes of geography and the imagination.

1 Essential Information

Before You Go

Visitor Information

A detailed book, *Discover the Californias*, is available free through the California Office of Tourism (tel. 800/862–2543). "The Californias" refers to a useful division of the Golden State into 12 segments; the book sketches in the attractions and the flavor of each area. Separate publications include: *Calendar of Events*, *Ski the Californias*, and *California Bed & Breakfast Inns*. In addition, the California Office of Tourism (801 K St., Sacramento, CA 95814, tel. 916/322–2881) can answer questions about travel in the state.

There are visitors bureaus and chambers of commerce throughout the state; see individual chapters for listings.

In the United Kingdom, contact the **U.S. Travel and Tourism Administration** (22 Sackville St., London W1X 2EA, tel. 071/439–7433).

Tour Groups

General-Interest Tours Most major airlines have sightseeing tours from San Francisco, Los Angeles, and San Diego. If you are flying into any of these cities, check with airlines about the possibilities.

Amtrak offers tours to major attractions in California. For a brochure and special information, tel. 800/872–7245 or 800/321–8684.

Other major providers of tours in California:

Domenico Tours (751 Broadway, Bayonne, NJ 07002, tel. 201/823–8687 or 800/554–8687) arranges seven- and eight-day tours of California as well as shorter tours organized around special events, such as the Rose Bowl Parade and game on New Year's Day.

Gadabout Tours (700 E. Tahquitz Way, Palm Springs, CA 92262, tel. 619/325–5556 or 800/952–5068) offers more than a dozen regional tours of California, including "Death Valley Holiday," "Lake Tahoe Tapestry," "Hearst Castle Cooler," "Redwood Ramble," and "California Wine Country."

Globus-Gateway/Cosmos (95-25 Queens Blvd., Rego Park, NY 11374, tel. 718/268–7000 or 800/221–0090) has a nine-day "Focus on California" tour that winds its way from San Francisco to Los Angeles. Highlights include Lake Tahoe, Yosemite, Monterey, and Carmel.

Maupintour (Box 807, Lawrence, KS 66044, tel. 913/843–1211 or 800/255–4266) offers tours of the California coast from San Francisco to San Diego and north from San Francisco to Portland.

Mayflower Tours (1225 Warren Ave., Downers Grove, IL 60515, tel. 708/960–3430 or 800/323–7604 outside IL) also traverses the California coast in eight days—from San Francisco to San Diego.

Talmage Tours (1223 Walnut St., Philadelphia, PA 19107, tel. 215/923–7100) hits the California highlights in nine days. The tour starts in San Diego and ends in San Francisco. Stops include Los Angeles, Monterey, and Yosemite.

Tauck Tours (11 Wilton Rd., Westport, CT 06881, tel. 203/226–

6911 or 800/468–2825) offers a 10-day tour that winds its way from San Francisco to Long Beach. The Napa and Sonoma valleys are also included.

Special-Interest Tours

Gold Prospecting

Gold Prospecting Expeditions (18170 Main St., Box 974, Jamestown 95327, tel. 209/984–4653) guides clients in gold panning, dredging, and prospecting in outings that range from one hour to one to two weeks, some involving river rafting and helicopter drop-ins. It has special family discount packages.

Rafting, Canoeing, Kayaking

Kiwi Kayak (10070 Old Redwood Hwy., Box 1140, Windsor 95492, tel. 707/838–7787) runs easy-water Kiwi Kayak trips on the Eel, Klamath, Russian, Petaluma, and Napa rivers lasting from a single summer evening to four days. In difficulty, they range from introducing new paddlers to the romance of paddling on easy waters to offering thrills for seasoned boaters.

O.A.R.S., Outdoor Adventure River Specialists (Box 67, Angels Camp 95222, tel. 209/736–4677) offers one- to four-day rafting trips at several gradations of difficulty in North California on the Salmon and Klamath rivers; in Central California on the three forks of the American River, the Tuolumne, Stanislaus, and the Merced; and in South California on the Kern River. The difficulty of the trips is rated on an international scale in terms of the roughest rapid, from I (easy) to VI (unrunnable); these California trips range from II to V. Some class III trips provide overnight accommodations at bed-and-breakfast inns instead of camping. One action-packed trip combines a day of white-water rafting, an overnight at a B&B, and a morning of hot-air ballooning.

Skiing

Heavenly Ski Resort (Box 2180, Stateline, NV 89449, tel. 702/588–4584) can book a complete ski vacation for a minimum of three nights.

SuperCities Escape (tel. 800/333–1234) packages include air flight, rental car, lodging, and an optional interchangeable lift ticket good at six North Tahoe resorts: Squaw Valley, Alpine Meadows, Northstar, Homewood, Ski Incline, and Mt. Rose.

Wineries

Viviani Touring Company, Inc. (500 Michael Dr., Sonoma 95476, tel. 707/938–2100 or 707/938–8687), offers customized tours for one person to 600 people of the Napa, Sonoma, and Russian River wineries. Transportation, tour director, and meals are included. Lodging can be arranged at the Silverado Country Club in Napa or the Sonoma Mission Inn near Sonoma (accommodations at both are in the Very Expensive category). This company also arranges one-day shopping tours of San Francisco or Napa and Sonoma and half-day art tours of Napa Valley galleries.

Package Deals for Independent Travelers

There is a wide range of packages for independent travelers. The large casino-hotels at Lake Tahoe (*see* Chapter 8), for example, will often include a show, cocktails, and breakfast with a special lodging rate. An innovative bed-and-breakfast inn (Murphy's Inn, Grass Valley: *see* Chapter 7) offers, in winter, a midweek ski package, a picnic lunch, downhill or cross-country tickets for two, and a spa to enjoy when you return; and in summer, a golf special that includes greens fees, an electric cart, and a carafe of wine.

Most airlines have packages that include car rentals and lodging along with your flight. Hotels in major cities often have packages for weekends or for off-season. Package possibilities sometimes cluster around major tourist attractions; hotels and motels near Disneyland in Anaheim or Marine World/Africa in Vallejo, for instance, offer lodging and admission tickets in a package.

America Fly AAway Vacations (tel. 817/355–1234 or 800/321–2121) offers city packages with discounts on hotels and car rental in San Francisco, Anaheim, and San Diego. The airline's "Funtime Adventure" packages to Anaheim includes admission to Disneyland. Also check with **United Airlines** (tel. 800/328–6877) and **Continental Airlines** (tel. 800/634–5555) for packages. **SuperCities West** (7855 Haskell Ave., 3rd floor, Van Nuys, CA 91406, tel. 818/988–7844 or 800/333–1234) offers similar city packages.

Packages are increasing in popularity as marketing strategies. Always ask about package options as you are making reservations or thinking about making them. Often chambers of commerce or convention and visitors bureaus will have information for you. Travel agents are good sources, too.

Tips for British Travelers

Passports You will need a valid 10-year passport. You do not need a visa if you are staying for 90 days or less, have a return ticket, are flying with a participating airline, and complete Visa Waiver Form I-94W, available at the airport or on the plane. There are some exceptions to this, so check with your travel agent or with the U.S. Embassy (Visa and Immigration Department, 5 Upper Grosvenor St., London W1A 2JB, tel. 071/499–3443). Note that the U.S. Embassy no longer accepts applications made in person.

No vaccinations are required for entry into the United States.

Customs If you are 21 or over, you can take into the U.S. (1) 200 cigarettes or 50 cigars or two kilograms of tobacco, (2) one liter of alcohol, and (3) duty-free gifts to a value of $100. You may not take in meat or meat products, seeds, plants, fruits, etc., and avoid drugs and narcotics.

Returning to Britain, you may bring home (1) 200 cigarettes or 100 cigarillos or 50 cigars or 250 grams of tobacco; (2) two liters of table wine and, in addition, (a) one liter of alcohol over 22% by volume (most spirits) or (b) two liters of alcohol under 22% by volume (fortified or sparkling wine) or (c) two more liters of table wine; (3) 60 milliliters of perfume and 250 milliliters of toilet water; and (4) other goods up to a value of £32, but not more than 50 liters of beer or 25 cigarette lighters.

Insurance We recommend that you insure yourself to cover health and motoring mishaps. **Europ Assistance** (252 High St., Croydon CR0 1NF, tel. 081/680–1234) is one company that offers this service. It is also wise to insure yourself against trip cancellations and loss of luggage. For free general advice on all aspects of holiday insurance contact the **Association of British Insurers** (51 Gresham St., London EC2V 7HQ, tel. 071/600–3333).

Tour Operators The price battle that has raged over transatlantic fares has led most tour operators to offer excellent budget packages to the

United States. Among those you might consider as you plan your trip are:

British Airways Holidays (Atlantic House, Hazelwick Ave., Three Bridges, Crawley, West Sussex RH10 1NP, tel. 0293/611611).

Cosmosair plc (Ground Floor, Dale House, Tiviot Dale, Stockport, Cheshire SK1 1TB, tel. 061/480–5799).

Jetsave (Sussex House, London Rd., East Grinstead, West Sussex RH19 1LD, tel. 0342–312033).

Key to America (15 Feltham Rd., Ashford, Middlesex TW15 1DQ, tel. 0784/248777).

Kuoni Travel Ltd. (Kuoni House, Dorking, Surrey RH5 4AZ, tel. 0306/76711).

Premier Holidays (Premier Travel Center, Westbrook, Milton Rd., Cambridge CB4 1YQ, tel. 0223/355977).

Airfares We suggest that you explore the current scene for budget-flight possibilities. A good source of these is the small ads found in daily and Sunday newspapers, or in the weekly magazine *Time Out*. Some of these fares can be extremely difficult to come by, so be sure to book well in advance. Also, check on APEX and other money-saving fares, since only business travelers who don't have to watch the price of their tickets fly full-price these days—and find themselves sitting right beside APEX passengers!

When to Go

Any time of the year is the right time to go to California, allowing of course for specific needs and inclinations. There won't be skiable snow in the mountains between Easter and Thanksgiving; there will usually be rain in December, January, and February in the lowlands, if that bothers you; it will be much too hot to enjoy Palm Springs or Death Valley in the summer.

San Francisco, Los Angeles, and San Diego are delightful year round; the Wine Country's seasonal variables are enticing; the coastal areas are almost always cool. You can plan an enjoyable and rewarding trip to California at any time of the year.

The climate varies amazingly in California, not only over distances of several hundred miles but occasionally within an hour's drive. A foggy, cool August day in San Francisco makes you grateful for a sweater, tweed jacket, or light wool coat. Head north 50 miles to the Napa Valley to check out the Wine Country, and you'll probably wear shirt-sleeves and thin cottons.

It's not only over distance that temperatures vary. Daytime and nighttime temperatures in some parts of the state swing widely apart, not only in the mountains where warm, sunny afternoons and cool evenings are expected but in other places as well. Take Sacramento, a city that is at sea level, but in California's Central Valley. In the summer, afternoons can be very warm indeed, in the 90s and occasionally over 100 degrees. But the nights cool down, often with a drop of 40 degrees; it makes for pleasant sleeping, and it also makes a sweater that was unnecessary at 2 PM seem welcome at 11 PM.

It's hard to generalize much about the weather in this varied state. Rain comes in the winter, and there is snow at higher elevations. Summers are dry everywhere. As a rule, if you're near the ocean, the climate will be cool year round, though as you move north, there is more fog. Inland is warmer in the summer and cooler in the winter. As you climb into the mountains, there are more distinct variations with the seasons: Winter brings snow, autumn is crisp, spring is variable, and summer is clear and warm.

Climate The following are average daily maximum and minimum temperatures for the major California cities.

Los Angeles

Jan.	64F	18C	May	69F	21C	Sept.	75F	24C
	44	7		53	12		60	16
Feb.	64F	18C	June	71F	22C	Oct.	73F	23C
	46	8		57	14		55	13
Mar.	66F	19C	July	75C	24C	Nov.	71F	22C
	48	9		60	16		48	9
Apr.	66F	19C	Aug.	75C	24C	Dec.	66F	19C
	51	11		62	17		46	8

San Diego

Jan.	62F	17C	May	66F	19C	Sept.	73F	23C
	46	8		55	13		62	17
Feb.	62F	17C	June	69F	21C	Oct.	71F	22C
	48	9		59	15		57	14
Mar.	64F	18C	July	73F	23C	Nov.	69F	21C
	50	10		62	17		51	11
Apr.	66F	19C	Aug.	73F	23C	Dec.	64F	18C
	53	12		64	18		48	9

San Francisco

Jan.	55F	13C	May	66F	19C	Sept.	73F	23C
	41	5		48	9		51	11
Feb.	59F	15C	June	69F	21C	Oct.	69F	21C
	42	6		51	11		50	10
Mar.	60F	16C	July	69F	21C	Nov.	64F	18C
	44	7		51	11		44	7
Apr.	62F	17C	Aug.	69F	21C	Dec.	57F	14C
	46	8		53	12		42	6

Current weather information on more than 750 cities around the world is only a phone call away. Dialing **WeatherTrak** at 900/370–8725 will connect you to a computer, with which you can communicate by touch tone—at a cost of 95¢ per minute. The number plays a taped message that tells you to dial the three-digit access code for the destination in which you're interested. The code is either the area code (in the United States) or the first three letters of the foreign city. For a list of all access codes, send a stamped, self-addressed envelope to Cities, 9B Terrace Way, Greensboro, NC 27403. For further information, call 214/869–3035 or 800/247–3282.

Festivals and Seasonal Events

January **East-West Shrine All-Star Football Classic,** Palo Alto, is America's oldest all-star sports event (1651 19th Ave., San Francisco 94122, tel. 415/661–0291).

Tournament of Roses Parade and Football Game, Pasadena. The 104th annual parade takes place on New Year's Day 1993, with lavish flower-decked floats, marching bands, and equestrian teams, followed by the Rose Bowl game. (Pasadena Tourna-

Pre-registration by April 1 required (Napa Valley Wine Auction, Box 141, St. Helena 94574, tel. 707/963–5246).

Nevada City Classic Bicycle Race, Nevada City. This event is held every year on Father's Day (Nevada City Chamber of Commerce, 132 Main St., Nevada City 95959, tel. 916/265–2692).

July   **Carmel Bach Festival,** Carmel. The works of Johann Sebastian Bach are performed for three weeks; events include concerts, recitals, seminars (Box 575, Carmel 93921, tel. 408/624–1521).

Gilroy Garlic Festival. Gilroy, the Garlic Capital of the World, celebrates its smelly but delicious product with a weekend of taste treats including such unusual concoctions as garlic ice cream (Gilroy Garlic Festival, Box 2311, Gilroy 95021, tel. 408/842–1625).

August   **California State Fair,** Sacramento. The agricultural showcase, with high-tech exhibits, rodeo, horse racing, carnival, big-name entertainment nightly, runs 18 days from August to Labor Day (Box 15649, Sacramento 95815, tel. 916/924–2000).

Old Spanish Days Fiesta, Santa Barbara. The coastal city's biggest event features costumes, a parade, carnival, fiesta breakfast, rodeo, dancers, and a Spanish marketplace (Old Spanish Days, 1121 N. Milpas St., Santa Barbara 93103, tel. 805/962–8101).

September   **Renaissance Pleasure Faire,** Novato. From Labor Day weekend through mid-October, 3,000 costumed revelers stage an Elizabethan harvest festival (Living History Centre, Box B, Novato 94948, tel. 415/892–0937).

Russian River Jazz Festival, Guerneville. Jazz fans and musicians jam at Johnson's Beach (Russian River Jazz Festival, tel. 707/869–3940).

Los Angeles County Fair, Pomona. The largest county fair in the world features entertainment, exhibits, livestock, horse racing, food (Box 2250, Pomona 91769, tel. 714/623–3111).

October   **Grand National Livestock Exposition, Rodeo, and Horse Show,** San Francisco. A world-class competition, with 3,000 top livestock and horses (Cow Palace, Box 34206, San Francisco 94134, tel. 415/469–6057).

Southern California Grand Prix, Del Mar. Vintage grand prix races, auto expo, and national sports car championship events are included (100 W. Broadway, Suite 760, Long Beach 90802, tel. 310/437–0341).

November   **Death Valley '49er Encampment,** Death Valley. Encampment at Furnace Creek commemorates historic crossing of Death Valley in 1849, with fiddlers' contest and an art show (Death Valley National Monument, Box 579, Death Valley 92328, tel. 619/786–2331).

Doo Dah Parade, Pasadena. A fun-filled spoof of the annual Rose Parade features the Briefcase Brigade and kazoo Marching Band (Box 2392, Pasadena 91102, tel. 818/796–2591).

December   **Christmas Boat Parade of Lights,** Newport Beach. More than 200 festooned boats parade through the harbor nightly December 17–23 (1470 Jamboree Rd., Newport Beach 92660, tel. 714/729–4400).

Miners' Christmas Celebration, Columbia. The fun includes a Victorian Christmas feast at the City Hotel, lamplight tours, Christmas theater, children's piñata, costumed carolers, and

ment of Roses, 391 S. Ora
818/449–4100.)
Whale-Watching. Hundred.
California coast from Decen.
fice of Tourism, 801 K St.,
2881).

February **AT&T Pebble Beach National Pi**
endary golf tournament, former.
January and ends in early Februai
tel. 408/649–1533).
Chinese New Year Celebration. San F
est concentration of Chinese-Americ
brates the Year of the Rooster for a
Golden Dragon Parade (Visitor Inf
429097, San Francisco 94142-9097, tel. 4
geles also has a Chinese New Year Parade
Commerce, 977 N. Broadway, Suite E, Lo.
213/617–0396).
National Date Festival, Indio. This is an exot
an Arabian Nights theme including camel and
Arabian Nights fantasy production, and date e
ings (46-350 Arabia St., Indio 92201, tel. 619/34
Snowfest Lake Tahoe (North Lake Tahoe). This
winter carnival in the West with skiing, food,
rades, and live music (Box 7590, Tahoe City 96145,
7625.)

March **Dinah Shore Invitational,** Rancho Mirage. The fine
golfers in the world compete for the richest purse on t
circuit (Nabisco Dinah Shore, 2 Racquet Club Dr., Ra
rage 92270, tel. 619/324–4546).
Mendocino/Fort Bragg Whale Festival (Mendocino and
Bragg). This event features whale-watching excursions,
rine art exhibits, wine and beer tastings, art exhibits, chow
contest (Fort Bragg–Mendocino Coast Chamber of Commerc
Box 1141, Fort Bragg 95437, tel. 707/961–6300).

April **Ramona Pageant,** Hemet. The poignant love story of Ramona
(based on the novel by Helen Hunt Jackson) is presented weekends in late April and early May by a large cast on a mountain-
side outdoor stage (Ramona Pageant Association, 27400
Ramona Bowl Rd., Hemet 92544, tel. 714/658–3111).

May **Jumping Frog Contest,** Angels Camp. Inspired by Mark
Twain's story "The Notorious Jumping Frog of Calaveras
County," this contest is for frogs and trainers who take their
competition seriously (39th District Agricultural Association,
Box 96, Angels Camp 95222, tel. 209/736–2561).
Dixieland Jazz Jubilee, Sacramento. The world's largest
Dixieland festival features 125 bands from around the world
(Sacramento Traditional Jazz Society, 2787 Del Monte St.,
West Sacramento 95691, tel. 916/372–5277).
Great Monterey Squid Festival (Monterey). The squirmy squid
is the main attraction for this two-day event featuring cleaning
and cooking demonstrations, taste treats, plus the usual festi-
val fare: entertainment, arts and crafts, educational exhibits
(2600 Garden Rd. 208, Monterey 93940, tel. 408/649–6547).

June **Napa Valley Wine Auction,** St. Helena. A wine event for serious
sippers, it features open houses, wine tasting, and the auction.

Los Posadas (Columbia Chamber of Commerce, Box 1824, Columbia 95310, tel. 209/532-4301).

The Shepherd's Play, San Juan Bautista. The annual production by the internationally acclaimed El Teatro Campesino is performed in the Old Mission (El Teatro Campesino, Box 1240, San Juan Bautista 95045, tel. 408/623-2444).

What to Pack

Clothing   The most important single rule to bear in mind in packing for a California vacation is to prepare for changes in temperature. An hour's drive can take you up or down many degrees, and the variation from daytime to nighttime in a single location is often marked. Take along sweaters, jackets, and clothes for layering as your best insurance for coping with variations in temperature. Include shorts and/or cool cottons unless you are packing for a midwinter ski trip. Always tuck in a bathing suit. You may not be a beach lover, but the majority of overnight lodgings include a pool, a spa, and a sauna; you'll want the option of using these facilities.

While casual dressing is a hallmark of the California lifestyle, in the evening men will need a jacket and tie for many good restaurants, and women will be more comfortable in something dressier than regulation sightseeing garb.

Considerations of formality aside, bear in mind that San Francisco can be chilly at any time of the year, especially in summer, when the fog is apt to descend and stay. Nothing is more pitiful than the sight of uninformed tourists in shorts, their legs blue with cold. Take along clothes to keep you warm, even if the season doesn't seem to warrant it.

Miscellaneous   Although you can buy supplies of film, sunburn cream, aspirin, and most other necessities almost anywhere in California (unless you're heading for the wilderness), it is a bother, especially if your time is limited, to have to search for staples. Take along a reasonable supply of the things you know you will be using routinely and save your time for sheer enjoyment.

An extra pair of glasses, contact lenses, or prescription sunglasses is always a good idea; the loss of your only pair can hamper a vacation.

It is important to pack any prescription medications you need regularly, as well as prescriptions that are occasionally important, such as allergy medications. If you know you are prone to certain medical problems and have good, simple ways of dealing with early manifestations, take along what you might need, even though you may never use it.

Cash Machines

An increasing number of the nation's banks belong to a network of ATMs (automatic teller machines), which gobble up bank cards and spit out cash 24 hours a day in cities throughout the country. There are eight major networks in the United States, the largest of which are Cirrus, owned by MasterCard, and Plus, affiliated with Visa. Some banks belong to more than one network. These cards are not automatically issued; you have to ask for them. If your bank doesn't belong to at least one network, you should consider moving your funds, for ATMs are becoming as essential as check cashing. Cards issued by Visa and MasterCard also may be used in the ATMs, but the fees are usually higher than the fees on bank cards and there is a daily interest charge on the "loan" even if monthly bills are paid on time. Each network has a toll-free number you can call to locate machines in a given city. The Cirrus number is 800/4–CIRRUS; the Plus number is 800/THE–PLUS. Check with your bank for fees and for the amount of cash you can withdraw in a day.

Traveling with Film

If your camera is new, shoot and develop a few rolls of film before leaving home. Pack some lens tissue and an extra battery for your built-in light meter. Invest about $10 in a skylight filter and screw it onto the front of your lens. It will protect the lens and also reduce haze.

Film doesn't like hot weather. If you're driving in summer, don't store the film in the glove compartment or on the shelf under the rear window. Put it behind the front seat on the floor, on the side opposite the exhaust pipe.

On a plane trip, never pack unprocessed film in check-in luggage; if your bags get X-rayed, you can say goodbye to your pictures. Always carry undeveloped film with you through security and ask to have it inspected by hand. (It helps to isolate your film in a plastic bag, ready for quick inspection.) Inspectors at American airports are required by law to honor requests for hand inspection; abroad, you'll have to depend on the kindness of strangers.

The old airport scanning machines—still in use in some Third World countries—use heavy doses of radiation that can turn a family portrait into an early morning fog. The newer models—used in all U.S. airports—are safe for anything from five to 500 scans, depending on the speed of your film. The effects are cumulative; you can put the same roll of film through several scans without worry. After five scans, though, you're asking for trouble.

If your film gets fogged and you want an explanation, send it to the **National Association of Photographic Manufacturers,** 550 Mamaroneck Avenue, Harrison, NY 10528. It will try to determine what went wrong. The service is free.

Car Rentals

All major car-rental agencies serve California, though not all have outlets in every city and airport. Two important suggestions for car rentals: Compare prices, and be sure you understand all the provisions of an agreement before you sign it. Often you will have to pay extra for the privilege of picking up a car in one location and dropping it off at another; know the difference in cost, and know how important it is to you. Differing requirements for filling gas tanks can change the cost of the rental. Ask questions.

It's always best to know a few essentials *before* you arrive at the car-rental counter. Find out what the collision-damage waiver (usually an $8 to $12 daily surcharge) covers and whether your corporate or personal insurance already covers damage to a rental car (if so, bring along a photocopy of the benefits section). More and more companies are holding renters responsible for theft and vandalism damages if they don't buy the CDW; in response, some credit-card and insurance companies are extending *their* coverage to rental cars.

Here are toll-free numbers for some of the car-rental agencies in California:

Agency Rent-A-Car, tel. 800/843–1143.
American International Rent a Car (AI), tel. 800/527–0202.
Avis, tel. 800/331–1212.
Budget Car and Truck Rental, tel. 800/527–0700.
Dollar Rent a Car, tel. 800/800–4000.
Hertz, tel. 800/654–3131.
National Car Rental, tel. 800/227–7368.
Thrifty Car Rental, tel. 800/367–2277.

Traveling with Children

The watchword for traveling with children is to plan ahead as much as possible. That way, the trip will be a lot more fun for all of you.

In many parts of California, bed-and-breakfast inns are growing in popularity. Small, charming, and usually old, they have a strong appeal for many people. However, if you are traveling with children, you may have to look carefully to find one that will give you a room at the inn. It's not too surprising; most of these places are furnished with antiques and decorative accessories that are definitely not childproof. Our research shows that you can travel with children in California and occasionally stay at a B&B, but you'll have to plan ahead; look at our listings.

Motels and hotels, with few exceptions, do welcome children. Often they can stay free in the same room with their parents, with nominal charges for cribs and $5–$10 charges for an extra bed. In addition, major hotels usually have lists of baby-sitters so that parents can leave for non-child-related activities.

If you have children, you won't need anyone to tell you to have a good supply of things to keep them busy in the car, on the airplane, on the train, or however you are traveling. If you're traveling by car, you'll have the option of stopping frequently. Just getting the children out of the confines of the car for a little while has an advantage; an even bigger advantage comes when you can stop at a park and the children can run or use a playground.

When you are sightseeing, try to plan some things that will be of special interest to your children. They may tolerate a museum and even show interest in a historic building or two, but put a zoo into the itinerary when you can.

In many ways California is made to order for traveling with children: Disneyland, the San Diego Zoo, the Monterey Aquarium, the San Francisco cable cars, the city-owned gold mine in Placerville, the caverns at Lake Shasta. . . . The list could go on and on.

Publications ***Family Travel Times,*** an 8- to 12-page newsletter published 10 times a year by TWYCH (Travel with Your Children, 45 W. 18 St., 7th Floor Tower, New York, NY 10011, tel. 212/206–0688). Subscription ($35) includes access to back issues and twice-weekly opportunities to call in for specific advice.

***Great Vacations with Your Kids: The Complete Guide to Family
Vacations in the U.S.,*** by Dorothy Ann Jordon and Marjorie
Adoff Cohen (E. P. Dutton, 375 Hudson St., New York, NY
10014; $12.95), details everything from city vacations to adven-
ture vacations to child-care resources.
Places to Go with Children in Southern California, by
Stephanie Kegan (Chronicle Books, 275 5th St., San Francisco,
CA 94103, tel. 800/722–6657; in CA, 800/445–7577; $9.95 plus $2
for shipping).
Places to Go with Children in Northern California, by
Elizabeth Pomada (Chronicle Books, same as above).
Eating Out with Kids in San Francisco, by Carole Terwilliger
Meyers (Carousel Press, $7.95). For Carousel Press's catalogue
of 100–150 family-oriented travel guides and activity books for
kids, send $1 for shipping or a business-size SASE with 45¢
postage to Carousel Press, Box 6061, Albany, CA 94706.
"Kidding Around in San Francisco," a free brochure available
from the San Francisco Convention & Visitors Bureau (Box
6977, San Francisco 94101, tel. 415/974–6900.

Hints for Disabled Travelers

California is a national leader in providing access for handicapped people to attractions and facilities. Since 1982 the state
building code has required that all construction for public use
include access for the disabled. State laws more than a decade
old provide special privileges, such as license plates allowing
special parking spaces, unlimited parking in time-limited
spaces, and free parking in metered spaces. Insignia from
states other than California are honored.

People with disabilities should plan ahead for travel; check
with providers when you make arrangements for transportation, lodging, and special sightseeing and events. Allow plenty
of time to meet bus, train, and plane schedules. Be sure your
wheelchair is clearly marked if it is carried with other luggage.

Greyhound-Trailways (tel. 800/752–4841; TDD 800/345–3109)
will carry a disabled person and companion for the price of a
single fare.

Amtrak (tel. 800/USA–RAIL) advises that you request Redcap
service, special seats, or wheelchair assistance when you make
reservations. Also note that not all stations are equipped to
provide these services. All handicapped passengers are enti-
tled to a 15% discount on the lowest available fare. A special
fare for handicapped children is also available. For a free copy
of Amtrak's *Access Amtrak,* which outlines all its services for
the elderly and handicapped, write to Amtrak (National Railroad Passenger Corp., 60 Massachusetts Ave., NE, Washington, DC 20002).

The **National Park Service** provides a Golden Access Passport
free to those who are medically blind or have a permanent disability; the passport covers the entry fee for the holder and anyone accompanying the holder in the same private vehicle and a
50% discount on camping and some other user fees. Apply for
the passport in person at a national recreation facility that
charges an entrance fee; proof of disability is required.

For additional information, write to the National Park Service
(Box 37127, Washington, DC 20013–7127).

Society for the Advancement of Travel for the Handicapped (347 5th Ave., Suite 610, New York, NY 10016, tel. 212/447–7284) is a good source for access information for the disabled. Annual membership is $45; for senior travelers and students, $25.

The Information Center for Individuals with Disabilities (Fort Point Pl., 1st floor, 27–43 Wormwood St., Boston, MA 02210, tel. 617/727–5540) offers useful problem-solving assistance, including lists of travel agencies that specialize in tours for the disabled.

Travel Industry and Disabled Exchange (TIDE, 5435 Donna Ave., Tarzana, CA 91356, tel. 818/368–5648) is an industry-based organization with a $15-per-person annual membership fee. Members receive a quarterly newsletter and information on travel agencies and tours.

Moss Rehabilitation Hospital Travel Information Service (1200 W. Tabor Rd., Philadelphia, PA 19141–3099, tel. 215/456–9600; TDD 215/456–9602) provides information on tourist sights, transportation, and accommodations for destinations around the world, for a small fee.

Mobility International USA (Box 3551, Eugene, OR 97403, tel. 503/343–1284) has information on accommodations, organized study, etc., around the world.

Hints for Older Travelers

Many discounts are available to older travelers: Meals, lodging, entry to various attractions, car rentals, tickets for buses and trains, and campsites are among the prime examples.

The age that qualifies you for these senior discounts varies considerably. The American Association of Retired Persons will accept you for membership at age 50, and your membership card will qualify you for many discounts. The state of California will reduce the cost of your campsite if you are at least 62.

If you are 50, our advice is to ask about senior discounts even if there is no posted notice. Ask at the time you are making reservations, buying tickets, or being seated in a restaurant. Carry proof of your age, such as a driver's license, and of course any membership cards in organizations that provide discounts for seniors. Many discounts are given solely on the basis of age, without membership requirement. A 10% cut on a bus ticket and $2 off a pizza may not seem like major savings, but they add up, and you can cut the cost of a trip appreciably if you remember to take advantage of these options.

The American Association of Retired Persons (AARP) (601 E St., NW, Washington, DC 20049, tel. 202/434–2277). The Purchase Privilege Program offers discounts on car rentals, sightseeing, hotels, motels, and resorts. AARP also arranges group tours through **AARP Travel Experience from American Express** (400 Pinnacle Way, Suite 450, Norcross, GA 30071, tel. 800/927–0111). These and other services are included in the annual dues of $5 per person or per couple. The AARP Motoring Plan offers emergency aid and trip routing information for an annual fee of $33.95 per couple.

Elderhostel (75 Federal St., Boston, MA 02110–1941, tel. 617/426–7788) is an innovative, low-cost educational program for people 60 or older (only one member of a traveling couple needs to be 60 to qualify). Participants live in dorms on 1,600 campuses in the United States and around the world. Mornings are devoted to lectures and seminars, afternoons to sightseeing and field trips. The fee includes room, board, tuition, and round-trip transportation.

National Council of Senior Citizens (1331 F St., NW, Washington, DC 20004, tel. 202/347–8800) is a nonprofit advocacy group with 5,000 local clubs across the country. Annual membership is $12 per person or per couple. Members receive a monthly newspaper with travel information and an ID card for reduced-rate hotels and car rentals.

Mature Outlook (6001 N. Clark St., Chicago, IL 60660, tel. 800/336–6330), a subsidiary of Sears, Roebuck & Co., is a travel club for people over 50, offering hotel and motel discounts and a bimonthly newsletter. Annual membership is $9.95 per couple. Instant membership is available at participating Holiday Inns.

September Days Club is run by the moderately priced Days Inns of America (tel. 800/241–5050). The $12 annual membership fee for individuals or couples over 50 entitles them to reduced car-rental rates and reductions of 15–50% at 95% of the chain's more than 350 motels.

Greyhound-Trailways (tel. 800/752–4841) and **Amtrak** (tel. 800/USA–RAIL) offer special fares for senior citizens.

Golden Age Passport is a free lifetime pass to all parks, monuments, and recreation areas run by the federal government. Permanent U.S. residents 62 and over may pick them up in person at any national park that charges admission. The passport covers the entrance fee for the holder and anyone accompanying the holder in the same private vehicle. It also provides a 50% discount on camping and various other user fees.

The California state park system includes more than 200 locations and provides a $2 discount on campsites (ask for this discount when you make advance reservations) for anyone 62 or over and others in the same private vehicle.

Publications **The Senior Citizen's Guide to Budget Travel in the United States and Canada** is available for $4.95, including postage, from Pilot Books (103 Cooper St., Babylon, NY 11702, tel. 516/422–2225).

Staying in California

Shopping

In California's big cities, opportunities abound to shop for internationally famed brands of clothing, jewelry, leather goods, and perfumes, often in shops or boutiques set up by French, Italian, British, or American designers. There are enough specialty shops and fine department stores to keep anyone "born to shop" busy and happy. *(Note:* San Francisco and Los Angeles are centers of clothing manufacture; if you're a bargain hunter, you'll want to explore the factory outlets in both cities.)

If you are shopping for something unique to California, look at the output of its artists. California is home to a great number of artists and craftspeople, and you can find their creations from one end of the state to the other in fine city galleries, in small neighborhood shops, in out-of-the-way mountain studios, at roadside stands, and at county fairs. Paintings, drawings, sculpture, wood carvings, pottery, jewelry, hand-woven fabrics, handmade baskets—the creativity and the output of California's artists and artisans seem endless. Whatever your taste and budget, you will probably have no trouble locating tempting shopping opportunities.

Another California specialty is wine. You can visit wineries in many parts of the state, not only in the Wine Country north of San Francisco. Wineries and good wine stores will package your purchases for safe travel or shipping.

Other possibilities range from antiques to souvenir T-shirts. If you're flying home from San Francisco, you can make one last purchase of the city's unique sourdough French bread at the airport.

Participant Sports

Almost any participant sport you can think of is available somewhere in California at some time of the year. A great many sports know no time limits and go on year round. Skiing, of course, depends on the snow and is limited for the most part to the period between Thanksgiving and April, but golf courses and tennis courts do a thriving business all year.

Swimming and surfing, scuba diving, and skin diving in the Pacific Ocean are favorite year-round California pleasures in the southern part of the state. On the coast from San Francisco and northward, the seasons play a limiting role.

California has abundant fishing options: deep-sea fishing expeditions, surf fishing from the shore, and freshwater fishing in streams, rivers, lakes, and reservoirs. There are many hunting opportunities as well. For information on fishing and hunting licenses and regulations, check with the **California Department of Fish and Game** (1416 9th St., Sacramento 95814, tel. 916/653–6420).

Hiking, backpacking, bicycling, and sailing are popular throughout the state, and you can readily arrange for rental of equipment. River rafting, white-water and otherwise, canoeing, and kayaking are popular, especially in the northern part of the state, where there are many rivers; see individual chapters for detailed information.

Hot-air ballooning is gaining in popularity, although it is not cheap: A ride costs in excess of $100. More and more of the large, colorful balloons drift across the valleys of the Wine Country, where the air drafts are particularly friendly to this sport, as well as in the desert, Temecula, and the Gold Country.

Beaches

With almost 1,000 miles of coastline, California is well supplied with beaches. They are endlessly fascinating: You can walk on them, lie and sun on them, watch seabirds and hunt for shells, dig clams, or spot seals and sea otters at play. From December through March you can watch the migrations of the gray whales.

What you can't always do at these beaches is swim. From San Francisco and northward, the water is simply too cold for any but extremely hardy souls. Some beaches, even along the southern half of the coast, are too dangerous for swimming because of undertows. Look for signs and postings and take them seriously. Park rangers patrol beaches and enforce regulations, such as those on pets (dogs must be on leash at all times), alcohol, dune buggies, and fires.

Access to beaches in California is generally excellent. The state park system includes many fine beaches, and oceanside communities have their own public beaches. In addition, through the work of the California Coastal Commission, many stretches of private property that would otherwise seal off the beach from outsiders have public-access paths and trails. Again, the best advice is to look for signs and obey them.

State and National Parks

State Parks California's state park system includes more than 200 sites; many are recreational and scenic, and some are historic or scientific. A sampling of the variety of state parks: Angel Island in San Francisco Bay, reached by ferry from San Francisco or Tiburon; Anza-Borrego Desert, 600,000 acres of the Colorado Desert northeast of San Diego; Big Basin Redwoods, California's first state redwood park, with 300-foot trees, near Santa Cruz; Empire Mine, one of the richest mines in the Mother Lode in Grass Valley; Hearst Castle at San Simeon; Leo Carrillo Beach north of Malibu; Pismo Beach, with surfing, clamming, and nature trails.

Reservations Most state parks are open year round. Parks near major urban areas and on beaches and lakes are often crowded, and campsite reservations are essential. MISTIX (tel. 800/444–7275) handles all state park reservations, which may be made up to eight weeks in advance.

For information on California's state parks, contact the **California State Park System** (Dept. of Parks and Recreation, Box 942896, Sacramento 94296, tel. 916/653–6995).

National Parks National parks are administered by the Department of the Interior, and the lands within their boundaries are preserved.

There are five national parks in California: Lassen, Redwood, Sequoia and Kings Canyon, Yosemite, and the Channel Islands. National monuments include Cabrillo, in San Diego; Death Valley; Devil's Postpile, 7,600 feet up in the eastern Sierra Nevada; Lava Beds, in northeastern California; Muir Woods, north of San Francisco; Joshua Tree in the desert near Palm Springs; and Pinnacles, in western central California.

There are three national recreation areas: Golden Gate, with 73,000 acres both north and south of the Golden Gate Bridge in San Francisco; Santa Monica Mountains, with 150,000 acres from Griffith Park in Los Angeles to the Ventura County line; and Whiskeytown-Shasta-Trinity, with 240,000 acres including four major lakes.

For information on specific parks, see the individual chapters or contact the **National Park Service** (Fort Mason, Bldg. 201, San Francisco, CA 94123, tel. 415/556–0560).

Dining

Restaurants are placed in one of four categories—Inexpensive, Moderate, Expensive, and Very Expensive—according to the price of a full dinner for one person. The full dinner includes soup or salad, an entrée, vegetables, dessert, and coffee or tea. The prices do not include drinks, tax, or tip.

Dining is more expensive in major cities than in rural areas. Since price levels vary from one part of California to another, check each chapter for the dollar amount denoted by the category.

Lodging

Overnight accommodations are placed in one of four categories—Inexpensive, Moderate, Expensive, and Very Expensive—according to the amount charged for two people in one room. Since lodging costs vary from one part of the state to another, check each chapter for the dollar amount denoted by the category.

Motel, hotel, and bed-and-breakfast accommodations are listed together in each chapter. Hotels are found primarily in cities and may or may not provide parking facilities. There is usually a charge for parking. Motels have parking space but may not have some of the amenities that hotels typically have: elevators, on-site restaurants, lounges, and room service.

Except for the parking, none of these generalizations is hard and fast. Many motels have restaurants, room service, and other services. Nor is size a distinction. Some hotels are small and have few rooms; some motels have more than 200 rooms.

Bed-and-breakfast inns have become more popular in California in recent years. Most typically, an inn is a large, older home, renovated and charmingly decorated with antiques, with a half-dozen guest rooms. The price usually includes breakfast. Baths may be private or shared. However, these are not hard-and-fast rules. Breakfast may be a four-course feast or Continental. Sometimes the inn is a renovated hotel from the last century with a dozen rooms; occasionally it is a Victorian farmhouse with only three guest rooms.

Few B&Bs allow smoking; virtually none take pets. Antique furniture, delicate fabrics, and the elaborate decorative accessories that are typical of these inns make these restrictions understandable.

On the matter of cost, there is no reliable way of distinguishing among hotels, motels, and B&Bs. A motel may be as lavish and luxurious as a hotel, and you don't necessarily economize by staying in a B&B.

Guest ranches and dude ranches are included in lodging listings, as are resorts. Their range of recreation options is greater than the usual, and this is noted.

Credit Cards

The following credit-card abbreviations are used: AE, American Express; D, Discover; DC, Diners Club; MC, MasterCard; V, Visa.

Camping

Camping facilities in the state parks are extensive, though you will need reservations. (*See* State Parks, above.) Many popular parks have all their spaces reserved several weeks ahead. *California RV Park and Campground Guide* gives information about nearly 300 private parks and campgrounds throughout the state. Send $2 to **California Travel Parks Association** (Box 5648, Auburn, CA 95604).

Smoking

Limitations on smoking are more and more common; if you smoke, be sensitive to restrictions. If you do not smoke, ask for and expect accommodations for nonsmokers on airplanes, in hotels, in restaurants, and in many other public places.

Smoking is prohibited on all airline routes within the 48 contiguous states, within the states of Hawaii and Alaska, on flights of under six hours to and from Hawaii and Alaska, and to and from the U.S. Virgin Islands and Puerto Rico. The rule applies to both domestic and foreign carriers.

Most hotels and motels have nonsmoking rooms; in larger establishments whole floors are reserved for nonsmokers. Most B&B inns do not allow smoking on the premises.

Most eating places have nonsmoking sections. Many cities and towns in California have ordinances requiring areas for nonsmokers in restaurants and many other public places.

The trend in California, a health-conscious state, is toward more "No Smoking" signs. Expect to see them in many places.

2 Portraits of California

Living with the Certainty of a Shaky Future

By John Burks

John Burks is a professor of journalism and humanities at San Francisco State University. He has served as editor-in-chief of two of the city's leading magazines, City and San Francisco Focus, was a Newsweek correspondent and managing editor of Rolling Stone, and currently edits the quarterly American Kite.

There's never been any question *whether* there will be another earthquake in San Francisco. The question is how soon. Even the kids here grow up understanding that it's just a matter of time, and from grade school on, earthquake safety drills become routine. *At the first rumble, duck under your desk or table or stand in a doorway,* they are instructed. *Get away from windows to avoid broken glass. When the shaking stops, walk—don't run—outdoors, as far away from buildings as possible.*

Sure as there are hurricanes along the Gulf of Mexico and blizzards in Maine, San Francisco's earthquakes are inevitable. Nobody here is surprised when the rolling and tumbling begins—it happens all the time. Just in the six months following the jarring 1989 earthquake, for instance, seismologists reported hundreds of aftershocks, ranging from the scarcely perceptible to those strong enough to bring down buildings weakened by October's jolt.

The Bay Area itself was created in upheaval such as this. Eons ago, a restless geology of shifting plates deep in the earth gave birth to the Sierra Mountains and the Pacific Coast Range. Every spring when the snows melted, the runoff rushed down from the mile-high Sierra peaks westward across what would eventually be known as California. Here, the runoff ran up against the coastal range, and a vast inland lake was formed.

The rampaging waters from the yearly thaw eventually crashed through the quake-shattered Coast Range to meet the Pacific Ocean, creating the gap now spanned by the Golden Gate Bridge. This breakthrough created San Francisco Bay, one of the world's great natural harbors, its fertile delta larger than that of the Mississippi River. What a fabulous setting for the city-to-be—surrounded on three sides by water, set off by dramatic mountainscapes to the north and south, and blessed by cool ocean breezes.

All this and gold, too. The twisting and rolling of so-called terra firma exposed rich veins of gold at and near ground level that otherwise would have remained hidden deep underground. The great upheaval pushed the Mother Lode to the surface and set the scene for the Gold Rush. But before the '49 miners came the Europeans. In the late 15th century, the Spanish writer Garci Ordóñez de Montalvo penned a fictional description of a place he called California, a faraway land ruled by Queen Califia, where gold and precious stones were so plentiful the streets were lined with them.

Montalvo's vision of wealth without limit helped fuel the voyages of the great 15th- and 16th-century European explorers in the New World. They never did hit pay dirt here, but the name California stuck nevertheless.

Northern California was eventually settled, and in 1848, the population of San Francisco was 832. The discovery of gold in the California hills brought sudden and unprecedented wealth to this coastal trading outpost and its population exploded; by the turn of the century San Francisco was home to 343,000 people.

En route to its destiny as a premier city of the West, San Francisco was visited by innumerable quakes. Yet while the city's very foundations shook, residents found that each new rattler helped to strengthen San Francisco's self-image of adaptability. Robert Louis Stevenson wrote of the quakes' alarming frequency: "The fear of them grows yearly in a resident; he begins with indifference and ends in sheer panic." The big shaker of 1865 inspired humorist Mark Twain to look at the quakes in a different light by writing an earthquake "almanac" for the following year, which advised:

Oct. 23—Mild, balmy earthquakes.
Oct. 26—About this time expect more earthquakes; but do not look for them . . .
Oct. 27—Universal despondency, indicative of approaching disaster. Abstain from smiling or indulgence in humorous conversation . . .
Oct. 29—Beware!
Oct. 31—Go slow!
Nov. 1—Terrific earthquake. This is the great earthquake month. More stars fall and more worlds are slathered around carelessly and destroyed in November than in any month of the twelve.
Nov. 2—Spasmodic but exhilarating earthquakes, accompanied by occasional showers of rain and churches and things.
Nov. 3—Make your will.
Nov. 4—Sell out.

On the whole, those who settled in San Francisco were more inclined toward Twain's devil-may-care attitude—those who succumbed to Stevenson's panic didn't stick around for long. Certainly the multitude of vices that saturated the metropolis were sufficient to distract many men from their fears; throughout Chinatown and the infamous Barbary Coast opium dens, gin mills, and bordellos operated day and night.

Money flowed. Money tempted. Money corrupted. The city was built on graft, and city hall became synonymous with corruption under the influence of political crooks like Blind Chris Buckley and Boss Ruef. The very building itself was a scandal. Planned for completion in six months at a cost of half a million dollars, the city hall ultimately took 29 years to build at a graft-inflated cost of $8 million, an astronomical sum at the dawning of the 20th century. When the San Andreas Fault set loose the 1906 earthquake, the most devastating ever to hit an American city, city hall was one of the first buildings to come crashing down. Its ruins exposed the shoddiest of building materials, an ironic symbol of the city's crime-ridden past.

The 1906 earthquake and fire has come to define San Francisco both for itself and the outside world. In the immediate aftermath of the catastrophe, San Franciscans wondered whether they ought to believe the preachers and reformers who declared that this terrible devastation had been wrought upon their wicked city by the avenging hand of God. San Franciscans asked themselves whether, somehow, they had earned it.

But the city was quick to prove its character. Fifty years earlier, six separate fires had destroyed most of San Francisco—yet each time it was rebuilt by a citizenry not ready to give up on either the gold or the city that gold had built. Now, in 1906, heroic firefighters dynamited one of the city's main thoroughfares to prevent the inferno from spreading all the way to the Pacific. The mood of San Franciscans was almost eerily calm, their neighborliness both heartwarming and jaunty. "Eat, drink, and be merry," proclaimed signs about town, "for tomorrow we may have to go to Oakland." No sooner had the flames died than rebuilding began—true to San Francisco tradition. Forty thousand construction workers poured into town to assist the proud, amazingly resilient residents.

The 1906 earthquake provided a chance to rethink the hodgepodge, get-rich-quick cityscape that had risen in the heat of Gold Rush frenzy. City fathers imported the revered urban planner Daniel Burnham, architect of the magnificent 1893 Chicago World's Fair, to re-invent San Francisco. "Make no little plans," Burnham intoned. "They have no power to stir men's souls."

The city's new Civic Center, built under Burnham's direction, was raised to celebrate the city's comeback and is regarded as one of America's most stately works of civic architecture. Its city hall stands as a monument to the city's will to prevail—from its colonnaded granite exterior to its exuberant interior, once described by Tom Wolfe as resembling "some Central American opera house. Marble arches, domes, acanthus leaves . . . quirks and galleries and gilt filigrees . . . a veritable angels' choir of gold." The inscription found over the mayor's office seems to sum it all up: "San Francisco, O glorious city of our hearts that has been tried and not found wanting, go thou with like spirit to make the future thine."

In 1915, San Francisco dazzled the world with its Panama–Pacific Exposition, designed to prove not only that it was back, but that it was back bigger and better and badder than ever before. An architectural wonderland, the Expo was built on 70 acres of marshy landfill, which later became the residential neighborhood called the Marina District. When the October 1989 earthquake struck, this neighborhood was badly damaged, and became a focus as the entire nation tuned in to see how San Francisco and its people would fare this time around.

Like the gold that surfaced in the Mother Lode, the 1989 quake once again brought out the best in this region's people. Out at Candlestick Park, 62,000 fans were waiting for the start of the World Series between the San Francisco Giants and the Oakland A's when everything started shaking. They cut loose with big cheer after the temblor subsided. One San Francisco fan quickly hand-lettered a sign and held it aloft: "That was Nothing—Wait Til the Giants Bat." When it became apparent that there would be no ball played that night, the fans departed from the ballpark, just like in a grade-school earthquake safety drill, quietly and in good order.

This was what millions of TV viewers across the nation first saw of the local response to this major (7.1) earthquake and, by and large, the combination of good humor and relative calm they observed was an accurate reflection of the prevailing mood around the city. San Franciscans were not about to panic. Minutes after the quake struck, a San Francisco couple spread a lace tablecloth over the hood of their BMW and, sitting in the driveway of their splintered home, toasted passersby with champagne. Simultaneously, across San Francisco Bay, courageous volunteers and rescue workers set to work digging through the pancaked rubble of an Oakland freeway in the search for survivors, heedless that they, too, could easily be crushed in an aftershock. Throughout the Bay Area, hundreds volunteered to fight the fires, clear away the mess, assist survivors, and donate food, money, and clothing.

San Francisco's city seal features the image of a phoenix rising from the flames of catastrophe, celebrating the city's fiery past and promising courage in the face of certain future calamity. The 1989 shake possessed only about one fortieth the force of the legendary 1906 quake, and all projections point to the inevitability of another Big One, someday, on at least the scale of '06. Often people from other, more stable, parts of the world have trouble understanding how it is possible to live with such a certainty.

The *San Francisco Bay Guardian*, shortly after the 1989 quake, spoke for many Bay Area residents: "We live in earthquake country. Everybody knows that. It's a choice we've all made, a risk we're all more or less willing to accept as part of our lives. We're gambling against fate, and last week our luck ran out. It was inevitable—as the infamous bumper sticker says, Mother Nature bats last."

Former San Francisco mayor Diane Feinstein explained it this way: "Californians seem undaunted. We [know] we'll never be a match for Mother Nature. But the principal thing that seems to arise from the ash and rubble of a quake is the strong resolve to rebuild and get on with life."

There Must Be a There Here Somewhere

"Hollywood is a town that has to be seen to be disbelieved"—Walter Winchell

By Jane E. Lasky

While hosting a British braodcaster-friend on his first trip to Los Angeles, I reluctantly took him to the corner of Hollywood and Vine. Driving toward the renowned street-corner, I explained (again) that this part of town isn't the "real" Hollywood. But he wasn't listening. He was on a pilgrimage and too filled with the anticipation of coming upon a sacred place to hear my warning. When we reached the intersection, his reaction was written all over his face: He was, as he later said, "gobsmacked."

As we pulled up to the light, a bedraggled hooker crossed Hollywood Boulevard. Otherwise, nothing was happening. Worse, this looked like someplace where nothing noteworthy or memorable ever had, would, or could happen. The area has been called squalid, but that gives it too much credit for being interesting. All there was to see were a few small and struggling businesses, the hulk of a long-defunct department store, and a couple of unremarkable office buildings.

To rescue the moment from disaster, I went into my standard routine: I pointed out that the northeast corner is where the Brown Derby restaurant once stood. I hoped this would conjure a strong enough image of movie stars dining in a giant hat to blot out the sun-bleached desolation before our eyes. I then recounted historian Richard Alleman's theory about how this unprepossessing street-corner got so famous. Alleman, who wrote *The Movie Lover's Guide to Hollywood*, believes that, because the radio networks, which maintained studios in the vicinity during the 1930s and 1940s, began their broadcasts with the words "brought to you from the corner of Hollywood and Vine . . ." the intersection became glamorous by association—at least to radio listeners who'd never seen it.

Any first-time visitor to Tinseltown is bound for some initial disappointment because, like a matinee idol, the place looks somehow smaller in person. Between the world-famous landmarks and the stars' names embedded in the sidewalks are long stretches of tawdriness that have resisted more than a decade of cleanup and restoration and look all the worse under the vivid glare of the Southern California sun. Even the best of Hollywood looks a little wan and sheepish in broad daylight, as if caught in the act of intruding upon a reality in which it does not belong.

Pressed to show my British friend the "real" Hollywood, I took him on a tour of the more outstanding architecture along Hollywood Boulevard. He was duly captivated by the lunatic exuberance of Hollywood's art-deco movie palaces, exemplified in the zigzaggy Moderne contours of the Pantages, and by the flamboyant absurdity of such thematically designed theaters as Mann's Chinese, the Egyptian, the baroque El Capitan, and other architectural treasures in and around Hollywood that have nothing directly to do with movies, yet are spiritual cousins. Among these are the Tail O' the Pup hotdog stand; the Capitol Records building, looking—deliberately, mind you—like a 14-story stack of 45s; and an assortment of mock Mayan-, Mission-, Moorish-, Moderne-, and made-up-style structures housing video stores, fast-food franchises, and offices.

Yet despite the grand movie houses, the famous names underfoot, and the impressively zany architecture, my friend still felt he'd missed the enchantment, the excitement . . . the movies.

I t's hard to fault the intrepid visitor for expecting a more dynamic, glitzier dream capital. Even seasoned locals, who understand that Hollywood is a state of mind more than a geographical location, can only just manage to intellectualize the concept, and still secretly hunger for evidence that all the magic and glamour come from an appropriately magical and glamorous place. But, except for the occasional gala premiere, you're not likely to see any movie stars in Hollywood. The workaday world of filmmaking and the off-duty hangouts of the movie crowd have largely moved elsewhere. There is only one movie studio—Paramount—still operating within Hollywood's city limits. Universal Studios and the Burbank Studios are both in the San Fernando Valley, across the hills to the north, as are most network-television studios. And, although firmly rooted in the spirit of Hollywood, Disneyland is a world away in Anaheim.

Even a cursory glance at Hollywood's history raises serious doubts that the town was ever as glamorous as we insist it no longer is, and pinning down exactly when its star-studded golden era was is a slippery business. Most people point to the 1930s and 1940s, and the images evoked by those days are irresistible: tan, handsome leading men posed, grinning, with one foot on the running board of a snazzy convertible; heartbreakingly beautiful actresses clad in slinky silk gowns and mink, stepping from long black limousines into the pop of photographers' flash bulbs. Hollywood was an industry—an entire city—whose purpose was to entertain and that further dazzled us with its glittering style of life. The view from ground zero, naturally, was a bit different: long hours; the tedium of the filmmaking process; the rarity of achieving and maintaining a successful career, much less stardom; and, for those who did achieve it, the precarious tightrope walk balancing publicity and privacy. Both sides of the equation are well known and much documented. Indeed, for a place so enamored of its own appeal, Hollywood has never been shy about depicting itself in an unflattering light. Some of the most memorable films ever are rather grim portrayals of the movie business: *A Star is Born*, *Sunset Boulevard*, and, most recently, *The Player*. That there is a very seamy side to the movie business is very old news and is as much a part of the legend as are fame and fortune. Scandal is a long-running subplot in Hollywood's epic history and has often proved as much a box-office draw as a liability.

The trick to seeing Hollywood is knowing *how* to look at it, as well as where to look for it. The magic of movies is that reality, at least on film, can be made to look any way the filmmakers want it to look. The problem with visiting Hollywood is that your own field of vision isn't as selective as a movie camera's lens, and you're working without a script. It may be helpful to think of Hollywood the town as something of a relic, a symbol of past grandeur (both real and imagined), an open-air museum of artifacts and monuments, but hardly the whole story. Tennessee Williams said, "Ravaged radiance is even better than earnest maintenance," and, as regards Hollywood, I couldn't agree more. It helps a bit to visit in the evening, when the neon, theater marquees, and orchestrated lighting show off the extravagant buildings' shapes to advantage.

It may be that in order to fully experience Hollywood, you have to go outside it.

Only after we'd driven through the canyons, Beverly Hills, and Bel Air and were rounding the last corner of Sunset that leads to the Pacific Coast Highway and out to Malibu did my British visitor feel truly satisfied. "Yes, well," he said finally, "this is really much more like it, then," and seemed almost physically relieved to have found someplace that matched his expectations of luxurious living. And these are physically lovely places, fitting backdrops for a Hollywood lifestyle, and, in fact, where successful movie people live.

The variety of fun and fanciful buildings you'll see throughout Los Angeles reveals, I think, the essence of Hollywood. How else to explain the incongruous jumble of architectural styles sitting side by side in almost any neighborhood? A '50s futuristic house next door to a Queen Anne Victorian, a Craftsman bungalow abutting a French château, a redbrick Georgian across the street from a tile-roof Spanish revival—all on the same block—can be viewed as an extrapolation of a movie-studio back lot, on which a New York street is steps from a Parisian sidewalk café, and both are just a stone's throw from an antebellum plantation house.

If it's celebrity sightings you want, you'll have to take your chances. Many Angelenos live long, happy, and productive lives without ever personally sighting a movie star, but, for the visitor, not seeing one can be a bigger letdown than a rainy week at the beach. Here are a few things you can do to greatly improve the odds of seeing somebody famous: Book a table (weeks in advance) at Spago, Wolfgang Puck's star-studded hot spot off Sunset; dine at Musso & Franks, Hollywood's oldest reataurant and a favorite celebrity hangout for more than 60 years; wander Rodeo Drive on a sunny afternon, paying close attention to Fred Hayman of Beverly Hills and the Alaia Chez Gallery, known for their high-profile clientele; stroll Melrose Avenue between La Brea and Fairfax during the dinner hour; stop by Tower Records on Sunset, especially if some blockbuster CD has just been released.

Although it's almost become an amusement-park thrill ride, Universal Studio's tour does give a good in-person approximation of the excitement you get from the movies, and, in the bargain, offers a fun look behind the scenes of filmmaking. Universal Studios aside, the business of Hollywood is making movies and getting people into theaters, not drumming up tourism for the town where it all started. And, besides, there are limits to what even movie magicians can do, especially in broad daylight. Given that the original appeal of Hollywood to moviemakers was the perpetual sunshine that allowed them to shoot outdoors on virtually any day of the year (and thereby make more movies and, therefore, more money) and the ready access to dozens of different landscapes, it is no small irony that over the years the most compelling reason to shoot a movie in Hollywood has become the ready access to soundstages in which the world (this one and others) can be recreated and the weather made to perform on cue. Hollywood has never hesitated to substitute reality with a more convenient or photogenic stand-in. This is an industry whose stock-in-trade is sleight of hand. Along with romance, car chases, and happy endings.

Whatever Hollywood is or isn't, I like the place just the way it is: flawed, scarred, energetic, and full of mysteries and contradictions. Living nearby and seeing it often haven't harmed my love of movies or taken any of the enchantment from the experience of sitting in a darkened theater and giving myself over to the doings on screen. After all, that's where to find the real Hollywood.

Idylling in San Diego

By Edie Jarolim

Edie Jarolim is a New York–born free-lance writer and editor who recently moved to Tucson, which is within easy driving distance of San Diego.

I've never been to Sea World; performing fish give me the willies. And during the two years I lived within striking distance of Balboa Park, I had to take visiting friends to the San Diego Zoo so many times I began having nightmares about koalas. But if I came to dislike various theme-park aspects of the city, I nevertheless loved San Diego. At first sight.

A typical easterner, I went out to San Diego in the late 1970s expecting to find a smaller version of Los Angeles. The freeways were there, along with a fair share of traffic congestion, but so was an oceanscape of surprisingly pristine beauty. The first drive I took from the University of California, where I was doing graduate research, knocked me for a loop: I rounded a curve on La Jolla Shores Drive to confront a coastline that could match any on the French Riviera.

I was also taken by the distinctiveness of the many shoreline communities. For one thing, the beaches tend to get funkier as you head south from the old-money enclave of La Jolla: Pacific Beach, with its Crystal Pier, looks like an aging Victorian resort taken over by teenagers, while transients and surfers share the turf at Ocean Beach. To the north, Del Mar has a strip of shops that rival those of Rodeo Drive, while Carlsbad and Oceanside show the democratizing influence of nearby Camp Pendleton.

Unlike Los Angeles, San Diego is still strongly defined by its relationship to the ocean—to some degree by default. During the latter half of the 19th century, the town was banking on a rail link to the East. A building boom in the 1880s was largely based on the assumption that San Diego would become the western terminus of the Santa Fe Railroad line; it hoped in this way to compete with Los Angeles, which was already connected by rail to San Francisco and thus to the national railroad network. The link was completed in 1885 but it proved unsuccessful for a variety of reasons, including the placement of the line through Temecula Canyon, where 30 miles of track were washed out repeatedly in winter rainstorms. The Santa Fe soon moved its West Coast offices to San Bernardino and Los Angeles, and to this day there is no direct rail service from San Diego to the eastern part of the United States.

Instead, San Diego's future was sealed in 1908, when President Theodore Roosevelt's Great White Fleet stopped here on a world tour to demonstrate U.S. naval strength. The Navy, impressed during that visit by the city's excellent harbor and temperate climate, decided to build a destroyer base on San Diego Bay in the 1920s; the newly developing aircraft industry soon followed (Charles Lindbergh's plane *Spirit of St. Louis* was built here). Over the years San Diego's economy became largely dependent on the military and its attendant enterprises, which provided jobs as well as a demand for local goods and services by those stationed here.

San Diego's character—conservative where Los Angeles's is cutting edge—was formed in large part by the presence of its military installations, which now occupy more than 165,000 acres of land in the area. And the city conducts most of its financial business in a single neighborhood, the district fronting San Diego Bay, in this way resembling New York more than its economic rival up the coast. San Diego has set some of its most prestigious scientific facilities on the water—Scripps Institute of Oceanography, naturally, but also Salk Institute. Jonas Salk didn't need the Pacific marine environment for his research, but his regular morning runs along Torrey Pines Beach no doubt cleared his head.

San Diego also has the ocean to thank for its near-perfect weather. A high-pressure system from the north Pacific is responsible for the city's sunshine and dry air; moderating breezes off the sea (caused by the water warming and cooling more slowly than the land) keep the summers relatively cool and the winters warm, and help clear the air of pollution. In the late spring and early summer the difference between the earth and water temperatures generates coastal fogs. This phenomenon was another of San Diego's delightful surprises: I never tired of watching the mist roll in at night, wonderfully romantic, as thick as any I'd ever seen in London and easier to enjoy in the balmy air.

If I loved San Diego from the start, I had a hard time believing in its existence. It was difficult to imagine that a functioning American city could be so attractive, that people lived and worked in such a place every day. Although I'd never considered myself a Puritan, I quickly came to realize that I'd always assumed work and leisure environments had to be separate, that one was supposed to toil in unpleasant surroundings in order to earn the time spent in idyllic settings.

I found that I could get used to working on sunny days, but that it was impossible to remain unaffected by the city's physical presence. Rampant nature conspires in a variety of ways to force you to let your guard down here. In northern East Coast cities, plants are generally orderly and prim: shrubs trimmed, roses demurely draped around railings, tulips in proper rows, the famed cherry blossoms of Washington, DC, profuse in neat columns. In San Diego, the flora, whimsical at best, sometimes border on obscenity. The ubiquitous palms come in comedic pairs: Short, squat trees that look like overgrown pineapples play Mutt to the Jeff of the tall, skinny variety. The aptly named bottle-brush bushes vie for attention with bright red flame trees, beaky orange birds of paradise, and rich purple bougainvillea spilling out over lush green lawns. Only in Hawaii had I previously encountered anthurium, a waxy red plant with a protruding white center that seems to be sticking its tongue out at you. "We're still on the mainland," I felt like telling them all on some days. "Behave yourselves."

Ironically, it was the Victorians who were largely responsible for this indecorous natural profusion. Difficult as it is to imagine now, it's the sparse brown vegetation of San Diego's undeveloped mesas that accurately reflects the climate of the region, technically a semiarid steppe. When Spanish explorer Juan Rodríguez Cabrillo sailed into San Diego Bay in 1542, looking for a shortcut to China, he and his crew encountered a barren, desolate landscape that did not inspire them to settle here, or even stop for very long.

I t wasn't until the late 19th century, when the Mediterranean in general and Italy in particular were all the rage among wealthy residents, that the vegetation now considered characteristic of Southern California was introduced to San Diego. In 1889, money raised by the Ladies Annex to the Chamber of Commerce was used to plant trees in Balboa Park, and between 1892 and 1903 a wide variety of exotic foliage was brought into the city: eucalyptus, cork oak, and rubber trees, to name a few. As homeowners in the area can attest, most of the landscaped local vegetation couldn't survive if it were not watered regularly.

No doubt both the natural setting and the relentlessly fine weather help contribute to the clash of cultures that exists here. The conservative traditionalism of the military presence in town is posed against the liberal hedonism of visiting sunseekers as well as a large local student population. Nude bathing is popular at Black's Beach in La Jolla, a spot that's reasonably private because it's fairly inaccessible: You have to hike down steep cliffs in order to get to the water. Rumor has it that every year a few Navy men are killed when they lose their footing on the cliffs, so intent are they at peering through their binoculars.

But I suspect it's the rare person of any political persuasion who can confront the Southern California attitude toward nudity with equanimity. I hadn't wanted to believe all the stereotypes, but the first time I went to a dinner party in town, the host asked the group if we wanted to adjourn to the hot tub after we ate. I hadn't brought my bathing suit, so I declined.

The next day, I consulted a local expert in matters of whirlpool etiquette. "What does one do?" I asked. "Undress in front of a group of relative strangers and jump into the water with them? Does one rip off one's clothes with abandon?

Fold them carefully afterward? Or go into another room and come out in the raw?" "All that's up to the individual," she answered. "Do whatever you feel comfortable with." "None of it," I asserted. "Where I come from, when people of different genders take their clothes off together they tend to have sex." "That's optional too," she said.

Nods to certain So-Cal conventions notwithstanding, San Diego has never come close to approaching the much-touted libertinism of Los Angeles. It has the porno theaters and sleazy clubs you'd expect in a liberty port, but little enter-tainment of a more sophisticated nature. Celebrities who came down from Hollywood in the 1920s and '30s sought out suites at the La Valencia Hotel and other chic La Jolla lo-cales for the privacy, not the nightlife; the gambling they did at Del Mar racetrack to the north was of the tony, gen-teel sort. Those who sought thrills—and booze during Prohibition—headed farther south to Mexico. Raymond Chandler, who spent most of his last 13 years in La Jolla and died there in 1959, wrote a friend that the town was "a nice place . . . for old people and their parents."

For all its conservatism, the one thing San Diego didn't conserve was its past—in some cases because there was little to save. When Father Junípero Serra ar-rived in 1769 to establish the first of the California mis-sions, he did not find the complex dwellings that characterized so many of the Native American settlements he had encountered in Mexico. Nor did his fellow Spaniards improve much upon the site during their stay; the town that the Mexicans took over in 1822 was rudimentary, consisting mostly of rough adobe huts. The mission church had been moved to a new site in 1774 and the original Spanish presid-io, abandoned in the 1830s, was in ruins by the next decade; some grass-covered mounds and a giant cross built in 1913 on Presidio Hill, incorporating the tiles of the original structure, are all that's left of it.

Though a romanticized version of the city during the Mexi-can period (1822–49), today's Old Town district gives a rough idea of San Diego's layout at that time, when some-what more impressive structures such as Casa Estudillo and the Bandini House were built. San Diego didn't really begin to flourish, however, until 1850, the year that Califor-nia became a state. At this point the dominant architectural influence came from the East Coast; their enthusiasm for becoming American caused San Diegans to reject their Spanish and Mexican roots as inappropriately "foreign." Thus the first brick structure in the state, the Whaley House (1856), was built in typical New England nautical style. Most of the original Old Town was destroyed by fire in 1872, and a good deal of what was left fell victim to the construction of I–5.

During the Victorian era (1880–1905), the site of the city's development moved south; entrepreneur Alonzo Horton may have miscalculated the success of the rail link to the East Coast but when he bought up a huge lot of land in 1867 for his "Addition," he knew the city's future lay on the harbor. It was in this area, now the city's financial district, that many of the neo-Gothic structures characteristic of the period were built. Perhaps it's perversely fitting that a number of the Victorian relics in downtown San Diego were removed in conjunction with the 15-block Horton Redevelopment Project, of which the huge Horton Plaza shopping complex is the center.

San Diego finally began to reject the East Coast architectural style at the turn of the century, and at the Panama–California Exposition of 1915 the city celebrated its Spanish roots—as well as a Moroccan and Italian past it never had—with a vengeance. The beautiful Spanish-style structures built for the occasion fit right into the Mediterranean landscape that had been cultivated in Balboa Park during the Victorian era; today these buildings house most of the city's museums. San Diego became even more thoroughly Hispanicized during the 1920s and '30s as Spanish Colonial–style homes became popular in new suburbs such as Mission Hills and Kensington, as well as in the beach communities that were developing. Downtown buildings began looking like Italian palaces and Moorish towers.

San Diego's landscape of ravines and hills is partly responsible for the city's sprawling development in the 20th century, and the popularization of the automobile in the 1930s helped ensure its continuing growth in an outward direction. The physical barriers have been overcome by an ever-expanding highway system—though not by a viable public transportation network—but the discrete, individual neighborhoods created by them remain, if their populations sometimes shift. For example, Kearny Mesa, formerly a middle-class suburban neighborhood, is now one of the many Southeast Asian communities in the city.

In some ways, as residents and visitors alike have long feared, San Diego is coming to look more like Los Angeles. Faceless developments are cropping up all over once-deserted canyons and mesas, and the huge, castlelike Mormon temple rising along I–5 north of La Jolla wouldn't look out of place in Disneyland. But in the years since I lived there, San Diego has also become more like a city—that is, what easterners know to be the city in its divinely ordained form.

As recently as 10 years ago, virtually no one went downtown unless required to. It was a desolate place after dark, and people who worked there during the day never stayed around in the evening to play. Gentrification of sorts began in the mid-1970s, as the low rents attracted artists and real-estate speculators. At about the same time the city designated the formerly rough Stingaree neighborhood as the Gaslamp Quarter, but revitalization, in the form of street-level shops and art galleries, didn't really take until Horton Plaza was completed in 1985, and for many years the newly installed gaslights illuminated only the homeless.

The poor and disenfranchised are still here—indeed, many lost their homes to various redevelopment projects—but now the staff at the recently renovated historic U.S. Grant Hotel offers to accompany its guests across the street to Horton Plaza at night so they won't be bothered by vagrants. For the first time there's a concentration of good restaurants, and a serious art and theater scene is developing in the district, too. The area is also a terminus for the San Diego Trolley. This inexpensive transportation link to Mexico has, among other things, allowed Mexican artists to bring their works to a wider market, and fostered a cultural as well as touristic exchange with Tijuana, which has cleaned up its own act considerably in recent years. I like the infusion of life into downtown San Diego, and I even like Horton Plaza, which, with its odd angles and colorful banners, looks like it was designed by Alice in Wonderland's Red Queen. But maybe I miss that spot of unadulterated blight that once helped me to believe in San Diego's reality.

Reality seems to be setting in on a large scale these days. San Diego's bad neighborhoods still don't look like slums as I know them, but gang-related crime is on the increase in the southeast part of the city. In 1992 a sewage spill closed a number of southern beaches, and the problem is likely to grow, as neither San Diego nor Tijuana has enacted any large-scale programs for effective waste disposal. Friends tell me that even the weather is changing for the worse, a fact they attribute to global warming.

Would I move back to San Diego? In a minute. Like many temporary residents, I left the city vowing to return; unlike many, I've never managed to do more than visit. I used to think that if I had the chance I'd live in Hillcrest, a close-knit inland community with lots of ethnic restaurants and theaters that show foreign films, but I've come to realize that would only be transplanting my East Coast life into the sun. Now I think I'll wait until I'm rich and can afford to move to La Jolla; no doubt I'll be old enough by then to fit in, so I'll fully enjoy that suite in the La Valencia Hotel overlooking the cove.

3 The North Coast

By Dan Spitzer

Updated and revised by Pam Hegarty

Within the nearly 400 miles of California coastline between the San Francisco Bay and the Oregon border are some of the most beautiful and rugged landscapes in America. Here in the aptly named Redwood Empire are primeval forests of the world's tallest trees, and the nearby shoreline holds a wealth of secluded coves and beaches from which you may well see gray whales migrating, seals sunning, and hawks soaring. The area is also rich in human history, having been the successive domain of Native American Miwoks and Pomos, Russian traders, Hispanic settlers, and more contemporary fishing folk and lumberjacks, all of whom have left legacies that can be seen today. For those in search of untamed natural beauty, great fishing, abundant wildlife, and elegant country inns, the vast panorama of the North Coast is a bit of heaven.

This region is sparsely populated, with only 10 towns of more than 700 inhabitants. Traditionally, residents have made their living from fishing and timber. But today these industries are depressed. Tourism, however, is doing well. Many fine restaurants have been founded to feed, and Victorian mansions restored to lodge, the increasing number of visitors.

Getting Around

By Plane **American Eagle,** linked with American Airlines (tel. 800/433–7300), has daily service to Eureka–Arcata from San Francisco with a plane change in San Jose. **United Express** (tel. 800/241-6522) offers regular nonstop flights from San Francisco to Eureka–Arcata. This is the fastest and most direct way to reach the redwood country. **Hertz** (tel. 800/654–3131) rents cars at the Eureka–Arcata airport.

By Car If Mendocino is your northernmost destination, the most scenic drive from San Francisco is via Highway 1, but with its twists and turns, it's slow going, and you should allow at least a full day to get there. Those who wish to explore Point Reyes National Seashore en route might consider an overnight stay at Inverness or another town along the way. You can return directly to San Francisco in about 3½ hours from Mendocino by taking Highway 1 south to Highway 128, which cuts inland and passes through picturesque farm and forest lands. At Cloverdale, Highway 128 intersects with U.S. 101, which continues south to San Francisco.

If Eureka or a point near the Oregon border is your destination, the quickest way from San Francisco is via U.S. 101. This takes a good six to seven hours if you drive straight through. Those with the time and inclination should opt for the more scenic but much slower Highway 1, which ultimately intersects with U.S. 101 at Legett. It would be backbreaking to cover the latter route in less than two days.

Although there are excellent services along Highway 1 and U.S. 101, gas stations and mechanics are few and far between on the smaller roads.

By Bicycle For the hardy rider who wishes to take in the full beauty of the North Coast by mountain bike, there are a number of rental services in San Francisco and the major North Coast towns. Some rental shops on the coast are **Point Reyes Pro-Cyclery** (Hwy. 1, Point Reyes Station, tel. 415/663–1046), **Catch-a-Canoe and Bicycles Too** (Stanford Inn by the Sea, Mendocino, tel.

707/937–5615), and **Mendocino Cyclery** (45040 Main St., Mendocino, tel. 707/937–4000). If you wish to go with a group, call **Backroads Bicycle Touring** (tel. 800/245–3874). There are plenty of campsites for long-distance bikers to stay at along the coast.

Important Addresses and Numbers

An excellent source of information on the North Coast is the **Redwood Empire Association.** Its San Francisco office is filled with brochures, and the staff is knowledgeable. For $2, the association will send you its visitor's guide to the region. Write, or stop at the office (785 Market St., 15th floor, San Francisco, CA 94103, tel. 415/543–8334; open weekdays 9–5).

For **emergency services** on the North Coast, dial 911.

Exploring

Exploring the Northern California coast is easiest in a car. Highway 1 is a beautiful, if sometimes slow and nerve-racking, drive. You'll want to stop frequently to appreciate the views, and there are many portions of the highway along which you won't drive faster than 30–40 mph. Even if you don't have much time, you can plan a fine trip, but be realistic and don't plan to drive too far in one day (*see* Getting Around, above).

We've arranged the exploring section for a trip from San Francisco heading north. The first section follows Highway 1 north past Fort Bragg to its intersection with U.S. 101. The second section follows U.S. 101 through the Redwood Empire.

The North Coast via Highway 1

Numbers in the margin correspond to points of interest on the North Coast maps.

To reach Highway 1 heading north from San Francisco, cross the Golden Gate Bridge and proceed north on U.S. 101 to the Stinson Beach/Route 1 exit. Follow Highway 1 north, and as it
❶ winds uphill, you will see a turnoff for **Muir Woods.**

Muir Woods National Monument and the adjoining Mt. Tamalpais State Park are described (as day trips) in Chapter 6, Excursions from San Francisco. Past this turnoff, the town
❷ of **Stinson Beach** has the most expansive sands (4,500 feet) in Marin County. Along Bolinas Lagoon, you will find the
❸ **Audubon Canyon Ranch,** a 1,000-acre wildlife sanctuary. In the spring, the public is invited to take to the trails to see great blue heron and great egret tree nestings. There is a small museum with displays on the geology and natural history of the region, a natural history bookstore, and a picnic area. *Tel. 415/ 868–9244. Donation requested. Open weekends and holidays mid–March—mid–July.*

At the northern edge of Bolinas Lagoon, a couple of miles beyond the Audubon Canyon Ranch, take the unmarked road running west from Highway 1, which leads to the sleepy town of **Bolinas.** Some residents of Bolinas are so wary of tourism that whenever the state tries to post signs, they tear them down.
❹ Birders should head down Mesa Road to the **Point Reyes Bird Observatory,** a sanctuary harboring nearly 225 species of bird

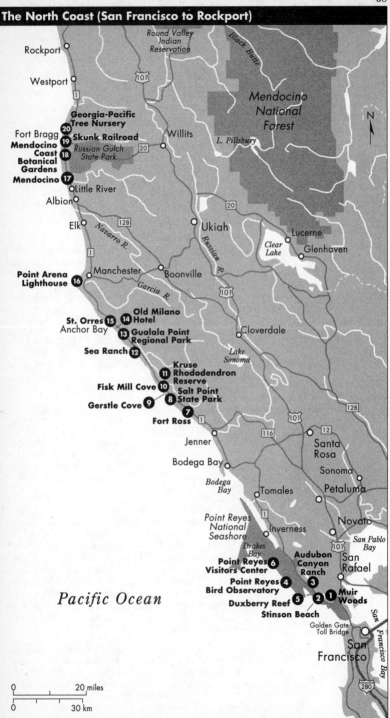

Rockport

Westport

101

Round Valley
Indian
Reservation

Black Butte

**Mendocino
National
Forest**

Georgia-Pacific
Tree Nursery

20 Skunk Railroad

19

Fort Bragg

Mendocino
Coast
Botanical
Gardens

18

Willits

L. Pillsbury

Russian Gulch
State Park

20

N

Mendocino 17

Little River

Albion

Elk

128

Ukiah

Clear
Lake

Lucerne

Glenhaven

Navarro R.

1

Manchester

Boonville

Garcia R.

Point Arena
Lighthouse 16

101

St. Orres 15

14 Old Milano
Hotel

Anchor Bay

13 Gualala Point
Regional Park

Cloverdale

Sea Ranch 12

11 Kruse
Rhododendron
Reserve

Lake
Sonoma

Fisk Mill Cove 10

Salt Point
State Park

8

Gerstle Cove 9

Fort Ross 7

1

128

Jenner

116

101

12

Santa
Rosa

Bodega Bay

Bodega
Bay

Tomales

Sonoma

Petaluma

Point Reyes
National
Seashore

Drakes
Bay

Inverness

1

Novato

San Pablo
Bay

San
Rafael

Point Reyes
Visitors Center

6

Audubon
Canyon
Ranch

101

Point Reyes
Bird Observatory

4

3

Muir
Woods

Duxberry Reef

5

2 1

Stinson Beach

Pacific Ocean

Golden Gate
Toll Bridge

San
Francisco

San
Francisco Bay

San

280

0   20 miles

0   30 km

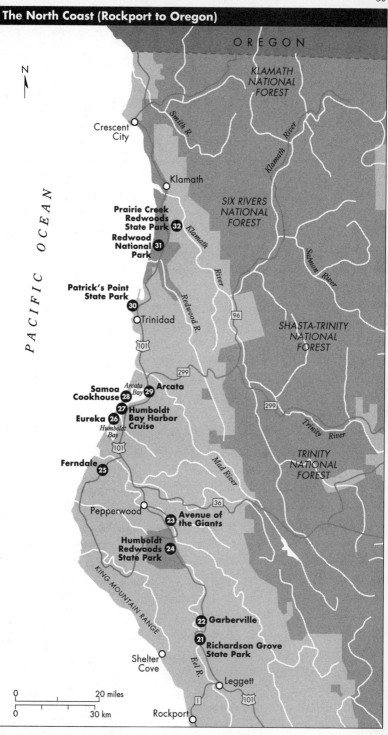

The North Coast (Rockport to Oregon)

OREGON

KLAMATH
NATIONAL
FOREST

Crescent
City

Smith R.

Klamath
River

Klamath

SIX RIVERS
NATIONAL
FOREST

Salmon River

Prairie Creek
Redwoods
State Park **32**
Redwood
National **31**
Park

Klamath River

96

Redwood R.

PACIFIC OCEAN

Patrick's Point
State Park
30
Trinidad

SHASTA-TRINITY
NATIONAL
FOREST

101

299

Samoa **28** Arcata Bay **29** Arcata
Cookhouse
27 Humboldt
Bay Harbor
Eureka **26** Cruise
Humboldt
Bay

299

Trinity River

Ferndale
25

101

Mad River

TRINITY
NATIONAL
FOREST

Pepperwood

36

23 Avenue of
the Giants

Humboldt
Redwoods **24**
State Park

KING MOUNTAIN RANGE

22 Garberville

21 Richardson Grove
State Park

Shelter
Cove

Eel R.

Leggett

0   20 miles
0   30 km

1

101

Rockport

life. *Tel. 415/868–0655. Admission free. Banding Apr. 1–Nov., daily, Dec. 1–Mar. 31, weekends and Wed. Visitor center open daily year round.*

On the way back to Bolinas, go right on Overlook Drive and ❺ right again on Elm Avenue until you come to **Duxberry Reef**, known for its fine tide pools.

Returning to Highway 1, you will pass pastoral horse farms. About ⅓-mile past Olema, look for a sign marking the turnoff ❻ for **Point Reyes National Seashore's Bear Valley Visitors Center** where there are exhibits of park wildlife, and helpful rangers who can advise you about beaches, visits to the lighthouse for whale watching (the season for gray-whale migration is mid-December through March), hiking trails, and camping. (Camping, for backpackers only, is free; reservations should be made through the visitors center.) No matter what your interests, the beauty of this wilderness is worth your time. A reconstructed Miwok Indian Village is a short walk from the visitors center. It provides insight into the daily lives of the first human inhabitants of this region. The lighthouse is a 30- to 40-minute drive from the visitors center, across rolling hills that resemble Scottish heath. On busy weekends during the season, parking near the lighthouse may be difficult. If you don't care to walk down—and then back up—the hundreds of steps from the clifftops to the lighthouse below, and choose to skip the descent altogether, console yourself with the fact that you can see whales from the cliffs, though most people find the lighthouse view worth the effort. *Tel. 415/663–1092. Admission free. Visitor Center open weekdays 9–5, weekends 8–5.*

If you choose to stay overnight in this area, there are good country inns and decent restaurants in and around the towns of **Inverness,** where the architecture and cuisine reflect the influence of the once-sizable Czech population, and in **Point Reyes Station.**

The Russian River empties into the Pacific at the fishing town of **Jenner.** If you are lucky, you may spot seals sunning themselves off the banks of the estuary. Travelers who wish to move on to the Wine Country from here can take Highway 116 east from Jenner.

What is perhaps the most dramatic stretch of North Coast shoreline is off Highway 1 between Jenner and Gualala. The road is one long series of steep switchbacks after another, so take your time, relax, and make frequent stops to enjoy the unparalleled beauty of this wild coast.

About 12 miles north of Jenner is a must-see for history buffs. Originally built in 1812, Russia's major fur-trading outpost in ❼ California, **Fort Ross,** has been painstakingly reconstructed by the state park service. The Russians brought Aleut sea-otter hunters down from their Alaskan bailiwicks to hunt pelts for the czar. In 1841, with the area depleted of seal and otter, the Russians sold their post to John Sutter, later of Gold Rush fame. After a local Anglo rebellion against the Mexicans, the land fell under U.S. domain, becoming part of the state of California in 1850. At Fort Ross, you will find a restored Russian Orthodox chapel, a redwood stockade, officers' barracks, a blockhouse, and an excellent museum. *Fort Ross State Historical Park, tel. 707/847–3286. Day use: $5. Open daily 10–4:30;*

closed Thanksgiving, Dec. 25, and Jan. 1. No dogs allowed past parking lot.

8 About 19 miles north of Jenner, the 6,000-acre **Salt Point State Park** offers a glimpse of nature virtually untouched by humans.
9 Begin at the park's **Gerstle Cove,** where you'll probably catch sight of seals sunning themselves on the beach's rocks, and deer roaming in the meadowlands. The unusual formations in the sandstone are called "tafoni," and are the product of hundreds of years of erosion. Next take the *very* short drive to Salt
10 Point's **Fisk Mill Cove,** where a five-minute walk following the trail uphill brings you to a bench from which there is a dramatic overview of Sentinel Rock and the pounding surf below. Part of the wonder of this spot is that it's all less than a mile off Highway 1. *Tel. 707/847–3221. Day use: $5, $4 for senior citizens; camping: $14 peak season; $12 off-season, $2 discount for senior citizens. Open daily sunrise to sunset.*

About 200 yards beyond Fisk Mill Cove, look for the sign to
11 **Kruse Rhododendron Reserve.** If you're around here in May, take this turnoff to see the towering pink flowers in this 317-acre reserve. *Admission free. Open daily.*

12 **Sea Ranch** is a development of pricey second homes, on 5,000 acres overlooking the Pacific about 10 miles south of Gualala. There was a great outcry by conservationists when this development was announced, and much controversy ensued. To appease the critics, Sea Ranch built publicly accessible trails down to the beaches. Even in the eyes of some militant environmentalists, architect Charles Moore's housing here is reasonably congruent with the surroundings; others find the weathered-wood buildings beautiful.

13 An excellent whale-watching spot is **Gualala Point Regional Park** (tel. 707/785–2377), where there is also picnicking and camping ($12 year-round). The park is right off Highway 1 and is well marked. Just north of the town of Gualala on Highway 1
14 are two inns worth a visit or a stay. The **Old Milano Hotel,** listed in the National Registry of Historic Places, is an elegant 1905
15 country inn overlooking Castle Rock. **St. Orres,** with its Russian-style turrets, is also a premier bed-and-breakfast inn and has one of the best restaurants on the North Coast. All along this stretch north to Mendocino are fine B&Bs and small hotels, perched in and around the coastal cliffs of tiny former lumber ports such as Elk, Albion, and Little River.

16 For a dramatic view of the surf, take the turnoff north of the fishing village of Point Arena to the **Point Arena Lighthouse** (tel. 707/882–2777). First constructed in 1870, the lighthouse was destroyed by the 1906 earthquake that also devastated San Francisco. Rebuilt in 1907, it towers 115 feet from its base, 50 feet above the sea. *Admission $2 adults; 50¢ children under 12. Tours daily 11–2:30, extended hours in summer and on holiday weekends.*

17 **Mendocino** is the tourism heartbeat on the north coast and has become a mecca for artists and visitors alike. The appeal is obvious: sweeping ocean views and a stately Victorian flavor, best exemplified by the gingerbread-like **MacCallum House** (45020 Albion St.) and the **Mendocino Hotel** (45080 Main St.). The town is most easily—and best—seen on foot, and there are numerous art galleries to peruse while walking around. The **Mendocino Art Center** (45200 Little Lake St., tel. 707/937–

5818) has exhibits, art classes, concerts, and a theater. The **Kelley House Museum** (45007 Albion St., tel. 707/937–5791, admission $1, open Fri.–Mon. 1–4) is a refurbished 1861 structure displaying historical photographs of Mendocino's logging days, antique cameras, Victorian-era clothing, furniture, and artifacts. Also on Albion Street is the **Chinese Joss Temple,** dating to 1871. Another restored structure, the **Ford House,** built in 1854, is on Main Street and serves as the visitors center for **Mendocino Headlands State Park** (tel. 707/937–5397, open winter, daily 11–4; summer, daily 10–5). The park itself consists of the cliffs that border the town; access is free.

Off Highway 1, between Mendocino and Fort Bragg, are the **18** **Mendocino Coast Botanical Gardens.** Started as a private preserve in 1962, the Mendocino Coast Park District acquired 17 acres of the gardens in 1982, and the Coastal Conservancy extended the gardens by another 30 acres in 1991. Along 2 miles of coastal trails, with ocean views and observation points for whale-watching, are a splendid array of flowers, with the rhododendron season at its peak from April to June, and perennials in bloom from May to September. Fuchsias, heather, and azaleas are resplendent here. This is a fine place to stop for a picnic. *Tel. 707/964–4352. Admission: $5 adults, $4 senior citizens, $3 children 13–17. Open Apr.–Oct., daily 9–5, Nov.–Mar. 9–4; closed Thanksgiving, Dec. 25, and Jan. 1.*

Fort Bragg is the commercial center of Mendocino County. Unless you are here on business, there is little reason to stay in this nondescript town. It is, however, the headquarters of the **19** famous and popular **Skunk Railroad,** on which you can take scenic half- or full-day tours through redwood forests inaccessible by automobile. A remnant of the region's logging days, the Skunk Railroad line dates from 1885, and travels a route from Fort Bragg on the coast to the town of Willits, 40 miles inland. A fume-spewing, self-propelled train car that shuttled passengers along the railroad got nicknamed the Skunk Train, and the entire line has been called that ever since. Excursions are now given on historic trains and replicas of the Skunk Train motorcar more aromatic than the original. In summer you have a choice of going part way to the Skunk's North spur, a three-hour round trip, or making the full 7½-hour journey to Willits and back. *California Western Railroad Inc., Fort Bragg, tel. 707/964–6371. Fort Bragg-Willits: Departs daily 9:20 AM. Admission: $23 adults, $11 children. Fort Bragg-North spur: second Sat. in June–third Sat. in Sept., departs daily 9:20 AM and 1:35 PM. Sept. 23–Dec. 4, Dec. 22–31, and March 25–June 7, departs daily 10 AM and 2 PM. Dec. 7–21 and Feb. 2–March 17, departs Sat. and Sun. 10 AM and 2 PM. Admission: $18.50 adults; $9 children.*

20 The **Georgia-Pacific Tree Nursery** (Main St. at Walnut St., tel. 707/964–5651) has a visitors center, picnic grounds, and a self-guiding nature trail (open daily 8–4). Those who like fishing can charter boats out of Noyo Harbor, at the southern end of town (*see* Sports, below).

North on Highway 1 from Fort Bragg, past the coastal mill town of **Westport,** the road cuts inland around the **King Range,** a stretch of mountain so rugged that it made constructing the intended major highway through it impossible. Highway 1 joins the larger U.S. 101 at the town of Legett and continues north into the redwood country of Humboldt and Del Norte counties.

The Redwood Empire

㉑ **Richardson Grove State Park,** north of Leggett, along U.S. 101, marks your first encounter with the truly giant redwoods, but there are even more magnificent stands farther north. A few

㉒ miles below **Garberville,** perched along Eel River, is an elegant Tudor resort, the **Benbow Inn.** Even if you are not staying here, stop in for a drink or meal and a look at the architecture and gardens.

㉓ For an unforgettable treat, take the turnoff for the **Avenue of the Giants** just north of Garberville. Along this stretch of two-lane blacktop you will find yourself enveloped by some of the tallest trees on the planet, the coastal redwoods. This road cuts

㉔ through part of the **Humboldt Redwoods State Park,** 51,222 acres of redwoods and waterways, and follows the south fork of the turquoise-colored Eel River. The visitors center near Weott (tel. 707/946–2311) is open in the spring and summer, and can provide information on the region's recreational opportunities, and flora and fauna. **Founders Grove** contains some of the tallest trees in the park. What was its tallest, at 362 feet, fell in 1991.

㉕ Detour 5 miles west of U.S. 101 from Fortuna to **Ferndale.** This stately town maintains some of the most sumptuous Victorian homes in California, many of them built by 19th-century timber barons and Scandinavian dairy farmers. The queen of them all is the **Gingerbread Mansion** (400 Berding St.), once a hospital and now refurbished as a bed-and-breakfast inn. Numerous shops carry a local map for self-guided tours of this lovingly preserved town.

The **Ferndale Museum** has a storehouse of antiques from the turn of the century. *515 Shaw Ave., tel. 707/786–4466. Admission: $1 adults, 50¢ children 6–16. Open Oct. 1–June 1, Wed.–Sat. 11–4, Sun. 1–4, also Tues. 11–4 in summer.*

㉖ With 25,000 inhabitants, **Eureka** ranks as the North Coast's largest city. It has gone through cycles of boom and bust, first with mining and later with timber and fishing. There are nearly 100 elegant Victorian buildings here, many of them well preserved or refurbished. The most splendid is the **Carson Mansion** (at M and 2nd Sts.), built in 1885 by the Newsom brothers for timber baron William Carson. Across the street is another Newsom extravaganza popularly known as **The Pink Lady.** For proof that contemporary architects still have the skills to design lovely Victoriana, have a look at the **Carter House** B&B inn (3rd and L Sts.) and keep in mind that it was built 10—not 100—years ago. The **Chamber of Commerce** can provide maps of the town and information on how to join organized tours. *2112 Broadway, tel. 707/442–3738. Open weekdays 9–5, also Sat. 10–5 and Sun. 11–3 in summer.*

Old Town Eureka is one of the most outstanding Victorian-era commercial districts in California, with buildings dating from the 1860s to 1915. The **Clarke Museum** has an extraordinary collection of northwestern California Native American basketry and contains artifacts from Eureka's Victorian, logging, and maritime heritage. *240 E. St., tel. 707/443–1947. Donations accepted. Open Tues.–Sat. noon–4 and July 4. Closed other major holidays.*

At the south end of Eureka stands **Fort Humboldt,** which guarded settlers against the Indians, and is now a state historic park. Ulysses S. Grant was posted here in 1854. On the fort's grounds are re-creations of the logging industry's early days, including a logging museum, some ancient steam engines, and a logger's cabin. *3431 Fort Ave., tel. 707/445–6567. Open daily 9–5. Closed Thanksgiving, Dec. 25, and Jan. 1.*

㉗ To explore the waters around Eureka, take a **Humboldt Bay Harbor Cruise.** You can observe some of the region's birdlife while sailing past fishing boats, oyster beds, and decaying timber mills. *The pier at C St., tel. 707/444–9440. Fare: $8.50 adults, $6.50 children 12–17, $5 children 6–11. Departs May–Sept., daily 1, 2:30, and 4 PM; Tues.–Sat.,5:30 PM cocktail cruise, fare: $5.50 adults; 7 PM cruise, fare: $8.50 adults.*

㉘ Across the bridge in Samoa is the **Samoa Cookhouse** (tel. 707/442–1659), an example from about the 1860s of the cookhouses that once stood in every lumber and mill town. There is a museum displaying antique culinary artifacts, and breakfast, lunch, and dinner are served family style at long wooden tables. (*See* Dining, below.)

㉙ Just north of Eureka is the pleasant college town of **Arcata,** home of Humboldt State University. One of the few California burgs that retain a town square, Arcata also has some restored Victorian buildings. For a self-guided tour, pick up a map from the **Chamber of Commerce.** *1062 G St., tel. 707/822–3619. Open year-round, Mon.–Fri. 9–5.*

After taking the turnoff for the town of **Trinidad,** follow the road a mile to one of the most splendid harbors on the West Coast. First visited by a Portuguese expedition in 1595, the waters here are now sailed by fishing boats trolling for salmon. Picturesque Trinidad Bay's harbor cove and rock formations look both raw and tranquil.

㉚ Twenty-five miles north of Eureka is **Patrick's Point State Park.** Set on a forested plateau almost 200 feet above the surf, the park affords good whale- and sea lion–watching. There are also tide pools and a small museum with natural history exhibits. *Tel. 707/677–3570. Day use: $5 per car, $4 senior citizens; camping, $12, $10 senior citizens.*

Those continuing north will pass through the 113,200 acres of **㉛** **Redwood National Park.** After 115 years of intensive logging, this vast region of tall trees came under government protection in 1968. This was the California environmentalists' greatest victory over the timber industry. The park encompasses three state parks (Prairie Creek Redwoods, Del Norte Coast Redwoods, and Jedediah Smith Redwoods), and is more than 40 miles long. *Redwood National Park Headquarters, 1111 2nd St., Crescent City, CA 95531, tel. 707/464–6101.*

Campground reservations for all state parks are usually necessary in summer. For reservations, call MISTIX, tel. 619/452–1950 or 800/444–7275 in CA.

For detailed information about the Redwood National Park, stop at the **Redwood Information Center** in Orick (tel. 707/488–3461). There you can also get a free permit to drive up the steep, 17-mile road (the last 6 miles are gravel) to reach the **Tall Trees Grove,** where a 3-mile round-trip hiking trail leads to the world's first-, third- and fifth-tallest redwoods. Whale-watchers will find the deck of the visitors center an excellent observation point, and birders will enjoy the nearby **Freshwater Lagoon,** a popular layover for migrating waterfowl.

Within **Lady Bird Johnson Grove,** just off Bald Hill Road, is a short circular trail to resplendent redwoods. This section of the park was dedicated by, and named for, the former first lady. For additional spectacular scenery, take Davison Road along a stunning seascape to **Fern Canyon.** This gravel road winds through 4 miles of second-growth redwoods, then hugs a bluff 100 feet above the pounding Pacific surf for another 4 miles.

32 Just opposite the entrance to Redwood's **Prairie Creek Redwoods State Park**, extra space has been paved alongside the parklands, providing fine vantage points from which to observe an imposing herd of **Roosevelt elk** grazing in the adjoining meadow. **Revelation Trail** in Prairie Creek is fully accessible to the disabled.

The route through the redwoods and sea views will ultimately lead past the Klamath River, home of the famous king salmon, to Del Norte County's largest town, **Crescent City.**

Travelers continuing north to the Smith River near the Oregon border will find fine trout and salmon fishing as well as a profusion of flowers. Ninety percent of America's lily bulbs are grown in this area.

Shopping

Most shops and galleries are open Monday–Saturday, 10–6. Some are open on Sunday during the summer.

In the charming town of Inverness, **Shaker Shops West** (5 Inverness Way, tel. 415/669–7256) has an exceptional array of reproduction Shaker furniture and gift items. There is a turn-of-the-century sensibility to the fine works exhibited here; open Tuesday–Saturday 11–5, Sunday noon–5. In Point Reyes Station, **Gallery Route One** (in the Creamery Bldg., tel. 415/663–1347) is a nonprofit cooperative of 24 area artists in all media, open Friday through Monday from 11 to 5.

Mendocino has earned a reputation as the artistic center of the North Coast. So many fine artists exhibit their wares here, and the streets of this compact town are so easily walkable, that it won't be long before you see a gallery with something that strikes your fancy. You might start at the **Mendocino Art Center** (45200 Little Lake St., tel. 707/937–5818), where artists teach courses and display their creations.

The Victorian village of Ferndale, in the Redwood Empire, is a magnet for fine painters, potters, and carpenters. Just walk down Main Street and stop in to browse at any of the stores along its three principal blocks.

Eureka has several fine art shops and galleries in the district running from C to I streets between 2nd and 3rd streets. One of note is the **Old Town Art Gallery** (233 F St., tel. 707/445–2315). Another recommended gallery is the **Humboldt Cultural Center** (422 1st St., tel. 707/442–2611 or 707/442–0278).

Sports

The following sporting attractions and facilities are listed in a south-to-north order.

Bicycling *See* Getting Around, above.

Canoeing Among the many canoe liveries of the North Coast are **Stanford Inn by the Sea** (Mendocino, tel. 707/937–5615) and **Benbow Inn** (Garberville, tel. 707/923–2124).

Golf Among others, there are courses open to the public at **Bodega Harbour** (Bodega Bay, tel. 707/875–3538), **Little River Inn** (Little River, tel. 707/937–5667), **Benbow Inn** (nine holes, Garberville, tel. 707/923–2124), and **Eureka Golf Course** (tel. 707/443–4808).

Fishing For ocean fishing, there are plenty of outfits from which you can charter a boat with equipment provided. Among them are **Bodega Bay Sportfishing** (tel. 707/875–3344), **Noyo Fishing Center** (Fort Bragg, tel. 707/964–7609), **Lost Coast Landing** (Shelter Cove, tel. 707/986–7624, closed winter), and **Blue Pacific Charters** (Eureka, tel. 707/442–6682). You can fish for salmon and steelhead in the rivers. There's particularly good *abalone diving* around Jenner, Fort Ross, Point Arena, Westport, Shelter Cove, and Trinidad.

Horseback Riding There are numerous stables and resorts that offer guided rides on the North Coast. Among them are **Five Brooks Stables** (Point Reyes, tel. 415/663–1570), **Sea Horse Guest Ranch** (Bodega Bay, tel. 707/875–2721), **Benbow Inn** (Garberville, tel. 707/923–2124), and **Lazy L Ranch** (Arcata, tel. 707/822–6736).

River and Ocean Rafting **Eel River Delta Tours** (Eureka, tel. 707/786–4187) emphasizes wildlife and history.

Whale-Watching There are any number of excellent observation points along the coast for watching whales during their annual migration season from December through March. Another option is a **whale-watching cruise.** Some cruises run June–November to the Farallon Islands to watch the Blue and Humpback whale migration. Possibilities include: **Oceanic Society Expeditions** (San Francisco, tel. 415/474–3385), **New Sea Angler and Jaws** (Bodega Bay, tel. 707/875–3495).

Beaches

Although the waters of the Pacific along the North Coast are fine for seals, most humans find the temperatures downright arctic. But when it comes to spectacular cliffs and seascapes, the North Coast beaches are second to none. So pack a picnic and take in the pastoral beauty of the wild coast. Explore tide pools, watch for seals, or dive for abalone. Don't worry about crowds: On many of these beaches you will have the sands largely to yourself. Day use is usually $5 or $6 per car, depending on the area.

The following beaches are particularly recommended and are listed in a south-to-north order:

Muir Beach. Located just off Highway 1, 3 miles from Muir Woods. Free.
Duxbury Reef. Tide pools. From Bolinas, take Mesa Road off

Olema-Bolinas Road; make a left on Overlook Drive and a right on Elm Avenue to the beach parking lot.

Point Reyes National Seashore. Limantour Beach is one of the most beautiful of Point Reyes sands. Free.

Tomales Bay State Park. Take Sir Francis Drake Boulevard off Highway 1 toward Point Reyes National Seashore, then follow Pierce Point Road to the park.

Fort Ross State Park. About 9 miles north of Jenner.

Sea Ranch Public Access Trails and Beaches. Off Highway 1 south of Gualala.

Manchester State Beach. About 9 miles north of Point Arena.

Agate Beach. Tide pools. Set within Patrick's Point State Park off U.S. 101 about 25 miles north of Eureka.

Dining

By Bruce Colen

Since 1974, Bruce David Colen has been the restaurant and food critic for Los Angeles Magazine. *He has also written on food and travel for* Town & Country, Architectural Digest, Bon Appétit, Connoisseur, Signature, and Endless Vacations.

For years, the better dining establishments of the North Coast specialized in fresh salmon and trout. With the growth of the tourist industry, a surprising variety of fare ranging from Japanese to Continental cuisine is now being served at good restaurants charging reasonable prices. Unless otherwise noted, dress is informal. During the winter months, December to mid-March, tourism slackens on the North Coast; consequently, restaurant days and/or hours are often reduced. It is best to call ahead to check the schedule.

Highly recommended restaurants are indicated by a star ★.

Category	Cost*
Very Expensive	over $35
Expensive	$25–$35
Moderate	$15–$25
Inexpensive	under $15

**per person, not including tax, service, or drinks*

Albion
Moderate–Expensive
★

The Albion River Inn. From its perch overlooking the site where the Albion River enters the Pacific, the glassed-in dining room offers spectacular views. The seafood, pasta, and meat dishes here are better than average. *Hwy. 1, few mi south of Mendocino, tel. 707/937–1919. MC, V. No lunch.*

Arcata
Moderate

Crosswinds. Recently rebuilt after a major fire, the restaurant offers good Continental cuisine in a comfortable, relaxed setting. Classical musicians provide the entertainment. *10th and I Sts., tel. 707/826–2133. Reservations advised on weekends. MC, V.*

Ottavio. This comfortable, polished restaurant offers Continental cuisine, from Italian gnocchi to Greek spanakopita, a spinach and cheese pie. *686 F St., tel. 707/822–4021. MC, V. No lunch Sat.–Mon.*

Bodega Bay
Expensive

The Inn at the Tides. The town's top restaurant is best known for its outstanding fish and meat dishes. *Hwy. 1, tel. 707/875–2751. AE, MC, V. No lunch. Closed Mon. and Tues.*

Crescent City
Moderate

Harbor View Grotto. This glassed-in dining hall overlooking the Pacific prides itself on fresh fish. *155 Citizen's Dock Rd., tel. 707/464–3815. No credit cards.*

Elk
Expensive
★
Harbor House. Continental cuisine is served in this dining room of the Harbor House Hotel that overlooks a dramatic seascape. *Rte. 1, 6 mi south of junction with Hwy. 128, tel. 707/877–3203. Reservations advised. Limited seating for non–hotel guests. No credit cards.*

Eureka
Expensive
Carter House. Comfortable, satisfying meals are served in the dining parlor of the contemporary-but-Victorian-style Carter House. The accent is on California cuisine, featuring only the freshest ingredients. *3rd and L Sts., tel. 707/444–8062. Reservations required. AE, MC, V. No lunch. Closed Mon.–Wed.*

Moderate–Expensive
Eureka Inn–Rib Room. In the dining hall of this Tudor manor, grilled meats are the specialty. *7th and F Sts., tel. 707/442–6441. AE, D, DC, MC, V.*

★
Lazio's. Long the premier restaurant in Eureka, Lazio's is chiefly noted for its seafood. *1st and C Sts., tel. 707/443–9717. D, MC, V.*

Moderate
Cafe Waterfront. This restaurant serves decent seafood at reasonable prices. *102 F St., tel. 707/443–9190. MC, V.*

OH's Townhouse. This is a good choice for reasonably priced grilled meats. *206 W. 6th St., tel. 707/443–4652. MC, V. No lunch.*

Samurai Japanese Cuisine. Decent Japanese fare at a good price is served here. *621 5th St., tel. 707/442–6802. MC, V. No lunch. Closed Sun. and Mon.*

Inexpensive
Mazzotti's. The local favorite for pizza and calzone. *305 F St., tel. 707/445–1912. AE, D, MC, V.*

Samoa Cookhouse. A local lumberman's watering hole dating back to the early years of the century, this eatery serves three substantial meals family style at long wooden tables. Meat dishes dominate the menu. *Short drive from Eureka, across Samoa Bridge, off Rte. 101 on Samoa Rd., tel. 707/442–1659. AE, D, MC, V.*

Fort Bragg
Moderate
The Restaurant. The name may be generic, but this place isn't. California cuisine is served in a dining room that doubles as an art gallery and features a jazz brunch on Sunday. *418 N. Main St., tel. 707/964–9800. Reservations advised. MC, V. No lunch Sun.–Tues. Closed Wed.*

Garberville
Moderate–Expensive
★
Benbow Inn. If you want to dine in style around here, this is the place. The resort's wood-paneled dining room, with fireplace ablaze, offers Continental cuisine, and fresh salmon and trout dishes. *445 Lake Benbow Dr., off U.S. 101, 2 mi south of Garberville, tel. 707/923–2124. Reservations advised. MC, V. Closed winter.*

Inexpensive–Moderate
Woodrose Cafe. This unpretentious eatery, a local favorite, serves fresh healthy food, with fish, pasta, and vegetarian specials. *911 Redwood Dr., tel. 707/923–3191. No credit cards. No dinner.*

Gualala
Expensive
Old Milano. In the dining room of this house, listed in the National Registry of Historic Places, adequate country meals are served five nights a week. *Hwy. 1, tel. 707/884–3256. Reservations advised. MC, V. Closed Mon. and Tues.*

★
St. Orres. From the Russian-style turrets that top this hotel to the hand-hewed timbers and stained-glass windows, the look and atmosphere clue you into the fact that this place is something special. This is one of the best restaurants on the North

Coast, and features intriguing cuisine. You have a choice of five
entrées (meat or fish), plus soup and salad, at a fixed price.
*Hwy. 1, just north of Gualala, tel. 707/884–3335. Reservations
advised. No credit cards. No lunch. Closed Wed.*
Sea Ranch Lodge Restaurant. Seafood and homemade desserts
are served in a dining room overlooking the Pacific. *North of
Gualala at 60 Sea Walk Dr., off U.S. 101 at Sea Ranch, tel. 707/
785–2371. MC, V.*

Inverness
Moderate–Expensive
★

Manka's. Excellent Czech cooking is served in a wood-paneled
dining room warmed by a fireplace. This is the best of Inverness's Eastern European restaurants. *30 Calendar Way, tel.
415/669–1034. Reservations advised in summer. MC, V. No
lunch. Closed Tues. and Wed.*

Inexpensive

Grey Whale. If you're driving through the area, this place is a
good stop for pizza, salad, pastries, and coffee. *Sir Francis
Drake Blvd., in center of town, tel. 415/669–1244. MC, V.*

Jenner
*Moderate–
Expensive*

River's End. The Continental/Germanic fare is very good, featuring seafood, venison, and duck dishes. The brunches here
are exceptional. *Hwy. 1, north end of Jenner, tel. 707/865–
2484. MC, V. Closed Mon., Tues., and Nov. 30–Mar. 15.*

Little River
Expensive
★

Heritage House. In a dining room with plate-glass windows
overlooking the sea, hearty American meat and fish dishes are
served prix fixe for breakfast and dinner. *Hwy. 1, south of Little River, tel. 707/937–5885. Reservations advised. Jacket required. MC, V.*
Little River Restaurant. This tiny restaurant across from the
Little River Inn is attached to the post office and gas station.
Despite appearances, this modest-looking eatery serves some
of the best dinners in the Mendocino area, featuring steaks and
the freshest of seafood. *Hwy. 1, tel. 707/937–4945. Reservations advised. No credit cards. No lunch. Closed Tues.–Thurs.*

Mendocino
Moderate–Expensive
★

Cafe Beaujolais. All the rustic charm of peaceful, backwoods
Mendocino is here, with great country cooking to boot. Owner
Margaret Fox is a marvelous baker, so be sure to take home several packages of her irresistible *panforte*, made with almonds,
hazelnuts, walnuts, or macadamia nuts. This is the best place in
town for breakfast, and the tree house–like second-story deck
is a splendid retreat for a leisurely lunch. If you don't order the
delicious chicken-apple sausages, you'll never forgive yourself.
*961 Ukiah St., tel. 707/937–5614. Reservations required. No
credit cards. No dinner Mon.–Wed. Closed Jan. and Feb.*
MacCallum House Restaurant. Set within a charming, period
bed-and-breakfast inn, the redwood-paneled dining room offers a Continental menu and lovely homemade desserts. *45020
Albion St., tel. 707/937–5763. Reservations advised. No credit
cards. No lunch. Closed Mon. and Jan.–Mar.*
Mendocino Hotel. A 19th-century ambience has been re-created in this wood-paneled dining room fronted by a glassed-in
solarium. Fine fish dishes and the best wild-berry cobblers in
California are served here. *45080 Main St., tel. 707/937–0511.
AE, MC, V.*

Muir Beach
Moderate–Expensive
★

Pelican Inn. Basic and sturdy English fare—from fish and
chips to prime rib and Yorkshire pudding—is served here,
along a wide selection of imported beers and ales. The atmosphere is wonderful and convivial: a wood-paneled dining room
warmed by a great stone fireplace and a glass-encompassed solarium, ideal for sunny lunches. *Hwy. 1 at Muir Beach, tel. 415/*

383–6005. Reservations advised for 6 or more. MC, V. Closed Mon.

Point Reyes Station
Moderate–Expensive

Chez Madeline. This restaurant features above-average French cooking and excellent seafood; its proprietor sometimes entertains diners by playing classical flute. *Hwy. 1, tel. 415/663–9177. MC, V. No lunch. Closed Mon.*

Station House Cafe. This modest local hangout serves breakfast, lunch, and dinner in a relaxing paneled dining room. Fresh fish and grilled meats highlight the dinner menu. *Hwy. 1, tel. 415/663–1515. MC, V.*

Stinson Beach
Moderate

Sand Dollar. This pleasant pub serves great hamburgers and other sandwiches for lunch and decent seafood for dinner. An added attraction is the outdoor dining deck. *Hwy. 1, tel. 415/868–0434. AE, D, MC, V.*

Trinidad
Moderate–Expensive
★

Larrupin Cafe. Actually in the town of Westhaven, close to Trinidad, Larrupin has earned a widespread reputation for its Cajun ribs and fish. *1150 Westhaven Dr., tel. 707/677–0230. Reservations required. No credit cards. No lunch. Closed Mon.–Wed.*

Moderate

Merryman's Dinner House. Fresh fish, naturally, is the main feature at this romantic oceanfront setting, perfect for hungry lovers. *On Moonstone Beach, tel. 707/677–3111. No credit cards. Closed Mon.–Thurs. and winter weekdays.*

Inexpensive–Moderate

Seascape. With its glassed-in main room, and a deck for alfresco dining, this is an ideal place to take in the splendor of Trinidad Bay over a good meal. The breakfasts are great, the lunches substantial, and the dinners feature good seafood. *At pier, tel. 707/677–3762. DC, MC, V.*

Lodging

The North Coast offers some of the most attractive lodging in the country, with a price range to accommodate virtually every pocketbook. You will find elaborate Victorian homes, grand old hotels, and modest motels. Many bed-and-breakfasts along the coast are sold out on weekends months in advance, so reserve early. Budget travelers will find youth hostels in Point Reyes National Seashore, Klamath, and Leggett (summer only).

Highly recommended hotels are indicated by a star ★.

Category	Cost*
Very Expensive	over $120
Expensive	$90–$120
Moderate	$50–$90
Inexpensive	under $50

**double room, not including tax*

Albion
Moderate–Very Expensive

Albion River Inn. Overlooking the sea, this attractive inn, built in 1987, has sizable rooms, some with fireplaces and Jacuzzis. The decor ranges from antique furnishings to big-backed willow chairs. A full breakfast is included. *3790 N. Hwy. 1, Box 100, 95410, tel. 707/937–1919. 20 rooms. Facilities: restaurant, horseback riding 15 mi away. MC, V.*

Arcata
Moderate–
Expensive
★

The Plough and the Stars. There's a truly Irish ambience at the Plough. It's hard to imagine a friendlier inn, as the warm hospitality of the hosts makes this Greek Revival farmhouse from the 1860s a wonderful place to stay. The house is in a truly pastoral setting, surrounded on three sides by farmland. The rooms are decorated according to a theme, such as the French country and English Victorian rooms. The suite has a wood stove. Breakfast is included. *1800 27th St., 95521, tel. 707/822–8236. 5 rooms, 3 with bath. Facilities: croquet lawn, spa. MC, V.*

Bodega Bay
Expensive–
Very Expensive

Inn at the Tides. This complex of modern condominium-style buildings offers spacious rooms with high, peaked ceilings, and uncluttered decor. All the rooms here have a view of the harbor and some have fireplaces. Continental breakfast is included. *800 Hwy. 1, Box 640, 94923, tel. 707/875–2751. 86 rooms. Facilities: room service, restaurant Thurs.–Sun., cable TV, refrigerator, pool, sauna, Jacuzzi, laundromat. AE, MC, V.*

Crescent City
Inexpensive

Curly Redwood Lodge. This lodge was built from a single, huge redwood tree, which produced 57,000 board feet of lumber. The decor in the guest rooms also makes the most of that tree, with paneling, platform beds, and dressers built into the walls. The rooms are a decent size, and there is a fireplace in the lobby. *701 Redwood Hwy. S, 95531, tel. 707/464–2137. 36 rooms. Facilities: color TV, phone. AE, DC, MC, V.*

Elk
Very Expensive

Harbor House. Constructed in 1916 by a timber company to entertain its guests, this redwood ranch-style house has a dining room with a view of the Pacific. Five of the six rooms in the main house have fireplaces, and some are furnished with antiques original to the house. There are also four smallish cottages with wood stove and decks. The path to the inn's private beach takes you through the lovely garden. Breakfast and dinner are included. *5600 S. Hwy. 1, 95432, tel. 707/877–3203. 10 rooms. No credit cards.*

Expensive–
Very Expensive
★

Elk Cove Inn. Private, romantic cottages are perched on a bluff above the pounding surf. One room's shower has a full-length window that shares this magnificent view of the Pacific. Skylights, wood-burning stoves, and hand-embroidered cloths are just some of the amenities. The 1883 Victorian home features three rooms with dormer windows and window seats, a parlor and ocean-view deck. A full gourmet breakfast is included. *6300 S. Hwy. 1, Box 367, 95432, tel. 707/877–3321. 4 cabin rooms (2 with wood stoves), 3 rooms in 1883 Victorian building, all with private bath. No credit cards.*

Eureka
Expensive–
Very Expensive

Eureka Inn. This striking Tudor-style manor, built in 1922 and now a National Historic Landmark, oozes charm and luxury. The elegant lobby is warmed by a fireplace. Guest rooms feature overstuffed wing chairs and 1930s reproduction furnishings. *Seventh and F Sts., 95501, tel. 707/442–6441. 105 rooms. Facilities: color TV, phone, pool, sauna, whirlpool. AE, D, DC, MC, V.*

Moderate–
Very Expensive
★

Carter House. For elegance coupled with warmth and hospitality, it's hard to beat Carter House. Owner Mark Carter has created a regal Victorian structure by employing a new design consistent with the Newsom architecture of the region. Some rooms have a view of the Carson Mansion as well as of the bay. There is a remarkable sense of airiness, with bay windows accenting two sizable parlors, each with a marble fireplace. Fine local artwork, in harmony with the interior's design, adorns the walls. The guest rooms are extraordinary, with Oriental carpets, generous windows, and fine wood furnishings. There is a two-room suite with fireplace and Jacuzzi. Four-course gourmet breakfast, voted the best in the state by *California* magazine, is included. *1033 3rd St., 95501, tel. 707/445-1390. 7 rooms. AE, MC, V.*

Hotel Carter. Across from the Carter House and a block from the Carson Mansion, this tastefully appointed hotel offers a spacious, elegant ambience at reasonable cost. The plush, contemporary decor and attentive service make this feel like an elegant, intimate cosmopolitan hotel. There are Jacuzzis in the deluxe room and suite. Gourmet Continental breakfast is included, and gourmet dinners are served Thurs.–Sun. *301 L St., 95501, tel. 707/444-8062. 20 rooms. Facilities: cable TV, telephones. AE, DC, MC, V.*

Ferndale
Moderate–
Very Expensive
★

The Gingerbread Mansion. Many visitors come expressly to stay in this spectacular Victorian home, one of the most romantic of the North Coast's bed-and-breakfast inns. The mansion's carved friezes set off its gables, and turrets dazzle the eye. Inside, the luxury continues with four comfortable parlors warmed by two fireplaces. The rooms seem designed for lovers. Some have fireplaces, some have views of the mansion's elegant English garden, and one has side-by-side bathtubs. Breakfast is included. Ask about off-season rates. *400 Berding St. Box 40, 95536, tel. 707/786-4000. 9 rooms with bath. Facilities: bicycles. MC, V.*

Fort Bragg
Moderate–
Very Expensive

Grey Whale Inn. Once a hospital, this comfortable, friendly abode doesn't look or feel anything like one today. Each room is individually decorated in a cozy style, with floral spreads or handcrafted quilts, and oak or white wicker beds. Three rooms have fireplaces, four have an ocean view, and the deluxe room has a private whirlpool tub and sundeck. Breakfast is included. *615 N. Main St., 95437, tel. 707/964-0640 or 800/382-7244. 14 rooms. Facilities: phones, billiards room. AE, D, MC, V.*

Garberville
Expensive–
Very Expensive
★

Benbow Inn. Set alongside the Eel River, this three-story Tudor-style manor resort is the equal of any in the region. A magnificent fireplace warms the bar/lobby of this National Historic Landmark, and all rooms are furnished with antiques. The most luxurious rooms are under the terrace, with fine views of the Eel River; some have fireplaces. *445 Lake Benbow Dr., 95440, tel. 707/923-2124. 55 rooms. Facilities: restaurant, VCR movies in lounge, 18 rooms with TV and VCR, 250-tape VCR library, swimming off private beach, canoeing, tennis, golf, fishing, horseback riding. MC, V. Closed Jan. 3–Apr. 21.*

Gualala
Moderate–
Very Expensive

Gualala Country Inn. In this contemporary, two-story, L-shape inn, all rooms have either ocean or river views. Most rooms are decorated with early American oak furnishings. Some rooms have fireplaces *and* ocean views, and two have two-person whirlpools; all have color TVs. Upstairs, the octagonal Horizon Room has a four-poster bed and a fireplace. *Hwy. 1, 95445, tel.707/884-4343. 20 rooms. MC, V.*

★

Old Milano Hotel. Overlooking the sea just north of Gualala, the Old Milano is one of California's premier bed-and-breakfast inns. Established in 1905, this elegantly rustic mansion is listed in the National Registry of Historic Places. Set amid English gardens, the estate overlooks Castle Rock and a spectacular coast. Tastefully furnished and appointed with exceptional antiques, five of the upstairs rooms look out over the ocean, and another looks over the gardens. The downstairs master suite has a private sitting room and a picture window framing the sea. Those in search of something different might consider the caboose with a wood-burning stove. A cottage also comes complete with wood stove. Breakfast is included, and dinners are offered Wednesday–Sunday. This hotel may not be appropriate for children. *38300 Hwy. 1, 95445, tel. 707/884–3256. 9 rooms. Facilities: hot tub. No smoking. MC, V.*

★ **St. Orres.** Located 2 miles north of Gualala, St. Orres is one of the North Coast's most eye-catching inns. Reflecting the area's Russian influence, St. Orres's main house is crowned by two onion-domed, Kremlinesque towers. The carved wood is accented by balconies and leaded-glass windows. Two of the rooms overlook the sea, while the other six are set over the garden or forest. Eleven wonderfully rustic cottages, built behind the main house in tranquil woods, provide excellent alternative lodging, eight with wood stoves or fireplaces. Those traveling with children are placed in the cottages. Breakfast is included with the room rate; for dinner, the inn's restaurant is considered one of the finest north of San Francisco. *Hwy. 1, Box 523, 95445, tel. 707/884–3303. 19 rooms. Facilities: private beach, hot tub, sauna. MC, V.*

Inverness
Expensive–
Very Expensive
★ **Blackthorne Inn.** Rising from the base of a tranquil wooded slope is one of the most striking North Coast bed-and-breakfasts. The Blackthorne is architecturally striking, with an octagonal wooden tower sitting above a turreted treehouse. It includes a glass-enclosed solarium and large fireplace as well as a penthouse, the Eagle's Nest, whose skylight provides a view of the stars. Breakfast is included. *266 Vallejo Ave., Box 712, Inverness Park, 94937, tel. 415/663–8621. 5 rooms, 2 with bath. Facilities: hot tub. MC, V.*

★ **Ten Inverness Way.** In a lovely 1904 shingle-style house, set on a quiet side street, you will find one of the most pleasant bed-and-breakfasts on the North Coast. The comfortable living room has a classic stone fireplace and player piano, and a weekend-cabin feel. The cozy rooms are highlighted by such homespun touches as patchwork quilts, lived-in-looking antiques, and skylighted dormer ceilings. The inn's proximity to Point Reyes hiking trails is a big draw for many guests. Full breakfast is included. *10 Inverness Way, Box 63, 94937, tel. 415/669–1648. 5 rooms. Facilities: hot tub. MC, V.*

Jenner
Moderate–
Very Expensive
Fort Ross Lodge. The lodge, about 1½ miles north of the old Russian fort, has all but four of its rooms equipped with fireplaces, and all have spectacular views of the Sonoma shoreline. *20705 Hwy. 1, 95450, tel. 707/847–3333. 22 rooms, some with private hot tub on back patio, plus 7 hill suites with sauna, in-room hot tub, VCR, and fireplace. Facilities: color TV and VCR. AE, MC, V.*

★ **Murphy's Jenner Inn.** Several units of this good-value inn have been built along the edge of the Russian River; some have partial ocean views. The large suite has a full kitchen, wood stove, and can accommodate up to six. Breakfast is included. *10400 Hwy. 1, Box 69, 95450, tel. 707/865–2377. 10 rooms. Facilities: hot tub available to 3 units. AE, MC, V.*

Timber Cove Inn. Set off Highway 1 about 3 miles north of the Russian fort, this attractive, weather-worn resort has sweeping views overlooking Timber Cove and no in-room phones or television to distract you. All but six of the rooms have both fireplaces and Jacuzzis or large sunken tubs, and the more expensive rooms have hot tubs. The lobby, bar, and dining hall are grand and rustic, and there is a Japanese pond at the entrance to the complex. There are also conference and seminar rooms. *21780 N. Coast Hwy. 1, 95450, tel. 707/847–3231. 49 rooms. AE, DC, MC, V.*

Inexpensive– Moderate **Stillwater Cove Ranch.** Sixteen miles north of Jenner, overlooking Stillwater Cove, this former boys' school has been transformed into a pleasant, reasonably priced place to lodge. Peacocks stroll the grounds. *22555 Hwy. 1, 95450, tel. 707/847–3227. 7 rooms. No credit cards.*

Klamath Inexpensive **DeMartin Redwood AYH Hostel.** The California coast's northernmost hostel, this turn-of-the-century inn (remodeled in 1987) is a stone's throw from the ocean, and is actually located within Redwood National Park, so hiking begins just beyond its doors. The living room is heated by a wood stove. Lodging is dormitory style. *14480 Hwy. 101 at Wilson Creek Rd., 95548, tel. 707/482–8265. No credit cards.*

Little River Very Expensive ★ **Heritage House.** This famous resort, where the movie *Same Time, Next Year* was filmed, has attractive cottages with stunning ocean views. There is a lovely dining room, also with fine Pacific views, serving breakfast and dinner, which are included with the room rate. Each room's decor is unique, but all are appointed with plush furnishings, and many have private decks, fireplaces, and whirlpool tubs. *Hwy. 1, 95456, tel. 707/937–5885. 72 rooms. Reserve well in advance. MC, V. Closed Dec. and Jan.*

Moderate– Very Expensive ★ **Glendeven.** For a touch of tranquillity, stay at this inn at the north end of Little River. The New England–style main house has six rooms, four with private bath, one with wood stove. The converted barn features a two-bedroom suite with kitchen and an art gallery. The 1986 Stevenscroft building has a high-peaked, gabled roof and weathered barnlike siding. The four rooms within all have fireplaces. The owners, both designers, have decorated the guest rooms with antiques, contemporary art, and ceramics. Breakfast is included. *8221 N. Hwy. 1, 95456, tel.707/937–0083. 11 rooms. MC, V.*

Mendocino Very Expensive ★ **Reed Manor.** One of Mendocino's newest inns, this luxurious property combines the elegant decor of rich floral fabrics and intimate feel of a fine B&B with the top-notch amenities of a modern hotel. Spacious rooms are enhanced by sumptuous furnishings, gas fireplaces, whirlpool tubs, televisions and VCRs, and private balconies (each with a telescope) overlooking Mendocino and the ocean. Each room is also equipped with a coffee maker, refrigerator, and a telephone with answering machine. A split of wine and Continental breakfast are included. *Off Palette Dr., Box 127, 95460, tel. 707/937-5446. 5 rooms. MC, V.*

★ **Stanford Inn by the Sea.** For those who wish to experience the quintessence of luxury on the Mendocino coast, this grand, two-story lodge is the place. In sumptuously appointed, wood-paneled rooms, each with a deck and fireplace, you can gaze out over the Pacific and the town of Mendocino. The Stanford is adjacent to a llama farm, a terraced organic garden, and is set along the estuary. Breakfast is included. *Just south of Mendocino, east on Comptche-Ukiah Rd., Box 487, 95460, tel. 707/ 937–5615 or 800/331–8884. 25 rooms. Facilities: canoes, color*

TV, stereo, VCRs, coffee makers, telephones, refrigerators, mountain bikes, indoor pool, hot tub. AE, D, DC, MC, V.

Expensive–
Very Expensive
★

Headlands Inn. A magnificently restored Victorian building erected in 1868, the inn combines 19th-century charm and contemporary comforts. All rooms have private baths and fireplaces; some overlook a garden and the pounding surf, others offer fine village views. There is also a private cottage on the premises. Gourmet breakfast is served in your room. *Howard and Albion Sts., Box 132, 95460, tel. 707/937-4431. 5 rooms. No credit cards.*

★ **Joshua Grindle Inn.** This homespun century-old Victorian inn has a reputation for friendliness. Laid-back and unpretentious, this place is most like Mendocino before it became a popular tourist destination. Some rooms have ocean views, and some have fireplaces. Three rooms are in a water tower. Two rooms in the backyard cottage are warmed by Franklin stoves. Full breakfast is included. *44800 Little Lake Rd., 95460, tel. 707/937-4143. 10 rooms. D, MC, V.*

Moderate–
Very Expensive
★

MacCallum House. The most artfully restored Victorian in Mendocino, this splendid 1882 inn, complete with gingerbread trim, transports you back to another era. Its comfortable period furnishings and antiques provide a turn-of-the-century ambience. In addition to the main house, individual cottages and barn suites are set around a garden with a gazebo. Continental breakfast is included (weekends only in winter). *45020 Albion St., Box 206, 95460, tel. 707/937-0289. 21 rooms. Facilities: restaurant, bar. MC, V.*

Mendocino Hotel. The exterior of this fine hotel creates a sense of the Wild West through its facade and its balcony that overhangs the raised sidewalk. Inside, an elegant atmosphere is achieved by stained-glass lamps, Remington paintings, polished wood, and Persian carpets. All but 14 of the rooms have private baths, and the 19th-century decor is appealing. There are also deluxe garden rooms with fireplaces on the property. *45080 Main St., Box 587, 95460, tel. 707/937-0511 or 800/548-0513. 51 rooms. Facilities: restaurant, bar, room service 8 AM–9 PM. AE, MC, V.*

Mendocino Village Inn. This refurbished 1882 Queen Anne–Victorian inn has a potpourri of styles, with one room providing a southwestern motif with Indian artifacts, such as Hopi beadwork on the wall and bent-willow furnishings. Another room is reminiscent of a whaling captain's quarters, and a third is an homage to Teddy Roosevelt. Many of the rooms have fireplaces, some have ocean views, and others look out on the garden. Breakfast is included. *44860 Main St., Box 626, 95460, tel. 707/937-0246; in CA, 800/882-7029. 12 rooms, 10 with bath. MC, V.*

Muir Beach
Very Expensive
★

Pelican Inn. An atmospheric Tudor-style B&B reminiscent of 16th-century England, the Pelican is a five-minute walk from Muir Beach. The rooms, filled with antiques, have half-canopied two- and four-poster beds. On the ground floor, there's an Old English pub complete with dart boards and a selection of British brews. The dining quarter consists of two sections: a romantic rustic wooden hall and a glassed-in solarium, both warmed by fireplaces. Includes full English breakfast. *Hwy. 1, 94965, tel. 415/383-6000. 7 rooms. MC, V.*

Point Reyes **National Seashore** *Inexpensive*	**Point Reyes Hostel.** Located within the national seashore and a mere 2 miles from Limantour Beach, this is the best deal for budget travelers. Lodging is dorm style in an old clapboard ranch house. The family room is limited to families with small children and must be reserved well in advance. *Box 247, Pt. Reyes Station, 94956, tel. 415/663-8811. Send $9 per adult per night with reservation request; state your gender. Facilities: shared kitchen. No credit cards.*

Sea Ranch
Very Expensive

Sea Ranch Lodge. South of Gualala, the lodge is set high on a bluff, affording ocean views. Some rooms have fireplaces, and some have hot tubs. Handcrafted wood furnishings and quilts create an earthy, contemporary look. Guests receive a complimentary wine and fruit basket upon arrival. It is close to beaches, trails, golf. *60 Sea Walk Dr., Box 44, 95497, tel. 707/785-2371. 20 rooms. AE, MC, V.*

Shelter Cove
Inexpensive–
Moderate

Beachcomber Inn. There are three good-size rooms in this converted private home. Two of the rooms have kitchenettes and wood-burning stoves, and ocean views. The decor doesn't get much beyond the basics of a brass bed and a wicker chair. The inn is near the marina and it's an easy walk to the beach. *Write c/o 7272 Shelter Cove Rd., Shelter Cove 95489, tel. 707/986-7733. 3 rooms. MC, V.*

Tomales Bay
Moderate

Tomales Country Inn. Secluded by trees and bordered by gardens, this Victorian house has a relaxed atmosphere. The previous owner, painter Byron Randall, filled the inn with his own turn-of-the-century, European-style paintings and other local art. Expanded Continental breakfast is included. *25 Valley St., Box 376, 94971, tel. 707/878-9992. 5 rooms, 2 with bath. No credit cards.*

Trinidad
Expensive–Very
Expensive
★

Trinidad Bed and Breakfast. Overlooking Trinidad Bay, this Cape Cod–style shingle house, built in 1949, gets our vote for having the most spectacular sea view on the North Coast. The innkeepers offer a wealth of information about the nearby wilderness, beach, and fishing habitats. The living room is warmed by a crackling fireplace. Upstairs, three comfortably furnished rooms offer fabulous seascapes which you can enjoy from a seat by a dormer window framed with white eyelet curtains. Breakfast is included. *560 Edwards St., Box 849, 95570, tel. 707/677-0840. 4 rooms and 1 first-floor, 180° ocean-view suite with fireplace. Reserve well in advance. D, MC, V.*

Westport
Moderate–Expensive

Howard Creek Ranch. This rustic redwood working ranch, complete with cows and horses, was built in 1871. Set within 300 yards of the beach, some rooms have ocean views. The three cabins on the property include one converted fishing boat set by the creek. Rooms in the main house are furnished with Victorian-era antiques. Breakfast is included. *40501 Hwy. 1, Box 121, 95488, tel. 707/964-6725. 8 rooms, 5 with bath. Facilities: hot tub, sauna. MC, V.*

Nightlife

If a swinging, raucous, after-dark scene is what you're hankering for, the North Coast is not the place for you. Nonetheless, there are some watering holes favored by locals and visitors that should meet the needs of those not quite ready for a good night's sleep after exploring the forest and sea.

The following are listed alphabetically by town.

Bolinas **Smiley's Schooner Saloon.** The *only* nightlife in Bolinas, Smiley's has a CD sound system and live music three nights a week. *41 Wharf Rd., tel. 415/868–1311.*

Garberville **Benbow Inn.** In this elegant Tudor mansion, you can hear a pianist nightly while you are warmed by a romantic fireplace. *445 Lake Benbow Dr., tel. 707/923–2124.*

Muir Beach **Pelican Inn.** Set just outside Muir Beach, this is an English-style pub and restaurant, with imported brews on tap, a dart board, a stone fireplace, a genial host, and friendly regulars. *Hwy. 1, tel. 415/383–6005.*

Point Reyes Station **Western Saloon.** If you are in town on the right Friday night, you can dance your jeans off at this favorite local pub. Other nights it's a friendly place to meet West Marinites. *Hwy. 1, tel. 415/663–1661.*

4 The Far North

While the rest of California was booming with high-tech industries and an influx of sun-seeking easterners and value-conscious developers, the Far North simply hung up its "gone fishin'" sign. You won't find many hot night spots or cultural enclaves here, but you will find some of the best hiking, fishing, and hunting the state has to offer. Some Bay Area families have been returning to this region of the state year after year. Many enjoy the outdoors from their own piece of paradise—a private houseboat. A good number of retirees have chosen to live out their golden years in the area.

The towering, snow-covered Mt. Shasta dominates the land. It can be seen for 100 miles, and qualifies the otherwise flat and fast trip through the valley along I–5 as a scenic drive. The 14,000-foot dormant volcano is surrounded by national and state parks. The natural and artificially created wonders include the sulfur vents and areas of bubbling mud of Lassen Volcanic National Park and the immense Shasta Dam.

Almost all of the towns in the Far North are small and friendly, made up of third- and fourth-generation descendants of '49ers who never cared to leave. Proud of their Gold Rush history, each town, no matter how small, has a museum filled with an impressive collection of artifacts donated by locals. This is the kind of place where people say hello to you as you walk down Main Street.

Getting Around

By Plane Redding Municipal Airport is served by **United Express** (tel. 800/241–6522) and **American Eagle** (tel. 800/433–7300), which flies daily from San Francisco. Major car-rental agencies are located at the airport.

By Train There are **Amtrak** stations in Redding and Dunsmuir (tel. 800/872–7245).

By Bus **Greyhound-Trailways** buses travel I–5, serving Red Bluff, Redding, Dunsmuir, and Mt. Shasta City (tel. 415/558–6789). In Redding, a city bus system, "The Ride" (tel. 916/241–2877), serves the local area daily except Sunday.

By Car I–5, an excellent four-lane divided highway, runs up the center of California through Red Bluff and Redding, and continues north to Oregon. Lassen Park can be reached by Highway 36 from Red Bluff or Highway 44 from Redding; Highway 299 leads from Redding to McArthur-Burney Falls. These are very good two-lane roads that are kept open year round. If you are traveling through this area in winter, however, always carry snow chains in your car.

Important Addresses and Numbers

Tourist Information **Mt. Shasta Convention and Visitors Bureau.** Information pavilion (300 Pine St., Mt. Shasta 96067, tel. 916/926–4865 or 800/926–4865).

Red Bluff–Tehama County Chamber of Commerce (100 N. Main St., Box 850, Red Bluff 96080, tel. 916/527–6220).

Redding Convention and Visitors Bureau (777 Auditorium Dr., Redding 96001, tel. 916/225–4100).

Shasta Cascade Wonderland Association. Visitor information for the entire region (1250 Parkview Ave., Redding 96001, tel. 916/243–2643).

Siskiyou County Visitors Bureau (325 W. Miner St., Yreka 96097, tel. 800/446–7475).

Emergencies The number for emergency assistance throughout the Far North is 911. This will put you in touch with police, fire, and medical help.

Exploring

Numbers in the margin correspond to points of interest on the Far North map.

The Far North covers a vast area, from the valleys east of the Coast Range to the Nevada border, and from the almond and olive orchards north of Sacramento to the Oregon border. The entire state of Ohio would fit into this section of California.

Redding is the urban center of the Far North. It offers the greatest selection of restaurants and the most luxurious accommodations. You'll experience the true flavor of this outdoor country at motels in the smaller towns. Many visitors make the outdoors their home for at least part of their stay. Camping, houseboating, and animal-pack trips into the wilderness are very popular.

This exploring section is arranged south-to-north, following the mostly flat and fast I–5 with the addition of two daylong side trips. The valley around Redding is hot, even in winter, but cooler temperatures prevail at the higher elevations to the east and north. Be aware that many restaurants and museums in this region have limited hours and sometimes close for stretches of the off-season.

Red Bluff

The turnoff for Red Bluff from I–5 will take you past a neon-lit motel row, but persevere and explore the roads to the left of the main drag, where you'll discover gracefully restored Victorian structures, a fine museum, and an Old West–style downtown.

1 The **Kelly-Griggs House Museum** is a restored 1880s Victorian dwelling with an impressive collection of antique furniture, housewares, and clothing arranged as though a refined Victorian family were still in residence: an engraved silver tea server waits at the end table; a "Self Instructor in Penmanship" teaching the art of graceful, flowing handwriting sits on the desk; and eerily lifelike mannequins seem frozen in conversation in the upstairs parlor.

The museum's collection also includes finely carved china cabinets, Native American basketry, and a turn-of-the-century painting by Thomas Hill, known for his western landscapes. The painting over the fireplace is by Sarah Brown, daughter of abolitionist John Brown, whose family settled in Red Bluff after his execution. The Brown home is part of the self-guided tour of Red Bluff Victoriana; maps are available here. *311 Washington St., tel. 916/527–1129. Donation suggested. Open Thurs.–Sun. 2–4. Closed major holidays.*

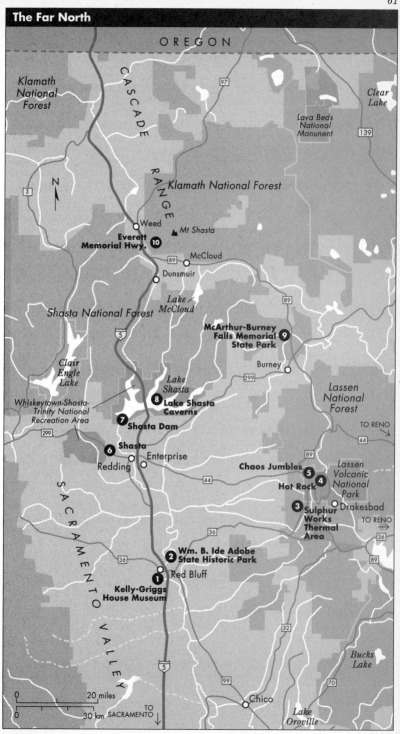

The Far North

North of town on the banks of the Sacramento River is the **William B. Ide Adobe State Historic Park,** which is a memorial to the man who was the first and only president of the short-lived California Republic of 1846. The Bear Flag Party proclaimed California a sovereign nation, no longer under the dominion of Mexico, and the republic existed for 25 days with Ide as chief executive before it was occupied by the United States. The flag concocted for the republic has survived, with only minor refinements, as California's state flag. Ide's adobe home was built in the 1850s, and now displays period furnishings and artifacts of the era. *21659 Adobe Rd., tel. 916/527–5927. Admission: $3 per vehicle. Home open 11–4 in summer; park and picnic facilities open year-round from 8 AM to sunset.*

Lassen Volcanic National Park

Take Highway 36 east from Red Bluff to Highway 89 to reach this still-active volcano. Highway 89 meanders north for 34 miles through Lassen Volcanic National Park, offering a look at three sides of the world's largest plug volcano. Except for the ski area, the park is largely inaccessible from late October to early June because of snow. Highway 89 through the park is closed to cars in winter but open to intrepid cross-country skiers.

In 1914 the 10,457-foot Mt. Lassen began a series of 300 eruptions that went on for seven years. Molten rock overflowed the crater; there were clouds of smoke and hailstorms of rocks and volcanic cinders. Proof of the volcano's volatility becomes evident shortly after you enter the park at the **Sulphur Works Thermal Area.** Boardwalks take you over bubbling mud and hot springs, and through the nauseating sulfur stink of steam vents. Five miles farther along Highway 89 you'll find the start of the **Bumpass Hell Trail,** a 3-mile round-trip hike to the park's most interesting thermal-spring area where you'll see hot and boiling springs, steam vents, and mud pots. The trail climbs and descends several hundred feet.

Back on the road, drive on through forests and past lakes, looking out for deer and wildflowers, to **Hot Rock.** This 400-ton boulder tumbled down from the summit during the volcano's active period, and was still hot to the touch when locals found it. Although cool now, it's still an impressive sight. Five miles on is **Chaos Jumbles,** created 300 years ago when an avalanche from the Chaos Crags lava domes spread hundreds of thousands of rocks 2 to 3 feet in diameter over 2 square miles.

An important word of warning: Stay on trails and boardwalks near the thermal areas. What may appear to be firm ground may be only a thin crust over scalding mud, and serious burns could result if you step through it. Be especially careful with children!

Lassen is a unique, lovely, and relatively uncrowded national park, but services are rather sparse. In the southwest corner of the park, at the winter-sports area, there is a year-round café and a gift shop that's open during the summer and the ski season. At the Manzanita Lake campground another store, open only in summer, offers gas and fast food. Admission to the park is $5 per vehicle.

There are seven campgrounds within Lassen Volcanic National Park. Reservations are not accepted; it's first come, first served. For campground and other information, contact Lassen Volcanic National Park (Mineral 96063, tel. 916/595–4444).

The only other lodging inside the park is the 100-year-old guest ranch at Drakesbad, near its southern border, and isolated from most of the park. Reservations should be made well in advance. *Booking office: 2150 Main St., Suite 5, Red Bluff 96080, tel. 916/529–1512. Open early June–early Oct.; closed winter.*

Shasta

A few miles west of Redding on Highway 299 are the ruins of the gold-mining town of **Shasta,** now a **state historic park** with a few restored buildings. A museum located in the old courthouse has an eclectic array of California paintings as well as memorabilia including period newspapers advertising "Gold Dust Bought and Sold," a "Prairie Traveler" guidebook with advice on encounters with Indians, and the 1860 census of this once-prosperous town. Continue down to the basement to see the iron-barred jail cells, and step outside for a look at the scaffold where murderers were hanged. *Tel. 916/243–8194. Admission: $2 adults, $1 children 6–17. Open Thurs.–Mon. 10–5. Closed New Year's, Thanksgiving, and Christmas days.*

Lake Shasta

Take the Dam/Project City exit west off I–5 about 12 miles north of Redding and follow the signs to **Shasta Dam.** You'll be able to see the mammoth construction from several points; this is the second-largest and the fourth-tallest concrete dam in the United States.

Whether you drive across the dam, or park at the landscaped visitors' area and walk across, you'll see three Shastas: the dam, the lake spreading before you, and the mountain presiding over it all. At twilight the sight is magical, with Mt. Shasta gleaming above the not-quite-dark water. The dam is lighted after dark, but there is no access from 10 PM to 6 AM. In addition to providing fact sheets, the **Visitor Information Center** (tel. 916/275–4463) offers photographic and historic displays (June–Aug., daily 7:30–4; Sept.–May, weekdays 7:30–4). The coffee shop is closed January through March.

Lake Shasta has 370 miles of shoreline and 21 varieties of fish. You can rent fishing boats, ski boats, sailboats, canoes, paddleboats, Jet Skis, and Windsurfer boards at one of the many marinas and resorts along the shore. But Lake Shasta is known as the houseboat capital of the world, and around here the houseboat is king.

Houseboats come in all sizes except small. The ones that sleep 12 to 14 people are 55 feet by 14 feet; the minimum size sleeps six. As a rule these moving homes come equipped with cooking utensils, dishes, and most of the equipment you'll need to set up housekeeping on the water. (You supply the food and linens.) Renters are given a short course in how to maneuver the boats before they set out on cruises; it's not difficult.

The houseboats are slow-moving, and life aboard is leisurely. You can fish, swim, sunbathe on the flat roof, or just sit on the deck and watch the world go by. The shoreline of Lake Shasta is beautifully ragged, with countless inlets; exploring it is fun, and it's not hard to find privacy. Be aware, however, that the recent drought has considerably diminished the volume of the lake, making some areas inaccessible.

Expect to spend a minimum of $170 a day for the six-sleeper-size houseboat. There is usually a three-night minimum in peak season. Contact the **Shasta Cascade Wonderland Association** (1250 Parkview Ave., Redding, CA 96001, tel. 916/243–2643) for specifics about the 10 marinas that rent houseboats.

8 Stalagmites, stalactites, odd flowstone deposits, and crystals entice visitors of all ages to the **Lake Shasta Caverns.** The two-hour tour includes a ferry ride across the McCloud arm of Lake Shasta and a bus ride up Grey Rock Mountain to the cavern entrance. The caverns are a constant 58°F year round, making them an appealingly cool retreat on a hot summer day. All cavern rooms are well lit, and the crowning jewel is the spectacular cathedral room. The guides are friendly, enthusiastic, and informative. *Take the Shasta Caverns Rd. exit from I–5. Tel. 916/238–2341. Admission: $12 adults, $6 children 4–12. Hourly tours May–Sept., daily 9–4; Oct.–Apr., at 10 AM, noon, and 2 PM. Closed Thanksgiving and Dec. 25.*

Burney Falls

9 Take the Highway 299 East exit off I–5 just north of Redding, past the town of Burney, and turn north on Highway 89 to get to **McArthur-Burney Falls Memorial State Park.** It's a two-hour round-trip drive from I–5, so you may want to plan to spend the day here. Just inside the southern boundary of the park, Burney Creek wells up from the ground and divides into two cascades that fall over a 129-foot cliff and into a pool below. The thundering water creates a mist at the base of the falls, often highlighted by a rainbow. Countless ribbonlike falls stream from hidden moss-covered crevices creating an ethereal backdrop to the main cascades. Each day, 100 million gallons of water rush over these falls; Theodore Roosevelt proclaimed them "the eighth wonder of the world." A self-guided nature trail descends to the foot of the falls. There is a lake and beach for swimming. A campground, picnic sites, trails, and other facilities are available. The camp store is open Memorial Day–Labor Day. *Rte. 1, Box 1260, Burney 96013, tel. 916/335–2777. Day use admission: $5 per vehicle; camping $14 per night. Campground reservations (necessary in summer) are made through MISTIX, Box 85705, San Diego, CA 92138–5705, tel. 800/365–2267 or 619/452–0150 for international callers.*

Mt. Shasta

If you drive up the valley on I–5, past the 130 million-year-old granite outcroppings of Castle Crags towering over the road, through the quaint old railroad town of Dunsmuir, you'll reach the town of Mt. Shasta, nestled at the base of the huge mountain. If you are interested in hiking on Mt. Shasta, stop at the **Forest Service Ranger Station** (204 W. Alma St., tel. 916/926–4511) as you come through town for the latest information on trail conditions, or call the **Fifth Season Mountaineering Shop** in Mt. Shasta City (tel. 916/926–3606), which also offers a recorded 24-hour climber/skier report (tel. 916/926–5555).

The central Mt. Shasta exit east leads out of town along the **Everett Memorial Highway.** This scenic drive climbs to almost 8,000 feet, and the views of the mountain and the valley below are extraordinary.

If you are wondering where all those eye-catching pictures of Mt. Shasta reflected in a lake are shot, take the central Mt. Shasta exit west and follow the signs to **Lake Siskiyou.** This is the only man-made lake in California created solely for recreational purposes. On the way, stop at the oldest **trout hatchery** in California. The pools there literally swarm with more than 100,000 trout.

What to See and Do with Children

Almost everything we've described above about the Far North of California offers something that children will enjoy: the bubbling mud at Lassen, the houseboats and caverns at Lake Shasta, and the falls at Burney. **Waterworks Park** in Redding has giant water slides, a raging-river inner-tube ride, and a children's water playground. *151 N. Boulder Dr., tel. 916/246-9550. Admission: $11.50 ages 12–65, $9.50 children 4–11. Open Memorial Day–Labor Day, daily 10–8.*

Off the Beaten Track

The hand-painted sign along Main Street in **McCloud** reads "Population 1,665, Dogs 462." To reach this time-capsule town, take the Highway 89 exit east from I–5 just south of the town of Mt. Shasta. McCloud began as a lumber-company town in the late 1800s, and was one of the longest-lived company towns in the country. In 1965, the U.S. Plywood Corp. acquired the town, its lumber mill, and the surrounding forest land, and allowed residents to purchase their homes. The immense mill has been cut back to a computerized operation, but the spirit of the townsfolk have kept McCloud from becoming a ghost town. Picturesque hotels, churches, a lumber baron's mansion, and simple family dwellings have been renovated, and the 60,000-pound Corliss steam engine that powered the original mill's machinery stands as a monument behind the town's small museum.

Sports

Fishing You'll need a California fishing license. State residents pay $23.65, but nonresidents must fork over $63.55 for a one-year license. Both residents and nonresidents can purchase a one-day license for $8.40. For information, contact the **Department of Fish and Game** (3211 S St., Sacramento 95816, tel. 916/739–3380).

For licenses, current fishing conditions, guides, or special fishing packages, contact **The Fly Shop** (4140 Churn Creek Rd., Redding 96002, tel. 916/222–3555), **The Fishin' Hole** (3844 Shasta Dam Blvd., Central Valley 96019, tel. 916/275–4123), or **Shasta Cascade Wonderland Association** (1250 Parkview Ave., Redding 96001, tel. 916/243–2643).

Golf **Churn Creek Golf Course** (8550 Churn Creek Rd., Redding, tel. 916/222–6353). Nine holes, par 36. Carts are available.

Gold Hills Country Club (1950 Gold Hills Dr., Redding, Oasis Rd. exit from I–5, tel. 916/246–7867). Eighteen holes, par 72. Carts, club rentals, driving range, pro shop, restaurant.

Lake Redding Golf Course (1795 Benton Dr., Redding, in Lake Redding Park, tel. 916/243–5531). Nine holes, par 31. Pull carts, electric carts, rentals.

Llama Pack Tours **Shasta Llamas** (Box 1137, Mt. Shasta 96067, tel. 916/926–3959) leads three- and five-day trips into the backcountry.

Raft and Canoe Rentals **Park Marina Watersports** (2515 Park Marina Dr., Redding, tel. 916/246–8388).

Skiing **Mt. Lassen Ski Park.** Inside the southwest entrance of Lassen Volcanic National Park is a ski area (and the only park facility open in winter), with a triple chair lift and two surface tows. The terrain is 40% beginner, 40% intermediate, 20% advanced. Mt. Lassen's top elevation is 7,200 feet; its base, 6,600 feet; its vertical drop, 600 feet. The longest run is ¾ mile. There is a ski school and a beginner's special: lift, rentals, lessons. The "Kids Are People Too" program for ages 5–11 includes rentals, lunch, lessons, lifts. Facilities include a cafeteria and rental shop. Cross-country skiing is allowed along Highway 89 through the park when the road is closed to car traffic because of the snow. *Hwy. 36 exit from I–5 at Red Bluff, tel. 916/595–3376. Snow phone: 916/595–4464.*

Mt. Shasta Ski Park. On the southeast flank of Mt. Shasta are three lifts on 300 acres. The terrain is 20% beginner, 60% intermediate, 20% advanced. Mt. Shasta's summit is 6,600 feet; its base, 5,500 feet; its vertical drop 1,100 feet. The longest run is 1.2 miles. Night skiing goes till 10 PM Wednesday–Saturday. There is a ski school with a beginner's special: lifts, rentals, lessons. The "Powder Pups" program is for ages 4–7. Lodge facilities include food and beverage, ski shop, and rentals. *Hwy. 89 exit east from I–5, just south of Mt. Shasta, tel. 916/926–8610. Snow phone 916/926–8686.*

Snowshoe Tours National Park Service rangers conduct snowshoe tours at Mt. Lassen Ski Park. A variety of natural history topics are covered. *Tel. 916/595–4444. No reservations. $1 donation for upkeep of snowshoes. Open weekends at 1:30 PM and daily through the Christmas and Easter holiday periods except Thanksgiving and Dec. 25.*

Dining

Cafés and simple, informal restaurants are ample in the Far North. Most of the fast-food restaurants are clustered in Redding, though they are also found along I–5 in some of the larger communities. The restaurants listed here are of special interest because of their food and/or unique atmosphere. Dress is always casual in the Far North; reservations aren't necessary except where noted.

Highly recommended restaurants are indicated by a star ★.

Category	Cost*
Very Expensive	over $25
Expensive	$20–$25

Moderate	$15–$20
Inexpensive	under $15

per person, not including tax, service, or drinks

Lake Shasta
Inexpensive–Moderate

Tail O' the Whale. Reminiscent of a ship's prow, this restaurant overlooking the lake is distinguished by its nautical decor. Seafood, beef, poultry, and Cajun pepper shrimp are the specialties. *10300 Bridge Bay Rd. (Bridge Bay exit from I–5), tel. 916/275–3021. Reservations advised for summer Sun. brunch. MC, V.*

Mt. Shasta
Inexpensive–Moderate
★

Bellissimo. This bright, Mediterranean-style café has an eclectic, creative menu with dishes that feature generous use of fresh herbs and healthful ingredients. Specialties change, but often include curry chicken with apple-raisin chutney, parsley-garlic fettuccine with clams, ravioli with acorn squash, cheeses, and nutmeg, and decadent desserts. There's a special Sunday brunch. *204A W. Lake St., tel. 916/926–4461. MC, V. Limited hrs. in winter.*

Inexpensive

Marilyn's. Everyone greets each other by name at this Mayberry-esque diner where all of 10¢ is charged for a cup of coffee. The local deputy sheriff is a regular here. The former stagecoach stop serves hearty breakfasts and sandwiches, as well as Italian specialties. Complete dinners including soup or salad cost less than $8. *1136 S. Mt. Shasta Blvd., tel. 916/926–2720. MC, V.*

Red Bluff
Inexpensive

The Snack Box. This renovated Victorian building is cheerfully decorated in country-French blue and dusty rose. The carved wooden murals, like the omelets, soups and sandwiches, are homemade by the owner. *257 Main St., 1 block from Kelly-Griggs Museum, tel. 916/529–0227. No credit cards. No dinner.*

Redding
Moderate–Expensive
★

Misty's. Two-story windows overlook the Red Lion Inn's pool area at this romantic dinner room with private booths. Specialties include steak Diane, whisky peppercorn steak, and wild-mushroom fettuccine. The meals are artistically presented, and there's a Sunday brunch. *Red Lion Inn, 1830 Hilltop Dr., tel. 916/221–8700. AE, D, DC, MC, V.*

Inexpensive–Moderate

Jack's Grill. Although it looks like a dive from the outside, this steak house is immensely popular with residents throughout the territory, who come in for the famous 16-ounce steaks. The place is usually jam-packed and noisy. *1743 California St., tel. 916/241–9705. AE, MC, V. No lunch. Closed Sun.*

Lodging

Motel chains, such as Best Western and Motel 6, have branches in many of the communities in the Far North, though Redding has the greatest selection by far. Luxury hotels are found only in Redding.

Highly recommended hotels are indicated by a star ★.

Category	Cost*
Very Expensive	over $100
Expensive	$75–$100

Moderate	$50–$75
Inexpensive	under $50

*double room, not including tax

Dunsmuir
Moderate

Railroad Park Resort. At this railroad buff's delight, antique cabooses have been converted to clean, playfully romantic motel rooms in honor of Dunsmuir's railroad legacy. There's also a restaurant in a restored, Orient Express–style dining car, and a full bar in a converted railcar. The lounge now features a Karaoke machine—the popular Japanese sing-along jukebox. The landscaped grounds feature a huge logging steam engine and restored water tower. *100 Railroad Park Rd., 96025, tel. 916/ 235–4440. 20 cabooses with bath, 4 cabins. Facilities: pool, Jacuzzi. AE, D, MC, V.*

Mt. Shasta
Inexpensive

Alpine Lodge. The clean, standard motel rooms here are decorated in a range of colors. Amenities include in-room coffee. *908 S. Mt. Shasta Blvd., 96067, tel. 916/926–3145. 8 rooms with bath, 5 family suites. Facilities: pool, spa with Jacuzzi jets. AE, DC, MC, V.*

Redding
Expensive–
Very Expensive
★

Red Lion Inn. Nicely landscaped grounds and a large, attractive patio area with outdoor food service are the highlights here. The rooms are spacious and comfortable. *1830 Hilltop Dr., Hwy. 44 and 299 exit east from I–5, 96002, tel. 916/221–8700 or 800/547–8010. 195 rooms with bath. Facilities: restaurant, coffee shop, lounge, pool, wading pool, whirlpool, putting green, room service, movies. Small pets are allowed; notify the clerk when booking rooms. AE, DC, MC, V.*

Moderate

Vagabond Inn. The clean, large rooms here feature a cheerful decor, with flowered drapes and spreads. Continental breakfast and weekday papers are on the house. *536 E. Cypress Ave., Cypress exit west from I–5, 96002, tel. 916/223–1600 or 800/ 522–1555. 71 rooms with bath. Facilities: coffee shop adjacent, pool, movies. Pets allowed for $3 fee. AE, DC, MC, V.*

Camping

There are an infinite number of camping possibilities in the Far North's national and state parks, forests, and recreation areas. You'll find every level of rusticity, too, from the well-outfitted campgrounds in McArthur-Burney State Park, which have hot water, showers, and flush toilets, to isolated campsites on Lake Shasta that can be reached only by boat. For information about camping in the region, contact the **Shasta Cascade Wonderland Association** (1250 Parkview Ave., Redding, CA 96001, tel. 916/ 243–2643).

Nightlife

Although the larger hotels in Redding usually have weekend dance bands geared to the younger set, there's not much nightlife in this outdoors country where the fish bite early. Rock-and-roll fans will enjoy the **Curiosity Club** (2655 Bechelli La., behind the bowling alley, Redding, tel. 916/223–3400), which features live music Monday through Saturday. There's a $2 cover charge on weekends.

5 The Wine Country

In 1862, after an extensive tour of the wine-producing areas of Europe, Count Agoston Haraszthy de Mokcsa reported to his adopted California with a promising prognosis: "Of all the countries through which I passed," wrote the father of California's viticulture, "not one possessed the same advantages that are to be found in California. . . . California can produce as noble and generous a wine as any in Europe; more in quantity to the acre, and without repeated failures through frosts, summer rains, hailstorms, or other causes."

The "dormant resources" that Haraszthy saw in the temperate valleys of Sonoma and Napa, with their balmy days and cool nights, are in full fruition today. While the wines produced here are praised and savored by connoisseurs throughout the world, the area continues to be a fermenting vat of experimentation, a proving ground for the latest techniques of grape-growing and wine-making.

In the Napa Valley, it seems that every available inch of soil is combed with neat rows of vines; would-be wine-makers with very little acreage can rent the cumbersome, costly machinery needed to stem and press the grapes. Many say making wine is a good way to turn a large fortune into a small one, but that hasn't deterred the doctors, former college professors, publishing tycoons, and airline pilots who come to try their hand at it.

Twenty years ago the Napa Valley had no more than 20 wineries; today there are almost 10 times that number. In Sonoma County, where the web of vineyards is looser, there are more than 100 wineries, and development is now claiming the cool Carneros region at the head of the San Francisco Bay, deemed ideal for growing the currently favored chardonnay grape.

All this has meant some pretty stiff competition, and the wine-makers are constantly honing their skills, aided by the scientific know-how of graduates of the nearby University of California at Davis, as well as by the practical knowledge of the grape-growers. They experiment with planting the vine stock closer together and with "canopy management" of the grape cluster, as well as with "cold" fermentation in stainless steel vats and new methods of fining, or filtering, the wine.

In the past the emphasis was on creating wines to be cellared, but today "drinkable" wines that can be enjoyed relatively rapidly are in demand. This has led to the celebration of dining as an art in the Wine Country. Many wineries boast first-class restaurants, which showcase excellent California cuisine and their own fine wines.

This stretch of highway from Napa to Calistoga rivals Disneyland as the biggest tourist draw in the state. Two-lane Highway 129 slows to a sluggish crawl on weekends throughout the year, and there are acres of vehicles parked at the picnic places, upscale gift shops, and restaurants in the area.

The pace in Sonoma County is less frenetic. While Napa is upscale and elegant, Sonoma is overalls-and-corduroy country, with an air of rustic innocence. But the county's Alexander, Dry Creek, and Russian River valleys are no less productive of award-winning vintages. The Sonoma countryside also offers excellent opportunities for hiking, biking, camping, and fishing.

In addition to state-of-the-art viticulture, the Wine Country also provides a look at California's history. In the town of Sonoma, you'll find remnants of Mexican California and the solid, ivy-covered, brick wineries built by Haraszthy and his disciples. The original attraction here was the water, and the rush to the spas of Calistoga, promoted by the indefatigable Gold Rush entrepreneur Samuel Brannan in the late-19th century, left a legacy of fretwork, clapboard, and Gothic architecture. More recent architectural details can be found at the Art Nouveau mansion of the Beringer brothers in St. Helena and the latter-day postmodern extravaganza of Clos Pegase in Calistoga.

The courting of the tourist trade has produced tensions, and some residents wonder whether projects like the Wine Train, running between Napa and St. Helena, brings the theme-park atmosphere a little too close to home. These fears may or may not be realized, but the natural beauty of the landscape will always draw tourists. Whether in the spring, when the vineyards bloom yellow with mustard flowers, or in the fall, when fruit is ripening, this slice of California has a feel reminiscent of the hills of Tuscany or Provence. Haraszthy was right: This is a chosen place.

Getting Around

By Plane The San Francisco and Oakland airports are closest to the Wine Country.

By Bus **Greyhound-Trailways** (tel. 415/558–6789) runs buses from the San Francisco Terminal at 7th and Mission streets to and from Sonoma (one each day) and to Santa Rosa (two each day). **Sonoma County Area Transit** (tel. 707/585–7516) and **The Vine** (tel. 707/255–7631), Napa's bus service, provide local transportation within towns in the Wine Country.

By Car Although traffic on the two-lane country roads can be heavy, the best way to get around in the Wine Country is by private car. Rental cars are available at the airports and in San Francisco, Oakland, Santa Rosa, and Napa.

The Rider's Guide (484 Lake Park Ave., Box 255, Oakland 94610, tel. 510/653–2553) produces tapes about the history, landmarks, and wineries of the Sonoma and Napa valleys that you can play in your car. The tapes are available for $11.95, plus $2 postage at Waldenbooks, Brentano's, and Books Inc. in San Francisco, as well as at selected locations (wineries and hotels) in the Wine Country itself. Call to inquire about current availability.

Guided Tours

Full-day guided tours of the Wine Country usually include lunch and cost about $50. The guides, some of whom are winery owners themselves, know the area well and may show you some lesser-known cellars.

Five-Oaks Farm (15851 Chalk Hill Rd., Healdsburg 95448, tel. 707/433–2422) offers horse-drawn vineyard tours through the Alexander Valley. The tours run Thursday–Sunday from April through November, weather permitting, and include lunch or dinner.

Gray Line Inc. (425 Mission St., San Francisco 94105, tel. 415/558–9400) has bright-red double-deckers that tour the Wine Country. Reservations are required.

Great Pacific Tour Co. (518 Octavia St., San Francisco 94102, tel. 415/626–4499) offers full-day tours, including a picnic lunch, to Napa and Sonoma, in passenger vans that seat 13.

HMS Tours (1057 College Ave. #206, Santa Rosa 95404, tel. 707/526–2922 or 800/367–5348) offers customized and regularly scheduled tours of the Wine Country.

Maxi Tours (545 Eddy St., Box 59046, San Francisco 94159, tel. 415/441–6294) provides air-conditioned van tours of the Wine Country.

Napa Valley Wine Train (1275 McKinstry St., Napa 94559, tel. 707/253–2111; 800/522–4142; 800/427–4124 in CA) allows you to enjoy lunch, dinner, or a weekend brunch on one of several restored 1915 Pullman railroad cars that now run between Napa and St. Helena on tracks that were formerly owned by the Southern Pacific Railroad. Round-trip fare is $29; a three-course brunch or luncheon costs $22, and a five-course dinner costs $45 (train fare is reduced to $14.50 for dinner parties of two or more). During the winter service is limited to Thursday through Sunday. There is a special car for families with children on the Saturday or Sunday brunch trip.

Superior Sightseeing (642 Alvarado St., Suite 100, San Francisco 94114, tel. 415/550–1352) limits its full-day excursions to 20 passengers. The company offers personalized itineraries on request and provides free hotel pickup as well as group and senior-citizen rates. Reservations are required.

Important Addresses and Numbers

Tourist Information

Redwood Empire Association (785 Market St., 15th floor, San Francisco 94103, tel. 415/543–8334). The Redwood Empire Visitors' Guide is available free at the office or for $2 by mail.

Napa Valley Conference and Visitors Bureau (1310 Napa Town Center, Napa 94558, tel. 707/226–7459).

Sonoma Valley Visitors Bureau (453 1st St. E, Sonoma 95476, tel. 707/996–1090).

Sonoma County Convention and Visitors Bureau (10 4th St., Suite 100, Santa Rosa 95401, tel. 707/575–1191 or 800/326–7666).

Calistoga Chamber of Commerce (1458 Lincoln Ave., Calistoga 94515, tel. 707/942–6333).

Healdsburg Chamber of Commerce (217 Healdsburg Ave., Healdsburg 95448, tel. 707/433–6935 or 800/648–9922 in CA).

St. Helena Chamber of Commerce (1080 Main St., Box 124, St. Helena 94574, tel. 707/963–4456 or 800/767–8528).

Emergencies The emergency number for fire, police, ambulance, and paramedics is 911; or dial 0 for the operator and ask to be connected with the appropriate agency.

Exploring

There are three major paths through the Wine Country: U.S. 101 north from Santa Rosa, Highways 12 and 121 through Sonoma County, and Highway 29 north from Napa.

From San Francisco, cross the Golden Gate Bridge and follow U.S. 101 to Santa Rosa and points north. Or cross the Golden Gate, go north on U.S. 101, east on Highway 37, and north on

Highway 121 into Sonoma. Yet another route runs over the San Francisco Bay Bridge and along I–80 to Vallejo, where Highway 29 leads north to Napa.

If you approach the Wine Country from the east, you'll travel along I–80 and then turn northwest on Highway 12 for a 10-minute drive through a hilly pass to Highway 29. From the north, take U.S. 101 south to Geyserville, turn southeast on Highway 128, and drive down into the Napa Valley.

Wineries

Choosing which of the 400 or so wineries to visit will be difficult, and the range of opportunities makes it tempting to make multiple stops. Being adventuresome will pay off. The wineries along the more frequented arteries of the Napa Valley tend to charge nominal fees for tasting, but in Sonoma County, where there is less tourist traffic, fees are the exception rather than the rule. In Sonoma, you are more likely to run into a wine-grower who is willing to spend part of an afternoon in convivial conversation than you are along the main drag of Napa Valley, where the waiter serving yards of bar has time to do little more than keep track of the rows of glasses.

Unless otherwise noted, visits to the wineries listed are free.

Highway 29 The town of **Napa** is the gateway into the famous valley, with its unrivaled climate and neat rows of vineyards. The towns in the area are small, and their Victorian Gothic architecture adds to the self-contained and isolated feeling that permeates the valley.

A few miles north of Napa is the small town of **Yountville**. Turn west off Highway 2 at the Veterans Home exit and then up California Drive to **Domaine Chandon**, owned by the French champagne producer Moët-Hennessy and Louis Vuitton. You can tour the sleek modern facilities of this beautifully maintained property and sample flutes of the *méthode champenoise* sparkling wine. Champagne is $4 per glass, the hors d'oeuvres are complimentary, and there is an elegant restaurant. *California Dr., Yountville, tel. 707/944–2280. Restaurant closed Mon. and Tues. Nov.–Apr. No dinner Mon.–Tues. May–Oct. Tours daily 11–5 except Mon.–Tues., Nov.–Apr. Closed major holidays.*

Vintage 1870, a 22-acre complex of boutiques, restaurants, and gourmet stores is on the east side of Highway 29. The vine-covered brick buildings were built in 1870 and originally housed a winery, livery stable, and distillery. The adjacent **Red Rock Cafe** is housed in the train depot Samuel Brannan built in 1868 for his privately owned Napa Valley Railroad. The remodeled railroad cars now accommodate guests at the Napa Valley Railway Inn (*see* Lodging, below).

Washington Square, at the north end of Yountville, is a new complex of shops and restaurants; **Pioneer Cemetery,** where the town's founder George Yount is buried, is across the street.

Many premier wineries lie along the route from Yountville to St. Helena.

At **Robert Mondavi,** tasters are required to take the 40- to 60-minute tour before they imbibe. There are concerts on the

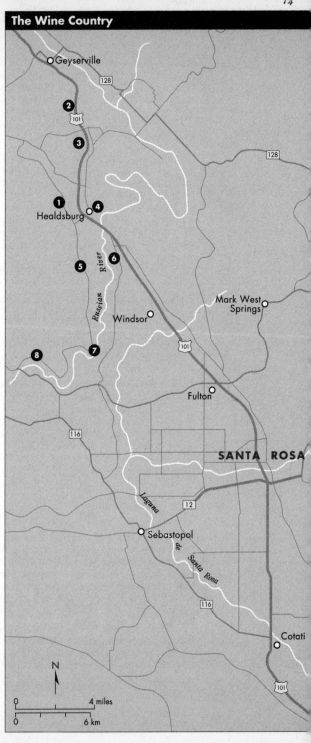

Beringer, **16**
Buena Vista, **27**
Charles Krug, **14**
Chateau Montelena, **9**
Christian Brothers, **15**
Clos du Bois, **4**
Clos du Val, **22**
Clos Pegase, **10**
Davis Bynum, **7**
Domaine Chandon, **20**
Freemark Abbey, **13**
Glen Ellen, **23**
Gloria Ferrer, **24**
Hans Kornell, **12**
Hop Kiln, **5**
Korbel, **8**
Lambert Bridge, **1**
Lytton Springs, **2**
Piper Sonoma, **6**
Robert Stemmler, **3**
Robert Mondavi, **19**
Rutherford Hill, **18**
Sebastiani, **26**
Stag's Leap
  Winery, **21**
Sterling, **11**
V. Sattui, **17**
Viansa, **25**

The Wine Country

Geyserville

128

101

128

Healdsburg

Russian River

Mark West
Springs

Windsor

101

Fulton

116

SANTA ROSA

Laguna

12

Sebastopol

de Santa Rosa

116

Cotati

101

N

0   4 miles

0   6 km

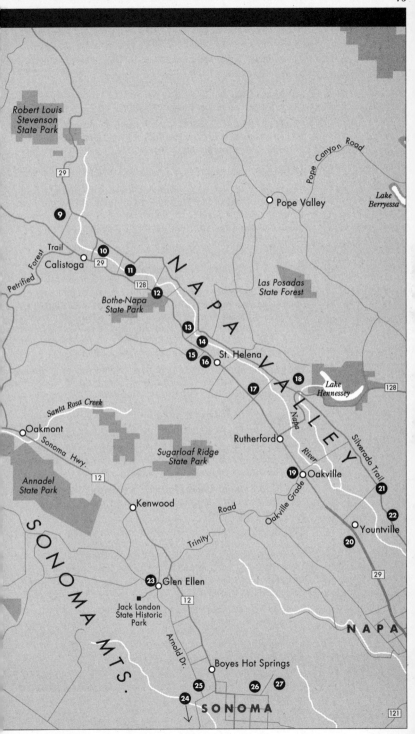

Robert Louis
Stevenson
State Park

29

Trail
Forest

Petrified Forest Trail

Calistoga

9

10

29

11

128

12

Bothe-Napa
State Park

13

14

15

16 St. Helena

17

18

Lake
Hennessey

128

N A P A   V A L L E Y

Pope Valley

Pope Canyon Road

Lake
Berryessa

Las Posadas
State Forest

Santa Rosa Creek

Oakmont

Sonoma Hwy.

Annadel
State Park

12

Kenwood

Sugarloaf Ridge
State Park

Trinity

Road

Rutherford

19 Oakville

Oakville Grade

Napa River

Silverado Trail

21

22

Yountville

20

29

S O N O M A   M T S .

23 Glen Ellen

Jack London
State Historic
Park

12

Arnold Dr.

Boyes Hot Springs

25

24

26

27

S O N O M A

121

N A P A

grounds during the summer. *7801 St. Helena Hwy., Oakville, tel. 707/963–9611. Open daily 10–4:30. Reservations advised in summer. Closed major holidays.*

The **Charles Krug Winery** opened in 1861 when Count Haraszthy lent Krug a small cider press. It is the oldest winery in the Napa Valley. Run by the Peter Mondavi family, it also has a gift shop. *2800 N. Main St., St. Helena, tel. 707/963–5057. Open daily 10–5. Closed major holidays.*

The wine made at **V. Sattui** is sold only on the premises; the tactic draws crowds, as does the huge delicatessen with its exotic cheeses. Award-winning wines include Dry Johannisberg Rieslings, Zinfandels, and Madeiras. *Main St. at White La., St. Helena, tel. 707/963–7774. Open daily 9–5. Closed Christmas.*

The town of St. Helena boasts many Victorian buildings. Don't overlook the **Silverado Museum,** two blocks east from Main Street on Adams Street. Its Robert Louis Stevenson memorabilia includes first editions, manuscripts, and photographs. *1490 Library La., tel. 707/963–3757. Admission free. Open Tues.–Sun. noon–4. Closed major holidays.*

Beringer Vineyards has been operating continually since 1876. Tastings are held in the Rhine House mansion, where handcarved oak and walnut and stained glass show Belgian Art Nouveau at its most opulent. The Beringer brothers, Frederick and Joseph, built the mansion in 1883 for the princely sum of $30,000. Tours include a visit to the deep limestone tunnels in which the wines mature. *2000 Main St., St. Helena, tel. 707/963–4812. Open daily 9:30–5. Closed major holidays.*

Christian Brothers Greystone Cellars is housed in an imposing stone building built in 1889 and recently renovated. There are tours every half hour, displays on wine-barrel making, and an unusual collection of corkscrews. *2555 Main St., St. Helena, tel. 707/967–3112. Open daily 10–5. Closed major holidays.*

Freemark Abbey Winery was founded in the 1880s by Josephine Tychson, the first woman to establish a winery in California. *3022 St. Helena Hwy. N, St. Helena, tel. 707/963–9694. Open daily 10–4:30. One tour daily at 2 PM.*

The **Hurd Beeswax Candle Factory** is next door, with two restaurants and a gift shop that specializes in handcrafted candles made on the premises.

The **Sterling Vineyards** sits on a hilltop to the east near Calistoga. The pristine white Mediterranean-style buildings are reached by an enclosed gondola from the valley floor; the view from the tasting room is superb. *1111 Dunaweal La., Calistoga, tel. 707/942–5151. Tram fee: $5 for adults, children under 16 free. Open daily 10:30–4:30. Closed major holidays.*

At **Clos Pegase,** neoclassicism sets the tone. The winery, designed by architect Michael Graves, the exemplar of postmodernism, and commissioned by Jan Schrem, a publisher and art collector, pays homage to art, wine, and mythology. *1060 Dunaweal La., Calistoga, tel. 707/942–4981. Open 10:30–4:30. Closed major holidays.*

Calistoga, at the head of the Napa Valley, is noted for its mineral water, hot mineral springs, mud baths, steam baths, and massages. The Calistoga Hot Springs Resort was founded in 1859 by that maverick entrepreneur Sam Brannan, whose ambition was to found "the Saratoga of California." He tripped up the pronunciation of the phrase at a formal banquet—it came out "Calistoga"—and the name stuck. One of his cottages, preserved as the Sharpsteen Museum, has a magnificent diorama of the resort in its heyday. *1311 Washington St., tel. 707/942–5911. Donations accepted. Open May–Oct., daily 10–4; Nov.–Apr., daily noon–4.*

Chateau Montelena is a vine-covered 1882 building set amid Chinese-inspired gardens complete with a lake, red pavilions, and arched bridges. It's a romantic spot for a picnic but you have to reserve in advance. *1429 Tubbs La., Calistoga, tel. 707/942–5105. Open daily 10–4. Tours at 11 and 2 by appointment only.*

The **Silverado Trail,** which runs parallel to Highway 29, takes you away from the madding crowd to some distinguished wineries as you travel north from Napa:

Clos du Val. Bernard Portet, the French owner, produces a celebrated Cabernet Sauvignon. *5330 Silverado Trail, tel. 707/252–6711. Open daily 10–4:30.*
Stag's Leap Wine Cellars. The Cabernet Sauvignon produced here was rated higher than many venerable Bordeaux wines at a blind tasting in Paris in 1976. *5766 Silverado Trail, tel. 707/944–2020. Open daily 10–4. Tours by appointment. Closed major holidays.*
Rutherford Hill Winery. The wine here is aged in French oak barrels stacked in more than 30,000 square feet of caves. You can tour the nation's largest such facility and picnic on the grounds. *200 Rutherford Hill Rd., Rutherford, tel. 707/963–7194. Open weekdays 10–4:30, weekends 10–5. Tours, which include the caves, are conducted on the half hour 11:30–3:30.*
Hanns Kornell Champagne Cellars. Kornell opened his winery in 1952, and still checks in on the operation, now run by his family. *1091 Larkmead La., just east of Hwy. 29, 4 mi north of St. Helena, tel. 707/963–1237. Open daily 10–4:30.*

The **Calistoga Soaring Center** will give you a bird's-eye view of the entire valley, offering rides in gliders and biplanes, as well as tandem skydiving. *1546 Lincoln Ave., tel. 707/942–5000. Fee: $70–$160. Open daily 9 AM–sunset, weather permitting.*

You don't have to be a registered guest at a spa to experience a mud bath. At **Dr. Wilkinson's Hot Springs** a $39 fee gets you "The Works": mud baths, individual mineral-water showers, and a mineral-water whirlpool, followed by time in the steam room, and a blanket wrap. For $59, you also get a half-hour massage. *Reservations are recommended. 1507 Lincoln Ave., Calistoga, tel. 707/942–4102. Open daily 8:30–3:30.*

Highway 12   Rustic Sonoma is anchored by its past. It is the site of the last and the northernmost of the 21 missions established by the Franciscan order of Fra Junípero Serra, and its central plaza includes the largest group of old adobes north of Monterey. The **Mission San Francisco Solano,** whose chapel and school labored to bring Christianity to the Indians, is now a museum that displays a collection of 19th-century watercolors. *114 Spain St. E, tel. 707/938–1519. Admission: $2 adults, $1 children 6–17; includes the Sonoma Barracks on the central plaza and General Vallejo's home, Lachryma Montis (see below). Open daily 10–5. Closed Thanksgiving, Christmas, New Year's Day.*

Time Out The four-block **Sonoma Plaza** is an inviting array of shops and food stores that look out onto the shady park and attract gourmets from miles around. You can pick up the makings for a first-rate picnic here. The **Sonoma French Bakery** (466 1st St. E) is famous for its sourdough bread and cream puffs. The **Sonoma Sausage Co.** (453 1st St. W) produces a mind-boggling selection of bratwurst, bologna, *boudin* (French blood sausage), bangers, and other Old World sausages. There are good cold cuts, too. The **Sonoma Cheese Factory** (2 Spain St.), run by the same family for four generations, makes Sonoma jack cheese and a tangy new creation, Sonoma Teleme. You can peer through the glass windows at the cheese-making process: great swirling baths of milk and curds and the wheels of cheese being pressed flat to dry.

A few blocks west (and quite a hike) is the tree-lined approach to **Lachryma Montis,** which General Mariano Vallejo, the last Mexican governor of California, built for his large family in 1851. The Victorian Gothic house is secluded in the midst of beautiful gardens; opulent Victorian furnishings, including a white marble fireplace in every room, are particularly noteworthy. The state purchased the home in 1933. *Spain St. W, tel. 707/938–1519. Admission: $2 adults, $1 children 6–17. Open Wed.-Sun. 10–5. Closed Thanksgiving, Christmas, New Year's Day.*

The **Sebastiani Vineyards,** originally planted by Franciscans of the Sonoma Mission in 1825 and later owned by General Vallejo, were bought by Samuele Sebastiani in 1904. The Sebastianis recently helped popularize "blush" wines, and Sylvia Sebastiani has recorded her good Italian home cooking in a family recipe book, *Mangiamo.* Tours include a look at an unusual collection of impressive carved oak casks. *389 4th St. E, tel. 707/938–5532. Open daily 10–5. Closed major holidays.*

The landmark **Buena Vista Winery** (follow signs from the plaza), set among towering trees and fountains, is a must-see in Sonoma. It was here, in 1857, that Count Agoston Haraszthy de Mokcsa laid the basis for modern California wine-making, bucking the conventional wisdom that vines should be planted on well-watered ground and planting instead on well-drained hillsides. Chinese laborers dug the cool aging tunnels 100 feet into the hillside, and the limestone they extracted was used to build the main house. Although the wines are produced elsewhere today, there are tours, a gourmet shop, art gallery, wine museum, and great picnic spots. *18000 Old Winery Rd., tel. 707/938–1266. Open daily 10–5.*

In the Carneros region of the Sonoma Valley, south of Sonoma, the wines at **Gloria Ferrer Champagne Caves** are aged in a "cava," or cellar, where several feet of earth maintain a constant temperature. *23555 Hwy. 121, tel. 707/996–7256. Tasting is $2.50–$4 by the glass, depending on the type of champagne. Open daily 10:30–5:30.*

The newest and perhaps most-talked-about winery in Sonoma Valley is **Viansa,** opened by a son of the famous Sebastiani family, who decided to strike out on his own. Looking like a transplanted Tuscan villa, the winery's ochre-colored building is surrounded by olive trees and overlooks the valley. Inside is an Italian food and gift market. *25200 Arnold Dr., Sonoma, tel. 707/935–4747. Open daily 10–5.*

Head north on Highway 12 through Sonoma Valley, in which writer Jack London lived for many years, and for whom much around here has been named. The drive along Highway 12 takes you through orchards and rows of vineyards, with oak-covered mountain ranges flanking the valley. Some 2 million cases of wine are bottled in this area annually, and the towns of Glen Ellen and Kenwood are rich in history and lore. **Glen Ellen,** with its century-old Jack London Bar, is nestled at the base of the hill leading to Jack London State Park and the Glen Ellen Winery. Nearby is Grist Mill Inn, a historic landmark with shops, and Jack London Village, with a charming bookstore filled with London's books and memorabilia. **Kenwood** is home to several important wineries, a historic train depot and several eateries and shops specializing in locally produced gourmet products.

In the hills above Glen Ellen is **Jack London State Historic Park.** The House of Happy Walls is a museum of London's effects, including his collection of South Sea artifacts. The ruins of Wolf House, which London designed and which mysteriously burned down just before he was to move in, are nearby, and London is buried on the property. *2400 London Ranch Rd., tel. 707/938–5216. Parking: $5 per car, $4 when driven by a senior citizen. Park open daily 8–sunset, museum 10–5. Museum closed Thanksgiving, Christmas, New Year's Day.*

The well-known **Glen Ellen Winery** uses watercolors painted by Jan Haraszthy, one of the count's descendants, on its labels. The originals hang in the tasting room. *1883 London Ranch Rd., Glen Ellen, tel. 707/935–3000. Open daily 10–4:30.*

U.S. 101   Santa Rosa is the Wine Country's largest city and your best bet for a moderately priced hotel room, especially if you haven't reserved rooms.

The **Luther Burbank Memorial Gardens** commemorate the great botanist, who lived and worked on these grounds for 50 years, single-handedly developing modern techniques of hybridization. Arriving as a young man from New England, he wrote: "I firmly believe . . . that this is the chosen spot of all the earth, as far as nature is concerned." The Santa Rosa plum, the Shasta daisy, and the lily of the Nile agapanthus are among the 800 or so plants he developed or improved. In the dining room of his house, a Webster's Dictionary of 1946 lies open to a page on which the verb "burbank" is defined as "to modify and improve plant life." *Santa Rosa and Sonoma Aves., tel. 707/524–5445. Gardens free, open daily 8–5. Home tours: $1, children under 12 free; open Apr.–Oct., Wed.–Sun. 10–3:30.*

The wineries of Sonoma County are located along winding roads and are not immediately obvious to the casual visitor; a tour of the vineyards that lie along the Russian River is a leisurely and especially bucolic experience. For a free map of the area, contact Russian River Wine Road (Box 46, Healdsburg, 95448, tel. 707/433–6782).

For a historical overview, start at the imposing **Korbel Champagne Cellars,** which displays photographic documents of the North West Railway in a former train stop on its property. *13250 River Rd., Guerneville, tel. 707/887–2294. Open Oct.–Apr., daily 9–4:30; May–Sept., daily 9–5. Tours on the hour from 10–3.*

Armstrong Woods State Reserve just outside of Guerneville contains 752 acres of virgin redwoods and is the best place in the Wine Country to see California's most famous trees. West of Guerneville along the Russian River Road (Highway 116) that leads to the Pacific Ocean and the rugged Sonoma coast is more redwood country and a string of small towns. **Duncans Mills** is an old logging and railroad town with a complex of shops and a small museum in an old train depot. At the coast is **Jenner,** where the Russian River meets the Pacific. A colony of harbor seals makes its home here March through June. There are several bed-and-breakfast inns here and restaurants specializing in seafood.

Traveling down the River Road east of Guerneville, turn left down Westside Road and follow it as it winds past a number of award-winning wineries.

Davis Bynum Winery is an up-and-coming label that offers a full line of varietal wines that have done well in recent competitions. *8075 Westside Rd., Healdsburg, tel. 707/433–5852. Open daily 10–5.*

The **Hop Kiln Winery** is located in an imposing hop-drying barn built during the early 1900s, which has been used as the backdrop for such films as the 1960 Lassie with James Stewart. *6050 Westside Rd., Healdsburg, tel. 707/433–6491. Open daily 10–5.*

Lambert Bridge produces some superbly elegant Cabernet Sauvignons and Merlots. *4085 W. Dry Creek Rd., Healdsburg, tel. 707/433–5855. Open daily 10–4:30.*

The **Robert Stemmler Winery** draws on German traditions of wine-making and specializes in Pinot noir. There are picnic facilities on the grounds. *3805 Lambert Bridge Rd., Healdsburg (Dry Creek Rd. exit from Hwy. 101, northwest 3 mi to Lambert Bridge Rd.), tel. 707/433–6334. Open daily 10:30–4:30.*

Lytton Springs Winery produces the archetype of the Sonoma Zinfandel, a dark, fruity wine with a high alcohol content. There is still dispute over its origin and whether it was transplanted from stock in New England, but the vines themselves are distinctive, gnarled, and stocky, many of them over a century old. *650 Lytton Springs Rd., Healdsburg, tel. 707/433–7721. Open daily 10–4.*

In Healdsburg, back on U.S. 101, is **Clos du Bois,** which features wine-making at its most high tech. You can take a tour by appointment, but you'd do better to concentrate on sampling the fine estate wines of the Alexander and Dry Creek valleys that are made here. *5 Fitch St., tel. 707/433–5576. Open daily 10–5.*

South of Healdsburg, off U.S. 101, are the **Piper Sonoma Cellars,** a state-of-the-art winery that specializes in *méthode champenoise* sparkling wines. *11447 Old Redwood Hwy., Healdsburg, tel. 707/433–8843. Open daily 10–5.*

Time Out Once you've seen, heard about, and tasted enough wine for one day, head over to **Kozlowski's Raspberry Farm** (5566 Gravenstein [Hwy. 116], tel. 707/887–1587), in Forestville, where jams are made from every berry imaginable. Also in Forestville, **Brother Juniper's** (6544 Front St. [Hwy. 116], tel. 707/ 887–7908 and at 463 Sebastopol Ave., Santa Rosa, tel. 707/542–

9012) makes a heavenly *Struan* bread of wheat, corn, oats, brown rice, and bran. *Open Mon.–Sat. 9–4:30.*

What to See and Do with Children

In the **Bale Grist Mill State Historic Park** there is a restored 1846 flour mill powered by a 36-foot overshot waterwheel. Hiking trails lead from the access road to the mill pond. *3 mi north of St. Helena on Hwy. 29, tel. 707/942–4575. Day use: $2 adults, $1 children 7–18. Open daily 10–5.*

Old Faithful Geyser of California blasts a 60-foot tower of steam and vapor about every 40 minutes; the pattern is disrupted if there's an earthquake in the offing. One of just three regularly erupting geysers in the world, it is fed by an underground river that heats to 350° F. The spout lasts three minutes. Picnic facilities are available. *1299 Tubbs La., 1 mi north of Calistoga, tel. 707/942–6463. Admission: $3.50 adults, $2 children 6–11. Open daily 9–6 during daylight saving time, 9–5 in winter.*

In the **Petrified Forest** you can see the result of volcanic eruptions of Mt. St. Helena 6 million years ago. The force of the explosion uprooted the gigantic redwoods, covered them with volcanic ash, and infiltrated the trees with silicas and minerals, causing petrification. There is a museum, and picnic facilities are available. *4100 Petrified Forest Rd., 5 mi west of Calistoga, tel. 707/942–6667. Admission: $3 adults, $2 senior citizens, $1 children 4–11. Open daily 10–6 in summer, 10–5 in winter.*

The Redwood Empire Ice Arena in Santa Rosa is not just another skating rink. It was built by local resident Charles Schulz, creator of *Peanuts.* The Snoopy Gallery and gift shop, with Snoopy books, clothing, and life-size comic-strip characters is delightful. *1667 W. Steele La., tel. 707/546–7147. Public skating in the afternoon.*

A scale steam train at **Train Town** runs for 20 minutes through a forested park with trestles, bridges, and small animals. *20264 Broadway, 1 mi south of Sonoma Plaza, tel. 707/938–3912. Admission: $2.60 adults, $1.90 senior citizens and children under 16. Open mid-June–Labor Day daily 10:30–5; Sept.–mid-June, weekends and holidays 10:30–5:30. Closed Christmas.*

Howarth Memorial Park, in Santa Rosa, has a lake where canoes, rowboats, paddleboats, and small sailboats can be rented for $3–$4 an hour. The children's area has a playground, pony rides, petting zoo, merry-go-round, and a miniature train. Fishing, tennis, and hiking trails are also available. *Summerfield Rd. off Montgomery Rd., tel. 707/539–1499. Amusements: 25¢–50¢. Park open daily; children's area open Wed.–Sun. in summer, weekends in spring and fall.*

Off the Beaten Track

You'll see breathtaking views of both the Sonoma and Napa valleys along the hairpin turns of the **Oakville Grade,** which twists along the range dividing the two valleys. The surface of the road is good, and if you're comfortable with mountain driving, you'll enjoy this half-hour excursion. Trucks are advised not to take this route.

Robert Louis Stevenson State Park, on Highway 53, 3 miles northeast of Calistoga, encompasses the summit of Mt. St. Helena. It was here, in an abandoned bunkhouse of the Silverado Mine, that Stevenson and his bride, Fanny Osbourne, spent their honeymoon in the summer of 1880. The stay inspired Stevenson's "The Silverado Squatters," and Spyglass Hill in *Treasure Island* is thought to be a portrait of Mt. St. Helena. The park's 3,000 acres are undeveloped except for a fire trail that leads to the site of the cabin, which is marked with a marble tablet, and on to the summit. Picnicking is permitted, but fires are not.

Shopping

Most wineries will ship purchases. Don't expect bargains at the wineries themselves, where prices are generally as high as at retail outlets. Residents report that the area's supermarkets stock a wide selection of local wines at lower prices. Gift shops in the larger wineries offer the ultimate in gourmet items—you could easily stock up on early Christmas presents.

Sports

Ballooning This sport has fast become part of the scenery in the Wine Country, and many hotels arrange excursions. Most flights take place soon after sunrise, when the calmest, coolest time of day offers maximum lift and soft landings. Prices depend on the duration of the flight, number of passengers, and services (some companies provide pickup at your lodging, champagne brunch after the flight, etc.). Expect to spend about $150 per person. Companies that provide flights include **Balloons Above the Valley** (Box 3838, Napa 94558, tel. 707/253–2222; in Northern CA, 800/464–6824), **Napa Valley Balloons** (Box 2860, Yountville 94599, tel. 707/253–2224; in CA 800/253–2224), and **Once in a Lifetime** (Box 795, Calistoga 94515, tel. 707/942–6541 or 800/722–6665 in CA).

Bicycling One of the best ways to experience the countryside is on two wheels, and the Eldorado Bike Trail through the area is considered one of the best. Reasonably priced rentals are available in most towns.

Golf Though the weather is mild year-round, rain may occasionally prevent your teeing off in the winter months. Call to check on greens fees at **Fountaingrove Country Club** (1525 Fountaingrove Pkwy., Santa Rosa, tel. 707/579–4653), **Oakmont Inn and Golf Course** (7025 Oakmont Dr., Santa Rosa, tel. 707/539–0415 or 707/548–2454), or **Silverado Country Club** (1600 Atlas Peak Rd., Napa, tel. 707/257–0200).

Dining

By Bruce David Colen

A number of the Wine Country's kitchens are the domains of nationally prominent chefs. The emphasis everywhere on fresh ingredients goes hand in hand with local bounty: vegetables and fruits, seafood, lamb, and poultry. Although a number of the restaurants are expensive (dinner at Auberge du Soleil or the Silverado Country Club may run more than $50 per person), the area has enough comfortably priced trattorias, cafés, and food-serving wine bars, as well as gourmet delis, to fit slim budgets.

With few exceptions (which are noted), dress is informal. Where reservations are indicated to be essential, you may need to reserve a week or more ahead during the summer and early fall harvest seasons.

The most highly recommended restaurants are indicated by a star ★.

Category	Cost*
Very Expensive	over $40
Expensive	$25–$40
Moderate	$16–$25
Inexpensive	under $16

per person, excluding drinks, service, and 8.25% sales tax

Calistoga
Moderate

Alex's. This family-style restaurant features prime rib and New York steaks. If you're not in the mood for beef, try one of the several fish entrées or the daily seafood special. Don't pass up the family-recipe cheesecake. *1437 Lincoln Ave., tel. 707/942–6868. AE, MC, V. No lunch. Closed Mon.*

Calistoga Inn. With the atmosphere and appeal of a village tavern and the talents of a big-city chef, this restaurant serves hearty California cuisine and excellent fish dishes. First-rate local wines are also featured. *1250 Lincoln Ave., tel. 707/942–4101. Reservations advised. Dress: casual. MC, V.*

Geyserville
Very Expensive
★

Château Souverain Restaurant at the Winery. There is a gorgeous view of the Alexander Valley vineyards from the dining room and terrace. The California/Continental menu is imaginative: Sonoma lamb loin with soy mustard ginger glaze; black peppercorn/rosemary/lamb essence and Japanese eggplant; grilled marinated quail with smoked pear puree, pancetta, and basil quail essence. *400 Souverain Rd. (Independence La. exit west from Hwy. 101), tel. 707/433–3141. Reservations advised. Jacket required at dinner. DC, MC, V. Closed Mon. and Tues.*

Healdsburg
Very Expensive

Madrona Manor. The chef uses a brick oven, smokehouse, orchard, and herb-and-vegetable garden to enhance other fresh produce and seafood on his California-cuisine menus. Dinners and Sunday brunch are served in the dining room and terrace of an 1881 Victorian mansion on a hilltop west of town. À la carte and prix fixe. *1001 Westside Rd., tel. 707/433–4231. Reservations advised. Jacket required. AE, D, DC, MC, V.*

Moderate

Jacob Horner. California cuisine with an emphasis on locally grown vegetables ("no more than 2 miles from the restaurant") and fresh seafood, lamb, and duck near at hand is the focus here. An enthusiastic owner-chef has put together a comfortable, good-looking restaurant on Healdsburg's charming town plaza. There is an extensive, award-winning wine list with 17 wines served by the glass. *106 Matheson St., tel. 707/433–3939. Reservations advised. AE, MC, V. No dinner Mon. Closed Sun.*

Inexpensive

Samba Java. Whether you decide it's a coffeehouse, a café, or a restaurant, one thing is for sure: This delightful hole-in-the-wall is a cozy, fun place to dine. Chef-owner Colleen McGlynn, late of San Francisco's super Stars, prepares bountiful California/Italian dishes at recession-era prices. Begin with the succulent, just shucked oysters, then eat your fill of pasta with artichokes and prosciutto, but save room for a truly great apple cobbler. *109A Plaza St., tel. 707/433-5282. No dinner Sun.– Thurs., no lunch Mon. D, MC, V.*

Napa
Very Expensive

Silverado Country Club. There are two dining rooms and a bar and grill at this large, famous resort. Vintner's Court, with California cuisine, serves dinner only—there is a seafood buffet on Friday night—and a champagne brunch on Sunday. Royal Oak serves steak, seafood, and lobster for dinner; in summer, it also serves lunch. The bar and grill is open for breakfast and lunch year-round. *1600 Atlas Peak Rd., 707/257-0200. Reservations advised. Jacket advised at dinner. AE, DC, MC, V.*

Expensive

French Laundry. Situated in a lovely old two-story house with wraparound balconies, and surrounded by an herb-and-flower garden, this is one of the restaurants that put Wine Country cuisine on the national map. The cooking is simple, pure French Provençal: braised tongue, veal loin, oxtails, and the house specialty, pasta with melon seeds. The prix fixe, five-course menu seems pricey at $45 but includes second helpings, and the excellent wine list is remarkably inexpensive. *Washington and Creek Sts., tel. 707/944-2380. Reservations advised. Dress: upscale casual. MC, V. Open Wed.–Sun., dinner only; open Sun. in summer.*

Moderate–Expensive
★

Table 29. Two of the best-known West Coast chefs, Alice Waters and Jonathan Waxman, have always preached that the nearer the source of produce, the better the food, and now they're proving it in a joint venture that's become the latest Napa Valley hit. The menu listings go on forever, and pretty much say it all: an appetizer of local goat cheese on a fennel bed, wild or locally raised pigeon with braised garlic, Vacaville quail, halibut from the North Coast wrapped in bacon, desserts galore featuring the region's fresh berries and fruits. There's something here for every palate. *4110 St. Helena Hwy., tel. 707/224-3300. Reservations advised. D, MC, V.*

Inexpensive

Jonesy's Famous Steak House. This longtime institution at the Napa County Airport is popular with private pilots throughout the West, as well as with locals who like a good steak. Steaks are prepared on an open grill, with large hot rocks placed on top of them while cooking. The building itself is nothing special: plain and businesslike. *2044 Airport Rd., tel. 707/255-2003. Reservations accepted for parties of 6 or more. AE, MC, V. Closed Mon., Thanksgiving, 1 wk. at Christmas, and New Year's Day.*

Rutherford
Moderate–Very Expensive
★

Auberge du Soleil. Sitting on the dining terrace of this hilltop inn, looking down across groves of olive trees to the Napa Valley vineyards, is the closest you can get to the atmosphere and charm of southern France without a passport. The mood is enhanced by a menu centered around light Provençal dishes, using the fresh produce of nearby farms. There is a moderately priced bar menu and a fine list of wines from California, France, and Italy. This place is also a 48-room inn (*see* Lodging, below). *180 Rutherford Hill Rd., tel. 707/963-1211. Reservations advised. Jacket advised. AE, MC, V.*

St. Helena
Very Expensive

Starmont at Meadowood. Three-course prix fixe dinners and an extensive Napa Valley wine list with some French wines are served in an elegantly casual 65-seat restaurant facing the outdoors, maximizing the view over the golf course and the stands of pine trees beyond. There is terrace service in warm weather and a piano bar. Lunch and Sunday brunch are served April–November. *900 Meadowood La., tel. 707/963-3646. Reservations required. Jacket advised. AE, DC, MC, V.*

Moderate–Expensive **Terra.** The delightful couple who own this lovely, unpretentious
★ restaurant, in a century-old stone foundry, learned their culinary skills at the side of chef Wolfgang Puck. Hiro Sone was head chef at L.A.'s Spago and Lissa Doumani was the pastry chef. The menu has an enticing array of American favorites, prepared with Hiro's Japanese-French-Italian finesse: addictive baked mussels in garlic butter; sautéed Miyagi oysters with jalapeño salsa; home-smoked salmon with golden caviar; grilled quail and polenta; and sweetbreads with asparagus and wild mushrooms. Save room for Lissa's desserts. *1345 Railroad Ave., tel. 707/963-8931. Reservations advised. Jacket required. AE, MC, V. Closed Tues.*

Moderate **Brava Terrace.** Another fine chef has swapped big-city hassle for a restaurant of his own in the bucolic Napa Valley. American-born, French-trained Fred Halbert offers the best of both culinary worlds, from a pork cassoulet with French lentils to grilled sirloin steak, and the juiciest prime beef burger north of San Francisco. The setting is stylish yet informal, with charming outdoor dining areas. *3010 St. Helena Hwy. (Hwy. 29), tel. 707/963-9300. Reservations advised. D, DC, MC, V. Closed Jan.*

Tra Vigne. A Napa Valley fieldstone building has been turned into a barn-size trattoria, serving good pizza, pasta, and traditional Italian grilled meat, fish, and fowl. There is terrace dining when weather permits. This is a popular meeting place for locals and tourists. *1050 Charter Oak Ave., tel. 707/963-4444. Reservations advised. Dress: casual. MC, V. Closed July 4, Thanksgiving, and Christmas.*

Inexpensive **Rissa Oriental Cafe.** Should you (and your wallet) care for a break from California/Italian/French cooking, this cheerful, sparkling-clean storefront restaurant is the perfect solution. Average check: $10 at lunch, $13 for dinner. The creation of Hiro Sone (*see* Terra, above), it has become the unofficial clubhouse of local winery folk. Dishes not to miss: shrimp chips with peanut sauce, Mongolian ribs, barbecued pork bun, five-spice calamari, steamed shellfish with sake and scallions, vegetarian Thai curry. *1420 Main St., tel. 707/963-7566. Dress: casual. MC, V. Closed Sun.*

Santa Rosa **John Ash & Co.** The thoroughly regional cuisine here empha-
Expensive sizes beauty, innovation, and the seasonal availability of food
★ products grown in Sonoma County. In spring, local lamb is roasted with hazelnuts and honey; in fall, farm pork is roasted with fresh figs and Gravenstein apples. There are fine desserts and an extensive wine list. Two dining rooms are in a vineyard setting next to Vintner's Inn. There is also a Sunday brunch. *4330 Barnes Rd. (River Rd. exit west from Hwy. 101), tel. 707/527-7687. Reservations advised. Jacket advised. MC, V. Closed Mon.*

Moderate **Equus.** In this handsome restaurant, the equestrian theme is carried out in redwood carvings, murals, and etched glass. A gallery of Sonoma County wines features nearly 300 bottles handpicked by their makers. The extensive menu features California cuisine, with everything made from organically grown local ingredients. *101 Fountaingrove Pkwy., tel. 707/578–6101. Reservations advised. Jacket advised. AE, DC, MC, V.*

Los Robles Lodge Dining Room. This elegant 120-seat dining room specializes in tableside presentations of chateaubriand, lamb, and flaming desserts. Seafood and sautéed dishes are also featured. Since its opening in 1964, this restaurant has developed a loyal following among locals. *9255 Edwards Ave. (Steele La. exit west from Hwy. 101), tel. 707/545–6330. Reservations advised. AE, DC, MC, V. No lunch on major holidays.*

Inexpensive **Omelette Express.** As the name implies, some 300 omelet varieties are offered in this old-fashioned restaurant in historic Railroad Square. *112 4th St., tel. 707/525–1690. No reservations. MC, V. No dinner. Closed Thanksgiving and Christmas.*

Sonoma **Sonoma Mission Inn.** There are two dining rooms as well as a
Expensive poolside terrace for alfresco meals at this attractive, "contemporary country" resort. The inn is also a spa, so the menu has a wide assortment of light dishes, with the accent on fresh salads, fish, and poultry, prepared in nouvelle California style. The annual Sonoma Wine Auction is held on the inn's grounds, so the extensive wine list comes as no surprise. *18140 Hwy. 12, Boyes Hot Springs, tel. 707/938–9000. Reservations advised. Jacket advised at dinner. AE, DC, MC, V.*

Moderate– **L'Esperance.** The dining room is small and pretty, with flow-
Expensive ered tablecloths, burgundy overcloths, and burgundy chairs.
★ There is a choice of classic French entrées, such as rack of lamb, plus a "menu gastronomique" that includes hot and cold appetizers, salad, entrée, dessert, and coffee. *464 1st St. E (down a walkway off the plaza, behind French bakery), tel. 707/996–2757. Reservations advised. AE, MC, V. Closed Mon. and Tues.*

Piatti. On the ground floor of the recently remodeled El Dorado Hotel, a 19th-century landmark building, this is the Sonoma cousin of the Napa Valley Piatti (*see* below). This very friendly trattoria features a nice selection of grilled northern Italian items. *405 1st St., tel. 707/996–3030. Dress: casual. MC, V.*

Moderate **Gino's Restaurant and Bar.** This relaxed, friendly eating and drinking establishment on Sonoma's plaza specializes in fresh seafood and pasta. *420 1st St., tel. 707/996–4466. Reservations advised on weekends. Dress: casual. AE, MC, V.*

La Casa. "Whitewashed stucco, red tile, serapes, and Mexican glass" describes this restaurant just around the corner from Sonoma's plaza. There is an extensive menu of traditional Mexican food: chimichangas, snapper Veracruz, sangria to drink, and flan for dessert. *121 E. Spain St., tel. 707/996–3406. Reservations advised. AE, DC, MC, V.*

Sonoma Hotel Dining Room. Seasonal produce and homemade ingredients are featured in this restaurant filled with antique oak tables and stained glass. The saloon boasts a magnificent old bar of oak and mahogany. There is dining in the garden patio in summer. *110 W. Spain St., tel. 707/996–2996. Reservations advised. Dress: casual. AE, MC, V. Closed Tues. and Wed. in winter.*

★ **Kenwood Restaurant & Bar.** This place's highest recommendation is the fact that when Napa and Sonoma chefs take their night off, they come here. Here the tastes and looks will remind you of a sunny hotel dining room in the South of France. Chef-owner Max Schacher's popular dishes include warm sweetbread salad, giant grape leaves stuffed with minced lamb, pasta of the day, and venison in a Cognac and pepper sauce. There is also terrace dining, weather permitting. *9900 Hwy. 12, tel. 707/833–6326. Reservations advised. MC, V. Closed Mon.*

Inexpensive **The Cafe.** This attractive, upscale diner adjacent to the Sonoma Mission Inn, is where hotel guests go when playing hooky from the spa cuisine, and where the natives congregate for high-calorie breakfasts, sandwiches and burgers, fresh salads, pasta and pizza. *18140 Sonoma Hwy. (Hwy. 12 north of Sonoma), tel. 707/938–9000, ext. 333. Reservations advised. AE, MC, V.*

Yountville **Domaine Chandon.** Nouvelle seafood, pasta, beef, and lamb are
Expensive– prepared imaginatively and presented beautifully. The archi-
Very Expensive tecturally dramatic dining room has views of vineyards and
★ carefully preserved native oaks. There is also outdoor service on a tree-shaded patio. *California Dr., tel. 707/944–2892. Reservations required. Jacket required. AE, D, DC, MC, V. No dinner Mon. or Tues., no lunch Mon. or Tues. Nov.–Apr.*

Moderate– **Anesti's Grill and Rotisserie.** Rotisserie-roasted lamb, duck,
Expensive and suckling pig are specialties of this small, cheerful restaurant with two mesquite grills. *6518 Washington St., tel. 707/944–1500. Reservations advised. AE, DC, MC, V.*
California Cafe & Grill. This is the Wine Country link of a small upscale chain serving bar and grill dishes, plus roast game and a variety of good pastas and salads. Also on the menu: chicken breast with red-pepper jam, *tapas* (Spanish appetizers), warm apple crisp, and an extensive wine selection served in a large, square room with an open kitchen. There is outdoor service on the terrace. Sunday brunch is also served. *6795 Washington St., tel. 707/944–2330. Reservations accepted. AE, DC, MC, V.*
Mama Nina's. This homey and old-fashioned restaurant serves homemade pasta and fresh grilled fish. There's also a children's menu. *6772 Washington St., tel. 707/944–2112. Reservations advised. D, MC, V. No lunch. Closed Easter, Thanksgiving, Christmas Eve, and Christmas Day.*
★ **Mustard's Grill.** Grilled fish, hot smoked meats, fresh local produce, and a good wine list are offered in a simple, unassuming dining room. It's very popular and crowded at prime meal- times. *7399 St. Helena Hwy. (Hwy. 29, 2 mi north of Yountville), tel. 707/944–2424. Reservations required. Dress: casual. MC, V.*
Piatti. A small, stylish trattoria with a pizza oven and open kitchen, this cheery place is full of good smells and happy people. Its authentic, light Italian cooking—from the antipasti to the grilled chicken to the tiramisu—is the perfect cure for a jaded appetite. The pastas are the best bet. *6480 Washington St., tel. 707/944–2070. Reservations advised. Jacket required at dinner. MC, V.*

Inexpensive **The Diner.** This is probably the best-known and most-appreciated stopover in the Napa Valley, especially for breakfast. Be sure to have the local sausages and the house potatoes. At night, many of the specials are Mexican. *6476 Washington St., tel. 707/944–2626. No reservations; expect to wait. No credit cards. Closed Mon.*

Lodging

Make no mistake, staying in the Wine Country is expensive. The inns, hotels, and motels are usually exquisitely appointed, and many are fully booked long in advance of the summer season. Since Santa Rosa is the largest population center in the area, it has the largest selection of rooms, many at moderate rates. Try there if you've failed to reserve in advance or have a limited budget. For those seeking romantic and homey atmosphere, check out the dozens of bed-and-breakfast inns that have been established in the Victorian homes and old hotels of the Wine Country (the tourist bureaus of Sonoma and Napa counties both provide information and brochures on B&Bs. Families should note, however, that small children are often discouraged as guests. Aside from the charm and romance, an advantage of B&Bs (which cost more than the average motel), is the often sumptuous breakfast that is included in the price. In the Wine Country, the morning meal often features local produce and specialties. For all accommodations in the area, rates are lower on weeknights and about 20% less in the winter.

Highly recommended hotels are indicated by a star ★.

Category	Cost*
Very Expensive	over $100
Expensive	$80–$100
Moderate	$50–$80
Inexpensive	under $50

All prices are for a standard double room, excluding 7% tax.

Calistoga
Expensive–
Very Expensive
★

Brannan Cottage Inn. This exquisite Victorian cottage with lacy white fretwork, large windows, and a shady porch is the only one of Sam Brannan's 1860 resort cottages still standing on its original site. The restoration is excellent and includes elegant stenciled friezes of stylized wildflowers. All rooms have private entrances. Full breakfast is included. *109 Wapoo Ave., 94515, tel. 707/942–4200. 6 rooms. MC, V.*

Mount View Hotel. This refurbished 1930s hotel provides live music and dancing on weekends. Continental breakfast in the lobby is included, and the restaurant features northern Italian cuisine. *1457 Lincoln Ave., 94515, tel. 707/942–6877. 34 rooms with bath. Facilities: restaurant, pool, Jacuzzi bar. MC, V.*

Moderate–
Expensive

Dr. Wilkinson's Hot Springs. This hot-springs spa resort has been in operation for more than 40 years. Reserve for weekends, when there are separate fees for mud baths, massages, facials, and steam rooms. Midweek packages include room and full spa services. *1507 Lincoln Ave., 94515, tel. 707/942–4102. 42 rooms. Facilities: 3 mineral pools. AE, MC, V.*

Moderate

Comfort Inn Napa Valley North. All the rooms in this recently opened motel have one king- or two queen-size beds, and many have vineyard views. Continental breakfast is included. There are rooms for nonsmokers and handicapped guests, and there are senior-citizen discounts. *1865 Lincoln Ave., 94515, tel. 707/942–9400 or 800/228–5150. 54 rooms with bath. Facilities: natural mineral-water pool, spa sauna, steam room, movies. AE, D, DC, MC, V.*

Mountain Home Ranch. This rustic ranch, built in 1913, is set on 300 wooded acres, with hiking trails, a creek, and a fishing lake. There is just one TV, in the dining room, and no phones. Families are welcome and there are special rates for children.

In summer, the modified American plan (full breakfast and dinner) is in effect; otherwise Continental breakfast is included. Six simple cabins without heat are available from mid-June to Labor Day. There is a separate shower facility, and you must bring your own linens. *3400 Mountain Home Ranch Rd., (north of town on Hwy. 128, left on Petrified Forest Rd., right on Mountain Home Ranch Rd., to end; 3 mi from Hwy. 128), 94515, tel. 707/942–6616. 14 rooms with bath, 6 cabins with ½ bath. Facilities: 2 pools, tennis. MC, V. Closed Dec.–Jan.*

Glen Ellen
Expensive–Very Expensive

Beltane Ranch. On a slope of the Mayacamas range on the eastern side of the Sonoma Valley is this 100-year-old house built by a retired San Francisco madam. The inn is part of a working cattle and grape-growing ranch (the nearby Kenwood Winery has a chardonnay made from the ranch's grapes, and named Beltane Ranch), and the family of innkeeper Rosemary Woods has lived here for 50 years. The inn's location is the big draw. There are miles of trails wandering through the oak-studded hills around the property. The comfortable living room has dozens of books on the area. The rooms all have private baths and antique furniture and open onto the building's wrap-around porch. *11775 Sonoma Hwy. (Hwy. 12) 95442, tel. 707/996–6501. 4 rooms. Facilities: tennis. No credit cards; personal checks accepted.*

Glenelly Inn. Just outside the hamlet of Glen Ellen is this sunny little establishment, built as an inn in 1916. Rooms are cozy and furnished with country antiques. Most bathrooms have claw-foot tubs. Mother-and-daughter innkeepers Ingrid and Kristi Hallamore serve breakfast in front of the common room's cobblestone fireplace, and local delicacies in the afternoons. The inn's hot tub is enclosed in a small garden. *5131 Warm Springs Rd., 95442, tel. 707/996–6720. 8 rooms. MC, V.*

Healdsburg
Very Expensive

Madrona Manor. A splendid, three-story, 1881 Gothic-style mansion, carriage house, and outbuildings sit on 8 wooded and landscaped acres. Mansion rooms are recommended: All nine have fireplaces, and five contain the antique furniture of the original owner. The approach to the mansion takes you under a stone archway and up a flowered hill; the house overlooks the valley and vineyards. Full breakfast is included, and there's a fine restaurant on the premises that serves dinner. Pets are allowed. *1001 Westside Rd., Box 818, 95448, tel. 707/433–4231 or 800/258–4003. 21 rooms with bath. Facilities: restaurant, pool. AE, DC, MC, V.*

Moderate–Very Expensive

Healdsburg Inn on the Plaza. This renovated 1900 brick building on the attractive town plaza has a bright solarium and a roof garden. The rooms are spacious, with quilts and pillows piled high on antique beds, and in the bathrooms, claw-foot tubs complete with rubber ducks. Full breakfast, afternoon coffee and cookies, and early evening wine and popcorn are included. *110 Matheson St., Box 1196, 95448, tel. 707/433–6991. 9 rooms. MC, V.*

Moderate

Best Western Dry Creek Inn. Movies, Continental breakfast, and a complimentary bottle of wine are included at this three-story motel in Spanish Mission style. There is a 24-hour coffee shop next door. Small pets are allowed; discounts are available for senior citizens. Direct bus service from San Francisco Airport is available. *198 Dry Creek Rd., 95448, tel. 707/433–0300; 800/528–1234; in CA, 800/222–5784. 102 rooms with bath. Facilities: pool, spa, laundry. AE, D, DC, MC, V.*

Napa
Very Expensive

Clarion. This modern, comfortable, and immaculately maintained motel has a restaurant and lounge on the premises, live music in the lounge, movies, and rooms for the handicapped. Pets are allowed with a $10 fee. *3425 Solano Ave., 94558 (1 block w. off Hwy. 29; take Redwood-Trancas exit), tel. 707/253–7433 or 800/333–7533. 191 rooms. Facilities: pool, spa, lighted tennis courts. AE, D, DC, MC, V.*

Silverado Country Club. This luxurious 1,200-acre resort in the hills east of the town of Napa offers cottages, kitchen apartments, and one- to three-bedroom efficiencies, many with fireplaces. There are also two dining rooms, a lounge, a sundries store, seven pools, 20 tennis courts, and two championship golf courses designed by Robert Trent Jones. Fees are charged for golf, tennis, and bike rentals. *1600 Atlas Peak Rd., 94558 (6 mi e. of Napa via Hwy. 121), tel. 707/257–0200 or 800/532–0500. 277 condo units. Facilities: restaurant. AE, D, DC, MC, V.*

Expensive

Chateau. There's a French country-inn atmosphere at this modern motel which provides Continental breakfast and a social hour with wine. Movies, in-room refrigerators, facilities for the handicapped, and senior-citizen discounts are available. *4195 Solano Ave., 94558 (w. of and adjacent to Hwy. 29; take W. Salvador Ave. exit), tel. 707/253–9300 or, in CA, 800/253–6272. 115 rooms. Facilities: pool, spa. AE, D, DC, MC, V.*

Moderate–
Very Expensive

Best Western Inn Napa. This immaculate modern redwood motel with spacious rooms has a restaurant on the premises and same-day laundry and valet service. There are suites as well as rooms for nonsmokers and the handicapped. Small pets are allowed. *100 Soscol Ave., 94558 (Imola Ave. Hwy. 121 exit e. from Hwy. 29 to Hwy. 121 and Soscol), tel. 707/257–1930 or 800/528–1234. 68 rooms. Facilities: pool, spa. AE, D, DC, MC, V.*

John Muir Inn. Continental breakfast and in-room coffee are included at this new, well-equipped, three-story motel that has kitchenettes, refrigerators, movies, valet service, and some whirlpool tubs. Senior-citizen discounts and rooms for nonsmokers and handicapped guests are available. *1998 Trower Ave., 94558 (adjacent to Hwy. 29, e. at Trower exit), tel. 707/257–7220; in CA, 800/522–8999. 59 rooms. Facilities: pool, spa. AE, D, DC, MC, V.*

Rutherford
Very Expensive

Auberge du Soleil. This luxurious French country–style inn has an excellent restaurant and a spectacular view over vineyards and hills. *180 Rutherford Hill Rd., 94573, tel. 707/963–1211 or 800/348-5406. 48 rooms. Facilities: pool, spa, tennis, masseuse. AE, MC, V.*

Rancho Caymus Inn. Early California–Spanish in style, this inn has well-maintained gardens and large suites with kitchens and whirlpool baths. There are home-baked breads, and an emphasis on decorative handicrafts, and there are unusual beehive fireplaces, tile murals, stoneware basins, and llama-hair blankets. *1140 Rutherford Rd., 94573 (Hwys. 29 and 128), tel. 707/963–1777 or 800/845–1777. 26 rooms. Facilities: restaurant. 2-night minimum Apr. 1–Nov. 30. MC, V.*

St. Helena
Very Expensive

Meadowood Resort. The resort is set on 256 wooded acres, with a golf course, croquet lawns, and hiking trails. The hotel is a rambling country lodge reminiscent of turn-of-the-century New England seaside cottages, and separate bungalow suites are clustered on the hillside. Half of the suites and some rooms have fireplaces. *900 Meadowood La., 94574, tel. 707/963–3646* *or 800/458–8080. 82 rooms. Facilities: 2 restaurants, lounge, room service, 2 pools, saunas, 9-hole and par golf courses, tennis, masseuse, wine school. AE, DC, MC, V.*

Expensive–
Very Expensive
Harvest Inn. This English Tudor–style inn with many fireplaces overlooks a 14-acre vineyard and an award-winning landscape. The furnishings are antiques, and there are wet bars, refrigerators, and fireplaces. Pets are allowed in certain rooms for a $10 fee. *1 Main St., 94574, tel. 707/963–9463 or 800/950–8466. 55 rooms. Facilities: 2 pools, 2 Jacuzzis. AE, D, MC, V.*

Hotel St. Helena. This restored 1881 stone hostelry, furnished with antiques and decorated in rich tones of burgundy, aims at Old World comfort. Continental breakfast is included. Smoking is discouraged. *1309 Main St., 94574, tel. 707/963–4388. 14 rooms with private bath, 4 rooms with shared bath. AE, DC, MC, V.*

Moderate–
Expensive
Cinnamon Bear Bed and Breakfast. Built in 1904 as a wedding gift, this house is decorated with a period flavor, from the antique quilts and toys to the claw-foot tubs. Full breakfast is included. Rooms for nonsmokers are available. *1407 Kearney St., 94574 (from Main St., Hwy. 29, turn west on Adams St., then 2 blocks to Kearney), tel. 707/963–4653. 4 rooms with bath. MC, V.*

Moderate
El Bonita Motel. This roadside motel was recently remodeled in an Art Deco style of white and gray, with streaks of flamingo and blue; a neon calla lily graces the north side. The small rooms have soft, smart furnishings. There are 16 rooms in the main motel and six garden rooms with kitchenettes. In 1992, 20 new rooms were added, most with whirlpool spas. *195 Main St., 94574, tel. 707/963–3216 or 800/541–3284. 42 rooms. Facilities: pool. AE, MC, V.*

Santa Rosa
Very Expensive
Vintner's Inn. Set on 50 acres of vineyards, this recently built inn has large rooms, French Provincial furnishings, and wood-burning fireplaces. Movies and breakfast are included, and there is an excellent restaurant on the premises. Rooms for the handicapped are available, as are VCRs for a small fee. *4350 Barnes Rd., 95403 (River Rd. exit w. from U.S. 101), tel. 707/575–7350 or, in CA, 800/421–2584. 44 rooms. Facilities: restaurant, spa. AE, DC, MC, V.*

Expensive
★
Fountaingrove Inn. This new, elegant, and comfortable inn boasts a redwood sculpture, *Equus III*, and a wall of cascading water in the lobby. Rooms have work spaces with modem jacks. Buffet breakfast is included, and there's an exceptional restaurant. Senior-citizen discounts and rooms for nonsmokers and the handicapped are available. *101 Fountaingrove Pkwy., 95403, tel. 707/578–6101 or, in CA, 800/222–6101. 85 rooms. Facilities: lap pool, spa, room service, movies. AE, DC, MC, V.*

Moderate–
Very Expensive
Doubletree Hotel. Many rooms in this large, modern, multistory hotel on a hilltop have views of the valley and vineyards; the Burgundy, Cabernet, Chardonnay, Chablis, and Riesling buildings have especially fine views. The spacious rooms have work-size desks and functional, comfortable furnishings. There are rooms for nonsmokers and the handicapped, and patio rooms overlooking the pool. Golf and tennis are available at the adjacent Fountaingrove Country Club for additional fees; there's a courtesy shuttle to Santa Rosa airport and a jogging path. *3555 Round Barn Blvd., 95401 (Old Redwood Hwy., exit*

e. from U.S. 101), tel. 707/523–7555 or 800/833–9595. 252 rooms with bath. Facilities: restaurant, bar, lounge, pool, spa, room service, valet service. AE, D, DC, MC, V.

Moderate–Expensive
★

Los Robles Lodge. This pleasant, relaxed motel has comfortable rooms overlooking a pool set into a grassy landscape. Rooms for the handicapped and nonsmokers are available. Pets are allowed, except in executive rooms, which have Jacuzzis. *925 Edwards Ave., 95401 (Steele La. exit w. from Hwy. 101), tel. 707/545–6330 or 800/522–1001. 105 rooms. Facilities: restaurant, coffee shop, lounge with nightly entertainment, pool, outdoor Jacuzzi, laundry. AE, D, DC, MC. V.*

Inexpensive

Best Western Hillside Inn. Some rooms at this cozy, nicely landscaped, small motel have balconies or patios. Kitchenettes and suites are available. Pets are allowed. *2901 4th St., 95409 (Farmers La., 2 mi e. off U.S. 101 on Hwy. 12), tel. 707/546–9353 or 800/528–1234. 35 rooms. Facilities: restaurant, pool, sauna, shuffleboard. AE, DC, MC, V.*

Sonoma
Very Expensive

El Dorado Hotel. in 1990, Claude Rouas, the owner of Napa's acclaimed Auberge du Soleil, entered the Sonoma scene with this fine small hotel and its popular restaurant, Piatti (*see* Dining, above). Rooms reflect Sonoma's Mission era, with Mexican tile floors and white walls. The best rooms are numbers 3 and 4 which have big balconies overlooking Sonoma Plaza. Only four of the rooms—the ones in the courtyard by the pool—have bathtubs; the others have showers only. *405 1st St. W (Sonoma Plaza), tel. 707/996–3030 or 800/289–3031. 27 rooms. Facilities: restaurant, heated pool. AE, MC, V.*

Sonoma Mission Inn. This elegantly restored 1920s resort blends Mediterranean and Old California architecture, for a result that's early Hollywood—you half expect Gloria Swanson to sweep through the lobby. The location is a surprise, off the main street of tiny, anything-but-posh Boyes Hot Springs. The grounds are nicely landscaped and the accommodations include suites that are larger and much nicer than the smallish standard rooms. This is the home of the *Spa Food* cookbook, and there are extensive spa facilities (fee for fitness classes and treatments). *18140 Sonoma Hwy. (Hwy. 12 n. of Sonoma), Box 1447, 95476, tel. 707/938–9000; 800/358–9022; in CA, 800/862–4945. 170 rooms. Facilities: restaurant, coffee shop, 2 bars, lounge, 2 pools, weights room, steam room, Jacuzzis, sauna, tennis. AE, DC, MC, V.*

Expensive

Thistle Dew Inn. Half a block from Sonoma Plaza is this turn-of-the-century Victorian home filled with collector-quality arts-and-crafts furnishings. Owners Larry and Norma Barnett live on the premises, with Larry cooking up creative, sumptuous breakfasts and serving hors d'oeuvres in the evenings. Each of the rooms has queen-size beds with antique quilts, private baths, and air-conditioning. There is a hot tub and bicycles are provided free to guests. Smoking is not permitted indoors. *171 W. Spain St., 95476, tel. 707/938–2909. 6 rooms. AE, MC, V.*

Moderate–Expensive

Best Western Sonoma Valley Inn. Just one block from the town plaza, this new motel features balconies, handcrafted furniture, wood-burning fireplaces, and whirlpool baths. Continental breakfast and a complimentary split of wine are included. Senior discounts, kitchenettes, and rooms for nonsmokers and the handicapped are available. *550 2nd St. W, 95476, tel. 707/*

938–9200 or, in CA, 800/334–5784. 72 rooms. Facilities: pool, whirlpool, laundry. AE, D, DC, MC, V.

Windsor
Moderate

Redwood Royale Hometel. This clean, no-frills motel is a bargain for an economy-minded family. Each unit has a bedroom, bath, kitchen, and living/dining area, and the rate is the same for one to four persons. Kitchen items are available for rent. The motel is on 2½ acres, and there is secured parking for RVs. *8900 Bell Rd., 95492, tel. 707/838–9771. 80 units. Facilities: pool, laundry. AE, MC, V.*

Yountville
Very Expensive

Vintage Inn. All the rooms at this luxurious new inn have fireplaces, whirlpool baths, refrigerators, private verandas or patios, hand-painted fabrics, window seats, and shuttered windows. Continental breakfast with champagne, a complimentary bottle of wine, and afternoon tea are provided. Bike rental in season and hot-air ballooning are available. *6541 Washington St., 94599, tel. 707/944–1112; 800/982–5539; in CA, 800/351–1133. 80 rooms with bath. Facilities: lap pool, spa, tennis. AE, DC, MC, V.*

Napa Valley Lodge. Spacious rooms overlook vineyards and the valley in this hacienda-style lodge with tile roofs, covered walkways, balconies, patios, and colorful gardens. Freshly brewed coffee is provided in rooms, as is Continental breakfast and the morning paper. Some rooms have fireplaces. Kitchenettes and rooms for nonsmokers and the physically disabled are available. *Madison St. and Hwy. 29, Box L, 94599, tel. 707/944–2468 or 800/368–2468. 55 rooms. Facilities: exercise room, pool, spa, sauna, valet service, refrigerators. AE, D, DC, MC, V.*

Expensive

Napa Valley Railway Inn. This unusual establishment is made up of nine vintage railcars set on the original track of the Napa Valley Railroad. Each car is now an air-conditioned suite, with sitting area, queen-size brass beds, skylights, bay windows, and full tiled baths. Wine and coffee are provided. *6503 Washington St., 94599, tel. 707/944–2000. 9 rooms with bath. MC, V.*

The Arts and Nightlife

Galleries throughout the Wine Country display the work of local artists: painters, sculptors, potters, and jewelry makers. The **Luther Burbank Performing Arts Center** in Santa Rosa (tel. 707/546–3600, box office open Mon.–Sat. noon–6) has a full calendar of concerts, plays, and other performances, with both locally and internationally known performers. Wineries often schedule concerts and music festivals during the summer.

Nightlife in the Wine Country is best savored with a leisurely, elegant dinner at one of the restaurants for which the area is justly famous. Many of the larger hotels and motels feature live music on weekends.

6 San Francisco

The Golden Gate, sailboats on the bay, the hills and the cable cars, restored Victorian "Painted Ladies," and the whiteness of the fog—if these are your dreams, they will come to life in San Francisco. In this last decade of the 20th century, however, the city is facing some hard realities: the shift of economic power to Southern California, the recession, the AIDS epidemic, and, most recently, a reminder that the forces of nature still reign supreme—the 1989 earthquake. The quake's most lingering effect is on traffic in the area. The Embarcadero Freeway in San Francisco and Interstate 880 in Oakland had to be demolished and permanent replacements are years away, with traffic diverted onto surface roads. Visitors planning on driving to and around the area should consult the AAA or the San Francisco Convention and Visitors Bureau for the latest word on road conditions.

Arriving and Departing

By Plane
Airports and Airlines

San Francisco International Airport is just south of the city, off U.S. 101. American carriers serving San Francisco are **Alaska Air, American, Continental, Delta, Southwest, TWA, United,** and **USAir.** International carriers include **Air Canada, Canadian Pacific, Japan Air Lines, British Airways, China Airlines, Qantas, Air New Zealand, Mexicana,** and **Lufthansa.** Many of these same airlines serve the Oakland Airport, which is across the bay but not much farther away from downtown San Francisco (via I–880 and I–80), although traffic on the Bay Bridge may at times make travel time longer.

From the Airport to Downtown

SFO Airporter (tel. 415/495–8404) provides bus service between downtown and the airport, making the round of downtown hotels. Buses run every 20 minutes from 5 AM to 11 PM, from the lower level outside the baggage claim area. The fare is $7 one way, $11 round-trip.

For $11, **Supershuttle** will take you from the airport to anywhere within the city limits of San Francisco. At the airport, after picking up your luggage, call 415/871–7800 and a van will pick you up within five minutes. To go to the airport, make reservations (tel. 415/558–8500) 24 hours in advance. The Supershuttle shops at the upper level of the terminal, along with several other bus and van transport services.

Taxis to or from downtown take 20–30 minutes and average $30.

By Train

Amtrak (tel. 800/USA–RAIL) trains (the *Zephyr*, from Chicago via Denver, and the *Coast Starlight*, traveling between San Diego and Seattle) stop at the Oakland Depot; from there buses will take you across the Bay Bridge to the Transbay Terminal at 1st and Mission streets in San Francisco.

By Bus

Greyhound-Trailways serves San Francisco from the Transbay Terminal at 1st and Mission streets (tel. 415/558–6789).

By Car

Route I–80 finishes its westward journey from New York's George Washington Bridge at the Bay Bridge, linking Oakland and San Francisco. U.S. 101, running north–south through the entire state, enters the city across the Golden Gate Bridge and continues south down the peninsula, along the west side of the bay.

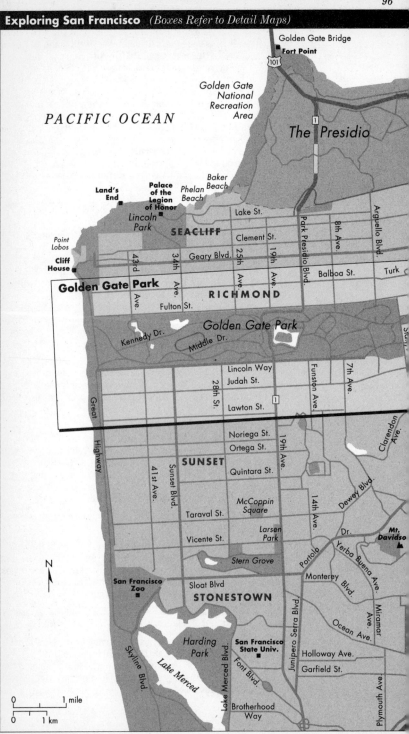

Golden Gate Bridge
■ **Fort Point**

101

*Golden Gate
National
Recreation
Area*

The Presidio

PACIFIC OCEAN

1

*Baker
Beach*

**Land's
End** ■

**Palace
of the
Legion
of Honor** ■

*Phelan
Beach*

Lake St.

Park Presidio Blvd.

8th Ave.

Arguello Blvd.

*Lincoln
Park*

SEACLIFF

Clement St.

*Point
Lobos*

43rd

34th

Geary Blvd.

25th

19th

Ave.

Ave.

Balboa St.

Turk

**Cliff
House** ■

Ave.

Golden Gate Park

Ave.

RICHMOND

Fulton St.

Kennedy Dr.

Middle Dr.

Golden Gate Park

Great

Lincoln Way

28th St.

Judah St.

Funston Ave.

7th Ave.

1

Lawton St.

Noriega St.

Ortega St.

19th Ave.

Clarendon Ave.

Highway

41st Ave.

Sunset Blvd.

SUNSET

Quintara St.

14th Ave.

Dewey Blvd.

*McCoppin
Square*

Taraval St.

Dr.

**Mt.
Davidso** ▲

Vicente St.

*Larsen
Park*

Portola

Yerba Buena Ave.

Miramar

Stern Grove

Monterey

Blvd.

Ave.

N

**San Francisco
Zoo** ■

Sloat Blvd

STONESTOWN

Junipero Serra Blvd

Ocean Ave.

*Harding
Park*

**San Francisco
State Univ.** ■

Lake Merced Blvd.

Font Blvd.

Holloway Ave.

Garfield St.

Plymouth Ave

Skyline Blvd.

Lake Merced

*Brotherhood
Way*

0 _____ 1 mile

0 _____ 1 km

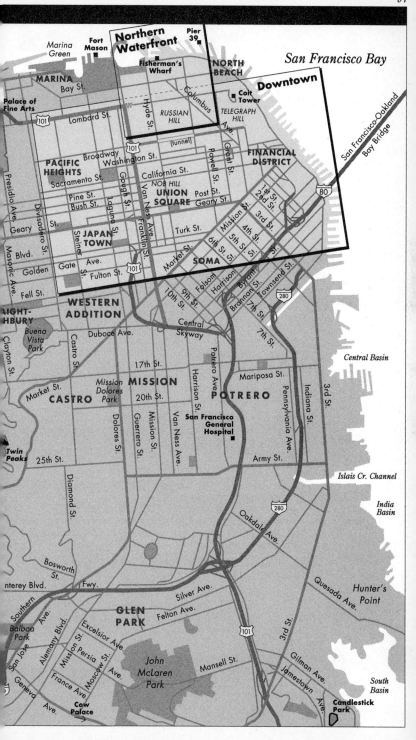

Marina Green

Fort Mason

Northern Waterfront

Pier 39

Fisherman's Wharf

NORTH BEACH

Downtown

San Francisco Bay

MARINA

Bay St.

Coit Tower

Palace of Fine Arts

[101]

Lombard St.

Hyde St.

RUSSIAN HILL

Columbus Ave.

TELEGRAPH HILL

Grant St.

San Francisco-Oakland Bay Bridge

(tunnel)

[101]

PACIFIC HEIGHTS

Broadway

Washington St.

FINANCIAL DISTRICT

Presidio Ave.

Sacramento St.

California St.

NOB HILL

Powell St.

[80]

Pine St.

UNION SQUARE

Post St.

Geary St.

2nd St.

Geary

Divisadero St.

Bush St.

Van Ness Ave.

Gough St.

Laguna St.

Steiner St.

Franklin St.

3rd St.

Masonic Ave.

Blvd.

JAPAN TOWN

Turk St.

Mission St.

4th St.

5th St.

6th St.

Golden

Gate

Ave.

Fulton St.

Market St.

SOMA

Folsom

Harrison

Bryant St.

Brannan St.

Townsend St.

[101]

Fell St.

WESTERN ADDITION

10th St.

9th St.

7th St.

[280]

AIGHT-HBURY

Buena Vista Park

Clayton St.

Duboce Ave.

Castro St.

Central Skyway

7th St.

Central Basin

Market St.

17th St.

Mission Dolores Park

MISSION

Potrero Ave.

Mariposa St.

Pennsylvania Ave.

Indiana St.

3rd St.

CASTRO

20th St.

Harrison St.

POTRERO

San Francisco General Hospital

Twin Peaks

Dolores St.

Guerrero St.

Mission St.

Van Ness Ave.

25th St.

Diamond St.

Army St.

Islais Cr. Channel

[280]

Oakdale Ave.

India Basin

Bosworth St.

Quesada Ave.

Hunter's Point

nterey Blvd.

Fwy.

Silver Ave.

Felton Ave.

3rd St.

Southern

Ave.

Balboa Park

San Jose Ave.

Alemany Blvd.

Excelsior Ave.

Mission St.

Persia Ave.

Moscow St.

GLEN PARK

John McLaren Park

Mansell St.

Gilman Ave.

Jamestown Ave.

South Basin

Geneva Ave.

France Ave.

Cow Palace

Quesada Ave.

Candlestick Park

Getting Around

By BART **Bay Area Rapid Transit** (tel. 415/788–BART) sends air-conditioned aluminum trains at speeds of up to 80 miles an hour across the bay to Oakland, Berkeley, Concord, Richmond, and Fremont. Trains also travel south from San Francisco as far as Daly City. Wall maps in the stations list destinations and fares (85¢–$3). Trains run Mon.–Sat. 6 AM–midnight, Sun. 9 AM–midnight.

A $2.60 excursion ticket buys a three-county tour. You can visit any of the 34 stations for up to four hours as long as you exit and enter at the same station.

By Bus The **San Francisco Municipal Railway System, or Muni** (tel. 415/673–MUNI), includes buses and trolleys, surface streetcars, and the new below-surface streetcars, as well as cable cars. There is 24-hour service, and the fare is 85¢ for adults, 15¢ for senior citizens, and 25¢ for children ages 5–17. Exact change is always required. Free transfers are available.

A $6 pass good for unlimited travel all day ($10 for three days) on all routes can be purchased from ticket machines at cable-car terminals and at the Visitor Information Center in Hallidie Plaza (Powell and Market Sts.).

By Cable Car "They turn corners almost at right angles; cross other lines, and for all I know, may run up the sides of houses," wrote Rudyard Kipling in 1889. In June 1984 the 109-year-old system returned to service after a $58.2 million overhaul. Because the cable cars had been declared a National Historic Landmark in 1964, renovation methods and materials had to preserve the historical and traditional qualities of Andrew Hallidie's system. The rehabilitated moving landmark has been designed to withstand another century of use.

The Powell–Mason line (No. 59) and the Powell–Hyde line (No. 60) begin at Powell and Market streets near Union Square and terminate at Fisherman's Wharf. The California Street line (No. 61) runs east and west from Market Street near the Embarcadero to Van Ness Avenue.

Cable cars are popular, crowded, and an experience to ride: Move toward one quickly as it pauses, wedge yourself into any available space, and hold on! The views from many cars are spectacular, and the sensation of moving up and down some of San Francisco's steepest hills in a small, open-air clanging conveyance is not to be missed.

The fare is $2 for adults, $1 for children 5–17. Exact change is required.

By Taxi Rates are high in the city, although most rides are relatively short. It is unfortunately almost impossible to hail a passing cab, especially on weekends. Either phone or use the nearest hotel taxi stand to grab a cab. See the Yellow Pages for numbers of taxi companies.

By Car Driving in San Francisco can be a challenge, what with the hills, the one-way streets, and the traffic. Take it easy, remember to curb your wheels when parking on hills, and use public transportation whenever possible. On certain streets, parking is forbidden during rush hours. Look for the warning signs; illegally parked cars are towed. This is a great city for walking and a terrible city for parking. Downtown parking lots are often full and always expensive. Finding a spot in North Beach at night, for instance, may be impossible.

Important Addresses and Numbers

Tourist Information The **San Francisco Convention and Visitors Bureau** maintains a visitors information center on the lower level at Hallidie Plaza (Powell and Market streets), just three blocks from Union Square, near the cable-car turnaround and the Powell Street entrance to BART. *Weekdays 9–5, Sat. 9–3, Sun. 10–2. Tel. 415/974–6900. Summary of daily events: tel. 415/391–2001.*

Emergencies **Police** or **ambulance,** telephone 911.

Doctors Two hospitals with 24-hour emergency rooms are **San Francisco General Hospital** (1001 Potrero Ave., tel. 415/821–8200) and the **Medical Center at the University of California, San Francisco** (500 Parnassus Ave. at 3rd Ave., near Golden Gate Park, tel. 415/476–1000).

Access Health Care provides drop-in medical care at two San Francisco locations, daily 8–8. No membership is necessary. *In Davies Medical Center, Castro St. at Duboce Ave., tel. 415/565–6600; and 26 California St. at Drumm St., tel. 415/397–2881.*

Pharmacies Several **Walgreen Drug Stores** have 24-hour pharmacies, including stores at 500 Geary Street near Union Square (tel. 415/673–8413) and 3201 Divisadero Street at Lombard Street (tel. 415/931–6417). Also try the Walgreen pharmacy on Powell Street near Market Street. *135 Powell St., tel. 415/391–7222. Open Mon.–Sat. 8 AM–midnight, Sun. 9 AM–8 PM. AE, MC, V.*

Guided Tours

Orientation Tours **Gray Line** offers a variety of tours of the city, the Bay Area, and Northern California. Its city tour, on regular or double-decker buses, lasts 3½ hours and departs from the Trans-Bay Terminal at 1st and Mission streets five to six times daily. Gray Line also picks up at centrally located hotels. *Tel. 415/558–9400. Tours daily. Make reservations the day before. Cost: $23.50 adults, $11.75 children.*
The Great Pacific Tour uses 13-passenger vans for its daily 3½-hour city tour. Bilingual guides may be requested. It picks up at major San Francisco hotels. Tours are available to Monterey, the Wine Country, and Muir Woods. *Tel. 415/626–4499. Tours daily. Make reservations the day before, or, possibly, the same day. Cost: $25 adults, $24 senior citizens, $20 children 5–11.*
San Francisco Scenic Route. Near Escapes (Box 193005, San Francisco 94119, tel. 415/386–8687) has produced an audiocassette with music and sound effects that will take you in your own car "where the tour buses can't go." It will guide you past Fisherman's Wharf, Chinatown, Golden Gate Park, Twin Peaks, Ghirardelli Square, Mission Dolores, the Civic Center, and other tourist attractions. Another cassette offers a detailed walking tour of Chinatown; both come with route maps. They are available in a few local outlets, or you can get them by mail order for $12.

Special-Interest Tours **Near Escapes** (Box 3005-K, 94119, tel. 415/386–8687) plans unusual activities in the city and around the Bay Area. Recent tours and activities included visits to a Hindu temple in the East Bay, the Lawrence Berkeley Laboratory, the aircraft-maintenance facility at the San Francisco Airport, and the quicksilver mines south of San Jose. The Julia Morgan Architectural Tour focuses on the work of one of the most prominent California architects of the early 20th century. Send $1 and a self-addressed, stamped envelope for a schedule for the month you plan to visit San Francisco.

Walking Tours **Castro District.** Trevor Hailey leads a 3½-hour tour focusing on the history and development of the city's gay and lesbian community, including restored Victorian homes, shops and cafés, and the NAMES Project, home of the AIDS memorial quilt. Tours depart at 10 AM most days from Castro and Market streets. *Tel. 415/550–8110. Cost: $25, including breakfast or lunch.*

Chinese Cultural Heritage Foundation (tel. 415/986–1822) offers two walking tours of Chinatown. The Heritage Walk leaves Saturday at 2 PM and lasts about two hours. *Cost: $12 adults, $2 children under 12.* The Culinary Walk, a three-hour stroll through the markets and food shops, plus a dim sum lunch, is held every Wednesday at 10:30 AM. *Cost: $25 adults, $10 children.*

Dashiell Hammett Tour. Don Herron gives four-hour, 3-mile literary walking tours designed around the life of Hammett and his character Sam Spade. Tours depart between May and August at Saturday noon from the main library at 200 Larkin Street. *Tel. 415/564–7021. Cost: $5.*

Golden Gate Park. The Friends of Recreation and Parks (tel. 415/221–1311) offer free, guided 1½- to 2-hour walking tours of the park, May–October.

Heritage Walks. The Foundation for San Francisco's Architectural Heritage, headquartered in the Hass-Lilienthal House at 2007 Franklin Street, sponsors architectural tours of nearby Pacific Heights, with excursions to Russian Hill and the Presidio. *Tel. 415/441–3004. Cost: $3.*

Exploring

Few cities in the world cram so much diversity into so little space. San Francisco is a relatively small city, with fewer than 750,000 residents nested on a 46.6-square-mile tip of land between San Francisco Bay and the Pacific Ocean.

San Franciscans cherish the city's colorful past, and many older buildings have been spared from demolition and nostalgically converted into modern offices and shops. For more than a century, the port city has been trafficking the peoples of the world. Today the city is again establishing strong commercial relations with the nations of the Pacific Rim. The unusually large number of residents with ties to other cultures flavors the cuisine, commerce, and charisma of the city. It also encourages a tolerance for deviations in customs and beliefs.

San Francisco is a maze of one-way streets and restricted parking zones. Public parking garages or lots tend to be expensive, as are the hotel parking spaces. The famed 40-plus hills can be a problem for drivers who are new to the terrain. People who know the city agree that one of the best ways to see and experience its many moods and neighborhoods is by foot. Those museums on wheels–the cable cars–or the numerous buses or trolleys can take you to or near many of the area's attractions. In the exploring tours that follow, we have often included information on public transportation.

Hills are a daily challenge to visitor and resident alike; good walking shoes are essential. Climate, too, is a consideration in deciding what to wear. There are dramatic temperature changes, especially in summer, when the afternoon fog rolls in. Winds are often a problem, both on the bay and cityside. Year-round, layered clothing best adapts to changing conditions; a cap or scarf and sunglasses are useful. Casual city togs are appropriate; shorts and tank tops are for Southern California's climate.

Union Square Area

Numbers in the margin correspond to points of interest on the Downtown San Francisco map.

Since 1850 Union Square has been the heart of San Francisco's downtown. Its name derives from a series of violent pro-Union demonstrations staged in this hilly area just prior to the Civil War. This is where you will find the city's finest department stores and its most elegant boutiques. There are 40 hotels within a three-block walk of the square, and the downtown theater district is nearby.

The square itself is a 2.6-acre oasis planted with palms, boxwood, and seasonal flowers, peopled with a kaleidoscope of characters: office workers sunning and brown-bagging, street musicians, always at least one mime, several vocal and determined preachers, and the ever-increasing parade of panhandlers. Smartly dressed women and camera-laden tourists usually hurry past the denizens. Throughout the year, the square hosts numerous public events: fashion shows, free noontime concerts, ethnic celebrations, and noisy demonstrations. Auto and bus traffic is often gridlocked on the four streets bordering the square. Post, Stockton, and Geary streets are one way, while Powell Street runs in both directions until it crosses Geary, where it then becomes a one-way street to Market Street. Union Square covers a convenient but costly four-story underground garage. Close to 3,000 cars are parked here on busy holiday shopping and strolling days.

❶ Any visitor's first stop should be the **San Francisco Visitors Information Center** (tel. 415/391–2000) on the lower level of Hallidie Plaza at Powell and Market streets. It is open daily, and the multilingual staff will answer specific questions as well as provide maps, brochures, and information on daily events. The office provides 24-hour recorded information (tel. 415/391–2001).

The cable-car terminus, also at Powell and Market streets, is the starting point for two of the three operating lines. Before 1900 there were 600 cable cars spanning a network of 100 miles. Today there are 39 cars in the three lines, and the network covers just 12 miles. Most of the cars date from the last century, although the cars and lines had a complete $58.2 million overhaul during the early 1980s. There are seats for about 30 passengers, with usually that number standing or strap-hanging. If possible, plan your cable-car ride for mid-morning or mid-afternoon during the week to avoid crowds. In summer-

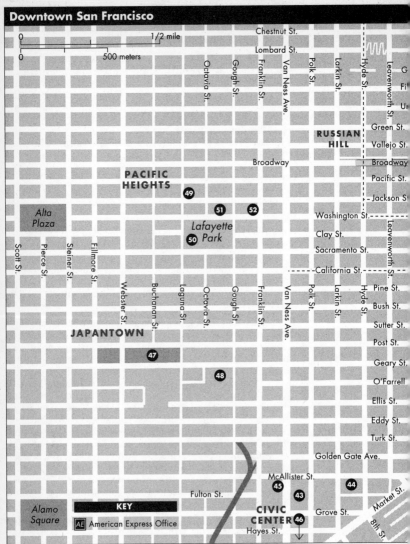

0   1/2 mile

0   500 meters

Chestnut St.

Lombard St.

Octavia St.

Gough St.

Franklin St.

Van Ness Ave.

Polk St.

Larkin St.

Hyde St.

Leavenworth St.

G
Fi
U

Green St.

RUSSIAN HILL

Vallejo St.

Broadway   Broadway

Pacific St.

Jackson S

PACIFIC HEIGHTS

49

51   52

Washington St.

Alta Plaza

50   *Lafayette Park*

Clay St.

Leavenworth St.

Sacramento St.

Scott St.

Pierce St.

Steiner St.

Fillmore St.

California St.

Webster St.

Buchanan St.

Laguna St.

Octavia St.

Gough St.

Franklin St.

Van Ness Ave.

Polk St.

Larkin St.

Hyde St.

Pine St.

Bush St.

Sutter St.

Post St.

JAPANTOWN

47

Geary St.

O'Farrell St.

48

Ellis St.

Eddy St.

Turk St.

Golden Gate Ave.

McAllister St.

45   43   44

Fulton St.

Alamo Square

KEY

AE American Express Office

CIVIC CENTER

46

Grove St.

Market St.

8th St.

Hayes St.

Ansel Adams Center, **20**

Bank of America, **11**

Cable Car Museum, **42**

Chinatown Gate, **21**

Chinese Cultural Center, **25**

Chinese Historical Society, **28**

Chinese Six Companies, **29**

Church of St. Francis of Assisi, **33**

City Hall, **43**

City Lights Bookstore, **34**

Coit Tower, **35**

Crocker Galleria, **8**

Curran Theater, **5**

Embarcadero Center, **18**

Fairmont Hotel, **38**

Ferry Building, **17**

450 Sutter Street, **9**

Geary Theater, **4**

Grace Cathedral, **37**

Grand Hyatt San Francisco, **6**

Haas-Lilienthal House, **52**

Hallidie Building, **16**

Huntington Hotel, **41**

Japan Center, **47**

Lafayette Park, **50**

Maiden Lane, **7**

Mark Hopkins Inter-Continental Hotel, **39**

Mills Building and Tower, **14**

Mission Dolores, **46**

Museum of Modern Art, **45**

Old Chinese Telephone Exchange, **26**

time there are often long lines to board any of the three systems. (*See* Getting Around, above.)

A two-block stroll north along bustling Powell Street leads
② to **Union Square** with its fashionable stores, fine hotels, and photogenic flower stalls. At center stage, the Victory Monument by Robert Ingersoll Aitken commemorates Commodore George Dewey's victory over the Spanish fleet at Manila in 1898. The 97-foot Corinthian column, topped by a bronze figure symbolizing naval conquest, was dedicated by President Theodore Roosevelt in 1903 and withstood the 1906 earthquake.

After the earthquake and fire in 1906, the square was dubbed "Little St. Francis" because of the temporary shelter erected for residents of the St. Francis Hotel. The actor John Barrymore was among the guests pressed into volunteering to stack bricks in the square. His uncle, thespian John Drew, remarked, "It took an act of God to get John out of bed and the United States government to get him to work."

③ **The Westin St. Francis Hotel**, on the southwest corner of Post and Powell streets, was built here in 1904 and was gutted by the 1906 disaster. The second-oldest hotel in the city was conceived by Charles Crocker and his associates as an elegant hostelry for their millionaire friends. Swift service and sumptuous surroundings were hallmarks of the property. A sybarite's dream, the hotel's Turkish baths had ocean water piped in. A new, larger, more luxurious residence was opened in 1907 to attract loyal clients from among the world's rich and powerful. Today you can relax over a traditional tea or opt for champagne and caviar in the dramatic Art Deco Compass Rose lounge in the lobby. Elaborate Chinese screens, intimate seating alcoves, and soothing background music make it an ideal time-out after frantic shopping or sightseeing. For dining, before or after the theater (within walking distance), visit the award-winning Victor's. After a breathtaking ride up 30-plus stories in an exterior, glass-walled elevator, guests enter a warm, wood-paneled lobby area with recessed bookshelves housing leather-bound classics. Floor-to-ceiling windows offer spectacular views of the bay and the city. Superb California cuisine is enhanced by a select list of California and French wines.

Both the Geary and Curran theaters are a few blocks west on Geary Street. The **Geary** (415 Geary St., tel. 415/749–2228) is
④ home of the American Conservatory Theatre. Now in its 26th season, A.C.T. is one of North America's leading repertory companies. The 1,300-seat house normally offers a 34-week season to 20,000 subscribers, presenting both classical and contemporary dramas. The theater was closed indefinitely as a result of the October 1989 earthquake, and currently productions are being run at the Stage Door theater (420 Mason St.) and elsewhere until repairs are completed. Its main box office
⑤ remains open. The **Curran** (445 Geary St., tel. 415/474–3800) is noted for showcasing traveling companies of Broadway shows.

The **San Francisco Ticket Box Office Service** (STBO, tel. 415/433–STBS) has a booth on the Stockton Street side of Union Square, opposite Maiden Lane. Open from noon till 7:30 PM, Tuesday through Saturday, it provides day-of-performance tickets (cash or traveler's checks only) to all types of performing-arts events at half price, as well as regular full-price box-office services. Telephone reservations are not accepted.

❻ Just a dash up from STBS, the newly renovated **Grand Hyatt San Francisco** (345 Stockton St.) offers exciting city views from its lounge, the Club 36. Stop and examine sculptor Ruth Asawa's fantasy fountain honoring the city's hills, bridges, and unusual architecture plus a wonder world of real and mythical creatures. Asawa was born in Los Angeles County but has lived in San Francisco since 1949. Children and friends helped the artist shape the hundreds of tiny figures created from baker's clay and then assembled on 41 large panels from which molds were made for the bronze casting. Asawa's distinctive designs decorate many public areas in the city. You can see her famous mermaid fountain at Ghirardelli Square.

❼ Pop around the corner into **Maiden Lane**, which runs from Stockton to Kearny streets. Known as Morton Street in the raffish Barbary Coast era, this red-light district reported at least one murder a week. But the 1906 fire destroyed the brothels and the street emerged as Maiden Lane. It has since become a chic and costly mall. The two blocks are closed to vehicles from 11 AM until 4 PM. During the day, take-out snacks can be enjoyed while resting under the gay, umbrella-shaded tables. Masses of daffodils and other bright blossoms and balloons bedeck the lane during the annual spring festival. A carnival mood prevails, with zany street musicians, artsy-craftsy people, and throngs of spectators.

Note **140 Maiden Lane:** This handsome brick structure is the only Frank Lloyd Wright building in San Francisco. With its circular interior ramp and skylights, it is said to have been a model for his designs for the Guggenheim Museum in New York. It now houses the Circle Gallery, a showcase of contemporary artists. Be sure to study the unique limited-edition art jewelry designed by internationally acclaimed Erté. *Open Mon.–Sat. 10–6, Sun. 11–5.*

❽ The **Crocker Galleria** (Post and Kearny Sts., tel. 415/392–0100) is an imaginatively designed three-level complex of fine dining and shopping establishments capped by a dazzling glass dome. One block north of Kearny, Sutter Street is lined by prestigious art galleries, antiques dealers, smart hotels, and noted designer boutiques. Art Deco aficionados will want to linger at the **❾** striking medical/dental office building at **450 Sutter Street.** Handsome Mayan-inspired designs are used in both exterior and interior surfaces of the 1930 terra-cotta-colored skyscraper.

Time Out   Most stores and shops here open at about 9:30–10 AM. Venturing out early and settling down to a leisurely breakfast before the day's traffic and shoppers hit in full force is a nice way to ease into a busy day of sightseeing. **Mama's** (398 Geary St.) has always been a favorite for either light- or full-breakfast selections. Or blow the day's meal budget at **Campton Place Hotel.** Wonderful breads and muffins, delicious hash, and out-of-season fruits are lavishly served. *340 Stockton St., tel. 415/781–5155. Reservations advised for brunch. Open weekdays 7–11 AM, Sat. 8–11:30 AM, Sun. brunch 8 AM–2:30 PM.*

The Financial District

The heart of San Francisco's financial district is Montgomery Street. It was here in 1848 that Sam Brannan proclaimed the historic gold discovery on the American River. At that time, all the streets below Montgomery between California Street and Broadway were wharves. At least 100 ships were abandoned by frantic crews and passengers all caught up in the '49 gold fever. Many of the wrecks served as warehouses or were used as foundations for new constructions.

The financial district is roughly bordered by Kearny Street on the west, Washington Street on the north, and Market Street on the southeast. On workdays it is a congested canyon of soaring skyscrapers, gridlock traffic, and bustling pedestrians. In the evenings and on weekends the quiet streets allow walkers to admire the distinctive architecture. Unfortunately, the museums in corporate headquarters are closed then.

⑩ The city's most photographed high rise is the 853-foot **Transamerica Pyramid** at 600 Montgomery Street, between Clay and Washington streets at the end of Columbus Avenue. Designed by William Pereira and Associates and erected in 1972, the $34 million controversial symbol has become more acceptable to local purists since gaining San Francisco instant recognition worldwide. There is a public viewing area on the 27th floor (open weekdays 8–4). You can relax in a redwood grove along the east side of the building.

⑪ The granite and marble **Bank of America** building dominates the territory bounded by California, Pine, Montgomery, and Kearny streets. The 52-story polished red granite complex is crowned by a chic cocktail and dining restaurant. As in almost all corporate headquarters, the interiors display impressive original art, while outdoor plazas include avant-garde sculptures. A massive abstract black granite sculpture designed by the Japanese artist Masayuki in the mall has been dubbed the "Banker's Heart" by local wags.

⑫ Diagonally across Montgomery Street is the **Wells Fargo Bank History Museum** (420 Montgomery St.). There were no formal banks in San Francisco during the early years of the Gold Rush, and miners often entrusted their gold dust to saloon keepers. In 1852 Wells Fargo opened its first bank in the city, and the company established banking offices in the Mother Lode camps using stagecoaches and Pony Express riders to service the burgeoning state. (California's population had boomed from 15,000 to 200,000 between 1848 and 1852.) The History Museum displays samples of nuggets and gold dust from major mines, a mural-size map of the Mother Lode, original art by western artists Charlie Russell and Maynard Dixon, mementos of the poet bandit Black Bart, and letters of credit and old bank drafts. The showpiece is the red, century-old Concord stagecoach, which in the mid-1850s carried 15 passengers from St. Louis to San Francisco in three weeks. *Admission free. Open banking days 9–5.*

⑬ The **Russ Building** (235 Montgomery St.) was called "the skyscraper" when it was built in 1927. The Gothic design was modeled after the Chicago Tribune Tower, and until the 1960s was San Francisco's tallest—at just 31 stories. Prior to the 1906 earthquake and fire, the site was occupied by the Russ House, considered one of the finest hostelries in the city.

⑭ The **Mills Building and Tower** (220 Montgomery St.) was the outstanding prefire building in the financial district. The 10-story all-steel construction had its own electric plant in the basement. The original Burnham and Root design of white marble and brick was erected in 1891–92. Damage from the 1906 fire was slight; its walls were somewhat scorched but were easily refurbished. Two compatible additions east on Bush Street were added in 1914 and 1918 by Willis Polk, and in 1931 a 22-story tower completed the design.

Ralph Stackpole's monumental 1930 granite sculptural groups, *Earth's Fruitfulness* and *Man's Inventive Genius*, flank anoth-
⑮ er imposing structure, the **Pacific Stock Exchange** (which dates from 1915), on the south side of Pine Street at Sansome Street. The Stock Exchange Tower around the corner at 155 Sansome Street is a 1930 modern classic by architects Miller and Pfleuger, featuring an Art Deco gold ceiling and black marble-walled entry. *Pacific Stock Exchange, 301 Pine St., 94104, tel. 415/393–4000. Reserve tours 2 weeks ahead; minimum 8 persons.*

Stroll down Sansome Street and turn right on Sutter Street.
⑯ The **Hallidie Building** (130 Sutter St. between Kearny and Montgomery Sts.) was built as an investment by the University of California Regents in 1918 and named for cable-car inventor and university regent Andrew S. Hallidie. It is believed to be the world's first all-glass curtain/wall structure. Architect Willis Polk's revolutionary design hangs a foot beyond the reinforced concrete of the frame. It dominates the block with its reflecting glass, decorative exterior fire escapes that appear to be metal balconies, the Venetian Gothic cornice, and horizontal ornamental bands of birds at feeders.

The Embarcadero and Lower Market Street

In one instance, the 1989 Loma Prieta earthquake changed San Francisco for the better: The Embarcadero Freeway had to be torn down, making the foot of Market Street clearly visible for the first time in 30 years. The trademark of the port is the
⑰ quaint **Ferry Building** that stands at the Embarcadero. The clock tower is 230 feet high and was modeled by Arthur Page Brown after the campanile of Seville's cathedral. The four great clock faces on the tower, powered by the swinging action of a 14-foot pendulum, stopped at 5:17 on the morning of April 18, 1906, and stayed that way for the following 12 months. The 1896 building survived the quake and is now the headquarters of the Port Authority and the World Trade Center. A waterfront promenade that extends from this point to the Oakland Bay Bridge is great for jogging, watching the sailboats on the bay (if the day is not too windy), or enjoying a picnic. Check out the beautiful new pedestrian pier adjacent to Pier 1, with its old-fashioned lamps, wrought-iron benches, and awe-inspiring views of the bay. Ferries from behind the Ferry Building sail to Sausalito, Larkspur, and Tiburon.

Strolling back up Market Street, one's attention is drawn to the
⑱ huge **Embarcadero Center** complex. Frequently called "Rockefeller Center West," its eight buildings include more than 100 shops, 40 restaurants, and two hotels, as well as high-rise resi-

dential towers and town-house condos. A three-tiered pedestrian mall links the buildings, and much attention has been given to attractive landscaping throughout the development. Louise Nevelson's dramatic 54-foot-high black-steel sculpture, *Sky Tree*, stands guard over Building 3. **The Hyatt Regency Hotel** (5 Embarcadero) was designed by John Portman and is noted for its spectacular lobby and 20-story hanging garden. Just in front of the hotel is the Justin Herman Plaza. There are arts and crafts shows, street musicians, and mimes here on weekends year-round. Kite-flying is popular here. A huge concrete sculpture, the Vaillancourt Fountain, has had legions of critics since its installation in 1971; most of the time the fountain does not work, and many feel it is an eyesore.

⑲ The **Old San Francisco Mint**, at 5th and Mission streets, reopened as a museum in 1973. The century-old brick-and-stone building exhibits a priceless collection of gold coins. Visitors tour the vaults and can strike their own souvenir medal on an 1869 press. *Admission free. Open weekdays 10–4.*

The vast tract of downtown land south of Market Street along the waterfront and west to the Mission district is now known by the acronym SoMa (patterned after New York City's south-of-Houston SoHo). This is the happening place after dark. The machine shops, printers, and warehouses are losing out to restaurants, bars, discos, and clubs.

⑳ The **Ansel Adams Center** (250 4th St., tel. 415/495–7000) showcases both historical and contemporary photography, with a permanent collection of Adams's own work. *Admission: $4 adults, $3 students, $2 senior citizens and youths 12–17, children under 12 free. Open Tues.–Sun. 11–6.*

Chinatown

A city within a city, this is the largest Chinese community outside of Asia. Approximately 100,000 Chinese live in a 24-block downtown area just south of North Beach (and in the Richmond district's "New Chinatown"). Chinatown has been revitalized by the fairly recent immigration of Southeast Asians, who have added new character and life to the neighborhood. Downtown Chinatown is officially defined as an area reaching from Bay Street south to California Street and from Sansome Street at the edge of downtown west to Van Ness Avenue; these boundaries actually include much of Russian Hill and Nob Hill.

㉑ Visitors usually enter Chinatown through the green-tiled dragon-crowned **Chinatown Gate** at Bush Street and Grant Avenue. To best savor this district, explore it on foot (it's not far from Union Square), even though you may find the bustling, noisy, colorful stretches of Grant and Stockton streets north of Bush difficult to navigate. Parking is extremely hard to find, and traffic is impossible. As in Hong Kong, most families shop daily for fresh meats, vegetables, and bakery products. This street world shines with much good-luck crimson and gold; giant beribboned floral wreaths mark the opening of new bakeries, bazaars, and banks. Nighttime is as busy as the daytime around here, what with almost 100 restaurants squeezed into a 14-block area.

㉒ The handsome brick **Old St. Mary's Church** at Grant and California streets served as the city's Catholic cathedral until 1891.

23 Granite quarried in China was used in the structure, which was dedicated in 1854. Diagonally across the intersection is **St. Mary's Park**, a tranquil setting for local sculptor Beniamino (Benny) Bufano's heroic stainless-steel and rose-colored granite Sun Yat Sen. The 12-foot statue of the founder of the Republic of China was installed in 1937. Bufano was born in Rome on October 14, 1898, and died in San Francisco on August 16, 1970. His stainless-steel and mosaic statue of St. Francis welcomes guests at San Francisco International Airport.

Shopping surrounds the stroller on **Grant Avenue.** Much of what is offered in the countless curio shops is worthless, and discerning visitors may be dismayed by the gaudy and glittery gimcrackery. In recent years, however, a growing number of large department store–type operations have opened. Most feature an ever-growing array of products from the People's Republic. You'll find, too, that visiting the Chinese markets, even just window-gazing, is fascinating. Note the dragon-entwined lampposts, the pagoda roofs, and street signs with Chinese calligraphy.

The city's first house was built in 1836 at the corner of Grant Avenue and Clay Street; it was later destroyed in the 1906 earthquake. Turn right here and a short walk will take you to **24** **Portsmouth Square**, the potato patch that became the plaza for Yerba Buena, the village that was to become the city of San Francisco. This is where Montgomery raised the American flag in 1846. Note the bronze galleon atop a 9-foot granite shaft. Designed by Bruce Porter, the sculpture was erected in 1919 in memory of Robert Louis Stevenson, who often visited the site during his 1879–80 residence. In the morning, the park is crowded with people performing solemn t'ai chi rituals.

25 From here you can walk to the **Chinese Cultural Center**, which frequently displays exhibits of Chinese-American art as well as traveling exhibits of Chinese culture. The center also offers $12 Saturday-afternoon walking tours of historic points in Chinatown. *In the Holiday Inn, 750 Kearny St., tel. 415/986–1822. Admission free. Open Tues.–Sat. 10–4.*

You're now on the edge of North Beach and could easily walk over to the **City Lights bookstore** or other North Beach sites.

The original Chinatown burned down after the 1906 earthquake; the first building to set the style for the new Chinatown is near Portsmouth Square, at 743 Washington Street. The **26** three-tiered pagoda called the **Old Chinese Telephone Exchange** was built in 1909. Also worth a visit is **Buddha's Universal Church**, 720 Washington Street, a five-story, hand-built temple decorated with murals and tile mosaics. *Open 2nd and 4th Sun. of the month, 1–3.*

Time Out Skip that Big Mac you've been craving; opt instead for dim sum, a variety of pastries filled with meat, fish, and vegetables, the Chinese version of a smorgasbord. More than a dozen Chinese restaurants feature this unusual lunch/brunch adventure from about 11 AM to 3 PM. In most places, stacked food-service carts patrol the premises; customers select from the varied offerings, and the final bill is tabulated by the number of different saucers on the table. Dim sum restaurants tend to be big, crowded, noisy, cheap, and friendly. Suggestions are often offered by nearby strangers as to what is inside the tempting morsels. Two favorites on Pacific Avenue, two blocks north of Washington Street, between Stockton and Powell streets, are **Hong Kong Tea House** (835 Pacific Ave.) and **Tung Fong** (808 Pacific Ave.). Many of the smaller, inexpensive Chinese restaurants and cafés do not accept credit cards; some serve beer and wine.

Waverly Place is noted for ornate painted balconies and Chi-
㉗ nese temples. **Tien Hou Temple**, at 125 Waverly Place, was dedicated to the Queen of the Heavens and Goddess of the Seven Seas by Day Ju, one of the first three Chinese to arrive in San Francisco in 1852.

㉘ The **Chinese Historical Society** traces the history of Chinese immigrants and their contributions to the state's rail, mining, and fishing industries. *650 Commercial St. (near Sacramento and Montgomery Sts.), tel. 415/391–1188. Admission free. Open Wed.–Sun. 12–4.*

The other main thoroughfare in Chinatown, where locals shop for everyday needs, is **Stockton Street**, which parallels Grant Avenue. This is the real heart of Chinatown. Housewives jostle one another as they pick among the sidewalk displays of Chinese vegetables. Double-parked trucks unloading crates of chickens or ducks add to the all-day traffic jams. You'll see excellent examples of Chinese architecture along this street.
㉙ Most noteworthy is the elaborate **Chinese Six Companies** (843 Stockton St.) with its curved roof tiles and elaborate cornices. Folk-art murals grace the walls of an apartment building at Stockton Street and Pacific Avenue. Displays of jade and gold glitter from jewelry windows—the Chinese value these items above all other ornaments. It's an easy ½-hour walk back down-
㉚ town to Union Square via the **Stockton Street Tunnel**, which runs from Sacramento Street to Sutter Street. Completed in 1914, this was the city's first tunnel to accommodate vehicular and pedestrian traffic.

North Beach and Telegraph Hill

Like neighboring Chinatown, North Beach, centered on Columbus Avenue north of Broadway, is best explored on foot. In the early days there truly was a beach. At the time of the Gold Rush, the bay extended into the hollow between Telegraph and Russian hills. North Beach, less than a square mile, is the most densely populated district in the city and is truly cosmopolitan. Much of the Old World ambience still lingers in this easygoing and polyglot neighborhood. Novelist Herbert Gold, a North Beach resident, calls the area "the longest running, most glorious American bohemian operetta outside Greenwich Village."

Among the first immigrants to Yerba Buena during the early 1840s were young men from the northern provinces of Italy. By 1848, the village, renamed San Francisco, had become an overnight boomtown with the discovery of gold. Thousands more poured into the burgeoning area, seeking the golden dream. For many the trail ended in San Francisco. The Genoese started the still-active fishing industry, as well as much-needed produce businesses. Later the Sicilians emerged as leaders of the fishing fleets and eventually as proprietors of the seafood restaurants lining Fisherman's Wharf. Meanwhile, their Genoese cousins established banking and manufacturing empires.

③ **Washington Square** may well be the daytime social heart of what was once considered "Little Italy." By mid-morning groups of conservatively dressed elderly Italian men are sunning and sighing at the state of their immediate world. Nearby, laughing Asian and Caucasian playmates race through the grass with Frisbees or colorful kites. Multinational denim-clad mothers exchange shopping tips and ethnic recipes. Elderly Chinese matrons stare impassively at the passing parade. Camera-toting tourists focus their lenses on the adjacent Roman-
③ esque splendor of **Sts. Peter and Paul**, often called the Italian Cathedral. Built in 1924, its twin-turreted terra-cotta towers are local landmarks. On the first Sunday of October, the annual Blessing of the Fleet is celebrated with a mass followed by a parade to Fisherman's Wharf. Another popular annual event is the Columbus Day pageant.

The 1906 earthquake and fire devastated this area, and the park provided shelter for hundreds of the homeless. **Fior d'Italia**, facing the cathedral, is San Francisco's oldest Italian restaurant. The original opened in 1886 and continued to operate in a tent after the 1906 earthquake until new quarters were ready. Surrounding streets are packed with Italian delicatessens, bakeries, Chinese markets, coffeehouses, and ethnic restaurants. Wonderful aromas fill the air. (Coffee beans roasted at **Graffeo** at 733 Columbus Avenue are shipped to customers all over the United States.) Stop by the **Panelli Brothers** deli (1419 Stockton St.) for a memorable, reasonably priced meat-and-cheese sandwich to go. **Florence Ravioli Factory** (1412 Stockton St.) features garlic sausages, prosciutto, and mortadella, as well as 75 tasty cheeses and sandwiches to go.

South of Washington Square and just off Columbus Avenue is
③ the **Church of St. Francis of Assisi** (610 Vallejo St.). This 1860 Victorian Gothic building stands on the site of the frame parish church that served the Gold Rush Catholic community.

Over the years, North Beach has attracted creative individualists, among them the members of what was to become known as the beat generation of the 1950s. Here it flourished, then faltered in what was then a predominantly Italian enclave. The Beat gathering places are gone, and few of the original leaders remain. Poet Lawrence Ferlinghetti still holds court at his
③ **City Lights Bookstore** (261 Columbus Ave.). The face of North Beach is changing. The bohemian community has migrated up Grant Avenue above Columbus Avenue. Originally called Calle de la Fundación, Grant Avenue is the oldest street in the city. Each June a street fair is held on the upper part of the avenue, where a cluster of cafés, boutiques, and galleries attract crowds.

Time Out The richness of North Beach lifestyle is reflected in the neighborhood's numerous cafés. Breakfast at **Caffe Roma** (414 Columbus Ave.) and create your own omelet from a list of 11 ingredients. Skip the main room with its pastel murals of cherubs and settle at one of the umbrella-shaded tables on the patio. Moviemaker Francis Ford Coppola is a regular, and the adjoining Millefiori Inn, a charming bed-and-breakfast, frequently hosts film celebrities.

Across the street is **Caffe Puccini** (411 Columbus Ave.). It could be Italy: Few of the staff speak English. Their *caffe latté* (coffee, chocolate, cinnamon, and steamed milk) and strains of

Italian operas recall *Roman Holiday*. A Saturday morning must is around the corner at **Caffe Trieste** (601 Vallejo St.). Get there at about 11; at noon, the Giotta family's weekly musical begins. The program ranges from Italian pop and folk music to favorite family operas. The Trieste opened in 1956 and became headquarters for the area's beatnik poets, artists, and writers. **Caffe Malvina** (1600 Stockton St.), ideal for people-watching along Washington Square, started during the 1950s and was among the first U.S. importers of Italian-made espresso machines.

Telegraph Hill residents command some of the best views in the city, as well as the most difficult ascent to their aeries. The Greenwich stairs lead up to Coit Tower from Filbert Street, and there are steps down to Filbert Street on the opposite side of Telegraph Hill. Views are superb en route, but most visitors should either taxi up to the tower or take the Muni bus No. 39 Coit at Washington Square. To catch the bus from Union Square, walk to Stockton and Sutter streets, board the Muni No. 30, and ask for a transfer to use at Washington Square (Columbus Ave. and Union St.) to board the No. 39 Coit. Public parking is very limited at the tower, and on holidays and weekends there are long lines of cars and buses winding up the narrow road.

Telegraph Hill rises from the east end of Lombard Street to about 300 feet and is capped with the landmark Coit Tower, dedicated as a monument to the city's volunteer firefighters. Early during the Gold Rush, an eight-year-old who would become one of the city's most memorable eccentrics, Lillie Hitchcock Coit, arrived on the scene. Legend relates that at age 17, "Miss Lil" deserted a wedding party and chased down the street after her favorite engine, Knickerbocker No. 5, clad in her bridesmaid finery. She was soon made an honorary member of the Knickerbocker Company, and after that always signed herself "Lillie Coit 5" in honor of her favorite fire engine. Lillie died in 1929 at the age of 86, leaving the city about $100,000 of her million-dollar-plus estate to "expend in an appropriate manner . . . to the beauty of San Francisco."

35 **Coit Tower** stands as a monument not only to Lillie Coit and the city's firefighters but also to the influence of the political radical Mexican muralist Diego Rivera. Fresco was Rivera's medium, and it was his style that unified the work of most of the 25 artists who painted the murals in the tower. The murals were commissioned by the U.S. government as a Public Works of Art Project. The artists were paid $38 a week. Some were fresh from art schools; others found no market for art in the dark Depression days of the early 1930s. An illustrated brochure for sale in the tiny gift shop explains the various murals dedicated to the workers of California. There is an elevator to the top that provides a panoramic view of both the Bay Bridge and Golden Gate Bridge; directly offshore is the famous Alcatraz and just behind it, Angel Island, a hikers' and campers' paradise. Be sure to carry a camera and binoculars. There are often artists at work in Pioneer Park, at the foot of the tower. Small paintings of the scene are frequently offered for sale at modest prices. The impressive bronze statue of Christopher Columbus, *Discoverer of America*, was a gift of the local Italian community.

At the foot of the hill you will come to the Levi Strauss headquarters, a carefully landscaped $150 million complex that appears so collegial and serene it is affectionately known as LSU (Levi Strauss University). Fountains and grassy knolls complement the stepped-back redbrick buildings and provide a stress-reducing environment perfect for brown-bag lunches.

Nob Hill

If you don't mind climbing uphill, Nob Hill is within walking distance of Union Square. Once called the Hill of Golden Promise, it became Nob Hill during the 1870s when "the Big Four"—Charles Crocker, Leland Stanford, Mark Hopkins, and Collis Huntington—built their hilltop estates. It is still home to many of the city's elite as well as four of San Francisco's finest hotels.

In 1882 Robert Louis Stevenson called Nob Hill "the hill of palaces." But the 1906 earthquake and fire destroyed all the palatial mansions. The shell of one survived. The Flood brownstone (1000 California St.) was built by the Comstock silver baron in 1886 at a reputed cost of $1.5 million. In 1909 the property was
36 purchased by the prestigious **Pacific Union Club.** The 45-room exclusive club remains the bastion of the wealthy and powerful. Adjacent is a charming small park noted for its frequent art shows.

37 Neighboring **Grace Cathedral** (1051 Taylor St.) is the seat of the Episcopal Church in San Francisco. The soaring Gothic structure took 53 years to build. The gilded bronze doors at the east entrance were taken from casts of Ghiberti's Gates of Paradise on the baptistery in Florence. The superb rose window is illuminated at night. There are often organ recitals on Sundays at 5 PM, as well as special programs during the holiday seasons.

38 What sets the **Fairmont Hotel** (California and Mason Sts.) apart from other luxury hotels is its legendary history. Since its dazzling opening in 1907, the opulent marble palace has hosted presidents, royalty, and local nabobs. The lobby sports as much red plush upholstery as anyone could ever want to see. The eight-room, $6,000-a-night penthouse suite was used frequently in the TV series *Hotel*, and the stunning Nob Hill Spa and Fitness Club is on the premises.

39 The stately **Mark Hopkins Inter-Continental Hotel,** across California Street, is remembered fondly by thousands of World War II veterans who jammed the Top of the Mark lounge before leaving for overseas duty. At California and Powell streets
40 stands the posh **Stouffer Stanford Court Hotel,** a world-class establishment known for service and personal attention. The
41 structure is a remodeled 1909 apartment house. The **Huntington** (1075 California St.) is impeccably British in protecting the privacy of its celebrated guests.

42 The **Cable Car Museum** (Washington and Mason Sts.) exhibits photographs, scale models, and other memorabilia from the cable car system's 115-year history. A new 17-minute film is shown continually. *Tel. 415/474–1887. Admission free. Open daily 10–5.*

Civic Center

San Francisco's Civic Center stands as one of the country's great city, state, and federal building complexes with handsome adjoining cultural institutions. It's the realization of the theories of turn-of-the-century proponents of the "City Beautiful." In recent years, it's also become the focal point for fine dining in San Francisco.

43 Facing Polk Street, between Grove and McAllister streets, **City Hall** is a Baroque masterpiece of granite and marble, modeled after the Capitol in Washington. Its dome is even higher than the Washington version, and it dominates the area. In front of the building are formal gardens with fountains, walkways, and seasonal flower beds. Brooks Exhibit Hall was constructed under this plaza in 1958 to add space for the frequent trade shows and other events based in the Civic Auditorium on Grove Street.

San Francisco's increasing numbers of homeless people are often seen in the city's green spaces. Visitors and residents should be aware of possible danger in strolling in park areas and deserted business sectors after dark.

Across the plaza from City Hall on Larkin Street is the main
44 branch of the **San Francisco Public Library.** (A new library is being built around the corner; when the library is completed in 1995,this site will become the new Asian Art Museum.) History buffs should visit the San Francisco History Room and Archives on the third floor. Historic photographs, maps, and other memorabilia are carefully documented for the layman or research scholar. *Tel. 415/557–4567. Open Tues., Fri. 12–6; Wed. 1–6; Thurs., Sat. 10–6.*

On the west side of City Hall, across Van Ness Avenue, are the Museum of Modern Art, the Opera House, and Davies Symphony Hall. The northernmost of the three is the Veterans' Build-
45 ing, whose third and fourth floors house the **Museum of Modern Art.** (A new MOMA is under construction as part of the downtown Yerba Buena development.) The museum's permanent collection was significantly enhanced in 1991 by the $40 million Haas bequest, which features Matisse's masterpiece, *Woman in a Hat*, as well as works by Derain, Manet, Monet, and Picasso. Traveling exhibitions bring important national and international paintings, photographs, graphics, and sculpture to the Bay Area. The Museum Store has a select offering of books, posters, cards, and crafts. The Museum Cafe serves light snacks as well as wine and beer. *At McAllister St. and Van Ness Ave., tel. 415/863–8800. Admission: $4 adults, $2 senior citizens and students 13 and over with ID; free 1st Tues. of the month. Open Tues., Wed., Fri. 10–5, Thurs. 10–9, Sat., Sun. 11–5. Closed major holidays.*

South of the Veterans' Building is the opulent **War Memorial Opera House**, which opened in 1932. Lotfi Mansouri has taken over as head of the San Francisco Opera, the largest opera company west of New York. Its regular season of world-class productions runs from September through December.

South of Grove Street, still on Van Ness Avenue, is the $27.5 million home of the San Francisco Symphony, the modern 3,000-plus-seat **Louise M. Davies Symphony Hall**, made of glass and granite. *Grove St. and Van Ness Ave., tel. 415/552–8338.*

Cost: $3 adults, $2 senior citizens and students. Tours of Davies Hall Wed. 1:30, 2:30, Sat. 12:30, 1:30. Tours of Davies Hall and the adjacent Performing Arts Center every ½ hour Mon. 10–2:30.

The **San Francisco Opera Shop**, up the street from Davies Hall, carries books, T-shirts, posters, and gift items associated with the performing arts. *199 Grove St., tel. 415/565–6414. Open Mon. 11–5, Tues.–Fri. 11–6, Sat. noon–6, Sun. noon–6 during matinees. (It frequently stays open till 8:30 during performances of the Opera and Symphony.)*

East of the Civic Center at Market and Fulton streets, the United Nations Plaza is the site of a bustling **farmers' market** on Wednesday and Sunday.

46 San Francisco's original civic center is **Mission Dolores,** founded in 1776 at what is now 16th and Dolores streets, about a mile south of City Hall. The sixth of 21 missions founded by the Franciscans and the oldest building in the city, it combines Moorish, Mission, and Corinthian styles. Until the Gold Rush, it was surrounded by farms, and a nearby creek flowed to the bay. It retains the appearance of a small-scale outpost, dwarfed by the towers of the adjacent basilica built in 1916. There is a small museum and cemetery garden. *Tel. 415/621–8203. Donation: $1. Open daily 9–4. Public transportation: Muni Metro J-Church train to 16th St.*

Japantown

Japanese-Americans began gravitating to the neighborhood known as the Western Addition prior to the 1906 earthquake. Early immigrants arrived about 1860, and they named San Francisco Soko. After the 1906 fire had destroyed wooden homes in other parts of the stricken city, many survivors settled in the Western Addition. By the 1930s the pioneers had opened shops, markets, meeting halls, and restaurants and established Shinto and Buddhist temples. Japantown was virtually disbanded during World War II when many of its residents, including second- and third-generation Americans, were "relocated" in camps. Today Japantown, or "Nihonmachi," is centered on the slopes of Pacific Heights, north of Geary Boulevard, between Fillmore and Laguna streets. The Nihonmachi Cherry Blossom Festival is celebrated two weekends every April with a calendar of ethnic events. Walking in Nihonmachi is more than just a shopping and culinary treat; it is a cultural and sensory experience.

To reach Japantown from Union Square, take the Muni bus No. 38-Geary or No. 2, 3, or 4 on Sutter Street, westbound to Laguna. Remember to have exact change—the fare is 85¢; free transfers are good for one direction and one change of vehicles.

We recommend visiting Japantown and the Western Addition during the day. Though the hotel, restaurant, and Kabuki movie complex are relatively safe in the evenings, it is often difficult to avoid long waits at isolated bus stops or to find a cruising cab when you want to get back to your hotel. The proximity of the often-hostile street gangs in the Western Addition could cause unpleasant incidents.

The buildings around the traffic-free **Japan Center Mall** between Sutter and Post streets are of the shoji screen school of architecture, and Ruth Asawa's origami fountain sits in the middle. (*See* Tour 1: Union Square, above, for more information on Ms. Asawa.)

47 The mall faces the three-block-long, 5-acre **Japan Center.** In 1968 the multimillion-dollar development created by noted American architect Minoru Yamasaki opened with a three-day folk festival. The cluster includes an 800-car public garage and shops and showrooms selling Japanese products: electronic products, cameras, tapes and records, porcelains, pearls, and paintings.

The center is dominated by its Peace Plaza and Pagoda located between the East and Kintetsu buildings. Designed by Professor Yoshiro Taniguchi of Tokyo, an authority on ancient Japanese buildings, the plaza is landscaped with traditional Japanese-style gardens and reflecting pools. A graceful *yagura* (wooden drum tower) spans the entrance to the plaza and the copper-roofed *Heiwa Dori* (Peace Walkway) at the north end connects the East and Kintetsu buildings. The five-tiered, 100-foot Peace Pagoda overlooks the plaza, where seasonal festivals are held. The pagoda draws on the tradition of miniature round pagodas dedicated to eternal peace by Empress Koken in Nara more than 1,200 years ago. It was designed by the Japanese architect Yoshiro Taniguchi "to convey the friendship and goodwill of the Japanese to the people of the United States." A cultural bridge modeled after Florence's Ponte Vecchio spans Webster Street.

Time Out At a sushi bar, sample the bite-size portions of lightly seasoned rice and seaweed topped with various kinds of seafood, usually raw. Try to manage the chopsticks, dip (don't drench) your portion into the soy sauce, and experience this typical Japanese favorite. Tea, sake, or excellent Japanese beer accompanies these morsels. One warning—the final bill is calculated by portion, and it is not unusual to run up a $20 tab per person. **Isobune**, in the Kentetsu Mall in Japan Center (tel. 415/563–1030), is unusual. The sushi chef prepares a variety of sushi, placing each small portion on a small wooden boat that floats on a "river" of water that circles the counter. The customer then fishes out a sampling.

An inexpensive and popular snack is ramen (noodle dishes). The noodles are either boiled and served in a broth or toss-fried with bits of greens and meat added for flavor. **Mifune**, also in the Kintetsu Mall, serves both hot and cold noodle dishes, including udon, which are thick noodles, and *soba*, which are made from buckwheat.

Walk back east on Geary Boulevard to Gough Street. This enclave of expensive high-rise residential towers is known as Cathedral Hill. The dramatic **St. Mary's Cathedral** was dedicated **48** in 1971 at a cost of $7 million. The impressive Catholic cathedral seats 2,500 people around the central altar. Above the altar is a spectacular cascade made of 7,000 aluminum ribs. Four magnificent stained-glass windows in the dome represent the four elements: the blue north window, water; the light-colored south window, the sun; the red west window, fire; and the green east window, earth. Designed by a team of local architects and Pier Nervi of Rome, the Italian travertine church is approached through a spacious plaza.

Pacific Heights

Pacific Heights forms an east–west ridge along the city's northern flank from Van Ness Avenue to the Presidio and from California Street to the bay. Some of the city's most expensive and dramatic real estate, including mansions and town houses priced at $1 million and up, are located here. Grand old Victorians, expensively face-lifted, grace tree-lined streets, although here and there glossy, glass-walled condo high rises obstruct the view.

Old money and some new, trade and diplomatic personnel, personalities in the limelight, and those who prefer absolute media anonymity occupy the city's most prestigious residential enclave. Rolls-Royces, Mercedeses, and security systems are commonplace.

Few visitors see anything other than the pleasing facades of Queen Anne charmers, English Tudor imports, and Baroque bastions, but strolling can still prove rewarding. The area encompasses a variety of great and small private homes. Many of the structures stand close together but extend in a vertical direction for two or more stories. A distinguishing feature of some of the grand residences is an ornate gate.

A good place to begin a tour of the neighborhood is at the corner of Webster Street and Pacific Avenue, deep in the heart of the heights. You can get here from Union Square by taking Muni bus No. 3 from Sutter and Stockton to Jackson and Fillmore streets. Turn right and walk one block east to Webster Street.

North on Webster Street, at 2550, is the massive Georgian brick mansion built in 1896 for William B. Bourn, who had inherited a Mother Lode gold mine. The architect, Willis Polk, was responsible for many of the most traditional and impressive commercial and private homes built from the prequake days until the early 1920s. (Be sure to see his 1917 Hallidie Bldg.; 130 Sutter St.; *see* Exploring the Financial District, above.)

Neighbors include a consulate and, on the northwest corner, two classic showplaces. **2222 Broadway** is the three-story Italian Renaissance palace built by Comstock mine heir James Flood. Broadway uptown, unlike its North Beach stretch, is big league socially. The former Flood residence was given to a religious order. Ten years later, the Convent of the Sacred Heart purchased the Baroque brick Grant house (2220 Broadway) and both serve as school quarters today. A second top-drawer school, the Hamlin (2120 Broadway), occupies another Flood property.

Go east on Broadway and at the next corner turn right onto Buchanan Street and continue south to 2090 Jackson Street. The **49** massive red sandstone **Whittier Mansion** was one of the most elegant 19th-century houses in the state, built so solidly that only a chimney toppled over during the 1906 earthquake. Next door at 2099 Pacific Avenue is the **North Baker Library of the California Historical Society.** The library houses a fine collection of local historical documents but is open only to researchers and has no public displays.

Proceed east another block to **Laguna Street.** The Italianate Victorians on the east side of the 1800 block of Laguna Street cost only $2,000 to $2,600 when they were built during the

1870s. This block is one of the most photographed rows of Victorians in the city.

50 One block south, at Washington Street, is **Lafayette Park,** a four-block-square oasis for sunbathers and dog-and-Frisbee teams. During the 1860s a tenacious squatter, Sam Holladay, had wood shipped round the Horn and built himself a big house in what is the center of the park. Holladay even instructed city gardeners as if the land were his own and defied all attempts to remove him. The house was finally torn down in 1936.

51 The most imposing residence is the formal French **Spreckels Palace** (2080 Washington St.). Sugar heir Adolph Spreckels's wife was so pleased with the structure that she commissioned architect George Applegarth to design the city's European museum, the California Palace of the Legion of Honor in Lincoln Park.

Continue south on Gough Street (pronounced "Goff"), which runs along the east side of the park. A number of Queen Anne Victorians here have been lovingly restored. Two blocks south and one east, at the corner of California and Franklin streets, is an impressive twin-turreted Queen Anne–style Victorian built for a Gold Rush mining and lumber baron. North on Franklin Street, at 1735, stands a stately brick Georgian, built during the early 1900s for a coffee merchant.

52 At 2007 Franklin Street is the handsome **Haas-Lilienthal Victorian.** Built in 1886, at an original cost of $20,000, this grand Queen Anne survived the 1906 earthquake and fire, and is the only fully furnished Victorian open to the public. The carefully kept rooms offer an intriguing glimpse into turn-of-the-century taste and lifestyle. A small display of photographs on the bottom floor proves that this elaborate house was modest compared with some of the giants that fell to the fire. It is operated by the Foundation for San Francisco's Architectural Heritage, and tours are given by docent volunteers. *Tel. 415/441-3004. Admission: $4 adults, $2 senior citizens and children under 12. Open Wed. noon-4, Sun. 11-4:30.*

By the mid-1970s, dozens of San Francisco's shabby gingerbreads were sporting psychedelic-colored facades, and the trend continues. Renovated treasures are found not only in the Haight-Ashbury district but increasingly in the Western Addition as well as in the working-class Mission area.

The Northern Waterfront

Numbers in the margin correspond to points of interest on the Northern Waterfront map.

For the sight, sound, and smell of the sea, hop on the Powell–Hyde cable car from Union Square to the end of the line. From the cable-car turnaround, Aquatic Park and the National Maritime Museum are immediately to the west; Fort Mason, with its several interesting museums, is just a bit farther west. If you're interested in exploring the more commercial attractions, Ghirardelli Square is behind you and Fisherman's Wharf to the east. We recommend you wear casual clothes, good walking shoes, and a jacket or sweater for mid-afternoon breezes or foggy mists.

Or you could begin your day with one of the early-morning boat tours that depart from the Northern Waterfront piers. On a clear day (almost always), the morning light casts a warm glow on the colorful homes on Russian Hill, the weather-aged fishing boats docked at Fisherman's Wharf, rosy Ghirardelli Square and its fairy-tale clock tower, and the swelling seas beyond the entrance to the bay.

San Francisco is famous for the arts and crafts that flourish on the streets. Each day more than 200 of the city's innovative jewelers, painters, potters, photographers, and leather workers offer their wares for sale. You'll find them at Fisherman's Wharf, Union Square, Embarcadero Plaza, and Cliff House. Be wary: Some of the items are from Mexican or other foreign factories, and some may be overpriced. If you can't live without the item, try to bargain.

1 The **National Maritime Museum** exhibits ship models, photographs, maps, and other artifacts chronicling the development of San Francisco and the West Coast through maritime history. *Aquatic Park, at the foot of Polk St., tel. 415/556-8177. Admission free. Open daily 10-5, till 6 in summer.*

2 The museum also includes the **Hyde Street Pier** (2 blocks east), where historic vessels are moored. The highlight is the *Balclutha*, an 1886 full-rigged, three-mast sailing vessel that sailed around Cape Horn 17 times. The *Eureka*, a sidewheel ferry, and the *C.A. Thayer*, a three-masted schooner, can also be boarded. *Tel. 415/ 556-6435. Admission: $3 adults, senior citizens and children free. Open daily 10-5, 10-6 in summer.*

The *Pampanito*, at Pier 45, is a World War II submarine. An audio tour has been installed. *Tel. 415/929-0202. Admission: $4 adults, $2 students 12-18, $1 senior citizens, active military, and children 6-11. Open Sun.-Thurs. 9-6, Fri.-Sat. 9-9, daily 9-9 in summer.*

3 Spend some time strolling through **Ghirardelli Square,** which is across Beach Street from the National Maritime Museum. This charming complex of 19th-century brick factory buildings has been transformed into specialty shops, cafés, restaurants, and galleries. Until the early 1960s, the Ghirardelli Chocolate Company's aromatic production perfumed the Northern Waterfront. One particularly noteworthy shop is **Xanadu Gallery**, which displays museum-quality tribal art from Asia, Africa, Oceania, and the Americas. Its array of antique and ethnic jewelry is peerless.

4 Just east of the Hyde Street Pier, **The Cannery** is a three-story structure built in 1894 to house the Del Monte Fruit and Vegetable Cannery. Shops, art galleries, and unusual restaurants ring the courtyard today, and the new **Museum of the City of San Francisco** can be found on the third floor. The first independent museum on the history of the city displays a number of significant historical items, maps, and photographs, including the eight-ton head of the *Goddess of Progress* statue that toppled from City Hall just before the 1906 earthquake. *2801 Leavenworth St., tel. 415/928-0289. Admission free. Open Wed.-Sun. 11-4.*

5 Just across the street, additional shopping and snacking choices are offered at the flag-festooned **Anchorage mall.**

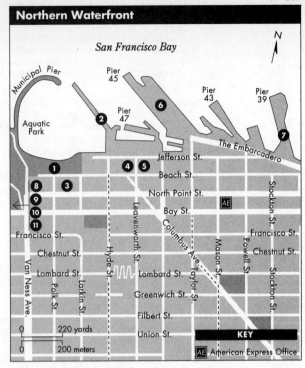

Northern Waterfront

➏ A bit farther down at Taylor and Jefferson streets is **Fisherman's Wharf.** Numerous seafood restaurants are located here, as well as sidewalk crab pots and counters that offer takeaway shrimp and crab cocktails. Ships creak at their moorings; seagulls cry out for a handout. By mid-afternoon, the fishing fleet is back to port. T-shirts and sweats, gold chains galore, redwood furniture, acres of artwork—some original—beckon visitors. Wax museums, fast-food favorites, amusing street artists, and the animated robots at Lazer Maze provide diversions for all ages.

Time Out   A great family spot on the wharf is **Bobby Rubino's** (245 Jefferson St.). It serves barbecued ribs, shrimp, chicken, and burgers—there is something tasty for everyone. A favorite of couples is crowded, noisy **Houlihan's** at the Anchorage mall. It is noted for fancy drinks, fantastic bay views, tasty pizza and pasta, plus nightly music and dancing.

Today's tourists have the daily opportunity of enjoying exhilarating cruising on the bay. Among the cruises of the **Red and White Fleet**, berthed at Pier 41, are frequent 45-minute swings under the Golden Gate Bridge and the Northern Waterfront. Advanced reservations are strongly recommended for the very popular Alcatraz Island tour, which enables passengers to take a self-guided tour through the prison and grounds. *Reservations for individuals from Ticketron, Box 26430, 94126, tel. 415/546–2896. Cost: $5; $8.50 with audio tour.*

The **Blue and Gold Fleet**, berthed at Pier 39, provides its passengers with validated parking across the street. The 1¼-hour tour sails under both the Bay and Golden Gate bridges. Dinner-dance cruises run April–mid-December. *Tel. 415/781–7877. Reservations not necessary. Bay Cruise: $14 adults, $7 senior citizens and children 5–18. Summertime dinner-dance cruise: $35 per person (group rates available). Daily departures.*

❼ **Pier 39** is the most popular of San Francisco's waterfront attractions, drawing millions of visitors each year to browse through its dozens of shops. Check out The Disney Store, with more Mickey Mouses than you can shake a stick at; Left Hand World, where left-handers will find all manner of gadgets designed with lefties in mind; and Only in San Francisco, the place for San Francisco memorabilia and the location of the Pier 39 information center. The myriad eateries confuse those seeking a traditional soda-and-burger stop. Ongoing free entertainment, accessible validated parking, and nearby public transportation ensure crowds most days.

The Marina and the Presidio

❽ San Francisco's rosy and Rococo **Palace of Fine Arts** is at the very end of the Marina, near the intersection of Baker and Beach streets. The palace is the sole survivor of the 32 tinted plaster structures built for the 1915 Panama–Pacific Exposition. Bernard Maybeck designed the Roman Classic beauty, and legions of sentimental citizens and a huge private donation saved the palace. It was reconstructed in concrete at a cost of $7 million and reopened in 1967. The massive columns, great rotunda, and swan-filled lagoon will be familiar from fashion layouts as well as many recent films. Recently, travelers on package tours from Japan have been using it as a backdrop for wedding-party photos, with the brides wearing Western-style finery.

The interior houses a fascinating hands-on museum, the **Exploratorium**. It has been called the best science museum in the world. The curious of all ages flock here to try to use and understand some of the 600 exhibits. Be sure to include the pitch-black, crawl-through Tactile Dome in your visit. *Tel. 415/563–7337. Prices and hours subject to change, so call ahead. Admission: $7 adults, $3 children under 17. Reservations required for Tactile Dome.*

If you have a car, now is the time to use it for a drive through the **Presidio.** (If not, Muni bus No. 38 from Union Square will take you to Park Presidio; from there use a free transfer to bus No. 28 into the Presidio.) A military post for more than 200 years, this headquarters of the U.S. Sixth Army may soon become a public park. A band of Spanish settlers claimed the area in 1776. It became a Mexican garrison in 1822 when Mexico gained its independence from Spain. U.S. troops forcibly occupied it in 1846.

The more than 1,500 acres of rolling hills, majestic woods, and attractive redbrick army barracks present an air of serenity in the middle of the city. There are two beaches, a golf course, and picnic sites. The **Officers' Club,** a long, low adobe, was the Spanish commandant's headquarters, built about 1776, and is ❾ the oldest standing building in the city. The **Presidio Army Museum** is housed in the former hospital and focuses on the role played by the military in San Francisco's development. *On the corner of Lincoln Blvd. and Funston Ave., tel. 415/561–4115. Admission free. Open Tues.–Sun. 10–4.*

10 Muni bus No. 28 will take you to the **Golden Gate Bridge** toll plaza. San Francisco celebrated the 50th birthday of the orange suspension bridge in 1987. Nearly 2 miles long, connecting San Francisco with Marin County, its Art Deco design is powerful, serene, and tough, made to withstand winds of over 100 miles per hour. Though frequently gusty and misty (walkers should wear warm clothing), the bridge offers unparalleled views of the Bay Area. The east walkway offers a glimpse of the San Francisco skyline as well as the islands in the bay. On a sunny day sailboats ply the water, and brave windsurfers test the often treacherous tides beneath the bridge. The view west consists of the wild hills of the Marin headlands, the curving coast south to Land's End, and the majestic Pacific Ocean. There's a vista point on the Marin side, where you can contemplate the city and its spectacular setting.

11 **Fort Point** was constructed during the years 1853–1861 to protect San Francisco from sea attack during the Civil War. It was designed to mount 126 cannons with a range of up to 2 miles. Standing under the shadow of the Golden Gate Bridge, the national historic site is now a museum filled with military memorabilia. Guided group tours are offered by National Park rangers, and there are cannon demonstrations. There is a superb view of the bay from the top floor. *Tel. 415/556–1693. Admission free. Open daily 10–5.*

From here, hardy walkers who elect to stroll about 3½ miles along the Golden Gate Promenade to Aquatic Park and the Hyde Street cable-car terminus will be rewarded with some particularly dramatic views of the bay.

Golden Gate Park

Numbers in the margin correspond to points of interest on the Golden Gate Park map.

It was a Scotsman, John McLaren, who became manager of Golden Gate Park in 1887 and transformed brush and sand into the green civilized wilderness we enjoy today. Here you can attend a polo game or a Sunday band concert and rent a bike, boat, or roller skates. On Sundays, some park roads are closed to cars and come alive with joggers, bicyclists, skaters, museum goers, and picnickers. There are tennis courts, baseball diamonds, soccer fields, and a buffalo paddock, and miles of trails for horseback riding in this 1,000-acre park.

Because it is so large, the best way for most visitors to see it is by car. Muni buses provide service, though on weekends there may be a long wait. On Market Street, board a west-bound No. 5-Fulton or No. 21-Hayes bus and continue to Arguello and Fulton streets. Walk south about 500 feet to John F. Kennedy Drive.

From May through October, free guided walking tours of the park are offered every weekend by the Friends of Recreation and Parks (tel. 415/221–1311).

1 The oldest building in the park and perhaps San Francisco's most elaborate Victorian structure is the **Conservatory,** a copy

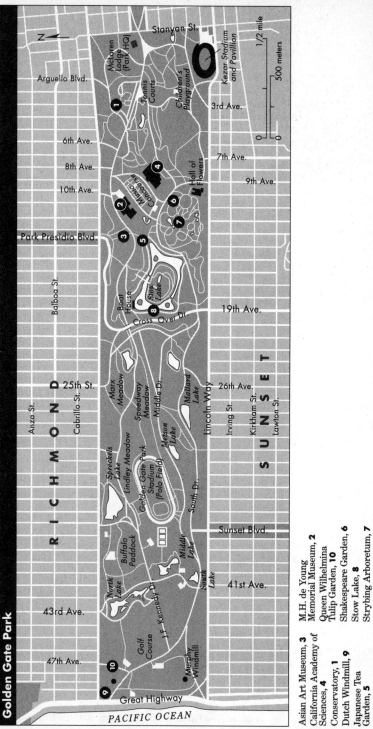

Golden Gate Park

Asian Art Museum, **3**
California Academy of Sciences, **4**
Conservatory, **1**
Dutch Windmill, **9**
Japanese Tea Garden, **5**

M.H. de Young Memorial Museum, **2**
Queen Wilhelmina Tulip Garden, **10**
Shakespeare Garden, **6**
Stow Lake, **8**
Strybing Arboretum, **7**

of London's famous Kew Gardens. The ornate greenhouse was originally brought around the Horn for the estate of James Lick in San Jose. The Conservatory was purchased from the Lick estate with public subscription funds and erected in the park. In addition to a tropical garden, there are seasonal displays of flowers and plants and a permanent exhibit of rare orchids.

❷ The eastern section of the park has three museums. The **M. H. de Young Memorial Museum** was completely reorganized in 1989. It now features American art, with collections of painting, sculpture, textiles, and decorative arts from Colonial times through the 20th century. Fifteen new galleries highlight the work of American masters including Copley, Eakins, Bingham, and Sargent. Don't miss the room featuring landscape paintings, dominated by Frederic Church's moody, almost psychedelic *Rainy Season in the Tropics*. There is a wonderful gallery of American still-life and trompe l'oeil art and a small selection of classic Shaker furniture. The de Young has also retained its dramatic collection of tribal art from Africa, Oceania, and the Americas, which includes pottery, basketry, sculpture, and ritual clothing and accessories. In addition to its permanent collections, the museum hosts selected traveling shows—often blockbuster events for which there are long lines and additional admission charges.

The museum has an outstanding shop with a wide selection of art objects. The Cafe de Young, which has outdoor seating in the Oakes Garden, serves a complete menu of light refreshments until 4 PM. *Tel. 415/863–3330 for 24-hour information. Admission: $5 adults, $3 senior citizens, $2 youths 12–17. Free 1st Wed. and Sat. morning of the month. Note: One entrance charge admits you to the de Young, Asian Art, and Legion of Honor museums on the same day. Open Wed.–Sun. 10–5.*

❸ The **Asian Art Museum** is located in galleries that adjoin the de Young. The world-famous Avery Brundage collection consists of more than 10,000 sculptures, paintings, and ceramics that illustrate major periods of Asian art. Very special are the Magnin Jade Room and the Leventritt collection of blue and white porcelains. On the second floor are treasures from Iran, Turkey, Syria, India, Tibet, Nepal, Pakistan, Korea, Japan, Afghanistan, and Southeast Asia. Both the de Young and Asian Art museums have daily docent tours. *Tel. 415/668–8921. Admission collected when entering the de Young. Open Wed.–Sun. 10–5.*

❹ The **California Academy of Sciences** is directly opposite the de Young Museum. It is one of the five top natural history museums in the country and has both an aquarium and a planetarium. Throngs of visitors enjoy its Steinhart Aquarium, with its dramatic 100,000-gallon Fish Roundabout, home to 14,000 creatures, and a living coral reef with colorful fish, giant clams, tropical sharks, and a rainbow of hard and soft corals. There is an additional charge for Morrison Planetarium shows ($2.50 adults, $1.25 senior citizens and students, tel. 415/750–7138 for daily schedule). The Space and Earth Hall has an "earthquake floor" that enables visitors to experience a simulated California earthquake. The Wattis Hall of Man presents lifelike habitat scenes that range from the icy terrain of the arctic to the lush highlands of New Guinea. Newly renovated is the Wild California Hall, with a 10,000-gallon aquarium showing underwater life at the Farallon (islands off the coast of Northern California), life-size elephant-seal models, and video information on the wildlife of the state. A stuffed great white shark, caught off the waters of Half Moon Bay, was added in 1989. The genuine 13½-foot, 1,500-pound "Jaws" is suspended in a tank. If you dare, you can look right into its gaping mouth. The innovative Life through Time Hall tells the story of evolution from the beginnings of the universe through the age of dinosaurs to the age of mammals. A cafeteria is open daily until one hour before the museum closes. The Academy Store offers a wide selection of books, posters, toys, and cultural artifacts. *Tel. 415/750-7145. Admission: $6 adults, $3 senior citizens and students 12-17, $1 children 6-11. $2 discount with Muni transfer. Free 1st Wed. of each month. Open daily July 4-Labor Day 10-7, Labor Day-July 3, 10-5.*

Time Out The **Japanese Tea Garden,** next to the Asian Art Museum, is
5 ideal for resting after museum touring. This charming 4-acre village was created for the 1894 Mid-Winter Exposition. Small ponds, streams, and flowering shrubs create a serene landscape. The cherry blossoms in spring are exquisite. The Tea House (tea, of course, and cookies are served) is popular and busy. *Tel. 415/752-1171. Admission: $2 adults, $1 senior residents of San Francisco and children 6-12. Free 1st Wed. of each month. Open daily 8:30-6:30.*

6 A short stroll from the Academy of Sciences will take you to the free **Shakespeare Garden.** Two hundred flowers mentioned by the Bard, as well as bronze panels engraved with quotations on a floral theme, are set throughout the garden.

7 **Strybing Arboretum** specializes in plants from areas with climates similar to that of the Bay Area, such as the west coast of Australia, South Africa, and the Mediterranean. There are many gardens inside the grounds, with 6,000 plants and tree varieties blooming seasonally. *9th Ave. at Lincoln Way, tel. 415/661-0668. Admission free. Open weekdays 8-4:30, weekends and holidays 10-5. Tours leave the bookstore weekdays at 1:30 PM, weekends at 10:30 AM and 1:30 PM.*

8 The western half of Golden Gate Park offers miles of wooded greenery and open spaces for all types of spectator and participant sports. Rent a paddleboat or stroll around **Stow Lake.** The Chinese Pavilion, a gift from the city of Taipei, was shipped in 6,000 pieces and assembled on the shore of Strawberry Hill Island in Stow Lake in 1981. At the very western end of the park, where Kennedy Drive meets the Great Highway, is the beauti-
9 fully restored 1902 **Dutch Windmill** and the photogenic **Queen Wilhelmina Tulip Garden.**

Lincoln Park and the Western Shoreline

No other American city provides such close-up views of the power and fury of the surf crashing on the shore. From Land's End in Lincoln Park you can look across the Golden Gate (the name was originally given to the opening of San Francisco Bay long before the bridge was built) to the Marin headlands. From Cliff House south to the San Francisco Zoo, the Great Highway and Ocean Beach run along the western edge of the city.

The wind is often strong along the shoreline, summer fog can blanket the ocean beaches, and the water is cold and usually too rough for swimming. Carry a sweater or jacket and bring binoculars.

At the northwest corner of the San Francisco Peninsula is Lincoln Park. At one time all the city's cemeteries were here, segregated by nationality. Today there is an 18-hole golf course with large and well-formed Monterey cypresses lining the fairways. There are scenic walks throughout the 275-acre park, with particularly good views from Land's End (the parking lot is at the end of El Camino del Mar). The trails out to Land's End, however, are for skilled hikers only: There are frequent landslides, and danger lurks along the steep cliffs.

Also in Lincoln Park is the **California Palace of the Legion of Honor**. The building itself—modeled after the 18th-century Parisian original—is architecturally interesting and spectacularly situated on cliffs overlooking the ocean and the Golden Gate Bridge. Rodin's famous *Thinker* towers over the entry court and serves as an introduction to one of the finest Rodin collections in the world. The exhibit spans centuries of European painting, sculpture, and the decorative arts, and includes works by Fra Angelico, Titian, El Greco, and Rembrandt. The museum closed in 1992 to undergo a two-year renovation: It is expected to reopen in April 1994. In the meantime, some of its collection is on display at the M.H. de Young Memorial Museum in Golden Gate Park.

Cliff House (1066 Point Lobos Ave.), where the road turns south along the western shore, has existed in several incarnations. The original, built in 1863, and several later structures were destroyed by fire. The present building has restaurants, a pub, and a gift shop. The lower dining room overlooks Seal Rocks (the barking marine mammals sunning themselves are sea lions).

An adjacent, free attraction is the **Musée Mécanique,** a collection of antique mechanical contrivances, including peep shows and nickelodeons. The museum carries on the tradition of arcade amusement at the Cliff House. *Tel. 415/386–1170. Open weekdays 11–7, weekends 10–7.*

Two flights below Cliff House is a fine observation deck and the **Golden Gate National Recreation Area Visitors Center** (tel. 415/556–8642; open daily 10–4:30). There are interesting historic photographs of Cliff House and the glass-roofed Sutro Baths. The baths covered 3 acres just north of Cliff House and comprised six enormous baths, 500 dressing rooms, and several restaurants. The baths were closed in 1952 and burned in 1966. You can explore the ruins on your own (the Visitors Center offers information on these and other trails) or take ranger-led walks on weekends.

Because traffic is often heavy in summer and on weekends, you might want to take the Muni system from the Union Square area out to Cliff House. On weekdays, take the Muni No. 38-Geary Limited to 48th Street and Point Lobos and walk down the hill. (On weekends and during the evenings, the Muni No. 38 is marked 48th Avenue.)

Time Out   Cliff House has several restaurants and a busy bar. The **Upstairs Room** (tel. 415/387–5847) features a light menu with a number of omelet choices. The lower dining room, the **Terrace Room** (tel. 415/386–3330), has a fabulous view of Seal Rocks. Reservations are recommended, but you may still have to wait for a table, especially at midday on Sunday.

Below the Cliff House are the **Great Highway** and **Ocean Beach**. Stretching for 3 miles along the western (Pacific) side of the city, this is a beautiful beach for walking, running, or lying in the sun—but not for swimming. Although dozens of surfers head to Ocean Beach each day, you'll notice they are dressed head to toe in wetsuits, as the water here is extremely cold. Across the highway from the beach is a new path that winds through landscaped sand dunes from Lincoln Avenue to Sloat Boulevard (near the zoo); this is an ideal route for walking and bicycling.

At the Great Highway and Sloat Boulevard is the **San Francisco Zoo**. The zoo was begun in 1889 in Golden Gate Park. At its present home there are 1,000 species of birds and animals, more than 130 of which have been designated endangered species. Among the protected are the snow leopard, Bengal tiger, red panda, jaguar, and the Asian elephant. One of the newest attractions is the greater one-horned rhino, next to the African elephants. Gorilla World, a $2 million exhibit, is the largest and most natural gorilla habitat in a zoo. The circular outer area is carpeted with natural African Kikuyu grass, while trees, shrubs, and waterfalls create communal play areas. The $5 million Primate Discovery Center houses 16 endangered species in atriumlike enclosures. One of the most popular zoo residents is Prince Charles, a rare white tiger and the first of its kind to be exhibited in the West.

There are 33 "storyboxes" throughout the zoo that, when turned on with the blue plastic elephant keys ($1.50), recite animal facts and basic zoological concepts in four languages (English, Spanish, Cantonese, and Tagalog).

The children's zoo has a minipopulation of about 300 mammals, birds, and reptiles, plus an insect zoo, a baby animal nursery, and a beautifully restored 1921 Dentzel Carousel. A ride astride one of the 52 hand-carved menagerie animals costs 75¢.

Zoo information, tel. 415/753–7083. Admission: $6 adults, $3 senior citizens and youths 12–15, under 12 free when accompanied by an adult. Free 1st Wed. of the month. Open daily 10–5. Children's zoo admission: $1, under 3 free. Open daily 11–4.

San Francisco for Free

This is not an inexpensive city to live in or visit. Lodging and dining are costly; museums, shopping, the opera, or a nightclub may set you back a bit. It is possible, however, to do much of your sightseeing very cheaply. Walking is often the best way to get around, and it's not very expensive to use the cable cars and buses. Exploring most of Golden Gate Park is absolutely free, and so is walking across the Golden Gate Bridge.

The Golden Gate National Recreation Area (GGNRA), consisting of most of San Francisco's shoreline, Alcatraz and Angel islands, and the headlands of Marin County, is the largest urban park in the world. The Golden Gate Promenade's 3.5-mile footpath runs from Fort Point at the base of the bridge along the shore to Hyde Street Pier. There's also a new 8-mile-long bicycle path along Ocean Beach from Cliff House south to Fort Funston, hugging sand dunes and providing ocean views. The GGNRA is San Francisco at its natural best.

From May through September, there are several popular neighborhood fairs held on weekends throughout the city. Among them are the Union Street Festival, the Fillmore Art and Jazz Festival, and the Grant Street Fair in North Beach. All are free and feature booths selling ethnic food, crafts from local artists, and musical performances. Check the "Sunday Datebook" section in the *San Francisco Examiner and Chronicle* to find out what's happening during your stay.

There are also free band concerts on Sunday and holiday afternoons at 1 in the music concourse in Golden Gate Park (opposite the de Young Museum and California Academy of Sciences, tel. 415/666–7107).

What to See and Do with Children

The attractions described in the above exploring sections offer a great deal of entertainment for children as well as their families. We suggest, for example, visiting the ships at the **Hyde Street Pier** and spending some time at **Pier 39**, where there is a double-decked Venetian carousel. (*See* the Northern Waterfront, above.)

Children will find much to amuse themselves with at **Golden Gate Park**, from the old-fashioned Conservatory to the expansive lawns and trails. There is another vintage carousel (1912) at the children's playground. The **Steinhart Aquarium** at the California Academy of Sciences has a Touching Tide Pool, from which docents will pull starfish and hermit crabs for children or adults to feel. The **Japanese Tea Garden**, although crowded, is well worth exploring; climbing over the high, humpbacked bridges is like moving the neighborhood playground toys into an exotic new (or old) world.

It is also possible to walk across the **Golden Gate Bridge.** The view is thrilling and the wind invigorating, if the children (and adults) are not overwhelmed by the height of the bridge and the nearby automobile traffic. (*See* the Marina and the Presidio, above.)

Many children may enjoy walking along crowded **Grant Avenue** and browsing in the many souvenir shops. Unfortunately, nothing—not even straw finger wrestlers, wooden contraptions to make coins "disappear," shells that open in water to release tissue paper flowers, and other true junk—is as cheap as it once was. (*See* Chinatown, above.)

The **San Francisco Zoo**, with a children's zoo, playground, and carousel, is not far from Ocean Beach. The weather and the currents do not allow swimming, but it's a good place for walking and playing in the surf. (*See* Lincoln Park and the Western Shoreline, above.)

The **Exploratorium** at the Palace of Fine Arts is a preeminent children's museum and is very highly recommended. (*See* the Marina and the Presidio, above.)

Finally, we remind you of the **cable cars.** Try to find time for a ride when the crowds are not too thick (mid-morning or afternoon). It's usually easier to get on at one of the turnarounds at the ends of the lines. (*See* Getting Around by Cable Car, above.)

If you're ready to spend a day outside of the city, consider a trip to Vallejo's **Marine World Africa USA.** (*See* Excursions, below.)

Shopping

San Francisco is a shopper's dream—major department stores, fine fashion boutiques, discount outlets, art galleries, and crafts stores are among the many offerings. Most accept at least Visa and MasterCard charge cards, and many also accept American Express and Diner's Club. A very few accept cash only. Ask about traveler's checks; policies vary. The *San Francisco Chronicle and Examiner* advertises sales; for smaller innovative shops, check the San Francisco *Bay Guardian.* Store hours are slightly different everywhere, but a generally trusted rule is to shop between 10 AM and 5 or 6 PM Monday through Saturday (until 8 or 9 PM on Thursday) and from noon until 5 PM on Sunday. Stores on and around Fisherman's Wharf often have longer summer hours.

If you want to cover most of the city, the best shopping route might be to start at Fisherman's Wharf, then continue on to Union Square and Crocker Galleria, the Embarcadero Center, Jackson Square, Chinatown, North Beach, Chestnut Street, Union Street, Fillmore and Sacramento streets, Japan Center, Haight Street, Civic Center, and South of Market (SoMa).

Major Shopping Districts
Fisherman's Wharf

San Francisco's Fisherman's Wharf is host to a number of shopping and sightseeing attractions: **Pier 39, the Anchorage, Ghirardelli Square,** and **The Cannery.** Each offers shops, restaurants, and a festive atmosphere as well as such outdoor entertainment as musicians, mimes, and magicians. Pier 39 includes an amusement area and a double-decked Venetian carousel. One attraction shared by all the centers is the view of the bay and the proximity of the cable-car lines, which can take shoppers directly to Union Square.

Union Square

San Francisco visitors usually head for shopping at Union Square first. It's centrally located in the downtown area and surrounded by major hotels, from the large luxury properties to smaller bed-and-breakfasts. The square itself is a city park (with a garage underneath). It is flanked by such large stores as **Macy's, Saks Fifth Avenue, I. Magnin,** and **Neiman Marcus. North Beach Leather** and **Gucci** are two smaller upscale stores. Across from the cable-car turntable at Powell and Market streets is the **San Francisco Shopping Centre,** with the fashionable **Nordstrom** store in the top five floors of shops. Nearby is **Crocker Galleria,** underneath a glass dome at Post and Kearny streets; 50 shops, restaurants, and services make up this financial district shopping center, which is topped by two rooftop parks.

Embarcadero Center

Five modern towers of shops, restaurants, and offices plus the Hyatt Regency Hotel make up the downtown Embarcadero Center at the end of Market Street. Like most malls, the center is a little sterile and falls short in the character department. What it lacks in charm, however, it makes up for in sheer quantity. The center's 175 stores and services include such nationally known stores as **The Limited, B. Dalton Bookseller,** and **Ann**

Taylor, as well as local and West Coast–based businesses such as the **Nature Company, Filian's European Clothing,** and **Lotus Designer Earrings.** Each tower occupies one block, and parking garages are available.

Jackson Square Jackson Square is where a dozen or so of San Francisco's finest retail antiques dealers are located. If your passion is 19th-century English furniture, for example, there's a good chance that something here will suit. Knowledgeable store owners and staffs can direct you to other places in the city for your special interests. The shops are along Jackson Street in the financial district, so a visit there will put you very close to the Embarcadero Center and Chinatown.

Chinatown The intersection of Grant Avenue and Bush Street marks "the Gateway" to Chinatown; here shoppers and tourists are introduced to 24 blocks of shops, restaurants, markets, and temples. There are daily "sales" on gems of all sorts—especially jade and pearls—alongside stalls of bok choy and gingerroot. Chinese silks and toy trinkets are for sale in most shops, as are selections of colorful pottery, baskets, and large figures of soapstone, ivory, and jade, including *netsuke* (carved figures).

North Beach The once largely Italian enclave of North Beach gets smaller each year as Chinatown spreads northward. It has been called the city's answer to New York City's Greenwich Village, although it's much smaller. Many of the businesses here tend to be small clothing stores, antiques shops, and such eccentric specialty shops as **Quantity Postcard** (1441 Grant Ave., tel. 415/986–8866), which has an inventory of 15,000 different postcards. If you get tired of poking around in the bookstores, you can relax at a number of cafés; there are also lots of Italian restaurants.

Union Street Out-of-towners sometimes confuse Union Street—a popular stretch of shops and restaurants five blocks south of the Golden Gate National Recreation Area—with downtown's Union Square. (*See* above.) Nestled at the foot of a hill between the neighborhoods of Pacific Heights and Cow Hollow, Union Street shines with contemporary fashion and custom jewelry. Union Street's feel is largely new and upscale, although there are a few antiques shops and some longstanding stores. Shopping here is not limited to wearing apparel, but includes a good bookstore, **Solar Light Books,** a place selling posters, **Union Street Graphics,** and several galleries that offer crafts, photographs, sculpture, and serigraphs.

Japantown Unlike Chinatown, North Beach, or the Mission, the 5-acre Japan Center (between Geary and Post Sts.) is contained under one roof. It is actually a mall of stores filled with antique kimonos, beautiful tansu chests, and both new and old porcelains. The center always feels a little empty, but the good shops here are well worth a visit. **Japan Center** occupies the three-block area between Laguna and Fillmore streets, and between Geary and Post streets.

Participant Sports

One great attraction of the Bay Area is the abundance of activities. Joggers, bicyclists, and aficionados of virtually all sports can find their favorite pastimes within driving distance, and often within walking distance, from downtown hotels. Golden

Gate Park has numerous paths for runners and cyclists. Lake Merced in San Francisco and Lake Merritt in Oakland are among the most popular areas for joggers.

For information on running races, tennis tournaments, bicycle races, and other participant sports, check the monthly issues of *City Sports* magazine, available free at sporting-goods stores, tennis centers, and other recreational sites.

Bicycling Two bike routes are maintained by the San Francisco Recreation and Park Department (tel. 415/666–7201). One route goes through Golden Gate Park to Lake Merced; the other goes from the south end of the city to the Golden Gate Bridge and beyond. Many shops along Stanyan Street rent bikes.

Boating and Sailing **Stow Lake** (tel. 415/752–0347) in Golden Gate Park has rowboat, pedalboat, and electric-boat rentals. The lake is open daily for boating, but the schedule varies according to the season; call for more information. San Francisco Bay offers year-round sailing, but tricky currents make the bay hazardous for inexperienced navigators. Boat rentals and charters are available throughout the Bay Area and are listed under "boat rentals" in the Yellow Pages. A selected charter is **A Day on the Bay** (tel. 415/922–0227). **Cass' Marina** (tel. 415/332–6789) in Sausalito has a variety of sailboats which can be rented or hired with a licensed skipper. Local sailing information can be obtained at **The Eagle Cafe** on Pier 39.

Fishing Numerous fishing boats leave from San Francisco, Sausalito, Berkeley, Emeryville, and Point San Pablo. They go for salmon outside the bay or striped bass and giant sturgeon within the bay. Temporary licenses are available on the charters. In San Francisco, lines can be cast from San Francisco Municipal Pier, Fisherman's Wharf, or Aquatic Park. Trout fishing is available at Lake Merced. Licenses can be bought at sporting-goods stores. The fishing licenses range from $5 for one day to $21.50 for a complete state license. For charters, reservations are suggested. Some selected sportfishing charters are listed below. Mailing addresses are given, but you're more likely to get a response if you call.

Capt. Fred Morini (Fisherman's Wharf; tel. 415/924–5575. Write to 138 Harvard Dr., Larkspur, CA 94939).
Muny Sport Fishing (3098 Polk St., 94109, across from Ghirardelli Sq.; tel. 415/871–4445). Leaves daily from Fisherman's Wharf.
Sea Breeze Sportfishing (Box 713, Mill Valley, CA 94942, tel. 415/381–3474). Departs daily from Fisherman's Wharf.
Wacky Jacky (Fisherman's Wharf; tel. 415/586–9800. Write Jacky Douglas at 473 Bella Vista Way, CA 94127).

Fitness Physical-fitness activities continue to be popular, but most clubs are private and visitors could have trouble finding a workout location. Several hotels have arrangements with neighborhood health clubs. A number of hotels have large health facilities of their own, including the Fairmont, Nikko, San Francisco Marriott, Mark Hopkins Inter-Continental, Ritz-Carlton, and Sheraton Palace Hotel. Of these, two are open to the public: the Fairmont charges a $15 drop-in fee and the Nikko $20.

Downtown, the **24-hour Nautilus** (1335 Sutter St., tel. 415/776–2200) is open to the public for a $10 drop-in fee. **Sante West Fit-**

ness (3727 Buchanan St., tel. 415/563–6222) offers aerobics, low- impact, stretching, and other exercise classes for a $9 drop-in fee. The **Embarcadero YMCA** (215 Fremont, tel. 415/ 392–2191), reopened in 1991 after a massive renovation, is now one of the finest facilities in San Francisco. For $12, visitors can exercise and use the sauna, whirlpool, and swimming pool, all while enjoying a view of the bay.

Golf San Francisco has four public golf courses, and visitors should call for tee times: **Harding Park**, an 18-hole, par-72 course (at Lake Merced Blvd. and Skyline Blvd., tel. 415/664–4690); **Lincoln Park**, 18 holes, par 69 (34th and Clement Sts., tel. 415/221–9911); **Golden Gate Park**, a "pitch and putt" 9-holer (47th and Fulton Sts., tel. 415/751–8987); and **Glen Eagles Golf Course**, a full-size 9-holer in McLaren Park (2100 Sunnydale Ave., tel. 415/587–2425). Another municipal course, the 18-hole, par 72 **Sharp Park**, is south of the city in Pacifica (tel. 415/355–8546).

Tennis The San Francisco Recreation and Park Department maintains 130 free tennis courts throughout the city. The largest set of free courts is at **Dolores Park**, 18th and Dolores streets, with six courts available on a first-come, first-served basis. There are 21 public courts in **Golden Gate Park**; reservations and fee information can be obtained by calling 415/753–7101.

Spectator Sports

For the sports fan, the Bay Area offers a vast selection of events—from yacht races to rodeo to baseball.

Baseball Plans to move the **San Francisco Giants** out of town or build them a new stadium in the Bay Area were still up in the air in late 1992; if the team sticks around they'll play at Candlestick Park (tel. 415/467–8000) until their new home is ready. The **Oakland A's** play at the Oakland Coliseum (tel. 415/638–0500). Game-day tickets are usually available at the stadiums. Premium seats, however, often do sell out in advance. City shuttle buses marked Ballpark Special run from numerous bus stops. Candlestick Park is often windy and cold, so take along extra layers of clothing. The Oakland Coliseum can be reached by taking BART trains to the Coliseum stop.

Basketball The **Golden State Warriors** play NBA basketball at the Oakland Coliseum Arena from October through April. Tickets are available through BASS (tel. 415/762–2277). Again, BART trains to the Coliseum stop are the easiest method of travel.

Football The **San Francisco 49ers** play at Candlestick Park, but the games are almost always sold out far in advance, so call first (tel. 415/468–2249).

Hockey The Bay Area welcomed the **San Jose Sharks** as its first National Hockey League team in 1991. Their games can be seen at the Cow Palace, at least until 1993 when they move to a new stadium in downtown San Jose. The team is a wild success, and though almost all their games sell out, try calling BASS (tel. 415/762–2277) for tickets.

Tennis The Civic Auditorium (999 Grove St.) is the site of the **Volvo Tennis/San Francisco tournament** in early February (tel. 415/ 239–4800). The **Virginia Slims women's tennis tour** visits the Oakland Coliseum Arena in October.

Yacht Racing There are frequent yacht races on the bay. The local papers will give you details, or you can be an uninformed but appreciative spectator from the Golden Gate Bridge or other vantage points around town.

Beaches

San Francisco's beaches are perfect for romantic sunset strolls, but don't make the mistake of expecting to find Waikiki-by-the-Metropolis. The water is cold, and the beach areas are often foggy; they are usually jammed on sunny days. They can be satisfactory for afternoon sunning, but treacherous currents make most areas dangerous for swimming. During stormy months, beachcombers can stroll along the sand and discover a variety of ocean treasures: glossy agates and jade pebbles, sea-sculptured roots and branches, and—rarely—glass floats.

Baker Beach Baker Beach is not recommended for swimming: Watch for larger-than-usual waves. In recent years, the north end of the beach has become popular with nude sunbathers. This is not legal, but such laws are seldom enforced. The beach is in the southwest corner of the Presidio and begins at the end of Gibson Road, which turns off Bowley Street. Weather is typical for the bay shoreline: summer fog, usually breezy, and occasionally warm. Picnic tables, grills, day-camp areas, and trails are available. The mile-long shoreline is ideal for jogging, fishing, and building sand castles.

China Beach From April to October, China Beach, south of Baker Beach, offers a lifeguard, gentler water, changing rooms, and showers. It is listed on some maps as Phelan Beach.

Ocean Beach South of Cliff House, Ocean Beach stretches along the western (ocean) side of San Francisco. It has a wide beach with scenic views and is perfect for walking, running, or lying in the sun—but not for swimming.

Dining

San Francisco probably has more restaurants per capita than any city in the United States, including New York. Practically every ethnic cuisine is represented. That makes selecting some 70 restaurants to list here from the vast number available a very difficult task indeed. We have chosen several restaurants to represent each popular style of dining in various price ranges, in most cases because of the superiority of the food, but in some instances because of the view or ambience.

Because we have covered those areas of town most frequented by visitors, this meant leaving out some great places in outlying districts such as Sunset and Richmond. The outlying restaurants we *have* recommended were chosen because they offer a type of experience not available elsewhere.

All the restaurants listed serve dinner and are open for lunch unless otherwise specified; restaurants are not open for breakfast unless the morning meal is specifically mentioned.

Parking accommodations are mentioned only when a restaurant has made special arrangements; otherwise you're on your own. There is usually a charge for valet parking. Validated parking is not necessarily free and unlimited; often there is a nominal charge and a restriction on the length of time.

Restaurants do change their policies about hours, credit cards, and the like. It is always best to make inquiries in advance.

The most highly recommended restaurants in each category are indicated by a star ★.

The price ranges listed below are for an average three-course meal. A significant trend among the more expensive restaurants is the addition of a bar menu, which provides light snacks—hot dogs, chili, pizza, and appetizers—often costing less than $10 for two.

Category	Cost*
Very Expensive	over $45
Expensive	$30–$45
Moderate	$18–$30
Inexpensive	under $18

*per person, excluding drinks, service, and 8.5% sales tax

American Before the 1980s, it was hard to find a decent "American" restaurant in the Bay Area. In recent years, however, the list has been growing and becoming more diversified, with fare that includes barbecue, Southwestern, all-American diner food, and that mix of Mediterranean-Asian-Latino dishes known as California cuisine.

Civic Center **Stars.** This is the culinary temple of Jeremiah Tower, the su-
★ perchef who claims to have invented California cuisine. Stars is a must stop on every traveling gourmet's itinerary, but it's also where many of the local movers and shakers hang out. It has become a popular place for post-theater dining and is open till the wee hours. The dining room has the ambience of a private club, and the food ranges from grills to ragouts to sautées—some daringly creative and some classical. Dinners here are pricey, but you can eat on a budget with a hot dog at the bar or by standing in line for a table at the informal Star's Cafe next door. *150 Redwood Alley, tel. 415/861–7827. Reservations accepted up to 2 wks. in advance, some tables reserved for walk-ins. Dress: casual. AE, DC, MC, V. No lunch weekends. Closed Thanksgiving and Christmas. Valet parking at night. Expensive.*

Embarcadero **Fog City Diner.** This is where the diner and grazing crazes began in San Francisco, and the popularity of this spot knows no end. The long, narrow dining room emulates a luxurious railroad car with dark wood paneling, huge windows, and comfortable booths. The cooking is innovative, drawing its inspiration from regional cooking throughout the United States. The sharable "small plates" are a fun way to go. *1300 Battery St., tel. 415/982–2000. Reservations advised several wks. in advance for peak hours. Dress: casual. DC, MC, V. Closed Thanksgiving and Christmas. Moderate.*

MacArthur Park. Year after year San Franciscans acclaim this as their favorite spot for ribs, but the oakwood smoker and mesquite grill also turn out a wide variety of all-American fare, from steaks, hamburgers, and chili, to seafood. Takeout is also available at this handsomely renovated pre-earthquake warehouse. *607 Front St., tel. 415/398–5700. Reservations advised. Dress: casual. AE, DC, MC, V. No lunch weekends and major* *holidays. Closed Thanksgiving and Christmas. Valet parking at night. Moderate.*

Financial District **Cypress Club.** Fans of John Cunin have flocked here since 1990 when Masa's longtime maître d' opened his own place, which he calls a "San Francisco brasserie." This categorizes the contemporary American cooking somewhat, but the decor defies description. It could be interpreted as anything from a parody of an ancient temple to a futuristic space war. *500 Jackson St., tel. 415/296–8555. Reservations advised. Dress: casual. AE, DC, MC, V. Closed for lunch Sat., and major holidays. Valet parking at night. Expensive.*

Nob Hill **Fournou's Ovens.** There are two lovely dining areas in the elegant Stanford Court Hotel. One is a multilevel room with tiers of tables facing the giant open hearth where many specialties are roasted. Under the direction of chef Lawrence Vito, the restaurant has become known for its imaginative contemporary American cuisine. Many people opt to have breakfast and lunch in the flower-filled greenhouses that flank the hotel and offer views of the cable cars clanking up and down the hill. Wherever you sit, you'll find excellent food and attentive service. *905 California St., tel. 415/989–1910. Reservations advised. Dress: casual. AE, DC, MC, V. Valet parking. Expensive.*

North Beach **Washington Square Bar & Grill.** You're apt to rub elbows with the city's top columnists and writers in this no-frills saloon. North Beach Italian pasta and seafood dishes mingle with basic bar fare, such as hamburgers and steaks. There is a pianist at night and it is open late. *1707 Powell St., tel. 415/982–8123. Reservations advised. Dress: casual. AE, DC, MC, V. Closed most major holidays. Validated parking at garage around corner on Filbert St. Moderate.*

South of Market **Asta.** Named after Nick and Nora's dog in "The Thin Man" series, this new spot is a time capsule of the '30s, with flicks of the famous sleuths on VCRs in the bar. The food, however, is in tune with the 1990s, with bright, creative versions of all-time American favorites and down-home desserts. Dancing Friday and Saturday nights. *Rincon Center, 101 Spear St., 415/495–2782. Reservations accepted. Dress: casual. AE, MC, V. Closed for lunch Sat., for dinner Mon., Sun. Validated parking at Rincon Center garage. Moderate.*

Union Square **Campton Place.** This elegant, ultrasophisticated small hotel ★ put new American cooking on the local culinary map. Although opening chef Bradley Ogden is now at his own place, the Lark Creek Inn, in Marin County, his successor at Campton Place, Jan Birnbaum, carries on Ogden's innovative traditions with great aplomb and has added his own touches from breakfast and Sunday brunch (one of the best in town) through the dinner hours. A bar menu offers some samplings of appetizers, plus a caviar extravaganza. *340 Stockton St., tel. 415/781–5155. Reservations advised, 2 wks. in advance on weekends. Jacket required at dinner, tie advised. AE, DC, MC, V. Valet parking. Expensive.*

★ **Postrio.** This is the place for those who want to see and be seen: there's always a chance to catch a glimpse of some celebrity, including Postrio's owner, superchef Wolfgang Puck, who periodically commutes from Los Angeles to make an appearance in the restaurant's open kitchen. A stunning three-level bar and dining area is highlighted by palm trees and museum-quality

Downtown San Francisco Dining

Jefferson St.
Beach St.
North St.
Bay St.
Francisco St.
Chestnut St.
Lombard St.
Embarcadero
Greenwich St.
Filbert St.
Union St.
Green St.
Vallejo St.
Broadway Tunnel
Pacific Ave.
Jackson St.
Pine St.
Bush St.
Sutter St.
Post St.
Geary St.
O'Farrell St.
Ellis St.
Eddy St.
Turk St.
Ave.

Leavenworth St.
Taylor St.
Jones St.
Leavenworth St.
Mason St.
Powell St.
Stockton St.
Grant St.
Kearny St.
Montgomery St.
Sansome St.
Battery St.
Front St.
Davis St.
Davis St.
Drumm St.
Front St.
Embarcadero
Steuart St.
Main St.
Spear St.
Beale St.
Fremont St.
1st St.
2nd St.
New Montgomery St.
Hawthorn St.
3rd St.
Market St.
Mission St.
4th St.
5th St.
Howard St.
6th St.
7th St.
Folsom St.
8th St.
9th St.
Harrison St.
Mission St.
Howard St.
Bryant St.
Brannan St.
King St.
Townsend St.
Columbus Ave.

0   1/2 mile
0   500 meters

KEY

AE American Express Office

contemporary paintings. The food is Puckish Californian with Mediterranean and Asian overtones, emphasizing pastas, grilled seafood, and house-baked breads. A substantial breakfast and bar menu are served here, too. *545 Post St., tel. 415/ 776–7825. Reservations advised. Jacket and tie advised. AE, DC, MC, V. Valet parking. Expensive–Very Expensive.*

Chinese For nearly a century, Chinese restaurants in San Francisco were confined to Chinatown and the cooking was largely an Americanized version of peasant-style Cantonese. The past few decades, however, have seen an influx of restaurants representing the wide spectrum of Chinese cuisine: the subtly seasoned fare of Canton, the hot and spicy cooking of Hunan and Szechuan, the northern style of Peking, where meat and dumplings replace seafood and rice as staples, and, more recently, some more esoteric cooking, such as Hakka and Chao Chow. The current rage seems to be the high-style influence of Hong Kong. These restaurants are now scattered throughout the city, leaving Chinatown for the most part to the tourists.

Embarcadero **Harbor Village.** Classic Cantonese cooking, dim sum lunches, ★ and fresh seafood from the restaurant's own tanks are the hallmarks of this 400-seat branch of a Hong Kong establishment, which sent five of its master chefs to San Francisco to supervise the kitchen. The setting is opulent, with Chinese antiques and teak furnishings. *4 Embarcadero Center, tel. 415/781–8833. Reservations not accepted for weekend lunch. Dress: casual. AE, DC, MC, V. Free validated parking in Embarcadero Center garage. Moderate.*

Financial District **Yank Sing.** This teahouse has grown by leaps and branches with the popularity of dim sum. The Battery Street location seats 300 and the older, smaller Stevenson Street site has recently been rebuilt in high-tech style. *427 Battery St., tel. 415/ 362–1640. 49 Stevenson St., tel. 415/495–4510. Reservations advised. Dress: casual. AE, MC, V. No dinner. Stevenson location closed weekends. Inexpensive.*

North Beach **Hunan.** Henry Chung's first café on Kearny Street had only six tables, but his Hunanese cooking merited six stars from critics nationwide. He has now opened this larger place on Sansome Street; it's equally plain but has 250 seats. Smoked dishes are a specialty, and Henry guarantees no MSG. *924 Sansome St., tel. 415/956–7727. Reservations advised. Dress: casual. AE, DC, MC, V. Inexpensive.*

Northern Waterfront **The Mandarin.** Owner Cecilia Chiang introduced San Franciscans to the full spectrum of Chinese cooking in 1961 in a tiny Post Street locale, then moved to this magnificent setting, decorated with paintings and embroideries from her family's palatial homes in Peking. Though Madam Chiang has retired, the new owners have expanded upon her traditions with the addition of a dim sum lunch. The finest offerings, such as Mandarin duck, beggar's chicken cooked in clay, and the Mongolian fire pot, must be ordered a day in advance. Some tables have bay views. *Ghirardelli Sq., tel. 415/673–8812. Reservations advised. Dress: casual. AE, DC, MC, V. Closed Thanksgiving and Christmas. Validated parking in Ghirardelli Sq. garage. Moderate–Expensive.*

Richmond **Hong Kong Flower Lounge.** Many Chinaphiles swear that this ★ outpost of a famous Asian restaurant chain serves the best Cantonese food in town. The seafood is spectacular, as is the dim sum. *5322 Geary Blvd., tel. 415/668–8998. Reservations advised. Dress: casual. AE, MC, V. Moderate.*

South of Market **Wu Kong.** Tucked away in the splashy Art Deco Rincon Center, Wu Kong features the cuisine of Shanghai and Canton. Specialties include dim sum; braised yellow fish; and the incredible vegetable goose, created from paper-thin layers of dried bean-curd sheets and mushrooms. *101 Spear St., tel. 415/957–9300. Reservations advised. Dress: casual. AE, DC, MC, V. Validated parking at Rincon Center garage. Moderate.*

French French cooking has gone in and out of vogue in San Francisco since the extravagant days of the Bonanza Kings. A renaissance of the classic haute cuisine occurred during the 1960s, but recently a number of these restaurants closed. Meanwhile, nouvelle cuisine went in and out of fashion, and the big draw now is the bistro or brasserie.

Civic Center **California Culinary Academy.** This historic theater houses one of the most highly regarded professional cooking schools in the United States. Watch the student chefs at work on the double-tiered stage while you dine on classic French cooking. Prix fixe meals and bountiful buffets are served in the main dining room; heart-healthy à la carte lunches are served at Cyril's on the balcony level, and there's a grill on the first floor. *625 Polk St., tel. 415/771–3500. Reservations advised (2–4 wks. in advance for Fri.-night buffet). Jacket and tie advised. AE, DC, MC, V. Closed weekends and major holidays. Moderate–Expensive.*

Financial District **Le Central.** This is the quintessential bistro: noisy and crowded, with nothing subtle about the cooking. But the garlicky pâtés, leeks vinaigrette, cassoulet, and grilled blood sausage with crisp french fries keep the crowds coming. *453 Bush St., tel. 415/ 391–2233. Reservations advised. Dress: casual. AE, MC, V. Closed Sun. and major holidays. Moderate.*

North Beach
★ **Ernie's.** This famous old-timer recently had a face-lift, and Alain Rondelli, one of France's most promising young chefs, is now in charge of the kitchen, preparing innovative light versions of French classics. Even so, Ernie's is still steeped with the aura of Gay Nineties San Francisco and is about the only place in town that offers tableside service. You will pay dearly for dinner, but the prix fixe, three-course lunch is a bargain. *847 Montgomery St., tel. 415/397–5969. Reservations advised. Jacket and tie required. AE, DC, MC, V. No lunch Sat.–Mon. Closed major holidays. Valet parking. Very Expensive.*

Union Square
★ **Masa's.** Chef Julian Serrano carries on the tradition of the late Masa Kobayashi. In fact, some Masa regulars even say the cooking is better. The artistry of the presentation is as important as the food itself in this pretty, flower-filled dining spot in the Vintage Court Hotel. *648 Bush St., tel. 415/989–7154. Reservations should be made precisely 21 days in advance. Jacket required. AE, DC, MC, V. No lunch. Closed Sun., Mon., 1st wk. in July, last wk. in Dec., 1st wk. in Jan. Valet parking. Very Expensive.*

★ **Fleur de Lys.** The creative cooking of chef/partner Hubert Keller is drawing rave reviews to this romantic spot that some now consider the best French restaurant in town. The menu changes constantly, but such dishes as lobster soup with lemon grass are signature offerings. The intimate dining room, like a sheik's tent, is encased with hundreds of yards of paisley. *777 Sutter St., tel. 415/673–7779. Reservations advised 2 wks. in* *advance for weekends. Jacket required. AE, DC, MC, V. No lunch. Closed Sun., Thanksgiving, Christmas, and New Year's Day. Valet parking. Very Expensive.*

Greek and Middle Eastern The foods of Greece and the Middle East have much in common: a preponderance of lamb and eggplant dishes, a widespread use of phyllo pastry, and an abundance of pilaf.

North Beach **Maykadeh.** Here you'll find authentic Persian cooking in a setting so elegant that the modest check comes as a great surprise. Lamb dishes with rice are the specialties. *470 Green St., tel. 415/362–8286. Reservations advised. Dress: casual. MC, V. Valet parking at night. Inexpensive–Moderate.*

South of Market **S. Asimakopoulos Cafe.** Terrific Greek food at reasonable prices keeps the crowds waiting for seats at the counter or at bare-topped tables in this storefront café. The menu is large and varied, but lamb dishes are the stars. It is near Showplace Square. *288 Connecticut St., Potrero Hill, tel. 415/552–8789. No reservations. Dress: casual. AE, MC, V. Closed for lunch weekends, and major holidays. Inexpensive–Moderate.*

Indian The following restaurants serve the cuisine of northern India, which is more subtly seasoned and not as hot as its southern counterparts. They also specialize in succulent meats and crispy breads from the clay-lined tandoori oven.

Northern Waterfront and Embarcadero **Gaylord's.** A vast selection of mildly spiced northern Indian food is offered here, along with meats and breads from the tandoori ovens and a wide range of vegetarian dishes. The dining rooms are elegantly appointed with Indian paintings and gleaming silver service. The Ghirardelli Square location offers bay views. *Ghirardelli Sq., tel. 415/771–8822. Embarcadero One, tel. 415/397–7775. Reservations advised. Dress: casual. AE, DC, MC, V. No lunch Sun. at Embarcadero. Closed Thanksgiving and Christmas. Validated parking at Ghirardelli Sq. garage and Embarcadero Center garage. Moderate.*

Pacific Heights **North India.** Small and cozy, this restaurant has a more limited menu and hotter seasonings than Gaylord's. Both tandoori dishes and curries are served, plus a range of breads and appetizers. Everything is cooked to order. *3131 Webster St., tel. 415/931–1556. Reservations advised. Dress: casual. AE, DC, MC, V. Closed for lunch weekends. Parking behind restaurant. Moderate.*

Italian Italian food in San Francisco spans the "boot" from the mild cooking of northern Italy to the spicy cuisine of the south. Then there is the style indigenous to San Francisco, known as North Beach Italian—such dishes as *cioppino* (a fisherman's stew) and Joe's special (a mélange of eggs, spinach, and ground beef).

Embarcadero **Il Fornaio.** An offshoot of the Il Fornaio bakeries, this handsome tile-floored, wood-paneled complex combines a café, bakery, and upscale trattoria with outdoor seating. The cooking is Tuscan, featuring pizzas from a wood-burning oven, superb house-made pastas and gnocchi, and grilled poultry and seafood. Anticipate a wait for a table, but once seated, you won't be disappointed—only surprised by the moderate prices. *Levi's Plaza, 1265 Battery St., tel. 415/986–0100. Reservations advised. Dress: casual. AE, MC, V. Closed Thanksgiving and Christmas. Valet parking. Moderate.*

Financial District **Blue Fox.** This landmark restaurant was revitalized in 1988 by Gianni Fassio, son of a former owner, who redecorated the place in a low-key, formal style. The classic cooking is from northern Italy, with a seasonally changing menu. Pasta and gnocchi are made on the premises, as are the luscious desserts. *659 Merchant St., tel. 415/981–1177. Reservations required. Jacket and tie required. AE, DC, MC, V. No lunch. Closed Sun. and major holidays. Valet parking. Expensive–Very Expensive.*

Marina **Ristorante Parma.** This is a warm, wonderfully honest trattoria with excellent food at modest prices. The antipasto tray, with a dozen unusual items, is one of the best in town, and the pastas and veal are exceptional. Don't pass up the spinach gnocchi when it is offered. *3314 Steiner St., tel. 415/567–0500. Reservations advised. Dress: casual. AE, MC, V. No lunch. Closed Sun. and some major holidays. Moderate.*

Midtown **Acquarello.** This exquisite restaurant is a venture of the former
★ chef and former maître d' at Donatello. The service and food are exemplary, and the menu covers the full range of Italian cuisine, from northern Italy to the tip of the boot. Desserts are exceptional. *1722 Sacramento St., tel. 415/567–5432. Reservations advised. Dress: casual. DC, MC, V. No lunch. Closed Sun. and Mon. Validated parking across street. Moderate–Expensive.*

Tutto Bene. Despite its dazzling decor, this upscale trattoria was off to a slow start until culinary wizard Tony Gulisano took over the kitchen in 1991. Now the pastas and polentas, grilled meats, and seafoods on the ever-changing menu have critics and the cognoscenti raving. There is live music at night. *2080 Van Ness Ave., tel. 415/673–3500. Reservations advised. Dress: casual. AE, DC, MC, V. No lunch. Closed Sun. and Mon. Valet parking. Moderate.*

North Beach **Buca Giovanni.** Giovanni Leoni showcases the dishes of his
★ birthplace: the Serchio Valley in Tuscany. Pastas made on the premises are a specialty, and the calamari salad is one of the best around. The subterranean dining room is cozy and romantic. *800 Greenwich St., tel. 415/776–7766. Reservations advised. Dress: casual. AE, DC, MC, V. No lunch. Closed Sun. and most major holidays. Moderate.*

Capp's Corner. One of the last of the family-style trattorias, diners sit elbow to elbow at long Formica tables to feast on bountiful five-course dinners. For the budget-minded or calorie-counters, a smaller dinner includes a tureen of soup, salad, and pasta. *1600 Powell St., North Beach, tel. 415/989–2589. Reservations advised. Dress: casual. DC, MC, V. Closed for lunch weekends, and Thanksgiving and Christmas. Credit with meal check for parking in garage across street. Inexpensive.*

South of Market **Etrusca.** The ancient Etruscan civilization inspired this popu-
★ lar showplace in Rincon Center. Onyx chandeliers cast a warm glow on Siena-gold walls, terrazzo floors, and ceiling frescoes. The dishes from the giant wood-fire oven that dominates the open kitchen, however, recall modern Tuscany more than ancient Etruria. In addition, there is a bar menu. *Rincon Center, 101 Spear St., tel. 415/777–0330. Reservations advised. Dress: casual. AE, MC, V. Closed for lunch weekends. Validated parking in Rincon Center garage, valet service at night. Moderate.*

Union Square **Donatello.** Much of the menu in this elegant restaurant in the Donatello Hotel is drawn from the Emilia–Romagna region of Italy, which is famous for its food, especially the Bolognese pastas. The intimate dining rooms are exquisitely appointed with silk-paneled walls, paintings, and tapestries. Service is superb and low-key. Donatello also serves breakfasts that combine typical American fare with Italian-accented dishes. *Post and Mason Sts., tel. 415/441–7182. Reservations advised. Jacket required. AE, DC, MC, V. No lunch. Validated parking in hotel garage. Expensive–Very Expensive.*

Japanese To understand a Japanese menu, you should be familiar with the basic types of cooking: *yaki,* marinated and grilled foods; *tempura,* fish and vegetables deep-fried in a light batter; *udon* and *soba,* noodle dishes; *domburi,* meats and vegetables served over rice; *ramen,* noodles served in broth; and *nabemono,* meals cooked in one pot, often at the table. Of course sushi bars are extremely popular in San Francisco; most restaurants offer a selection of *sushi,* vinegared rice with fish or vegetables, and *sashimi,* raw fish. Western seating refers to conventional tables and chairs; *tatami* seating is on mats at low tables.

Chinatown **Yamato.** The city's oldest Japanese restaurant is by far its most beautiful, with inlaid wood, painted panels, a meditation garden, and a pool. Both Western and tatami seating, in private shoji rooms, are offered, along with a fine sushi bar. Come primarily for the atmosphere; the menu is somewhat limited, and more adventuresome dining can be found elsewhere. *717 California St., tel. 415/397–3456. Reservations advised. AE, DC, MC, V. Closed for lunch weekends, and Mon., Thanksgiving, Christmas, and New Year's Day. Moderate.*

Japantown **Sanppo.** This small place has an enormous selection of almost every type of Japanese food: yaki, nabemono dishes, domburi, udon, and soba, not to mention feather-light tempura and interesting side dishes. Western seating only. *1702 Post St., tel. 415/346–3486. No reservations. Dress: casual. No credit cards. Closed Mon. and major holidays. Validated parking in Japan Center garage. Inexpensive.*

Mediterranean In its climate and topography, its agriculture and viticulture, and the orientation of many of its early settlers, Northern California resembles the Mediterranean region. But until quite recently no restaurant billed itself as "Mediterranean." Those that do so now primarily offer a mix of southern French and northern Italian food, but some include accents from Spain, Greece, and more distant ports of call.

Civic Center **Zuni Cafe Grill.** Zuni's Italian–Mediterranean menu and its un-
★ pretentious atmosphere pack in the crowds from early morning to late evening. A balcony dining area overlooks the large bar, where both shellfish and drinks are dispensed. A second dining room houses the giant pizza oven and grill. Even the hamburgers have an Italian accent: They're served on herbed focaccia buns. *1658 Market St., tel. 415/552–2522. Reservations advised. Dress: casual. AE, MC, V. Closed Mon., Thanksgiving, and Christmas. Moderate–Expensive.*

Embarcadero **Splendido's.** Mediterranean cooking is the focus at this handsome new restaurant. Diners here are transported to the coast of southern France or northern Italy by the pleasant decor. Among the many winners are the shellfish soup, warm goat cheese and ratatouille salad, *pissaladière* (the pizza of Provence), and pan-roasted quail with white truffle pasta. Desserts are truly *splendido*. Bar menu. *Embarcadero Four, tel. 415/986–3222. Reservations advised. Dress: casual. AE, DC, MC, V. Closed for lunch weekends. Validated parking at Embarcadero Center garage. Moderate.*

Union Square **Lascaux.** Despite its Gallic name (after the caves in France), the cuisine at this smart new restaurant is primarily Mediterranean, with a contemporary Italian accent. Of particular note are the appetizers (such as sun-dried tomato and mascarpone torta, or the various takes on polenta), spit-roasted meats, and grilled seafood with zesty sauces. A huge fireplace cheers the romantically lighted subterranean dining room. There is live jazz at night. *248 Sutter St., tel. 415/391–1555. Reservations advised. Dress: casual. AE, DC, MC, V. Closed for lunch Sat., and Sun., Thanksgiving, and Christmas. Moderate.*

Mexican/Latin In spite of San Francisco's Mexican heritage, until recently
American most south-of-the-border eateries were locked into the Cal-Mex taco-enchilada-mashed-beans syndrome. But now some newer places offer a broader spectrum of Mexican and Latin American cooking.

South of Market **Chevys.** This first San Francisco branch of a popular Mexican minichain is decked out with funky neon signs and "El Machino" turning out flour tortillas. "Stop gringo food" is the motto here, and the emphasis is on the freshest ingredients and sauces. Of note are the fabulous fajitas and the grilled quail and seafood. *4th and Howard Sts., tel. 415/543–8060. Reservations accepted for parties of 8 or more. Dress: casual. MC, V. Closed Christmas. Validated parking evenings and weekends at garage under bldg. (enter from Minna St.). Inexpensive.*

Union Square **Corona Bar & Grill.** The ever-changing menu offers light ver-
★ sions of regional Mexican dishes. Corona's paella, laden with shellfish and calamari, is sensational, as is the chocolate-coated flan. The atmosphere is a mix of old San Francisco (pressed tin ceilings and an antique bar) and old Mexico (hand-painted masks and Aztec motifs). *88 Cyril Magnin St., tel. 415/392–5500. Reservations advised. Dress: casual. AE, DC, MC, V. Closed Thanksgiving and Christmas. Moderate.*

Old San Francisco Several of the city's landmark restaurants just don't fit neatly into any ethnic category. Some might call them Continental or French or even American. But dating back to the turn of the century or earlier, these places all exude the traditions and aura of old San Francisco. The oldest one of them all, Tadich Grill, is listed under Seafood.

Financial District **Garden Court, Palace Hotel.** After a massive, two-year, multi-million-dollar renovation, the Garden Court of the Sheraton Palace has reemerged as the ultimate old San Francisco experience. From breakfast through lunch, teatime, and the early dinner hours, light splashes through the $7 million stained-glass ceiling against the towering Ionic columns and crystal chandeliers. The classic European menu highlights many famous dishes devised by Palace chefs during the early years of this century, and the extravagant Sunday buffet brunch again takes center stage as one of the city's great traditions. *Market and New Montgomery Sts., tel. 415/546–5000. Reservations advised. Jacket and tie required at dinner. AE, DC, MC, V. Expensive.*

Jack's. Little has changed in more than 100 years at this bankers' and brokers' favorite. The menu is extensive, but regulars opt for the simple fare—steaks, chops, seafood, and stews. The dining room has an old-fashioned, no-nonsense aura, and private upstairs rooms are available for top-secret meetings. *615 Sacramento St., tel. 415/986–9854. Reservations advised. Jacket required. AE. Closed for lunch weekends, and major holidays. Moderate.*

Union Square **Bardelli's.** Founded in 1906 as Charles' Oyster House, this turn-of-the-century showplace boasts high-vaulted ceilings, massive marble columns, and stained glass. The menu mixes French, Italian, and American fare with superb fresh seafood. *243 O'Farrell St., tel. 415/982–0243. Reservations accepted. Dress: casual. AE, DC, MC, V. No Sat. lunch. Closed Sun. Validated parking at Downtown Center garage. Moderate.*

Seafood Like all port cities, San Francisco takes pride in its seafood, even though less than half the fish served here is from local waters. In winter and spring look for the fresh Dungeness crab, best served cracked with mayonnaise. In summer, feast upon Pacific salmon, even though imported varieties are available year round. A recent development is the abundance of unusual oysters from West Coast beds and an outburst of oyster bars.

Civic Center **Hayes Street Grill.** Eight to 15 different kinds of seafood are
★ chalked on the blackboard each night at this extremely popular restaurant. The fish is served simply grilled, with a choice of sauces ranging from tartar to a spicy Szechuan peanut concoction. Appetizers are unusual, and desserts are lavish. *320 Hayes St., tel. 415/863–5545. Reservations required precisely 1 wk. in advance. Dress: casual. AE, MC, V. Closed for lunch Sat., and Sun. and major holidays. Moderate.*

Financial District **Aqua.** This quietly elegant and ultrafashionable spot is the
★ most important new San Francisco restaurant of the 1990s, and possibly the city's most important seafood restaurant ever. Chef-owner George Morrone has a supremely original talent for creating contemporary versions of French, Italian, and American classics: Expect mussel, crab or lobster soufflés; lobster gnocchi with lobster sauce; shrimp and corn madeleines strewn in a salad; and ultra rare ahi tuna paired with foie gras. Desserts are miniature museum pieces. *252 California St., tel. 415/956–9662. Reservations required. Dress: casual. AE, DC, MC, V. Closed for lunch Sat., and Sun. Valet parking at night. Expensive.*

Sam's Grill. Sam's and Tadich (below) are two of the city's oldest restaurants and so popular for lunch that you must arrive before 11:30 to get a table. No frills here. The aura is starkly old-fashioned; some booths are enclosed and curtained. Although the menu is extensive and varied, those in the know stick with the fresh local seafood and East Coast shellfish. *374 Bush St., tel. 415/421–0594. Reservations accepted for parties of 6 or more. Dress: casual. AE, DC, MC, V. Closed weekends and holidays. Moderate.*

Tadich Grill. Owners and locations have changed many times since this old-timer opened during the Gold Rush era, but the 19th-century atmosphere remains, as does the kitchen's special way with seafood. Seating is at the counter or in private booths; there are long lines for a table at lunchtime. *240 California St., tel. 415/391–2373. No reservations. Dress: casual. MC, V. Closed Sun. and holidays. Moderate.*

Northern Waterfront **McCormick & Kuleto's.** This new seafood emporium in Ghirardelli Square is a visitor's dream come true: a fabulous view of the bay from every seat in the house; an old San Francisco atmosphere; and some 30 varieties of fish and shellfish prepared in some 70 globe-circling ways, from tacos, pot stickers, and fish cakes to grills, pastas, and stew. The food does have its ups and downs, however, but even on foggy days you can count on the view. *Ghirardelli Sq., tel. 415/929–1730. Reservations advised. Dress: casual. AE, DC, MC, V. Closed major holidays. Validated parking in Ghirardelli Sq. garage. Moderate.*

Pacific Heights **Pacific Heights Bar & Grill.** This is unquestionably the best oyster bar in town, with at least a dozen varieties available each day and knowledgeable shuckers to explain the mollusks' origins. In the small dining rooms, grilled seafood and shellfish stews head the bill of fare. Paella is a house specialty. *2001 Fillmore St., tel. 415/567–3337. Reservations advised. Dress: casual. AE, DC, MC, V. No lunch. Closed Thanksgiving and Christmas. Moderate.*

Southeast Asian In recent years San Franciscans have seen tremendous growth in the numbers of restaurants specializing in the foods of Thailand, Vietnam, and, most recently, Cambodia. The cuisines of these countries share many features, and one characteristic in particular: The cooking is always spicy and often very hot.

Civic Center **Monsoon.** This brilliant new restaurant combines the cuisines ★ of China and Southeast Asia, most notably Thailand. The concept of a pan-Asian menu is common in many of China's coastal cities, and was adapted here by Monsoon founder Bruce Cost, one of the foremost authorities on Asian food in the United States. The subtle surroundings are highlighted by contemporary Asian ceramics. *Opera Plaza, 601 Van Ness Ave., tel. 415/441–3232. Reservations advised. Dress: casual. MC, V. Closed Mon. Moderate.*

Thepin. It seems as if there's a Thai restaurant on every block now, but this is the jewel in the crown. The stylish dining room sparkles with linen napery, fresh flowers, Thai artworks, and a wine list that surpasses the Asian norm. Notable are the duck dishes and the curries, each prepared with its own mixture of freshly blended spices. *298 Gough St., tel. 415/863–9335. Reservations advised. Dress: casual. MC, V. Closed for lunch weekends. Inexpensive–Moderate.*

Marina **Angkor Palace.** This is one of the loveliest Cambodian restaurants in town and also the most conveniently located for visitors. The extensive family-style menu offers such exotic fare as fish-and-coconut mousse baked in banana leaves. You'll have questions, of course, but you'll find the staff eager to explain the contents of the menu. *1769 Lombard St., tel. 415/931–2830. Reservations advised. Dress: casual. AE, MC, V. No lunch. Inexpensive.*

South of Market **Manora.** When Passarin Prassl opened this homey Thai café way out on Mission Street, she named it after her daughter, Manora. Soon crowds from all over town were lined up for a table to try the extensive selection of carefully prepared dishes. Now Manora has her own spot on Folsom Street, not far from the Performing Arts Center, with the same great food. *3226 Mission St., tel. 415/550–0856. 1600 Folsom St., tel. 415/861–6224. Dress: casual. MC, V. Closed for lunch weekends, and Labor Day and Thanksgiving. Inexpensive.*

Steak Houses Although San Francisco traditionally has not been a meat-and-potatoes town, the popularity of steak is on the rise. Following are some of the best steak houses, but you can also get a good piece of beef at some of the better French, Italian, and American restaurants.

Marina **Izzy's Steak & Chop House.** Izzy Gomez was a legendary San Francisco saloonkeeper, and his namesake eatery carries on the tradition with terrific steaks, chops, and seafood, plus all the trimmings—such as cheesy scalloped potatoes and creamed spinach. A collection of Izzy memorabilia and antique advertising art covers almost every inch of wall space. *3345 Steiner St., tel. 415/563-0487. Reservations accepted. Dress: casual. AE, DC, MC, V. No lunch. Closed Thanksgiving and Christmas. Validated parking at Lombard Garage. Moderate.*

Midtown **Harris'.** Ann Harris knows her beef. She grew up on a Texas
★ cattle ranch and was married to the late Jack Harris of Harris Ranch fame. In her own elegant restaurant she serves some of the best dry-aged steaks in town, but don't overlook the grilled seafood or poultry. The bar menu is extensive. *2100 Van Ness Ave., tel. 415/673-1888. Reservations advised. Dress: casual. AE, DC, MC, V. No lunch Thurs.–Tues. Closed Christmas and New Year's Day. Valet parking. Expensive.*

Vegetarian Aside from the restaurant mentioned below, vegetarians should also consider Gaylord's (*see* Indian restaurants, above), which offers a wide variety of meatless dishes from the Hindu cuisine.

Marina **Greens at Fort Mason.** This beautiful restaurant with its bay
★ views is a favorite of carnivores as well as vegetarians. Owned and operated by the Tassajara Zen Center of Carmel Valley, the restaurant offers a wide, eclectic, and creative spectrum of meatless cooking, and the bread promises nirvana. Dinners are à la carte on weeknights, but only a five-course prix fixe dinner is served Friday and Saturday. *Bldg. A, Fort Mason, tel. 415/771-6222. Reservations advised. Dress: casual. MC, V. Closed for dinner Sun., and Mon., Thanksgiving, Christmas, and New Year's Day. Public parking at Fort Mason Center. Moderate.*

Lodging

Few cities in the United States can rival San Francisco's variety in lodging. There are plush hotels ranked among the finest in the world, renovated older buildings that have the charm of Europe, bed-and-breakfast inns in the city's Victorian "Painted Ladies," and popular chain hotels and low-rise motels that are found in most cities in the United States.

Because San Francisco is one of the top destinations in the United States for tourists as well as business travelers and convention goers, reservations are always advised, especially during the May–October peak season.

San Francisco's geography makes it conveniently compact. No matter their location, the hotels listed below are on or close to public transportation lines. Some properties on Lombard Street and in the Civic Center area have free parking, but a car is more of a hindrance than an asset in San Francisco.

Although not as high as New York, San Francisco hotel prices may come as a surprise to travelers from less urban areas. Average rates for double rooms downtown and at the wharf are in the $110 range. Adding to the expense is the city's 11% transient occupancy tax, which can significantly boost the cost of a lengthy stay. The good news is that because of the hotel building boom of the late 1980s there is now an oversupply of rooms, which has led to much discounting of prices. Check for special rates and packages when making reservations.

An alternative to hotels, inns, and motels is staying in privately owned homes and apartments, available through three companies: **American Family Inn/Bed & Breakfast San Francisco** (Box 420009, San Francisco, CA 94142, tel. 415/931–3083), **Bed & Breakfast International–San Francisco** (1181–B Solano Ave., Albany, CA 94706, tel. 415/696–1690 or 800/872–4500), and **American Property Exchange** (170 Page St., San Francisco, CA 94102, tel. 415/863–8484 or 800/747–7784).

The **San Francisco Convention and Visitors Bureau** (tel. 800/ 677–1550) each year publishes a free lodging guide with a map and listing of all hotels. Send $1 for postage and handling to the SFCVB, Box 6977, San Francisco, CA 94101-6977. The bureau also makes hotel reservations for visitors.

If you are looking for truly budget accommodations (under $50), consider the Adelaide Inn (see Union Square/Downtown, below) and the **YMCA Central Branch**. *220 Golden Gate Ave., 94102, tel. 415/885–0460. 102 rooms, 3 with bath. Facilities: health club, pool, sauna. MC, V.*

The most highly recommended hotels are indicated by a star ★.

Lodgings are listed by geographical area and price range.

Category	Cost*
Very Expensive	over $175
Expensive	$110–$175
Moderate	$75–$110
Inexpensive	under $75

*All prices are for a standard double room, excluding 11% tax.

Civic Center/Van Ness The governmental heart of San Francisco has been undergoing a renaissance that has made it come alive with fine restaurants, trendy night spots, and renovated small hotels.

Expensive **Cathedral Hill Hotel.** Guest rooms were renovated in 1988 at this popular convention hotel. *1101 Van Ness Ave., 94109, tel. 415/776–8200; 800/227–4730; in CA, 800/622–0855. 400 rooms. Facilities: 2 restaurants, lounge, free parking, pool. AE, DC, MC, V.*

★ **Inn at the Opera.** A music or ballet lover's heart may quiver at the sight of this lovely small hotel, where musicians and singers stay when they appear at San Francisco's performing-arts centers a block away. There are comfortable pillows, terry-cloth robes, and microwave ovens in each room. *333 Fulton St., 94102, tel. 415/863–8400; 800/325–2708; in CA, 800/423–9610. 48 rooms. Facilities: restaurant, lounge. AE, DC, MC, V.*

Miyako. In the heart of Japantown is this elegant, recently ren-

Downtown San Francisco Lodging

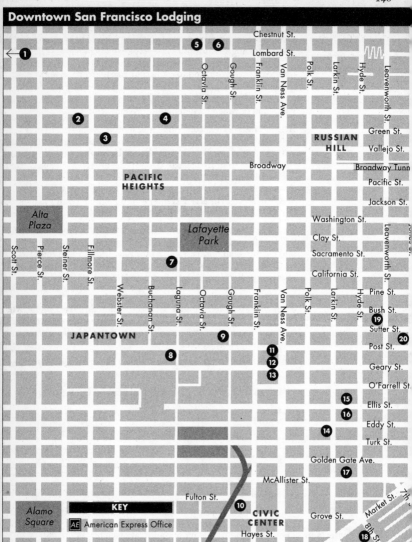

Abigail Hotel, **17**
Adelaide Inn, **52**
Amsterdam, **21**
Aston Pickwick Hotel, **56**
Atherton Hotel, **16**
Bed and Breakfast Inn, **4**
Beresford Arms, **20**

Best Western Americana, **54**
Campton Place Kempinski, **39**
Cathedral Hill Hotel, **11**
Cartwright, **35**
Chancellor Hotel, **36**
Columbus Motor Inn, **23**

Essex Hotel, **15**
Fairmont Hotel and Tower, **25**
Four Season Clift, **49**
Grand Hyatt, **40**
Grant Plaza, **28**
Handlery Union Square, **44**
Holiday Inn--Civic Center, **18**

Holiday Inn--Financial District, **29**
Holiday Inn--Union Square, **37**
Hotel Britton, **55**
Hotel Diva, **47**
Hotel Nikko--San Francisco, **50**
Huntington Hotel, **24**
Hyatt Regency, **32**

Inn at the Opera, **10**
Inn at Union
Square, **43**
Kensington Park, **41**
King George, **46**
Lombard Hotel, **12**
Majestic Hotel, **9**
Mandarin Oriental, **31**
The Mansion, **7**
Marina Inn, **5**

Marina Motel, **1**
Mark Hopkins Inter-
Continental, **26**
Miyako, **8**
New Richelieu, **13**
Park Hyatt, **30**
Petite Auberge, **34**
Phoenix Inn, **14**
Prescott Hotel, **53**
The Raphael, **45**

San Franciso Hilton on
Hilton Square, **51**
San Remo Hotel, **22**
Sheraton Palace, **33**
Sherman House, **3**
Sir Francis Drake, **38**
Stouffer Stanford
Court, **27**
Town House Motel, **6**
Union Street Inn, **2**
Warwick Regis
Hotel, **48**
Westin St. Francis, **42**
York Hotel, **19**

ovated hotel. The Japanese ambience is established by a greeting from a kimono-clad hostess. Traditional Japanese rooms with tatami mats are available. *1625 Post St. at Laguna St., 94115, tel. 415/922–3200 or 800/533–4567. 218 rooms. Facilities: restaurant, 2 lounges, Japanese baths, saunas. AE, DC, MC, V.*

Moderate
★ **Abigail Hotel.** A former B&B inn, this hotel retains its homey atmosphere with an eclectic mix of English antiques and mounted hunting trophies in the lobby. Hissing steam radiators and sleigh beds set the mood in the antiques-filled rooms. Room 211—the hotel's only suite—is the most elegant and spacious. *246 McAllister St., 94102, tel. 415/861–9728 or 800/243–6510. 62 rooms. AE, DC, MC, V.*

Best Western Americania. This hotel is distinguished by its pink-and-turquoise Moorish facade. Rooms overlook inner courtyards with fountain or swimming pool. *121 7th St., 94103, tel. 415/626–0200 or 800/444–5816. 142 rooms. Facilities: coffee shop, outdoor pool, sauna, free parking, nonsmoking rooms, evening shuttle to Union Sq. AE, DC, MC, V.*

Holiday Inn–Civic Center. A 1989 renovation has added a touch of elegance. The location is good—three blocks from the Civic Center and two blocks from Brooks Hall/Civic Auditorium. *50 8th St., 94103, tel. 415/626–6103 or 800/465–4329. 390 rooms. Facilities: restaurant, lounge, outdoor pool. AE, DC, MC, V.*

★ **Lombard Hotel.** This is a European-style hotel with a handsome marble-floor lobby flanked on one side by the Gray Derby restaurant. Many of the rooms were refurbished in 1989 with blondwood furniture and new self-serve bars. Quiet rooms are in the back. Complimentary evening cocktails and chauffeured limousine downtown are offered. *1015 Geary St., 94109, tel. 415/673–5232 or 800/227–3608. 100 rooms. Facilities: restaurant. AE, DC, MC, V.*

Majestic Hotel. One of San Francisco's original grand hotels, the Majestic was meticulously restored and reopened in 1985 with even more stately elegance. Romantic rooms have French and English antiques and four-poster canopy beds. Many have fireplaces and original claw-foot bathtubs. *1500 Sutter St., 94109, tel. 415/441–1100 or 800/869–8966. 60 rooms. Facilities: restaurant, lounge. AE, DC, MC, V.*

The Mansion. This twin-turreted Queen Anne Victorian was built in 1887 and today houses one of the most unusual hotels in the city. Rooms contain an oddball collection of furnishings and vary from the tiny Tom Thumb room to the opulent Josephine suite, the favorite of such celebrities as Barbra Streisand. Owner Bob Pritikin's pig paintings and other "porkabilia" are everywhere. *2220 Sacramento St., 94115, tel. 415/929–9444. 28 rooms. Facilities: dining room, weekend concerts, garden. AE, DC, MC, V.*

New Richelieu Hotel. The Richelieu's rooms acquired new beds, furniture, and carpeting in an extensive 1988 renovation. Rooms in the back building are larger and have new bathrooms. The lobby has been spruced up with an elegant gray-and-blue color scheme. *1050 Van Ness Ave., 94109, tel. 415/673–4711 or 800/227–3608. 150 rooms. Facilities: adjacent restaurant, nonsmoking rooms, gift shop and tour desk in lobby. AE, DC, MC, V.*

The Phoenix Inn. Resembling a '50s-style beachside resort more than a hotel in San Francisco's government center, the Phoenix bills itself aptly as an "urban retreat." Bungalow-style rooms, decorated with casual Filipino bamboo and original art by San Francisco artists, all face a pool courtyard and sculpture garden. *601 Eddy St., 94109, tel. 415/776–1380. 44 rooms. Facilities: lounge, free parking, heated pool. AE, DC, MC, V.*

Inexpensive   **The Atherton Hotel.** This clean, low-price hotel has a bilevel Mediterranean-style lobby. *685 Ellis St., 94109, tel. 415/474–5720 or 800/227–3608. 75 rooms. Facilities: restaurant, bar. AE, DC, MC, V.*

The Essex Hotel. New Italian marble floors in the lobby give this otherwise simple tourist hotel a touch of class. The friendliness of the Australian couple who own it is also a big plus. Popular with German and English tourists. *684 Ellis St., 94109, tel. 415/474–4664; 800/453–7739; in CA, 800/443–7739. 100 rooms, 52 with bath. AE, MC, V.*

★ **Hotel Britton.** This hotel is clean and comfortable, with reasonable rates, and is close to the Civic Center. Rooms are attractively furnished, and color TVs offer in-room movies. *112 7th St. at Mission St., 94103, tel. 415/621–7001 or 800/444–5819. 80 rooms. Facilities: coffee shop. AE, DC, MC, V.*

Financial District   High-rise growth in San Francisco's financial district has turned it into mini-Manhattan, a spectacular sight by night.

Very Expensive   **Hyatt Regency.** The stunning atrium-lobby architecture is the highlight here. Major renovations took place in late 1989 to upgrade the rooms and the lobby. *5 Embarcadero Center, 94111, tel. 415/788–1234 or 800/233–1234. 803 rooms. Facilities: 2 restaurants, coffee shop, lounge, 24-hour room service, shopping arcade. AE, DC, MC, V.*

Mandarin Oriental. The third-highest building in San Francisco's skyline is topped by a luxurious 11-story hotel on its 38th–48th floors. It's the best for spectacular views, especially from the bathrooms in the Mandarin rooms with floor-to-ceiling windows flanking the tubs. *222 Sansome St., 94104, tel. 415/885–0999 or 800/622–0404. 160 rooms. Facilities: restaurant, lounge. AE, DC, MC, V.*

Park Hyatt. This is the Hyatt chain's candidate for competing with the ultraluxury of some of the city's best hotels. Service is highly personal and attentive and rooms are plush, with such goodies as gourmet chocolates and imported soaps. Many rooms have balconies and bay views. The hotel caters to corporate executives and the like. *333 Battery St., tel. 415/392–1234 or 800/323–7275. 360 rooms. Facilities: restaurant, lounge, library. AE, DC, MC, V.*

Expensive   **Sheraton Palace.** One of the city's grand old hotels, the Sheraton reopened in 1991 after a $150 million reconstruction. New features include air-conditioning, a business center, health club, and pool. Happily, the Garden Court restaurant, famous for its leaded-glass ceiling, and the Pied Piper lounge, featuring Maxfield Parrish's painting of that name, were restored. *2 New Montgomery St., 94105, tel. 415/392–8600 or 800/325–3535. 550 rooms. Facilities: 2 restaurants, 2 lounges, 24-hour room service, fitness center. AE, DC, MC, V.*

Fisherman's Wharf/ North Beach   Fisherman's Wharf, San Francisco's top tourist attraction, is also the most popular area for accommodations. All are within a couple of blocks of restaurants, shops, and cable-car lines. Because of city ordinances, none of the hotels exceeds four stories; thus, this is not the area for fantastic views of the city or bay. Reservations are always necessary, sometimes weeks in advance during the peak summer months (when hotel rates rise by as much as 30%). Some streetside rooms can be noisy.

Moderate **Columbus Motor Inn.** This is an attractive motel between the wharf and North Beach with suites that are ideal for families. *1075 Columbus Ave., 94133, tel. 415/885–1492. 45 rooms. Facilities: free parking. AE, DC, MC, V.*

Inexpensive **San Remo Hotel.** This cozy hotel is reminiscent of a European-
★ style pension. Renovated during recent years, its smallish rooms and narrow corridors are freshly painted and decorated with plants and antiques. It offers a good location on the border of Fisherman's Wharf and North Beach. *2237 Mason St., 94133, tel. 415/776–8688. 62 rooms with shared baths. Facilities: restaurant. Daily and weekly rates. AE, DC, MC, V.*

Lombard Lombard Street, a major traffic corridor leading to the Golden
Street/Cow Hollow Gate Bridge, is sandwiched between two of San Francisco's poshest neighborhoods, Cow Hollow and the Marina district.

Very Expensive **The Sherman House.** In the middle of an elegant residential dis-
★ trict is this magnificent landmark mansion, the most luxurious small hotel in San Francisco. Each room is individually decorated with Biedermeier, English Jacobean, or French Second-Empire antiques, with tapestrylike canopies covering four-poster beds. Marble-top, wood-burning fireplaces and black granite bathrooms with whirlpool baths complete the picture. There is an in-house restaurant for guests only. *2160 Green St., 94123, tel. 415/563–3600. 15 rooms. Facilities: dining room, sitting rooms. AE, DC, MC, V.*

Moderate **The Bed and Breakfast Inn.** The first of San Francisco's B&Bs, this is an ivy-covered renovated Victorian located in an alleyway off Union Street. Romantic, cheery rooms with flowery wallpaper include The Mayfair, a flat with a spiral staircase leading to a sleeping loft. Some rooms are more modest and share baths. *4 Charlton Ct., 94123, tel. 415/921–9784. 10 rooms with baths. Facilities: breakfast room. No credit cards.*
★ **Marina Inn.** Here cute B&B-style accommodations are offered at motel prices. Dainty-flowered wallpaper, poster beds, country pine furniture, and fresh flowers give the rooms an English country air. Continental breakfast is served in the cozy central sitting room. Turned-down beds and chocolates greet guests at the end of the day. No parking. *3110 Octavia St. at Lombard St., 94123, tel. 415/928–1000. 40 rooms. Facilities: lounge. AE, MC, V.*
Union Street Inn. A retired schoolteacher has transformed this 1902 Edwardian home into a cozy inn. Antiques and fresh flowers are found throughout. *2229 Union St., 94123, tel. 415/346–0424. 6 rooms with bath. Facilities: garden, breakfast room. AE, MC, V.*

Inexpensive **Marina Motel.** This quaint Spanish-style stucco complex is one of the oldest motels on Lombard Street, but it is well kept. Each room has its own garage. *2576 Lombard St., 94123, tel. 415/921–9406. 45 rooms, some with kitchen. Facilities: free parking. AE, MC, V.*
★ **Town House Motel.** A very attractive motel with recently redecorated rooms, this is one of the best values on Lombard Street. *1650 Lombard St., 94123, tel. 415/885–5163 or 800/255–1516. 24 rooms. Facilities: free parking. AE, DC, MC, V.*

Nob Hill Synonymous with San Francisco's high society, Nob Hill contains some of the city's best-known luxury hotels. All offer spectacular city and bay views and noted gourmet restaurants. Cable-car lines that cross Nob Hill make transportation a cinch.

Very Expensive **Fairmont Hotel and Tower.** The regal grande dame of Nob Hill, the Fairmont has one of the most spectacular lobbies and public rooms in the city. All guest rooms are spacious and finely decorated. Those in the modern tower have the best views, while those in the old building have the stately ambience of another era. *950 Mason St., 94108, tel. 415/772–5000 or 800/527–4727. 596 rooms. Facilities: 5 restaurants, 5 lounges, health club and spa, gift shops, 24-hour room service. AE, DC, MC, V.*

★ **Huntington Hotel.** Understated class is found in this little jewel atop Nob Hill. Sumptuous rooms and suites are individually decorated. *1075 California St., 94108, tel. 415/474–5400; 800/227–4683; in CA, 800/652–1539. 143 rooms. Facilities: restaurant, lounge with entertainment. AE, DC, MC, V.*

Mark Hopkins Inter-Continental. Another Nob Hill landmark, "The Mark" is lovingly maintained. Rooms were redone in late 1987 in dramatic neoclassical furnishings of gray, silver, and khaki and with bold leaf-print bedspreads. Bathrooms are lined with Italian marble. Even-numbered rooms have views of the Golden Gate Bridge. *999 California St., 94108, tel. 415/392–3434 or 800/327–0200. 392 rooms. Facilities: restaurant, 2 lounges, gift shops. AE, DC, MC, V.*

Stouffer Stanford Court Hotel. Since taking over three years ago, Stouffer has spent $10 million upgrading this acclaimed hotel. In 1992, it installed a dramatic mural—depicting scenes of early San Francisco—in the lobby under the lovely stained-glass dome. One of the city's finest restaurants, Fournou's Ovens, is located here. *905 California St., 94108, tel. 415/989–3500 or 800/227–4726. 402 rooms. Facilities: 2 restaurants, 2 lounges, gift shops. AE, DC, MC, V.*

Union Square/Downtown The largest variety and greatest concentration of hotels are centered in the city's lovely downtown hub, Union Square, where hotel guests find the best shopping, the theater district, and transportation to every spot in San Francisco.

Very Expensive **Campton Place Kempinski.** Steps away from Union Square is ★ one of San Francisco's most elegant and highly rated hotels. Campton Place came under the mangament of the Kempinski organization, a German hotel company, in 1991. However, the attentive, personal service that begins from the moment uniformed doormen greet guests outside the marble-floor lobby has not changed. *340 Stockton St., 94108, tel. 415/781–5555, 800/647–4007, 800/235–4300 in CA. 126 rooms. Facilities: restaurant, bar. AE, DC, MC, V.*

★ **Four Seasons Clift.** Probably San Francisco's most acclaimed hotel, this stately landmark is the first choice of many celebrities and discriminating travelers for its attentive personal service. Special attention is given to children, with fresh cookies and milk provided at bedtime. All rooms are sumptuously decorated—the suites in elegant black and gray, others in bright beige and pink—in a somewhat updated contemporary style. *495 Geary St., 94102, tel. 415/775–4700 or 800/332–3442. 329 rooms. Facilities: restaurant, lounge. AE, DC, MC, V.*

Grand Hyatt. This hotel overlooks Union Square and Ruth Asawa's fantasy fountain in the garden (*see* Union Square tour, below). The hotel, formerly the Hyatt on Union Square, underwent a $20 million renovation in 1990. *345 Stockton St., 94108, tel. 415/398–1234 or 800/233–1234. 693 rooms. Facilities: 2 restaurants, 2 lounges, shopping arcade. AE, DC, MC, V.*

Hotel Nikko–San Francisco. Trickling waterfalls and walls of white marble set a quiet, subtle mood at this fine Japanese Airlines–owned hotel. The rooms are pink and gray contemporary with an Oriental touch. *222 Mason St., 94102, tel. 415/394–1111 or 800/645–5687. 525 rooms. Facilities: 2 restaurants, lounge, indoor pool, health club and spa. AE, DC, MC, V.*

San Francisco Hilton on Hilton Square. A huge expansion and renovation in 1988 made this by far the largest hotel in San Francisco. Popular with convention and tour groups. *1 Hilton Sq. (O'Farrell and Mason Sts.), tel. 415/771–1400 or 800/445–8667. 1,907 rooms. Facilities: 4 restaurants, 2 lounges, pool, shopping arcade. AE, DC, MC, V.*

Westin St. Francis. This is one of the grand hotels of San Francisco and a Union Square landmark. Rooms in the original building have been redecorated but still retain some of the 1904 moldings and bathroom tiles. Rooms in the modern tower have brighter, lacquered furniture. In 1991, three 40-foot trompe l'oeil murals were installed in the renovated tower lobby, and the main lobby received new marble floors. *335 Powell St., 94102, tel. 415/397–7000 or 800/228–3000. 1,200 rooms. Facilities: 5 restaurants, 5 lounges, shopping arcade. AE, DC, MC, V.*

Expensive **Warwick Regis Hotel.** This is one of the finest examples of the new generation of small, renovated hotels. Rooms are large and elegant, decorated in Louis XVI style with French and Oriental antiques and canopy beds. *490 Geary St., 94102, tel. 415/928–7900 or 800/827–3447. 86 rooms. Facilities: restaurant, lounge. AE, DC, MC, V.*

Holiday Inn–Union Square. This hotel enjoys a good location on the cable-car line only a block from Union Square. The decor of the Sherlock Holmes Lounge is 221B Baker Street all the way. *480 Sutter St., 94108, tel. 415/398–8900 or 800/465–4329. 400 rooms. Facilities: restaurant, lounge. AE, DC, MC, V.*

Hotel Diva. This hotel attracts the avant-garde set with a high-tech look that sets it apart from any other hotel in San Francisco. *440 Geary St., 94102, tel. 415/885–0200 or 800/553–1900. 125 rooms. Facilities: restaurant, lounge. AE, DC, MC, V.*

Inn at Union Square. The individually decorated rooms with goosedown pillows and four-poster beds here are sumptuous. Continental breakfast and afternoon tea are served before a fireplace in the cozy sitting areas on each floor. *440 Post St., 04102, tel. 415/397–3510 or 800/288–4346. 30 rooms. AE, DC, MC, V.*

Kensington Park. A handsome, high-ceilinged lobby sets the mood of this fine hotel, where afternoon tea and sherry are served. The rooms are decorated with English Queen Anne–style furniture. *450 Post St., 94102, tel. 415/788–6400 or 800/553–1900. 90 rooms. AE, DC, MC, V.*

★ **Petite Auberge.** The French countryside was imported to downtown San Francisco to create this charming bed-and-breakfast inn. Calico-printed wallpaper, fluffy down comforters, and French reproduction antiques decorate each room. Most have wood-burning fireplaces. Next door is its sister hotel, the 27-room White Swan, similar in style but with an English country flavor. *845 Bush St., 94108, tel. 415/928–6000. 26 rooms. Facilities: breakfast rooms, parlors. AE, MC, V.*

The Prescott Hotel. One of the plushest of the city's renovated old hotels, the Prescott may be better known as the home of Wolfgang Puck's Postrio restaurant. The hotel's emphasis is on personalized service, such as complimentary limousine service to the financial district. *545 Post St., tel. 415/563–0303 or 800/283–7322. 167 rooms. Facilities: restaurant, lounge. AE, DC, MC, V.*

Sir Francis Drake. The rooms in this popular San Francisco hotel, famous for its Beefeater-costumed doormen, got a face-lift in 1986 during a multimillion-dollar renovation. They are decorated in an old-English style, with mahogany furniture. The Starlight Roof is a lovely place for a drink. *450 Powell St., 94102, tel. 415/392–7755; 800/227–5480; in CA, 800/652–1668. nationwide. 415 rooms. Facilities: restaurant, lounge, exercise room. AE, DC, MC, V.*

Moderate **The Cartwright.** This is a family-owned hotel with a friendly,
★ personal touch in an ideal location. Renovated in 1986 after a five-year program to instill elegance and charm into the surroundings, this hotel offers rooms with brass or wood-carved beds, small refrigerators, and newly tiled bathrooms. *524 Sutter St., 94102, tel. 415/421–2865 or 800/227–3844. 114 rooms. Facilities: coffee shop. AE, DC, MC, V.*

★ **Chancellor Hotel.** This venerable hotel has been attracting a loyal clientele since it opened in 1924. Renovated in 1986, rooms have a new, elegant appearance with polished cherry-wood furniture. It is one of the best buys on Union Square. *433 Powell St., 94102, tel. 415/362–2004 or 800/428–4748. 140 rooms. Facilities: restaurant, lounge. AE, DC, MC, V.*

Handlery Union Square Hotel. The former Handlery Motor Inn and Stewart Hotel were combined and refurbished at a cost of $5 million in early 1988. The suitelike Handlery Club rooms are larger and more expensive. *351 Geary St., 94102, tel. 415/781–7800 or 800/223–0888. 378 rooms. Facilities: restaurant, outdoor heated pool, nonsmoking rooms. AE, DC, MC, V.*

Holiday Inn–Financial District. This hotel boasts an excellent location in Chinatown and is five minutes from Union Square and North Beach. Rooms on the 12th floor and above have city and bay views. *750 Kearny St., 94108, tel. 415/433–6600 or 800/465–4329. 556 rooms. Facilities: restaurant, lounge, pool, free parking. AE, DC, MC, V.*

★ **King George.** This charming midsize hotel was renovated in 1988 and 1989 to give it a more elegant, sophisticated look. The hotel's quaint Bread and Honey Tearoom serves traditional afternoon high tea. *334 Mason St., 94102, tel. 415/781–5050 or 800/288–6005. 144 rooms. Facilities: tearoom, lounge. AE, DC, MC, V.*

The Raphael. A favorite among repeat visitors to San Francisco, the Raphael was one of the first moderately priced European-style hotels in the city. Rooms were redecorated in 1988. The location is excellent. *386 Geary St., 94102, tel. 415/986–2000 or 800/821–5343. 151 rooms. Facilities: restaurant, lounge, in-room HBO. AE, DC, MC, V.*

York Hotel. This very attractive, renovated old hotel is known for its Plush Room cabaret and as the site of a scene in Alfred Hitchcock's *Vertigo. 940 Sutter St., 94109, tel. 415/885–6800 or 800/227–3608. 96 rooms. Facilities: nightclub, fitness center, complimentary chauffeured limousine. AE, DC, MC, V.*

Inexpensive **Adelaide Inn.** The bedspreads may not match the drapes or carpets and the floors may creak, but the rooms are clean and cheap (less than $50 for a double room) at this friendly small hotel that is popular with Europeans. Continental breakfast is complimentary. *5 Isadora Duncan Ct., off Taylor St. between Geary and Post Sts., 94102, tel. 415/441–2474. 16 rooms with shared baths. Facilities: sitting room, refrigerator for guest use. AE, MC, V.*

Amsterdam. This European-style pension is in a Victorian building two blocks from Nob Hill. Rooms were renovated in 1988. *749 Taylor St., 94108, tel. 415/673–3277 or 800/637–3444. 30 rooms, 8 with shared bath. Facilities: breakfast room for complimentary breakfast, cable TV in rooms, reading room. AE, MC, V.*

Aston Pickwick Hotel. A renovation in 1991 dramatically upgraded the rooms in this tourist-class hotel across from the San Francisco Mint and a block from the cable-car turnaround. Rooms are clean and attractively furnished, and have in-room voice mail. *85 5th St. at Mission St., 94103, tel. 415/421–7500 or 800/922–7866. 189 rooms. Facilities: cocktail lounge, coffee shop, parking. AE, MC, V.*

Beresford Arms. Complimentary pastries and coffee are served in the hotel's grand old lobby. The suites with full kitchens are a good bargain for families. Standard rooms contain queen-size beds and small refrigerators. *701 Post St., 94109, tel. 415/673–2600 or 800/533–6533. 90 rooms. Facilities: some rooms have whirlpool baths. AE, DC, MC, V.*

★ **Grant Plaza.** This bargain-price hotel at the entrance of Chinatown has small but clean and attractively furnished rooms. There is no restaurant, but plenty of dining nearby. *465 Grant Ave., 94103, tel. 415/434–3883; 800/472–6899; in CA, 800/472–6805. 72 rooms. AE, MC, V.*

The Arts and Nightlife

The best guide to arts and entertainment events in San Francisco is the "Datebook" section, printed on pink paper, in the Sunday *Examiner and Chronicle.* The *Bay Guardian* and *S.F. Weekly,* free and available in racks around the city, list more neighborhood, avant-garde, and budget-priced events. For up-to-date information about cultural and musical events, call the Convention and Visitors Bureau's Cultural Events Calendar (tel. 415/391–2001).

The Arts Half-price tickets to many local and touring stage shows go on sale (cash only) at noon Tuesday–Saturday at the **STBS** booth on the Stockton Street side of Union Square, between Geary and Post streets. STBS is also a full-service ticket agency for theater and music events around the Bay Area (open until 7:30 PM). While the city's major commercial theaters are concentrated downtown, the opera, symphony, and ballet perform at the Civic Center. For recorded information about STBS tickets, call 415/433–7827.

The city's charge-by-phone ticket service is **BASS** (tel. 415/762–2277), with one of its centers in the STBS booth mentioned above and another at **Tower Records** (Bay St. at Columbus Ave.) near Fisherman's Wharf. Other agencies downtown are the **City Box Office,** 141 Kearny Street in the Sherman-Clay store (tel. 415/392–4400), and **Downtown Center Box Office** in the parking garage at 320 Mason Street (tel. 415/775–2021). The opera, symphony, the ballet's *Nutcracker*, and touring hit musicals are often sold out in advance; tickets are usually available within a day of performance for other shows.

Theater San Francisco's "theater row" is a single block of Geary Street west of Union Square, but a number of commercial theaters are located within walking distance, along with resident companies that enrich the city's theatrical scene. The three major commercial theaters are operated by the Shorenstein-Nederlander organization, which books touring plays and musicals, some of them before they open on Broadway. The most venerable is the **Curran** (445 Geary St., tel. 415/673–4400), which is used for plays and smaller musicals. The **Golden Gate** is a stylishly refurbished movie theater (Golden Gate Ave. at Taylor St., tel. 415/474–3800), primarily a musical house. The 2,500-seat **Orpheum** (1192 Market St. near the Civic Center, tel. 415/474–3800) is used for the biggest touring shows.

The smaller commercial theaters, offering touring shows and a few that are locally produced, are the **Marines Memorial Theatre** (Sutter and Mason Sts., tel. 415/441–7444) and **Theatre on the Square** (450 Post St., tel. 415/433–9500). For commercial and popular success, nothing beats *Beach Blanket Babylon*, the zany revue that has been running for years at **Club Fugazi** (678 Green St. in North Beach, tel. 415/421–4222). Conceived by imaginative San Francisco director Steve Silver, it is a lively, colorful musical mix of cabaret, show-biz parodies, and tributes to local landmarks. (*See* Cabarets in Nightlife, below.)

The city's major theater company is the **American Conservatory Theatre (ACT)**, which quickly became one of the nation's leading regional theaters when it was founded during the mid-1960s. It presents a season of approximately eight plays in rotating repertory from October through late spring. The ACT's ticket office is at the **Geary Theatre** (415 Geary St., tel. 415/749–2228), though the theater itself was closed following the 1989 earthquake. During reconstruction ACT is performing at the nearby **Stage Door Theater** (420 Mason St.) and the **Theatre on the Square** (450 Post St.).

At the next level are several established theaters in smaller houses and with lower ticket prices which specialize in contemporary plays. The most reliable are the **Eureka Theatre** (2730 16th St. in the Mission district, tel. 415/558–9898) and the **Magic Theatre** (Bldg. D, Fort Mason Center, Laguna St. at Marina Blvd., tel. 415/441–8822).

The city boasts a wide variety of specialized and ethnic theaters that work with dedicated local actors and some professionals. Among the most interesting are **The Lamplighters**, the delightful Gilbert and Sullivan troupe that often gets better reviews than touring productions of musicals, performing at **Presentation Theater** (2350 Turk St., tel. 415/752–7755); the **Lorraine Hansberry Theatre**, which specializes in plays by black writers (620 Sutter St., tel. 415/474–8800); the **Asian American Theatre** (405 Arguello Blvd., tel. 415/346–8922); and the gay and lesbian **Theatre Rhinoceros** (2926 16th St., tel. 415/861–5079). The **San Francisco Shakespeare Festival** offers free performances on summer weekends in Golden Gate Park (tel. 415/221–0642).

Music The completion of Davies Symphony Hall at Van Ness Avenue and Grove Street finally gave the San Francisco Symphony a home of its own. It solidified the base of the city's three major performing-arts organizations—symphony, opera, and ballet—in the Civic Center. The symphony and other musical groups also perform in the smaller, 928-seat Herbst Theatre in the opera's "twin" at Van Ness Avenue and McAllister Street, the War Memorial Building. Otherwise the city's musical ensembles can be found all over the map: in churches and museums, in restaurants and outdoors in parks, and in outreach series in Berkeley and on the peninsula.

San Francisco Symphony (Davies Symphony Hall, Van Ness Ave. at Grove St., tel. 415/431–5400; tickets at the box office or through BASS, tel. 415/762–2277). The city's most stable performing-arts organization plays from September to May, with music director Herbert Blomstedt conducting for about two thirds of the season. Guest conductors often include Michael Tilson Thomas, Edo de Waart, and Riccardo Mutti. Guest soloists include artists of the caliber of Andre Watts, Leontyne Price, and Jean-Pierre Rampal. The symphony has stayed with the standard repertoire in recent years as Blomstedt concentrates on the ensemble's stability and focus. Special events include a Mostly Mozart festival during the spring, a Beethoven festival during the summer, a New and Unusual Music series during the spring in the more intimate Herbst Theatre, and summer Pops Concerts in the nearby Civic Auditorium. Throughout the season, the symphony presents a Great Performers Series of guest soloists and orchestras.

Opera **San Francisco Opera** (Van Ness Ave. at Grove St., tel. 415/864–3330). Founded in 1923, and the resident company at the War Memorial Opera House in the Civic Center since it was built in 1932, the opera has expanded to a fall season of 13 weeks. Approximately 70 performances of 10 operas are given, beginning on the first Friday after Labor Day. For many years the Opera was considered a major international company and the most artistically successful operatic organization in the United States. International opera stars frequently sing major roles here, but the Opera is also well known for presenting the American debuts of singers who have made their name in Europe. In the same way, the company's standard repertoire is interspersed with revivals of rarely heard works. Ticket prices range from about $28 to a high of about $90, and many performances are sold out far in advance. Standing-room tickets are always sold, however, and patrons often sell extra tickets on the Opera House steps just before curtain time.

Dance **San Francisco Ballet** (War Memorial Opera House, Van Ness Ave. at Grove St., tel. 415/621–3838). The ballet has regained much of its luster under artistic director Helgi Tomasson, and both classical and contemporary works have won admiring reviews. The company's primary season runs February–May; its repertoire includes such full-length ballets as *Swan Lake* and a new production of *Sleeping Beauty*. The company is also intent on reaching new audiences with bold new dances, what it likes to call "cutting-edge works that will make you take a second look." Like many dance companies in the nation, the ballet presents *The Nutcracker* in December, and its recent production is one of the most spectacular.

Film The San Francisco Bay Area, including Berkeley and San Jose, is considered to be one of the nation's most important movie markets. If there is a film floating around the country or around the world in search of an audience, it is likely that it will eventually turn up on a screen in San Francisco. The Bay Area is also a filmmaking center: Documentaries and experimental works are being produced on modest budgets, feature films and television programs are shot on location, and some of Hollywood's biggest directors prefer to live here, particularly in Marin County. In San Francisco, about a third of the theaters regularly show foreign and independent films. The city is also one of the last strongholds of "repertory cinema," showing older American and foreign films on bills that change daily.

San Francisco's traditional movie-theater center, downtown on Market Street, is pretty much given over to sex and action movies nowadays. First-run commercial movie theaters are now scattered throughout the city, although they are concentrated along Van Ness Avenue, near Japantown, and in the Marina district. All are accessible on major Muni bus routes, as are the art-revival houses. Several of the most respected and popular independent theaters have been taken over by chains recently, and their policies could change. The San Francisco International Film Festival (tel. 415/931–3456), the oldest in the country, continues to provide an extensive selection of foreign films each spring. The Pacific Film Archive in Berkeley is an incomparable source for rare American and foreign films.

Nightlife   Although San Francisco is a compact city with the prevailing influences of some neighborhoods spilling into others, the following generalizations should help you find the kind of entertainment you're looking for. **Nob Hill** is noted for its plush piano bars and panoramic skyline lounges. **North Beach**, infamous for its topless and bottomless bistros, also maintains a sense of its beatnik past and this legacy lives on in atmospheric bars and coffeehouses. **Fisherman's Wharf**, while touristy, is great for people-watching and provides plenty of impromptu entertainment from street performers. **Union Street** is home away from home for singles in search of company. **South of Market** (SoMa, for short) has become a hub of nightlife, with a bevy of highly popular nightclubs, bars, and lounges in renovated warehouses and auto shops. Gay men will find the **Castro** and **Polk Street** scenes of infinite variety, while lesbian bars abound on and around **Valencia Street**.

Rock, Pop, Folk,   **Freight and Salvage Coffee House.** This is one of the finest folk
and Blues   houses in the country; it's worth a trip across the bay. Some of the most talented practitioners of folk, blues, Cajun, and bluegrass perform at the Freight, among them U. Utah Phillips and Rosalie Sorrels. *1111 Addison St., Berkeley, tel. 510/548–1761. Shows weeknights 8, Fri. and Sat. 8:30. Cover: $6–$10. No credit cards.*

Great American Music Hall. This is one of the great eclectic nightclubs not only in San Francisco but in the entire country. Here you will find truly top-drawer entertainment, running the gamut from the best in blues, folk, and jazz to rock with a sprinkling of outstanding comedians. This colorful marble-pillared emporium also accommodates dancing to popular bands. Past headliners here include Carmen McCrae, B. B. King, Tom Paxton, and Doc Watson. *859 O'Farrell St. between Polk and Larkin Sts., tel. 415/885–0750. Shows usually at 8 PM, but this may vary, so call. Cover: $5–$20. No credit cards.*

I-Beam. One of the most popular of San Francisco's rock dance clubs, the I-Beam features new-wave bands and high-energy rock 'n' roll in a spacious setting. Spectacular lights and lasers enhance your dancing pleasure here. *1748 Haight St., tel. 415/ 668–6006. Open nightly 9. Cover: $5–$10; occasionally free. No credit cards.*

Last Day Saloon. In an attractive setting of wooden tables and potted plants, this club offers some major entertainers and a varied schedule of blues, Cajun, rock, and jazz. Some of the illustrious performers who have appeared here are Taj Mahal, the Zazu Pitts Memorial Orchestra, Maria Muldaur, and Pride and Joy. *406 Clement St. between 5th and 6th Aves. in the Richmond district, tel. 415/387–6343. Shows nightly 9. Cover: $4– $20. No credit cards.*

Slim's. One of the most popular nightclubs on the SoMa scene, Slim's specializes in what it labels "American roots music"— blues, jazz, classic rock, and the like. Co-owner Boz Scaggs helps bring in the crowds and famous headliners. *333 11th St., tel. 415/621–3330. Shows nightly 9. Cover $10–$20. AE, MC, V.*

The Saloon. Some locals consider the historic Saloon the best spot in San Francisco for the blues. Headliners here include local blues favorite Roy Rogers. *1232 Grant St. near Columbus Ave. in North Beach, tel. 415/989–7666. Shows nightly 9:30. Cover: $5–$8 Fri. and Sat. No credit cards.*

The Warfield. This old Art Deco theater was completely renovated in 1988 to become a showcase for mainstream rock 'n' roll. There are tables and chairs downstairs, and theater seating upstairs. Such contemporary acts as Robert Palmer, Simply Red, and k.d. Lang have played here recently. *982 Market St., tel. 415/775–7722. Shows most nights at 8. Tickets $15–$20. V.*

Jazz **Jazz at Pearl's.** This club is one of the few reminders of North Beach's days as a hot jazz night spot. Sophisticated and romantic, the club's picture windows look over City Lights Bookstore across the street. *256 Columbus Ave. near Broadway, tel. 415/ 291–8255. Live music Tues.–Sat. at 9:30 PM. Cover: $5 on weekends. MC, V.*

Kimball's East. This three-year-old club in a new shopping complex in Emeryville, just off Highway 80 near Oakland, hosts jazz greats such as Dizzy Gillespie and popular vocalists such as Lou Rawls and Patti Austin. With an elegant interior and fine food, this is one of most luxurious supper clubs in the Bay Area. *5800 Shellmound St., Emeryville, tel. 510/658–2555. Shows Fri. and Sat. at 9 and 11, Wed. and Thurs. at 8 and 10. Sun. brunch with live performances by local jazz groups, 11–2. Cover: $12–$24 with $5 minimum. $5 cover for Sun. brunch. Advance ticket purchase advised for big-name shows. MC, V.*

Cabarets **Club Fugazi.** *Beach Blanket Babylon Goes around the World* is a wacky musical revue that has become the longest-running show of its genre in the history of the theater. It has run now for well over a decade, outstripping the Ziegfeld Follies by years. While the choreography is colorful and the songs witty, the real stars of the show are the exotic costumes—worth the price of admission in themselves. Order tickets as far in advance as possible; the revue has been sold out up to a month in advance. *678 Green St., 94133, tel. 415/421–4222. Shows Wed.–Thurs. 8 PM, Fri.–Sat., 8 and 10:30 PM, Sun. 3 and 7:30 PM. Cover: $17–$40, depending upon date and seating location. Note: those under 21 are admitted only to the Sun. matinee performance. MC, V.*

Finocchio's. Are you ready for the truly outrageous? You will redefine "queen" once you see Finocchio's female impersonators—among the finest on the planet. Finocchio's has been generating general confusion for 50 years. *506 Broadway, North Beach, tel. 415/982-9388. Note: those under 21 not admitted. Shows nightly at 8:30, 10, and 11:30, closed Mon. and Wed. Cover: $15. MC, V.*

Comedy Clubs **Holy City Zoo.** Robin Williams ascended like a meteor from an improv group that gained fame here, and terrific stand-up comics, such as local favorite Michael Prichard, headline now. The Zoo features comedy nightly, with an open mike for pros and would-be comedians every Tuesday. *408 Clement St. in the Richmond district, tel. 415/386-4242. Shows Sun.-Thurs. 9 PM, Fri.-Sat. 9 and 11 PM. Cover: $3 Sun.-Thurs., $8 Fri. and Sat., 2-drink minimum. MC, V.*

The Punch Line. A launching pad for the likes of Jay Leno and Whoopie Goldberg, the Punch Line features some of the top talents around—several of whom are certain to make a national impact. Note that weekend shows often sell out, and it is best to buy tickets in advance at BASS outlets (tel. 415/762-BASS). *444-A Battery St. between Clay and Washington Sts., tel. 415/ 397-PLSF. Shows Sun.-Thurs. 9 PM, Fri. 9 and 11 PM, Sat. 7, 9, and 11:30 PM. Cover: $8 Tues.-Thurs., $10 Fri. and Sat.; special $5 showcases Mon. and Sun.; 2-drink minimum. MC, V.*

Dancing **Cesar's Palace.** Salsa-style Latin music attracts all kinds of
Emporiums dancers to this popular club in the city's Hispanic Mission district. Note: no alcohol is served here. *3140 Mission St., tel. 415/ 648-6611. Open Fri.-Sun. 9 PM-5 AM. Cover: $7.*

Club DV8. One of the largest of the trendy SoMa clubs, DV8 attracts scores of stylish young people to its 25,000 square feet (two levels) of dance floors. *540 Howard St., tel. 415/957-1730. Open Wed.-Sat. 9 PM-3 AM. Cover: $5-$10.*

Club O. This dance spot gets its name from the swimming pool adjacent. It was the original SoMa crossover bar. The cover charge varies. Note: You must be 21 to enter. *278 11th St., South of Market, tel. 415/621-8119. Opens 9:30.*

Oz. The most popular upscale disco in San Francisco, the land of Oz is reached via a glass elevator. Then, surrounded by a splendid panorama of the city, you dance on marble floors and recharge on cushy sofas and bamboo chairs. The fine sound system belts out oldies, disco, Motown, and new wave. *335 Powell St. between Geary and Post Sts. on the top floor of the Westin St. Francis Hotel, tel. 415/397-7000. Open nightly 9 PM-2 AM. Cover: $8 Sun.-Thurs., $15 Fri.-Sat.*

Piano Bars **Act IV Lounge.** A popular spot for a romantic rendezvous, the focal point of this elegant lounge is a crackling fireplace. *At the Inn of the Opera, 333 Fulton St. near Franklin St., tel. 415/ 863-8400. Pianist nightly 6-9. No cover.*

Washington Square Bar and Grill. A favorite of San Francisco politicians and newspapermen, the "Washbag," as it is affectionately known, hosts pianists performing jazz and popular standards. *On North Beach's Washington Sq., 1707 Powell St., tel. 415/982-8123. Music Mon.-Sat. from 9 PM. No cover.*

Skyline Bars **Carnelian Room.** At 781 feet above the ground, enjoy dinner or cocktails here on the 52nd floor, where you may drink from the loftiest view of San Francisco's magnificent skyline. Reservations are a must for dinner here. *Top of the Bank of America Bldg., 555 California St., tel. 415/433-7500. Open Mon.- Thurs. 3 PM-midnight, Fri. 3 PM-1 AM, Sat. 4 PM-1 AM, Sunday 10 AM-midnight.*

Crown Room. Just ascending to the well-named Crown Room is a drama in itself as you take the Fairmont's glass-enclosed Skylift elevator to the top. Some San Franciscans maintain that this lounge is the most luxurious of the city's skyline bars. Lunches, dinners, and Sunday brunches are served as well as drinks. *29th floor of the Fairmont Hotel, California and Mason Sts., tel. 415/772–5131. Open daily 11 AM–1 AM.*

Equinox. What's distinctive about the Hyatt Regency's sky-line-view bar is its capacity to revolve atop its 22nd-floor perch, offering 360-degree views to guests from their seats. *At the Hyatt Regency, 5 Embarcadero Center, tel. 415/788–1234. Open Mon.–Sat. 11 AM–2:30 PM and 6 PM–1:30 AM, Sun. 11 AM–3:30 PM.*

Top of the Mark. This fabled landmark affords fabulous views in an elegant 19th-floor setting. *In the Mark Hopkins Hotel, California and Mason Sts., tel. 415/392–3434. Open nightly 4 PM–1:30 AM.*

San Francisco's Favorite Bars

Buena Vista. Even though the Buena Vista's claim of having introduced Irish Coffee to the New World may be dubious, this is the wharf area's most popular bar. Usually packed with tourists, it has a fine view of the waterfront. *2765 Hyde St. near Fisherman's Wharf, tel. 415/474–5044.*

Edinburgh Castle. This is a delightful Scottish drinking emporium, with a jukebox that breathes Scottish airs and live bag-pipes on weekends. The decor is Scottish, the bartender is Scottish, and there are plenty of Scottish brews from which to choose. You can work off the fish-and-chips variety fare with a turn at the dart board. *950 Geary St. near Polk St., tel. 415/885–4074.*

House of Shields. For a taste of an authentic old-time San Francisco saloon, try this bar, which attracts an older, financial district crowd after work. It closes at 8 PM. *39 New Montgomery St., tel. 415/392–7732.*

John's Grill. Located on the fringe of the Tenderloin, this bar was featured in *The Maltese Falcon* and mystery fans will revel in its Hammett memorabilia. *63 Ellis St., tel. 415/986–0069.*

Vesuvio Cafe. Near the legendary City Lights Bookstore, this quintessentially North Beach bar is little altered since its hey-day as a haven for the beat poets. *255 Columbus Ave. between Broadway and Pacific Ave., tel. 415/362–3370.*

Gay Bars

Kimo's. This relaxed establishment affords an elegant ambience. *1351 Polk St., tel. 415/885–4535.*

The Midnight Sun. This is one of Castro's longest-standing and most popular bars, with giant video screens riotously programmed. *4067 18th St., tel. 415/861–4186.*

Twin Peaks. A pleasant, mirrored fern bar, Twin Peaks is a tranquil place in which to drink and converse. *401 Castro St., tel. 415/864–9470.*

Excursion to Sausalito

The San Francisco Convention and Visitors Bureau describes Sausalito's location as "the Mediterranean side of the Golden Gate." With its relatively sheltered site on the bay in Marin County, just 8 miles from San Francisco, it appeals to Bay Area residents and visitors for the same reason: It is so near and yet so far. As a hillside town with superb views, an expansive yacht harbor, the aura of an artists' colony, and ferry service,

Sausalito might be a resort within commuting distance of the city. It is certainly the primary excursion for visitors to San Francisco, especially those with limited time to explore the Bay Area. Mild weather encourages strolling and outdoor dining, although afternoon winds and fog can roll over the hills from the ocean, funneling through the central part of town once known as Hurricane Gulch.

There are substantial homes, including Victorian mansions, in Sausalito's heights, but the town has long had a more colorful and raffish reputation. Discovered in 1775 by Spanish explorers and named Saucelito (Little Willow) for the trees growing around its springs, Sausalito was a port for whaling ships during the 19th century. In 1875, the railroad from the north connected with ferryboats to San Francisco and the town became an attraction for the fun-loving. Even the chamber of commerce recalls the time when Sausalito sported 25 saloons, gambling dens, and bordellos. Bootleggers flourished during Prohibition in the 1920s, and shipyard workers swelled the town's population during the 1940s, when tour guides divided the residents into "wharf rats" and "hill snobs." Ensuing decades brought a bohemian element with the development of an artists' colony and a houseboat community. Sausalito has also become a major yachting center, and visitors are attracted by the fresh seafood offered at restaurants as well as the spectacular views. Sausalito remains a friendly and casual small town, although summer traffic jams can fray nerves. If possible, visit Sausalito on a weekday—and take the ferry.

Arriving and Departing

By Car Cross the Golden Gate Bridge and go north on U.S. 101 to the Sausalito exit, then go south on Bridgeway to municipal parking near the center of town. The trip takes ½ hour–45 minutes one way. (You will need change for the parking lots' meters.)

By Bus **Golden Gate Transit** (tel. 415/332–6600) travels to Sausalito from 1st and Mission streets and other points in the city.

By Ferry **Golden Gate Ferry** (tel. 415/332–6600) crosses the bay from the Ferry Building at Market Street and the Embarcadero; **Red and White Fleet** (tel. 415/546–2896) leaves from Pier 41 at Fisherman's Wharf. The trip takes 15–30 minutes.

Guided Tours

Most tour companies include Sausalito on excursions north to Muir Woods and the Napa Valley Wine Country. Among them are **Gray Line** (tel. 415/558–9400) and **Great Pacific Tour Co.** (tel. 415/626–4499).

Exploring

Numbers in the margin correspond to points of interest on the Sausalito map.

Bridgeway is the prime destination in Sausalito, as well as its main thoroughfare. The bay, yacht harbor, and waterfront restaurants are on one side, and more restaurants, shops, hillside homes, and hotels on the other. It is only a few steps from the ferry terminal to the tiny landmark park in the center of town: ❶ the **Plaza Vina del Mar,** named for Sausalito's sister city in

Alta Mira Hotel, **5**
Bay Model, **7**
Plaza Vina del Mar, **1**
Sausalito Hotel, **2**
Sausalito Yacht
Club, **3**
Valhalla, **4**
Village Fair, **6**

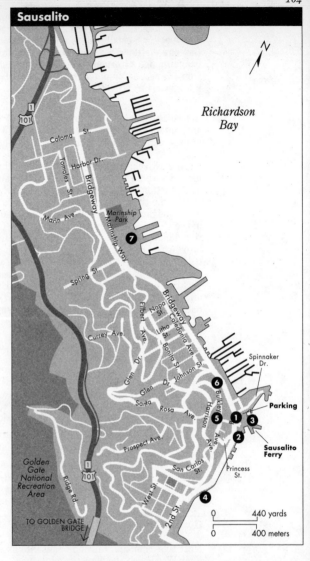

Chile. The park features a fountain and two 14-foot-tall statues of elephants created for the 1915 Panama–Pacific International Exposition in San Francisco.

2 Across the street to the south is the Spanish-style **Sausalito**
3 **Hotel,** which has been refurbished and filled with Victorian antiques. Between the hotel and the **Sausalito Yacht Club** is another unusual historic landmark, a drinking fountain with the invitation "Have a Drink on Sally." It's in remembrance of Sally Stanford, the former San Francisco madam who later ran Sausalito's Valhalla restaurant and became the town's mayor. Actually, the monument is also in remembrance of her dog. There is a sidewalk-level bowl that suggests "Have a Drink on Leland."

South on Bridgeway, toward San Francisco, there is an esplanade along the water with picture-perfect views. Farther south are a number of restaurants on piers, including—near the end of Bridgeway at Richardson Street—what was the ❹ **Valhalla**, the oldest restaurant in Sausalito. Built in 1893 as "Walhalla," it was one of the settings for the 1940s film *The Lady from Shanghai*, Sally Stanford's place in the 1950s, and most recently a Chart House restaurant.

North on Bridgeway from the ferry terminal are yacht harbors and, parallel to Bridgeway a block to the west, the quieter Caledonia Street, with its own share of cafés and shops. There is a pleasant, grassy park with a children's playground at Caledonia and Litho streets, with a food shop nearby for picnic provisions.

Here and there along the west side of Bridgeway are flights of steps that climb the hill to Sausalito's wooded, sometimes rustic and sometimes lavish, residential neighborhoods. The stairway just across the street from Vina del Mar Park is named ❺ Excelsior, and it leads to the **Alta Mira**, a popular Spanish-style hotel and restaurant with a spectacular view. However, there are vistas of the bay from all these streets.

Where there isn't a hillside house or a restaurant or a yacht in Sausalito, there is a shop. Most are along Bridgeway and Princess Street, and they offer a wide assortment of casual and sophisticated clothing, posters and paintings, imported and handcrafted gifts, and the expected variety of T-shirts, ice ❻ cream, cookies, and pastries. The **Village Fair** (777 Bridgeway) is a four-story former warehouse that has been converted into a warren of clothing, craft, and gift boutiques. Crafts workers often demonstrate their talents in the shops, and a winding brick path—Little Lombard Street—connects various levels. The shopping complex is a haven during wet weather.

Sausalito's reputation as an art colony is enhanced by the **Art Festival** held during the three-day Labor Day weekend in September. It attracts more than 35,000 visitors to the waterfront area, and there are plans to expand the site and offer direct ferry service from San Francisco. Details are available from the Sausalito Chamber of Commerce (333 Caledonia St., 94965, tel. 415/332–0505).

❼ North on Bridgeway, within a few minutes' drive, is the **Bay Model,** a re-creation in miniature of the entire San Francisco Bay and the San Joaquin–Sacramento River delta. It is actually nearly 400 feet square and is used by the U.S. Army Corps of Engineers to reproduce the rise and fall of tides, the flow of currents, and the other physical forces at work on the bay. It is housed in a former World War II shipyard building, and there is a display of shipbuilding history. At the same site is the *Wapama*, a World War I–era steam freighter being restored by volunteers. *2100 Bridgeway, tel. 415/332–3871. Open Tues.–Fri. 9–4, weekends 10–6. Closed Sun. in winter.*

Along the shore of Richardson Bay, between the Bay Model and U.S. 101, are some of the 400 houseboats that make up Sausalito's "floating-homes community." In the shallow tidelands, most of them float only about half the time, but they are always a fanciful collection of the rustic, the eccentric, the flamboyant, and the elegant.

Dining

Restaurants and cafés line Bridgeway, Sausalito's main street, and specialize in seafood. A variety of sandwiches, salads, and snack foods are also available. The favored restaurants are directly on the bay or on Sausalito's hillside.

Restaurants are listed according to price category.

Category	Cost*
Very Expensive	over $30
Expensive	$20–$30
Moderate	$10–$20
Inexpensive	under $10

*per person, excluding drinks, service, and 6.5% sales tax

Moderate–Expensive **Alta Mira.** This is a smart restaurant, with a more formal atmosphere than the downtown cafés, in a Spanish-style hotel a block above Bridgeway. The Alta Mira serves three meals a day, and the specialties are fresh scallops and Pacific salmon, grilled meats, and large crab and shrimp salads. The terrace offers one of Sausalito's best views and is popular for lunch and Sunday brunch. *125 Bulkley Ave., tel. 415/332–1350. Reservations advised. AE, DC, MC, V.*

Casa Madrona. Another restaurant in a charming hotel, this is a Victorian surrounded by a landscaped walk and newer rooms stepping down the hill to Bridgeway. Casa Madrona serves American cuisine, with an appealing selection of breakfast and brunch dishes. *801 Bridgeway, tel. 415/331–5888. MC, V. No lunch Sat.*

Moderate **The Spinnaker.** Seafood specialties and homemade pastas are offered in a quietly contemporary building in a spectacular setting on a point beyond the harbor, near the yacht club. You may see a pelican perched on one of the pilings just outside. *100 Spinnaker Dr., tel. 415/332–1500. AE, DC, MC, V.*

Inexpensive–Moderate **Winship Restaurant.** Here seafood, pasta, steaks, burgers, and salads are served in a casual nautical setting directly on the Bridgeway shopping strip. *670 Bridgeway, tel. 415/332–1454. AE, DC, MC, V. No dinner Sun.–Wed.*

Excursion to Muir Woods

One hundred and fifty million years ago, ancestors of redwood and sequoia trees grew throughout the United States. Today the *Sequoia sempervirens* can be found only in a narrow, cool coastal belt from Monterey to Oregon. (*Sequoiadendron gigantea* grows in the Sierra Nevada.) **Muir Woods National Monument,** 17 miles northwest of San Francisco, is a 550-acre park that contains one of the most majestic redwood groves in the world. Some redwoods in the park are nearly 250 feet tall and 1,000 years old. This grove was saved from destruction in 1908 and named after naturalist John Muir, whose campaigns helped to establish the National Park system. His response: "This is the best tree-lover's monument that could be found in all of the forests of the world. Saving these woods from the axe and saw is in many ways the most notable service to God and man I have heard of since my forest wandering began."

Arriving and Departing

By Car Take U.S. 101 north to the Mill Valley–Muir Woods exit. The trip takes 45 minutes one-way when the roads are open, but traffic can be heavy on summer weekends, so allow more time.

Guided Tours

Most tour companies include Muir Woods on excursions to the Wine Country, among them **Gray Line** (tel. 415/558–9400) and **Great Pacific** (tel. 415/626–4499).

Exploring

Muir Woods is a park for walking; no cars are allowed in the redwood grove itself. There are 6 miles of easy trails from the park headquarters. The paths cross streams and pass through ferns and azaleas as well as magnificent stands of redwoods such as Bohemian Grove and the circular formation called Cathedral Grove. No picnicking or camping is allowed, but snacks are available at the visitor center. The weather is usually cool and often wet, so dress warmly and wear shoes appropriate for damp trails. *Tel. 415/388–2595. Open daily 8 AM–sunset.*

Excursion to Berkeley

Berkeley and the University of California are not synonymous, although the founding campus of the state university system dominates the city's heritage and contemporary life. The city of 100,000 facing San Francisco across the bay has other interesting features for visitors. Berkeley is culturally diverse and politically adventurous, a breeding ground for social trends, a continuing bastion of the counterculture, and an important center for Bay Area writers, artists, and musicians. The city's liberal reputation and determined spirit have led detractors to describe it in recent years as the People's Republic of Berkeley. Wooded groves on the university campus, neighborhoods of shingled bungalows, and landscaped hillside homes temper the environment.

The city was named after George Berkeley, the Irish philosopher and clergyman who crossed the Atlantic to convert the Indians and who wrote "Westward, the course of empire takes its way." The city grew with the university, which was created by the state legislature in 1868 and established five years later on a rising plain of oak trees split by Strawberry Canyon. The central campus occupies 178 acres of the scenic 1,282-acre property, with most buildings located from Bancroft Way north to Hearst Street and from Oxford Street east into the Berkeley Hills. The university has more than 30,000 students and a full-time faculty of 1,600. It is considered one of the nation's leading intellectual centers and a major site of scientific research.

Note that the telephone area code for Berkeley, Oakland, and other cities on the east side of San Francisco Bay changed from 415 to 510 in 1991.

Arriving and Departing

By Car Take I–80 east across the Bay Bridge, then the University Avenue exit through downtown Berkeley to the campus, or take the Ashby Avenue exit and turn left on Telegraph Avenue to the traditional campus entrance; there is a parking garage on Channing Way. The trip takes ½ hour one way (except in rush hour).

By Public Transportation **BART** (tel. 415/788–2278) trains run under the bay to the downtown Berkeley exit; transfer to the Humphrey GoBart shuttle bus to campus. The trip takes from 45 minutes to one hour one way.

Exploring

Numbers in the margin correspond to points of interest on the Berkeley map.

1 The Visitors Center (tel. 510/642–5215), in **University Hall** at University Avenue and Oxford Street, is open weekdays 8–5. There are maps and brochures for self-guided walks; student-guided tours leave Mondays, Wednesdays, and Fridays at 10 AM and 1 PM.

2 The throbbing heart of the University of California is **Sproul Plaza,** just inside the campus at Telegraph Avenue and Bancroft Way. It's a lively panorama of political and social activists, musicians, food vendors along Bancroft Way, children, and dogs, and students on their way to and from classes at this "university within a park."

The university's suggested tour circles the upper portion of the central campus, past buildings that were sited to take advantage of vistas of the Golden Gate across the bay. The first campus plan was proposed by Frederick Law Olmsted, who designed New York's Central Park, and over the years the university's architects have included Bernard Maybeck and Julia Morgan (who designed Hearst Castle at San Simeon). Beyond **3** Sproul Plaza is the bronze **Sather Gate,** built in 1909 and the south entrance to the campus until expansion during the 1960s. **4** Up a walkway to the right is vine-covered **South Hall,** one of the two remaining buildings that greeted the first students in 1873.

5 Just ahead is **Sather Tower,** popularly known as the Campanile, the campus landmark that can be seen for miles. The 307-foot tower was modeled on St. Mark's tower in Venice and was completed in 1914. The carillon, which was cast in England, is played three times a day. In the lobby of the tower is a photographic display of campus history. An elevator takes visitors 175 feet up to the observation deck. *Open daily except university holidays 10–4:30. Admission: 50¢.*

6 Opposite the Campanile is **Bancroft Library,** with a rare-book collection and a changing series of exhibits that may include a Shakespeare first folio or a Gold Rush diary. On permanent display is a gold nugget purported to be the one that started the rush to California when it was discovered on January 24, 1848.

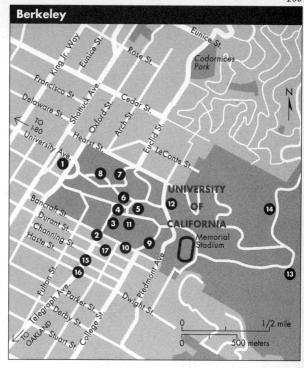

7 Across University Drive to the north is the **Earth Sciences Building,** with a seismograph for measuring earthquakes. The **8** building also contains the **Paleontology Museum,** which has displays of dinosaur bones and the huge skeleton of a plesiosaur. *Open when the university is in session, weekdays 8–5, weekends 1–5.*

The university's two major museums are on the south side of **9** campus near Bancroft Way. **The Lowie Museum of Anthropology,** in Kroeber Hall, has a collection of more than 4,000 artifacts. Items on display may cover the archaeology of ancient America or the crafts of Pacific Islanders. The museum also houses the collection of artifacts made by Ishi, the lone survivor of a California Indian tribe who was brought to the Bay Area in 1911. *Tel. 510/642–3681. Open Tues.–Fri. 10–4:30, weekends noon–4:30.*

10 **The University Art Museum** is a fan-shaped building with a spiral of ramps and balcony galleries. It houses a collection of Asian and Western art, including a major group of Hans Hofmann's abstract paintings, and also displays touring exhibits. On the ground floor is the Pacific Film Archive, which offers daily programs of historic and contemporary films. *2626 Bancroft Way, tel. 510/642–0808. Museum open Wed.–Sun. 11–5. Free museum admission. Film-program information, tel. 415/642–1124.*

Many of the university's notable attractions are outdoors. Just **11** south of the Campanile near the rustic Faculty Club is **Faculty Glade** on the south fork of Strawberry Creek, one of the best examples of the university's attempt to preserve a parklike atmosphere. East of the central campus, across Gayley Road, is **(12)** the **Hearst Greek Theatre,** built in 1903 and seating 7,000. Sarah Bernhardt once performed here; now it is used for major musical events.

Above the Greek Theatre in Strawberry Canyon is the 30-acre **(13)** **Botanical Garden,** with a collection of some 25,000 species. It's a relaxing gathering spot with benches and picnic tables. *Open daily 9–5, except Christmas.*

Perched on a hill above the campus on Centennial Drive is the **(14)** fortresslike **Lawrence Hall of Science,** which is a laboratory, a science-education center, and—most important to visitors—a dazzling display of scientific knowledge and experiments. Displays are updated regularly. On weekends there are additional films, lectures, and demonstrations, especially for children. *Tel. 510/642–5132. Nominal admission charge. Open weekdays 10–4:30, weekends 10–5.*

Berkeley is a rewarding city to explore beyond the university. Just south of the campus on **Telegraph Avenue** is the busy, student-oriented district, full of cafés, bookstores, poster shops, and street vendors with traditional and trendy crafts items. Shops come and go with the times, but among the neighbor- **(15)** hood landmarks are **Cody's Books** (2454 Telegraph Ave.), with **(16)** its adjacent café; **Moe's** (2476 Telegraph Ave.), with a huge se- **(17)** lection of used books; and **Leopold Records** (2518 Durant Ave.). This district was the center of student protests during the 1960s, and on the street it sometimes looks as if that era still lives. People's Park, one of the centers of protest, is just east of Telegraph Avenue between Haste Street and Dwight Way.

Downtown Berkeley around University and Shattuck avenues is nondescript. However, there are shops for browsing along College Avenue near Ashby Avenue south of campus and in the Walnut Square development at Shattuck Avenue and Vine Street northwest of campus. Berkeley's shingled houses can be seen on tree-shaded streets near College and Ashby avenues. Hillside houses with spectacular views can be seen on the winding roads near the intersection of Ashby and Claremont avenues, around the Claremont Hotel (*see* Excursion to Oakland, below). At the opposite side of the city, on Fourth Street north of University Avenue, an industrial area has been converted into a pleasant shopping street with popular eateries such as Bette's Oceanview Diner and the Fourth Street Grill.

Dining

Berkeley's major restaurants, including those on Shattuck Avenue north of the university, are known for their innovative use of fresh local produce. There is an eclectic variety of low-cost international cafés and snack stands in the student area along Telegraph Avenue and more cafés downtown on Shattuck Avenue near the central Berkeley BART station.

Restaurants are listed according to price category.

Category	Cost*
Very Expensive	over $30
Expensive	$20–$30
Moderate	$10–$20
Inexpensive	under $10

per person, excluding drinks, service, and 6.5% sales tax

Moderate– Expensive **Cafe at Chez Panisse.** Fresh and innovative light meals (lunch and dinner) are served, including pasta, pizza, salads, and light grilled dishes, upstairs from the mecca for California cuisine. *1517 Shattuck Ave., n. of University Ave., tel. 510/548–5525. Same-day reservations accepted. AE, DC, MC, V. Closed Sun.*

Moderate **Spenger's Fish Grotto.** This is a rambling, boisterous seafood restaurant, with daily specials and hearty portions. *1919 Fourth St., near University Ave. and I–80, tel. 510/845–7771. Reservations accepted for parties of 5 or more. AE, DC, MC, V.*

Inexpensive **Kip's.** This is a student hangout but it is open to everyone, upstairs near Telegraph Avenue, with big wooden tables and burgers, pizza, and—of course—beer on tap. *2439 Durant Ave., tel. 510/848–4340. No reservations. No credit cards.*
New Delhi Junction. A popular Indian restaurant, New Delhi Junction offers tandoori-roasted meats, curries, and regional specialties. *2556 University Ave., tel. 510/486–0477. MC, V.*

Excursion to Oakland

Originally the site of ranches, farms, a grove of redwood trees, and, of course, clusters of oaks, Oakland has long been a warmer and more spacious alternative to San Francisco. By the end of the 19th century, Mediterranean-style homes and gardens had been developed as summer estates. With swifter transportation, Oakland became a bedroom community for San Francisco; then it progressed to California's fastest-growing industrial city. In recent decades, Oakland has struggled to redefine its identity. However, the major attractions remain: the parks and civic buildings around Lake Merritt, which was created from a tidal basin in 1898; the port area, now named Jack London Square, where the author spent much of his time at the turn of the century; and the scenic roads and parks along the crest of the Oakland-Berkeley hills. Also in the hills is the castlelike Claremont Resort Hotel, a landmark since 1915, as well as more sprawling parks with lakes and miles of hiking trails.

Arriving and Departing

By Car Take I–80 across the Bay Bridge, then I–580 to the Grand Avenue exit for Lake Merritt. To reach downtown and the waterfront, take the I–980 exit from I–580. The trip takes 45 minutes.

By Public Transportation Take the BART to Oakland City Center station or to Lake Merritt station for the lake and Oakland Museum. The trip takes 45 minutes one way.

Exploring

Numbers in the margin correspond to points of interest on the Oakland map.

If there is one reason to visit Oakland, it is to explore the
❶ **Oakland Museum,** an inviting series of landscaped buildings
that display the state's art, history, and natural science. It is
the best possible introduction to a tour of California, and its
dramatic and detailed exhibits can help fill the gaps on a brief
visit. The natural-science department displays a typical
stretch of California from the Pacific Ocean to the Nevada border, including plants and wildlife. There is a breathtaking film,
Fast Flight, that condenses the trip into five minutes. The museum's sprawling history section includes everything from
Spanish-era artifacts and a gleaming fire engine that battled
the flames in San Francisco in 1906 to 1960s souvenirs of the
"summer of love." The "California Dream" exhibit recalls a century of inspirations. The museum's art department includes
mystical landscapes painted by the state's pioneers, as well as
contemporary visions. There is a pleasant museum café for
lunch and outdoor areas for relaxing. *1000 Oak St. at 10th St.,
tel. 510/834–2413. Admission free. Open Wed.–Sat. 10–5, Sun.
noon–7.*

❷ Near the museum, **Lake Merritt** is a 155-acre oasis surrounded
by parks and paths, with several outdoor attractions on the
❸ north side. The **Natural Science Center and Waterfowl Refuge**
attracts birds by the hundreds during winter months. *At the
foot of Perkins St., tel. 510/273–3739. Open Mon. noon–5,
Tues.–Sun. 10–5.*

❹ **Children's Fairyland** is a low-key amusement park with a puppet theater, small merry-go-round, and settings based on nursery rhymes. *Grand Ave. at Park View Terr., tel. 510/832–3609.
Open daily in summer, 10–4:30. Closed weekdays in winter.*

❺ The **Lakeside Park Garden Center** includes a Japanese garden
and many native flowers and plants. *666 Bellevue Ave., tel. 510/
273–3208. Open daily 10–3 or later in summer. Closed Thanksgiving, Christmas, New Year's Day.*

Jack London, although born in San Francisco, spent his early
years in Oakland before shipping out for adventures that inspired *The Call of the Wild, The Sea Wolf, Martin Eden,* and
The Cruise of the Snark. He is commemorated with a bronze
❻ bust on what is now called the **Jack London Waterfront** at the
❼ foot of Broadway. A livelier landmark is **Heinhold's First and
Last Chance Saloon,** one of his hangouts. Next door is the reas-
sembled Klondike cabin in which he spent a winter. The square
is mainly for drinking and dining. Next door, Jack London Village has specialty shops and restaurants. The best local collection of the author's letters, manuscripts, and photographs is in
the Jack London Room at the Oakland Main Library (125 14th
St., tel. 510/273–3134).

Oakland's downtown has been undergoing redevelopment for
many years. More stable and pleasant areas for shopping and
browsing, with a selection of cafés, can be found on Lake Shore
Avenue northeast of Lake Merritt, Piedmont Avenue near the
Broadway exit from I–580, and College Avenue west of Broadway in North Oakland. College Avenue is lined with antiques
stores, boutiques, and cafés. The neighborhood surrounds

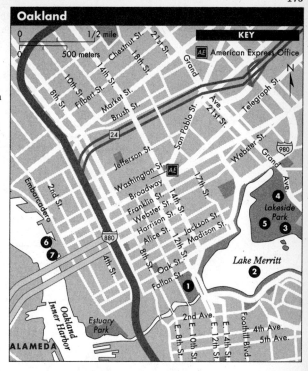

BART's Rockridge station. Transferring there to the local No. 51 bus will take visitors to the University of California campus, about 1½ miles away in Berkeley.

Time Out   A drive through the Oakland Hills is spectacular, although a wide area north from Broadway is still recovering from the devastating 1991 firestorm. One landmark that was saved is the **Claremont Hotel** (Ashby and Domingo Aves., tel. 510/843–3000), which offers fine views, a spot in which to relax, and good food. Drive north on Claremont Avenue to Ashby Avenue and on up the hill to the hotel. From a distance, this sprawling white building with towers and gables looks like a castle. Surrounded by 22 acres of lush grounds tucked into the south Berkeley hills, the Claremont is on the Oakland–Berkeley border, and for years both cities have claimed it. When a new entrance was built on a different side of the building, the address changed from Berkeley to Oakland. The 1915 hotel has been restored and refurbished and turned into a resort spa facility. The dining room is large and elegant, with pressed linen, large contemporary paintings, and views across the bay to San Francisco and the peninsula and north to Mt. Tamalpais. Meals, which fall into the Moderate–Expensive category, feature California cuisine, with seasonal fresh seafood for Sunday brunch and creative sandwiches for lunch.

The East Bay Regional Park District (tel. 510/531–9300) offers 46 parks in an area covering 60,000 acres to residents and visitors. In the Oakland hills is **Redwood Regional Park,** accessible from Joaquin Miller Road off Highway 13, to which Ashby Avenue will lead you. In the Berkeley hills is the 2,000-acre **Tilden Park,** which includes a lake and children's playground and is accessible from Grizzly Peak Boulevard off Claremont Avenue. There are scenic views of the Bay Area from roads that link the hilltop parks: Redwood Road, Skyline Boulevard, and Grizzly Peak Boulevard. Parks are open daily during daylight hours.

Dining

Oakland's ethnic diversity is reflected in its restaurants and cafés. There is a thriving Chinatown a few blocks northwest of the Oakland Museum, a number of seafood restaurants at Jack London Square, and a variety of international fare on Piedmont and College Avenues.

Restaurants are listed according to price category.

Category	Cost*
Very Expensive	over $30
Expensive	$20–$30
Moderate	$10–$20
Inexpensive	under $10

per person, excluding drinks, service, and 6.5% sales tax

Moderate–
Expensive

The Bay Wolf. French inspiration and fresh, regional specialties mark one of the city's best restaurants, in a converted home. *3853 Piedmont Ave., tel. 510/655–6004. Reservations advised. Dress: casual. MC, V. No weekend lunch.*

Moderate

Pacific Coast Brewing Co. This pub/restaurant/brewery serves a fine selection of sandwiches and salads. *906 Washington St., tel. 510/836–2739. MC, V.*

Inexpensive

Ratto's. Salads, sandwiches, soups, and pasta are served in a big, cheerful room adjacent to one of the Bay Area's best international grocery stores, in the Old Oakland Victorian Row restoration. *821 Washington St., tel. 510/832–6503. No credit cards. Weekday lunch; take-out orders prepared Mon.–Sat. in deli.*

Excursion to Marine World Africa USA

This wildlife theme park is one of Northern California's most popular attractions. It has been a phenomenal success since moving in 1986 from a crowded site south of San Francisco to Vallejo, about an hour's drive northeast. The 160-acre park features animals of the land, sea, and air performing in shows, roaming in natural habitats, and accompanying their trainers to stroll among park visitors. Among the "stars" are killer whales, dolphins, a dozen Bengal tigers, elephants, sea lions, chimpanzees, and a troupe of human waterskiers. There are cockatoos, macaws, flamingos, cranes, and ostriches. There is a whale and dolphin show, a sea-lion show, a tiger and lion show, and an elephant and chimpanzee show.

The park is owned by the Marine World Foundation, a nonprofit organization devoted to educating the public about the world's wildlife. The shows and close-up looks at exotic animals serve that purpose without neglecting entertainment. The park is a family attraction, so it's not just for youngsters. For additional sightseeing, visitors can reach the park on a high-speed ferry from San Francisco, a trip that offers unusual vistas of San Francisco Bay and San Pablo Bay. *Marine World Pkwy., Vallejo, tel. 707/643-6722. Admission: $15-$20; tickets at Ticketron outlets. Open daily (9:30-5), Wed.-Sun. rest of year and some school holidays (or later in summer).*

Arriving and Departing

By Car Take I-80 east to Marine World Parkway in Vallejo. The trip takes one hour one way.

By Bus **Greyhound Lines** (tel. 415/558-6789) from 1st and Mission streets, San Francisco, to Vallejo, or the **BART** train (415/781-BART) to El Cerrito Del Norte Station; transfer to **Vallejo Transit** line (tel. 707/643-7663) to the park.

By Ferry **Red and White Fleet's** (tel. 415/546-2896) high-speed ferry departs mornings each day that the park is open from Pier 41 at Fisherman's Wharf. It arrives in Vallejo an hour later. Round-trip service allows five hours to visit the park. Excursion tickets are $20-$38 and include park admission.

7 The Gold Country

By Vicky Elliott

Before the Gold Rush, California looked toward the coast: The Spanish colonizers, despite their hunger for precious metal, had neglected the Sierras. When gold was discovered at Coloma in 1848, everybody headed for the hills, starting the greatest mass migration since the Crusades. It lured people from everywhere in the world, and when it was all over, California was a very different place.

The boom towns of the Sierra foothills were virtually abandoned when the gold ran out, and today, the Gold Country lies waiting to be discovered again, once more off the well-beaten track, and ripe with hidden treasure. You can still join a prospecting expedition and try your hand at panning for the flakes deposited by millennia of trickling streams, but the chief reward here is the chance to walk a bit back into the past.

At one point in the 1850s, Nevada City was as big a place as Sacramento and San Francisco. It still stands out for its sophistication among its neighbors, but, like almost all the towns along Highway 49, which winds the 200-mile length of the historic mining area, its population is in the five-digit range. Time has washed over the Mother Lode; economic opportunities are limited, and consequently there is an unspoiled, homey feel to it that attracts those who are content to live modestly amid the natural beauty of these rolling hills.

Travelers can experience that lifestyle at bed-and-breakfast inns, many in exquisite Victorian buildings that have been taken down to the studs and lovingly restored. Their sumptuous breakfasts and period atmosphere offer a comfortable and romantic base from which to explore the tumbledown villages and historic sites that speak of the 19th century.

In the frenzy of the Gold Rush, as tents and flimsy wooden buildings sprang up around promising "diggings," comfort was in short supply. Especially during the early years, this was a man's world. After the hard journey around the Horn by ship, or the wearying trek across the continent, everyday life in the claims, under blazing sun or in freezing streams, was tough.

Saloonkeepers and canny merchants realized that the real gold was to be made from the 49ers' pockets. Nothing came cheap. This was a market where potatoes and onions could command $1 apiece, and in which entrepreneurs like storekeeper Samuel Brannan became millionaires.

The labor of panning made way for the crude wooden stamp mill and the arrastre, which were used to break up the gold-bearing rock, as well as for a host of mining techniques imported from all over the world. Hydraulic mining washed whole hillsides away, and as the industry matured, the exploration for and exploitation of quartz-bearing hard-rock lodes demanded organization and capital that superseded the rough-and-tumble self-government of the first arrivals.

The story of this extraordinary episode in American history, vividly described by Mark Twain and Bret Harte, comes alive in mining towns in various stages of decay, as well as in careful reconstructions including Columbia State Historic Park. The Gold Country may be a backwater, but it bountifully repays leisurely exploration.

Getting Around

By Plane Sacramento Metropolitan Airport is the major airport closest to the Gold Country (it's an hour's drive from Placerville, and a little closer to Auburn). San Francisco International Airport is about two hours from Sacramento. Car rentals are available at both airports.

By Bus **Greyhound-Trailways** serves Sacramento, Auburn, Grass Valley, and Placerville from San Francisco. The **Sacramento Transit Authority** buses service points of major interest in downtown Sacramento.

By Car This is the most convenient way to see the Gold Country, since most of its towns are too small to provide a base for public transportation. I–80 intersects with Highway 49 at Auburn; U.S. 50 intersects with Highway 49 at Placerville.

By Train Shuttle buses leave San Francisco's Transbay Terminal for the Oakland Amtrak station three times daily. From here, pick up **CalTrain**'s (tel. 415/557–8661) Capitol train service to Sacramento, which stops for passengers in Berkeley, Richmond, Martinez and Davis.

Guided Tours

Gold Prospecting Expeditions (18170 Main St., Box 974, Jamestown 95327, tel. 209/984–4653). Specialists in the field, this outfit offers one-hour gold-panning excursions, two-week prospecting trips, and a good deal in between.

Outdoor Adventure River Specialists (O.A.R.S.) (Box 67, Angels Camp 95222, tel. 209/736–4677 or 800/346–6277). A wide range of white-water rafting trips on the Stanislas, American, Merced, and Tuolumne rivers are offered from late March through early October.

Capital City Cruises (1401 Garden Hwy., Suite 125, Sacramento 95833, tel. 916/921–1111) runs two-hour narrated cruises, as well as brunch, dinner-dance, and murder-mystery cruises on the Sacramento River year round on the *River City Queen* and the steamer *Elizabeth Louise*.

Spirit of Sacramento (Channel Star Excursions, 1207 Front St., No. 18, Sacramento 95814, tel. 916/522–2933 or 800/433–0263). This paddlewheel riverboat, successor to the *Matthew McKinley*, offers a variety of excursions, including a one-hour narrated cruise, happy hour, dinner, and luncheon cruises, and a champagne brunch.

Important Addresses and Numbers

Tourist Information **Amador County Chamber of Commerce** (30 S. Hwy. 49–88, Box 596, Jackson 95642, tel. 209/223–0350).

Auburn Area Visitors and Convention Bureau (601 Lincoln Way, Auburn 95603, tel. 916/885–5616 or 800/427–6463 in CA).

Columbia State Historic Park (Box 151, Columbia 95310, tel. 209/532–4301 or 209/532–0150).

El Dorado County Chamber of Commerce (542 Main St., Placerville 95667, tel. 916/621–5885).

Golden Chain Council of the Mother Lode (Box 7046, Auburn 95604).

Nevada City Chamber of Commerce (132 Main St., Nevada City 95959, tel. 916/265–2692 or 800/655–NJOY).

Nevada County Chamber of Commerce (248 Mill St., Grass Valley 95945, tel. 916/273–4667 or 800/655–4667 in CA). The Nevada County Chamber is housed in a reproduction of the home owned on this site by the notorious dancer Lola Montez when she moved to Grass Valley in the early 1850s; her bathtub is still there.

Sacramento Convention and Visitors Bureau (1421 K St., Sacramento 95814, tel. 916/264–7777).

Old Sacramento Visitor Information Center (1104 Front St., Old Sacramento, tel. 916/442–7644).

Tuolumne County Visitors Bureau (Box 4020, 55 W. Stockton St., Sonora 95370, tel. 209/533–4420 or 800/446–1333).

Emergencies Dial 911 for emergencies throughout the Gold Country to reach police, fire, and medical personnel.

There are several hospitals with 24-hour emergency room service in Sacramento: **Mercy Hospital of Sacramento Promptcare** (4001 J St., tel. 916/453–4424), **Sutter General Hospital** (2801 L St., tel. 916/733–3003), and **Sutter Memorial Hospital** (52nd and F Sts., tel. 916/733–1000).

Exploring

From San Francisco, I–80 runs toward the Gold Country via Sacramento; at Auburn, it intersects with Highway 49, which links many of the old Gold Rush communities. Alternatively, you can pick up U.S. 50 at Sacramento; it intersects Highway 49 at Placerville.

Although Highway 49 is winding and almost entirely two-lane, it is excellent and takes you through spectacular scenery. But, while it is possible to travel the length of Highway 49 in a single day, such a tight timetable wouldn't allow for the fun of wandering through ghost towns and exquisitely restored villages, stopping by the roadside to read historical markers, poking through antiques shops and craft stores, and visiting the foothill vineyards to sample the wines. This is a region where it pays to slow down and take your time.

Highway 49

Numbers in the margin correspond to points of interest on the Gold Country map.

❶ A two-hour drive from Sacramento to the northern end of Highway 49 brings you to **Downieville,** one of the prettiest of the Gold Rush towns. Stone, brick, and frame buildings seem to cling to the mountainsides, or hug the banks of the fast-moving Yuba River. Along the quiet streets, lovely old houses have been well maintained or restored. The spare and elegant Methodist church, which dates from 1865, is the oldest Protestant church in continuous use in the state. Drive out Main Street past the last bridge and take a short walk past the PG&E Station to the crystal-clear Yuba River. The river forms pools as it

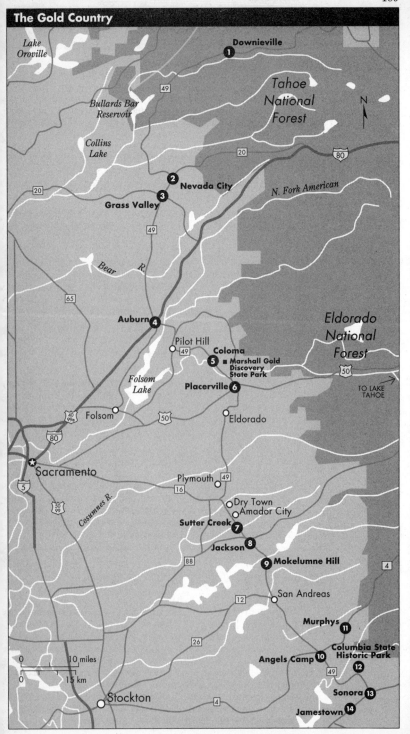

rushes over boulders, and it's a favorite swimming spot. *An information booth in the center of town is open from May to Sept.*

② Wind back down Highway 49 and drive the 50 miles to **Nevada City,** a Gold Rush town reminiscent of New England with its white houses and picket fences. The **Nevada Theatre** on Broad Street, built in 1865, is California's oldest theater in continuous use, and when not playing host to dramatic productions—a thriving business hereabouts—it is used by the town as a community center.

Behind the theater is the **Miners Foundry,** also built in 1865, a cavernous building that now serves as a cultural center offering plays, concerts, and a wide range of events that include a Victorian Christmas fair, a teddy-bear convention, a winefest, and antiques shows, as well as themed period parties. *325 Spring St., tel. 916/265–5040. Open daily 9:30–5.*

Shopping is a big draw in Nevada City. You'll find an enticing selection of antiques, brass, crystal, books, and toys. The town also boasts some of the best restaurants in the Gold Country.

Time Out | **Sierra Mountain Coffee Roasters** is a cozy and appealing refreshment stop. Excellent coffee, coffee drinks, and homemade pastries are served until late afternoon. It's an informal place—there's a pile of daily papers to read in a booth or outdoors on the quiet patio. *316 Commercial St., corner of York St., tel. 916/265–5282.*

③ South along Highway 49, **Grass Valley** is worth a full day's browsing. More than half of California's total gold production was extracted from the mines of Nevada County, and some of the area's most interesting exhibits on gold mining are to be found here.

The **Empire Mine** was worked from 1850 right up to 1956, and was one of California's richest quartz mines. An estimated 5.8 million ounces of gold were brought up from its 367 miles of underground passages. The mine is now a State Historic Park, and its buildings and grounds are open year round. Tours allow you to peer into the deep recesses of the mine and to view the owner's "cottage," with its exquisite woodwork. The visitors' center has films and exhibits on mining and a picnic area. *10791 E. Empire St. (Empire St. exit south from Hwy. 49), tel. 916/ 273–8522. Admission: $2 adults, $1 children 6–12. Open summer, daily 9–6; winter, daily 10–5. Tours and lectures daily in summer on the hour 11–4; weekends only in winter at 1 and 2.*

The **North Star Power House and Pelton Wheel Exhibit** boasts a 32-foot-high Pelton wheel, the largest ever built. It was used to power mining operations, and is a forerunner of the modern water turbines that generate hydroelectricity. Period mining equipment and a stamp mill are also on display, as well as the largest operational Cornish pumps in the country, part of the legacy of the tin miners who migrated here from Cornwall in England. There are hands-on displays for children and a picnic area. *Allison Ranch Rd. and Mill St. (Empire St. exit north from Hwy. 49), tel. 916/273–4255. Donation requested. Open May–Oct. 10–5.*

Time Out | A more palpable reminder of the mining past can be had at **Marshall's Pasties,** which still purveys handmade beef and potato pies like those taken down into the shafts in lunch buckets by the Cornish miners who came to work in the hard-rock mines. The apple pasties are good, too. *203B Mill St., tel. 916/272–2844. Open Mon.–Sat. 9:30–6.*

❹ **Auburn,** at the intersection of Highway 49 and I–80 (after 49 crosses under I–80, turn right on Lincoln St. and follow the signs), is a small old town with narrow, climbing streets, cobblestones, wooden sidewalks, and many original buildings. The **Bernhard Museum Complex,** built in 1851 as the Traveler's Hotel, now offers a glimpse of family life in the late-Victorian era, with a carriage house displaying several period conveyances. *291 Auburn-Folsom Rd., tel. 916/889–4156. Admission: $1 adults, 50¢ senior citizens over 65 and children 6–16. Open Tues.–Fri. 11–3, weekends noon–4.*

❺ Twenty-five miles farther on is **Coloma,** where the California Gold Rush got started. John Sutter erected a sawmill here on the banks of the American River, and it was in the millrace that one of his employees, a wagon-builder named James Marshall, discovered gold in January 1848. "My eye was caught with the glimpse of something shining in the bottom of the ditch," he recalled later. Unfortunately, Marshall himself never found any more "color," as it came to be called.

Most of Coloma lies within **Marshall Gold Discovery State Historic Park.** Within six months of Marshall's discovery, 2,000 prospectors arrived in the area, and Coloma became the first Gold Rush town. Its population swelled rapidly to 10,000, but when reserves of the precious metal dwindled, the prospectors left as quickly as they had come. A replica of Sutter's mill, based on Marshall's drawings, now stands here, with Marshall's cabin and museum. There are picnic areas, and along the south fork of the American River are campgrounds, good fishing spots, and rafting. *Tel. 916/622–3470. Day use: $5 per car, $4 senior citizens. Park open daily 8 AM–sunset. Museum open summer, daily 10–5; Labor Day–Memorial Day, daily 10:30–4:30. Closed Thanksgiving, Christmas, and New Year's Day.*

❻ Follow Highway 49 south 10 miles into **Placerville,** which shed its former name of Hangtown, a graphic allusion to the summary nature of frontier justice. Placerville today has the distinction of being one of the only cities in the world to own a gold mine. The **Gold Bug Mine** has two fully lighted shafts that can be toured. One of the mine's shafts dead-ends at a gold-flecked vein, and the other follows an uphill trail. A shaded stream runs through the park, and there are picnic facilities. *Bedford exit north from Hwy. 49 to Gold Bug Park, tel. 916/642–5232. Admission free, 50¢ for self-guided tour of mine. Park open daily 8 AM–sunset; mine open May–Sept., daily 10–4; March 16–April 29 and Oct. 5–Nov. 10, weekends 10–4.*

Placerville is the largest town on Highway 49. Driving south through rolling countryside, you'll pass villages such as Plymouth, Drytown, and Amador City, which amount to little more than a few antiques stores and perhaps a café, which crumbling brick buildings and the ubiquitous historical markers.

❼ **Sutter Creek** is another matter. The town is well kept and totally unspoiled, its white homes carefully restored, with green shutters and picket fences. The stores clustered along Highway 49 are worth a closer look, and the raised wood sidewalks recall the muddy 19th century roads that made them necessary.

A detour here along Shake Ridge Road to **Volcano** will take you past Daffodil Hill, which, from March to mid-April, comes alive with color. Dutch colonists planted the bulbs here, and the daffodils have propagated themselves riotously since. The village of Volcano, once a bustling town of 5,000 people, with 17 hotels and 35 saloons, is a faithful reflection of a vanished age: Nothing has been tampered with, and its general store and theater are still in use, as they have been for more than 140 years.

8 Driving south from Sutter Creek, Highway 49 climbs sharply, twists and turns, and then rewards you with a wonderful view of the mining town of **Jackson.** An old white church sits on a knoll, its small cemetery spread out around it, and from this vantage point, the brick buildings below cluster tightly. Seen up close, however, the town is a motley assortment of modern businesses and buildings in various states of repair; it also has the dubious distinction of closing its bordellos only as recently as 1956.

9 Seven miles south along Highway 49 is the town of **Mokelumne Hill,** known as Moke Hill. Unlike busy Jackson, the county seat, this little village is frozen in an earlier time. Many of the buildings are constructed of light-brown rhyolite tuff, a stone common in much of the Gold Country. Where there are sidewalks, they are wooden, as are the small, frail-looking houses on the hilly side streets.

10 A further 20 miles along the highway is **Angels Camp,** famed chiefly for its jumping-frog contest held each May, based on Mark Twain's "The Jumping Frog of Calaveras County." It was one of his first stories to attract public notice, but Twain was not impressed by the hospitality he experienced during his stay here in 1865, describing the coffee as "day-before-yesterday dishwater." At the north end of town is a museum with a collection of minerals and early artifacts. *Tel. 209/736–2963. Open Mar.–Labor Day, daily 10–3, Labor Day–Mar., Wed.–Sun. 10–3.*

11 East on Highway 4, and less than 10 miles up the road, is **Murphys,** a town of white picket fences and Victorian houses. In **Murphys Hotel,** opened in 1856 as the Sperry & Perry and still operating, is a guest register recording the visits of Horatio Alger and Ulysses S. Grant, who joined the 19th-century swarms who came to visit the giant sequoias in **Calaveras Big Trees State Park,** about 15 miles farther east on Highway 4. *Tel. 209/795–2334. Day use: $5 per car. Open daily.*

Another spectacle of nature, 4 miles out of Murphys, on the Vallecito–Columbia highway, is **Moaning Cavern,** a vast underground chamber with ancient crystalline rock formations. *Tel. 209/736–2708. Admission: $5.75 adults, $2.75 children 6–12. Open summer daily 9–6, winter 10–5.*

Back on Highway 49 driving south, there is a breathtaking ride across the bridge over the Melones Reservoir and an indication of the rugged terrain in a part of California where the rivers have dug deep canyons. Horse-drawn wagons must have found it rough going.

12 A well-marked turnoff leads to **Columbia State Historic Park,** a pleasingly executed mix of preservation and restoration. The

"Gem of the Southern Mines" comes as close to a Gold Rush town in its heyday as you can get, although there are far more ice-cream parlors than saloons today. You can ride a stagecoach and pan for gold; street musicians give lively performances on the banjo, the fiddle, and the stump; and there is a blacksmith working at his anvil. Elegant lodging can be found at the City Hotel or Fallon House, both dating from the 1850s, and the Fallon Theater presents plays year round. Columbia's candy store makes its own old-fashioned confectionery: licorice sticks, horehound drops, and fudge. *Tel. 209/532-4301; exhibits and demonstrations daily 10-6. Museum open 8-5.*

⑬ Highway 49 is the main street in **Sonora.** Don't miss the beautiful **St. James Episcopal Church,** built in 1860, the second-oldest frame church in California. In winter, the ski traffic passes through Sonora on the way along Highway 108 to Lake Tahoe 30 miles east.

The road turns west for a few miles out of Sonora, and heads to **⑭** **Jamestown** whose **Railtown 1897 State Historic Park** includes 26 acres of trains, a station, a roundhouse, and facilities for maintaining trains. There are slide presentations, guided tours, and train excursions on the weekends. *Tel. 209/984-3953. Admission: $2 adults, $1.25 children; train excursions $9 adults, $4.50 children. Open daily 10-4.*

Sacramento

Numbers in the margin correspond to points of interest on the Sacramento map.

The gateway to the Gold Country, Sacramento has its own slice of Gold Rush history, as the point from which gold prospectors fanned out to seek their fortunes. Sacramento predates the Gold Rush, but came into its own as a center for financial transactions and the shipping of provisions to the gold fields, ultimately becoming the western terminus of the Pony Express, the transcontinental railroad, and the telegraph. One of the largest restoration projects in the United States has spruced up the old city, an airy island marooned on its plot to one side of the state capital's extravagant high rises. Today, its cobbled streets are paced by horse-drawn carts laden with visitors, and covered walkways frame magnificent commercial buildings whose tall windows and high ceilings offer a revealing glimpse into 19th-century shopping.

❶ The **visitor's center** (1104 Front St., tel. 916/442-7644) is housed in a former depot for passengers and freight bound down the river to San Francisco by steamship. *Open daily 9-5.*

❷ The **Eagle Theater** (925 Front St.) was built in 1849, and was California's first. A reconstruction was completed in 1976, and the theater is in regular use today. The building housing the **❸** **Sacramento History Museum** was once the nerve center of the town, containing the mayor's offices, council chambers, jail, and policemen's quarters, among other things. It now offers a streamlined, well-presented introduction to the history of Sacramento and its surroundings, complete with gold pans with which you can sift, an Indian thatched hut, memorabilia from the world wars, and a colorful stack of turn-of-the-century cans of local produce. *101 I St., tel. 916/264-7057. Admission: $3*

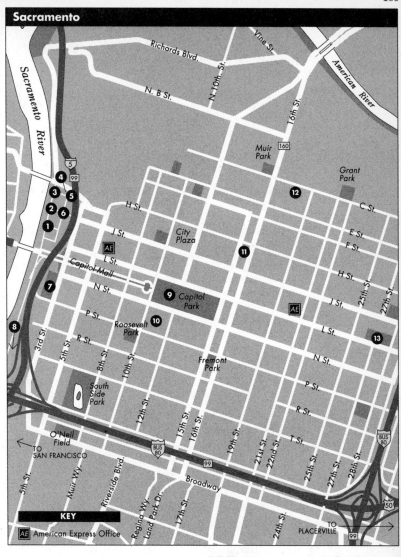

Sacramento

KEY

AE American Express Office

B.F. Hastings
Building, **6**

Blue Diamond
Growers' Store, **12**

California State
Archives, **10**

California State
Railroad Museum, **4**

Crocker Art
Museum, **7**

Eagle Theater, **2**

Governor's
Mansion, **11**

Huntington, Hawkins
& Co. Store, **5**

Sacramento History
Museum, **3**

State Capitol, **9**

Sutter's Fort, **13**

Towe Ford
Museum, **8**

Visitor's Center, **1**

adults, $1.50 children 6–17. Open Tues.–Sun. 10–4:30. Closed Thanksgiving, Christmas, and New Year's Day.

❹ Old Sacramento's biggest draw is the **California State Railroad Museum,** 100,000 square feet exhibiting 21 restored locomotives and railroad cars in perfect working order, including the *Governor Stanford,* the Central Pacific locomotive that steamed from Sacramento to Promontory Point to mark the completion of the transcontinental railroad. You can walk through a post-office car and peer into the cubbyholes and canvas bags of mail, or go through a sleeping car that simulates the swaying on the roadbed and the flashing lights of a passing town at night. On weekends from May through Labor Day, a steam-powered excursion train runs several miles down the river, from the depot on Front Street to Miller Park, every hour on the hour from 10 to 5. *125 I St., at 2nd and I Sts., tel. 916/448–4466. Admission: $5 adults, $2 children 6–12. Open daily 10–5. Closed Thanksgiving, Christmas and New Year's Day.*

❺ The **Huntington, Hawkins & Co. Store** hardware exhibit at 111 I Street gives a good idea of the kind of store that supplied prospectors during the Gold Rush, is open daily 11–5, and still **❻** stocks a variety of merchandise typical of the period. The **B. F. Hastings Building** (2nd and J sts.) includes the first Sacramento chambers of the California State Supreme Court, built in 1854. *Open daily 10–5.*

❼ The **Crocker Art Museum,** a few blocks from old Sacramento, is the oldest art museum in the American West, with a collection of European, Asian, and Californian art, including *Sunday Morning in the Mines,* a large canvas depicting the mining industry of the 1850s. The museum's lobby and magnificent ballroom retain the original 1870s woodwork, plaster moldings, and imported tiles. *216 O St., tel. 916/264–5423. Admission: $3 adults, $1.50 children 7–17. Open Thurs. 10–9, Wed.–Sun. 10–5. Closed Dec., July 4, Thanksgiving, Christmas, and New Year's Day.*

❽ The **Towe Ford Museum** contains a collection of more than 150 vintage cars, including every year and model manufactured by the Ford company for 50 years, starting from 1903. *2200 Front St., tel. 916/442–6802. Admission: $5 adults, $4.50 senior citizens, $2.50 young adults 14–18, $1 children 5–13. Open daily 10–6; closed Thanksgiving, Christmas and New Year's Day.*

❾ The California **state capitol building** was built in 1869 and recently underwent extensive restoration. The lacy plasterwork of the rotunda, 120 feet high, has the complexity and color of a Fabergé Easter egg. There are free guided tours of the building, as well as of the well-kept grounds, two blocks wide and five blocks long, whose plants and shrubs from all over the world are clearly identified. *Capitol Ave. and 10th St., tel. 916/324–0333. Admission free. Tours daily every hour on the hour from 9–4. Closed Thanksgiving, Christmas, and New Year's Day.*

❿ The **California State Archives** has a wealth of documents on the history of the state, including the oldest collection of Western newspapers and a catalogue of all those eligible to vote at the turn of the century. *1020 O St., tel. 916/653–0066. Open weekdays 8–5. Closed major holidays.*

⑪ The historic **Governor's Mansion** was originally the palatial residence of Albert Gallatin, one of the partners in the Central Pacific Railroad, and subsequently home to 13 California governors—until Ronald Reagan turned it down in 1967. *16th and H Sts., tel. 916/323-3047. Admission: $2 adults, $1 children 6–12. Tours on the hour 10–4. Closed major holidays.*

⑫ Well worth visiting also is the Blue Diamond cooperative's **Blue Diamond Growers' Store,** the world's largest almond-processing factory, with tours that fill you in on the myriad uses of the almond—as butter, powder, paste, and oil. The variety of almond delicacies on sale in the gift shop is amazing. *1701 C St., tel. 916/446-8439 or 800/225-6887 to order. Open weekdays 10–5, gift shop also Sat. 10–4. Tours by appointment at 10 AM and 1 PM.*

⑬ **Sutter's Fort** is the settlement from which Sacramento grew. Founded in 1839 by the Swiss immigrant John Augustus Sutter, its thick walls now surround an adobe house and workshops for gunsmiths, blacksmiths, and candlemakers. Behind the fort is the State Indian Museum, displaying local Native American artifacts. *27th and L Sts., tel. 916/445-4422. Admission: $2 adults, $1 children 6–12. Open daily 10–5. Closed Thanksgiving, Christmas, and New Year's Day.*

Dining

Given the small population of the Gold Country (only two towns, Auburn and Placerville, even approach a population of 10,000), there is a disproportionate number of good restaurants, especially in Nevada City. Many of the menus are ambitious: In addition to standard American, Italian, and Mexican fare, there is Continental, French, and California cuisine, with an emphasis on innovation and the freshest ingredients. The national fast-food chains are few and far between—there just aren't enough people here to support them. It's not difficult, though, to find the makings for a good picnic in most Gold Country towns.

Sacramento has recently enjoyed a period of expansion, and offers a wide range of eating places for its growing population; restaurants listed are all located in Old Sacramento or downtown. Unless otherwise noted, dress is informal.

Highly recommended restaurants are indicated by a star ★.

Category	Cost*
Very Expensive	over $50
Expensive	$30–$50
Moderate	$15–$30
Inexpensive	under $15

per person, not including tax, service, or drinks

Auburn
Moderate

Butterworth's. Housed in a handsome Victorian mansion on a hillside overlooking Old Auburn, this restaurant features California cuisine with a Continental flair, with copious servings and a Sunday brunch. *1522 Lincoln Way, tel. 916/885-0249. Reservations accepted. AE, MC, V. Closed for lunch weekends.*

Harris Restaurant and Lounge. This is an informal but nicely appointed restaurant with a pleasant atmosphere, offering an American menu for lunch, dinner, and breakfast. Beef, lamb, and seafood are emphasized, as well as some Italian specialties. *13480 Lincoln Way, tel. 916/885–3090. Reservations advised on weekends. AE, DC, MC, V.*

★ **Headquarter House.** This restaurant is set on a hilltop within the Dunipace Angus Ranch, with a lounge on the top floor overlooking pine trees, and a nine-hole golf course. The varied menu emphasizes California cuisine, with a good choice of fresh seafood. *14500 Musso Rd., tel. 916/878–1906. Reservations advised. AE, D, DC, MC, V. Closed Mon. and Tues.*

Inexpensive **CafeDelicias.** Located in a picturesque building in Old Auburn, this Mexican restaurant has an extensive menu, and the helpings are generous. One dinner choice is *carne asada a la Tampiqueña*—steak grilled with spices, onions, and bell peppers, served with a cheese enchilada, rice, and beans. *1591 Lincoln Way, tel. 916/885–2050. AE, D, MC, V.*

Coloma **Vineyard House.** In this Victorian country inn, dating from
Moderate 1878, the small dining rooms have fireplaces or wood-burning stoves, flower-painted chandeliers, and early California memorabilia. Four-course dinners of country-style fare are offered, with chicken, beef, seafood, and pasta. Chicken and dumplings are a house specialty. Sunday brunch is served. *Cold Springs Rd., off Hwy. 49, tel. 916/622–2217. Reservations advised. AE, MC, V. No lunch. Closed Mon.*

Columbia **City Hotel.** This authentically restored 1850s hotel and dining
Expensive room serves California cuisine, using fresh local produce stylishly prepared, and served with flair. The California wine list is comprehensive, and brunch is offered on weekends. An adjoining bar, also restored, is called the What Cheer Saloon, after the liquor store of that name that once operated here. *Columbia State Park, Main St., tel. 209/532–1479. Reservations advised. AE, MC, V. Closed Mon.; in winter, no weekday lunch and no dinner Mon.–Wed.*

Cool **The Nugget.** Started by a German émigré, this unassuming res-
Inexpensive taurant not far from Auburn offers an array of German specialties lovingly prepared, including some delectable goulash, tender Wiener schnitzels, and an excellent pork roast. *Hwy. 49, tel. 916/823–1294. Reservations advised on weekends. No credit cards. Closed for dinner Mon.*

Downieville **Cirino's at the Forks.** This small, cheerful restaurant on the
Inexpensive– banks of the Downie River provides outdoor service in summer
Moderate on a flagstone patio at the water's edge. The menu features mainly Italian cuisine, with beef, chicken, homemade soup, salads, sandwiches, and 12 varieties of tea. There is a short, very reasonably priced California wine list. *Main St., tel. 916/289–3479 or 800/540–2099. Reservations advised in summer. MC, V.*

Grass Valley **Holbrooke Hotel.** The recently opened restaurant in an 1851
Moderate– hotel is Victorian in decor, with a saloon and some of the ori-
Expensive ginal brick walls, archways, and beams. The cuisine is French-inspired and the chef's creations include salmon with light mussel sauce, blackened sea scallops nantua, and an award-winning chocolate hazelnut cake with crème anglaise. There is also an elegant Sunday brunch. *212 W. Main St., tel. 916/273–*

1353 or 800/933–7077. Reservations advised. AE, MC, V. Closed for lunch Sat., for dinner Sun.

Jackson
Inexpensive

Teresa's. This long-established Italian restaurant has a local clientele. The menu features daily specials and includes homemade ravioli, fresh minestrone daily, and a fine selection of veal, scampi, and other Italian classics. *1235 Jackson Gate Rd., tel. 209/223–1786. Reservations advised. AE, MC, V. Closed for lunch Sun., and Wed. and Thur.*

Jamestown
Moderate

Jamestown Hotel. The old oak sideboards, cut-glass lamps, and rocking chairs in the lobby set the tone in this restored Gold Rush hotel. The accent is on fresh seasonal produce with a country flair, including ragouts, cassoulets, and seafood dishes at dinner; salads, sandwiches, and omelets are offered at lunch. Service is in the dining room or the garden patio. Sunday brunch is served. *18153 Main St., tel. 209/984–3902. Reservations advised. AE, D, MC, V.*

Nevada City
Moderate

Country Rose Cafe. The exterior of this old brick and stone building, complete with the original iron shutters from Gold Rush days, harmonizes well with the antiques inside this French country restaurant. A lengthy menu features seafood, beef, lamb, chicken, and ratatouille. In the summer, there is outdoor service on a leafy patio. *300 Commercial St., tel. 916/265–6248. Reservations advised. AE, MC, V. Closed for lunch Sun.*

National Hotel. This is the oldest continuously operating hotel west of the Rockies (and perhaps the Mississippi), founded in 1856. The menu has a down-home Victorian feel to it, featuring prime rib, steaks, and other hearty offerings. *211 Broad St., tel. 916/265–4551. Reservations advised. AE, MC, V.*

Peter Selaya's California Restaurant. Stained glass, lace curtains, antique sideboards, and old-fashioned high-back oak dining chairs set the mood in this venerable dinner house. The menu features California cuisine, with Italian and French detours and an emphasis on seafood. Desserts are a specialty. *320 Broad St., tel. 916/265–5697. Reservations advised. AE, MC, V. No lunch. Closed Mon.*

Inexpensive

Cirino's. Fine American-Italian food in an informal bar and grill atmosphere is offered in the popular restaurant, housed in a 19th-century building with a handsome period Brunswick back bar. The menu features seafood, pasta, and veal. *309 Broad St., tel. 916/265–2246. Reservations advised. AE, MC, V.*

Posh Nosh. They bake their own bread every day at this restaurant, which offers deli fare and California cuisine. Everything on the lunch menu is available for takeout: sandwiches, salads, and bagel baskets. There's a good wine list, as well as 20 varieties of imported beer and a dozen domestic brands. Dinner features fresh seafood, as well as vegetarian selections. You can dine on the garden patio in nice weather. *318 Broad St., tel. 916/265–6064. Reservations advised for dinner. AE, MC, V.*

Trolley Junction Cafe. The expansive view from the windows of this sparkling new restaurant take full advantage of the setting beside a creek, waterfall, and waterwheel. The menu features prime rib and scampi, as well as good home food, with hearty breakfast choices and salads and sandwiches for lunch. *400 Railroad Ave., tel. 916/265–5259. Reservations advised. AE, DC, MC, V.*

Placerville
Moderate

Smokehouse 1898. An airy two-level restaurant with garden decor offers traditional American food, including barbecued chicken, steak, and ribs, as well as Continental selections. *311 Main St., tel. 916/622–1898. Reservations advised. AE, MC, V. Closed Mon.*

Inexpensive

Apple Cafe. This light, spacious coffee shop has a superb setting, looking out over valleys and mountains. It features homemade dishes including biscuits and gravy, and soup. Breakfast is served all day. *2740 U.S. 50, tel. 916/626–8144. No reservations. No credit cards. No dinner.*

★ **Powell Bros. Steamer Co.** This seafood restaurant sports a nautical-theme decor, old brick walls, and dark wood. The menu is primarily shellfish, served in stews, pastas, chowders, cocktails, and sandwiches, and cooked in big steamers—nothing is fried. *425 Main St., tel. 916/626–1091. No reservations. MC, V.*

Sacramento
Very Expensive

The Firehouse. A restored firehouse, dating from 1853, this opulent restaurant offers fine cuisine, with elaborate Continental entrées. Less formal, but highly appealing, are the outdoor lunches served in the leafy cobbled courtyard to the tinkle of fountains, weather permitting, from April through September. *1112 2nd St., tel. 916/442–4772. Reservations advised. Jacket and tie advised at dinner. AE, MC, V. Closed for lunch Sat., and Sun. and major holidays.*

Expensive

Biba's. Biba Caggiano, a native of Bologna, Italy, and an authority on Italian cuisine with several cookbooks to her name, runs this restaurant that has become a great favorite of leading lights in the state legislature. In addition to such delicate pasta dishes as her baked spinach lasagne and homemade tortelloni, Caggiano offers a great *osso buco* in a marsala sauce with red peppers. The fresh whitefish of the day, baked in parchment with prawns and scallops, is excellent. There are also regional specialties, and the desserts, including a delectable *tiramisu*, are all made on the premises. There is a full bar and extensive wine list. *2801 Capitol Ave., tel. 916/455–2422. Reservations advised. AE, MC, V. Closed for lunch Sat., and Sun.*

Moderate

California Fat's. The ultimate in postmodern decor, this restaurant is built on three levels with a splashy, two-story waterfall, and a menu featuring dishes from the Pacific Rim. Its banana cream pie is famous. *1015 Front St., tel. 916/441–7966. Reservations advised. AE, MC, V. Closed Thanksgiving and Christmas Day.*

Fat City. Once Sam Brannan's general merchandise store, it's now a study in Art Deco, incorporating the Leadville, Colorado, bar behind which the unsinkable Molly Brown served customers before she made off on the *Titanic*. *1001 Front St., tel. 916/446–6768. No reservations. AE, MC, V. Closed Thanksgiving and Christmas.*

Inexpensive

The Virgin Sturgeon. This restaurant is rustic and casual, and right on the Sacramento River; you can dine on the deck and watch the water rush by. The simple American menu offers seafood, steaks, chicken, and salads, but no desserts. *1577 Garden Hwy., tel. 916/921–2694. No reservations. MC, V. Closed Thanksgiving and Christmas.*

★ **The Old Spaghetti Factory.** An old Western Pacific Railroad station has been transformed into an Italian family restaurant, complete with fringed lampshades and velvet settees. Menu highlights are the pasta specialties, crusty bread, and spumoni. *1910 J. St., tel. 916/443–2862. No reservations. MC, V. Closed for lunch weekends, and Christmas Day.*

Sonora
Moderate
★

Hemingway's Cafe Restaurant. The menu here, starting from Continental-Californian, is eclectic and downright exotic, with such delicacies as Mongolian lamb chops, Cajun shrimp, gourmet pizzas, and sherry trifle: The chef does not lack for imagination. There is live music, and a dinner theater on occasion as well. The wine list features award-winning selections, and many unusual imported beers are stocked. *362 S. Stewart St., tel. 209/532–4900. Reservations advised. AE, MC, V. Closed Mon. and Sun. most of winter.*

Sutter Creek
Expensive

Pelargonium. An old California bungalow has been renovated as a restaurant. The walls of the small dining rooms are crowded with art. The California cuisine features seafood and new specials weekly, such as trout stuffed with crab, or roast lamb served with three-cheese polenta and tomato-basil topping. *Hwy. 49 at Hanford St., tel. 209/267–5008. Reservations advised. No lunch. Closed Sun.*

Moderate

Ron and Nancy's Palace. This popular, unpretentious restaurant offers Continental cuisine, with daily specials such as chicken marsala and veal piccata. The lunch menu includes quiches and crepes. Senior citizens receive discounts. *76 Main St., tel. 209/267–1355. Reservations advised. AE, MC, V. Closed Mon. and Tues.*

Lodging

Among the treasures of the Gold Country today are its inns, many of them beautifully restored buildings dating back to the 1850s and 1860s and furnished with period pieces. If you came here for the history, there's no better way to get a taste of it. In Sacramento, most of the lodgings listed are all in the downtown area, close to Old Sacramento, the capitol, and Sutter's Fort.

Highly recommended hotels are indicated by a star ★.

Category	Cost*
Expensive	over $80
Moderate	$45–$80
Inexpensive	under $45

*double room, not including tax

Amador City
Moderate

Mine House Inn. On a steep hillside overlooking tiny Amador City, the headquarters of the Keystone Consolidated Mining Co., more than a century old, have been transformed into an inn furnished with Victorian antiques. Continental breakfast is included. *Box 245, Hwy. 49, 95601, tel. 209/267–5900. 7 rooms. Facilities: pool (open Memorial Day–late Sept.). No pets. No credit cards.*

Angels Camp
Moderate

Gold Country Inn. This modern, air-conditioned two-story motel provides queen-size beds and a coffee maker in each room. There is also a coffee shop next door. *Box 188, 720 S. Main St., Hwy. 49, 95222, tel. 209/736–4611. 40 rooms. Facilities: cable TV. AE, D, MC, V.*

Auburn
Moderate

Auburn Inn. This beige and brown multistory inn, built in 1984, is exceptionally well maintained. The decor is contemporary, in teal and pastel colors. There are king- and queen-size beds, suites, nonsmoking rooms, and rooms with facilities for the handicapped. *1875 Auburn Ravine Rd., Foresthill exit north from I–80, 95603, tel. 916/885–1800 or 800/272–1444. 81 rooms. Facilities: pool, spa, laundry, cable TV. AE, DC, MC, V.*

Inexpensive–
Moderate

Country Squire Inn. This three-story motel is built around a spacious central area and has modern rooms decorated in browns and blues. Suites are available. There is a restaurant next door. *13480 Lincoln Way, Foresthill exit east off I–80, 95603, tel. 916/885–7025. 80 rooms. Facilities: pool, spa, cable TV. Pets allowed. AE, D, DC, MC, V.*

Coloma
Expensive

Coloma Country Inn. A restored Victorian bed-and-breakfast that was built in 1852, this inn is set on 5 acres and offers fishing and canoeing on its own pond. The rooms have antique double beds and private sitting areas; the decor features quilts, stenciled friezes, and fresh flowers. Country breakfasts are served. Hot-air ballooning and white-water rafting can be arranged. Reservations recommended. *Box 502, 345 High St., 95613, tel. 916/622–6919. 5 rooms, 2 with shared bath. Advance notice needed for children. No pets. No smoking. No credit cards.*

Moderate–
Expensive
★

Vineyard House. This 1878 country inn, outfitted with handsome antiques and thick carpets, is built on the site of a prizewinning winery, whose owner turned to wine making when the Gold Rush petered out. The setting is romantic; the ruins of the wine cellars lie behind flower gardens. Full breakfast is included. The restaurant and lounge are open every evening from May through September and Friday, Saturday, and Sunday in winter. *Box 176, Cold Springs Rd., off Hwy. 49, 95613, tel. 916/622–2217. 7 rooms, 6 with shared baths. No pets. No smoking. AE, MC, V.*

Columbia
Moderate–
Expensive

City Hotel. The rooms in this restored 1856 hostelry are elaborately furnished with period antiques. Two rooms have balconies overlooking Main Street, and the four parlor rooms open onto a second-floor sitting room. Rooms have private half-baths with showers nearby; robes and slippers are provided. Continental breakfast is served in the upstairs parlor, and a dining room is open for lunch and dinner. There are weekend packages including dinner and theater tickets. *Main St., Columbia State Park, Box 1870, 95310, tel. 209/532–1479. 9 rooms with ½ bath. Facilities: saloon. No pets. AE, MC, V.*

Fallon Hotel. The state of California recently restored this 1857 hotel to Victorian grandeur. The lobby and rooms are furnished with 1890s antiques. Each accommodation has a private half-bath; there are also men's and women's showers. Continental breakfast is served; if you occupy one of the five balcony rooms, you can sit outside with your coffee and watch the town wake up. One room is equipped for the handicapped. *Washington St., Columbia State Park, next to Fallon House Theater, Box 1870, 95310, tel. 209/532–1470. 14 rooms with ½ bath. No smoking. AE, MC, V.*

Inexpensive–Moderate

Columbia Gem Motel. The rustic cottages and six simple air-conditioned motel rooms here are set among pine trees. Senior citizens receive discounts. *Columbia Hwy., 1 mi from Columbia State Park, Box 874, 22131 Parrot's Ferry Rd., 95310, tel. 209/532–4508. 12 rooms. Facilities: cable TV. MC, V.*

Downieville
Moderate–Expensive

Saundra Dyer's Resort and Bed and Breakfast. The enterprising owner of this small, cheerful, spotlessly clean establishment on the Yuba River has recently given the place a Victorian makeover, and now offers package weekend package deals including dinner at the local eatery, Cirino's at the Forks. Some kitchenettes are available. *9 River St., 1st right from Hwy. 49, Box 406, 95936, tel. 916/289–3308 or 800/696–3308. 14 rooms. Facilities: pool. AE, MC, V.*

Grass Valley
Expensive
★

Murphy's Inn. An immaculate white house in a leafy setting (there is a giant sequoia in the back yard and some eye-catching topiaries), this outstanding bed-and-breakfast, built in 1866, was once the mansion of a gold-mine owner. Some guest rooms have the original wallpaper, four have fireplaces, and many have gas chandeliers. The spacious veranda is festooned with ivy. There are award-winning full breakfasts; Belgian waffles and eggs Benedict are specialties. *318 Neal St., Colfax Hwy. 174 exit from Hwy. 49, left on S. Auburn St., 95945, tel. 916/ 273–6873. 8 rooms. Facilities: pool, swim spa. No pets (kennel facilities nearby). No smoking. AE, MC, V.*

Moderate–Expensive

Holbrooke Hotel. Founded in 1851, this Gold Rush hostelry has hosted the likes of Mark Twain, actress Lola Montez, Ulysses S. Grant, and a stream of presidents over the years. The hotel was lovingly polished to its Victorian luster and reopened in 1989. Its saloon is one of the oldest operating west of the Mississippi. The Holbrooke offers a varied selection of rooms furnished with antiques, some with balconies and sitting areas. Service is old-fashioned friendly, and complimentary Continental breakfast is dished up in the cozy library room. *1212 W. Main St., 95945, tel. 916/273–1353 or 800/933–7077. 27 rooms. Facilities: restaurant, saloon. No pets. AE, MC, V.*

Moderate

Best Western Gold Country Inn. This well-kept two-story motel has a contemporary decor in warm colors; 58 rooms have small refrigerators, and 16 have kitchens. Some rooms adjoin each other. Complimentary Continental breakfast is included. *11972 Sutton Way, Brunswick Rd. exit east from Hwy. 49, 95945, tel. 916/273–1393 or 800/528–1234. 84 rooms. Facilities: pool, spa. Small pets allowed. AE, D, DC, MC, V.*

Jackson
Moderate

Best Western Amador Inn. An up-to-date motel with rooms decorated in blue, rose, and light brown colors. Some rooms have fireplaces, and a few kitchenettes are available. *200 S. Hwy. 49, Box 758, 95642, tel. 209/223–0211 or 800/528–1234. 119 rooms. Facilities: restaurant, lounge, pool, cable TV. Pets allowed. AE, D, DC, MC, V.*

Jamestown
Moderate

Jamestown Hotel. Each room in this old brick building with Gold Rush-era furnishings is individually decorated with comforters, iron beds, rocking chairs, flags, and other 19th-century artifacts, as well as a private Victorian bath. Continental breakfast is included. From October through April rates are discounted 20%. *18153 Main St., Box 539, 95327, tel. 209/984– 3902. 8 rooms with bath. No pets. AE, D, MC, V.*

Sonora Country Inn. This three-story motel, opened in 1986, is decorated in subdued pastel colors. Continental breakfast is included. Half the rooms are for nonsmokers; there are facilities for the handicapped. *Hwy. 108 between Jamestown and Sonora, 18755 Charbroullian La., 95327, tel. 209/984–0315 or, in CA, 800/847–2211. 60 rooms. Facilities: pool. AE, D, DC, MC, V.*

Murphys
Expensive

Dunbar House. This restored 1880 home in a pleasant setting is filled with antiques and quilts, and offers refreshments, complimentary wine, and a full country breakfast. *271 Jones St., 95247, tel. 209/728-2897. 4 rooms. No pets. No smoking. MC, V.*

Moderate

Murphys Hotel. The rooms are rustic in this restored 1855 hotel, which was visited by Mark Twain and Ulysses S. Grant. It has retained its period charm, but the modern rooms in the adjoining motel are more comfortable. Children are welcome. *457 Main St., 95247, tel. 209/728-3454. 28 rooms. Facilities: restaurant, lounge. No pets. AE, D, MC, V.*

Nevada City
Very Expensive

Grandmere's Bed and Breakfast Inn. This large, white, wedding cake of a house was built in 1856 and restored in 1985 in a country French style. The antiques, fabrics, and flower arrangements are superb, and the gardens beautifully landscaped. Full breakfast is included. *449 Broad St., 95959, tel. 916/265-4660. 7 rooms. No smoking. MC, V.*

Expensive–
Very Expensive

The Red Castle Inn. A state landmark, this 1860 Gothic Revival mansion stands on a hillside overlooking Nevada City. Its brick exterior is trimmed with white icicle woodwork, and its porches and gardens add to the charm. The rooms, some of which look over the town, have antique furnishings and are elaborately decorated. A full buffet breakfast is served. *109 Prospect St., 95959, tel. 916/265-5135. 6 rooms with bath, 2 with shared bath. No pets. MC, V.*

Moderate

Northern Queen. This bright, pleasant, two-story motel has a lovely creekside setting. Accommodations include new or remodeled motel units; eight two-story chalets and eight rustic cottages with efficiency kitchens are located in a secluded, wooded area. Rooms have small refrigerators. Facilities for the handicapped are available. *400 Railroad Ave., Sacramento St. exit off Hwy. 49, 95959, tel. 916/265-5824. 85 rooms. Facilities: restaurant, heated pool, spa, cable TV. No pets. AE, DC, MC, V.*

Placerville
Inexpensive–
Moderate

Days Inn. The clean and comfortable rooms here have bright flowered bedspreads and curtains. Continental breakfast is included, and there is a coffee shop next door. *1332 Broadway, Hwy. 50 east from Hwy. 49, then Schnell School exit south, 95667, tel. 916/622-3124 or 800/325-2525. 45 rooms. Facilities: cable TV. AE, D, DC, MC, V.*

Sacramento
Expensive

Aunt Abigail's. This beautifully appointed Colonial Revival mansion near the center of town bills itself as a home-away-from-home since 1912. There is a piano, and games are available to play in the elegant living room, and the decor is soothingly Edwardian. A copious breakfast includes home-baked breads and an entrée, and each bedroom has books, flowers, and an old-fashioned radio. *2120 G St., 95816, tel. 916/441-5007 or 800/858-1568. 6 rooms. D, DC, MC, V.*

Holiday Inn Capitol Plaza. This high-rise hotel offers fine views of the Sacramento River and the capitol building from its upper-floor rooms and top-floor restaurant and lounge. Old Sacramento is just across the road, and the capitol is eight blocks away. The modern rooms and suites are furnished in pastels and accented with brass. *300 J St., 95814, tel. 916/446-0100 or 800/465-4329. 370 rooms, 5 suites. Facilities: 2 restaurants, 2 lounges, pool, sauna, health club, gift shop, garage. Pets allowed. AE, D, DC, MC, V.*

★ **Hotel El Rancho Resort.** This 17-acre resort offers outstanding recreational facilities; the rooms and suites are decorated in contemporary pastels with wicker accents. There is an excellent restaurant and lounge. *1029 W. Capitol Ave., Jefferson Blvd. exit north off Business Loop 80, West Sacramento, 95691, tel. 916/371–6731 or 800/952–5566 in CA. 245 rooms. Facilities: limited room service; kitchenettes; pool; sauna; lighted tennis courts; racquetball; fitness center with aerobics, Nautilus, and free weights; 1.2-mi par course; massage. AE, D, DC, MC, V.*

Sterling House. The former Carter Hawley Hale mansion, the handsome residence of the famous Weinstock's department store's founding family, was built in 1895 and turned into a hotel in 1989, with no expense spared. Opulent details include the lobby's marble floors and Oriental rugs, as well as the four-poster and canopy beds and marble bathrooms. *1300 H St., 95814, tel. 916/448–1300 or 800/365–7660. 12 rooms. Facilities: full room service, whirlpool baths. No pets. No smoking. AE, DC, MC, V.*

Moderate **Best Western Sandman.** The contemporary rooms are decorated in shades of rose, teal, and paprika in this two-story motel on the banks of the Sacramento River. The location is convenient, at a freeway exit out of Old Sacramento. Senior citizens receive a discount. *236 Jibboom St., Richards Blvd. exit west from I–5, 95814, tel. 916/443–6515 or 800/528–1234. 115 rooms. Facilities: restaurant, pool, Jacuzzi. AE, D, DC, MC, V.*

Inexpensive **Motel Orleans.** This is a bright, well-maintained two-story economy hotel with simple contemporary rooms, just one freeway exit from Old Sacramento. A coffee shop is adjacent. *228 Jibboom St., Richards Blvd. exit west from I–5, 95814, tel. 916/443–4811. 70 rooms. Facilities: pool. Dogs allowed with refundable $25 deposit. AE, D, DC, MC, V.*

Sonora **Best Western Sonora Oaks Motor Hotel.** This 1984 motel is located away from Sonora's crowded central area. The style is modern, with print bedspreads accenting the blue, green, or burgundy colors of the rooms and suites. *19551 Hess Ave., 3 mi from Hwy. 49 on Hwy. 108, 95730, tel. 209/533–4400 or 800/528–1234. 72 rooms. Facilities: restaurant, lounge, pool, spa. AE, D, DC, MC, V.*

Moderate

Gunn House Bed & Breakfast. The original adobe house on this site was built in 1850. It was the first two-story building in town, the home of a newspaperman from Philadelphia who championed the rights of Chinese laborers. It has since been enlarged, restored, and furnished with antiques and air-conditioning. Continental breakfast is served in the old-fashioned lounge on the premises. *286 S. Washington St., 95370, tel. 209/532–3421. 24 rooms. Facilities: pool. No pets. AE, D, MC, V.*

Ryan House Bed and Breakfast Inn. Rose gardens add to the pleasure of this 1855 farm homestead, furnished with antiques and wood-burning stoves. There are two parlors, and a full breakfast is served. *153 S. Shepherd St., 95370, tel. 209/533–3445 or 800/831–4897. 3 rooms with bath. AE, D, MC, V.*

Sonora Inn. This inn stands on the site of the first hotel established by a woman in the Gold Country; its original Victorian facade was plastered over in the 1920s when Spanish Mission architecture came into fashion. The roomy lobby, restaurant, and lounge have tiled floors. Some rooms are in the attached newer motel building. *160 S. Washington St., 95370, tel. 209/*

532–7468 or 800/321–5261. 61 rooms. Facilities: pool. AE, MC, V.

Sutter Creek
Expensive
★

The Foxes Bed & Breakfast. The rooms in this house, built in 1857, are handsome, with high ceilings, antique beds, and lofty armoires topped with floral arrangements. All rooms have queen-size beds; three have wood-burning fireplaces. A menu allows guests to select a full breakfast, cooked to order and brought to each room on a silver service. *Box 159, 77 Main St., 95685, tel. 209/267–5882. 6 rooms. No pets. No smoking. D, MC, V.*

Hanford House Bed & Breakfast. A modern brick building that evokes an earlier period with its California antiques and spacious rooms. The beds are queen-size, and a hearty Continental breakfast is served. One room offers wheelchair access, and there is a rooftop deck. *61 Hanford St., Hwy. 49, Box 1450, 95685, tel. 209/267–0747. 9 rooms with bath. No pets. No smoking. D, MC, V.*

Moderate–
Expensive
★

Sutter Creek Inn Bed & Breakfast. This white and green New England–style house, dating from the 1850s, is something of a legend in the bed-and-breakfast business for its painstaking attention to detail. The rooms are comfortable and individually decorated, furnished with a homey melange of antiques, woodburning fireplaces, and unique hanging beds, suspended on chains from the ceiling. The gardens are spacious, with a variety of tables, chairs, and chaises, and the parlor is stocked with books and games. Breakfast, served family style, is lavish. *Box 385, 75 Main St., 95685, tel. 209/267–5606. 19 rooms. No credit cards.*

8 Lake Tahoe

With a shoreline more than 6,000 feet above sea level in the Sierra Nevada, Lake Tahoe is one of California's most spectacular natural attractions—even if a third of the lake is in Nevada. Visitors to the 482-square-mile Lake Tahoe Basin are also divided. About half of them arrive intent on sightseeing, hiking, fishing, camping, and boating, while the rest head directly for the casinos on the Nevada side of the lake where gambling is legal. During some summer weekends it seems that absolutely every tourist—100,000 at peak periods—is in a car on the 72-mile shoreline, looking for historic sites and uncrowded beaches, or parking places, restaurants, motels. But the crowds and congestion don't exist at a vantage point overlooking Emerald Bay early in the morning, or on a trail in the national forests that ring the basin, or on a sunset cruise on the lake itself, which is 22 miles long and 12 miles wide.

Placid vistas contrast with the lake's violent formation and dramatic history. About 25 million years ago the Tahoe Basin sank between the uplifting Sierra Nevada and an eastern offshoot of the Carson Range. Lava flowing from Mt. Pluto on the north blocked the basin's outlet. During the Ice Age, glaciers scoured the landscape. Now mountains rise 4,000 feet above the lake, and as much as 500 inches of snow falls in the winter at upper elevations. Sixty-three streams flow into the lake, but only the Truckee River flows out, and it never reaches the ocean. The lake's deepest point is 1,645 feet, and the brilliant blue and blue-green color can be breathtaking. Protecting its clarity is a continuing and often controversial campaign.

For centuries, before the lake was sighted by explorers Kit Carson and John C. Fremont in 1844, it was a summer gathering place and sacred site for Washoe Indians. The California Gold Rush lured emigrants over the treacherous Sierra north and south of the lake, and Nevada's silver bonanza enticed prospectors east from California a few years later. Hotels and resorts sprang up in the 1850s and 1860s, but the Tahoe Basin's forests were nearly stripped of trees for silver-mining operations. By the turn of the century wealthy Californians were building lakeshore estates, some of which survive. Improved roads brought the less affluent in the 1920s and 1930s, when modest, rustic bungalows began to fill the wooded shoreline. The first casinos opened in the 1940s, and ski resorts also brought a development boom as the lake became a year-round attraction. Road construction and other building projects, however, washed soil and minerals into the lake, leading to a growth of algae that threatened its fabled clarity. (Objects can still be seen to a depth of 75 feet.) The environmental movement gained strength in the 1970s, resulting in a moratorium on new construction on the lakeshore and development of a master plan for future growth. A major redevelopment program has been approved that gradually will add new accommodations to the lakeshore while retaining its natural beauty.

The lake has long been a summer refuge from California's hot Central Valley and the Nevada desert. July and August daytime temperatures are in the 70s, with nighttime lows in the 40s. In the winter, the average daytime high is 36 degrees, the nighttime low 18. Ski resorts open at the end of November, sometimes with machine-made snow, and operate as late as May. Organized summer activities begin at the end of May, when the Desolation Wilderness Area U.S. Forest Service Visitors Center opens on the south shore. Most accommodations, restaurants, and some parks are open year-round, although September and October, when crowds have thinned but the weather is still pleasant, may be the most satisfying time to visit Lake Tahoe.

Getting Around

By Plane Two airports provide good access. **Reno Cannon International,** 58 miles northeast of the lake, is served by a number of national and regional airlines. Rental cars are available from the major agencies. There is shuttle bus service to the lake during peak travel periods, and the largest hotel/casinos offer their own transportation, for a fee. **Lake Tahoe Airport** on Highway 50, 3 miles south of the lake's shore, is served by American Airlines' **American Eagle** service (tel. 800/433–7300) with smaller jet planes from San Francisco, San Jose, and Los Angeles. Rental cars are also available.

By Train There is an **Amtrak** station in Truckee (tel. 800/USA–RAIL).

By Bus **South Tahoe Area Ground Express (STAGE;** tel. 916/573–2080) runs 24 hours along U.S. 50 and through the neighborhoods of South Lake Tahoe. On the lake's west and north shores, **Tahoe Area Regional Transit, known as TART** (tel. 916/581–6365 or 800/736–6365), runs between Tahoma (from Meeks Bay in summer) and Incline Village daily from 6:30 AM to 6:30 PM. **Greyhound Bus** lines (tel. 916/587– 3822 or 702/322–4511 for 24-hour fare and schedule information) run among Sacramento, Truckee, and Reno and between Sacramento and South Lake Tahoe. Free shuttle buses run among the casinos, major ski resorts, and motels of South Lake Tahoe.

By Car Lake Tahoe is 198 miles northeast of San Francisco, a four- to five-hour drive, depending on weather and traffic. The major route is I–80, which cuts through the Sierra Nevada about 14 miles north of the lake; from there state Highways 89 and 267 reach the north shore. U.S. 50, which begins at I–80 in Sacramento, is the more direct highway to the south shore. U.S. 395 runs south toward the lake from Reno. These are all-weather highways, although there may be delays as snow is cleared during major storms. Tire chains should be carried, and are provided by car-rental agencies, from October to May. Avoid the heavy traffic leaving the San Francisco area for Tahoe on Friday afternoons and returning on Sunday afternoons.

By Taxi Taxi service is plentiful in South Lake Tahoe. On the north shore, try **North Shore Taxi** (tel. 916/546–3181) and **Truckee Taxi Service** (Truckee, tel. 916/587–6336).

Guided Tours

Gray Line (tel. 702/329–1147) runs daily tours to Emerald Bay, South Lake Tahoe, Carson City, and Virginia City. Other tour providers are **Showboat Lines** (Box 12119, Zephyr Cove, NV 89448, tel. 702/588–6688) and **Tahoe Limousine Service** (Box 9909, South Lake Tahoe 96158, tel. 916/577–2727).

Important Addresses and Numbers

Tourist
Information

Lake Tahoe Visitors Authority (Box 16299, South Lake Tahoe 95706, tel. 916/544–5050 or 800/288–2463 for information and lodging reservations).
North Lake Tahoe Chamber of Commerce (Box 884, Tahoe City 96145, tel. 916/581–6900).
Tahoe North Visitors and Convention Bureau (Box 5578, Tahoe City 96145, tel. 916/583–3494 or 800/824–6348) for airline, car-rental, and lodging information and reservations, as well as honeymoon and ski packages.
Ski Phone (tel. 415/864–6440) for around-the-clock ski reports and weather information.
Road Conditions (tel. 916/577–3550).

Emergencies

The emergency number throughout the Tahoe area is 911. This will put you in touch with police, fire, and medical help. Make a point of knowing your location.

Exploring

Numbers in the margin correspond to points of interest on the Lake Tahoe map.

The most common way to explore the Lake Tahoe area is to drive the 72-mile road that follows the shore, through wooded flatlands and past beaches, climbing to vistas on the rugged west side of the lake and descending to the busiest commercial developments and casinos. It takes about three hours, but it can be frustrating to drive during peak visiting periods, such as summer holiday weekends when the road is clogged with tourist traffic. Obviously, it's best to stop at parks, picnic areas, and scenic lookouts rather than sightseeing entirely from a car. There are many hiking trails, some of them easy, paved paths; with access from the shoreline highway, they offer a quick escape from the traffic. Free maps and information are available at the U.S. Forest Service Visitors Center (*see* below). The scenic highway around the lake is marked as Highway 28 on the north and northeast shore, U.S. 50 on the south, and Highway 89 on the southwest and west. Highway 89 may be closed at D. L. Bliss State Park when there is a heavy snowfall.

❶ We'll begin a tour around the lake at **Stateline** on the California–Nevada border. Traveling west along U.S. 50, turn
❷ left at Ski Run Boulevard and drive up to the **Heavenly Ski Resort.** Whether you're a skier or not, you'll want to ride 2,000 feet up on the 50-passenger Heavenly Tram partway up the mountain to 8,200 feet. There you'll find a memorable view of Lake Tahoe and the Nevada desert. The Top of the Tram restaurant, open daily during tram hours, offers basic American food and cafeteria service. It serves lunch, dinner, and Sunday brunch in summer, lunch only in winter. *Tram information, tel. 702/586–7000. Dinner reservations, tel. 702/586–7000 ext. 6347. Tram hours, June–Sept., daily 10–10; Nov.–May 9–4. Round trip: $10.50 adults, $6.50 senior citizens and children under 12.*

Return to U.S. 50 and turn left, heading west toward South Lake Tahoe, the largest community on the lake. As the lakeshore route becomes Highway 89 in Tahoe Valley, commercial development gives way to more wooded national forest lands.

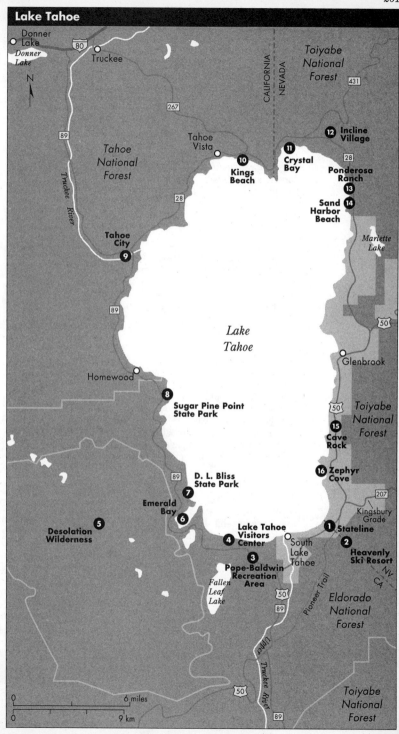

Lake Tahoe

❸ You'll notice pleasant bike trails well off the road. At **Pope-Baldwin Recreation Area,** take in the Tallac Historic Site. Three grand mansions built as summer cottages for wealthy San Franciscans almost 100 years ago have been restored. Guided tours of the Pope House and a museum at the Baldwin Estate are available in the summer. *Tel. 916/541–5227. Admission free, tour $2. Tours given daily Memorial Day–Labor Day.*

❹ The **Lake Tahoe Visitors Center** on Taylor Creek is operated by the U.S. Forest Service and offers far more than answers to questions. This stretch of lakefront is a microcosm of the area's natural history. You can visit the site of a Washoe Indian settlement; walk self-guided trails through meadow, marsh, and forest; and inspect the Stream Profile Chamber, an underground, underwater display with windows so that visitors can look in to Taylor Creek (in the fall you may see spawning salmon digging their nests). *Tel. 916/573–2674 in season; at other times of the year, 916/573–2600. Open June–Sept. daily, Oct. weekends.*

❺ To the west is the vast **Desolation Wilderness,** a 63,473-acre preserve of granite peaks, glacial valleys, subalpine forests, and more than 80 lakes. Access for hiking, fishing, and camping is by trail from outside the wilderness preserve; Meeks Bay and Echo Lake are two starting points. Permits (free) are required for access at any time of the year from the Forest Service Visitors Center or headquarters (870 Emerald Bay Rd., Suite 1, South Lake Tahoe, CA 96150, tel. 916/573–2600).

❻ The winding road next takes you to **Emerald Bay,** famed for its jewellike shape and colors. The road is high above the lake at this point; from Emerald Bay Lookout you can survey the whole scene, which includes Tahoe's only island. From the lookout a steep, mile-long trail leads down to **Vikingsholm,** a 38-room estate built in the 1920s by Lora Knight, who was inspired by Norwegian and Swedish castles of the 11th century. A rugged stone building with a partial sod roof, it is furnished with Scandinavian antiques and reproductions. Be warned: the hike back up is steep. *Tel. 916/525–7277. Admission: $2 adults, $1 children under 18. Open July–Labor Day daily 10–4.*

Another way to see Emerald Bay close up is to take one of the daily cruises across its waters. The *Tahoe Queen,* a glass-bottom sternwheeler, travels year-round on 2½-hour cruises from Ski Run Marina off U.S. 50 in South Lake Tahoe. (Tel. 916/541–3364. Daytime cruise $14 adults, $5 children under 12; sunset/dinner cruise fare: $18 adults, $9.50 children under 12. Fares do not include food or beverages.) From late April through early November the **MS** *Dixie* sails from Zephyr Cove Marina to Emerald Bay. (Tel. 702/588–3508. Daytime, breakfast, brunch, dinner, and cocktail cruises. Fare: $12 to $31 adults, $4 to $9.50 children 4–12, depending on type of cruise; food and beverages included in fares.) **Tahoe Cruises** offers a winter ski shuttle, including bus to ski areas, from the south shore to Tahoe City. (Tel. 916/541–3364. Fare: $18 adults, $9 children.)

❼ Beyond Emerald Bay is **D. L. Bliss State Park,** which shares 6 miles of shoreline and 168 family campsites with the bay. At the north end of the park is Rubicon Point, which overlooks one of the lake's deepest spots. *Tel. 916/525–7277; day use fee: $5 per vehicle, $14 per campsite; closed in winter.*

8 The main attraction at **Sugar Pine Point State Park** is the **Ehrman Mansion,** a stately, stone-and-shingle 1903 summer home that displays the "rustic" aspirations of the era's wealthy residents. It is furnished in period style. *Tel. 916/525–7232 or 916/525–7982 in season. Admission free. State Park day use fee: $5 per vehicle. Open July–Labor Day, daily 11–4.*

9 At **Tahoe City,** Highway 89 turns north from the lake to Squaw Valley; Highway 28 continues around the lake. You'll cross the Truckee River, the lake's only outlet. Fanny Bridge is the best observation point to see the river's giant trout and the rows of visitors leaning over the railing, which gave the bridge its name. The **Gatekeeper's Log Cabin Museum** in Tahoe City provides one of the best records of the area's past, and displays Washoe and Paiute Indian artifacts as well as late-19th- to early 20th-century settlers' memorabilia. *130 W. Lake Blvd., tel. 916/583–1762. Admission free. Open May 15–Oct. 1, daily 11–5.*

The museum also oversees the nearby **Watson Cabin,** a 1909 log cabin, built by Robert M. Watson and his son, with turn-of-the-century furnishings and costumed docents who act out the daily life of a typical pioneer family. *560 N. Lake Blvd., tel. 916/ 583–8717 or 916/583–1762. Admission free. Open June 15–Labor Day, daily noon–4.*

10 Traveling east on Highway 28 you will reach the 28-acre **Kings Beach State Recreation Area,** one of the lakeshore parks open **11** year-round; **Crystal Bay** just over the Nevada border, with the towering Cal-Neva hotel/casino; and the affluent residential **12** community of **Incline Village.**

13 The **Ponderosa Ranch** is east of Incline Village on Highway 28. The site of the popular television series "Bonanza" includes the Cartwrights' ranch house, a western town, and a saloon; pony rides and hayrides are available. *Tel. 702/831–0691. Admission: $7.50 adults, $5.50 children 5–11. Open late April–Oct., daily 9:30–5.*

14 **Sand Harbor Beach** is one of the lake's finest, and so popular it's sometimes filled to capacity by 11 AM on summer weekends. A pop music festival is held here in July, and in August there's a Shakespeare festival. *Festival information, tel. 916/583–9048.*

Now you meet U.S. 50 again and travel past scenic vistas. The **15** road passes through **Cave Rock,** through 25 yards of solid stone. **16** Six miles farther, you'll come to **Zephyr Cove,** with a beach and a marina that is home to tour boats. Just ahead you'll see the towers of the casinos at Stateline, and you'll have come full circle.

What to See and Do with Children

Except for gambling and the floor shows in Nevada, most attractions and activities around the lake are family-oriented. The Forest Service is the best resource, and the Visitors Center at Taylor Creek the prime site. In the summer, the center has discovery walks and nighttime campfires with singing and marshmallow roasts. There are Native American exhibits at the Visitors Center and at the Gatekeeper's Museum in Tahoe City. Other options range from bike rentals to flashy video arcades in many casinos.

In the winter **Granlibakken** (tel. 916/583–6203), just south of Tahoe City on Highway 89, rents saucers. Ski areas have classes for children as young as three. **Borges Carriage and Sleigh Rides** in South Lake Tahoe (tel. 916/541–2953) and some ski resorts have sleigh rides.

Off the Beaten Track

For a new perspective that goes above the mountain trams, **CalVada Seaplanes Inc.** (tel. 916/525–7143) provides rides over the lake for $43–$77 per person, depending on the length of the trip. For a closer look at the area's scenery, **Tahoe Sierra Recreation** (tel. 916/583–0123) rents mountain bikes for $10 (2 hours), $15 (½-day), and $20 (full day), including helmets. A 4-mile paved trail follows the Truckee River to River Ranch. A 15-mile trail runs along the lake shore.

There's never a shortage of ice at the top of Squaw Valley where the **Olympic Ice Pavillion** (tel. 916/583–6985) offers year-round ice skating with a view daily 10–9. Skate rentals are available.

A tragic reminder of the High Sierra's past is **Donner Memorial State Park** just off I–80, 2 miles west of Truckee. During the ferocious winter of 1846–47 a westbound party led by George Donner was trapped here. The Pioneer Monument stands on a pedestal 22 feet high, the depth of the snow that winter. Of 89 people in the group, only 47 lived; some survived by eating animal hides and some resorted to cannibalism. The Immigrant Museum offers a slide show hourly about the Donner Party's plight; other displays include the history of other settlers, and railroad development through the Sierra. *Tel. 916/587–3841. Admission: $2 adults, $1 children 6–17. Open daily 10–4, closed noon–1 early Sept.–late-Nov. Closed Jan. 1, Thanksgiving, Dec. 25.*

Old West facades line the main street of nearby **Truckee.** This is a favorite stopover for people traveling from San Francisco to the north shore of Lake Tahoe. Fine art galleries and upscale boutiques are plentiful, but you will also find low-key diners, discount skiwear, and an old-fashioned five-and-dime store. For a map outlining a walking tour of historic Truckee, stop by the information booth in the Amtrak depot.

Participant Sports

For most of the popular sports at Lake Tahoe, summer or winter, you won't have to bring much equipment with you, an important factor if you're traveling by air or have limited space. Bicycles and boats are readily available for rent at Lake Tahoe. Golf clubs can be rented at several area courses. Most of the ski resorts have rental shops.

Golf These courses in the Lake Tahoe area have food facilities, pro shops, cart rentals, and putting greens.

Edgewood Tahoe. 18 holes, par 72. Driving range. Cart mandatory. *U.S. 50 and Lake Pkwy., behind Horizon Casino, Stateline, tel. 702/588–3566. Open 7–6.*
Incline Championship. 18 holes, par 72. Driving range. Cart mandatory. *955 Fairway Blvd., Incline Village, tel. 702/832–1144. Open 6 AM–6:30 PM.*

Incline Executive. 18 holes, par 58. Cart mandatory. *690 Wilson Way, Incline Village, tel.702/832–1150. Open 7:30–5:30.*

Lake Tahoe Golf Course. 18 holes, par 71. Driving range. *U.S. 50 between South Lake Tahoe Airport and Meyers, tel. 916/ 577–0788. Open 6 AM–8 PM.*

Northstar-at-Tahoe. 18 holes, par 72. Driving range. Cart mandatory before 12:30. *Hwy. 267 between Truckee and Kings Beach, tel. 916/587–0290. Open 7:30 AM–dark.*

Tahoe City Golf Course. 9 holes, par 33. Pull carts. *Hwy. 28, Tahoe City, tel. 916/583–1516.*

Skiing The Tahoe Basin ski resorts boast the largest concentration of skiing in the country and its most breathtaking winter scenery. There are 12 downhill ski resorts and eight Nordic ski centers, with more cross-country skiing available on thousands of acres of public forests and parklands. Among the resorts are Heavenly Ski Resort, the nation's largest, covering 20 square miles, and Squaw Valley, site of the 1960 Winter Olympics. There are many ski packages: lodging and lift tickets; lift tickets, rentals, and lessons; airline tickets, lodging, skiing, and auto rental. Ask questions when you are planning an excursion and you may find some bargains. Many resorts at Tahoe offer free or discounted skiing to beginners.

Free shuttle-bus service is available between most ski resorts and hotels and lodges.

Alpine Meadows Ski Area. The high base elevation and a variety of sun exposures give Alpine the longest season in Tahoe, mid-November to Memorial Day. Of its 2,000 acres, 25% are beginner, 40% intermediate, 35% advanced. Its 12 lifts handle 16,000 skiers per hour. The summit elevation is 8,637 feet; base, 6,835 feet; vertical drop, 1,800 feet. The longest run is 2.5 miles. There is a ski school and a children's snow school for three- to six-year-olds. The expansive day lodge has a large sundeck, restaurant, bar, and cafeteria. There is an overnight RV area. *North shore, between Truckee and Tahoe City on Hwy. 89, Box 5279, Tahoe City 96145, tel. 916/583–4232 or 800/824–6348 for lodging reservations. Snow information, tel. 916/583–6914.*

Diamond Peak at Ski Incline. This north-shore resort at Incline Village specializes in family skiing. The terrain is 20% beginner, 55% intermediate, 25% advanced. Its seven lifts can handle 3,700 skiers per hour. The summit is 8,540 feet; base, 6,700 feet; vertical drop, 1,840 feet. The longest run is 2.5 miles. Family ticket rates and special all-inclusive "Learn-to-Ski" packages are available. The Child Ski Development Center is for ages 4–7. The full-facility base lodge has a mountaintop barbecue. *1210 Ski Way, Incline Village, NV 89451, tel. 702/832–1177 or 800/468–2463.*

Diamond Peak Cross Country. This high-elevation cross-country ski area, opened in 1989, offers spectacular views of Lake Tahoe. Its 2,600 acres of rolling terrain are 15% beginner, 70% intermediate, 15% advanced. There are 22 miles of groomed trails. Elevation is 8,200 feet; the longest trail, 3.5 miles. Besides a ski school, there is a beginner special that includes trail pass, rentals, and lesson. *5 mi up Mt. Rose Hwy. from Incline Village, tel. 702/832–1177 or 800/468–2463. Snow conditions, tel. 702/831–3211.*

Heavenly Ski Resort. Located in the heart of the South Lake Tahoe area, this is America's largest ski resort, with nine mountain peaks and 20 square miles of ski terrain of which 25%

is beginner, 50% intermediate, and 25% advanced. Its 24 lifts carry 31,000 skiers each hour. The summit is 10,100 feet; base, 6,550 feet (CA) and 7,200 feet. (NV); vertical drop, 3,600 feet. Its longest run is 5.5 miles. The resort has a ski school, three base lodges, and four on-mountain lodges. *Ski Run Blvd., Box 2180, Stateline, NV 89449, tel. 916/541–1330 or 800/243–2836. Snow information, tel. 916/541–7544.*

Kirkwood Ski Resort. Thirty-five miles south of Lake Tahoe, this large resort has extensive trails and the highest base elevation in Northern California. Its 2,000 acres are 15% beginner, 50% intermediate, 35% advanced. There are 11 lifts. Kirkwood's summit is 9,800 feet; its base, 7,800 feet; vertical drop, 2,000 feet, and longest run, 2.5 miles. Facilities include a ski school, Mighty Mountain for children 4–12, licensed child care, and two base lodges with restaurants and bars. Also available are a beginner special, shuttle bus from Lake Tahoe ($2), and hotel packages. *On Hwy. 88, Box 1, Kirkwood, CA 95646, tel. 209/258–6000. Lodging information, tel. 209/258–7000. Snow information, tel. 209/258–3000.*

Northstar-at-Tahoe. Northstar is a complete resort, with lodging and full amenities. Its 1,700 acres of tree-lined ski runs are 25% beginner, 50% intermediate, 25% advanced, with 9 lifts. The summit is 8,600 feet; base, 6,400 feet; vertical drop, 2,200 feet and longest run, 2.9 miles. Northstar has a ski school; adult and children's beginner package; all-day junior lesson program ("Starkids," for ages 5–12). It has 40 miles of groomed and tracked wilderness trails for cross-country; beginner 30%, intermediate 40%, advanced 30%. The base is 6,800 feet; vertical drop, 800 feet and longest trail, 12 miles. Lessons, guided tours, and rentals are available. Packages may include air tickets, lodging, lifts, ski school, ski rental, child care, rental car. *Off Hwy. 267 between Truckee and North Shore, Box 129, Truckee 96160, tel. 916/562–1010 or 800/533–6787 for lodging reservations. Snow information, tel. 916/562–1330.*

Sierra Ski Ranch. This is a little farther away, but the slopes are usually uncrowded and it has spectacular views of the lake. Of 2,000 acres, 20% are beginner, 60% intermediate, 20% advanced, and there are nine lifts. The summit is 8,852 feet; base, 6,640 feet; vertical drop, 2,212 feet. The longest run is 3.5 miles. Ski school and children's snow school are available. Base lodge has three cafeterias, rental and retail shops; plus a lodge and café on top of mountain. Beginner specials are available. There is free shuttle bus service from South Lake Tahoe hotels. *On U.S. 50, 12 mi west of South Lake Tahoe, 9921 Sierra Ski Ranch Rd., Twin Bridges 95735, tel. 916/659–7453. Snow information, tel. 916/659–7475.*

Squaw Valley USA. There are vast, open slopes here, at the site of the 1960 Winter Olympics on 8,300 acres of skiable terrain, which includes 25% beginner, 45% intermediate, 30% advanced. Its 32 lifts have an uphill lift capacity of 47,370 skiers per hour. The summit of the highest of five peaks is 9,050 feet; base, 6,200 feet; vertical drop, 2,850 feet and longest run, 3.5 miles. Ten Little Indians day care is available for children six months to two years old; Papoose Snow School offers ski instruction for children three to five years old. First-time skiers ski free midweek during nonholiday periods. Base facilities and both Gold Coast and High Camp Complex on upper mountain have a variety of food and beverages. Ski rentals and a wide range of packages are available. *Between Truckee and Tahoe City on Hwy. 89, Squaw Valley 96145, tel. 916/583–6985. Lodg-*

*ing reservations 800/545–4350. Snow information, tel. 916/
583–6955.*

Tahoe Nordic Ski Center. This cross-country center north of
Tahoe City offers 2,000 acres, 41.5 miles of trails, 30% beginner, 40% intermediate, 30% advanced. Its summit is 7,880 feet;
base, 6,550 feet; vertical drop, 1,000 feet and longest trail, 15.5
miles. Facilities include a ski school and beginners' special: trail
pass, rentals, lesson. *Off Hwy. 28, north of Tahoe City, Box
1632, Tahoe City 95730, tel. 916/583–9858 or 916/583–0484.*

Swimming There are 36 public beaches on Lake Tahoe. Swimming is permitted at many of them, but since Tahoe is a high mountain lake
with fairly rugged winters, only the hardiest will be interested, except in midsummer. Even then the water warms to
only 68°F. Lifeguards are on duty at some of the swimming
beaches, and yellow buoys mark safe areas where motorboats
are not permitted. Opening and closing dates for beaches vary
with the climate and available park service staffing. There may
be a parking fee of $1 or $2.

Gambling

You don't need a roadside marker to know when you've crossed
from California into Nevada. The lake's water and the pine
trees may be identical, but the flashing lights and elaborate
marquees of the casinos announce legal gambling with a bang.
Nevada got gambling in 1931, and nearby Reno soon proclaimed itself "the biggest little city in the world." In 1944,
Harvey's Wagon Wheel Saloon and Gambling Hall, little more
than a rustic cabin, brought gambling to Lake Tahoe, and competition soon flourished in the Stateline area. Now, in addition
to the big casinos, visitors will find slot machines in every con-
ceivable location, from gas stations to supermarkets.

The major casinos are also hotels and, more recently, resorts.
Four are clustered on a strip of Highway 50 in Stateline, two
others on the north shore at Crystal Bay and Incline Village.
They are open 24 hours a day, 365 days a year, and offer craps,
blackjack, roulette, baccarat, poker, keno, pai gow, bingo, and
vast armies of slot machines—1,750, for instance, at Harrah's.

The hotel/casinos compete by offering shows starring celebrity
entertainers, and restaurants and lounges open around the
clock; frequent refurbishing has eliminated western decor in
favor of the contemporary international look. Some casino restaurants are elegant places designed to attract upscale visitors; Bill's Casino in Stateline has installed a McDonald's to
reach a younger crowd.

Dining

Restaurants at Lake Tahoe range from rustic rock-and-wood
decor to elegant French, with stops along the way for Swiss
chalet and spare modern. The food, too, is varied: delicate Continental sauces, mesquite-broiled fish, and wild boar in season.

Separate listings are given here for the north and south shores.
Casino restaurants are described under lodging. There are also
many fast-food restaurants and coffee-shop chains in South
Lake Tahoe and some in Tahoe City. Unless otherwise noted,
dress is informal for all restaurants. Even the most elegant and
expensive Tahoe eating places welcome customers in the casual

clothes that are considered appropriate in this year-round mecca for vacationers.

Highly recommended restaurants are indicated by a star ★.

Category	Cost*
Very Expensive	over $30
Expensive	$20–$30
Moderate	$16–$20
Inexpensive	under $16

per person, not including tax, service, or drinks

North Shore
Moderate–
Expensive

Captain Jon's. The dining room is small and cozy, with linen cloths and fresh flowers on the tables. On chilly evenings diners are warmed by a fireplace with a raised brick hearth. The lengthy dinner menu is country French, with two dozen daily specials; the emphasis is on fish. The restaurant's lounge is in a separate building on the water, with a pier where guests can tie up their boats. In summer, lunch is served in the lounge and on the deck. *7220 N. Lake Blvd., Tahoe Vista, tel. 916/546–4819. Reservations advised. AE, DC, MC, V. Closed for lunch in winter (usually Nov.–May), Mon.*

La Playa. This restaurant right on the lake features a Continental menu, with outdoor service an option in the summer. Seafood is a specialty. *7046 N. Lake Blvd., Tahoe Vista, tel. 916/546–5903. Reservations advised. AE, D, DC, MC, V.*

Le Petit Pier. The view from this lakeside restaurant, along with the French Provincial decor within, make this a romantic dining spot. The menu features French classics, such as roast duckling with a blueberry sauce. There is an award-winning wine list. *7250 N. Lake Blvd., Tahoe Vista, tel. 916/546–4464. Reservations advised. AE, DC, MC, V. Closed for lunch.*

Moderate
★

Sunnyside Restaurant and Lodge. An expansive lakefront deck with steps down to the beach and the water fronts this handsome wooden lodge. The large lounge features rock fireplaces, comfortable sofas, a seafood bar, and snacks. The dining room is decorated in a trim and sleek nautical style: in mahogany, with carpets and upholstery in maroon and blue. Seafood is a specialty of the Continental menu. *1850 W. Lake Blvd., Tahoe City, tel. 916/583–7200. Reservations accepted. AE, MC, V. Closed for lunch and brunch in winter.*

★

Wolfdale's. An intimate dinner house on the lake, Wolfdale's offers Japanese/California cuisine. The menu changes weekly and features a small number of imaginative entrées such as grilled Chinese pheasant with plum sauce and shiitake mushrooms, and baked Norwegian salmon with saffron scallop sauce. *640 N. Lake Blvd., Tahoe City, tel. 916/583–5700. Reservations advised. MC, V. Closed for lunch, and Tues.*

Inexpensive–
Moderate

Gar Woods Grill and Pier. This elegant but casual lakeside restaurant recalls the lake's past, with wood paneling, a river-rock fireplace, and boating photographs. It specializes in grilled foods, along with pasta and pizza. It also serves Sunday brunch. *5000 N. Lake Blvd., Carnelian Bay, tel. 916/546–3366. Reservations accepted. MC, V.*

★

Jake's on the Lake. Continental food is served in spacious, handsome rooms featuring oak and glass, on the water at the

Boatworks Mall. There is an extensive seafood bar and a varied menu that includes meat and poultry but emphasizes fresh fish. *780 N. Lake Blvd., Tahoe City, tel. 916/583–0188. Reservations accepted. Dress: collared shirts for men in evening. AE, MC, V. Closed for lunch in winter.*

★ **River Ranch.** You can almost get your feet wet from the terrace of this old-fashioned lodge set beside the Truckee River. The food is decidedly American, with fresh fish, smoked herb chicken and barbecued ribs from a wood-burning oven, and wild-game specials: pheasant, chukar partridge, rabbit, quail, goose, elk, venison, wild boar, and buffalo. In the summer there is terrace dining, and appetizers are served from 3:30 PM. *Hwy. 89 between Truckee and Tahoe City, at Alpine Meadows turn, tel. 916/583–4264. Reservations accepted. AE, MC, V.*

Tahoe House. Combining Swiss and California cuisine, this casual, somewhat rustic dinner house features an elegant menu: veal, lamb, beef, fresh pasta and seafood, fresh-baked breads, and a large selection of homemade desserts. In season, try the strawberry torte with white chocolate mousse. A children's menu is available. *625 W. Lake Blvd., Tahoe City, tel. 916/ 583–1377. Reservations advised. AE, MC, V.*

Inexpensive **Cafe Cobblestone.** A basically American menu is featured at breakfast and lunch (and dinner on winter weekends and during the summer high season) in a casual Tyrolean decor. Salads are a specialty, and there is a good variety of quiches, omelets, and sandwiches. *475 N. Lake Blvd., Tahoe City, tel. 916/583–2111. No reservations. MC, V.*

South Shore **The Summit.** On the 16th floor of Harrah's, this intimate res-
Very Expensive taurant offers romantic dining with spectacular views. A tuxe-
★ do-clad pianist plays the grand by candlelight while a fire crackles in the immense hearth. The creative menu includes quail with prune sauce and fritters as an appetizer, as well as artfully presented salads; lamb, venison; or seafood entrées with delicate sauces; and such sensuous desserts as soufflé with vanilla cream sauce. *Harrah's Hotel/Casino, Stateline, NV 89449, tel. 702/588–6606 or 800/648–3773. Reservations advised. AE, DC, MC, V.*

Moderate– **The Chart House.** The American menu of steak and seafood is
Expensive presented in a room with a panoramic lake view. There is a children's menu. *Kingsbury Grade, tel. 702/588– 6276. Reservations accepted. AE, D, DC, MC, V. No lunch.*

Christiania Inn. Located at the base of Heavenly Ski Resort's tram, this inn offers fireside dining in a Swiss country decor filled with antiques. The American/Continental menu emphasizes fresh seafood, prime beef, and veal. There is an extensive wine list. Midday buffets are served on holidays. Appetizers, soups, and salads are available in the lounge daily after 2 PM. *3819 Saddle Rd., South Lake Tahoe, tel. 916/544–7337. Reservations advised. MC, V.*

Moderate **Zackary's Restaurant.** The ambience here is casual and intimate. The menu is Continental, offering fresh fish and traditional dishes. *4130 Lake Tahoe Blvd., tel. 916/544–5400. AE, D, DC, MC, V.*

Swiss Chalet. The Swiss decor is carried out with great consistency. The Continental menu features Swiss specialties, veal dishes, fresh seafood, and home-baked pastries. Seasonal specials change daily. There is also a children's menu. *2540 Tahoe Blvd., South Lake Tahoe, tel. 916/544–3304. Reservations ad-*

vised. *AE, MC, V. Closed Mon., Easter, Nov. 23–Dec. 5, and Christmas.*

Inexpensive–
Moderate

The Greenhouse. Hanging plants, white linen cloths, a brick fireplace, and a coppertop bar create the ambience here. The Continental menu includes veal marsala, tournedos of lamb, and prawns à la cognac. *4140 Cedar Ave., Box RRR, South Lake Tahoe 95729, tel. 916/541–5800. Reservations advised. AE, DC, MC, V. No lunch.*

Tahoe Seasons Restaurant. Located at the Tahoe Seasons Resort in Heavenly Valley, this comfortable restaurant is warmed by eight fireplaces. The dinner menu is Continental, with some American fare. Breakfast is also served. *3901 Saddle Rd., South Lake Tahoe, tel. 916/541–6700. Reservations advised. AE, MC, V.*

Lodging

Accommodations at Lake Tahoe are as varied as everything else at this prime vacation spot. Quiet inns on the water, motel rooms in the heart of the casino area, rooms at the casinos themselves, lodges close to the ski runs—the most deluxe of lodgings and inexpensive bases for your vacation are all here. Just remember that during the summer months and the ski season, the lake is crowded; plan in advance. Spring and fall give you a little more leeway and lower—sometimes significantly lower—rates. Price categories listed below reflect high-season rates. Lake Tahoe has two telephone reservation services: Tahoe North Visitors and Convention Bureau (tel. 800/824–6348); and, for the south shore, Lake Tahoe Visitors Authority, (tel. 800/288–2463).

The listing of lodgings is divided between the north and south shores. The large hotel/casinos are listed at the end of each geographical section.

Highly recommended hotels are indicated by a star ★.

Category	Cost*
Very Expensive	over $100
Expensive	$75–$100
Moderate	$50–$75
Inexpensive	under $50

double room, not including tax

North Shore Hotels
Very Expensive

Hyatt Lake Tahoe Resort Hotel/Casino. Some of the rooms in this luxurious hotel on the lake have fireplaces. A children's program and rental bicycles are available. The restaurants are Hugo's Rotisserie, Ciao Mein Trattoria (Oriental/Italian), and Sierra Cafe (open 24 hours). *Lakeshore and Country Club Dr., Box 3239, Incline Village 89450, tel. 702/831–1111 or 800/233–1234. 460 rooms. Facilities: casino, beach, pool, spa, sauna, tennis, pay movies, health club, laundry, valet parking, entertainment. AE, DC, MC, V.*

Tahoe Vista Inn & Marina. Located at the northern tip of Lake Tahoe, this small, luxurious inn has suites only. Each has a living room, fireplace, kitchen, whirlpool bathtub, separate bedroom, and private lanai overlooking the lake. The decor is opulently modern, with white sofas, glass coffee tables, blond wood, and fieldstone gas-jetted fireplaces. *7220 N. Lake Blvd., Tahoe Vista 96148, tel. 916/546–7662 or 800/662–3433. 7 suites. Facilities: restaurant, lounge, beach. MC, V.*

Expensive–Very Expensive ★ **Sunnyside Lodge.** This modern mountain lodge, located so that it soaks up the sun, has large lakefront decks and a marina. Rooms are decorated in a crisp, nautical style with prints of boats hanging on the pin-striped wallcoverings, and sea chests as coffee tables. Each room has its own deck, with lake and mountain views. Continental breakfast is provided. *1850 W. Lake Blvd., Tahoe City 96145, tel. 916/583–7200; 800/822–2754 in CA. 23 rooms. MC, V.*

Moderate–Expensive **Tahoe City TraveLodge.** Overlooking Lake Tahoe and the Tahoe City Golf Course, the motel rooms here offer king-size beds with flowered spreads, desks, and high-nap carpets; there is fresh-ground coffee in each room. A restaurant and lounge are adjacent. Senior citizens receive a discount. *455 N. Lake Blvd., Box 84, Tahoe City 96145, tel. 916/583–3766 or 800/255–3050. 47 rooms with bath and shower massage. Facilities: heated pool, whirlpool. AE, DC, MC, V.*

★ **River Ranch.** This small, cozy old lodge is beautifully situated right on the Truckee River, close to Alpine Meadows and Squaw Valley skiing. Some rooms have balconies overlooking the river, and all are furnished with antiques. There is a good restaurant and lounge on the first floor. *Box 197, Tahoe City 96145, tel. 916/583–4264 or 800/535–9900 in CA. 21 rooms. AE, MC, V.*

North Shore Hotel/Casinos *Expensive–Very Expensive* **Cal Neva Lodge Resort Hotel/Casino.** All of the rooms in this hotel on Highway 28 at Crystal Bay have views of Lake Tahoe and the mountains. There is an arcade with video games for children, cabaret entertainment, and 22 cabins with living rooms. The restaurants are Lake View (coffee shop) and Sir Charles Fine Dining. *Box 368, Crystal Bay 89402, tel. 702/832–4000 or 800/225–6382. 220 rooms. Facilities: cable TV, pool, sauna, whirlpool, tennis courts, 3 wedding chapels. AE, DC, MC, V.*

South Shore Hotels *Very Expensive* ★ **Embassy Suites.** In this grand Bavarian-style hotel fountains and water wheels splash in soaring, nine-story atriums where cooked-to-order buffet breakfasts and complimentary evening cocktails are served daily. Glass elevators rise to guest rooms, each is a suite with living room, dining area, and separate bedroom. Zachary's, and Pasquale's Pizza restaurants are on the premises, as is Julie's Deli. Turtles nightclub is on the ground floor. *4130 Lake Tahoe Blvd., South Lake Tahoe 96150, tel. 916/ 544–5400 or 800/362–2779. 400 suites. Facilities: indoor pool, spa, exercise room, room service, valet parking. AE, MC, V.*

Expensive–Very Expensive ★ **Inn by the Lake.** This luxury motel across the road from the beach is far from the flashy casinos, but convenient to them by free shuttle bus. The rooms and bathrooms are spacious and comfortable, furnished in contemporary style (blond oak, pale peach). All rooms have balconies; some have lake views, wet bars, and in-room kitchens. Continental breakfast is served. A senior-citizen discount is available. *3300 Lake Tahoe Blvd., South Lake Tahoe 96150, tel. 916/542–0330 or 800/877–1466. 100 rooms. Facilities: heated pool, 2-level spa, sauna, movies, laundry. AE, DC, MC, V.*

Tahoe Seasons Resort. This resort, built among pine trees on the side of a mountain across from the Heavenly ski area, has outfitted each room with a fireplace, immense whirlpool, and minikitchen. The newly refurbished rooms are done in teal blues and contemporary decor; all beds are queen-size. *3901 Saddle Rd., South Lake Tahoe 96157, tel. 916/541-6700 or 916/541-6010. 160 rooms. Facilities: restaurant, lounge, room service, pool, whirlpool, tennis, indoor parking, valet garage, free Lake Tahoe Airport and casino shuttle. AE, MC, V.*

Expensive **Best Western Station House Inn.** This pleasant inn has won de-
★ sign awards for its exterior and interior. The rooms are subtly decorated in mauve and are nicely appointed, with king- and queen-size beds and double vanity baths. The location is good, near a private beach and yet close to the casinos. American breakfast is complimentary October 1–May 31. A senior-citizen discount is available. *901 Park Ave., South Lake Tahoe 96157, tel. 916/542-1101; in CA, 800/822-5953. 102 rooms. Facilities: restaurant, lounge, pool, hot tub, shuttle to casinos. AE, D, DC, MC, V.*

Moderate– **Best Western Lake Tahoe Inn.** Located near Harrah's Casino on
Expensive U.S. 50, this large motel is nicely situated on 6 acres of grounds, with gardens and the Heavenly Ski Resort directly behind. Rooms are modern, decorated in pastel pinks, purple, and mauve. *4110 Lake Tahoe Blvd., South Lake Tahoe 96150, tel. 916/541-2010 or 800/528-1234. 400 rooms. Facilities: restaurants, lounge, 2 heated pools, hot tub, 1-day valet service. AE, DC, MC, V.*

Flamingo Lodge. This motel has completely refurbished rooms decorated in contemporary blues and tans, all with refrigerators and in-room fresh-ground coffee, and some with wet bars. The lodge's grounds are spacious. There is an adjacent coffee shop. *3961 Lake Tahoe Blvd., South Lake Tahoe 96150, tel. 916/544-5288. 90 rooms. Facilities: pool, steam room, sauna, hot tub, laundry. AE, D, DC, MC, V.*

Lakeland Village Beach and Ski Resort. A town house-condominium complex located along 1,000 feet of private beach, Lakeland Village has a wide range of accommodations: studios, suites, and town houses, all with kitchens and fireplaces. *3535 Lake Tahoe Blvd., South Lake Tahoe 96156, tel. 916/542-1101 or 800/822-5696. 260 units. Facilities: beach, boating and fishing pier, 2 pools, wading pool, spa, saunas, laundry. AE, MC, V.*

Royal Valhalla Motor Lodge. On the lake at Lakeshore Boulevard and Stateline Avenue, this motel has simple modern rooms decorated in earth tones with queen-size beds. There is some covered parking. A senior-citizen discount is available. *Box GG, South Lake Tahoe 96157, tel. 916/544-2233. 80 rooms, 29 with kitchenettes. Facilities: pool, laundry. AE, DC, MC, V.*

Inexpensive– **Best Tahoe West Inn.** A long-established motel that is proud of
Moderate its repeat business, Tahoe West is three blocks from the beach
★ and the downtown casinos. The exterior is rustic in appearance. The rooms are neatly furnished, and the beds are queen-size. Coffee and doughnuts are served in the lobby. *4107 Pine Blvd., South Lake Tahoe 96157, tel. 916/544-6455 or 800/522-1021. 59 rooms, 12 with kitchenettes. Facilities: pool, sauna, spa, private beach privileges, shuttle to casinos and ski areas. AE, DC, MC, V.*

South Shore **Harrah's Tahoe Hotel/Casino.** Harrah's is a luxurious 18-story
Hotel/Casinos hotel/casino on U.S. 50 in the casino area. All guest rooms have
Very Expensive refrigerators, private bars, and two full bathrooms, each with
a television and telephone. All rooms have views of the lake and
the mountains, but the least-obstructed views are from rooms
on the higher floors. There is an enclosed children's arcade on
the lower level. Harrah's has a four-star Mobil rating and a
four-diamond rating from the American Automobile Association. Top-name entertainment is presented in the South Shore
Room and Stateline Cabaret. There are more than 150 table
games (blackjack, craps, baccarat, pai gow, keno, roulette,
poker, big six, bingo), and 1,750 slot machines. Race and sports
book are also available. Restaurants include The Summit (Continental), The Forest (buffet), Cafe Andreotti (Italian bistro),
North Beach Deli (New York style), Asia (Pacific Rim), Friday's Station (steaks and seafood), Sierra Restaurant (24-hour
breakfast, lunch, and dinner), and Bentley's Ice Cream Parlor.
*Box 8, Stateline, NV 89449, tel. 702/588–6606 or 800/648–3773.
534 rooms. Facilities: heated indoor pool, hot tubs, health club,
valet garage, parking lot, 24-hour room and valet service, pet
kennel. AE, DC, MC, V.*

Caesars Tahoe. This luxurious 16-story hotel/casino, built in
1980, is on U.S. 50 in the casino area. Each room has a view of
Lake Tahoe or the encircling mountains and a massive bathtub
"reminiscent of ancient Rome." There is top-name entertainment in the 1,600-seat Circus Maximus and the Cabaret.
Games include dice, 21, roulette, big six, French roulette, baccarat, poker, sic bo, pai gow, and hundreds of slot machines.
Race and sports book are also available. Restaurants include
Empress Court (Chinese), Cafe Roma (24-hour meals), Le Posh
(French-Californian, and Continental, with tableside service),
Primavera (Italian), Broiler Room, and Yogurt Palace. *Box
5800, South Lake Tahoe, CA 89449, tel. 702/588–3515 or 800/
648–3353 for reservations and show information. 440 rooms.
Facilities: heated indoor pool, saunas, whirlpool, tennis (fee),
health club (fee), movies, valet garage, parking lot. AE, DC,
MC, V.*

Harvey's Resort Hotel/Casino. Harvey's started out as a small
service station in the 1940s; today it's the largest Tahoe resort.
A luxurious mirrored 18-story structure on U.S. 50 in the casino area, it has well-appointed rooms, six restaurants, 10 cocktail lounges, and a complete health spa. Cabaret revues and
contemporary bands perform in the Theatre Lounge. Games
include blackjack, craps, roulette, baccarat, pai gow, red dog,
poker and many slot machines. Restaurants include Cafe
Metro, Carriage House Restaurant, The Garden Buffet, Sage
Room Steak House, Llewelynns (Continental), El Vaquero
(Mexican), and Seafood Grotto (seafood and Chinese). *Box 128,
Stateline, NV 89449, tel. 702/588–2411 or 800/648–3361. 575
rooms. Facilities: tennis, valet parking, garage. AE, DC, MC,
V.*

Expensive–Very **Horizon Casino Resort.** Formerly called the High Sierra, this
Expensive hotel underwent a $15 million renovation in a bid to attract up-
scale patrons. Decor is contemporary in the guest rooms, and
many have beautiful lake views. The casino follows a French
Beaux Arts design, and is brightened by pale molded wood and
mirrors. Games include blackjack, craps, roulette, keno, mini
baccarat, and many slot machines. The Grand Lake Theater
showcases celebrity performers. The Golden Cabaret features

revues, magicians, and other nightclub entertainment. The Aspen Lounge presents soloists. Restaurants include Josh's (fine but still casual dining), Four Seasons (24-hour service), Gregory's (steak and seafood), and Le Grande Buffet. *Box C, Stateline, NV 89449, tel. 702/588–6211; outside NV, 800/322–7723. 539 rooms. Facilities: pool, wading pool, 3 hot tubs. AE, DC, MC, V.*

Nightlife

Major nighttime entertainment is found at the casinos. The top venues are the **Circus Maximus** at Caesars Tahoe, the **Emerald Theater** at Harvey's, and the **South Shore Room** at Harrah's. Each theater is as large as a Broadway house. Typical headliners are Jay Leno, Dionne Warwick, Willie Nelson, Kenny Rogers, and Johnny Mathis; their shows are more like concerts than the extravaganzas typical in Las Vegas. The big showrooms also present performances of Broadway musicals, put on by touring Broadway companies or by casts assembled specifically for the casino's production.

Reservations are almost always required for superstar shows. Depending on the act, cocktail shows usually cost $19–$40, including Nevada's sales and entertainment tax. Smaller casino cabarets sometimes have a cover charge or drink minimum. There are also lounges with no admission charge, featuring jazz and pop music soloists and groups. Even these performers don't try to compete all night with gambling; the last set usually ends at 2:30 or 3 AM.

Lounges around the lake may offer pop and country music singers and musicians, and in the winter the ski resorts do the same. Summer alternatives are outdoor music events, from chamber quartets to jazz bands and rock performers, at Sand Harbor and the Lake Tahoe Visitors Center amphitheater.

9 The Sierra National Parks

By Barbara Elizabeth Shannon and Pam Hegarty

Yosemite, Sequoia, and Kings Canyon national parks are famous throughout the world for their unique sights and experiences. Yosemite, especially, should be on your "don't miss" list. Unfortunately, it's on everyone else's as well, so making advance reservations is essential. We recommend allowing several days to explore the parks; day trips simply won't do them justice. Save them for your next trip to California if you don't have time now. We also recommend that you make your plans far enough in advance so you can stay in the parks themselves, not in one of the "gateway cities" in the foothills or Central Valley. You'll probably be adjusting to a higher altitude, dealing with traffic, and exercising a fair amount, so save your energy for exploring the park, not driving to and from it.

Yosemite, Sequoia, and Kings Canyon all celebrated their centennial as national parks in 1990, and many of the lodgings, restaurants, and exhibits were spiffed up for the occasion.

Yosemite National Park

Yosemite Valley is one of the most famous sights (or collection of sights) in California. The surrounding granite peaks and domes, such as El Capitan and Half Dome, rise more than 3,000 feet above the valley floor; two of the five waterfalls that cascade over the valley's rim are among the world's 10 highest; and the Merced River, placid here, runs through the valley. Millions of people visit Yosemite every year, most of them in the summer, and it can get very crowded. Such extravagant praise has been written of this valley (by John Muir and others) and so many beautiful photographs taken (by Ansel Adams and others) that you may wonder if the reality can possibly measure up. For almost everyone, it does; Yosemite is a reminder of what "breathtaking" and "marvelous" really mean.

Yosemite Valley includes only seven of the more than 1,000 square miles of national park in the Sierra. The western boundary dips as low as 2,000 feet in the chaparral-covered foothills; the eastern boundary rises to 13,000 feet at points along the Sierra crest. Much of this country is accessible only to backpackers and horseback riders (and thus beyond the scope of this guide), but there are many sites to be explored by visitors who do not want to range too far from their cars.

The falls are at their most spectacular in May and June. By the end of the summer, however, some may have dried up, or very nearly so. They begin flowing again in late fall with the first storms, and during the winter, they may be dramatically hung with ice. Yosemite Valley is open year round. Because the valley floor is only 4,000 feet high, snow does not stay long, and it is possible to camp even in the winter (January highs are in the mid-40s, lows in the mid-20s). Tioga Pass Road is closed in winter (roughly from late October through May), so you can't see Tuolumne Meadows then. The road to Glacier Point beyond the turnoff for Badger Pass is also not cleared in winter.

Admission to the park is $5 per car for a week's stay; $2 per person if you don't arrive in a car.

Getting Around

Thanks to the free shuttle bus that runs around Yosemite Valley (8 AM–11 PM in the summer, 10–10 the rest of the year), it is possible to visit the park without your own car. From 9–5 in the summer, another free shuttle runs from Wawona to Big Trees. Campers are not allowed on this road.

By Plane You can fly into one of the large California airports (San Francisco or Los Angeles) or one of the smaller Central Valley airports (Sacramento, Fresno) and then either rent a car or take public transportation to Yosemite.

By Bus **Yosemite Via** (tel. 209/722–0366) and **Yosemite Gray Line** (tel. 209/443–5240 or 800/640–6306 in CA) run buses from Merced and Fresno, both on Highway 99, to Yosemite Valley. Both buses make connections with Greyhound and Amtrak.

By Car Yosemite is a four- to five-hour drive from San Francisco and a six-hour drive from Los Angeles. From the west, three highways come to Yosemite; all intersect with Highway 99, which runs north–south through the Central Valley. Highway 120 is the northernmost route—the one that travels farthest and slowest through the foothills. If you are exploring the Gold Country along Highway 49, you may want to come this way. The more-traveled routes are Highway 140 from Merced and Highway 41 from Fresno. Highway 140 is the major route; Highway 41 provides the most dramatic first view of the valley, after you come out of the Wawona Tunnel.

If you are coming from the east, you could cross the Sierra from Lee Vining on Highway 120 (Tioga Pass). This route takes you over the Sierra crest, past Tuolumne Meadows, and down the west slope of the range. It's scenic but the mountain driving may be stressful for some, and it's open only in the summer. You should have tire chains when you drive in these mountains at any time of the year; the eastern entrance to the park at Tioga Pass is at nearly 10,000 feet.

Road Conditions **Yosemite Area Road Conditions** (tel. 209/372–0200).

Northern California Road Conditions (tel. 619/873–6366).

Guided Tours

California Parlor Car Tours (Cathedral Hill Hotel, 1101 Van Ness Ave., San Francisco 94109, tel. 415/474–7500 or 800/227–4250) offers several tours that include Yosemite (along with Monterey or Hearst Castle) and depart from either San Francisco or Los Angeles. Some tours are one way. Lodging and some meals are included; you can choose to stay in either Yosemite Lodge or the Ahwahnee (there's a difference in price, of course). We recommend that you not consider any tour that leaves you less than one full day in the valley (and that is cutting it very short!).

Important Addresses and Numbers

General Information **National Park Service, Information Office** (Box 577, Yosemite National Park, CA 95389, tel. 209/372–0265; 209/372–0264 for a 24-hour recording) or **National Park Service, Fort Mason** (Bldg. 201, San Francisco, CA 94123, tel. 415/556–0560).

Reservations **Camping and Recreation Information** (tel. 209/372–4845).

Yosemite Park and Curry Company (Central Reservations, 5410 E. Home, Fresno, CA 93727, tel. 209/252–4848).

Exploring

Numbers in the margin correspond to points of interest on the Yosemite National Park map.

Although there is more to see in Yosemite National Park than the valley, this is the primary, if not only, destination for many visitors, especially those who won't be making backpack or pack-animal trips. Because the valley is only 7 miles long and averages less than 1 mile wide, you can visit sites in whatever order you choose and return to your favorites at different times of the day.

At Yosemite Village, near the east end of the valley, you'll find the park headquarters, a restaurant, store, and gas station, the Ahwahnee Hotel, Yosemite Lodge, a medical clinic, and the
❶ Visitors Center, where park rangers provide information and wilderness permits (necessary for overnight backpacking). There are exhibits on natural and human history as well as an adjacent Indian Cultural Museum, and a re-created Ahwahneechee village. *Tel. 209/372–0299 or 209/372–0265. Open daily 9–5, with extended hours in summer.*

Another visitor center is open at Tuolumne Meadows from late June to early September, 8 AM–7:30 PM daily, and a Yosemite Association Bookstore at Mariposa Grove is open from Memorial Day through Labor Day, usually from 9:30 to 4:30.

❷ Yosemite Falls is the highest waterfall in North America and the fifth-highest in the world. The upper falls (1,430 ft.), the middle cascades (675 ft.), and the lower falls (320 ft.) combine for a total of 2,425 feet and, when viewed from the valley, appear as a single waterfall. From the parking lot there is a ¼-mile trail to the base of the falls. The Yosemite Falls Trail is a strenuous 3½-mile climb rising 2,700 feet, taking you above the top of the falls. It starts from Sunnyside Campground.

If you arrive in Yosemite via the Wawona Road, your first view of the valley (in John Muir's words "a revelation in landscape
❸ affairs that enriches one's life forever") will include **Bridalveil Fall,** a filmy fall of 620 feet that is often diverted as much as 20 feet one way or the other by the breeze. Indians called it Pohono ("puffing wind"). There is a very short (⅛-mi) trail from a parking lot on the Wawona Road to the base of the fall.

❹ Across the valley, **Ribbon Fall** (1,612 ft.) is the valley's highest single fall, but it is also the first one to dry up in the summer.

Vernal and Nevada falls are on the Merced River at the east end
❺ of the valley. **Vernal Fall** (317 ft.) is bordered by fern-covered
❻ black rocks, and rainbows play in the spray at the base. **Nevada Fall** (594 ft.) is the first major fall as the river comes out of the high country. Both falls can be viewed from Glacier Point or visited on foot from Happy Isles nature area, east of Yosemite Village. The roads at this end of the valley are now closed to private cars, but a free shuttle bus runs frequently from the village. From late June through early September, the Happy Isles nature area is open daily 9–5, and features exhibits on ecology.

The hike on a paved trail from Happy Isles to the bridge at the base of Vernal Fall is only moderately strenuous and less than 1 mile long. It's another steep ¾-mile along the Mist Trail up to the top of the fall, and then an additional 2½ miles to the top of Nevada Falls. The top of this trail at Nevada Falls is the beginning of the famous John Muir Trail, which leads south for more than 200 miles through the High Sierra to Mt. Whitney, in the southeastern section of Sequoia/Kings Canyon.

Most famous among Yosemite's peaks are El Capitan and Half Dome. **El Capitan** is the largest exposed granite monolith in the world, almost twice the height of the Rock of Gibraltar. It rises 3,593 feet above the valley, with an apparently vertical front thrust out from the valley's rim. **Half Dome** is the most distinctive rock in the region: The west side of the dome is fractured vertically and cut away to form a 2,000-foot cliff. Rising 4,733 feet from the valley floor, the top is at an altitude of 8,842 feet above sea level.

9 **Glacier Point** offers what may be the most spectacular view of the valley and the High Sierra that you can get without hiking. The Glacier Point Road leaves Highway 41 about 23 miles southwest of the valley; it's then a 16-mile drive, with fine views into higher country. From the parking area, walk just a few hundred yards and you'll be able to see Nevada, Vernal, and Yosemite falls as well as Half Dome and other peaks. This road is closed beyond the turnoff for Badger Pass Ski Area in the winter.

10 At the **Pioneer Yosemite History Center** in Wawona (on Hwy. 41) are local historic buildings moved here from their original sites. A living history program in summer re-creates Yosemite's past. The center is open Wednesday through Sunday from late June to early September.

11 Farther down the Wawona Road (36 mi from the valley) is the **Mariposa Grove of Big Trees.** This fine grove of *Sequoiadendron gigantea* can be visited on foot or on the one-hour tram rides in summer (May–Oct. 9–6; $5.25 adults, $4.50 for those 62 and older, $2.50 children 4–12). The Grizzly Giant is the oldest tree here; its age is estimated to be 2,700 years; its base diameter is 30.7 feet, its circumference 96.5 feet, and its height 210 feet. The Wawona Tunnel Tree—that granddaddy of Yosemite giants that was the centerpiece of many a vacation photo opportunity featuring family, car, and tree base—fell during the winter of 1968–69 (did anyone hear it?), but two other tunnel trees nearby remain. A museum presents information on the big trees.

12 **Hetch Hetchy Reservoir** is about 40 miles from Yosemite Valley, via Big Oak Flat Road and Highway 120. The reservoir supplies water and power (some of which is sold at a profit) to San Francisco. Some say John Muir died of heartbreak when this beautiful valley was dammed and buried beneath 300 feet of water in 1913.

13 The Tioga Pass Road (Highway 120) crosses the Sierra Nevada and meets U.S. 395 at Lee Vining. This scenic route (open only in summer) will take you past **Tuolumne Meadows,** the largest alpine meadow in the Sierra. There are campgrounds, a gas station, store, stables, lodge, and visitor center. This is the trailhead for many backpack trips into the High Sierra, but there are also shorter day hikes you can take. Remember,

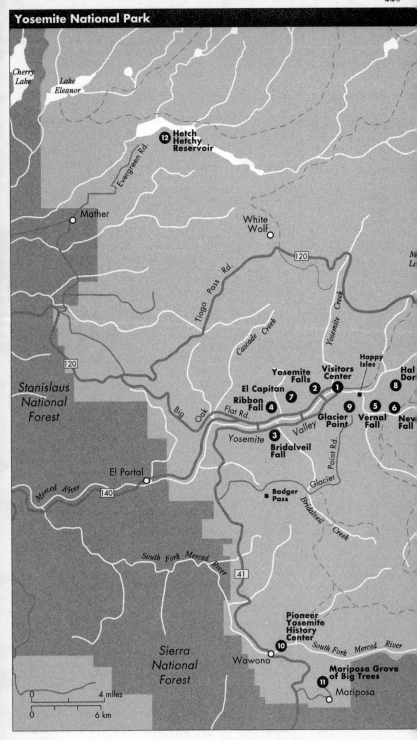

Yosemite National Park

Cherry Lake

Lake Eleanor

12 Hetch Hetchy Reservoir

Evergreen Rd.

Mather

White Wolf

120

Tioga Pass Rd.

Cascade Creek

Yosemite Creek

120

Stanislaus National Forest

Yosemite Creek

Happy Isles

Visitors Center

Yosemite Falls **2** **1**

El Capitan **7**

Ribbon Fall **4**

Big Oak Flat Rd.

Glacier Point **9** **5** **Vernal Fall**

8 Hal Dor

6 Nev Fall

Yosemite Valley

3 **Bridalveil Fall**

Glacier Point Rd.

El Portal

Merced River

140

Badger Pass

Glacier

Bridalveil Creek

South Fork Merced River

41

Sierra National Forest

Pioneer Yosemite History Center

10

Wawona

South Fork Merced River

Mariposa Grove of Big Trees

11

Mariposa

0   4 miles

0   6 km

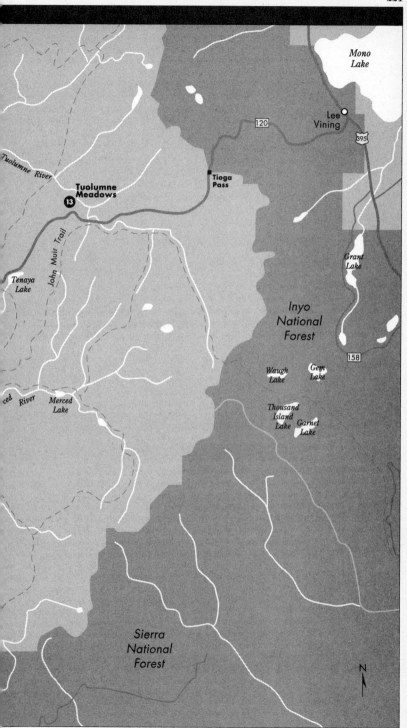

though, to give yourself time (a day or two, at least) to get acclimated to the altitude: 8,575 feet. From Yosemite Valley, it's 55 miles to Tuolumne Meadows and 74 miles to Lee Vining.

Off the Beaten Track

From early May to late October and during the Christmas holiday week, actor Lee Stetson portrays noted naturalist John Muir, bringing to life Muir's wit, wisdom, and storytelling skill. Stetson's programs—"An Evening with a Tramp" and "The Spirit of John Muir"—are two of the park's best-loved shows. Locations and times are listed in the *Yosemite Guide,* the newspaper handed to you upon entering the park (and also found at the Visitors Center and at many local stores). Stetson, as John Muir, also leads free interpretive walks twice a week; the walks start at the Visitors Center (tel. 209/372-0298).

Sports

Bicycling Bicycles can be rented at **Yosemite Lodge** or **Curry Village.**

Fishing You will have to buy a fishing license if you want to angle. State residents pay $23.65 for a year's license. Nonresidents must fork over $63.55; residents and nonresidents may purchase a one-day license for $8.40.

Hiking Hiking is the primary sport here. If you are hiking up any of the steep trails, remember to stay on the trail. Consider also the effect of the altitude on your endurance. If you plan to backpack overnight, you'll need a wilderness permit (they're free), available at visitor centers or ranger stations.

Rock Climbing **Yosemite Mountaineering** (tel. 209/372-1244 Sept.–May, 209/372-1335 June–Aug.) conducts beginner through intermediate rock climbing and backpacking classes. A one-day session includes a hands-on introduction to climbing. Classes are held April through September.

Winter Sports Cross-country and downhill skiing are at **Badger Pass,** off the Glacier Point Road (tel. 209/372-1330). There is an outdoor skating rink at Curry Village.

Dining

With precious few exceptions, the best meals available in our national parks are probably those cooked on portable grills at the various campgrounds—which is fine: After all, one doesn't visit wilderness preserves expecting to find gourmet restaurants. Moreover, there is a snack bar in Yosemite Village, as well as coffee shops and a cafeteria at the Ahwahnee and Yosemite Lodge. Even so, if you are just there for a day, you will not want to waste precious time hunting about for food; instead, stop at a grocery store on the way in and fill up your hamper and ice chest with the makings of a picnic to enjoy under the umbrellas of giant fir trees. Price categories are based on the cost of a full dinner for one, excluding drinks, tax, and tip.

Highly recommended restaurants are indicated by a star ★.

Expensive **Ahwahnee Hotel.** With the huge sugar-pine log beams and sup-
($15–$35) ports, and the big, roaring fireplace, you can imagine you're
★ dining in a hunting lodge, built by one of the railroad or silver barons of the last century. Stick with what they would have

eaten: steak, trout, prime rib, all competently prepared. Generations of Californians have made a ritual of spending Christmas and New Year's here, so make reservations well in advance. *Yosemite Village, tel. 209/372–1489. Reservations advised. Jacket and tie required. AE, DC, MC, V.*

★ **Erna's Elderberry House.** As a special treat on the way into, or leaving, Yosemite, stop at this countryside gem, where the owner, Vienna-born Erna Kubin, offers bountiful Continental-California cuisine, along with dishes from whatever country she's visited recently. Prix fixe, six-course dinners change nightly. *48688 Victoria La., Oakhurst, tel. 209/683–6800. Reservations advised. Jacket advised. MC, V. Sun. brunch. Closed lunch Sat.–Tues., dinner Mon. and Tues., and first 3 wks. of Jan.*

Moderate ($10–$20) **Mountain Room Broiler.** The food becomes secondary when you see the spectacular Yosemite Falls through the dining room's window-wall. Best bets are steaks, chops, roast duck, and a fresh herb-basted roast chicken. *Yosemite Village, tel. 209/372–1281. Reservations advised. Dress: casual. AE, DC, MC, V. Closed lunch.*

Inexpensive ($5–$15) **Four Seasons Restaurant.** The upscale rustic setting here features high-finish natural wood tables and lots of potted representatives of the local greenery and flora. The breakfast is hearty and all-American; dinner offerings cover the beef, chicken, and fish spectrum, plus vegetarian fare. *Yosemite Lodge, Yosemite Village, tel. 209/372–1269. Reservations advised. Dress: casual. AE, DC, MC, V. Closed lunch.*

Lodging

There is a wide range of accommodations in Yosemite, from simple tent cabins to the luxurious but still rustic Ahwahnee Hotel. Most rooms are in the valley, but there are also tent cabins at Tuolumne Meadows and White Wolf (on Tioga Pass Rd.). White Wolf also has a few cabins with private baths (but no electricity). Reservations should be made well in advance, especially for summer travel. At other times, you can always call and try; you might get a room for the next week.

All reservations are made through the **Yosemite Park & Curry Company** (Central Reservations, 5410 E. Home Ave., Fresno, CA 93727, tel. 209/252–4848). Price categories are based on the cost of a room for two people.

Very Expensive ($180–$200) **Ahwahnee Hotel.** This grand, 1920s-style mountain lodge is constructed of rocks and sugar-pine logs, with exposed timbers and spectacular views. The Grand Lounge and Solarium are decorated in a style that is a tribute to the local Miwok and Paiute Indians. The decor in the rooms continues that motif; modern facilities include TVs. The Ahwahnee was renovated for the park's 1990 centennial. *123 rooms. Facilities: restaurant, lounge, pool, tennis. DC, MC, V.*

Moderate ($26–$85) **Housekeeping Camp.** These are also rustic tent cabins, set along the Merced River, but you can cook here on gas stoves rented from the front desk. These cabins are usually rented for several weeks at a time and are difficult to get; reserving at least a year in advance is advised. *282 tent cabins with no bath (maximum 4 per cabin). Toilet and shower facilities in central shower house. DC, MC, V.*

Yosemite Lodge. The lodge has various rooms, from fairly rustic motel-style rooms with two double beds, decorated in rust and green, to very rustic cabins with no baths—all within walking distance of Yosemite Falls. *495 rooms. Facilities: restaurant, lounge, pool. DC, MC, V.*

Inexpensive–
Moderate
($25–$72)

Curry Village. These are plain accommodations: cabins with bath and without, tent cabins with rough wood frames and canvas walls and roofs. It's a step up from camping (linens and blankets are provided), but food or cooking are not allowed because of the animals. If you stay in a cabin without bath, the showers and toilets are centrally located, as they would be in a campground. *180 cabins, 426 tent cabins, 8 hotel rooms. Facilities: cafeteria, pool, rafting (fee), skating (fee), horseback riding (fee). DC, MC, V.*

Camping

Reservations for camping are required year-round in Yosemite Valley and from spring through fall at two campgrounds outside the valley. They are strongly recommended at any time. Reservations for all campgrounds in Yosemite are made through MISTIX (Box 85705, San Diego, CA 92138–5705, tel. 619/452–0150 or 800/365–2267, TDD 209/255–8345). You can reserve campsites no sooner than eight weeks in advance, and should indicate the name of the park, the campground, and your first, second, and third choice of arrival dates. Campsites cost $12 per night. If space is available, you can also make reservations in person at the Campground Reservations Office in Yosemite Valley, but we strongly recommend making them ahead of time. The campgrounds outside the valley that are not on the reservation system are first come, first served.

Sequoia and Kings Canyon National Parks

The other two Sierra national parks are usually spoken of together. These adjacent parks share their administration and a main highway. Although you may want to concentrate on either Kings Canyon or Sequoia, most people visit both parks in one trip.

Like Yosemite, Sequoia and General Grant national parks were established in 1890. The General Grant National Park was added to over the years to include the Redwood Canyon area and the drainages of the south and middle forks of the Kings River, and eventually renamed Kings Canyon National Park. Both Sequoia and Kings Canyon now extend east to the Sierra crest. The most recent major addition was to Sequoia in 1978, to prevent the development of the Mineral King area as a ski resort.

The major attractions of both parks are the big trees (*Sequoiadendron gigantea*—the most extensive groves and the most impressive specimens are found here) and the spectacular alpine scenery. These trees are the largest living things in the world. They are not as tall as the coast redwoods (*Sequoia sempervirens*), but they are much more massive and older. The exhibits at the visitors centers and the interpretive booklets that you can get there and take with you along the trails will explain the special relationship between these trees and fire (their thick, squishy bark protects them from fire and insects), and how they live so long and grow so big.

The parks encompass land from only 1,200 feet above sea level to more than 14,000 feet. Mt. Whitney, on the eastern side of Sequoia, is the highest mountain (14,495 ft.) in the contiguous United States. The greatest portion of both parks is accessible only by foot or pack animal. The Generals Highway (46 mi from Hwy. 180 in Kings Canyon National Park to the Ash Mountain Entrance in Sequoia National Park) links the major groves in the two parks and is open year round.

Summer is the most crowded season, but even then it is much less crowded than at Yosemite. Snow may remain on the ground in the sequoia groves into June, but is usually gone by mid-month. The flowers in the Giant Forest meadows hit their peak in July. Fall is an especially good time to visit. The rivers will not be as full, but the weather is usually warm and calm, and there are no crowds.

The entrance fee is $5 per car for a week's stay in both parks. A Golden Eagle pass ($25) will get you into all national parks and monuments for a year.

Getting Around

By Car From the south, enter Sequoia National Park via Highway 198 from Visalia; from the north, enter Kings Canyon National Park via Highway 180 from Fresno. Both highways intersect with Highway 99, which runs north–south through the Central Valley. If you are driving up from Los Angeles, take Highway 65 north from Bakersfield to Highway 198 east of Visalia.

Highways 198 and 180 are connected through the parks by the Generals Highway, a paved two-lane road that is open year round but may be closed temporarily during heavy snowstorms (carry chains in winter). Drivers of RVs and drivers who are not comfortable on mountain roads should probably avoid the southern stretch between the Ash Mountain Entrance and Giant Forest. These 16 miles of narrow road rise almost 5,000 feet and are very twisty, but with care and without undue haste, this is a spectacular drive. Few roads up the west slope of the Sierra rise so quickly through the foothills and offer such spectacular views up into the high country. The rest of the Generals Highway is a well-graded, wide two-lane road and a pleasure to drive.

Highway 180 beyond Grant Grove to Cedar Grove and the road to Mineral King are open only in summer. Both roads, especially the latter, which is unpaved in sections, may present a challenge to inexperienced drivers. Don't expect to drive quickly, particularly into Mineral King. Campers and RVs more than 30 feet long are not allowed on the Mineral King road. Trailers are not allowed in Mineral King campgrounds.

Guided Tours

For those who must see but not necessarily savor, **Sequoia-Yosemite Tours** leads one-day trips in vans from Visalia (in the Central Valley) to Giant Forest and Grant Grove. They visit

Crescent Meadows, Tharp's Log, and Moro Rock, and stop for lunch at the cafeteria at Giant Forest Village before heading on to the General Sherman Tree and Grant Grove. The tours leave at 8 AM and return at 5:30–6 PM. That's a lot of driving and a lot to see in one day, so we recommend these tours only for those who want to see the largest living things, but can't spend more than a day in the mountains. It also offers tours from Fresno for six or more people. *Tel. 209/685–0100 or 800/333–8571. Tours daily May–Oct. Fare: $24.95 adults, $19.95 children 3–17.*

Within the park, you can take van tours with Sequoia Guest Services (tel. 209/565–3381) of Giant Forest ($9 adults, $8 senior citizens, $4.50 children under 12) or of Kings Canyon ($21 adults, $19 senior citizens, $10.50 children). You can sign up for either tour at the Giant Forest Lodge.

Important Addresses and Numbers

General Information   **Sequoia and Kings Canyon National Parks** (Three Rivers, CA 93271, tel. 209/565–3456, daily 8–4:30 or 209/565–3351 for road and weather conditions) or **National Park Service, Fort Mason** (Bldg. 201, San Francisco, CA 94123, tel. 415/556–0560).

Reservations   **Sequoia Guest Services** (Box 789, Three Rivers, CA 93271, tel. 209/561–3314 for both parks).

Exploring

Numbers in the margin correspond to points of interest on the Sequoia and Kings Canyon National Parks map.

If you take Highway 180 to the parks, you come into Kings Canyon National Park at the Big Stump Entrance, just southwest ❶ of Wilsonia (a private community) and **Grant Grove.** This is the grove (or what remained of a larger grove decimated by logging) that was designated as General Grant National Park in 1890, and is now the most highly developed area of Kings Canyon National Park. A walk along the 1-mile Big Stump Trail, starting near the park entrance, graphically demonstrates the effects of heavy logging on these groves.

At Grant Grove Village, you will find a visitor center, gas station, grocery store, campground, coffee shop, and lodging. The visitor center has exhibits on *Sequoiadendron gigantea* and the area. Books and maps describing the region are available for purchase. Trail maps for this and the other major areas of the two parks may be purchased for $1 each here and at all the visitor centers.

A spur road leads west less than 1 mile to the General Grant Grove. An easy ⅓-mile trail leads through the grove and is accessible to disabled travelers. The most famous tree here is the General Grant. In total mass it is not as large as the General Sherman Tree in Sequoia, but it is nearly as tall and just as wide at its base. The Gamlin Cabin is one of several pioneer cabins that can be visited in the parks. A large sequoia was cut for display at the 1876 Philadelphia Exhibition; the Centennial Stump still remains.

❷ Actually in Sequoia National Forest, **Hume Lake** is a reservoir built early this century by loggers; today it is the site of many Christian camps, as well as a public campground. This is a pretty, small lake with views of high mountains in the distance. If

Sequoia and Kings Canyon National Parks

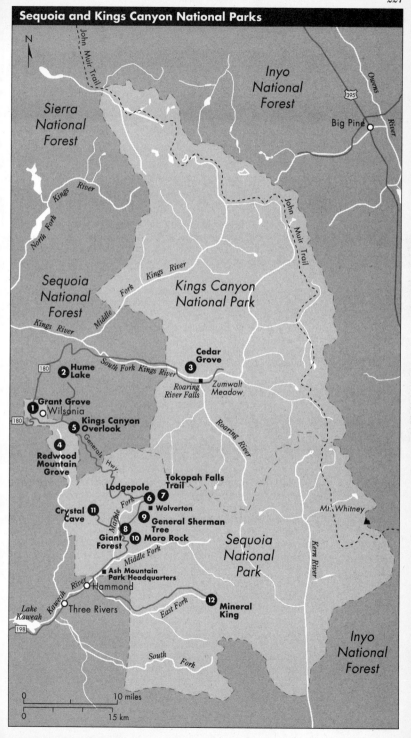

N

Sierra National Forest

Inyo National Forest

John Muir Trail

Owens River

395

Big Pine

North Fork Kings River

Kings River

Middle Fork

Sequoia National Forest

Kings River

Kings Canyon National Park

John Muir Trail

180 **2** **Hume Lake**

South Fork Kings River

3 **Cedar Grove**

Roaring River Falls

Zumwalt Meadow

1 **Grant Grove**
Wilsonia

180

5 **Kings Canyon Overlook**

Roaring River

4 **Redwood Mountain Grove**

Generals Hwy.

Tokopah Falls Trail

Lodgepole

Marble Fork

6 **7**

Wolverton

Mt. Whitney

Crystal Cave **11**

8 **9** **General Sherman Tree**

10 **Moro Rock**

Giant Forest

Middle Fork

Sequoia National Park

Kern River

Ash Mountain
Park Headquarters

Kaweah River

Hammond

Three Rivers

Lake Kaweah

198

East Fork

12 **Mineral King**

South Fork

Inyo National Forest

0 —— 10 miles
0 —— 15 km

it's hot and you're desperate for a place to swim, you might want to make this side trip. It's accessible by side roads off the Generals Highway east of—or off Highway 180 north of—Grant Grove. There are fine views of Kings Canyon from either road, but the route from the Generals Highway is easier to drive.

Beyond the turnoff for Hume Lake, Highway 180 (Kings River Hwy.) is closed in winter (usually Nov.–Apr.). In the summer, ❸ you can take this for a spectacular drive to the **Cedar Grove** area, a valley along the south fork of the Kings River. It's a one-hour drive from Grant Grove to the end of the road where you turn around for the ride back. Although it is steep in places, this is not a difficult road to drive. Built by convict labor in the 1930s, the road clings to some dramatic cliffs along the way, and you should watch out for falling rocks. The highway passes the scars where large groves of big trees were logged at the beginning of the century, and it runs through dry foothills covered with yuccas that bloom in the summer, and along the south fork itself. There are amazing views down into what may be the deepest gorge on the continent, at the confluence of the two forks, and up the canyons to the High Sierra.

Cedar Grove, named for the incense cedars that grow there, has campgrounds and lodging, a small ranger station, snack bar, convenience market, and gas station. Horses are available here, and they are a good way to explore this country. There are also short trails (one around Zumwalt Meadow, one to the base of Roaring River Falls), and Cedar Grove is the trailhead for many backpackers. If you're staying at Grant Grove or Giant Forest, Cedar Grove makes for a lovely day trip.

The **Generals Highway** begins south of Grant Grove and runs through this smaller portion of Kings Canyon National Park, through a part of Sequoia National Forest, and then through Sequoia National Park to the Giant Forest and on to the southern entrance to these parks at Ash Mountain.

❹ The **Redwood Mountain Grove** is the largest grove of big trees in the world. There are several paved turnouts (about 4 mi from the beginning of the highway) from which you can look out over the grove (and into the smog of the Central Valley), but the grove is accessible only on foot or horseback. Less than 2 miles ❺ farther, on the north side of the road, a large turnout, **Kings Canyon Overlook,** offers spectacular views into the larger portion of Kings Canyon National Park (the backcountry). You can peer into the deep canyons of the south and middle forks of the Kings River. If you drive east on Highway 180 to Cedar Grove along the south fork, you will see these canyons at much closer range.

❻ **Lodgepole,** in a U-shape canyon on the Marble Fork of the Kaweah River, is a developed area with campground, snack bars, grocery store, gas station, and a market complex including a deli, grocery store, gift shop, ice-cream parlor, public showers, public laundry, and post office. Lodgepole pines, rather than sequoias, grow here because the canyon conducts air down from the high country that is too cold for the big trees but is just right for lodgepoles. The visitor center (open July–Labor Day, daily 10–5) here has the best exhibits in Sequoia or Kings Canyon, a small theater that shows films about the parks, and the Lodgepole Nature Center, which features hands-on exhibits and activities that are geared toward children.

A very short marked nature trail leads from behind the visitor center down to the river. Except when the river is flowing fast (be very cautious), this is a good place to rinse one's feet in cool water, because the trail runs past a "beach" of small rocks along the river.

❼ The **Tokopah Falls Trail** is a more strenuous, 2-mile hike up the river from the campground (pick up a map at the visitor center), but it is also the closest you can get to the high country without taking a long hike. This is a lovely trail, but remember to bring insect repellent during the summer, when the mosquitoes can be ferocious.

❽ Four miles beyond Lodgepole you will come to the **Giant Forest.** This area has the greatest concentration of accommodations, although plans call for moving these to the Clover Creek area. In the meantime, this is a magical place to stay because of the numerous and varied trails through a series of sequoia groves. There are a grocery store, cafeteria, and two gift shops at Giant Forest Village and a wide range of accommodations at Giant Forest Lodge. The lodge also runs a full-service dining room and a gift shop during the summer.

Whether you are staying here or elsewhere in the parks, get the map of the local trails and start exploring. The well-constructed trails range in length from 1 to 5 miles. They are not paved, crowded, or lined with barricades, so you quickly get the feeling of being on your own in the woods, surrounded by the most impressive trees you are ever likely to see.

Be sure to visit one of the meadows. They are lovely, especially in July when the flowers are in full bloom, and you can get some of the best views of the big trees from across them. Round Meadow, behind Giant Forest Lodge, is the most easily accessible, with its ¼-mile, wheelchair-accessible "Trail For All People." Crescent and Log meadows are accessible by slightly longer trails. Tharp's Log, at Log Meadow, is a small and rustic pioneer cabin built in a fallen sequoia. There is also a log cabin at Huckleberry Meadow that children will enjoy exploring.

❾ The most famous tree here is the **General Sherman Tree.** If you aren't up for hiking at all, you can still get to this tree. There is usually a ranger nearby to answer questions, and there are benches so you can sit and contemplate one of the largest living things in the world. The tree is 274.9 feet tall and 102.6 feet around at its base, but what makes this the biggest tree is the fact that it is so wide for such a long way up: The first major branch is 130 feet up.

The Congress Trail starts here and travels past a series of large trees and younger sequoias. This is probably the most popular trail in the area, and it also has the most detailed booklet, so it is a good way to learn about the ecology of the groves. The booklet costs 50¢ and can be bought from a vending machine that takes quarters near the General Sherman Tree.

A 2½-mile spur road takes off from the Generals Highway near the village and will lead you to other points of interest in the Giant Forest area as well as to the trails to Crescent and Log meadows. The road actually goes through the Tunnel Log (there is a bypass for RVs that are too tall—7 ft. 9 in. and more—to fit). Auto Tree is merely a fallen tree onto which you can drive your car for a photograph (if that seems like a reasonable idea to you).

⑩ This is also the road to **Moro Rock,** a granite monolith 6,725 feet high, which rises from the edge of the Giant Forest. During the Depression, the Conservation Corps built a fabulous trail to the top. There are 400 steps and, although there is a railing along most of the route, the trail often climbs along narrow ledges over steep drops. The view from the top is spectacular. Southwest you look down the Kaweah River to Three Rivers, Lake Kaweah, and—on clear days—the Central Valley. Northeast you look up into the High Sierra. Below, you look down thousands of feet to the middle fork of the Kaweah River.

⑪ **Crystal Cave** is the best-known of Sequoia's many caves, but it will be closed for the summer of 1993 because of repairs being made to the access road. For information about other caves in Sequoia in which you can see the stalagmites and stalactites, call 209/565-3758.

⑫ The **Mineral King** area is a recent addition to the parks. In the 1960s the U.S. Forest Service planned to have Walt Disney Productions develop a winter-sports resort here, but the opposition of conservation groups led to its incorporation in Sequoia National Park in 1978. It is accessible in summer only by a narrow, twisty, and steep road that takes off from Highway 198 at Hammond. The road is only 25 miles long, but budget 90 minutes each way from Highway 198. This is a tough but exciting drive to a beautiful high valley. There are campgrounds and a ranger station; facilities are limited but some supplies are available. Many backpackers use this as a trailhead, and there are a number of fine trails for strenuous day hikes.

Off the Beaten Track

Montecito-Sequoia Resort (tel. 800/227-9900), off the Generals Highway between the two parks, offers year-round family-oriented recreation. In winter, there are 21 miles (35 km) of groomed cross-country ski trails, 50 miles (84 km) of back-country trails, ski rentals, and lessons. Rates include all meals, lodging, and trail use ($89 per person, per night, 2-night minimum). In summer guests stay for six nights in this Club Med atmosphere with access to canoeing, sailing, waterskiing (fee), horseback riding (fee), a preschool program, volleyball, horseshoes, tennis, archery, nature hikes, and a heated pool ($525 per adult, less for children, includes meals, lodging and all activities and instruction).

Sports

Fishing Fishing licenses are required for all anglers. State residents pay $23.65 for a year's license, nonresidents are charged $63.55. A one-day license costs $8.40 for everybody.

Hiking As in Yosemite, hiking is the primary sport in these two parks. Talk to the rangers at the visitor centers about which trails they recommend when you are there. Keep in mind that you will have to become acclimated to the altitude (over 6,000 ft. at Giant Forest) before you can exert yourself fully.

Horseback Riding Horseback riding is available at **Grant Grove, Cedar Grove, Wolverton Pack Station** (between Lodgepole and Giant Forest), and **Mineral King.** Ask at the visitor centers for specifics.

Swimming If you get hot and need a swim, try **Hume Lake** (*see* Exploring, above). Don't try to swim in the fast-running Sierra rivers.

Winter Sports In the winter, there is skiing and snowshoeing. You can ski cross-country at Grant Grove and Giant Forest. Rentals, lessons, and tours are offered by **Sequoia Ski Touring Center** (tel. 209/565–3435) at Wolverton and Grant Grove.

Rangers lead snowshoe walks through Grant Grove and Giant Forest on winter weekends. You can also use the shoes on the cross-country trails at these two areas. Snowshoes can be rented from Sequoia Ski Touring at Wolverton.

Dining

Dining in Sequoia and Kings Canyon national parks is even less of a gourmet experience than in Yosemite, but acceptable food is available. Again, we suggest that you bring food (especially snacks, fresh fruit, and beverages) with you. It will give you more freedom in planning your day. Still, there are places to get a meal inside the parks, and the food is not expensive and will satisfy hunger pangs. All of the restaurants within the park are managed by Guest Services (tel. 209/565–3381).

Food should not be left overnight in cars, because bears might be tempted to try to break in and get it.

Giant Forest Lodge Dining Room. This is the fanciest restaurant in the two parks, with cloth tablecloths, soft lighting, and a quiet atmosphere. The cuisine is basic American, featuring chicken, fish, and prime rib, and a Sunday buffet brunch. *MC, V. No lunch. Moderate. Open year-round.*

Cedar Grove Restaurant. This fast-food restaurant serves hamburgers, hot dogs, and sandwiches for lunch and dinner; eggs, bacon and toast for breakfast. *MC, V. Inexpensive. Closed Oct.–early May.*

Giant Forest Cafeteria. Fish, chicken, and a veggie stir-fry are served in a cafeteria-style setting. Open for breakfast, lunch, and dinner, the cafeteria is where to feed a family on a budget without getting heartburn in the bargain. *MC, V. Inexpensive. Open year round.*

Grant Grove Restaurant. This spacious family-style restaurant, with wood tables and chairs and a long counter, serves American standards for breakfast, lunch and dinner: eggs, burgers, and steak. There are also chef's salads, fruit platters, and seasonal fish specials. *MC, V. Inexpensive. Open year-round.*

Lodging

All of the park's lodges and cabins are open during the summer months, but in winter only some of those in Giant Forest and Grant Grove remain open. A variety of accommodations is offered at Giant Forest and Grant Grove, from rustic cabins without baths to deluxe motels. From November through April, excluding holiday periods, low season rates are in effect, resulting in savings of 20% to 30%.

Lodging facilities within the park are operated by Sequoia Guest Services (Box 789, Three Rivers, CA 93271, tel. 209/561–3314. MC, V.). Reservations are recommended for visits at any time of the year because it's a long way out if there's no room at these inns.

Giant Forest. There are seven different types of accommodations in this area, including rustic cabins without bathrooms, family cabins that sleep six, and a deluxe motel. Facilities and decor vary in a big way: Some cabins have only kerosene lamps and propane heat; motel rooms have carpeted floors and double and queen-size beds. Prices range accordingly—from $28.50 to $97.50 per night. The lower-priced cabins are not available in winter.

Grant Grove. The most luxurious accommodations here are the carpeted cabins with private baths, electric wall heaters, and double beds. Other cabins are simpler, with wood stoves providing heat, and kerosene lamps providing light. A central rest room and shower facility is nearby. Rates range from $23 in low season to $51.50 in summer.

Cedar Grove. At the bottom of Kings Canyon, in one of the prettiest areas of the parks, this is a good location for those who plan on staying a few days and doing a lot of day-hiking. Although accommodations are close to the road and there is quite a bit of traffic through here, Cedar Grove manages to retain a quiet atmosphere. Those who don't want to camp out will have to book way in advance—the motel/lodge has only 18 rooms. Each room is air-conditioned and carpeted and has a private shower and two queen-size beds. *Open late May through Sept. $27 per night.*

Camping

Campgrounds are by far the most economical accommodations in Sequoia and Kings Canyon, and probably the most fun. Located near each of the major tourist centers, the park's campgrounds are equipped with tables, fire grills, drinking water, garbage cans, and either flush or pit toilets. The only campground that takes reservations is Lodgepole in Sequoia (contact MISTIX, tel. 800/365–2267). All others assign sites on a first-come, first-served basis, and on weekends in July and August they are often filled up by Friday afternoon. Most campgrounds permit a maximum of one vehicle and six persons per site.

Potwisha, Grant Grove, Lodgepole, Dorst, and Cedar Grove campgrounds are the only areas where trailers and RVs are permitted. Sanitary disposal stations are available year-round in the Potwisha and Azalea (snow permitting) areas; from Memorial Day to mid-October in Lodgepole; and from May to mid-October in Sheep Creek. There are no hookups in the parks, and only a limited number of campsites can accommodate vehicles longer than 30 feet.

Lodgepole, Potwisha, and Azalea campsites stay open all year. Other campgrounds open some time from Mid-April to Memorial Day or later in September or October. Some campgrounds in Sequoia National Forest (such as Landslide, a very small campground 3 mi from Hume Lake) are just about as convenient as those within the two national parks. Campers should be aware that the nights, and even the days, can be chilly into early June.

10 Monterey Bay

By Maria Lenhart and Vicky Elliott

"The interest is perpetually fresh. On no other coast that I know shall you enjoy, in calm, sunny weather, such a spectacle of ocean's greatness, such beauty of changing color or such degrees of thunder in the sound." What Robert Louis Stevenson wrote of the Monterey Peninsula in 1879 is no less true today—it still provides a spectacle that is as exciting on the first visit as on the 23rd.

A semicircle about 90 miles across, Monterey Bay arcs into the coast at almost the exact halfway point between California's northern and southern borders. Santa Cruz sits at the top of the curve, and the Monterey Peninsula, including Monterey, Pacific Grove, and Carmel, occupies the lower end. In between, Highway 1 cruises along the coastline, passing windswept beaches piled high with sand dunes. Along the route are fields of artichoke plants, the towns of Watsonville and Castroville, and Fort Ord, the army base where millions of GIs got their basic training.

The bay is blessed by nature in a number of unique ways. Here are deep green forests of Monterey cypress, oddly gnarled and wind-twisted trees that grow nowhere else. Here also is a vast undersea canyon, larger and deeper than the Grand Canyon, that supports a rich assortment of marine life, from fat, barking sea lions to tiny plantlike anemones.

The Monterey Peninsula especially holds a unique place in California history that is evident in its carefully preserved adobe houses and missions. With the arrival of Father Junípero Serra and Commander Don Gaspar de Portola from Spain in 1770, Monterey became both the military and ecclesiastical capital of Alta California. Portola established the first of California's four Spanish presidios, while Serra founded the second of 21 Franciscan missions, later moving it from Monterey to its current site in Carmel.

When Mexico revolted against Spain in 1822, Monterey remained the capital of California under Mexican rule. The town grew into a lively seaport, drawing Yankee sea traders who added their own cultural and political influence. Then, on July 7, 1846, Commodore John Sloat arrived in Monterey and raised the American flag over the Custom House, claiming California for the United States.

Monterey's political importance in the new territory was short-lived, however. Although the state constitution was framed in Colton Hall, the town was all but forgotten in the excitement caused by the discovery of gold at Sutter's Mill near Sacramento. After the Gold Rush, the state capital moved from Monterey and the town became a sleepy backwater.

At the turn of the century, however, the Monterey Peninsula began to draw tourists with the opening of the Del Monte Hotel, the most palatial resort the West Coast had ever seen. Writers and artists also discovered the peninsula, adding a rich legacy that remains to this day.

For visitors, the decline of Monterey as California's most important political and population center can be seen as a blessing. The layers of Spanish and Mexican history remain remarkably undisturbed, while the land and sea continue to inspire and delight.

Getting Around

By Plane Monterey Peninsula Airport (tel. 408/373–3731) is 3 miles from downtown Monterey and is served by **American Eagle** (tel. 800/433–7300), **Sky West/Delta** (tel. 800/453–9417), **United Airlines** and **United Express** (tel. 800/241–6522) with daily service from San Francisco and Los Angeles. **USAir** (tel. 800/428–4322) has daily service from Los Angeles and San Francisco.

By Car The drive south from San Francisco to Monterey can be made comfortably in three hours or less. The most scenic way is to follow Highway 1 down the coast, past pumpkin and artichoke fields and the seaside communities of Half Moon Bay and Santa Cruz. Unless the drive is made on sunny weekends when locals are heading for the beach, the two-lane coast highway takes no longer than the freeway.

Of the freeways from San Francisco, a fast but enjoyable route is I–280 south to Highway 17, just south of San Jose. Highway 17 heads south over the redwood-forested Santa Cruz mountains, and connects with Highway 1 in Santa Cruz. Another option is to follow U.S. 101 south through San Jose to Salinas, then take Highway 68 west to Monterey. If your route of choice takes you through San Jose, avoid the rush hour, which starts early and can be horrendous.

From Los Angeles, the drive to Monterey can be made in less than a day by heading north on U.S. 101 to Salinas and then heading west on Highway 68. The spectacular but slow alternative is to take U.S. 101 to San Luis Obispo and then follow the hairpin turns of Highway 1 up the coast. Allow at least three extra hours if you do.

The Rider's Guide (Suite 255, 484 Lake Park Ave., Oakland 94610, tel. 510/653–2553) produces a tape you can play in your car about the history, landmarks, and attractions of the Monterey peninsula and Big Sur, for $11.95 plus $2 postage.

By Train The closest train connection to the Monterey Peninsula is Amtrak's *Coast Starlight*, which makes a stop in Salinas on its run between Los Angeles and Seattle (tel. 800/USA–RAIL).

By Bus From San Francisco, **Greyhound-Trailways** (tel. 415/558–6789) serves Monterey five times daily on a trip that takes up to four hours.

For getting around on the peninsula by bus, **Monterey-Salinas Transit** (tel. 408/424–7695) provides frequent service between towns and many major sightseeing spots and shopping areas for $1.25 per ride, with an additional $1.25 for each zone you travel into.

Scenic Drives

17-Mile Drive Although some sightseers balk at the $6-per-car fee, most agree that it is well worth the price to explore this 8,400-acre microcosm of the Monterey coastal landscape. The main entrance gates are off Lighthouse Avenue in Pacific Grove and off Highway 1 and North San Antonio Avenue in Carmel.

Once inside, the drive presents primordial nature preserved in quiet harmony with palatial estates. Among the natural treasures here are many prime examples of the rare Monterey cypress, trees so gnarled and twisted that Robert Louis

Stevenson once described them as "ghosts fleeing before the wind." The most photographed of them all is the **Lone Cypress,** a weather-sculpted tree growing out of a rocky outcropping above the waves. A turnout parking area makes it possible to stop for a view of the Lone Cypress, but walking out to it on the precipitous outcropping is no longer allowed. Two other landmarks to note are **Seal Rock** and **Bird Rock,** two islands of bird and marine life teeming with harbor seals, sea lions, cormorants, and pelicans.

As enticing as the natural landscapes are along the drive, those created by man are a big part of the attraction as well. Perhaps no more famous concentration of celebrated golf courses exists anywhere in the world, particularly the **Pebble Beach Golf Links,** with its famous 18th hole, around which the ocean plays a major role. Even if you're not a golfer, views of impeccable greens can be enjoyed over a drink or lunch at the **Lodge at Pebble Beach** or the **Inn at Spanish Bay,** the two resorts located along the drive.

Among the stately homes, many of which reflect the classic Monterey or Spanish Mission style typical of the region, a standout is the **Crocker Marble Palace,** a waterfront estate designed after a Byzantine castle. Located near the Carmel entrance to the drive, this baroque mansion is easily identifiable by its dozens of marble arches. The estate's grounds feature a beach area with water heated by underground pipes.

Carmel Valley Road A world away from the cypress forests and tide pools of the coast are the pastoral ranchlands of Carmel Valley. The rolling meadows studded with oak trees are especially compelling during the spring, when the grass is lush, green, and blooming with bright gold California poppies and blue lupines.

Carmel Valley Road, which turns inland at Highway 1 just south of Carmel, is the main thoroughfare through this secluded enclave of horse ranchers and other well-heeled residents who prefer the valley's perpetually dry, sunny climate to the fog and wind on the coast. A pleasant couple of hours can be spent rambling up the road and back. Or, if you want to stay longer, you can go to **Garland Ranch Regional Park** (tel. 408/659–4488), 10 miles east of Carmel Valley, which has hiking trails and picnic facilities; or spend some time in tiny Carmel Valley village, where there are several crafts shops and art galleries.

A popular stop along this road is the tasting room at the beautiful **Château Julien** winery, known for its chardonnay and merlot. Tours are given at 10:30 AM and 2.30 PM but must be arranged by calling ahead. *Tel. 408/624–2600. Open weekdays 8:30–5, weekends 11–5.*

An enjoyable loop drive can be added by turning off Carmel Valley Road onto **Los Laureles Grade,** a 6-mile winding road that heads over the mountains to Highway 68, ending at a point about halfway between Monterey and Salinas. Located along Highway 68 is the award-winning **Ventana Vineyards,** which has a tasting room. *Tel. 408/372–7415. Open daily noon–5.*

Guided Tours

Seacoast Safaris (tel. 408/372–1288) offers both custom tours and half-day tours of the Monterey Peninsula, which include the 17-Mile Drive, Carmel shopping, Cannery Row, and wine tasting. Rates include minivan transportation and sightseeing with guides who are longtime area residents.

Motorcoach tours departing from San Francisco that feature the Monterey Peninsula in their Northern California itineraries include **California Parlor Car Tours** (tel. 415/474–7500 or 800/227–4250) and **Gray Line** (tel. 415/558–9400).

Important Addresses and Numbers

Tourist Information **The Monterey Peninsula Chamber of Commerce** (Box 1770, 380 Alvarado St., Monterey 93942, tel. 408/649–1770) and the **Salinas Chamber of Commerce** (119 E. Alisal St., Salinas 93901, tel. 408/424–7611) are both open weekdays 8:30–5. **The Santa Cruz County Conference and Visitors Council** (701 Front St., 95060, tel. 408/425–1234 or 800/833-3494) is open daily 9–5.

Emergencies Dial 911 for **police** and **ambulance** in an emergency.

Doctors The **Monterey County Medical Society** (tel. 408/373–4197) will refer doctors on weekdays, 9–5. For referrals at other times, call **Community Hospital of Monterey Peninsula** (23625 Holman Hwy., Monterey, tel. 408/624–5311). The hospital has a 24-hour emergency room.

Pharmacies There are no all-night pharmacies, but for emergencies there is the Pharmacy Department at the Community Hospital of Monterey Peninsula (*see* above). **Surf 'n' Sand** in Carmel at Sixth and Junipero streets (tel. 408/624–1543) has a pharmacy open weekdays 9–6:30, Saturday, Sunday, and holidays 9–2.

Exploring

Despite its compact size, the Monterey Peninsula is packed with many and varied diversions, and would require more than a weekend to just get beyond the surface. Although most of the region's communities are situated only a few minutes' drive away from each other, each is remarkably different in flavor and in attractions.

If you have an interest in California history and historic preservation, the place to start is in Monterey, where you need at least two full days to explore the adobe buildings along the Path of History, a state historic park encompassing much of the downtown area. Fans of Victorian architecture will want to allow extra time to explore Pacific Grove, where many fine examples have been preserved, and often house restaurants or bed-and-breakfast inns.

In Carmel you can shop till you drop, although one day's worth of fighting the summer and weekend hordes through boutiques, art galleries, houseware outlets, and gift shops is usually enough for most people. After that, the incomparable loveliness of the Carmel coast can restore the spirit if not the pocketbook.

The climate can also vary on the peninsula. A sweater or windbreaker is nearly always necessary along the coast, where a cool breeze is usually blowing and the fog is on the way in or out. Inland is very different, however, particularly during the summer, when temperatures in Salinas or Carmel Valley can be a good 15 or 20 degrees warmer than those in Carmel and Monterey.

Although a car is handy for getting from town to town, most of the Monterey Peninsula can be seen on foot. Parking is especially difficult in Carmel and in the vicinity of the Monterey Bay Aquarium on Cannery Row. Take comfortable shoes for negotiating village streets, ambling along the shoreline, and hiking through nature preserves. A good pair of binoculars is also highly recommended; you never know when a playful otter or even a migrating gray whale may splash into sight.

Santa Cruz

The beach town of **Santa Cruz** is sheltered by the surrounding mountains from the coastal fog to the north and south, and from the smoggy skies of the San Francisco Bay Area. The climate here is mild, and it is usually warmer and sunnier than elsewhere along the coast this far north. Something of a haven for those opting out of the rat race, and a bastion of '60s-style counterculture values, Santa Cruz is less manicured than its up-market neighbors to the south, but more urban than the agricultural towns between it and the Monterey Peninsula. Having been at the forefront of such very Californian trends as health food, recycling, and environmentalism, the city takes great pride in continuing to experiment with new ideas.

Making an art of the makeshift has been a necessity here since the earthquake of 1989, which laid low much of Pacific Garden Mall, in the historic downtown section. The epicenter of the quake was only a few miles away, in the Santa Cruz mountains, and the unreinforced masonry of the town's older buildings proved extremely vulnerable. Rebuilding has been a long process, and there are still gaping lots behind wire fencing, especially along Pacific Avenue, in the heart of the downtown area, but the spirit of the place is alive and well even in the temporary quarters into which many of the local businesses had to be decanted.

The town gets something of its youthful ambience from the nearby **University of California at Santa Cruz.** The school's harmonious redwood buildings are perched on the forested hills above the town, and the campus is tailor-made for the contemplative life, with a juxtaposition of sylvan settings and sweeping vistas over open meadows onto the bay. The humanities faculty offers a major in the "History of Consciousness," and this does seem to be the perfect spot for it.

Santa Cruz has been a seaside resort since the mid-19th century, and its **Boardwalk's** 1911 **Merry-Go-Round** and **Giant Dipper** monster roller-coaster are national historic landmarks. Elsewhere along the Boardwalk the **Casino Arcade** has its share of video-game technology, as does **Neptune's Kingdom**, which features a state-of-the-art miniature golf course with robotics and fiber-optics special effects, but this is still primarily a place of good old-fashioned fun. The colonnades of the turn-of-the-century **Cocoanut Grove**, now a convention center and banquet hall, host lavish weekend brunches beneath the glass dome of its Sun Room. *Boardwalk, tel. 408/423–5590. Day pass for unlimited rides, $16.95. Open Memorial Day–Labor Day, daily from 11 AM (evening closing times vary between dusk, 9 PM, and*

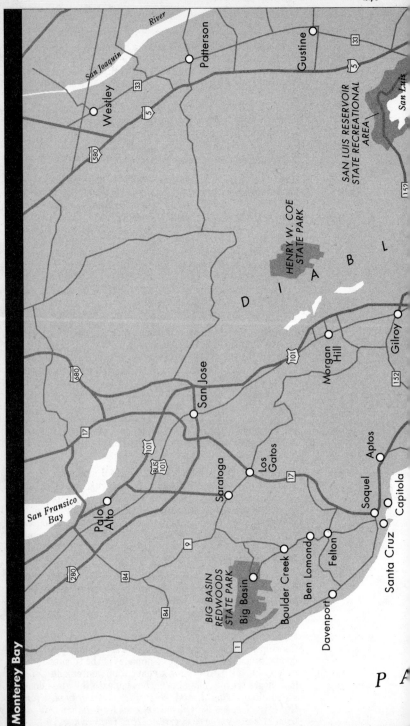

Monterey Bay

San Joaquin River

Patterson

Gustine

33

5

Westley

33

5

580

SAN LUIS RESERVOIR
STATE RECREATIONAL
AREA

San Luis

152

HENRY W. COE
STATE PARK

D I A B L

Gilroy

680

San Jose

Morgan
Hill

101

152

17

101

BUS
101

Saratoga

Los
Gatos

17

Aptos

Soquel

San Fransico
Bay

Palo
Alto

9

Capitola

280

84

84

1

BIG BASIN
REDWOODS
STATE PARK

Big Basin

Boulder Creek

Ben Lomond

Felton

Davenport

Santa Cruz

P A

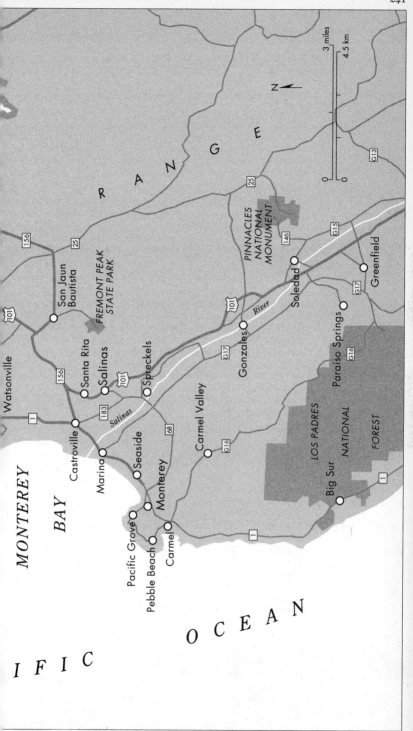

11 PM throughout the year), weekends and holidays rest of year. Cocoanut Grove, tel. 408/423-2053. Brunch Sun. 9:30 AM-1:30 PM. MC, V.

The **Santa Cruz Municipal Wharf** is lined with restaurants and is enlivened from below by the barking and baying of the sea lions that lounge in communal heaps under the wharf's pilings and shamelessly accept any seafood offerings tossed their way.

Fishing and whale-watching trips from the wharf from December through April are offered by the Stagnaro family, which owns the lion's share of the businesses on the wharf (*see* Fishing, and Participant Sports, *below*). The "super yacht" *Chardonnay II,* which can accommodate 49 passengers, also organizes cruises on the bay (1661 Pine Flat Rd., 95060, tel. 408/423-1213).

Down West Cliff Dr. along the promontory, one comes upon **Seal Rock**, another favored pinniped hangout, and the **Lighthouse**, which has a surfing museum (tel. 408/429-3429; open Wed.-Mon. noon-4). The road continues on to **Natural Bridges State Park,** famous for its tide pools and a colony of Monarch butterflies. *2531 W. Cliff Dr., tel. 408/423-4609. Open 8 AM-sunset. Parking fee.*

A visible local subspecies are the surfers, who seem to live only for the spectacular waves and sunsets at such spots as **Pleasure Point** (East Cliff Dr. and 41st Ave.) and **New Brighton State Beach** (1500 Park Ave., Capitola), which also has campsites. **Manresa State Beach** (San Andreas Rd. Watsonville, tel. 408/688-3241), farther south, offers premium surfing conditions, and those who surf here tend to be very good, but, although there is a lifeguard on duty during most of the summer season, the waters off this beach are notorious for treacherous currents and riptides, and we recommend it as a spot for sunning and spectating.

Santa Cruz's temperate climate has attracted some fine wineries, producing chiefly chardonnay, cabernet sauvignon, and Pinot Noir. Information on the region's 30-or-so family-owned wineries can be obtained from **Santa Cruz Winegrowers** (303 Potrero St. 35, Santa Cruz, 95060, tel. 408/458-5030).

Time Out | **Caffè Pergolesi**, not far from the downtown area, is a Victorian residence that has become a humming coffeehouse with a very European flair. You can read the newspaper and enjoy a pastry at one of the veranda tables, or have a light meal inside, surrounded by local artists' work and under the elegant molded ceilings. *418A Cedar St., tel. 408/426-1775. Closed major holidays. No credit cards.*

Monterey

Numbers in the margin correspond to points of interest on the Monterey map.

A good way to begin exploring the Monterey Peninsula is to start at the beginnings of the town of Monterey—the beautifully preserved collection of adobe buildings contained in the **Monterey State Historic Park** (tel. 408/649-7118). Far from being a hermetic period museum, the park facilities are an integral part of the day-to-day business life of the town, with some of the buildings still serving as government offices, restaurants, banks, and private residences. Others are museums illustrating life in the raw, early seaport as it developed from a colonial Spanish outpost to its brief heyday as California's political center.

The best way to enjoy the park is on a 2-mile self-guided walking tour outlined in a brochure called the **"Path of History,"** available at the Chamber of Commerce or at many of the landmark buildings contained in the park. *Tour package for multiple sites: $4 adults, $3 children 6–12.*

1 A logical beginning to the walking tour is at the **Custom House** across from Fisherman's Wharf. Built by the Mexican government in 1827 and considered the oldest government building west of the Rockies, this two-story adobe was the first stop for sea traders whose goods were subject to duty. Its grandest day in Monterey's history came at the beginning of the Mexican-American War in 1846, when Commodore John Sloat raised the American flag over the building and claimed California for the United States. Now the lower floor displays examples of a typical cargo from a 19th-century trading ship. *1 Custom House Plaza, tel. 408/649–7118. Admission free. Open Sept.–May, Wed.–Sun. 10–4; June–Aug., daily 10–5.*

2 The next stop along the path is **Pacific House,** a former hotel and saloon, and now a museum of early California life. There are Gold Rush relics, historic photographs of old Monterey, and a costume gallery displaying lacy Mexican shawls and tiny kid slippers from the colonial days. *10 Custom House Plaza, tel. 408/649–2907. Admission: $2, $1 for children 6–12. Open Sept.–May, Wed.–Sun. 10–4; June–Aug., Wed.–Sun. 10–5.*

3 Monterey's most historic gift shop is the **Joseph Boston Store,** located in the Casa del Oro adobe. It first opened for business in 1849, and was built from wood from a shipwrecked Portuguese whaler. Now staffed with volunteers from the Monterey History and Art Association, the shop is stocked with antiques, tea, and a variety of gift items. *Scott and Oliver Sts. Open Wed.–Sat. 10–5, Sun. noon–5.*

4 Farther along the Path of History is the **Larkin House,** one of the most architecturally significant homes in California. Built in 1835, this two-story adobe with a veranda encircling the second floor is a blend of Mexican and New England influences that became known as the Monterey style. The rooms are furnished with period antiques, many of them brought from New Hampshire to Monterey by the Larkin family. *Jefferson St. and Calle Principal. Admission: $2 adults, $1 children 6–12. Open weekends. Tours on the hour 10–3 (June–Aug. 10–4).*

5 Next door, the **Allen Knight Maritime Museum** is devoted to the private collection of maritime artifacts of former Carmel mayor Allen Knight. The highlight among the exhibits of ship models, scrimshaw items, and nautical prints is the enormous multifaceted Fresnel Light from the Point Sur Lighthouse. *550 Calle Principal, tel. 408/375–2553. Open Sept. 15–June 15, Tues.–Fri. 1–4, Sat.–Sun. 2–4; June 16–Sept. 14, Tues.–Fri. 10–4, Sat.–Sun. 2–4.*

The largest site along the Path of History is the restored **6** **Cooper-Molera Adobe,** a 4-acre complex that includes an early California house dating from the 1820s, a gift shop, a screening

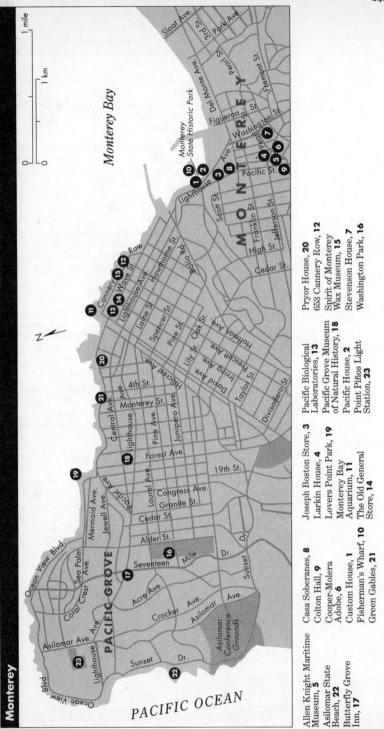

Monterey

Allen Knight Maritime Museum, **5**

Asilomar State Beach, **22**

Butterfly Grove Inn, **17**

Casa Soberanes, **8**

Colton Hall, **9**

Cooper-Molera Adobe, **6**

Custom House, **1**

Fisherman's Wharf, **10**

Green Gables, **21**

Joseph Boston Store, **3**

Larkin House, **4**

Lovers Point Park, **19**

Monterey Bay Aquarium, **11**

The Old General Store, **14**

Pacific Biological Laboratories, **13**

Pacific Grove Museum of Natural History, **18**

Pacific House, **2**

Point Piños Light Station, **23**

Pryor House, **20**

653 Cannery Row, **12**

Spirit of Monterey Wax Museum, **15**

Stevenson House, **7**

Washington Park, **16**

room where an introductory slide presentation is shown, and a large garden enclosed by a high adobe wall. The tile-roofed house is filled with antiques and memorabilia, mostly from the Victorian era, that illustrate the life of a prosperous pioneer family. *Polk and Munras Sts. Admission: $2, $1 for children 6–12. Tours on the hour 10–3 (June–Aug. 10–4). Closed 1–2.*

7 For literary and history buffs, one of the path's greatest treasures is the **Stevenson House,** named in honor of Robert Louis Stevenson, author of *Treasure Island* and other classics, who boarded there briefly in a tiny upstairs room. In addition to Stevenson's room, which is furnished with items from his family's estate, there is a gallery of the author's memorabilia and several charming period rooms, including a children's nursery stocked with Victorian toys and games. *530 Houston St. Admission: $2 adults, $1 for children 6–12. Open weekends. Tours on the hour 10–3, June–Aug. 10–4. Closed noon–1 PM.*

8 A historic house with an entirely different feel is the low-ceilinged **Casa Soberanes,** a classic adobe structure that once housed the commander of the Spanish Presidio. *336 Pacific St. Admission: $2, $1 for children 6–12. Open weekends. Tours on the hour 10–3, June–Aug. 10–4; Closed 1–2.*

9 California's equivalent of Independence Hall is **Colton Hall,** a white edifice where a convention of delegates met in 1849 to draft the first state constitution. Now the historic building, which has served as a school, courthouse, and county seat, is a museum furnished as it was during the constitutional convention. The extensive grounds outside the hall also include a more notorious building, the Old Monterey Jail, where inmates languished behind thick granite walls. *Pacific St. between Madison and Jefferson Sts., tel. 408/375–9944. Admission free. Open March–Oct., daily 10–5; Nov.–Feb., 10–4. Closed noon–1 weekends, major holidays.*

Although not on the Path of History, the **Monterey Peninsula Museum of Art** is just across the street from Colton Hall. The museum is especially strong on artists and photographers who have worked in the area, a distinguished lot that includes Ansel Adams and Edward Weston. Another focus of the museum is folk art from around the world; the collection ranges from Kentucky hearth brooms to Tibetan prayer wheels. *559 Pacific St., tel. 408/372–7591. $2 donation requested. Open Tues.–Sat. 10–4, Sun. 1–4.*

Fisherman's Wharf and Cannery Row

Inevitably, visitors are drawn toward the waterfront in Monterey, if only because the mournful barking of sea lions that can be heard throughout the town makes its presence impossible to ignore. The whiskered marine mammals are best enjoyed while
10 walking along **Fisherman's Wharf,** an aging pier crowded with souvenir shops, fish markets, seafood restaurants, and popcorn stands.

Although tacky and touristy to the utmost, the wharf is a good place to visit, especially with children. For years, an organ grinder with a costumed monkey has entertained crowds at the entrance to the wharf. Farther down, you can buy a bag of squid to feed the sea lions that beg from the waters below.

From the wharf, a footpath along the shore leads to **Cannery Row,** a street that has undergone several transformations since it was immortalized in John Steinbeck's 1944 novel of the same name. The street that Steinbeck wrote of was crowded with sardine canneries processing, at their peak, nearly 200,000 tons of the smelly silver fish a year. During the mid-1940s, however, the sardines mysteriously disappeared from the bay, causing the canneries to close.

Over the years the old tin-roof canneries have been converted to restaurants, art galleries, and minimalls with shops selling T-shirts, fudge, and plastic otters. A recent trend, however, has been toward a more tasteful level of tourist development along the row, including several attractive inns and hotels. The Monterey Plaza Hotel (400 Cannery Row) is a good place to relax over a drink and watch for otters.

The most important recent development on Cannery Row has
⓫ been the opening of the spectacular **Monterey Bay Aquarium,** a $50 million window on the sea waters just outside its back doors. The aquarium has proved so popular that visitors should expect long lines and sizable crowds on weekends, especially during the summer. Braving the crowds is worth it, however, especially to see the three-story Kelp Forest exhibit, the only one of its kind in the world, and a re-creation of the sea creatures and vegetation found in Monterey Bay. Among other standout exhibits are a bat-ray petting pool, where the flat velvetlike creatures can be touched as they swim by; a 55,000-gallon sea otter tank; and an enormous outdoor artificial tide pool that supports anemones, crabs, sea stars, and other colorful creatures. *886 Cannery Row, tel. 408/649–6466. Admission: $9.75 adults, $7.25 senior citizens and students, $4.50 children 3–12. Open daily 10–6, 9:30–6 on holidays; closed Christmas. AE, MC, V.*

Although Steinbeck would have trouble recognizing the street today, there are still some historical and architectural features
⓬ from its colorful past. One building to take note of is **653 Cannery Row,** with its tiled Chinese dragon roof that dates from 1929. A weathered wooden building at 800 Cannery Row was
⓭ the **Pacific Biological Laboratories,** where Edward F. Ricketts, the inspiration for Doc in Steinbeck's novel, did much of his marine research. Across the street, the building now called
⓮ **The Old General Store** is the former Wing Chong Market that Steinbeck called Lee Chong's Heavenly Flower Grocery.

On a more kitschy note, characters from the novel *Cannery*
⓯ *Row* are depicted in wax at **Steinbeck's Spirit of Monterey Wax Museum,** which also features a 25-minute description of the history of the area over the past 400 years, with a recorded narration by Steinbeck himself. *700 Cannery Row, tel. 408/375–3770. Admission: $4.95 adults, $3.95 senior citizens and students, $2.95 children 6–12. Open daily 8:45 AM–10 PM.*

Pacific Grove

If not for the dramatic strip of coastline in its backyard, Pacific Grove could easily pass for a typical small town in the heartland. Beginning as a summer retreat for church groups a century ago, the town has retained some of its prim and proper Victorian heritage in the host of tiny board and batten cottages and stately mansions lining its streets.

Even before the church groups migrated here, however, Pacific Grove had been receiving thousands of annual guests in the form of bright orange and black monarch butterflies. Known as "Butterfly Town USA," Pacific Grove is the winter home of the monarchs that migrate south from Canada and the Pacific Northwest and take residence in the pine and eucalyptus groves between October and March. The site of a mass of butterflies hanging from the branches like a long fluttering veil is unforgettable.

Although many of their original nesting grounds have vanished, two good spots for viewing butterflies remain. The largest is **Washington Park** at the corner of Pine Avenue and Alder Street; the other is a grove adjoining the **Butterfly Grove Inn** at 1073 Lighthouse Avenue.

If you are in Pacific Grove when the butterflies aren't, an approximation of this annual miracle is on exhibit at the **Pacific Grove Museum of Natural History.** In addition to a finely crafted butterfly-tree exhibit, the museum features a collection of 400 mounted birds native to Monterey County and a film presentation about the monarch butterfly. *165 Forest Ave., tel. 408/648–3116. Admission free. Open Tues.–Sun. 10–5.*

A prime way to enjoy Pacific Grove is to walk or bicycle along its 3 miles of city-owned shoreline, a clifftop area following Ocean View Boulevard that is landscaped with succulents and native plants and has plenty of park benches on which to sit and gaze at the sea. A variety of marine and bird life can be spotted here, including colonies of cormorants that are drawn to the massive rocks rising out of the surf. **Lovers Point Park,** located midway along the waterfront, is a pleasant grassy area in which to stop and picnic.

Although it is difficult to turn away from the gorgeous coast, the other side of Ocean View Boulevard has a number of imposing turn-of-the-century mansions that are well worth your attention. One of the finest is the **Pryor House** at number 429, a massive shingled structure with a leaded and beveled glass doorway built in 1909 for an early mayor. At the corner of 5th Street and Ocean View is **Green Gables,** a romantic Swiss Gothic-style mansion, now a bed-and-breakfast inn, with steeply peaked gables and stained-glass windows.

Another beautiful coastal area in Pacific Grove is **Asilomar State Beach,** on Sunset Drive between Point Piños and the Del Monte Forest. The 100 acres of dunes, tide pools, and pocket-size beaches form one of the region's richest areas for marine life. The deep tide pools support 210 species of algae and are alive with sea urchins, crabs, and other creatures.

The oldest continuously operating lighthouse on the West Coast is also a museum open to the public, the **Point Piños Light Station.** Visitors can learn about the lighting and foghorn operations and wander through a small museum containing historical memorabilia from the U.S. Coast Guard. *Ocean View Blvd. at Point Piños, tel. 408/648–3116. Admission free. Open weekends 1–4 PM.*

Carmel

Numbers in the margins correspond to points of interest on the Carmel map.

Although the community has grown quickly over the years and its population quadruples with tourists on weekends and during the summer, Carmel retains its identity as a quaint "village" where buildings have no street numbers and live music is banned in the local watering holes. Indeed, there is still a villagelike ambience for visitors wandering the side streets at their own pace, poking into hidden courtyards and stopping at a Hansel-and-Gretel-like café for tea and crumpets.

Carmel has its share of hokey gift emporiums, but most of the wares in its hundreds of shops are distinctive and of high quality. Classic sportswear, gourmet cookware, and original art are among the best buys to be found along the main street, Ocean Avenue, and its cross streets. Just as notable is the architecture of many of the shops, a charming mishmash of ersatz English Tudor, Mediterranean, and other styles.

In recent years, the popularity of shopping in Carmel has led to the creation of several attractive, nicely landscaped shopping malls. **Carmel Plaza,** in the east end of the village proper, consists of more than 50 shops, restaurants, and small branches of major department stores. **The Barnyard** and **the Crossroads** are just southeast of the village off Highway 1.

Time Out | **Patisserie Boissiere,** a Carmel Plaza café reminiscent of a country French inn, is the perfect place to take a break from shopping. Light entrées and French pastries are offered. *On Mission Ave. between Ocean and 7th Aves., tel. 408/624–5008. AE, MC, V. Open daily except on Christmas Day.*

Before it became an art colony in the early 20th century and long before it became a shopping and browsing mecca, Carmel was an important religious center in the early days of Spanish California. That heritage is preserved in one of the state's loveliest historic sites, the Mission San Carlos Borromeo del Rio Carmelo, more commonly known as the **Carmel Mission.** Founded in 1770 and serving as headquarters for the mission system in California under Father Junípero Serra, the Carmel Mission exists today with its stone church and tower dome beautifully restored. Adjoining the church is a tranquil garden planted with California poppies and a series of museum rooms that depict an early kitchen, Father Serra's spartan sleeping quarters, and the oldest college library in California. *Rio Rd. and Lasuen Dr., tel. 408/624–3600. Donations suggested. Open Mon.–Sat. 9:30–4:30, Sun. 10:30–4:30.*

Scattered throughout the pines in Carmel are the houses and cottages that were built for the steady stream of writers, artists, and photographers who discovered the area decades ago. Among the most impressive dwellings is **Tor House,** a stone cottage built by the poet Robinson Jeffers in 1918 on a craggy knoll overlooking the sea. The low-ceilinged rooms are filled with portraits, books, and unusual art objects, such as a white stone from the Great Pyramid in Egypt. The highlight of the small estate is Hawk Tower, a detached edifice set with stones from the Great Wall of China and a Roman villa, which served as a retreat for the poet's wife, Una, an accomplished musician. The docents who lead tours are very well informed about the poet's work and life. Jeffers's home and life present a fascinating story, even if you are not a fan of his poetry. *26304 Ocean View Ave., tel. 408/624–1813 or 408/624–1840. Admission: $5 adults,*

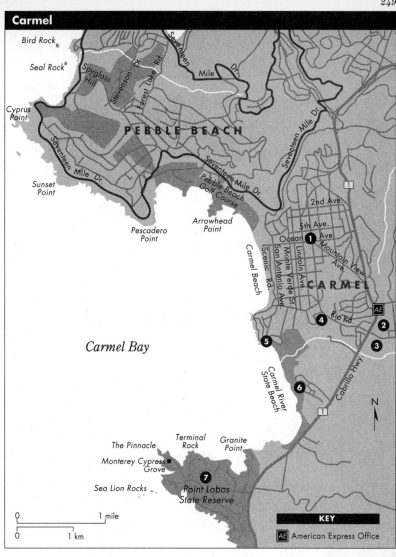

Carmel

Bird Rock
Seal Rock
Spyglass Hill
Stevenson Dr.
Forest Lake Rd.
Seventeen Mile Dr.
Cyprus Point
Seventeen Mile Dr.
PEBBLE BEACH
Seventeen Mile Dr.
Sunset Point
Pescadero Point
Pebble Beach Golf Course
Seventeen Mile Dr.
Arrowhead Point
Carmel Beach
Scenic Rd.
Monte Verde St.
San Antonio Ave.
Lincoln Ave.
Ocean Ave.
2nd Ave.
5th Ave.
Mountain View Ave.
CARMEL
Rio Rd.
AE
Carmel Bay
Carmel River State Beach
Cabrillo Hwy.
N
The Pinnacle
Monterey Cypress Grove
Sea Lion Rocks
Terminal Rock
Granite Point
Point Lobos State Reserve

0   1 mile
0   1 km

KEY
AE American Express Office

The Barnyard, **2**
Carmel Mission, **4**
Carmel Plaza, **1**
Carmel River State Park, **6**
The Crossroads, **3**
Point Lobos State Reserve, **7**
Tor House, **5**

$3.50 college students, $1.50 high-school students. Tours by appointment on Fri. and Sat. 10–3.

Carmel's greatest beauty, however, is not to be found in its historic and architectural landmarks. Nature has done the most impressive work here, particularly in forming the rugged coastline with its pine and cypress forests and countless inlets. Happily, much of the coastal area has been set aside for public enjoyment.

❻ Carmel River State Park stretches for 106 acres along Carmel Bay. On sunny days the waters appear nearly as turquoise as those of the Caribbean. The park features a sugar-white beach with high dunes and a bird sanctuary that is a nesting ground for pelicans, kingfishers, hawks, and sandpipers. *Off Scenic Rd., south of Carmel Beach, tel. 408/649–2836. Open daily 9 AM–½ hour after sunset.*

❼ The park is overshadowed by **Point Lobos State Reserve,** a 1,250-acre headland just south of Carmel. Roads have been kept to a minimum, and the best way to explore is to walk along the extensive network of hiking trails. Especially good choices are the Cypress Grove Trail, which leads through a forest of rare Monterey cypresses clinging to the rocks above an emerald-green cove, and Sea Lion Point Trail, where sea lions, otters, harbor seals, and (during certain times of year) migrating whales can be observed. Part of the reserve is an undersea marine park open to qualified scuba divers. *Hwy. 1, tel. 408/624–4909, or 800/444–7275 to reserve for scuba diving. Admission: $6 per car, $5 if senior citizen is traveling. Open May–Sept., daily 9–6:30; Oct.–Apr., daily 9–4:30.*

Salinas

While Monterey turns its face toward the sea, Salinas, a half-hour inland and a world away in spirit, is deeply rooted as the population center of a rich agricultural valley. This unpretentious town may lack the sophistication and scenic splendors of the coast, but it is of interest to literary and architectural buffs.

The memory and literary legacy of Salinas native John Steinbeck are well honored here. The author's birthplace, a Victorian frame house, has been converted to a lunch-only restaurant called—what else—the **Steinbeck House,** and is run by the volunteer Valley Guild. The restaurant contains some Steinbeck memorabilia and presents a menu featuring locally grown produce. *132 Central Ave., tel. 408/424–2735. Reservations requested. Open weekdays for 2 sittings at 11:45 AM and 1:15 PM.*

Steinbeck did much of his research for *East of Eden,* a novel partially drawn from his Salinas boyhood, at what is now called the **Steinbeck Library.** The library features tapes of interviews with people who knew Steinbeck and a display of photos, first editions, letters, original manuscripts, and other items pertaining to the novelist. *110 W. San Luis, tel. 408/758–7311. Admission free. Open Mon.–Thurs. 10–9, Fri.–Sat. 10–6.*

Salinas's turn-of-the-century architecture has been the focus of an ongoing renovation project, much of which is centered on the original downtown area on South Main Street, with its handsome stone storefronts. One of the finest private residences from this era is the **Harvey-Baker House,** a beautifully preserved redwood house built in 1868 for the city's first mayor.

238 E. Romie La., tel. 408/757–8085. Admission free. Open Sun. 1–4 PM, and weekdays by appointment.

Of even earlier vintage is the **Jose Eusebio Boronda Adobe,** the last unaltered adobe home from Mexican California open to the public in Monterey County. Located in the meadows above the Alisal Slough, the house, which suffered some damage in the 1989 earthquake, contains furniture and artifacts from the period. *333 Boronda Rd., tel. 408/757–8085. Admission free. Open weekdays 10–2, Sun. 1–4, Sat. by appointment.*

San Juan Bautista

A sleepy little hamlet tucked off U.S. 101 about 20 miles north of Salinas, San Juan Bautista is a nearly unaltered example of a classic California mission village. Protected from development since 1933, when much of it became **San Juan Bautista State Historic Park,** the village is about as close to early 19th-century California as you can get. On the first Saturday of each month, on Living History Day, costumed volunteers entertain visitors with such period events as quilting bees, making tortillas, or churning butter, and refreshments are served in the hotel's bar. *Tel. 408/623–4881. Admission: $2 adults; $1 children 6–17. Open Wed.–Sun. 10–4:30.*

The centerpiece for the village is the wide green plaza ringed by historic buildings that include a restored blacksmith shop, a stable, a pioneer cabin, and jailhouse. Running along one side of the square is **Mission San Bautista,** a long, low colonnaded structure founded by Father Lasuen in 1797. A poignant spot adjoining it is **Mission Cemetery,** where more than 4,300 Indian converts are buried in unmarked graves.

After the mission era, San Juan Bautista became an important crossroads for stagecoach travel. The principal stop in town was the **Plaza Hotel,** a collection of adobe buildings with furnishings from the 1860s. Next door, the **Castro-Breen Adobe,** once owned by survivors from the Donner party and furnished with Spanish colonial antiques, presents a view of domestic life in the village.

More contemporary pursuits in San Juan Bautista include poking around in the numerous antiques shops and art galleries lining the side streets. Every August the village holds a popular flea market.

What to See and Do with Children

Beaches. While local waters are generally too cold and turbulent for children (or adults, for that matter), the Monterey Municipal Beach east of Wharf No. 2 has shallow waters that are warm and calm enough for wading. Another good beach for kids is Lovers Point Park on Ocean View Boulevard in Pacific Grove, a sheltered spot with a children's pool and picnic area. Glass-bottom boat rides, which permit viewing of the plant and sea life below, are available during the summer.

Dennis the Menace Playground (Fremont St. and Camino El Estero, Monterey). Delightful Lake El Estero Park is the setting for this imaginative playground whose name pays tribute to one of its developers, cartoonist and longtime local resident Hank Ketcham. Among the features are a maze made from hedges, free-form play equipment, and a Southern Pacific steam locomotive. Rowboats and paddleboats can be rented on Lake El Estero, a U-shaped lake that is home to a varied assortment of ducks, mud hens, and geese.

Edgewater Packing Co. (640 Wave St., Monterey, tel. 408/649–1899). The centerpiece of this converted sardine cannery and processing plant is an antique carousel with hand-carved animals and mermaids that is as much fun to ride now as it was in 1905. A candy store and game arcade are among the other attractions.

Roller Skating. Roller skates can be rented from the old-fashioned rink at Del Monte Gardens. *2020 Del Monte Ave., Monterey, tel. 408/375–3202. Closed Mon. and Tues.*

Children will enjoy the Monterey Bay Aquarium, the Museum of Natural History, and the Point Piños Lighthouse (*see* Exploring, above). Also popular is whale-watching (*see* Participant Sports, below).

Off the Beaten Track

A few miles north of Monterey near the tiny harbor town of Moss Landing is one of only two federal research reserves in California, the **Elkhorn Slough** from the visitors center at the National Estuarine Research Reserve. There are 2,500 acres of tidal flats and salt marshes that form a complex environment supporting more than 300 species of birds and fish. A 1-mile walk along the meandering canals and wetlands can reveal swans, pelicans, loons, herons, and egrets, and sharks may be observed in the summer months. You can wander at leisure or, on weekends, take a guided walk (10 AM and 1 PM) to the heron rookery. *1700 Elkhorn Rd., Hwy. 1, Moss Landing, tel. 408/728–2822. Admission: $2.50 over 16. Open Wed.–Sun. 9–5.*

Shopping

Art Galleries   Although few artists can afford the real estate anymore, Carmel's heritage as a thriving art colony lives on in dozens of galleries scattered throughout the town. A wide and eclectic assortment of art—everything from 19th-century watercolors to abstract metal sculpture—is available for browsing and purchase in galleries in Carmel and elsewhere on the peninsula.

The Coast Gallery Pebble Beach presents the work of contemporary wildlife and marine artists in forms that range from etchings to bronze sculpture. *The Lodge at Pebble Beach, 17-Mile Dr., Pebble Beach, tel. 408/624–2002. Open daily 9–5.*

The **Masterpiece Gallery** features early California Impressionists, Bay Area figurative art, and the work of local artist Roger Blum. *Dolores St. and 6th Ave., Carmel, tel. 408/624–2163. Open daily 11–5.*

Classic impressionism and traditional realism are the focus of the **Cottage Gallery.** *Mission St. and 6th Ave., Carmel, tel. 408/624–7888. Open daily 10–5.*

The **Bill W. Dodge Gallery** features one of the largest collections of contemporary folk art in the West, including Dodge's own turn-of-the-century-style paintings, posters, and prints.

Dolores St. between 5th and 6th Aves., Carmel, tel. 408/625–5636. Open daily 10–5.

At **GWS Galleries,** which features the work of nationally recognized artists, the primary themes and styles are western, wildlife, marine, aviation, Americana, and landscape. Museum-quality framing is offered. *26390 Carmel Rancho La., Carmel, tel. 408/625–2288. Open Mon.–Sat. 10–5:30, Sun. 11–4.*

The **Highlands Sculpture Gallery** is devoted to indoor and outdoor sculpture, primarily work done in stone, bronze, wood, and metal by West Coast artists. *Dolores St. between 5th and 6th Aves., Carmel, tel. 408/624–0535. Open 10:30–4:30.*

Photography West Gallery exhibits a changing spectrum of well-known 20th-century photography and features the work of Ansel Adams, who lived and worked in the region for many years. *Ocean Ave. and Dolores St., Carmel, tel. 408/625–1587. Open Mon.–Thurs. 11–5, Fri. 11–6, Sat. 10–6, Sun. 10–5.*

Gift Ideas   In a region known for superb golf courses, one can find the ultimate in golf equipment and accessories. At **John Riley Golf** customers can get custom-made golf clubs manufactured on the premises. *601 Wave St., Monterey, tel. 408/373–8855. Open Mon.–Sat. 9–5, Sun. noon–5.*

Unusual gifts for golfers can be found at **Golf Arts and Imports,** which features antique golf prints and clubs, rare golf books, and other golfing memorabilia. *Dolores St. and 6th Ave., Carmel, tel. 408/625–4488. Open Mon.–Sat. 10–5, Sun. 10–3.*

The illustrations of Beatrix Potter are in evidence everywhere at **Peter Rabbit and Friends,** which offers toys, nursery bedding, books, music boxes, party supplies, and other items embellished with characters and scenes from Potter's children's tales. *Lincoln Ave. between 7th and Ocean Aves., Carmel, tel. 408/624–6854. Open Mon.–Sat. 10–5, Sun. 11–5.*

One of the best places for books on marine life and attractive gifts with a marine-life theme is the **Monterey Bay Aquarium Gift Shop,** which offers everything from posters and art prints to silk-screened sweatshirts and lobster-shaped wooden napkin rings. *886 Cannery Row, Monterey, tel. 408/649–6466. Open daily 10–6.*

Participant Sports

Bicycling   The Monterey Peninsula is wonderful biking territory, with bicycle paths following some of the choicest parts of the shoreline, including the 17-Mile Drive and the waterfront of Pacific Grove. Bikes can be rented from **Bay Bikes** (640 Wave St., Monterey, tel. 408/646–9090). Pickup and delivery to hotels is possible in the summer season.

Adventures by the Sea Inc. (299 Cannery Row, tel. 408/372–1807) has biking packages that combine rentals with restaurant vouchers or with tickets good for the Monterey Bay Aquarium. Tour packages for groups as well as for walking tours are available.

Mopeds can be rented from **Monterey Moped Adventures** (1250 Del Monte Ave., tel. 408/373–2696). A free practice lesson is included in the rental price; a driver's license is required.

Fishing Rock cod is a relatively easy catch in Monterey Bay, with salmon and albacore tuna also among the possibilities. Most fishing trips are a half day or a full day in duration, leave from Fisherman's Wharf in Monterey, and can include options such as equipment rental, bait, fish cleaning, and a one-day license. Boat charters for groups and trips for individuals are available.

Fishing trips in Monterey are offered by **Monterey Sport Fishing** (96 Fisherman's Wharf, tel. 408/372–2203), **Randy's Fishing Trips** (66 Fisherman's Wharf, tel. 408/372–7440), and **Sam's Fishing Fleet** (84 Fisherman's Wharf, tel. 408/372–0577). In Santa Cruz try **Stagnaro Fishing Trips** (center of the wharf, tel. 408/425–7003).

Golf With 19 golf courses, most of them commanding strips of choice real estate, it is not surprising that the Monterey Peninsula is sometimes called the golf capital of the world. Beginning with the opening of the Del Monte Golf Course in 1897, golf has been an integral part of the social and recreational scene in the area.

Many hotels will help with golf reservations or offer golf packages; inquire when you make lodging reservations.

Several of the courses are within the exclusive confines of the 17-Mile Drive, where the Del Monte Forest and the surging Pacific help make the game challenging as well as scenic. The most famous of these courses is **Pebble Beach Golf Course** (17-Mile Dr., tel. 408/624–3811), which takes center stage each winter during the AT&T Pro-Am (known for years as the "Crosby"), where show-business celebrities and pros team up for what is perhaps the world's most glamorous golf tournament. Such is the fame of this course that golfers from around the world make it one of the busiest in the region, despite greens fees that are well over $100. (You do get a refund of the $6 fee for the 17-Mile Drive.) Reservations are essential.

Another famous course in Pebble Beach is **Spyglass Hill** (Spyglass Hill Rd., tel. 408/624–3811), where the holes are long and unforgiving to sloppy players. With the first five holes bordering on the Pacific, and the rest reaching deep into the Del Monte Forest, the views offer some consolation.

A newer addition to the Pebble Beach scene is **Poppy Hills** (17-Mile Dr., tel. 408/625–2035), a 1986 creation of Robert Trent Jones, Jr., that has been named by *Golf Digest* as one of the top 20 courses in the world.

The newest course in Pebble Beach is the **Spanish Bay Golf Links** (tel. 408/624–3811), which opened on the north end of the 17-Mile Drive in 1987. Spanish Bay, which hugs a choice stretch of shoreline, is designed in the rugged manner of a traditional Scottish course with sand dunes and coastal marshes interspersed among the greens.

Less experienced golfers and those who want to sharpen their iron shots can try the shortest course in Pebble Beach, the nine-hole **Peter Hay** (17-Mile Dr., tel. 408/624–3811).

Just as challenging as the Pebble Beach courses is the **Old Del Monte Golf Course** (1300 Sylvan Rd., tel. 408/373–2436) in Monterey, the oldest course west of the Mississippi. The greens fees are among the most reasonable in the region.

Another local favorite, with greens fees only a fraction of those in Pebble Beach, is **Pacific Grove Golf Links** (Asilomar Blvd., tel. 408/648–3177). Designed by Jack Neville, who also designed the Pebble Beach Golf Links, the course features a back nine with spectacular ocean views and iceplant-covered sand dunes that make keeping on the fairway a must.

Although lacking ocean views, golf courses in Carmel Valley offer the company of deer and quail wandering across the greens. One of the choicest is **Rancho Cañada Golf Club** (Carmel Valley Rd., tel. 408/624–0111) with 36 holes, some of them overlooking the Carmel River.

Up the road a few miles is the **Golf Club at Quail Lodge** (8000 Valley Greens Dr., tel. 408/624–2770), which has a course made beautiful and challenging by several lakes incorporated into its design. The course is private but is open to guests at the adjoining Quail Lodge and by reciprocation with other private clubs.

Guests at the nearby Carmel Valley Ranch resort have access to the private Peter Dye–designed **Carmel Valley Ranch Resort** course (1 Old Ranch Rd., tel. 408/626–2510), which has a front nine running along the Carmel River and a back nine reaching well up into the mountains for challenging slopes and spectacular views.

Seven miles inland from Monterey, off Highway 68, is **Laguna Seca Golf Club** (1 York Rd., tel. 408/373–3701), a course with an 18-hole layout designed by Robert Trent Jones, Jr., and open to the public.

Horseback Riding   A great way to enjoy the Del Monte Forest, which has more than 34 miles of bridle trails, is by reserving a horse from the **Pebble Beach Equestrian Center** (Portola Rd. and Alva La., tel. 408/624–2756). You can ride in a group of four people, between 10 AM and 2 PM, Tues.–Sun.

Kayaking   Sea kayaking is an increasingly popular sport in Monterey Bay, giving paddlers a chance to come face to face with otters, sea lions, and harbor seals. Kayak rentals, basic instruction, and escorted tours are offered by **Monterey Bay Kayaks** (693 Del Monte Ave., Monterey, tel. 408/373–5357 or 800/649–5357 in CA).

Scuba Diving   Although the waters are cold, the marine life and kelp beds attract many scuba divers to Monterey Bay. Diving lessons, rental equipment and guided dive tours are offered at **Aquarius Dive Shops** (2240 Del Monte Ave., Monterey, tel. 408/375–1933 and 32 Cannery Row, Suite #4, tel. 408/375–6605).

Tennis   Public courts are available in Monterey and Pacific Grove; information is available through **Monterey Tennis Center** (tel. 408/372–0172) and **Pacific Grove Municipal Courts** (tel. 408/648–3129). Nonmembers are eligible to play on the courts for a small fee at the **Carmel Valley Inn Swim and Tennis Club** (Carmel Valley Rd. and Los Laureles Grade, Carmel Valley, tel. 408/659–3131).

If tennis is a top vacation priority, you may want to stay at a resort where instruction and facilities are part of the scene. Among the resorts most geared for tennis are the Lodge at Pebble Beach, the Inn at Spanish Bay, Hyatt Regency Monterey, Holiday Inn Resort of Monterey, Quail Lodge, and Carmel Valley Ranch Resort. *See* the Lodging section below for details.

Whale-Watching On their annual migration between the Bering Sea and Baja California, 45-foot gray whales can be spotted not far off the Monterey coast. Although they sometimes can be seen with binoculars from shore, a whale-watching cruise is the best way to see these magnificent mammals up close. The migration south takes place between December and March, while the migration north is from March to June. Late January is considered the prime viewing time, when their numbers in Monterey Bay peak.

Even if no whales are in sight, however, the bay cruises nearly always include some unforgettable marine-life encounter that can range from watching a cluster of sea lions hugging a life buoy to riding the waves alongside a group of 300 leaping porpoises. Whale-watching cruises, which usually last about two hours, are offered by **Monterey Sport Fishing** (96 Fisherman's Wharf, Monterey, tel. 408/372–2203), **Randy's Fishing Trips** (66 Fisherman's Wharf, Monterey, tel. 408/372–7440, and **Sam's Fishing Fleet** (84 Fisherman's Wharf, tel. 408/372–0577). In Santa Cruz, try **Stagnaro Fishing Trips** (center of the wharf, tel. 408/425–7003).

Spectator Sports

Car Racing Four major races take place each year on the 2.2-mile, 11-turn **Laguna Seca Raceway** (SCRAMP, Box 2078, Monterey 93942, tel. 408/648–5100 or 800/367–9939). They range from Indianapolis 500–style CART races to a historic car race featuring more than 300 restored race cars from earlier eras.

Rodeo One of the oldest and most famous rodeos in the West is the annual **California Rodeo** (Box 1648, Salinas 93902, tel. 408/757–2951) in Salinas, which takes place during a week of festivities starting in mid-July.

Dining

By Bruce David Colen There is little question that the Monterey area is the best and richest area for dining along the coast between Los Angeles and San Francisco. The surrounding waters abound with a variety of fish, there is wild game in the foothills, and the inland valleys are the vegetable basket of California, while nearby Castroville prides itself on being the Artichoke Capital of the World. The region also takes pride in producing better and better wines. San Francisco's conservative streak extends this far south, when it comes to dress—"casual" tends to mean attractive resort wear.

Highly recommended restaurants are indicated by a star ★.

Category	Cost*
Very Expensive	over $50
Expensive	$35–$50
Moderate	$20–$35
Inexpensive	under $20

per person, not including tax, service, or drinks

Carmel   **The Covey at Quail Lodge.** Continental cuisine is served at this
Expensive   elegant restaurant in a romantic lakeside setting. Specialties
include swordfish with avocado in a curried cream sauce, black-
currant duck, and sea scallop mousse. *8205 Valley
Greens Dr., tel. 408/624–1581. Reservations advised. Jacket
and tie required. AE, DC, MC, V. No lunch.*

French Poodle. The service is attentive in this intimate dining
room with framed maps of French wine regions on the walls.
Specialties on the traditional French menu include duck breast
in port. *Junipero and 5th Aves., tel. 408/624–8643. Reservations advised. Dress: casual. AE, DC, MC, V. No lunch.
Closed Sun. and Wed.*

★ **Pacific's Edge.** This restaurant's dramatic views of ancient cypress trees and pounding surf combine with a staff headed by
renowned chef Brian Whitmer to create one of the most memorable dining experiences along the California coast. *Hwy. 1,
Carmel-by-the-Sea, tel. 408/624–3801. Reservations advised.
Jacket required. AE, DC, MC, V.*

Raffaello. A sparkling, elegant rendezvous in one of the loveliest parts of Carmel, this restaurant's menu offers very good
northern Italian dishes with French overtones. There's excellent pasta, Monterey Bay prawns with garlic butter, local sole
poached in champagne, and the specialty of the house, chicken
alla Fiorentina. *Mission St. between Ocean and 7th Aves., tel.
408/624–1541. Reservations advised. Jacket and tie required.
AE, DC, MC, V. No lunch. Closed Tues.*

Moderate   **Crème Carmel.** This bright and airy small restaurant has a California-French menu that changes according to season. Specialties include sea bass stuffed with Dungeness crab, and beef
tenderloin in cabernet sauce. *San Carlos St., near 7th Ave., tel.
408/624–0444. Reservations advised. DC, MC, V.*

Flaherty's Seafood Grill & Oyster House. This is a bright blue-
and-white-tiled fish house that serves bowls of steamed mussels, clams, cioppino, and crab chowder. Seafood pastas and
daily fresh fish selections are also available. *6th Ave. and San
Carlos St., tel. 408/624–0311. No reservations. MC, V.*

Hog's Breath Inn. Former mayor Clint Eastwood's place provides a convivial publike atmosphere in which to enjoy no-
nonsense meat and seafood entrées with sautéed vegetables.
*San Carlos St. and 5th Ave., tel. 408/625–1044. Reservations
advised. AE, DC, MC, V.*

Piatti. Here's one more link in this statewide chain of friendly,
attractive trattorias that serve authentic, light Italian cuisine.
Junipero and 6th Sts., tel. 408/625–1766. MC, V.

Pine Inn. An old favorite of locals, this Victorian-style restaurant offers traditional American fare, including pork loin, roast
duck, and beef Stroganoff. At lunch you can opt for dining outdoors at tables set up around the gazebo. *Ocean Ave. and Monte Verde St., tel. 408/624–3851. Reservations advised. AE, DC,
MC, V.*

Q Point of Carmel. The cuisine here might best be called Cali-
fornia/Continental, and features such dishes a sautéed sea scallops and Gulf prawns with basil; chicken breast, rolled and
stuffed with mushrooms; pasta with the catch of the day; and
rack of Sonoma lamb. *Ocean Ave. between 3rd Ave. and Delores
St., tel. 408/624–2569. Reservations advised. AE, DC, MC, V.
No weekend lunch.*

★ **Rio Grill.** The best bets in this attractive Santa Fe–style setting are the meat and seafood (such as fresh tuna) cooked in an

oakwood smoker. There's also a good California wine list. *Hwy. 1 and Rio Rd.*, *tel. 408/625-5436. Reservations advised. AE, MC, V.*

Inexpensive **Friar Tuck's.** This busy, wood-paneled coffee shop serves huge omelets at breakfast, and at lunch offers 17 varieties of hamburgers, including one topped with marinated artichoke hearts. *5th Ave. and Dolores St.*, *tel. 408/624-4274. No reservations. No credit cards. No dinner.*

Shabu Shabu. Light meat and seafood dishes, cooked at your table, are the specialties in this country-style Japanese restaurant. *Ocean and 7th Aves.*, *tel. 408/625-2828. Reservations advised. AE, MC, V.*

Birgit Dagmar. This quaint café with a fireplace and Scandinavian decor features Swedish pancakes, homemade rye bread, and—yes, Swedish—meatballs for breakfast and lunch. *Dolores St. and 7th Ave.*, *tel. 408/624-3723. No reservations. No credit cards. No dinner.*

Thunderbird Bookstore and Restaurant. This well-stocked bookstore is also a good place to enjoy a light lunch or dinner and browse among the books. A hearty beef soup, sandwiches, and cheesecake are the best sellers. *3600 The Barnyard, Hwy. 1 at Carmel Valley Rd.*, *tel. 408/624-1803. MC, V.*

Monterey **Bindel's.** In this historic old pink Sanchez adobe the menu is Re-
Expensive gional California, with the emphasis on whatever the local fishing fleet brings back each day. Don't miss the crab and salmon ravioli with pesto sauce. *500 Hartnell St.*, *tel. 408/373-3737. Reservations advised. AE, DC, MC, V. No weekend lunch.*

Delfino. This elegant dining room in the Monterey Plaza Hotel is built over the waterfront on Cannery Row. Fresh seafood, veal medallions, and angel-hair pasta with prawns are among the standouts on the California-Italian menu. *400 Cannery Row*, *tel. 408/646-1700. Reservations advised. AE, D, DC, MC, V.*

★ **Fresh Cream.** Ask local residents where to go for pleasant, light, imaginative California cuisine, and nine out of 10 will recommend this charming little restaurant in Heritage Harbor. Be sure to try the squab and quail from nearby farms. *100 Pacific St.*, *tel. 408/375-9798. Reservations advised. Dress: casual. D, DC, MC, V. No lunch. Closed Mon.*

Sardine Factory. The interior of this old processing plant on Cannery Row has been turned into five separate dining areas, including a glass-enclosed garden room. The decor is from the gaslight era with lots of Gay Nineties touches. The menu stresses fresh seafood, prepared in an elegant, Italian manner. There's a great wine list. *701 Wave St.*, *tel. 408/373-3775. Reservations advised. Jacket required. AE, DC, MC, V. No lunch.*

★ **Whaling Station Inn.** A pleasing mixture of rough-hewn wood and sparkling white linen makes this restaurant both a festive and a comfortable place in which to enjoy some of the best mesquite- grilled fish and meats in town. There are excellent artichoke appetizers and fresh salads. *763 Wave St.*, *tel. 408/373-3778. Reservations advised. AE, DC, MC, V. No lunch.*

Moderate **Clock Garden.** The eclectic decor here is highlighted by a collection of antique clocks. There's a Continental menu, with a variety of fresh fish, veal, pork, lamb, and chicken dishes that can be followed by wonderful, rich desserts. *565 Abrego St.*, *tel. 408/375-6100. Reservations advised. AE, MC, V.*

Ferrante's. Gorgeous views of both the town and the bay can be seen from this northern Italian restaurant at the top of the nine-story Monterey Sheraton. The pasta and seafood combinations here, such as spinach fettuccine with clams, are especially good. *350 Calle Principal, tel. 408/649-4234. Reservations advised. AE, D, DC, MC, V. No lunch.*

★ **The Fishery.** Popular with locals, this restaurant features a mixture of Asian and Continental influences, in both food and decor. Specialties include broiled swordfish with saffron butter and fresh Hawaiian tuna with macadamia-nut butter. *21 Soledad Dr., tel. 408/373-6200. MC, V. No lunch. Closed Sun. and Mon.*

Mara's Restaurant. Greek and Armenian dishes such as hummus, shish kebab, moussaka, and a chicken and lemon soup called *avgolemono* are featured at this family restaurant. *570 Lighthouse Ave., tel. 408/375-1919. Reservations advised. MC, V. No lunch.*

Steinbeck Lobster Grotto. Pacific views on three sides highlight this long-established Cannery Row spot known for its Maine lobster and local catches. Also good are the bouillabaisse, the cioppino, and the seafood casseroles. *720 Cannery Row, tel. 408/373-1884. Reservations advised. AE, DC, MC, V. No lunch.*

Surdi's. Meals at this pleasant stucco restaurant start with an impressive antipasto salad bar. Along with traditional pasta dishes, a house specialty is chicken Monterey baked with cream and artichoke hearts. *2030 Fremont St., tel. 408/646-0100. Reservations advised. Dress: casual. AE, DC, MC, V.*

Inexpensive **Abalonetti.** From a squid-lover's point of view, this casual wharfside restaurant is the best place in town. You can get your squid served in a variety of ways: deep-fried, sautéed with wine and garlic, or baked with eggplant. *57 Fisherman's Wharf, tel. 408/373- 1851. No reservations. AE.*

Beau Thai. Located across from the Monterey Bay Aquarium, this plant-filled local favorite features such dishes as beef curry with tamarind sauce and spicy noodle dishes. *807 Cannery Row, tel. 408/373-8811. Reservations advised. AE, DC, MC, V.*

Old Monterey Cafe. Breakfast here, which is served all day, can include fresh-baked muffins and eggs Benedict. This is also a good place to relax with a cappuccino or coffee made from freshly ground beans. *489 Alvarado St., tel. 408/646-1021. No reservations. MC, V.*

Sancho Panza. Although the basic Mexican dishes here are not extraordinary, the setting, in the low-ceilinged 1841 Casa Gutierrez adobe along the Path of History, definitely is. *590 Calle Principal, tel. 408/375-0095. AE, DC, MC, V.*

Pacific Grove **Gernot's.** The ornate Victorian-era Hart Mansion that now
Expensive houses this restaurant is a delightful setting in which to dine on seafood and game served with light sauces. California-French specialties include pheasant with green peppercorns and roast venison. *649 Lighthouse Ave., tel. 408/646-1477. Reservations advised. Dress: casual. AE, MC, V. No lunch. Closed Mon.*

★ **Old Bath House.** A romantic, nostalgic atmosphere permeates this converted bathhouse overlooking the water at Lovers Point. The seasonal Continental menu here makes the most of local seafood and produce. When they're available, the salmon and Monterey Bay prawns are particularly worth ordering. *620 Ocean View Blvd., tel. 408/375-5195. Reservations advised. Jacket required. AE, D, DC, MC, V. No lunch.*

Moderate **Fandango.** With its stone walls and country furniture, this restaurant has the earthy feel of a southern European farmhouse. Complementing the ambience are the cuisine's robust flavors from southern France, Italy, Spain, Greece, and North Africa. The menu ranges from couscous and paella to canneloni. *223 17th St., tel. 408/373-0588. Reservations advised. AE, D, DC, MC, V.*

Inexpensive **Peppers.** This pleasant white-walled café offers fresh seafood and traditional dishes from Mexico and Latin America. The red and green salsas are excellent. *170 Forest Ave., tel. 408/373-6892. Reservations advised. AE, MC, V. Closed Tues.*

The Tinnery. The simple, clean lines of this contemporary dining room are framed by picture-window views of Monterey Bay. The eclectic menu ranges from Japanese teriyaki chicken to Mexican burritos to English fish and chips. *Ocean View Blvd. and 17th St., tel. 408/646-1040. Reservations advised. AE, DC, MC, V.*

Pebble Beach **The Bay Club.** This restaurant along the 17-Mile Drive is deco-
Expensive rated in pleasant pastels, and overlooks the coastline and the Inn at Spanish Bay's golf links. Continental specialties include truffle ravioli in lobster sauce, and veal chop with rosemary butter. *2800 17-Mile Dr., tel. 408/647-7500. Reservations advised. Jacket required. AE, DC, MC, V. No lunch.*

★ **Club XIX.** Classic French dishes are served in this intimate, café-style restaurant at the Lodge at Pebble Beach, with views of Carmel Bay and the 18th green. *17-Mile Dr. and Portola Rd., tel. 408/624-3811. Reservations advised. Jacket required. AE, DC, MC, V.*

Santa Cruz **Chez Renee.** This small and elegant retreat, owned by a hus-
Moderate–Expensive band-and-wife team, serves French-inspired cuisine. Special-
★ ties include sweetbreads with two sauces, Madeira and mustard; duck and home-preserved brandied cherries; deep-sea scallops garnished with smoked salmon and dill. Save room for the excellent dessert soufflés. *9051 Soquel Dr., Aptos, 408/688-5566. Reservations required. MC, V. No lunch Sat.*

Moderate **The Veranda.** In this refurbished Victorian dining room in the Bayview Hotel, the cordial surroundings and service enhance such appetizers as corn fritters with Smithfield ham and scallion pancakes with gravlax. Main-course offerings include cassoulet of local shellfish, baked salmon with a mustard-and-herb sauce, and roast rack of lamb with juniper berries. The best-selling dessert is the white-chocolate macadamia cheesecake. *8041 Soquel Dr., 408/685-1881. Reservations advised. MC, AE, V. No lunch weekends.*

Inexpensive **O Mei Szechwan Chinese Restaurant.** Not your run-of-the-mill chop-suey joint, this sophisticated, attractive place offers some unusual dishes: *gan pund*, boneless chicken crisp-fried and served with a spicy garlic sauce; *gan bian*, dried sautéed beef with hot pepper and ginger on crisp rice noodles; and snapper prepared Taiwan style. *3216 Mission, Rte. 1, Santa Cruz, 408/425-8458. Reservation advised. AE, MC, V. No lunch weekends.*

El Palomar. This restaurant near the Municipal Wharf, in the old Santa Cruz train station, provides a variety of good Mexican food. You'll find your favorites plus some off beat, south-of-the-border-style offerings. *123 Washington St., Santa Cruz, 408/425-7575. AE, MC, V.*

Lodging

A recent hotel and resort boom on the Monterey Peninsula has given travelers a far greater choice of accommodations, especially on the most deluxe level, than ever before. The luxury resort scene is particularly flourishing in Carmel Valley and Pebble Beach, whose country clublike spreads have recently been attracting Japanese investors.

In Monterey, the trend has been toward sophisticated hotels, some with the same range of services and amenities offered by top hotels in San Francisco. Some of the newer hotels are a bit impersonal and clearly designed for conventions, but others pamper the individual traveler in grand style.

While large resorts and hotels have been opening elsewhere on the peninsula, Pacific Grove has quietly turned itself into the bed-and-breakfast capital of the region. Many of the town's landmark Victorian houses, some more than a century old, have been converted to charming inns with brass beds and breakfast buffets laden with cranberry muffins and baked pears.

Rates in the Monterey area are often as high as in a major city, especially during the April–October high season, when even modest motels may charge $100 a night for a double room.

Highly recommended hotels are indicated by a star ★.

Category	Cost*
Very Expensive	over $150
Expensive	$100–$150
Moderate	$70–$100
Inexpensive	under $70

double room, not including tax

Capitola
Expensive

The Inn at Depot Hill. This inventively designed hotel in a former rail depot has taken the Orient Express as its theme, and then run with it. Each room is unique, inspired by such European destinations as Delft, the Netherlands; Portofino, Italy; Sissinghurst, England; the Cote d'Azur; Paris. One is decorated like a Pullman car for a railroad baron. *250 Monterey Ave., Capitola-by-the-Sea, 95010, tel. 408/462–3376. 8 rooms. AE, MC, V.*

Carmel
Very Expensive
★

Highlands Inn. The hotel's unparalleled location on high cliffs above the Pacific just south of Carmel gives it views that stand out even in a region famous for them. Accommodations are in plush condominium-style units with wood-burning fireplaces, ocean-view decks; some have spa tubs and full kitchens. *Hwy. 1, Box 1700, 93921, tel. 408/624–3801 or 800/538–9525, 800/682–4811 in CA. 142 rooms. Facilities: 2 restaurants, lounges, pool, whirlpools, entertainment. AE, D, DC, MC, V.*

Expensive–Very Expensive

Carriage House Inn. This attractive small inn with a rustic wood-shingled exterior has rooms with open-beam ceilings, fireplaces, down comforters, and sunken Japanese baths. Continental breakfast, wine and hors d'oeuvres are included. *Junipero Ave. between 7th and 8th Aves., Box 1900, 93921, tel. 408/625–2585 or 800/422–4732. 13 rooms. AE, D, DC, MC, V.*

★ **Cobblestone Inn.** Recent renovations in this former motel have created an English-style inn with stone fireplaces in the guest rooms and in the sitting-room area. Quilts and country antiques, along with a complimentary gourmet breakfast buffet and afternoon tea, contribute to the homey feel. *8th and Junipero Aves., Box 3185, 93921, tel. 408/625–5222. 24 rooms. AE, DC, MC, V.*

Tally Ho Inn. This is one of the few inns in Carmel's center that has good views out over the bay. There are suites and penthouse units with fireplaces and a pretty English garden courtyard. Continental breakfast and after-dinner brandy are included. *Monte Verde St. and 6th Ave., tel. 408/624–2232, 800/624–2290 in CA. 14 rooms. MC, V.*

Tickle Pink Country Inn. Just up the road from the Highlands Inn, this small, secluded inn also features spectacular views. Simple but comfortable accommodations include Continental breakfast. *155 Highland Dr., 93923, tel. 408/624–1244 or 800/635–4774. 34 rooms. AE, MC, V.*

Expensive **Carmel Mission Inn.** Located on the edge of Carmel Valley, this attractive modern inn has a lushly landscaped pool and Jacuzzi area and is close to the Barnyard and Crossroads shopping centers. Rooms are large, some with spacious decks. *Hwy. 1 and Rio Rd., 3665 Rio Rd., 92923, tel. 408/624–1841 or 800/348–9090. 165 rooms. Facilities: restaurant, bar, pool, Jacuzzi. AE, D, DC, MC, V.*

Moderate– **Pine Inn.** This traditional favorite of generations of Carmel vis-
Expensive itors features Victorian-style decor complete with grandfather clock, flocked wallpaper, and marble-topped furnishings. Located in the heart of the shopping district, the inn has its own brick courtyard of specialty shops. *Ocean Ave. and Lincoln St., Box 250, 93921, tel. 408/624–3851 or 800/228–3851. 49 rooms. Facilities: dining room. AE, DC, MC, V.*

Wayside Inn. Within easy walking distance of shops and restaurants, this attractive brick and wood inn has some units with fireplaces and full kitchens; all come with Continental breakfast and morning paper. *Mission St. and 7th Ave., Box 1900, 93921, tel. 408/624–5336 or 800/422–4732. 21 rooms. AE, D, DC, MC, V.*

Moderate **Lobos Lodge.** Pleasant white stucco units in an oak and pine
★ setting on the edge of the business district feature fireplaces and private brick patios. Continental breakfast is included. *Monte Verde St. and Ocean Ave., Box L–1, 93921, tel. 408/624–3874. 30 rooms. AE, MC, V.*

Carmel Valley **Carmel Valley Ranch Resort.** This new addition to the resort
Very Expensive scene is a stunning mix of contemporary California architec-
★ ture with such down-home touches as handmade quilts, wood-burning fireplaces, and watercolors by local artists. Rooms feature cathedral ceilings, oversize decks, and fully stocked wet bars. *1 Old Ranch Rd., 93923, tel. 408/625–9500 or 800/4CARMEL. 100 suites. Facilities: restaurant, pool, golf (fee), tennis club and courts, saunas, Jacuzzis. AE, DC, MC, V.*

Quail Lodge. One of the area's most highly regarded resorts is beautifully situated on the grounds of a private country club where guests have access to golf and tennis. There are also 853 acres of wildlife preserve, including 11 lakes, frequented by deer and migratory fowl. The rooms, which are clustered in several low-rise buildings, are spacious and modern, with a mixture of Oriental and European decor. *8205 Valley Greens Dr., Carmel 93923, tel. 408/624–1581 or 800/538–9516, 800/682–9303 in CA. 100 rooms. Facilities: restaurant, 2 lounges, piano bar, 2 pools, Jacuzzi, putting green, golf (fee), tennis. AE, DC, MC, V.*

Stonepine Resort. The former estate of the Crocker banking family has been converted to an ultradeluxe inn nestled in 330 pastoral acres with riding trails and an equestrian center. The main house, richly paneled and furnished with antiques, offers eight individually decorated suites and a private dining room for guests only. Less formal but still luxurious suites are also available in the ranch-style Paddock House. *150 E. Carmel Valley Rd., Box 1543, 93924, tel. 408/659–2245. 14 rooms. Facilities: dining room, pool, tennis, weight room, archery, mountain bikes, horseback riding. AE, MC, V.*

Moderate–Expensive **Robles Del Rio Lodge.** This pine-paneled charmer in a gorgeous setting of rolling meadows and oak forests dates from 1928. Rooms and cottages feature country-style decor with Laura Ashley prints, and the grounds include a large pool and sunbathing area, and hiking trails. Complimentary breakfast buffet is included. *200 Punta del Monte, 93924, tel. 408/659–3705 or 800/833–0843. 31 rooms. Facilities: restaurant, lounge, pool, tennis, sauna, hot tub. MC, V.*

Valley Lodge. In this small, pleasant inn, there are rooms surrounding a garden patio and separate one- and two-bedroom cottages with fireplaces and full kitchens. Continental breakfast and morning paper are included. *Carmel Valley Rd. at Ford Rd., Box 93, 93924, tel. 408/659–2261 or 800/641–4646. 31 rooms. Facilities: pool, Jacuzzi, sauna, small fitness center. AE, MC, V.*

Monterey
Very Expensive **Hyatt Regency Monterey.** While the rooms and general atmosphere are less glamorous than at some other resorts in the region, the Hyatt does offer excellent golf and tennis facilities, two pools, a Jacuzzi, and a fitness room. *1 Old Golf Course Rd., 93940, tel. 408/372–1234l, 800/824–2196 in CA. 579 rooms. Facilities: restaurant, lounge, sports bar, 2 pools. AE, D, DC, MC, V.*

★ **Monterey Plaza.** This sophisticated full-service hotel commands a superb waterfront location on Cannery Row, where frolicking sea otters can be observed from the wide outdoor patio and from many of the room balconies. The architecture and decor, a blend of early California and Oriental styles that retains a little of the old cannery design, harmonizes well with the site. *400 Cannery Row, 93940, tel. 408/646–1700 or 800/631–1339, 800/334–3999 in CA. 290 rooms. Facilities: restaurant, bar, cable TV, garage (fee). AE, D, DC, MC, V.*

★ **Spindrift Inn.** This elegant small hotel on Cannery Row boasts the street's only private beach and a rooftop garden overlooking Monterey Bay. Indoor pleasures include spacious rooms with sitting areas, Oriental rugs, fireplaces, canopied beds, down comforters, and other luxuries. Continental breakfast brought to the room on a silver tray and afternoon tea are included. *652 Cannery Row, 93940, tel. 408/646–8900 or 800/225–2901, 800/841–1879 in CA. 41 rooms, valet parking (fee). AE, D, DC, MC, V.*

Expensive–Very Expensive **Doubletree Hotel.** Adjacent to the downtown conference center, this hotel is geared more toward convention groups and business travelers than toward vacationers seeking local ambience. Rooms, some with good views of Fisherman's Wharf and the bay, are attractively furnished. Resort amenities include three tennis courts and a round swimming pool with adjoining Jacuzzi. *2 Portola Plaza, 93940, tel. 408/649–4511 or 800/528–0444. 374 rooms. Facilities: 2 restaurants, pool, tennis (fee), parking (fee). AE, D, DC, MC, V.*

★ **Hotel Pacific.** Unlike other new hotels in downtown Monterey that clash with the early California architecture and small-town ambience, the Hotel Pacific is an attractive adobe-style addition that fits right in. All rooms are suites, handsomely appointed with four-poster feather beds, hardwood floors, Indian rugs, fireplaces, wet bars, and balconies or patios. Continental breakfast and afternoon tea are included. *300 Pacific St., 93940, tel. 408/373–5700, 800/554–5542 in CA. 104 rooms. Facilities: garage, 2 Jacuzzis. AE, D, DC, MC, V.*

Monterey Hotel. Originally opened in 1904, this quaint, small, downtown hotel reopened in 1987 after an extensive restoration that left its oak paneling and ornate fireplaces gleaming. Standard rooms are small but well appointed with antiques; master suites have fireplaces. Complimentary Continental breakfast, afternoon tea, and wine and cheese in the evening are included. *406 Alvarado St., 93940, tel. 408/375–3184 or 800/727–0960. 44 rooms, parking (fee). AE, D, DC, MC, V.*

Monterey Marriott. This large, convention-oriented hotel sticks out like a pale pink nine-story sore thumb in the middle of Monterey's quaint downtown. Rooms are small, but many have good views of the town and bay. *350 Calle Principal, 93940, tel. 408/649–4234 or 800/372–2968. 338 rooms. Facilities: restaurant, lounge, Jacuzzi, pool, health club, garage (fee). AE, DC, MC, V.*

Holiday Inn Resort. The rooms are Monterey contemporary style, and have large private decks, some overlooking the pool area. Resort amenities include tennis courts, saunas, as well as rooms with access for the handicapped, and a large indoor whirlpool. *1000 Aguajito Rd., 93940, tel. 408/373–6141 or 800/234–5697. 204 rooms. Facilities: restaurant, pool, tennis, sauna, Jacuzzi, putting green. AE, D, DC, MC, V.*

Victorian Inn. Under the same ownership as the Spindrift Inn, this hotel two blocks above Cannery Row has a more casual feel but also offers such in-room comforts as fireplaces, private balconies or patios, and Continental breakfast. A few rooms have ocean views. Wine and cheese are served in the antique-filled lobby during the afternoon. *487 Foam St., 93940, tel. 408/373–8000 or 800/225–2902, 800/232–4141 in CA. 68 rooms. Facilities: garage. AE, D, DC, MC, V.*

Moderate–Expensive

★ **Arbor Inn.** This unusually attractive motel has a friendly, country-inn atmosphere. Continental breakfast is served in a pine-paneled lobby with a tile fireplace. There is an outdoor Jacuzzi, and rooms are light and airy, some with fireplaces and some with accessibility for the handicapped. *1058 Munras Ave., 93940, tel. 408/372–3381; in CA, 800/351–8811. 56 rooms. Facilities: hot tub. AE, D, DC, MC, V.*

Best Western Monterey Beach. This Best Western offers a great waterfront location about 2 miles north of town with panoramic views of the bay and the Monterey skyline. The rooms are nondescript, but the grounds are pleasantly landscaped and feature a large pool with a sunbathing area. *2600 Sand Dunes Dr., 93940, tel. 408/394–3321 or 800/528–1234. 195 rooms. Facilities: restaurant, lounge, pool. AE, D, DC, MC, V.*

Cannery Row Inn. This is a modern small hotel on a street above Cannery Row with bay views from the private balconies of many rooms. Gas fireplaces and complimentary Continental breakfast are among the amenities. *200 Foam St., 93940, tel. 408/649–8580. 32 rooms. Facilities: Jacuzzi, garage. AE, MC, V.*

Otter Inn. This low-rise hotel with a rustic shingle exterior is two blocks above Cannery Row and has bay views from most of the rooms. Coffee and pastries are provided in rooms, which are spacious, with fireplaces and private hot tubs in some. *571 Wave St., 93940, tel. 408/375–2299. 31 rooms. AE, MC, V.*

Moderate
★ **Monterey Motor Lodge.** A pleasant location on the edge of Monterey's El Estero park gives this motel an edge over its many competitors along Munras Avenue. Indoor plants and a large secluded courtyard with pool are other pluses. Continental breakfast is included. *55 Aguajito Rd., 93940, tel. 408/372–8057 or 800/558–1900. 45 rooms. Facilities: restaurant, pool. AE, D, DC, MC, V.*

Pacific Grove
Very Expensive **Centrella Hotel.** A handsome century-old Victorian mansion and garden cottages with claw-foot bathtubs and wicker and brass furnishings house the Centrella Hotel. Depending on the time of day, a sideboard in the large parlor is laden with breakfast treats, cookies and fruit, sherry and wine, or hors d'oeuvres. *612 Central Ave., 93950, tel. 408/372–3372, 800/235–3372 outside CA. 26 rooms, 24 with bath. AE, MC, V.*

Expensive–
Very Expensive **Martine Inn.** While most bed-and-breakfasts in Pacific Grove are Victorian houses, this one is a pink stucco Mediterranean-style villa overlooking the water. The rooms, most of which have ocean views, are individually decorated with such unique items as a mahogany bedroom set featured at the 1969 World's Fair. Full breakfast, wine, and hors d'oeuvres are included. *255 Oceanview Blvd., 93950, tel. 408/373–3388. 19 rooms. MC, V.*

Expensive
★ **Green Gables Inn.** Originally built a century ago by a Pasadena judge to house his mistress, this Swiss Gothic bed-and-breakfast retains an air of Victorian romance. Stained-glass windows framing an ornate fireplace and other details compete with the spectacular bay views. The breakfast buffet is tempting, as are afternoon hors d'oeuvres served with wine, sherry, or tea. *104 5th St., 93950, tel. 408/375–2095. 11 rooms, 7 with bath. AE, MC, V.*

Moderate–
Expensive **Gosby House Inn.** This lovely yellow Victorian bed-and-breakfast in the town center has 22 individually decorated rooms, al-
★ most all with private bath and some with fireplaces. Breakfasts and afternoon hors d'oeuvres are served in a sunny parlor or before the fireplace in the living room. *643 Lighthouse Ave., 93950, tel. 408/375–1287 or 800/527–8828. 22 rooms, 20 with bath. AE, D, DC, MC, V.*

Inexpensive–
Moderate **Asilomar Conference Center.** A pleasant summer camplike at-
★ mosphere pervades this assortment of 28 rustic but comfortable lodges in the middle of a 100-acre state park across from the beach. Lodging is on the American plan. Reservations should be made at least a month before arrival. *800 Asilomar Blvd., Box 537, 93950, tel. 408/372–8016. 315 rooms. Facilities: cafeteria, pool. No credit cards.*

Pebble Beach
Very Expensive

The Inn at Spanish Bay. Under the same management as the Lodge at Pebble Beach, this 270-room resort sprawls on a breathtaking stretch of shoreline along 17-Mile Drive. The resort has a slightly more casual feel, although the 600-square-foot rooms are no less luxurious. The inn is adjacent to its own tennis courts and golf course, but guests also have privileges at all the Lodge facilities. *Box 1589, 2700 17-Mile Dr., 93953, tel. 408/647–7500 or 800/654–9300. 270 rooms. Facilities: 4 restaurants, tennis, pool. AE, DC, MC, V.*

★ **The Lodge at Pebble Beach.** A renowned resort since 1916, the Lodge features quietly luxurious rooms with fireplaces and wonderful views. The golf course, tennis club, and equestrian center are also highly regarded. Guests of the lodge have privileges at the Inn at Spanish Bay. *17-Mile Dr., Box 1418, Pebble Beach 93953, tel. 408/624–3811 or 800/654–9300. 161 rooms. Facilities: 3 restaurants, coffee shop, lounge, pool, sauna, beach club, golf (fee), tennis (fee), riding (fee), weights, massage, bikes for rent. AE, DC, MC, V.*

Santa Cruz
Expensive
★

The Darling House Bed and Breakfast by the Sea. This superb 1910 mansion on the promontory overlooking the Boardwalk was built as a summer house for a rich Colorado family by William Weeks, architect of Santa Cruz's Cocoanut Grove. The decor, including antique furnishings and beveled glass, is authentic. Modern plumbing and electricity are among the few concessions made to the 1990s; in all other ways, the house retains an atmosphere of turn-of-the-century leisurely elegance. Continental breakfast is offered. No pets; smoking outdoors only. *1314 Cliff Dr., Santa Cruz 96060, tel. 408/458–1958 or 800/458–1958. 7 rooms with shared bath. AE, D, MC, V.*

Moderate–Expensive
★

Casablanca Motel. Of the many waterfront motels along here, this is perhaps the most interesting. The main building was once the Cerf Mansion, built in 1918 in the Mediterranean style for a federal judge, and every room—each complete with ocean view—is individually decorated. There are brass beds, velvet drapes and fireplaces, and the Latrelle family sets great store in maintaining the tranquillity of the place amid the hurly-burly of the waterfront. The restaurant here serves innovative cuisine, and has spectacular views. *101 Main at Beach, Santa Cruz 95060, tel. 408/423–1570. 27 rooms. Facilities: restaurant. AE, DC, MC, V.*

The Arts and Nightlife

The area's top venue for the performing arts is the **Sunset Community Cultural Center** (San Carlos, between 8th and 10th Aves., tel. 408/624–3996) in Carmel, which presents music and dance concerts, film screenings, and headline performers throughout the year. Facilities include the cathedral-domed Sunset Theater and the Forest Theater, the first open-air amphitheater built in California.

The Arts
Special Events

Performing-arts festivals have a long tradition in the Monterey area, with the most famous drawing thousands of spectators. Ordering tickets as far in advance as possible is often essential. The oldest performing-arts festival on the peninsula is the **Carmel Bach Festival** (Box 575, Carmel, 93921, tel. 408/624–1521), which has presented the work of Johann Sebastian Bach and his contemporaries in concerts and recitals for more than 50 years. The highlight of the three-week event, starting in mid-July, is a candlelit concert held in the chapel of the Carmel Mission Basilica.

Nearly as venerable is the celebrated **Monterey Jazz Festival** (Box JAZZ, Monterey, 93942, tel. 408/373–3366), which attracts jazz and blues greats from around the world to the Monterey Fairgrounds for a weekend of music each September.

Another popular jazz event is **Dixieland Monterey** (177 Webster St., Suite A-206, Monterey, 93940, tel. 408/443–5260), held on the first full weekend of March, which features Dixieland bands performing in cabarets, restaurants, and hotel lounges throughout Monterey, as well as a Saturday-morning jazz parade downtown.

For blues fans, there is the **Monterey Bay Blues Festival** (tel. 408/394–2652), which is held in June at the Monterey Fairgrounds, featuring entertainment and soul food.

The Custom House Plaza in downtown Monterey is the setting for free afternoon performances outdoors, and, in the evenings, shows held in a tent (admission is charged) during the **Monterey Bay Theatrefest** (tel. 408/649–6852), which is held on weekend afternoons and evenings during most of the summer.

The **Cabrillo Music Festival** in Santa Cruz (9053 Soquel Dr., Aptos 95003, tel. 408/662–2701, or box office 408/429–3444), one of the longest-running new music festivals, showcases contemporary sounds, particularly by American composers, for two weeks in late July and early August.

Concerts   One of the nation's most highly regarded metropolitan symphonies, the **Monterey County Symphony** (Box 3965, Carmel 93921, tel. 408/624–8511) performs a series of concerts throughout the year in Salinas and Carmel. Programs range from classical to pop and include guest artists.

The **Chamber Music Society of the Monterey Peninsula** (Box 6283, Carmel 93921, tel. 408/625–2212) presents a series of concerts featuring guest artists such as the Juilliard String Quartet and the New York Philomusica. Dance, classical music, and operatic concerts are sponsored by the **Salinas Concert Association** (318 Catharine St., Salinas 93901, tel. 408/758–5027), which presents a series of featured artists between October and May at the Sherwood Hall in Salinas.

Film   The **Monterey Institute of Foreign Study** (440 Van Buren St., Monterey, tel. 408/626–1730) sponsors regular screenings of notable foreign films. Classic films are also shown on Thursdays once a month in the community room of the **Monterey Public Library** (625 Pacific St., Monterey, tel. 408/646–3930).

Theater   **California's First Theater** (Scott and Pacific Sts., Monterey, tel. 408/375–4916) is home to the Troupers of the Gold Coast, who perform 19th-century melodramas year round in the state's oldest operating little theater, a historic landmark dating from 1846 on Monterey's Path of History.

Specializing in contemporary works, both comedy and drama, is the **GroveMont Theater**, an acclaimed repertory company that has two theaters, the Grovemont Arts Center (320 Hoffman Ave., Monterey, tel. 408/649–6852) and the refurbished Monterey Playhouse (425 Washington St., tel. 408/655–PLAY). Also part of the GroveMont Center is the **Poetic Drama Insti-**

tute, which often features solo dramatic performances and poetry readings.

American musicals, both old and new, are the focus of the **New Wharf Theater** (Fisherman's Wharf, Monterey, tel. 408/649–2332), where a local cast is sometimes joined by Broadway actors, directors, and choreographers.

Shakespeare Santa Cruz (Performing Arts Complex, University of California at Santa Cruz, 95064, tel. 408/459–2121) puts on a six-week Shakespeare festival in July and August that also includes 20th-century works.

Nightlife
Cabaret

Kalisa's (851 Cannery Row, Monterey, tel. 408/372–8512). This long-established, freewheeling café in a Cannery Row landmark building offers a potpourri of entertainment that can include belly dancing, flamenco, jazz, folk dancing, and magic.

Bars and Nightclubs

Boiler Room (625 Cannery Row, Monterey, tel. 408/373–1449). Most nights it features comedy shows, followed by dancing to live rock music. There is occasional country and western dancing and entertainment.

The Club (Alvarado and Del Monte Sts., Monterey, tel. 408/646–9244). This popular night spot has dancing to Top-40 music Friday through Monday, plus changing entertainment that includes performances by rock and reggae bands, and male stripteasers.

Doc Ricketts' Lab (95 Prescott St., Monterey, tel. 408/649–4241). Live rock bands perform nightly one block above Cannery Row.

Doubletree Hotel (2 Portola Plaza, Monterey, tel. 408/649–4511). Popular music entertainment is offered nightly except Sundays in the Brasstree Lounge.

Highlands Inn (Hwy. 1, Carmel, tel. 408/624–3801). There is piano music nightly in the Lobos Lounge; dancing on weekends in the Fireside Lounge.

Lodge at Pebble Beach (17-Mile Dr., Pebble Beach, tel. 408/624–3811). You'll find easy listening entertainment in the Cypress Room and Terrace Lounge; there's a jazz band on Friday and Saturday evenings.

Mark Thomas Outrigger (700 Cannery Row, Monterey, tel. 408/372–8543). Rock 'n' roll and rhythm and blues from the 1960s, '70s and '80s is played by live bands on Friday and Saturday night.

Monterey Plaza Hotel (400 Cannery Row, Monterey, tel. 408/646–1700). Piano music and a guitarist can be heard in a romantic setting overlooking the bay in the hotel's Delfino Lounge.

Monterey Marriott (350 Calle Principal, Monterey, tel. 408/649–4234). Live jazz is offered nightly (except Sunday) in the Monterey Bay Club.

Sly McFlys (700 Cannery Row, Monterey, tel. 408/649–8050). This popular local watering hole has a pub atmosphere.

Discos

Brick House (220 N. Fremont St., Monterey, tel. 408/375–6116) is Monterey's country and western spot.

Safari Club (1425 Munras Ave., Monterey, tel. 408/649–1020). Again, there is dancing to Top-40 music with the local DJ at the Ramada Inn. Open Friday and Saturday 9 to 2 AM.

11 The Central Coast

The coastline between Carmel and Santa Barbara, a distance of just over 200 miles, is one of the most popular stretches of scenery in California. Maybe anywhere. It is what many visitors to the state have come to see, and a drive that many Californians will take whenever the opportunity presents itself. Except for a few smallish cities—Ventura and Santa Barbara in the south and San Luis Obispo in the north—the area is sparsely populated, with only a few small towns whose inhabitants relish their isolation among the redwoods at the sharp edge of land and sea. Between settlements, the landscape is dotted with grazing cattle and hillsides of wild flowers. Around Big Sur, the Santa Lucia mountains drop down to the Pacific with dizzying grandeur, but as you move south, the shoreline gradually flattens into the long sandy beaches of Santa Barbara and Ventura.

Big Sur has long attracted individualists—novelist Henry Miller comes to mind—drawn by the intractability of the terrain. But even the less precipitous junction of land and sea farther south has pulled in its share, most notably—and visibly—William Randolph Hearst, whose monumental home is the biggest single tourist attraction along the coast.

Throughout the region are bed-and-breakfast inns, and pleasant little towns, such as Cambria and Ojai, where resident artists and artisans create and sell their work. In the rolling hills of the Santa Ynez Valley are a growing number of wineries with steadily rising reputations. The Danish town of Solvang is a popular stopover for hearty Scandinavian fare and an architectural change of pace.

Santa Barbara is your introduction to the sand, surf, sun, and unhurried hospitality and easy living of Southern California. Only 90 miles from Los Angeles, Santa Barbara works hard to maintain its relaxed atmosphere and cozy scale. Wedged as it is between the Pacific and the Santa Ynez Mountains, it's never had much room for expansion, and the city's setting, climate, and architecture combine for a Mediterranean feel that permeates not only its look but its pace.

Highway 1, which runs through most of this region, was the first in the country to be declared a scenic highway, in 1966. Barring fog or rain, the coast is almost always in view from the road. In some sections, the waves break on rocks 11,200 feet below; in other places, the highway is just 20 feet above the surf. The two-lane road is kept in good repair, but it twists, and traffic, especially in the summer months, can be very slow. Allow plenty of time and sit back and enjoy the unfolding scenery that is both breathtaking and serene.

Getting Around

By Plane **American** and **American Eagle** (tel. 800/433–7300), **Skywest/ Delta** (tel. 800/453–9417), and **United** and **United Express** (tel. 800/241–6522) fly into Santa Barbara Municipal Airport (tel. 805/967–5608), 8 miles from downtown on Marxmiller Road.

Santa Barbara Express Airbus (tel. 805/964–7374) runs to and from the airport and shuttles travelers between Santa Barbara and Los Angeles Airport. **Aero Airport Limousine** (tel. 805/ 965–2412) serves Los Angeles Airport (by reservation only).

Metropolitan Transit District (tel. 805/963–3364) bus No. 11 runs from the airport to the downtown transit center.

By Car   The only way to see the most dramatic section of the central coast, the 70 miles between Big Sur and San Simeon, is by car. Heading south on Highway 1, you'll be on the ocean side of the road and will get the best views. Don't expect to make good time along here. The road is narrow and twisting with a single lane in each direction, making it difficult to pass slower traffic or the many lumbering RVs that favor this route, and, in fog or rain, the drive can be downright nerve-wracking. U.S. 101 from San Francisco to San Luis Obispo is the quicker, easier alternative, but it misses the coast entirely. U.S. 101 and Highway 1 join north of Santa Barbara. Both, eventually dividing, continue south through Southern California.

By Bus   Major bus lines avoid Highway 1, preferring the speedier inland routes. There is, however, local service in several towns. From Monterey and Carmel, **Monterey–Salinas Transit** (tel. 408/899–2555) operates daily bus runs to Big Sur April–September. From San Luis Obispo, **North Coastal Transit** (tel. 805/541–BUSS) runs buses around the town and out to the coast on regular schedules. Local service is also provided by the Santa Barbara Metropolitan Transit District (tel. 805/963–3364).

By Train   Amtrak (tel. 800/USA-RAIL) runs the *Coast Starlight* train along the coast from Santa Barbara to San Luis Obispo, but there it heads inland for the rest of the route to the San Francisco Bay Area and Seattle. Local numbers are, in Santa Barbara, tel. 805/687–6848; in San Luis Obispo, tel. 805/541–0505.

Guided Tours

California Parlour Car Tours (Cathedral Hill Hotel, 1101 Van Ness Ave., San Francisco 94109, tel. 415/474–7500 or 800/227–4250) offers a number of tours that include the central coast area. Lasting three to 11 days, these are one-way trips from San Francisco to Los Angeles (or vice versa) that travel along the coast in 36-passenger buses, visit Hearst Castle, Santa Barbara, and Monterey, and may also include time in Yosemite or Lake Tahoe. While there are advantages to such organized touring, especially in a region where driving is so demanding, there are also disadvantages, such as not being able to choose how long you visit any given site or attraction. (We recommend that you steer clear of any tour that takes you to Yosemite for less than one full day; readers have been disappointed in the past. Save Yosemite for a trip when you have enough time.)

Santa Barbara Trolley Co. (tel. 805/965–0353) has five daily, regularly scheduled runs in Santa Barbara. Motorized San Francisco–style cable cars deliver visitors to major hotels, shopping areas, and attractions. Stop or not as you wish and pick up another trolley when you're ready to move on. All depart from and return to Stearns Wharf. *Fare: $5 adults, $3 children and senior citizens.*

Walking Tours Through History (tel. 805/967–9869). Longtime Santa Barbara resident Elias Chiacos takes small groups on walking tours of gardens and historic buildings. Morning and afternoon tours begin at the courthouse lobby. Call to reserve.

Important Addresses and Numbers

Tourist Information
Free pamphlets on accommodations, dining, sports, and entertainment are available at the **Visitors Information Center** (1 Santa Barbara St. at Cabrillo Blvd., tel. 805/965–3021. Open Mon.–Sat. 9–5, Sun. 10–4). Before arriving, contact **Santa Barbara Conference and Visitors Bureau** (510A State St., 93101, tel. 805/966–9222; or 800/927–4688 to receive publications by mail).

Information on other towns along the central coast is available from:

Big Sur Chamber of Commerce (Box 87, 93920, tel. 408/667–2100).
San Luis Obispo Chamber of Commerce (1039 Chorro St., 93401, tel. 805/543–1323 or 800/756–5056).
Cambria Chamber of Commerce, (767 Main St., 93428, tel. 805/927–3624).
San Simeon Chamber of Commerce (Box 1, 9190 Hearst St., 93452, tel. 805/927–3500 or 800/342–5613).
Solvang Visitors Bureau (Box 70, 1593 Mission Dr., 93464, tel. 805/688–6144 or 800/468–6765).
California Dept. of Parks and Recreation (in Big Sur, tel. 408/667–2315.)

Emergencies
Dial 911 for **police** and **ambulance** in an emergency.

Doctors
Emergency care is available at **St. Francis Hospital** (601 E. Micheltorena St., Santa Barbara, tel. 805/568–5712 or 962–7661).

Road Conditions
Dial 408/757–2006 for information.

Exploring

For the 90 miles from Big Sur to Morro Bay, plan on spending three to four hours on the road. This is not a freeway, and chances are you'll want to stop at some of the 300 scenic turnouts along this route. Once you start south from Carmel, there is no route off until Highway 46 heads inland from Cambria to connect with U.S. 101. Most of the major sights and attractions of the region are right along the coastal route, or just a short detour away. Highway 1 and U.S. 101 run more or less parallel, with Route 1 hugging the coast and 101 remaining a few miles inland. Along some stretches the two roads join and run together for a stretch. At Morro Bay, Highway 1 moves inland for 13 miles and connects with U.S. 101 at San Luis Obispo. From here, south to Pismo Beach, the two highways run concurrently, and dramatic coastal scenery is replaced by driving ease. The roads go their separate ways again near Gaviota, just north of Santa Barbara.

The entire distance from Big Sur to Santa Barbara *could* be tackled in one long day of driving, but that would rather defeat the purpose of taking the slower, scenic coastal route. A better option is to plan on taking several days, and to allow time for exploring Big Sur, Hearst Castle, the beaches, and Santa Barbara, and for savoring the changing scenery of the shoreline. You can drive up to Santa Barbara from Los Angeles in just a couple of hours. If you fly into town, and don't intend to stray far beyond the city limits, a car is not absolutely necessary.

South Along Highway 1

Numbers in the margin correspond to points of interest on the Central Coast map.

❶ Just 13 miles south of Carmel is one of the quintessential views of California's coast, the elegant concrete arc of **Bixby Creek Bridge.** This view is a photographer's dream, and there is a small parking area on the north side from which to take a photo or to start a walk across the 550-foot span.

❷ Five miles south is the **Point Sur Light Station,** standing watch from atop a sandstone cliff. The century-old beacon is open to the public on ranger-led tours on Saturday at 9:30 and 1:30, and Sunday mornings at 9:30. The Big Sur State Park District (tel. 408/667–2315 or 625–4419) can provide further information.

The small developed area of the Big Sur valley begins a few miles south. Pfeiffer Big Sur State Park, gas, groceries, hotels, and restaurants are all clustered along the next 7 miles of the highway.

❸ One of the few places where you may actually set foot on the coastline you have been viewing from the road is at **Pfeiffer Beach.** The road to the beach turns off Highway 1 immediately past the Big Sur Ranger Station; follow it for 2 miles. The picturesque beach is at the foot of the cliffs, and a hole in one of the big sea-washed rocks lets you watch the waves break first on the sea side and then again on the beach side. The water is too cold and the surf too dangerous for swimming much of the year, however.

❹ On the ocean side of Highway 1, a towering 800 feet above the water, is **Nepenthe,** a favorite hangout of tourists and locals. The restaurant's deck can be an excellent place to take a break from the rather stressful—though very beautiful—drive. Rita Hayworth and Orson Welles spent their honeymoon at the inn here. Downstairs is a craft and gift shop, displaying among other items the work of Kaffe Fassett, the famous knitting designer who grew up at Nepenthe.

❺ A few miles south is **Julia Pfeiffer Burns State Park** (tel. 408/667–2315), where a short and popular hike is a nice way to stretch your legs. The trail leads up a small, redwood-filled valley to a waterfall. You can go back the same (easier) way or continue on the trail and take a loop that leads you along the valley wall, with views out into the tops of the redwood trees you were just walking among. There are picnic and camping areas as well as access to the beach.

❻ For the next dozen miles' drive, it is just you, the road, and the coast, and the gas station at Lucia is the first sign that you're returning to civilization. Among the many picnic areas and campgrounds between here and San Simeon is **Jade Cove,** one of the best-known areas on the coast in which to hunt for jade. Rock hunting is allowed on the beach, but you may not remove anything from the walls of the cliffs.

❼ It's another 30 miles to the **Hearst San Simeon State Historical Monument.** One of California's most popular tourist attractions, "Hearst Castle" sits in solitary splendor atop *La Cuesta Encantada* (the Enchanted Hill), and its buildings and gardens spread over the 123 acres that were the heart of newspaper magnate William Randolph Hearst's 250,000-acre ranch.

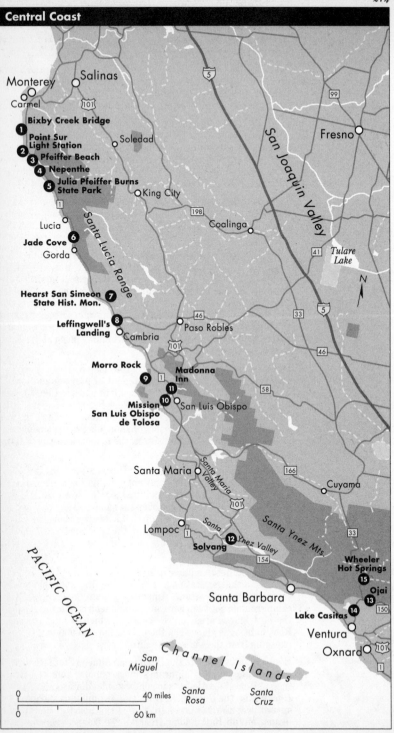

Central Coast

You'll forget the indignity of being herded into buses at the bottom of the hill once you reach the neoclassical extravaganza above. Hearst devoted nearly 30 years and some $10 million to the building of this elaborate mansion, commissioning renowned architect Julia Morgan—who was also responsible for many of the buildings at U.C. Berkeley—to erect a "shrine of beauty." The result is a pastiche of Italian, Spanish, Moorish, and French styles; a fitting showcase of Hearst's vast collection of European artwork. The majestic marble halls and art-filled main building, and the three guest "cottages," are connected by terraces and staircases, and surrounded by reflecting pools, elaborate gardens, and statuary at every turn. In its heyday, this place was a playground for Hearst and the Hollywood celebrities, and the rich and powerful who were frequent guests here. On the way up or down the hill, you may catch a glimpse of a zebra, one of the last descendants of Hearst's magnificent private zoo.

Although construction began in 1919, the project was never officially completed, and work was halted in 1947 when Hearst had to leave San Simeon due to failing health. The Hearst family presented the property to the state of California in 1958.

There are four tours available (the garden tour, however, is offered only from April through October), ranging from ½- to three hours in length, and all involve covering a considerable distance on foot. A new, free visitors center offers an introduction to the life of this master of yellow journalism and inspiration for Orson Welles's film *Citizen Kane*—something about which Hearst was none too pleased. Reservations for the tours are a virtual necessity. *San Simeon State Park, 750 Hearst Castle Rd., tel. 805/927–2020 or 800/444–7275. Tours daily 8:20 AM–3 PM (later in summer). Admission: $12.20 adults, $6.20 children 6–12, plus $1.80 charge for booking, closed Thanksgiving, Christmas, and New Year's Day. Reservations may be made up to 8 weeks in advance. AE, D, MC, V.*

Cambria, an artists' colony full of turn-of-the-century homes, is located a few minutes south of San Simeon and is becoming a popular weekend getaway spot for people from Los Angeles. The town is divided into the newer West Village and the original East Village, each with its own personality, and full of B&Bs, fine restaurants, art galleries, and shops selling unusual wares. You can still detect traces of the heritage of the Welsh miners who settled here in the 1890s. Moonstone Beach Drive, ❽ which runs along the coast, is lined with motels, and **Leffingwell's Landing,** a state picnic ground at its northern end, is a good place for examining tide pools and watching otters as they frolic in the surf.

The coastal ribbon of Highway 1 comes to an end at Morro Bay. The bay is separated from the ocean by a 4½-mile sandspit and the causeway built in the 1930s that leads to the huge monolith ❾ of **Morro Rock.** It's a quick drive to the rock (actually an extinct volcano) from town, and then a short walk around the base of the rock to the breakwater where you can stand with the calm, sheltered harbor (home of a large fishing fleet) on one side and the crashing waves of the Pacific on the other. The breakwater and the area around the ocean side base of Morro Rock are composed of huge boulders piled on top of one another, so walking around here involves stepping carefully and making occasional leaps. Morro Bay is also a wildlife preserve, protecting the nesting areas of endangered peregrine falcons, and you don't have to get too close to see that the rock is alive with birds. The town is dominated by the tall smokestacks of the PG&E plant just behind the waterfront, which can be seen from anywhere in the bay. Also in town is a huge chessboard with human-size pieces.

South from Morro Bay, Highway 1 turns inland on its way to San Luis Obispo, the halfway point between San Francisco and Los Angeles, and home to two decidedly different institutions: California Polytechnic State University, known as Cal Poly, and the exuberantly goofy, garish Madonna Inn. The town has several restored Victorian-era homes, and the chamber of commerce offers a list of self-guided historic walks. Among the places to see is the **Mission San Luis Obispo de Tolosa** (tel. 805/543–6850) at the heart of the downtown. Nearby, several old warehouses along a stream have been renovated as shops. The Ah Louis Store (800 Palm St., tel. 805/543–4332) was established in 1884 to serve the Chinese laborers building the Pacific Coast and Southern Pacific railroads, and is still in business. If you're in town on Thursday night, don't miss the weekly farmers' market and street fair along Higuera Street. Highway 1 and U.S. 101 run concurrently from San Luis Obispo to Pismo Beach.

Even if you're not staying at the **Madonna Inn,** drop by the café and shops for a look at the gilt cherubs, pink bar stools, pink trash cans, pink lampposts, and all the other assorted outrageous kitsch that has put this place in a class by itself—a place way beyond any notions of "good" or "bad" taste. You'll first notice that something is up when, outside the inn, you come across the "Flintstone"–style gas station made entirely of huge boulders. Begun in 1958 by Alex Madonna, a local highway contractor, and his wife, Phyllis, each of the more than 100 rooms of the inn now has its own played-to-the-hilt theme. The cave rooms, complete with waterfalls for showers, are among the most popular. *100 Madonna Rd. (take the Madonna Rd. exit from U.S. 101), tel. 805/543–3000.*

Avila Beach, just a short detour off Highway 1/U.S. 101, is a usually quiet beach town, but it comes alive on weekends when Cal Poly students take over. A bit farther down the highway, 20 miles of wide sandy beaches begin at the town of Pismo Beach, where U.S. 101 and Highway 1 again go their separate ways. The action at this busy community centers on the shops and arcades near the pier, and there is camping near the beach.

Along the roads in and around Lompoc from May through August, you'll see vast fields of brightly colored flowers in bloom, and you will have little trouble believing the town's boast of being the "Flower-Seed Capital of the World." Lompoc hosts a flower festival each June, and many of the petunias, poppies, marigolds, and other flowers grown here wind up on Rose Parade floats.

From Lompoc, take Highway 246 east to Mission Gate Road which leads to the mission **La Purisima** (2295 Purisima Rd., Lompoc 93436, tel. 805/733–3713). Founded in 1787, this is the most fully restored mission in the state, and its still-remote setting in this stark and serene landscape powerfully evokes the life of the early Spanish settlers in California. Costumed docents demonstrate crafts, and displays illustrate the secular as well as religious life of the mission. A corral near the parking area holds several farm animals, including sheep that are descendants of the original mission stock.

12 Southeast of Lompoc, inland along Highway 246 (or U.S. 101 to the turnoff for 246 at Buellton), is the Danish town of **Solvang**. You'll know when you've reached Solvang: the architecture suddenly turns to half-timbered buildings, windmills, and flags galore. Although aimed squarely at tourists, there is a genuine Danish heritage here, and more than two thirds of the town is of Danish descent. The 300 or so shops selling Danish goods and an array of knickknacks and specialty gift items are all within easy walking distance, many along Copenhagen Drive and Alisal Road. Stop by the narrow and jammed coffee shop attached to the Solvang Bakery, on Alisal Road, to try the Danish pastry. It is only one of a half-dozen aroma-filled bakeries in town.

At the Bethania Lutheran Church, on Atterdag Road at Laurel Avenue, everything but the palm trees outside is traditional; the Danish services are open to the public.

From Buellton, U.S. 101 heads back to the coast, where it joins Highway 1 again and runs east to Santa Barbara, about 30 miles away.

13 A half-hour drive east of Santa Barbara over the narrow and winding Highway 150 will put you in **Ojai**, a surprisingly rural town reminiscent of California's early agricultural days. You'll see acres of ripening orange and avocado groves that look like the picture-postcard images of Southern California from decades ago. In recent years the area has seen an influx of show-biz types and other Angelenos who've opted for a life out of the fast lane. Moviemaker Frank Capra used the Ojai Valley as a backdrop for his 1936 classic, *Lost Horizon*. Be aware that the valley sizzles in the summer when temperatures routinely reach 90 degrees.

The works of local artists can be seen in the Spanish-style shopping arcade along the main street. On Sundays they display their paintings and crafts at the outdoor exhibition in the Security Bank parking lot (205 W. Ojai Ave.). The Art Center (113 S. Montgomery, tel. 805/646–0117) features art exhibits, theater, and dance.

A stroll around town should include a stop at **Bart's Books** (302 W. Matilija St., tel. 805/646–3755), an outdoor store sheltered by native oaks and overflowing with used books. *Open Tues.– Sun. 10–5:30.*

14 Nearby **Lake Casitas** on Highway 150 offers boating, fishing, and camping. It was the venue for the 1984 Summer Olympic rowing events.

15 One of the attractions in Ojai is a hot spring that makes use of natural mineral water in the hills nearby. The spa at **Wheeler Hot Springs** emerges like an oasis 7 miles north of town on Highway 33. Its tall palms and herb gardens are fed by an adjacent stream, and natural mineral waters fill the four redwood hot tubs and a large pool at the well-kept spa. Massage is also available. A restaurant on site offers dinner and live entertainment Thursday through Sunday and brunch on weekends. *16825 Maricopa Hwy., tel. 805/646–8131 or 800/227–9292. Res-*

ervations advised at least a week in advance, especially for spa. Open Mon.–Thurs. 10–9, Fri.–Sun. 9 AM–10 PM.

Santa Barbara

Numbers in the margin correspond to points of interest on the Santa Barbara map.

Santa Barbara's attractions begin with the ocean, with most everything along Cabrillo Boulevard. In the few miles between the beaches and the hills, you pass the downtown and then reach the old mission and, a little higher up, the botanic gardens. A few miles farther up the coast, but still very much a part of Santa Barbara, is the exclusive residential district of Hope Ranch. To the east is the district called Montecito, where Charlie Chaplin built the Montecito Inn to house his guests in the days when he made his movies in Santa Barbara before moving to Hollywood. Montecito is also where the exclusive San Ysidro Ranch is located.

Because the town is on a jag in the coastline, the ocean is to the south, and directions can be confusing. "Up" the coast is west, and "down" toward Los Angeles is actually east, and the mountains are north.

Everything in town is so close that the 8-mile drive to the airport seems like a long trip. A car is handy, but not essential, if you're planning on staying pretty much in town. The beaches and downtown are easily explored by bicycle or on foot, and the Santa Barbara Trolley takes visitors to most of the major hotels and sights, which can also be reached on the local buses.

The Visitors Information Center publishes a free guide to a scenic drive that circles the town with a detour into the downtown. It passes the harbor, beaches, Hope Ranch, and the old mission, offers fine views on the way to Montecito, then returns you to the beaches. You can pick up the drive, marked with blue "Scenic Drive" signs, anywhere along the loop. A free guide to the downtown, the "Red Tile Walking Tour," is also available free from the tourist office. It hits historical spots in a 12-block area.

The town of Goleta, the home of the University of California at Santa Barbara, is located a few miles up the coast via U.S. 101.

❶ If you start at the Pacific and move inland, one of the first spots to visit is **Stearns Wharf** on Cabrillo Boulevard at the foot of State Street. You can drive out and park on the pier, then wander through the shops or stop for a meal at one of the wharf's restaurants or at the snack bar. The **Sea Center,** a recent addition to the pier, is a branch of the Museum of Natural History that specializes in exhibits of marine life. Originally built in 1872, and reconstructed in 1981 after a fire, the wharf extends the length of three city blocks into the Pacific. The view from here back toward the city gives you a sense of the town's size and general layout.

❷ The nearby **Santa Barbara Yacht Harbor** is sheltered by a man-made breakwater at the west end of Cabrillo Boulevard. You can take a ½-mile walk along the paved breakwater, check out the tackle and bait shops, or hire a boat from here.

❸ Planted in 1877, the **Moreton Bay Fig Tree,** at Chapala Street and Highway 101, is so huge it reportedly can provide shade for

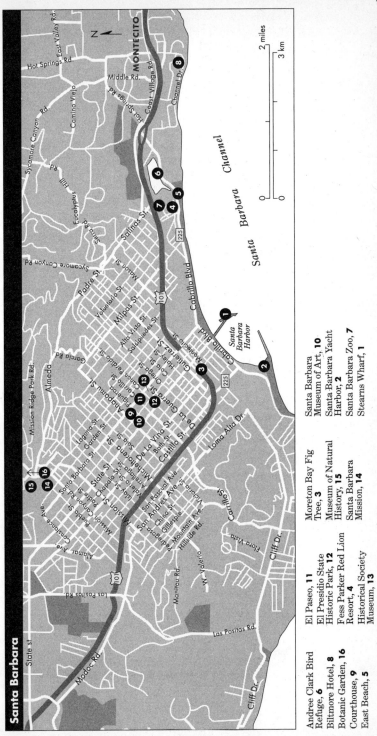

Santa Barbara

Andree Clark Bird
Refuge, **6**
Biltmore Hotel, **8**
Botanic Garden, **16**
Courthouse, **9**
East Beach, **5**

El Paseo, **11**
El Presidio State
Historic Park, **12**
Fess Parker Red Lion
Resort, **4**
Historical Society
Museum, **13**

Moreton Bay Fig
Tree, **3**
Museum of Natural
History, **15**
Santa Barbara
Mission, **14**

Santa Barbara,
Museum of Art, **10**
Santa Barbara Yacht
Harbor, **2**
Santa Barbara Zoo, **7**
Stearns Wharf, **1**

10,000 people. In recent years, however, the tree has become a gathering place for an increasing number of homeless people.

Back along Cabrillo, sandy beaches stretch for miles. The sprawling reddish Spanish-style hotel across from the beach is **❹** the **Fess Parker Red Lion Resort.** Parker, the actor who played Davy Crockett and Daniel Boone on television, owned the oceanfront acreage for many years, and spent several more years trying to convince city fathers to allow him to develop a hotel. He finally did, and the hotel opened in 1987 as the largest in Santa Barbara.

❺ Just beyond the hotel is the area's most popular beach, **East Beach,** a wide swatch of sand at the east end of Cabrillo. Near-**❻** by is the **Andree Clark Bird Refuge,** a peaceful lagoon and gardens. *1400 E. Cabrillo Blvd. Admission free.*

❼ Adjoining the lagoon is the **Santa Barbara Zoo,** a small, lushly landscaped home to big-game cats, elephants, and exotic birds. *500 Ninos Dr., tel. 805/962–6310. Admission: $5 adults, $3 senior citizens and children 2–12. Open daily in winter 10–5; daily in summer 9–6.*

Where Cabrillo Boulevard ends at the lagoon, Channel Drive **❽** picks up and, a short distance east, passes the **Biltmore Hotel,** now owned by the Four Seasons chain. For more than 60 years, Santa Barbara's high society, and the visiting rich and famous, have come here to indulge in quiet California-style elegance.

To reach the downtown area, return to Cabrillo Boulevard and **❾** head inland along State Street. **The Courthouse,** in the center of downtown, has all the grandeur of a Moorish palace. As you wander the halls admiring the brilliant hand-painted tiles and spiral staircase, you might just forget that you're in a courthouse until you spot a handcuffed group of offenders being marched by. This magnificent building was completed in 1929 as part of the rebuilding of Santa Barbara made necessary by a 1925 earthquake that destroyed much of the downtown. At the time the city was also in the midst of a cultural awakening, and the trend was toward an architecture appropriate to the area's climate and history. The result is the harmonious Mediterranean-Spanish look of much of Santa Barbara's downtown area, especially its municipal buildings. An elevator to the Courthouse tower takes visitors to a lovely arched observation area with a panoramic view of the city, and a fine spot from which to take photos. In the supervisors' ceremonial chambers on the Courthouse's second floor are murals painted by an artist who did backdrops for Cecil B. DeMille's silent films. *1100 block of Anacapa St., tel. 805/962–6464. Open weekdays 8–5, weekends 9–5. Free 1-hour guided tours Tues.–Sat. 2 PM, Wed. and Fri., 10:30 AM.*

❿ One block down Anapamu Street past the Spanish–style **Public Library** is the **Santa Barbara Museum of Art.** This fine small museum houses a permanent collection featuring ancient sculpture, Oriental art, a collection of German expressionist paintings, and a sampling of the work of American artists such as Grandma Moses. *1130 State St., tel. 805/963–4364. Admission: $3 adults, $2.50 senior citizens, $1.50 children 6–16. Open Tues.–Sat. 11–5 (9 PM Thurs. eve.), Sun. noon–5. Tours are led Tues.–Sat. at 2 PM, Sun. at 1 PM.*

⑪ Walking south you'll pass **El Paseo,** a shopping arcade built around an old adobe home. There are several such arcades in this area as well as many small art galleries. A few blocks north **⑫** is the **El Presidio State Historic Park.** Built in 1782, the presidio was one of four military strongholds established by the Spanish along the coast of California. The guardhouse, El Cuartel, is one of the two original adobe buildings that remain of the complex, and is the oldest building owned by the state. *123 E. Cañon Perdido St., tel. 805/966–9719. Admission free. Open daily 10:30–4:30.*

⑬ A block away is the **Historical Society Museum,** with an array of items from the town's past, including a silver-clad riding saddle and a collection of ladies' fancy fans. *136 E. De la Guerra St., tel. 805/966–1601. Admission free. Open Tues.–Sat. 10–5, Sun. noon–5.*

A short distance from downtown (take State St. north and **⑭** make a right on Los Olivos) at the base of the hills is the **Santa Barbara Mission,** the gem of the chain of 21 missions established in California by Spanish missionaries in the late 1700s. One of the best-preserved of the missions, it is still active as a Catholic church. *Laguna St., tel. 805/682–4713. Admission: adults $2, children under 16 free. Open daily 9–5.*

⑮ Continuing north a block you pass the **Museum of Natural His-** **⑯** **tory** (2559 Puesta del Sol), and then the **Botanic Garden,** 1½ miles north of the mission. The 60 acres of native plants are particularly beautiful in the spring. *1212 Mission Canyon Rd., tel. 805/682–4726. Admission $3 adults, $2 senior citizens, $1 children 5-12. Open 8 AM–sunset. Guided tours (10:30 AM and 2 PM) Thurs., Sat., and Sun.*

What to See and Do with Children

Santa Barbara Zoo. Youngsters particularly enjoy the scenic railroad and barnyard petting zoo (*see* Exploring, above).

Beach playground. For children who tire of the beach quickly, there is an elaborate Jungle Gym play area at Santa Barbara's East Beach, next to the Cabrillo Bath House.

Whale bones. Outside the Museum of Natural History in Santa Barbara is the skeleton of a blue whale, the world's largest creature. Kids are dwarfed by the bones and invited to touch them (they just can't climb on them) (*see* Exploring, above).

Off the Beaten Track

Channel Islands Hearty travelers should consider a day visit or overnight camping trip to one of the five Channel Islands that often appear in a haze off the Santa Barbara horizon. The most often visited is Anacapa Island, 11 miles off the coast. The islands' remoteness and unpredictable seas protected them from development, and now provide a nature enthusiast's paradise—both underwater and on land. In 1980 the islands became the nation's 40th national park, and the water a mile around each is protected as a marine sanctuary.

On a good day, you'll be able to view seals, sea lions, and an array of birdlife. From December through March, migrating whales can be seen close up. On land, tide pools alive with sea life are often accessible. Underwater, divers can view fish, giant squid, and coral. Off Anacapa Island, scuba divers can see the remains of a steamship that sank in 1853. Frenchy's Cove, on the west end of the island, has a swimming beach and fine snorkeling.

The waters of the channel are often rough and can make for a rugged trip out to the islands. You can charter a boat and head out on your own, but most visitors head to Ventura Harbor, a 40-minute drive south from Santa Barbara. From here a park-district concessionaire carries small groups to the islands for day hikes, barbecues, and primitive overnight camping.

Boat trips. *Island Packers* provides day trips to the islands and overnight camping to three of them. Boats link up with national park naturalists for hikes and nature programs. A limited number of visitors is allowed on each island and unpredictable weather can limit island landings. *1867 Spinnaker Dr., Ventura 93001, tel. 805/642–7688. Reservations are essential in the summer.*

Wineries   Centered in the Solvang area, and spreading north toward San Luis Obispo, is a California wine-making region with much of the variety but none of the glitz or crowds of the Napa Valley in Northern California. Most of the region's 30 wineries are located in the rolling hills in either the Santa Maria or Santa Ynez valleys. A leisurely tour of the entire area could take all day, but many wineries are just a short jog off U.S. 101. They tend to be fairly small, and only a few offer guided tours, but most have tasting rooms run by helpful staff, and wine makers will often act as your tour guide. Several of the wineries also have picnic areas on their properties.

Pamphlets with detailed maps and listings of each winery are readily available at motels and tourist centers all along the coast. A map for a self-guided driving tour is available free from the Santa Barbara County Vintners' Association (Box 1558, Santa Ynez, 93460, tel. 805/688–0881).

Shopping

Antiques   In Santa Barbara a dozen antiques and gift shops are clustered in restored Victorian buildings on Brinkerhoff Avenue, two blocks west of State Street at West Cota Street.

Arcade   In all, 32 shops, art galleries, and studios share the courtyard and gardens of El Paseo, a shopping arcade rich in history. Lunch at the outdoor patio is a nice break from a downtown tour. *Between State and Anacapa Sts. at Cañon Perdido St. in Santa Barbara.*

Beachwear   If you want to go home with the absolutely latest in California beachwear, stop by **Pacific Leisure,** which specializes in volleyball fashions, shorts, tops, and beach towels. *808 State St., Santa Barbara, tel. 805/962–8828. Open Mon.–Sat. 10–6, Sun. 11–5.*

Participant Sports

Bicycling   In Solvang you'll see people pedaling along on quadricycles, or in four-wheel carriages. Those and other bikes are available at **Surrey Cycle Rental** (486 1st St., tel. 805/688–0091 and 2164 Center St., tel: 805/653–0449).

Santa Barbara's waterfront boasts the level, two-lane Cabrillo Bike Lane. In just over 3 easy miles, you pass the zoo, a bird refuge, beaches, and the harbor. There are restaurants along the way, or you can stop for a picnic along the palm-lined path looking out on the Pacific. Rent bikes from **Beach Rentals** (8 W. Cabrillo Blvd., tel. 805/963–2524; open 8 AM–sunset in winter, and 8 AM–dusk in summer). It also has roller skates for hire. Bikes and quadricycles can also be rented from the **Cycles 4 Rent** concession near the pool at Fess Parker's Red Lion Resort (633 E. Cabrillo, tel. 805/564–4333, ext. 444).

Boating Charter or rent 14- to 50-foot sailboats and powerboats from **Sailing Center of Santa Barbara,** which also has a sailing school (Harbor at the launching ramp, tel. 805/962–2826 or 800/350–9090).

Camping There are many campsites along Highway 1, but they can fill up early any time but winter. In Big Sur, campsites are at Pfeiffer Big Sur and Julia Pfeiffer Burns state parks. Near Hearst Castle, camping is available at several smaller state parks (San Simeon, Atascadero, Morro Bay, Montana de Oro, Avila Beach, and Pismo Beach). Most of the sites require reservations from MISTIX reservation service (tel. 800/444–7275 or 619/452–1950).

Fishing There is access to freshwater- and surf-fishing spots all along the coast. For deep-sea trips, **Virg's Fish'n** (tel. 805/772–1222) offers day trips out of Morro Bay all year. Also in Morro Bay is **Bob's Sportfishing** (tel. 805/772–3340).

At Santa Barbara, surface and deep-sea fishing are possible all year. Fully equipped boats leave the harbor area for full- and half-day trips, dinner cruises, island excursions, and whale-watching from **SEA Landing** (Cabrillo Blvd. at Bath, tel. 805/963–3564).

Glider Rides Scenic rides of 15–20 minutes are offered weekends, 10–5, at the Santa Ynez Airport near Solvang (tel. 805/688–8390).

Golf Play nine or 18 holes at the **Santa Barbara Golf Club** (Las Positas Rd. and McCaw Ave., tel. 805/687–7087). **Sandpiper Golf Course,** 15 miles west in Goleta, offers a challenging course that used to be a stop on the women's professional tour (7925 Hollister Ave., Goleta, tel. 805/968–1541).

Hiking There are miles of hiking trails in the Ventana Wilderness, with trailheads at state parks and picnic areas on Highway 1 from Big Sur to San Simeon. Twelve miles east of Solvang is Cachuma Lake, a jewel of an artificial lake offering hiking as well as fishing and boating.

Horseback Riding San Ysidro Ranch hotel offers trail rides for parties of no more than six into the foothills by the hour (900 San Ysidro La., Montecito, tel. 805/969–5046. Reservations required; hotel guests only on Sat.).

Tennis Many hotels have their own courts, but there are also excellent public courts. Day permits, for $3, are available at the courts. **Las Positas Municipal Courts,** 1002 Las Positas Road, has six lighted courts. Large complexes are also at the **Municipal Courts,** near Salinas Street and Highway 101, and **Pershing Park,** Castillo and Cabrillo Blvds.

Volleyball   The east end of East Beach has more than a dozen sandlots. There are some casual, pickup games, but if you get into one, be prepared—these folks play serious volleyball.

Spectator Sports

Polo   The public is invited to watch the elegant game at the **Santa Barbara Polo Club**, 7 miles east in Carpinteria. *Take the Santa Claus La. exit from Hwy. 101, turn left under the freeway and then left again onto Via Real. The polo grounds are ½ mi farther, surrounded by high hedges. Tel. 805/684–6683. Admission $6, children under 12 free. April–Oct., Sun.*

Beaches

Santa Barbara's beaches don't have the big surf of the beaches farther south, but they also don't have the crowds. A short walk from the parking lot can usually find you a solitary spot. Be aware that fog often hugs the coast until about noon in May and June.

East Beach. At the east end of Cabrillo Boulevard, this is *the* beach in Santa Barbara. There are lifeguards, volleyball courts, a jogging and bike trail, and the Cabrillo Bath House with a gym, showers, and changing rooms open to the public.

Arroyo Burro Beach. Located just west of the harbor on Cliff Drive at Las Positas Road, this state beach has a small grassy area with picnic tables and sandy beaches below the cliffs. The Brown Pelican Restaurant on the beach serves a delicious breakfast.

Goleta Beach Park. To the north of Santa Barbara, in Goleta, this is a favorite with the college students from the nearby University of California campus. The easy surf makes it perfect for beginning surfers and families with young children.

State Beaches. West of Santa Barbara on Highway 1 are *El Capitan, Refugio,* and *Gaviota* state beaches, each with campsites, picnic tables, and fire pits. East of the city is the state beach at *Carpinteria,* a sheltered, sunny and often crowded beach.

Dining

By Bruce David Colen   Although you will find some chain restaurants in the bigger towns, the central coast from Big Sur to Solvang is far enough off the interstate rush to ensure that each restaurant and café has its own personality—from chic to down-home and funky. You'll find a few burger places, but they won't come with golden arches. In almost all cases, the restaurants will be right off Highway 1.

There aren't many restaurants along the coast from Big Sur until you reach Hearst Castle, where there is a large, new snack bar in the visitors center. From there south, however, the commercial fishing industry ensures daily fresh fish in many of the restaurants. The stretch of Highway 1 in and around San Simeon is a popular tour-bus route, and restaurants catering to large groups offer solid, if routine, American fare. Generous quantities of prime rib for dinner and bacon and eggs for breakfast can always be found. Cambria, true to its British-Welsh flavor, provides a taste of English cooking complete with peas and Yorkshire pudding, but the offerings range far beyond that. In Solvang, where the tone turns to Danish, count on traditional smorgasbord and sausages.

The variety of good food in Santa Barbara is astonishing for a town its size. Menu selections range from classic French to Cajun to fresh seafood, and the dining style from tie-and-jacket and necessary reservations to shorts-and-T-shirt hip. A leisurely brunch or lunch will take the best advantage of the beach and harbor views afforded by many restaurants and cafés. At the Biltmore's acclaimed and expensive Sunday brunch, however, all attention is on the spread of fresh fruits, seafood, and pastries. Served in the hotel's airy glass-roofed courtyard, it is a perfect choice for special occasions.

A tasty and satisfying meal certainly doesn't have to cost a fortune. If it is good, cheap food with an international flavor you are after, follow the locals to Milpas Avenue on the east edge of downtown. A recent count there found three Thai restaurants, Hawaiian, Greek, and New Mexican eateries. Freshly made tortillas are easily found in the markets on Milpas, particularly at La Super Rica, reputedly one of Julia Child's favorites for a quick, authentic Mexican snack.

Highly recommended restaurants are indicated by a star ★. Casual dress is acceptable, unless otherwise noted.

Category	Cost*
Very Expensive	over $50
Expensive	$40–$50
Moderate	$15–$40
Inexpensive	under $15

per person, without tax, service, or drinks

Big Sur
Expensive
★

Ventana Restaurant. The low, wide, modern/rustic stone and wood dining room is attractive; the terrace, with views over golden hills down to the ocean, is spectacular. Even if it's foggy along the highway, it may be sunny and warm up here. Noted for its handling of the light touches of California cuisine, the menu features grilled veal chops, sliced duck, occasional and unexpected game dishes, and some creative sandwiches. Weekend brunches on the patio are a real event. *Off Hwy. 1, near south end of town, tel. 408/667–2331. Reservations advised on weekends. AE, DC, MC, V.*

Moderate

Deetjen's Big Sur Inn. The restaurant is in the main house of the old, funky inn. There are four small dining rooms, none with more than four tables. Classical music enhances the stylish fare that includes roast duckling for dinner and wonderfully light and flavorful whole-wheat pancakes for breakfast (there is no lunch). *Hwy. 1, south end of Big Sur, tel. 408/667–2378. Reservations required. No credit cards.*

Glen Oaks Restaurant. Food critics praise the originality of the food served in this small, simply decorated dining room. The restaurant, owned by a husband-and-wife team, emphasizes fresh ingredients, mesquite grilling, fish, and pasta. *Hwy. 1, north end of town, tel. 408/667–2623. MC, V. No lunch Mon.*

Inexpensive– **Nepenthe.** You'll not find a more spectacular coastal view be-
Moderate tween Los Angeles and San Francisco than from here. The 800-
★ foot-high cliff site, overlooking lush meadows to the ocean below, was once owned by Orson Welles and Rita Hayworth. The
food is adequately average—from roast chicken with sage to
sandwiches and hamburgers—so it is the one-of-a-kind location, in the one and only magnificent Big Sur, that rates the
star. An outdoor café serves lunch until nightfall. *Hwy. 1, south
end of town, tel. 408/667–2345. Reservations for large parties
only. AE, MC, V.*

Cambria **Brambles Dinner House.** This is the best-known restaurant in
Moderate Cambria, but it can be hit-or-miss. Specialties include fresh
salmon cooked over a seasoned oak fire, blackstrap molasses
bread, prime rib, and Yorkshire pudding. *4005 Burton Dr., tel.
805/927–4716. Reservations advised. AE, MC, V. No lunch.*
Sylvia's Rigdon Hall. Delicate pink floral china sets the tone for
this dinner house with a British flavor. The Spencer steak marinated in Jack Daniel's is a favorite; also featured are a chicken
curry mulligatawny soup and prime rib. *4022 Burton Dr., tel.
805/927–5125. Reservations advised. MC, V. No lunch. Closed
Christmas Day.*

Inexpensive– **The Hamlet at Moonstone Gardens.** This is in the middle of a
Moderate plant nursery. The enchanting patio garden is perfect for
★ lunch. The upstairs dining room—sleek chrome and lavender
with fireplace and grand piano—looks over the Pacific or the
gardens. Service can be slow, but no one seems to mind. Fish of
the day comes poached in white wine; other entrées range from
hamburgers to rack of lamb. Downstairs is the Central Coast
Wine Center, where you can taste wines from more than 50
wineries. *East side Hwy. 1, tel. 805/927–3535. Reservations
accepted. MC, V. Closed Dec.*
Mustache Pete's. This lively, upbeat place with overhead fans
and baskets of flowers features Italian food, with seafood, pasta, and poultry selections. *4090 Burton Dr., tel. 805/927–8589.
Reservations unnecessary. AE, MC, V.*

Morro Bay **Dorn's.** This very pleasant seafood café overlooks the harbor
Moderate and main square. It looks like a Cape Cod cottage, with blue
walls, wainscoting, awnings, and bay windows. Breakfast,
lunch, and dinner are served; dinner features excellent fish and
native abalone. *801 Market St., tel. 805/772–4415. Weekend reservations advised. No credit cards.*

Inexpensive **Margie's Diner.** This clean and attractive, Mom-and-Pop type
★ diner-café serves generous portions of all-American favorites:
ham or steak and eggs, three-egg omelets, chili, nine versions
of hamburger, hot and cold sandwiches, fried chicken steak,
deep-dish apple pie—you name it, but don't forget the milkshakes. Top quality produce is used and service is excellent.
*1698 N. Main St., tel. 805/772–2510. No reservations. No credit
cards.*

Ojai **Wheeler Hot Springs Restaurant.** The menu changes weekly but
Moderate always features herbs and vegetables grown in the spa's garden. It's in Ojai, 6 miles north on Highway 33. The restaurant
serves brunch on Sunday. *16825 Maricopa Hwy., tel. 805/646–
8131. Reservations advised. AE, MC, V. No lunch. Closed
Mon.–Wed.*

San Luis Obispo
Inexpensive–
Moderate

Madonna Inn. This visual fantasy has to be seen to be believed. It is the ultimate in kitsch, from rococo bathrooms to pink-on-pink, frou-frou dining areas. You come to ogle, not necessarily to dine, although the latter is perfectly adequate, stop-by cooking, with decor-matching desserts. *100 Madonna Rd., tel. 805/543–3000. Reservations advised. Dress: casual. No credit cards.*

San Simeon
Moderate

Europa. A Hungarian touch brings egg dumplings and paprika to the unexpected menu in an area of traditional fare. Crisp linen tablecloths brighten the small dining room. Steaks are featured as well as specialties from Italy and Vienna. Weekend brunch is served. *9240 Castillo Dr. (Hwy. 1), tel. 805/927–3087. Reservations accepted. MC, V. No lunch. Closed Sun.*

Inexpensive–
Moderate

San Simeon Restaurant. This restaurant makes the most of its proximity to Hearst Castle, with a mind-boggling decor of imitation Greek columns, statues, and tapestries. There is a standard American menu; prime rib is the big draw. The dark dining room opens to views of the Pacific across the highway. *East side Hwy. 1, tel. 805/927–4604. Reservations advised in summer. AE, MC, V.*

Santa Barbara
Moderate–
Expensive

The Harbor Restaurant. Still sparkling fresh from a complete renovation in 1989, this on-the-wharf spot is where locals like to take out-of-town guests. The upstairs, now a bar and grill, offers an extensive menu of fresh seafood, sandwiches, large salads, and a huge variety of appetizers. The spacious room boasts nautical decor and a complete new video system. Head downstairs for healthy portions of fresh seafood, prime rib, or steaks, and order one of the house's specialty drinks; every seat in the remodeled restaurant has a harbor view. *210 Stearns Wharf, tel. 805/963–3311. Some reservations accepted. Dress: casual. AE, MC, V.*

★ **The Stonehouse.** The restaurant is in a turn-of-the-century, granite farmhouse, part of the San Ysidro Ranch resort. The California-French cooking is very good, but the real drawing card is the pastoral setting. Be sure to have lunch—seafood salads, pastas, pizzas with paper-thin crust—on the treehouselike outdoor patio. At night, the candle-lighted interior becomes even more romantic and the cuisine more serious, with game, roasts, and fresh fish entrées. *900 San Ysidro La., 805/969–5046. Reservations required. Jacket required. AE, D, MC, V.*

Moderate
★

Citronelle. This offspring of Michel Richard's famed Citrus in Los Angeles has brought Santa Barbara folk some of the best California-French cuisine they've ever had this close to home. The accent is on Riviera-style dishes: light, delicate, but loaded with intriguing good tastes. The desserts here are unmatched anywhere in Southern California. There are splendid, sweeping views of the harbor from the second-story dining room's picture windows. *901 E. Cabrillo Blvd., tel. 805/963–0111. Full bar. Reservations advised. Dress: casual but neat. AE, D, DC, MC, V.*

Pane & Vino. This tiny trattoria, and its equally small sidewalk dining terrace, is in a tree-shaded, flower-decked shopping center in Montecito, just east of Santa Barbara. The cold antipasto is very good, as are grilled meats and fish, pastas, and salads. There's a nearby water trough and hitching post for the visiting horsey set. *1482 E. Valley Rd., Montecito, tel. 805/969–9274. Reservations advised. No credit cards. Closed Sun.*

The Palace Cafe. A stylish and lively restaurant, the Palace has won acclaim for its Cajun and Creole dishes such as blackened redfish and jambalaya with dirty rice. Caribbean fare here includes Bahamian Slipper Lobster Tails—tender lobster sautéed with garlic, mushrooms, and tomatoes, then flambéed in a Madeira sauce. Just in case the dishes aren't spicy enough for you, each table has a bottle of hot sauce. The Palace offers dinner only; be prepared for a wait. *8 E. Cota St., tel. 805/966–3133. Reservations accepted for 5:30 seating Fri. and Sat. Dress: casual. MC, V.*

Inexpensive **Castagnola Bros. Fish Galley.** This is an unassuming spot just two blocks from the beach where wonderfully good, fresh fish is served on paper plates. Newly expanded indoor space and the outdoor patio provide ample seating. *205 Santa Barbara St., tel. 805/962–8053. No reservations. No credit cards. Closes Tues.–Thurs. and Sun. 6 PM, Fri. and Sat. 9 PM.*

East Beach Grill. Watch the waves break and the action on the sand from a surprisingly pleasant outdoor café right on this busy beach. It's a step above a fast-food joint, with its friendly table service and pleasant shoreline view. You'll find basic breakfast fare served with real plates and cutlery, and hot dogs and burgers for lunch. *Cabrillo Bath House, East Beach, tel. 805/965–8805. No reservations. No credit cards. Closes fall–spring 3 PM, summer 5 PM.*

Joe's Cafe. The vinyl checked tablecloths and simple round stools at the hefty wooden counter tell the story: nothing fancy, but solid café fare in generous portions. Joe's is a popular hangout and drinking spot, particularly of the younger crowd. *536 State St., tel. 805/966–4638. AE, MC, V. No lunch Sun.*

La Super Rica. A tiny, tacky food stand serving the best and hottest Mexican dishes between Los Angeles and San Francisco. Fans drive for miles to fill up on the soft tacos. *622 N. Milpas Ave. at Cota St., tel. 805/963–4940. Dress: casual. No credit cards.*

Solvang
Moderate–Expensive **Danish Inn.** The smorgasbord here is popular, but there are also steaks and many Continental–style items to choose from. The atmosphere is more formal than what you'll find in most other Solvang restaurants, but the fireplace and lace curtains keep it cozy. *1547 Mission Dr., tel. 805/688–4813. Reservations advised. AE, MC, V.*

Inexpensive–Moderate **Restaurant Mollen-Kroen.** A busy upstairs dining room serves smorgasbord and other Danish specialties. It has a cheerful, light setting, with fresh flowers on the tables and booths. The local folks come here when they want a good meal at a good price. *435 Alisal Rd., tel. 805/688–4555. AE, DC, MC, V.*

★ **Royal Scandia Restaurant.** Despite the size (there are three dining rooms), this restaurant is decorated like a quaint old Danish cottage, with vaulted ceilings, rafters, and lots of brass and frosted glass. There is also dining on an enclosed patio. The menu caters to traditional American tastes, with a few Danish items. *420 Alisal Rd., tel. 805/688–8000. Reservations advised. AE, DC, MC, V. No lunch.*

Lodging

The lodging choices in Big Sur, though few in number, range from the dramatic Ventana Inn to the rustic and funky Deetjen's Big Sur Inn. Neither caters to children, but the Big

Sur Lodge is the perfect place for them. You won't find many hotels or motels between Big Sur and San Simeon. In castle country—from San Simeon to San Luis Obispo—there are many moderately priced hotels and motels, some nicer than others, but mostly just basic lodging. Only the Madonna Inn, the all-pink, one-of-a-kind motel in San Luis Obispo, is worthy of a stay for its own sake. Make your reservations ahead of time, well ahead in the summer. Remember that there may not be another town just down the road with more lodging options.

Bargain lodging is hard to come by in Santa Barbara, where high-end resorts are more the style. Long a favorite getaway for congestion-crazed Los Angeles residents, the resorts promise, and usually deliver, pampering and solitude in romantic settings. The beach area is certainly the most popular locale for lodging. It is also where you will find the largest concentration of moderately priced motels. Many places offer discounts in the winter season. Come summer weekends, when 90% of the town's 46,000 motel and hotel rooms are filled, reservations well in advance are strongly advised.

Highly recommended lodgings are indicated by a star ★.

Category	Cost*
Very Expensive	over $150
Expensive	$100–$150
Moderate	$60–$100
Inexpensive	under $60

for a double room, not including tax

Big Sur

Very Expensive
★

Ventana Inn. This getaway is essential California chic—restful and hip. Rooms are in buildings that are scattered in clusters on a hillside above the Pacific, done in natural woods with cool tile floors. Activities here are purposely limited to sunning at poolside—there is a clothing-optional deck—and walks in the hills nearby. Rates include an elaborate Continental breakfast and afternoon wine and cheese (featuring California wines). *Hwy. 1, 93920, tel. 408/667–2331, 800/628–6500 in CA. 59 rooms. Facilities: restaurant, 2 pools, spa, gift shop. AE, D, DC, MC, V. Minimum stay 2 nights on weekends, 3 on holidays.*

Moderate

Big Sur Lodge. Located inside Pfeiffer Big Sur State Park, this is the best place in Big Sur for families. Motel-style cottages are set around a meadow surrounded by redwood and oak trees. Some have fireplaces, some kitchens. *Hwy. 1, Box 190, 93920, tel. 408/667–2171. 61 rooms. Facilities: pool, sauna. MC, V.*

Deetjen's Big Sur Inn. Built in bits and pieces in the '20s and '30s, this place has a certain rustic charm, at least for travelers not too attached to creature comforts. There are no locks on the doors (except from the inside), the heating is by wood-burning stove in half of the rooms, and your neighbor can often be heard through the walls. Still, it's a special place, set among redwood trees with each room individually decorated and given a name like "Château Fiasco." *Hwy. 1, south end of town, 93920, tel. 408/667–2377. 19 rooms, 13 with bath. Facilities: restaurant. No credit cards.*

Cambria
Moderate
★

Best Western Fireside Inn. This modern motel has spacious rooms decorated in cream and peach tones, with sofas and upholstered lounge chairs (plus refrigerators and coffee makers). Some have whirlpools. All the rooms have fireplaces and an ocean view. Continental breakfast is served in a room adjacent to the pool. The gardens are beautifully maintained, and the inn is just across from the beach, with fishing nearby. *6700 Moonstone Beach Dr., 93428, tel. 805/927–8661 or 800/528– 1234. 46 rooms. Facilities: heated pool, spa. AE, D, DC, MC, V.*

Cambria Pines Lodge. The lodge's buildings, from rustic cabins to fireplace suites, are set among 25 acres of pine trees above the town, with peacocks wandering the grounds. There is a big stone fireplace in the lounge, and all the furnishings—new and old—fit the decor of the 1920s, when the original lodge was established. *2905 Burton Dr., 93428, tel. 805/927–4200 or 800/ 445–6868. 125 rooms. Facilities: restaurant, bar, pool, Jacuzzi, weight room. AE, D, MC, V.*

★ **San Simeon Pines Resort Motel.** Set on 10 acres of pines and cypresses, this motel didn't tack the word "resort" onto its name just to keep up with the competition: It has its own golf gourse, and is directly across from Leffingwell Landing, a state picnic area on the rocky beach. The accommodations include cottages with their own landscaped backyards, and there are areas set aside for adults and families. *7200 Moonstone Beach Dr., Box 117, San Simeon 93452, tel. 805/927–4648. 60 rooms. Facilities: children's playground, 9-hole golf course, pool, shuffleboard. AE, MC, V.*

Inexpensive **Bluebird Motel.** Located between the east and west villages, this older motel was recently fully redecorated, and includes a homey lounge for hanging out. *1880 Main St., 93428, tel. 805/ 927–4634 or 800/553–5434. 31 rooms. AE, D, DC, MC, V.*

Morro Bay
Moderate

The Breakers. Rooms in this motel, ½ block from the waterfront, are decorated in pastel colors—each with a different wallpaper—and traditional furniture. Most have ocean views, some have fireplaces, all have coffee makers and refrigerators. *Morro Bay Blvd. at Market St., Box 1447, 93443, tel. 805/772– 7317. 25 rooms. Facilities: heated pool, spa, cable TV. AE, D, DC, MC, V.*

Ojai
Very Expensive

Oaks at Ojai. This is a well-known, comfortable health spa with a solid fitness program that includes lodging, three nutritionally balanced, low-calorie meals (surprisingly good), complete use of spa facilities, and 16 optional fitness classes. *122 E. Ojai Ave., 93023, tel. 805/646–5573 or 800/753–6257. 88 rooms. Facilities: spa with pool, Jacuzzis, sauna, weight room. D, MC, V.*

★ **Ojai Valley Inn and Country Club.** Reopened in 1988 after a $40 million renovation, the hotel is set in landscaped grounds lush with flowers. The peaceful setting comes with hillside views in nearly all directions. Some of the nicer rooms are in the original adobe building, which has been totally remodeled, but that preserved such luxurious features as huge bathrooms and the original tiles. Suites in the cabanas are more expensive than other rooms. The decor is southwestern style, and works by local artists are featured throughout the resort. *Country Club Rd., 93023, tel. 805/646–5511 or 800/422–OJAI. 218 units. Facilities: 2 restaurants, bar, golf course, lighted tennis*

courts, 2 pools, men's and women's sauna and steam room, bicycles. AE, D, DC, MC, V.

Inexpensive **Los Padres Inn.** On the main street of town, across from the
Soule Park Golf Course, is this spacious, modern hotel with a
red-tiled, Spanish-style roof. *1208 E. Ojai Ave. 93023, tel. 805/
646–4365, 800/228–3744 in CA. 31 units. Facilities: pool,
Jacuzzi. AE, D, DC, MC, V.*

San Luis Obispo **Apple Farm.** The interior design is the strong point at this coun-
Moderate– try-style hotel, where everything is meant to be soothing to the
Expensive eye, and no detail has been overlooked. Decorated to the hilt
★ with floral bedspreads and wallpaper, and with watercolors by
local artists, each room is individually appointed, some of them
with canopy beds and cozy window seats. Complimentary coffee is served in the rooms. The adjoining restaurant serves such
hearty country fare as chicken with dumplings and smoked
ribs, and the breakfasts are copious. *2015 Monterey St., 93401,
tel. 805/544–2040, 800/255–2040 in CA. 101 rooms. Facilities:
bakery, gift shop, adjacent Mill House. AE, MC, V.*

★ **Madonna Inn.** A designer's imagination run amok, this place is
as much a tourist attraction as a place to stay. Each room is
unique, to say the least. "Rock Bottom" is all stone, even the
bathroom. The "Safari Room" is decked out in animal skins.
"Old Mill" features a water wheel that powers cuckoo-clock-like
figurines. *100 Madonna Rd., 93405, tel. 805/543–3000 or 800/
543–9666. 109 rooms. Facilities: 2 restaurants, ballroom, wine
cellar, 2 gift shops, gourmet shop, and bakery. No credit cards.*

Inexpensive **Motel Inn.** If it's nostalgia rather than comfort you seek, this
place, built in 1925, bills itself as the world's first motel. The
small stucco and red-tile-roof bungalows set around the auto
court will make you feel like you are on the set of an old B movie. The place is old, but the rooms are clean, and the grounds
well-kept and lush. *2223 Monterey St., 93401, tel. 805/543–
4000. Facilities: bar, pool. AE, MC, V.*

San Simeon **San Simeon Lodge.** This unpretentious motel is right across
Inexpensive– from the ocean, and many of its rooms have sea views. And,
Moderate aside from the location, there's nothing fancy here. Built in
1958, the place has a straightforward stucco facade with wood
trim. *9520 Castillo Dr. (Hwy. 1), 93452, tel. 805/927–4601. 63
rooms. Facilities: restaurant, bar, lounge, pool. AE, DC, MC,
V.*

Inexpensive **Motel 6.** This is a newish two-story motel with comfortable
rooms opening on an interior corridor. The rooms are standard
Holiday Inn style, decorated in blue and rust. *9070 Castillo
Ave. (Hwy. 1), 93452, tel. 805/927–8691. 100 rooms. Facilities:
heated pool, room service. AE, D, DC, MC, V.*

Santa Barbara **Four Seasons Biltmore.** Santa Barbara's grande dame got a
Very Expensive $15 million sprucing-up by its new Four Seasons owners. The
decor of muted pastels and bleached woods gives the cabanas a
light, airy touch without sacrificing the hotel's reputation for
understated elegance. It's a bit more formal than elsewhere in
town, with lush gardens and palm trees galore. *1260 Channel
Dr., 93108, tel. 805/969–2261 or 800/332–3442. 236 rooms. Facilities: 2 restaurants, bar, 2 Olympic pools, whirlpool, croquet, shuffleboard, racquet ball, health club, casino, putting
green, tennis courts. AE, DC, MC, V.*

San Ysidro Ranch. At this luxury "ranch" you can feel at home
in jeans and cowboy boots, but be prepared to dress for dinner.

A hideout for the Hollywood set, this romantic place hosted John and Jackie Kennedy on their honeymoon. Guest cottages, some with antique quilts and all with wood-burning stoves or fireplaces, are scattered among 14 acres of orange trees and flower beds. There are 500 acres more of open space to roam at will on foot or horseback. The hotel welcomes children and pets. *900 San Ysidro La., Montecito, 93108, tel. 805/969–5046 or 800/368–6788. 45 rooms. Facilities: restaurant, pool, tennis courts, horseback riding, croquet, badminton. AE, MC, V. Minimum stay: 2 days on weekends, 3 on holidays.*

Expensive–Very Expensive ★ **Fess Parker's Red Lion Resort.** This is a sprawling resort complex with a slightly Spanish flair. Two- and three-story stucco buildings are located directly across the street from the beach. A showplace for this chain of hotels, this is Santa Barbara's newest luxury resort. There is a huge and lavishly appointed lobby, and the guest rooms are spacious, furnished with light wood furniture, and decorated in pastel colors. All have either private patio or balcony, and many have ocean views. *633 E. Cabrillo Blvd., 93103, tel. 805/564–4333 or 800/879–2929. 360 rooms. Facilities: 2 restaurants, bar lounge with dance floor, pool, sauna, tennis courts, exercise room, Jacuzzi, gift shop, putting green, shuffleboard, basketball court, bike rentals, hair salon. AE, D, DC, MC, V.*

Santa Barbara Inn. This three-story motel, directly across the street from East Beach, has recently been spruced up, with a crisp new exterior and a sophisticated interior decor featuring light woods, teal accents, and subdued tones. Many rooms have ocean views, and the lower-priced rooms have mountain views but also look over the parking lot. The inn's new restaurant, Citronelle, is presided over by French chef Michel Richard, who rustles up California cuisine and has become a favorite of local residents. *901 E. Cabrillo Blvd., 93103, tel. 805/966–2285 or 800/231–0431. 71 rooms. Facilities: restaurant, pool, whirlpool. AE, DC, MC, V.*

Moderate–Expensive **Ambassador by the Sea.** The wrought-iron trim and mosaic tiling on this Spanish-style building near the harbor and Stearns Wharf make this seem the quintessential California beach hotel. The rooms have verandas, and there are sundecks that overlook the ocean and the bike path. *202 W. Cabrillo Blvd., 93101, tel. 805/965–4577. 32 units. Facilities: pool, 2 units with kitchenettes. AE, D, DC, MC, V.*

Old Yacht Club Inn. Built in 1912 as a private home, this inn near the beach was one of Santa Barbara's first bed-and-breakfasts. The rooms feature turn-of-the-century furnishings and Oriental rugs. Guests receive complimentary full breakfast and evening wine, along with the use of bikes and beach chairs. No smoking. *431 Corona del Mar Dr., 93103, tel. 805/962–1277, 800/549–1676 in CA. 9 rooms. Facilities: dining room open Sat. for guests only, airport shuttle. AE, D, MC, V.*

Villa Rosa. Inside this hotel, a 60-year-old, red-tile roofed Spanish-style house of stucco and wood, the rooms and intimate lobby in this hotel are decorated in an informal southwestern style. The Villa Rosa is just one block from the beach. Rates include Continental breakfast and wine and cheese in the afternoon. *15 Chapala St., 93101, tel. 805/966–0851. 18 rooms. Facilities: pool, spa. AE, MC, V.*

Inexpensive **Motel 6.** The low price and location near the beach are the pluses for this no-frills place. Reserve well in advance all year.

443 Corona del Mar Dr., 93103, tel. 805/564–1392. 52 units. Facilities: heated pool. AE, D, DC, MC, V.

Pacific Crest Inn. A block from East Beach on a quiet residential street, this motel has clean and comfortable rooms, without the austerity of some budget operations. Kitchens are available in some rooms. *433 Corona del Mar Dr., 93103, tel. 805/966–3103. 26 rooms. Facilities: pool, coin laundry. AE, D, DC, MC, V. Minimum stay: 2 nights on weekends, 3 on holidays.*

Solvang
Moderate

Chimney Sweep Inn. All the rooms are pleasant, but it is the cottages in the backyard that are extra special (and expensive) here. Built in a half-timbered style, they were inspired by the C. S. Lewis children's book, *The Chronicles of Narnia.* The cottages have kitchens and fireplaces. In the garden are a waterfall and fish pond. Complimentary Continental breakfast includes hot apple cider. *1554 Copenhagen Dr., 93463, tel. 805/688–2111 or 800/824–6444. 28 rooms. Facilities: spa, garden. AE, MC, V.*

Solvang Royal Scandinavian Inn. This follows the Danish theme of the town, and its rooms—Scandinavian modern style, of course—have nice touches, like hand-painted furniture. The large, brick, and darkly timbered lobby has a fireplace and overstuffed chairs. *400 Alisal Rd., 93464, tel. 805/688–8000 or 800/624–5572. 133 rooms. Facilities: restaurant, lounge, pool, Jacuzzi. AE, D, DC, MC, V.*

Inexpensive

Solvang Gaard Lodge. This was Solvang's first motel and is still as comfortable and friendly as you could want, with old-Danish–style rooms and a tranquil atmosphere, just beyond the center of things. *293 Alisal Rd., 93463, tel. 805/688–4404. 21 units. AE, MC, V.*

The Arts and Nightlife

The Arts

Santa Barbara prides itself on being a top-notch cultural center. It supports a professional symphony and chamber orchestra and an impressive art museum. Its proximity to the University of California at Santa Barbara ensures an endless stream of visiting artists and performers.

The performing arts find a home in two theaters that are themselves works of art. The enormous Moorish-style **Arlington Theater** on State Street is home to the Santa Barbara Symphony. You can also catch a first-run movie there. The **Lobero,** at the corner of Anacapa and Cañon Perdido streets, is a state landmark, built in 1923, and named after José (Giuseppe) Lobero, an Italian impresario who, failing to make his fortune in the Gold Rush, set up an opera company here instead. Nowadays, its stage is shared among community theater groups and touring professionals.

The works housed in the **Museum of Art** range from collections of Greek and Roman antiquities to Grandma Moses's American folk-art vistas. There's also a fine collection of antique dolls. *1130 State St., tel. 805/963–4364 or 800/552–5434. Admission $3 adults, $2.50 senior citizens, $1.50 children 6–16. Open Tues.–Sat. 11–5, Sun. noon–5, Thurs. 11–9. Tours are led Tues.–Sat. 2 PM, Sun. 1 PM.*

For a more casual art experience, catch the beachfront display of wares local artists and craftspeople exhibit each Sunday from 10 AM to dusk along Cabrillo Boulevard.

Music Since 1971, the **San Luis Obispo Mozart Festival** (Box 311, San Luis Obispo, 93406, tel. 805/543–4580) has been held early in August. The settings include the Mission San Luis Obispo de Tolosa and the Cal Poly Theater. There are afternoon and evening concerts and recitals—by professionals and well-known visiting artists—as well as seminars and workshops. Not all the music is Mozart; you'll hear Haydn and other composers. The Festival Fringe offers free concerts outdoors.

Theater Boo and hiss the villains year round at the **Great American Melodrama** (Hwy. 1, tel. 805/489–2499) in the small town of Oceano, south of San Luis Obispo.

The **Pacific Conservatory of the Performing Arts** (Box 1700, Santa Maria, 93456, tel. 805/922–8313, or 800/221–9469 in CA) presents a full spectrum of theatrical events, from classical to contemporary, with a few musicals thrown in, in different theaters in Solvang and Santa Maria. The Solvang Festival Theater has open-air performances.

Film The **Santa Barbara International Film Festival** (1216 State St. #201, 93101, tel. 805/963–0023), held each March, pulls in the Hollywood crowd, with premieres and screenings of American and international films.

Nightlife Most of the major hotels offer nightly entertainment during the summer season and live weekend entertainment all year. To see what's scheduled at the hotels and many small clubs and restaurants, pick up a copy of the free weekly *Santa Barbara Independent* newspaper for an extensive rundown.

Dancing **Zelo.** This is a high-energy restaurant that doubles as a progressive rock and punk dance club featuring offbeat videos and innovative lighting. *630 State St., Santa Barbara. tel. 805/966–5792. Closed Mon.*

You've Let Your Imagination Go, Now Get Up And Follow Your Dreams.

For The Vacation You're Dreaming Of, Call
American Express® Travel Agency At 1-800-YES-AMEX.*

American Express will send more than your imagination soaring. We'll
fly you, sail you, drive you to any Fodor's destination and beyond.
Because American Express believes the best vacations happen
from Europe to the Orient, Walt Disney® World to Hawaii
and everywhere in between.

For dependable service, expert advice, and value wherever
your dreams take you, call on American Express. After all,
the best traveling companion
is a trustworthy friend.

It's easy to recognize a good place when you see one.

American Express Cardmembers have been doing it for years.

The secret? Instead of just relying on what they see in the window,

they look at the door. If there's an American Express Blue Box on it, they

know they've found an establishment that cares about high standards.

Whether it's a place to eat, to sleep, to shop, or simply meet, they

know they will be warmly welcomed.

So much so, they're rarely taken in by anything else.

Always a good sign.

12 Los Angeles

By Jane E. Lasky

A syndicated newspaper columnist and the author of several travel books, Jane Lasky also publishes articles in many national magazines, such as Vogue, Connoisseur, Travel & Leisure, and Esquire.

You're preparing for your trip to Los Angeles. You're psyching up with Beach Boys CDs and some Hollywood epics on the VCR. You've pulled out your Hawaiian shirts and tennis shorts. You've studied the menu at Taco Bell. You're even doing a crash regimen at your local tanning salon and aerobics studio so you won't *look* so much like a tourist when you hit the coast.

Well, relax. *Everybody's* a tourist in LaLa Land. Even the stars are star-struck (as evidenced by the celebrities watching the other celebrities at Spago). Los Angeles is a city of ephemerals, of transience, and above all, of illusion. Nothing here is quite real, and that's the reality of it all. That air of anything-can-happen—as it often does—is what keeps thousands moving to this promised land each year and millions more vacationing in it. Not just from the East or Midwest, mind you, but from the Far East, Down Under, Europe, and South America. It's this influx of cultures that's been the lifeblood of Los Angeles since its Hispanic beginning.

We cannot predict what *your* Los Angeles will be like. You can laze on a beach or soak up some of the world's greatest art collections. You can tour the movie studios and stars' homes or take the kids to Disneyland, Magic Mountain, or Knott's Berry Farm. You can shop luxurious Beverly Hills' Rodeo Drive or browse for hipper novelties on boutique-lined Melrose Avenue. The possibilities are endless—rent a boat to Catalina Island, watch the floats in Pasadena's Rose Parade, or dine on tacos, sushi, goat cheese pizza, or just plain hamburgers, hot dogs, and chili.

None of this was imagined when Spanish settlers founded their Pueblo de la Reina de Los Angeles in 1781. In fact, no one predicted a golden future for desert-dry Southern California until well after San Francisco and Northern California had gotten a head start with their own Gold Rush. The dusty outpost of Los Angeles eventually had oil and oranges, but the golden key to its success came on the silver screen: the movies. Although, if the early pioneers of Hollywood—religiously conservative fruit farmers—had gotten their way, their town's name would never have become synonymous with cinema and entertainment.

The same sunshine that draws today's visitors and new residents drew Cecil B. DeMille and Jesse Lasky in 1911 while searching for a place to make movies besides New York City. Lesser filmmakers had been shooting reels for the nickelodeons of the day in Hollywood, but DeMille and Lasky were the first to make a feature-length movie here. It took another 15 years to break through the sound barrier in cinema, but the silent-film era made Hollywood's name synonymous with fantasy, glamour, and, as the first citizens would snicker in disgust, with sin.

Outrageous partying, extravagant homes, eccentric clothing, and money, money, money have been symbols of life in Los Angeles ever since. Even the more conservative oil, aerospace, computer, banking, and import/export industries on the booming Pacific Rim have enjoyed the prosperity that leads inevitably to fun living. But even without piles of money, many people have found a kindred spirit in Los Angeles for their colorful lifestyles, be they spiritually, socially, or sexually unusual.

Tolerance reigns; live and let live—which explains why you, too, will fit in.

The distance between places in Los Angeles explains why the ethnic enclaves have not merged, regardless of the melting-pot appearance of the city. Especially since the rioting in the spring of 1992, which—among other things—brought to the surface much long-simmering tension between various ethnic groups, it is imposssible to gloss over the disparities of race, economics, and social mobility between neighborhoods, and to think of any given part of town as quite so distinct and separate from any other. Nonetheless, at its best, and most notable for visitors, is the rich cultural and culinary diversity this mix of peoples creates.

Arriving and Departing

By Plane Los Angeles International Airport or LAX (tel. 310/646–5252) is the largest airport in the area. Departures are from the upper level and arrivals on the lower level. Over 85 major airlines are serviced by LAX, the third-largest airport in the world in terms of passenger traffic.

Airlines Among the major carriers that serve LAX are **Air Canada** (tel. 800/776–3000), **America West** (tel. 800/228–7862), **American** (tel. 800/433–7300), **British Airways** (tel. 800/247–9297), **Continental** (tel. 800/525–0280), **Delta** (tel. 800/221–1212), **Japan Air Lines** (tel. 800/525–3663), **Northwest** (tel. 800/225–2525), **Southwest** (tel. 800/531–5601), **TWA** (tel. 800/221–2000), **United** (tel. 800/241–6522), and **USAir** (tel. 800/428–4322).

From the Airport to the Hotels A dizzying array of ground transportation is available from LAX to all parts of Los Angeles and its environs. A taxi ride to downtown Los Angeles can take 20 minutes—*if* there is no traffic. But in Los Angeles, that's a big if. Visitors should request the flat fee ($24 at press time) to downtown or choose from the several ground-transportation companies that offer set rates.

SuperShuttle offers direct service between the airport and hotels. The trip to downtown hotels runs about $11. The seven-passenger vans operate 24 hours a day. In the airport, phone 310/417–8988 or use the SuperShuttle courtesy phone in the luggage area; the van should arrive within 15 minutes. To be picked up anywhere in the Los Angeles area, phone 310/338–1111. **L.A. Top Shuttle** (9100 S. Sepulveda Blvd., No. 128, tel. 310/670–6666) features door-to-door service and low rates ($10 per person from LAX to hotels in the Disneyland/Anaheim area).

The following limo companies charge a flat rate for airport service, ranging from $65 to $75: **Jackson Limousine** (tel. 213/734–9955), **West Coast Limousine** (tel. 213/756–5466), and **Dav-El Livery** (tel. 310/550–0070). Many of the cars have bars, stereos, televisions, and cellular phones.

Flyaway Service (tel. 818/994–5554) offers transportation between LAX and the central San Fernando Valley for around $6. For the western San Fernando Valley and Ventura area, contact **The Great American Stage Lines** (tel. 800/287–8659). **RTD** (tel. 213/626–4455) also offers limited airport service.

Other Airports The greater Los Angeles area is served by several other local airports. **Ontario Airport** (tel. 714/988–2700), located about 35

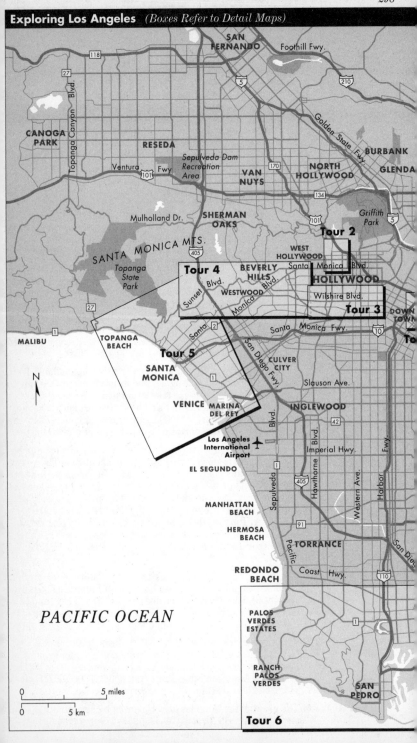

298

Exploring Los Angeles *(Boxes Refer to Detail Maps)*

SAN FERNANDO

Foothill Fwy.

CANOGA PARK

RESEDA

Topanga Canyon Blvd.

Ventura Fwy.

Sepulveda Dam Recreation Area

VAN NUYS

NORTH HOLLYWOOD

BURBANK

GLENDA

Golden State Fwy.

Mulholland Dr.

SHERMAN OAKS

Griffith Park

SANTA MONICA MTS.

Topanga State Park

Tour 2

WEST HOLLYWOOD

Santa Monica Blvd.

HOLLYWOOD

Tour 4

BEVERLY HILLS

Sunset Blvd.

WESTWOOD

Monica Blvd.

Wilshire Blvd.

Tour 3

DOWN TOWN

MALIBU

TOPANGA BEACH

Santa Monica Fwy.

Santa Monica Fwy.

To

Tour 5

SANTA MONICA

CULVER CITY

Slauson Ave.

N

VENICE

MARINA DEL REY

San Diego Fwy.

INGLEWOOD

Los Angeles International Airport

EL SEGUNDO

Imperial Hwy.

Sepulveda

Hawthorne Blvd.

Western Ave.

Harbor Fwy.

MANHATTAN BEACH

HERMOSA BEACH

TORRANCE

San Dieg

PACIFIC OCEAN

REDONDO BEACH

Coast Hwy.

Pacific

PALOS VERDES ESTATES

0   5 miles

0   5 km

RANCH PALOS VERDES

SAN PEDRO

Tour 6

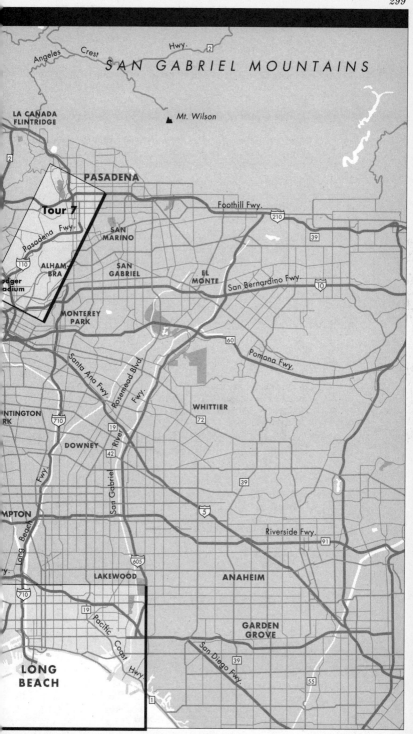

SAN GABRIEL MOUNTAINS

Hwy. 2

Angeles Crest

LA CAÑADA
FLINTRIDGE

Mt. Wilson

2

PASADENA

Foothill Fwy.

210

39

Tour 7

SAN
MARINO

Pasadena Fwy.

110

ALHAM-
BRA

SAN
GABRIEL

SAN
dger
adium

EL
MONTE

San Bernardino Fwy.

10

MONTEREY
PARK

60

Pomona Fwy.

Santa Ana Fwy.

Rosemead Blvd.

Fwy.

WHITTIER

72

NTINGTON
RK

710

19

DOWNEY

42

River

San Gabriel

39

5

MPTON

Long Beach

Fwy.

Riverside Fwy.

91

605

LAKEWOOD

ANAHEIM

710

19

GARDEN
GROVE

Pacific

LONG
BEACH

Coast

Hwy.

1

San Diego Fwy.

39

55

miles east of Los Angeles, serves the San Bernardino–Riverside area. Domestic flights are offered by Air LA, Alaska Airlines, American, America West, Continental, Delta, Northwest, SkyWest, Southwest, TWA, United, United Express, and USAir. Ground-transportation possibilities include Super-Shuttle as well as Inland Express (tel. 714/626–6599), Empire Airport Transportation (tel. 714/884–0744), and Southern California Coach (tel. 714/978–6415).

Burbank Airport (tel. 818/840–8847) serves the San Fernando Valley with commuter, and some longer, flights. Alaska Airlines, Alpha Air, USAir, American, America West, TWA, United, Delta, LA Helicopter, SkyWest, States West, and United Express are represented.

John Wayne Airport, in Orange County (tel. 714/252–5006), is served by TWA, SkyWest, American, Northwest, Alaska, American West, Continental, Delta, United, USAir, and States West.

By Car Three main interstate routes take drivers into the Los Angeles area. **I–5** runs from Canada to Mexico, through Seattle, Sacramento, and San Diego. It is known as the Golden State or Santa Ana Freeway here. **I–10** crosses the country from Florida to Los Angeles and is known locally as the Santa Monica Freeway. **I–15** comes into the area from the northeast, from Montana through Las Vegas and San Bernardino.

By Train Los Angeles can be reached by **Amtrak** (tel. 800/USA–RAIL). The *Coast Starlight* is a superliner that travels along the spectacular California coast. It offers service from Seattle–Portland and Oakland–San Francisco down to Los Angeles. Amtrak's *San Joaquin* train runs through the Central Valley from Oakland to Bakersfield, where passengers transfer to a bus to Los Angeles. The *Sunset Limited* goes to Los Angeles from New Orleans, the *Eagle* from San Antonio, and the *Southwest Chief* and the *Desert Wind* from Chicago.

Union Station in Los Angeles is one of the grandes dames of railroad stations, and is a remnant of the glory days of the railroads. It is located at 800 North Alameda Street.

By Bus The Los Angeles **Greyhound** terminal (tel. 213/620–1200) is located at 208 East 6th Street, on the corner of Los Angeles Street.

Getting Around Los Angeles

By Bus A bus ride on the **Southern California Rapid Transit District (RTD)** (tel. 213/626–4455) costs $1.10, with 25¢ for each transfer.

By Taxi You probably won't be able to hail a cab on the street in Los Angeles. Instead, you should phone one of the many taxi companies. The metered rate is $1.60 per mile. Two of the more reputable companies are **Independent Cab Co.** (tel. 213/385–8294 or 385–TAXI) and **United Independent Taxi** (tel. 213/653–5050). United accepts MasterCard and Visa.

By Limousine Limousines come equipped with everything from a full bar and telephone to a hot tub and a double bed—depending on your needs. Reputable companies include **Dav-El Livery** (tel. 310/550–0070), **First Class** (tel. 213/476–1960), and **Le Monde Limousine** (tel. 213/271–9270 or 818/887–7878).

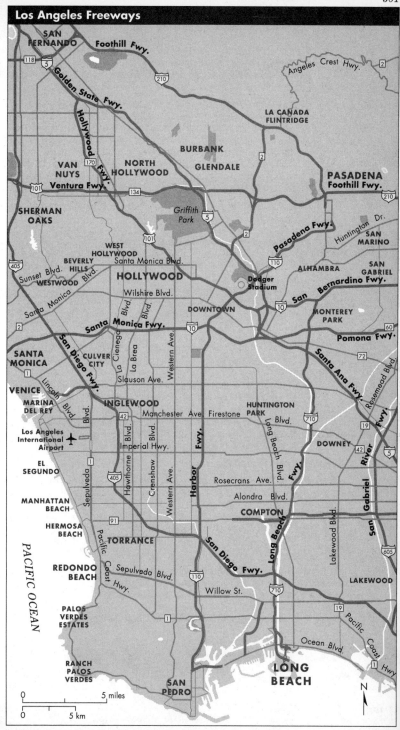

Los Angeles Freeways

SAN FERNANDO

Foothill Fwy.

118

5

Golden State Fwy.

210

Angeles Crest Hwy.

2

LA CANADA FLINTRIDGE

BURBANK

GLENDALE

170

NORTH HOLLYWOOD

Hollywood Fwy.

VAN NUYS

101

Ventura Fwy.

134

2

PASADENA
Foothill Fwy.

210

SHERMAN OAKS

Griffith Park

5

Huntington Dr.

SAN MARINO

Pasadena Fwy.

110

SAN GABRIEL

WEST HOLLYWOOD

101

Santa Monica Blvd.

ALHAMBRA

San Bernardino Fwy.

405

BEVERLY HILLS

Sunset Blvd.

WESTWOOD

Santa Monica Blvd.

HOLLYWOOD

Wilshire Blvd.

DOWNTOWN

Dodger Stadium

MONTEREY PARK

10

60

Pomona Fwy.

SANTA MONICA

2

Santa Monica Fwy.

10

72

La Cienega Blvd.

La Brea Blvd.

Western Ave.

Santa Ana Fwy.

San Diego Fwy.

CULVER CITY

VENICE

Slauson Ave.

Rosemead Blvd.

MARINA DEL REY

1

INGLEWOOD

42

Manchester Ave.

Firestone

HUNTINGTON PARK

Blvd.

710

19

DOWNEY

Los Angeles International Airport

Lincoln Blvd.

Imperial Hwy.

Crenshaw Blvd.

Harbor Fwy.

Long Beach Blvd.

River Fwy.

42

San Gabriel River

5

EL SEGUNDO

1

Sepulveda

405

Hawthorne Blvd.

Western Ave.

Rosecrans Ave.

MANHATTAN BEACH

Alondra Blvd.

HERMOSA BEACH

91

COMPTON

Lakewood Blvd.

605

TORRANCE

Pacific Coast Hwy.

San Diego Fwy.

Long Beach Fwy.

LAKEWOOD

REDONDO BEACH

Sepulveda Blvd.

110

Willow St.

710

PALOS VERDES ESTATES

1

19

Pacific Coast Hwy.

PACIFIC OCEAN

Ocean Blvd.

RANCH PALOS VERDES

SAN PEDRO

LONG BEACH

1

0 ___ 5 miles

0 ___ 5 km

N

By Car It's almost a necessity to have a car in Los Angeles. Rental agencies are listed in Planning Your Trip in Chapter 1. The accompanying map of the freeway system should help you. If you plan to drive extensively, consider buying a *Thomas Guide*, which contains detailed maps of the entire county. Despite what you've heard, traffic is not always a major problem outside of rush hours (7–9 and 3–7).

To the Airport **SuperShuttle** (tel. 310/338–1111) will pick you up at your hotel or elsewhere and take you to the Los Angeles airport. The cost varies; it's about $11 from downtown. **Funbus Airlink Airport Service** (tel. 800/962–1975 nationwide or 800/772–5299 in CA) provides regular service from hotels to LAX. From the valley, try **Flyaway Service** (Van Nuys, tel. 818/994–5554) or the **Great American Stage** (Woodland Hills, Thousand Oaks, Oxnard, Van Nuys, tel. 800/287–8659).

If you're driving, leave time for heavy traffic; it really is unpredictable.

Important Addresses and Numbers

Tourist **Visitor Information Center,** Arco Plaza, Level B, 6th and S.
Information Flower Sts., 90071, tel. 213/689–8822. Open Mon.–Sat. 8–5.
Los Angeles Convention and Visitors Bureau, 515 S. Figueroa St., 90071, tel. 213/624–7300.
Beverly Hills Visitors Bureau, 239 S. Beverly Dr., 90212, tel. 310/271–8174. Open weekdays 8:30–5.
Long Beach Area Convention and Visitors Council, 1 World Trade Center, Suite 300, Long Beach 90831, tel. 310/436–3645.
Santa Monica Visitors Center, 1400 Ocean Ave. (in Palisades Park 90401), tel. 310/393–7593. Open daily 10–4.
Hollywood Visitors Center, 6541 Hollywood Blvd., 90028, tel. 213/461–4213. Open Mon.–Sat. 9–5.
Pasadena Convention and Visitors Bureau. 171 S. Los Robles Ave., 91101, tel. 818/795–9311. Open weekdays 9–5, Sat. 10–4.
Surf and Weather Report, tel. 310/451–8761.
Community Services, tel. 800/339–6993 (24 hours).

Emergencies Dial 911 for **police** and **ambulance** in an emergency.

Doctors **Los Angeles Medical Association Physicians Referral Service,** tel. 213/483–6122. Open weekdays 8:45–4:45. Most larger hospitals in Los Angeles have 24-hour emergency rooms. A few are: **St. John's Hospital and Health Center** (1328 22nd St., tel. 310/829–5511), **Cedar-Sinai Medical Center** (8700 Beverly Blvd., tel. 310/855–5000), **Hollywood Presbyterian Medical Center** (1300 N. Vermont Ave., tel. 213/413–3000).

24-hour **Horton and Converse Pharmacy,** 6625 Van Nuys Blvd., Van
Pharmacies Nuys, tel. 818/782–6251, is open until 2 AM.
Bellflower Pharmacy, 9400 E. Rosecrans Ave., Bellflower, tel. 310/920–4213.
Horton and Converse, 11600 Wilshire Blvd., tel. 310/478–0801, is open until 2 AM.

Guided Tours

Orientation Tours Los Angeles is so spread out and has such a wealth of sightseeing possibilities that an orientation bus tour may prove useful. The cost is about $25.

Gray Line (1207 W. 3rd St., 90017, tel. 213/933–1475), one of the best-known tour companies in the country, picks passengers up from more than 140 hotels. There are more than 24 tours to Disneyland, Universal Studios, the *Queen Mary*, Catalina Island, and other attractions.

All tours are fully narrated by a driver-guide. Reservations must be made in advance. Many hotels can book them for you.

StarLine Sightseeing Tours (6845 Hollywood Blvd., Hollywood 90028, tel. 213/463–3131) has been showing people around Los Angeles since 1935, with an emphasis on the homes of the stars.

A more personalized look at the city can be had by planning a tour with **Casablanca Tours** (Roosevelt Hotel, 7000 Hollywood Blvd., Cabana 4, Hollywood 90028, tel. 213/461–0156), which offers an insider's look at Hollywood and Beverly Hills. The four-hour tour, which can be taken in the morning or afternoon, starts in Hollywood or in centrally located hotels. Tours are in minibuses with a maximum of people, and prices are equivalent to the large bus tours—about $29. Guides are college students with a high-spirited view of the city.

Special-Interest Tours
So much of Los Angeles is known to the world through Hollywood, it is fitting that many of the special-interest tours feature Hollywood and its lore.

Grave Line Tours (Box 931694, Hollywood 90093, tel. 213/469–3127) digs up the dirt on notorious suicides and visits the scenes of various murders, scandals, and other crimes via a luxuriously renovated hearse: a clever, definitely off-the-beaten-track tour in the true sensationalist spirit of Hollywood. *Tours daily at noon for 2 hours; $30 per person reserved, $25 standby.*

Hollywood Fantasy Tours (6773 Hollywood Blvd., Hollywood 90028, tel. 213/469–8184) has one tour that takes you through Beverly Hills, down Rodeo Drive, around Bel Air, and up and down colorful Sunset Strip, then on to exclusive Holmby Hills, home of *Playboy* magazine's founder Hugh Hefner. If you're interested only in Hollywood, ask about a tour of that area, pointing out television and film studios as well as famous stores, such as Frederick's of Hollywood.

Visitors who want something dramatically different should check with Marlene Gordon of **The Next Stage** (Box 35269, Los Angeles 90035, tel. 213/939–2688). This innovative tour company takes from four to 46 people, on buses or vans, in search of ethnic L.A., Victorian L.A., Underground L.A. (in which all the places visited are underground), and so on. The "Insomniac Tour" visits the flower market and other places in the wee hours of the morning. Marlene Gordon, who is a member of the L.A. Conservancy and the California Historical Society, also plans some spectacular tours outside Los Angeles. Among them are a bald-eagle tour to Big Bear with a naturalist; a whale-watching and biplane adventure; and a glorious garlic train, which tours Monterey and Carmel, and takes in the Gilroy Garlic Fest.

LA Today Custom Tours also has a wide selection of offbeat tours, some of which tie in with seasonal and cultural events, such as theater, museum exhibits, and the Rose Bowl. Groups range from 8 to 50, and prices from $6 to $50. The least expensive is a walking tour of hotel lobbies in downtown Los Angeles. The two-hour tour costs $6. For further information contact

Elinor Oswald (LA Today, 14964 Camarosa Dr., Pacific Palisades 90272, tel. 310/454–5730).

Architecture in Los Angeles is rich and varied. Guided and self-guided tours of the many design landmarks are becoming increasingly popular. Buildings run the gamut from the Victorian Bradbury Building in the downtown core to the many fine examples of Frank Lloyd Wright's works—the Ennis-Brown House, Hollyhock House, and Snowden House among them. On the last Sunday of April each year the Los Angeles County Museum of Art (tel. 213/857–6500) holds a fund-raising tour of a selection of special houses in the city.

Personal Guides Perhaps the best way to see Los Angeles, or any city, is with a guide who knows the city well and can gear sightseeing to your interests. One such service, **Tour Elegante** (15446 Sherman Way, Van Nuys, tel. 818/786–8466), offers the perk of a personal guide without the usual expense (under $50 per person). Tours run from three to six hours.

Elegant Tours for the Discriminating (tel. 213/472–4090) is a personalized sightseeing and shopping service for the Beverly Hills area. Joan Mansfield offers her extensive knowledge of Rodeo Drive to one, two, or three people at a time. Lunch is included.

L.A. Nighthawks (Box 10224, Beverly Hills 90210, tel. 310/392–1500) will arrange your nightlife for you. For a rather hefty price, you'll get a limousine, a guide, and a gourmet dinner, as well as immediate entry into L.A.'s hottest night spots. For a group of eight, prices come down considerably because vans or tour buses are used. Nighthawks proprietor Charles Andrews, a music writer and 20-year entertainment-business veteran, has been featured on "Eye on LA" and other television shows for this innovative approach to nighttime entertainment.

Exploring Los Angeles

By Ellen Melinkoff

Updated and revised by Rosemary Freskos, Mary Jane Horton, Mimi Kmet, and Jane E. Lasky

In a city where the residents think nothing of a 40-mile commute to work, visitors have their work cut out for them. To see the sites—from the Huntington Library in San Marino to the Getty Museum in Malibu—requires a decidedly organized itinerary. Be prepared to put miles on the car. It's best to view Los Angeles as a collection of destinations, each to be explored separately, and not to jump willy-nilly from place to place. In this guide, we've divided up the major sightseeing areas of Los Angeles into eight major tours: Downtown; Hollywood; Wilshire Boulevard; the Westside; Santa Monica, Venice, Pacific Palisades, and Malibu; Palos Verdes, San Pedro, and Long Beach; Highland Park, Pasadena, and San Marino; and the San Fernando Valley.

Each takes visitors to the major sites, augmented with bits of history and comments on the area, and occasional Time Out suggestions for meals. These main attractions are listed and numbered on the accompanying maps.

Downtown Los Angeles

Numbers in the margin correspond to points of interest on the Downtown Los Angeles map.

All those jokes about Los Angeles being a city without a downtown are simply no longer true. They might have had some ring of truth to them a few decades ago when Angelenos ruthlessly turned their backs on the city center and hightailed to the suburbs. There *had* been a downtown, once, when Los Angeles was very young, and now the city core is enjoying a resurgence of attention from urban planners, real-estate developers, and intrepid downtown office workers who have discovered the advantages of living close to the office.

Downtown Los Angeles can be explored on foot, or better yet, on DASH (Downtown Area Short Hop). This minibus service travels in a loop past most of the attractions listed here. Every ride costs 25¢, so if you hop on and off to see attractions, it'll cost you every time. But the cost is worth it, since you can travel quickly and be assured of finding your way. Whether you begin your tour at ARCO, as suggested, or decide to start at Olvera Street in Chinatown, DASH will get you around. The bus stops every two blocks or so. DASH (tel. 213/689–8822) runs weekdays and Saturday 6:30 AM–10 PM.

Begin your walk in the Los Angeles of today. The new downtown is a collection of east-side streets, paralleling the Harbor Freeway. Your walk will take you from the most modern buildings back in time past Art Deco movie palaces to the very oldest adobe in the city.

1 ARCO Plaza is hidden directly under the twin ARCO towers. This subterranean shopping mall is jam-packed with office workers during the week, nearly deserted on weekends. The **Los Angeles Visitor and Convention Bureau** is nearby. It offers free information about attractions as well as advice on public transportation. *685 Figueroa St., between 7th St. and Wilshire Blvd., tel. 213/689–8822. Open weekdays 8–6, Sat. 8:30–5.*

One block from the ARCO Plaza, at the corner of Flower and 7th streets, is the downtown L.A. terminus of the Metrorail Blue Line trains that run from here to Long Beach.

2 Just north of ARCO, the **Westin Bonaventure Hotel** (404 S. Figueroa St., tel. 213/624–1000) is unique in the L.A. skyline: five shimmering cylinders in the sky, without a 90-degree angle in sight. Designed by John Portman in 1974, the building looks like science-fiction fantasy. Nonguests can use only one elevator, which rises through the roof of the lobby to soar through the air outside to the revolving restaurant and bar on the 35th floor. The food here is expensive; a better bet is to come for a drink (still overpriced) and nurse it for an hour as Los Angeles makes a full circle around you.

In the 19th century, Bunker Hill was the site of many stately mansions. Thanks to bulldozers, there's not much of a hill left, but this downtown area is being redeveloped, and two major sites here showcase visual arts (painting, sculpture, and environmental work) and media and performing arts.

3 The **Museum of Contemporary Art** houses a permanent collection of international scope, representing modern art from 1940 to the present. Included are works by Mark Rothko, Franz Kline, and Susan Rothenberg. The red sandstone building was designed by renowned Japanese architect Arata Isozaki, and opened in 1986. Pyramidal skylights add a striking geometry to the seven-level, 98,000-square-foot building. Don't miss the

Downtown Los Angeles

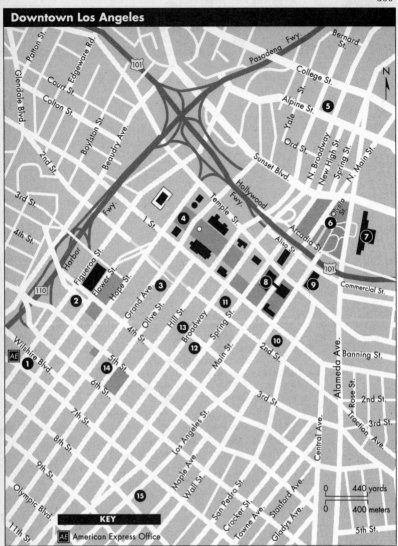

KEY

AE American Express Office

Biltmore Hotel, **14**

Bradbury Building, **12**

Chinatown, **5**

El Pueblo State Historic Park, **6**

Garment District, **15**

Grand Central Market, **13**

Greater Los Angeles Visitor and Convention Bureau, **1**

Little Tokyo, **10**

Los Angeles Children's Museum, **9**

Los Angeles City Hall, **8**

Los Angeles *Times*, **11**

Museum of Contemporary Art, **3**

Music Center, **4**

Union Station, **7**

Westin Bonaventure Hotel, **2**

gift shop or the lively Milanese-style café. *250 S. Grand Ave.,
tel. 213/626–6222. Admission: $4 adults, children under 12
free; free to all after 5 PM Thurs. Open Tues., Wed., Fri., Sat.,
and Sun. 11–5, Thurs. 11–8. Closed Mon.*

❹ Walk north to the **The Music Center,** which has become the cultural center for Los Angeles since it opened in 1969. For years,
it was the site of the Academy Awards each spring: The limousines arrived at the Hope Street drive-through and celebrities
were whisked through the crowds to the Dorothy Chandler Pavilion, the largest and grandest of the three theaters. It was
named after the widow of the publisher of the Los Angeles
Times, who was instrumental in fund-raising efforts to build
the complex. The round, center building, the Mark Taper Forum, seats only 750 and seems almost cozy. Most of its offerings
are of an experimental nature, many of them on a pre-Broad-
way run. The Ahmanson, at the north end, is the venue for
many musical comedies. The plaza has a fountain and sculpture
by Jacques Lipchitz. *First St. and Grand Ave., tel. 213/972–
7211. Free 1-hr, 10-min tours are offered Tues.–Sat. 10–1:30.
Schedule subject to change; call for reservations.*

❺ L.A.'s **Chinatown** runs a pale second to San Francisco's Chinatown but still offers visitors an authentic slice of life, beyond
the tourist hokum. The neighborhood is bordered by Yale, Bernard, and Ord streets, and Alameda Avenue. The main drag is
North Broadway, where, every February, giant dragons snake
down the center of the pavement during Chinese New Year celebrations. More than 15,000 Chinese and Southeast Asians
(mostly Vietnamese) actually live in the Chinatown area, but
many times that regularly frequent the markets (filled with exotic foods unfamiliar to most Western eyes) and restaurants
(dim sum parlors are currently the most popular).

❻ **El Pueblo State Historic Park** preserves the "birthplace" of Los
Angeles (no one knows exactly where the original 1781 settlement was), the oldest downtown buildings, and some of the
only remaining pre-1900 buildings in the city. The state park,
comprising 44 acres and including the Plaza and Olvera Street,
is bounded by Alameda, Arcadia, Spring, and Macy streets.
*The Visitors Center is in Sepulveda House, 622 N. Main St.,
tel. 213/628–1274. Open weekdays 10–4, Sat. 10–4:30. Most
shops and restaurants in the park are open daily 10–9.*

Olvera Street is the heart of the park and one of the most popular tourist sites in Los Angeles.

With its cobblestone walkways, piñatas, mariachis, and authentic Mexican food, Olvera Street should not be dismissed as
merely some gringo approximation of the real thing. Mexican-
American families come here in droves, especially on weekends
and Mexican holidays—to them it feels like the old country.

Begin your walk of the area at the plaza, between Main and Los
Angeles streets, a wonderful Mexican-style park with shady
trees, a central gazebo, and plenty of benches and walkways for
strolling. On weekends there are often mariachis and folk-
dance groups here. You can have your photo taken in an oversize velvet sombrero, astride a stuffed donkey (a takeoff of the
zebra-striped donkeys that are a tradition on the streets of Tijuana).

Head north up Olvera Street proper. Mid-block is the Sepulveda House, site of the Visitors Center; it now undergoing renovations. The Eastlake Victorian was built in 1887 as a hotel and boardinghouse. Pelanconi House, built in 1855, was the first brick building in Los Angeles and has been home to the La Golondrina restaurant for more than 50 years. During the 1930s, famed Mexican muralist David Alfaro Siqueiros was commissioned to paint a mural on the south wall of the Italian Hall building. The patrons were not prepared for—and certainly not pleased by—this anti-imperialist mural depicting the oppressed workers of Latin America held in check by a menacing American eagle. It was promptly whitewashed into oblivion, and remains under the paint to this day. While preservationists from the Getty Conservation Trust work on ways of restoring the mural, copies can be seen at the Visitors Center.

Walk down the east side of Olvera Street to mid-block, passing the only remaining sign of Zanja Ditch (mother ditch), which supplied water to the area in the earliest years. Avila Adobe (open weekdays 10–4:30), built in 1818, is generally considered the oldest building still standing in Los Angeles. This graceful, simple adobe is designed with the traditional interior courtyard and is furnished in the style of the 1840s.

On weekends, the restaurants are packed, and there is usually music in the plaza and along the street. Two Mexican holidays, Cinco de Mayo (May 5) and Independence Day (September 16), also draw huge crowds—and long lines for the restaurants. To see Olvera Street at its quietest and perhaps loveliest, visit on a late weekday afternoon. The long shadows heighten the romantic feeling of the street and there are only a few strollers and diners milling about.

South of the plaza is an area that has undergone recent renovation but remains, for the most part, only an ambitious idea. Except for docent-led tours, these magnificent old buildings remain closed, awaiting some commercial plan (à la Ghirardelli Square in San Francisco) that never seems to come to fruition. Buildings seen on tours include the Merced Theater, Masonic Temple, Pico House, and the Garnier Block—all ornate examples of the late-19th-century style. Under the Merced and Masonic Temple are the catacombs, secret passageways, and old opium dens used by Chinese immigrants. Tours depart Tuesday–Saturday 10–1, on the hour. Meet at the Old Firehouse (south side of plaza, tel. 213/625–3741), an 1884 building that contains early fire-fighting equipment and old photographs.

Time Out   The dining choices on Olvera Street range from fast-food stands to comfortable, sit-down restaurants. The most authentic Mexican food is at **La Luz del Dia** (tel. 213/628–7495), at the southwest corner of the street. Served here are traditional favorites like barbecued goat and pickled cactus as well as standbys such as tacos and enchiladas. Best of all are the handmade tortillas. You haven't tasted real tortillas until you've tried these (the only ones on the street), which are patted out in a practiced rhythm by the women behind the counter. **La Golondrina** (tel. 213/628–4349) and **El Paseo** (tel. 213/626–1361) restaurants, across from each other in mid-block, have delightful patios and extensive menus.

⑦ Union Station (800 N. Alameda St.), directly east of Olvera Street across Alameda Street, is one of those quintessentially Californian buildings that seemed to define Los Angeles to movie goers all over the country in the 1940s. Built in 1939, its Spanish Mission style is a subtle combination of Streamline Moderne and Moorish. The majestic scale of the waiting room alone is worth the walk over. The place is so evocative of its heyday that you'll half-expect to see Carole Lombard or Groucho Marx or Barbara Stanwyck step onto the platform from a train and sashay through.

⑧ Los Angeles City Hall is another often-photographed building and well-known from its many appearances on "Dragnet," "Superman," and other television shows. Opened in 1928, the 27-story City Hall remained the only building to break the 13-story height limit (earthquakes, you know) until 1957. There is a 45-minute tour and ride to the top-floor observation deck, and, although some newer buildings (e.g., the Bonaventure) offer higher views, City Hall has a certain landmark panache. *200 N. Spring St., tel. 213/485–4423. Tours are by reservation only, weekday mornings at 10 and 11.*

⑨ Los Angeles Children's Museum was the first of several strictly-for-kids museums now open in the city. All the exhibits here are hands-on, from Sticky City (where kids get to pillow-fight with abandon in a huge pillow-filled room) to a TV studio (where they can put on their own news shows). *310 N. Main St., tel. 213/687–8800. Admission: $5, children under 2 free. Open during school sessions Wed.–Thurs. 2–4 and weekends 10–5; during summer vacations, open weekdays 11:30–5, weekends 10–5.*

⑩ Little Tokyo is the original ethnic neighborhood for Los Angeles's Japanese community. Most have deserted the downtown center for suburban areas such as Gardena and West Los Angeles, but Little Tokyo remains a cultural focal point. Nisei (the name for second-generation Japanese) Week is celebrated here every August with traditional drums, obon dancing, a carnival, and huge parade. Bound by First, San Pedro, Third, and Los Angeles streets, Little Tokyo has dozens of sushi bars, tempura restaurants, trinket shops, and even a restaurant that serves nothing but eel. The Japanese American Cultural and Community Center presents such events as kabuki theater straight from Japan.

⑪ The **Los Angeles *Times*** complex is made up of several, supposedly architecturally harmonious, buildings, and combines several eras and styles, but looks pretty much like a hodge-podge. *202 W. 1st St., tel. 213/237–5000. Two public tours given weekdays: 35-min. tour of old plant and 45-min. tour of new plant. Tour times vary. Call for information. Reservations required.*

Broadway between First and Ninth streets is one of Los Angeles's busiest shopping thoroughfares. The shops and sidewalk vendors cater primarily to the Hispanic population with bridal shops, immigration lawyers, and cheap stereo equipment. First-floor rental space is said to be the most expensive in the city, even higher than in Beverly Hills. This can be an exhilarating slice-of-life walk, past the florid old movie theaters like the Mayan and the Million Dollar and the perennially classy Bradbury Building.

⑫ The five-story 1983 **Bradbury Building** (304 S. Broadway, tel. 213/626–1893) remains a marvelous specimen of Victorian-era commercial architecture, serenely anchoring the southeast corner of Third Street and Broadway and keeping its nose above the hustle and bustle of the street like a grand dowager. Once the site of turn-of-the-century sweatshops, it now houses somewhat more genteel law offices. The interior courtyard with its glass skylight and open balconies and elevator is picture perfect, and, naturally, a popular movie locale. The building is open only during the week, and its owners prefer that you not wander too far past the lobby.

⑬ **Grand Central Market** (317 S. Broadway, tel. 213/624–2378) is the most bustling market in the city and a testimony to the city's diversity. This block-through marketplace of colorful and exotic produce, herbs, and meat draws a faithful clientele from the Hispanic community, senior citizens on a budget, along with Westside matrons for whom money is no object seeking rare foodstuffs for their recipe adventures. Even if you don't plan to buy so much as one banana, Grand Central Market is a delightful place in which to browse: The butcher shops display everything from lamb heads and bulls' testicles, to pigs' tails; the produce stalls are piled high with the ripest, reddest tomatoes; and the herb stalls promise remedies for all your ills. Mixed among them are fast-food stands (one Chinese but most Mexican). *317 S. Broadway. Open Mon.–Sat. 9–6, Sun. 10–4.*

⑭ The **Biltmore Hotel** (515 S. Olive St.), built in 1923, rivals Union Station for sheer architectural majesty in the Spanish Revival tradition. The public areas have recently been restored; the magnificent, hand-painted wood beams brought back to their former glory.

⑮ **The Garment District** (700–800 blocks of Los Angeles St.) is an enclave of jobbers and wholesalers that sell off the leftovers from Los Angeles's considerable garment-industry production. The Cooper Building (860 S. Los Angeles St.) is the heart of the district and houses several of what local bargain-hunters consider to be the best pickings.

Hollywood

Numbers in the margin correspond to points of interest on the Hollywood map.

"Hollywood" once meant movie stars and glamour. The big film studios were here; starlets lived in sororitylike buildings in the center of town; and movies premiered beneath the glare of klieg lights at the Chinese and the Pantages theaters.

Those days are long gone. Paramount is the only major studio still physically located in Hollywood; and though some celebrities may live in the Hollywood Hills, there certainly aren't any in the "flats." In short, Hollywood is no longer "Hollywood." These days it is, even to its supporters, a seedy town that could use a good dose of urban renewal (some projects are, in fact, finally under way). So why visit? Because the legends of the golden age of the movies are heavy in the air. Because this is where the glamour of Hollywood originated, and where those who made it so worked and lived. Judy Garland lived here and so did Marilyn Monroe and Lana Turner. It is a tribute to Hollywood's powerful hold on the imagination that visitors are able to look past the junky shops and the lost souls who walk the streets to get a sense of the town's glittering past. Besides, no visit to Los Angeles is truly complete without a walk down Hollywood Boulevard.

❶ Begin your tour of Hollywood simply by looking to the **Hollywood sign** in the Hollywood Hills that line the northern border of the town. Even on the smoggiest days, the sign is visible for miles. It is on Mt. Lee, north of Beachwood Canyon, which is approximately 1 mile east of Hollywood and Vine. The 50-foot-tall letters, originally spelling out "Hollywoodland," were erected in 1923 as a promotional scheme for a real-estate development. The "land" was taken down in 1949.

❷ **Hollywood and Vine** was once considered the heart of Hollywood. The mere mention of this intersection still inspires images of a street corner bustling with movie stars, starlets, and moguls passing by, on foot, or in snazzy convertibles. But these days, Hollywood and Vine is far from the action, and pedestrian traffic is, well, pedestrian. No stars, no starlets, no moguls. The Brown Derby restaurant that once stood at the northeast corner is long gone, and the intersection these days is little more than a place for visitors to get their bearings.

❸ **Capitol Records Building** (1756 N. Vine St.). When Capitol decided to build its new headquarters just north of Hollywood and Vine, two of the record company's big talents of the day (singer Nat King Cole and songwriter Johnny Mercer) suggested that it be done in the shape of a stack of records. It was, and it opened in 1956, the very picture of '50s chic. Compared with much of what's gone up in L.A. since then, this building doesn't seem so odd.

❹ **The Palace** (1735 N. Vine St., tel. 213/467–4571), just across the street from the Capitol Building, was opened in 1927 as the Hollywood Playhouse. It has played host to many shows over the years, from Ken Murray's "Blackouts" to Ralph Edwards's "This Is Your Life." It is now the site of popular rock concerts and late-night weekend dancing.

❺ When the **Pantages Theater,** at 6233 Hollywood Boulevard, just east of Vine Street, opened in 1930, it was the very pinnacle of movie-theater opulence. From 1949 to 1959, it was the site of the Academy Awards, and today hosts large-scale Broadway musicals.

❻ **The Hollywood Walk of Fame** is at every turn along the sidewalks as you make your way through downtown Hollywood. The name of one or other Hollywood legend is embossed in brass, at the center of a pink star embedded in a dark gray terrazzo circle. The first eight stars were unveiled in 1960 at the northwest corner of Highland Avenue and Hollywood Boulevard. Some of these names have stood the test of time better than others: The eight were Olive Borden, Ronald Colman, Louise Fazenda, Preston Foster, Burt Lancaster, Edward Sedgwick, Ernest Torrence, and Joanne Woodward. In the 30 years since, 1,800 others have been added. Being walked on, day after day, may be a celebrity's dream, but this kind of immortality doesn't come cheap. The personality in question (or, far more likely, the personality's movie studio or record company) must pay $3,500 for the honor. Walk a few blocks and you'll quickly find that not all the names are familiar. Many are stars from the earliest days of Hollywood. The celebrities are identi-

Hollywood

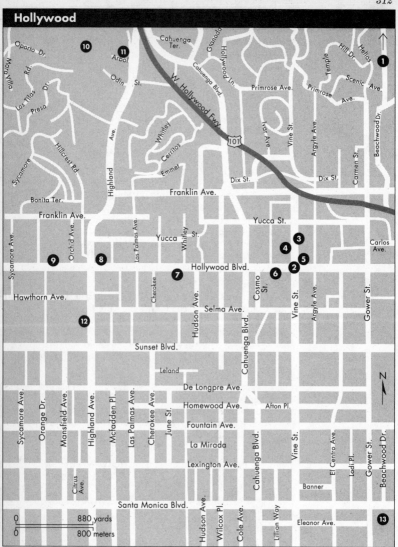

Capitol Records
Building, **3**

Frederick's of
Hollywood, **7**

Hollywood Bowl, **10**

Hollywood High
School, **12**

Hollywood Memorial
Cemetery, **13**

Hollywood sign, **1**

Hollywood Studio
Museum, **11**

Hollywood and Vine, **2**

Hollywood Walk of
Fame, **6**

Hollywood Wax
Museum, **8**

Mann's Chinese
Theater, **9**

The Palace, **4**

The Pantages
Theater, **5**

fied by one of five logos: a motion-picture camera, a radio microphone, a television set, a record, or theatrical masks. Here's a guide to a few of the more famous stars on the Walk of Fame: Marlon Brando at 1765 Vine, Charlie Chaplin at 6751 Hollywood, W. C. Fields at 7004 Hollywood, Clark Gable at 1608 Vine, Marilyn Monroe at 6774 Hollywood, Rudolph Valentino at 6164 Hollywood, and John Wayne at 1541 Vine.

❼ Frederick's of Hollywood (6608 Hollywood Blvd., tel. 213/466–8506) is one of Hollywood's more infamous spots. After decades of sporting a gaudy lavender paint job, the store's exterior has been restored to its original understated Art Deco look. Fear not, however, that the place has suddenly gone tasteful; inside is all the risqué and trashy lingerie that made this place famous. There is also a bra museum that features the undergarments of living and no longer living Hollywood legends. This is a popular tourist spot, if only for a good giggle.

❽ Hollywood Wax Museum. It's not the same as seeing celebrities in the flesh, but the museum can offer visitors sights that real life no longer can (Mary Pickford, Elvis Presley, and Clark Gable) and a few that even real life never did (Rambo and Conan). Recently added living legends on display include actors Kevin Costner and Patrick Swayze. A short film on Academy Award winners is shown daily. *6767 Hollywood Blvd., tel. 213/462–8860. Admission: $7.50 adults, $6.50 senior citizens, $5 children. Children under 6 admitted free if accompanied by an adult. Open Sun.–Thurs. 10 AM–midnight, Fri.–Sat. 10 AM–2 AM.*

❾ Most residents finally no longer call **Mann's Chinese Theater** (6925 Hollywood Blvd., tel. 213/464–8111) "Grauman's Chinese," and the new owners seem to have a firm hold on the place in the public's eye. The theater opened in 1927 with the premiere of Cecil B. DeMille's *King of Kings*. The architecture is a fantasy of Chinese pagodas and temples as only Hollywood could turn out. Although you'll have to buy a movie ticket to appreciate the interior trappings as well as the exterior's excess, the famous courtyard is open for browsing. You'll see the well-known cement hand- and footprints. The tradition is said to have begun at the premiere itself, when actress Norma Talmadge accidentally stepped into the wet cement. Now more than 160 celebrities have added their footprints and handprints, along with a few oddball prints like the one of Jimmy Durante's nose. Space has pretty much run out and, unlike the Walk of Fame, these etched-in-stone autographs are by invitation only.

❿ Summer evening concerts at the **Hollywood Bowl** have been a tradition since 1922, although the bandshell has been replaced several times. The 17,000-plus seating capacity ranges from boxes (where local society matrons put on incredibly fancy alfresco preconcert meals for their friends) to concrete bleachers in the rear. Some people actually prefer the back rows for their romantic appeal.

The Bowl's official concert season begins in early July and runs through mid-September. Performances are given on Tuesdays, Thursdays, and weekends. The program ranges from jazz to pop to classical. Evenings can be chilly (even on 90-degree days), so bring a sweater and wear comfortable shoes. A night at the Bowl involves considerable walking. *2301 N. Highland*

Ave., tel. 213/850–2000. Grounds open daily summer, 9–sunset. Call for program schedule.

⑪ The **Hollywood Studio Museum** sits in the Hollywood Bowl parking lot, east of Highland Boulevard. The building, recently moved to this site, was once called the Lasky–DeMille Barn and it was where Cecil B. DeMille produced the first feature-length film, *The Squaw Man*. In 1927, the barn became Paramount Pictures, with the original company of Jesse Lasky, Cecil B. DeMille, and Samuel Goldwyn. The museum shows the origin of the motion-picture industry. There's a re-creation of DeMille's office, with original artifacts and a screening room offering vintage film footage of Hollywood and its legends. A great gift shop sells such quality vintage memorabilia as autographs, photographs, and books. *2100 N. Highland Ave., tel. 213/874–2276. Admission: $3.50 adults, $2.50 children. Free parking. Open weekends 10–4.*

⑫ Such stars as Carol Burnett, Linda Evans, Rick Nelson, and Lana Turner attended **Hollywood High School** (1521 N. Highland Ave.). Today the student body is as diverse as Los Angeles itself, with every ethnic group represented.

⑬ Many of Hollywood's stars, from the silent-screen era on, are buried in **Hollywood Memorial Cemetery,** a few blocks from Paramount Studios. Walk from the entrance to the lake area and you'll find the crypt of Cecil B. DeMille and the graves of Nelson Eddy and Douglas Fairbanks, Sr. Inside the Cathedral Mausoleum is Rudolph Valentino's crypt (where fans, the press, and the famous Lady in Black turn up every August 23, the anniversary of his death). Other stars interred in this section are Peter Lorre and Eleanor Powell. In the Abbey of Palms Mausoleum, Norma Talmadge and Clifton Webb are buried. *6000 Santa Monica Blvd., tel. 213/469–1181. Open daily 8–5.*

Wilshire Boulevard

Wilshire Boulevard begins in the heart of downtown Los Angeles and runs west, through Beverly Hills and Santa Monica, ending at the cliffs above the Pacific Ocean. In 16 miles it moves through fairly poor neighborhoods populated by recent immigrants, solidly middle-class enclaves, and through a corridor of the highest-priced high-rise condos in the city. Along the way, and all within a few blocks of each other, are many of Los Angeles's top architectural sites, museums, and shops.

This linear tour can be started at any point along Wilshire Boulevard but to really savor the cross-section view of Los Angeles that this street provides, take the Bullocks-west-to-the-sea approach. If you have only limited time, it would be better to skip Koreatown and Larchmont and pare down the museum time than to do only one stretch. All these sites are on Wilshire or within a few blocks north or south.

One Wilshire, at the precise start of the boulevard in downtown Los Angeles, is just another anonymous office building. Begin, instead, a few miles westward, past the Harbor Freeway. As Wilshire Boulevard moves from its downtown genesis, it quickly passes through neighborhoods now populated by recent immigrants from Central America. Around the turn of the century, however, this area was home to many of the city's wealthy citizens, as the faded Victorian houses on the side streets attest.

As the population crept westward, the distance to downtown shops began to seem insurmountable and the first suburban department branch store, **I. Magnin Bullocks Wilshire** (3050 Wilshire Blvd., tel. 213/382–6161), was opened in 1929. It remains in excellent condition today and is still operating. To appreciate the real splendor of the store, enter from the rear door. The behind-the-store parking lot was quite an innovation in 1929 and the first accommodation a large Los Angeles store made to the automobile age. On the ceiling of the porte cochere, a mural depicts the history of transportation. Inside, the store remains a well-preserved monument to the Art Deco age. The walls, the elevators, and the floors are the height of late-1920s style. The Los Angeles Conservancy gives monthly tours or makes arrangements for special group tours. The fee of about $5 goes to building preservation. Information: 213/623-CITY.

Koreatown begins almost at I. Magnin Bullocks Wilshire's back door. Koreans are one of the latest and largest groups in this ethnically diverse city. Settling in the area south of Wilshire Boulevard, along Olympic Boulevard between Vermont and Western avenues, the Korean community has slowly grown into a cohesive neighborhood with active community groups and newspapers. The area is teeming with Asian restaurants (not just Korean but also Japanese and Chinese, because Koreans are fond of those cuisines). Many of the signs in this area are in Korean only. Although some businesses in this neighborhood were damaged in the riots in the spring of 1992, most were rebuilding and reopening within a few weeks.

At the southwest corner of Wilshire and Western Avenue sits **Wiltern Theater** (3780 Wilshire Blvd.), part of the magnificent Wiltern Center and one of the city's best examples of full-out Art Deco architecture. The 1930s zigzag design was recently restored to its splendid turquoise hue. Inside, the theater is full of opulent detail at every turn. Originally a movie theater, the Wiltern is now a multi-use arts complex.

Continuing west on Wilshire, the real-estate values start to make a sharp climb. The mayor of Los Angeles has his official residence in **Getty House** (605 S. Irving Blvd.), one block north of Wilshire in the Hancock Park district. This is one of the city's most genteel neighborhoods, remaining in vogue since its development in the 1920s. Many of L.A.'s old-money families live here in English Tudor homes with East Coast landscaping schemes that defy the local climate and history. The white-brick, half-timber mayor's residence was donated to the city by the Getty family.

Miracle Mile, the strip of Wilshire Boulevard between La Brea and Fairfax avenues, was so dubbed in the 1930s as a promotional gimmick to attract shoppers to the new stores. The area went into something of a decline in the '50s and '60s, but is now enjoying a comeback, as Los Angeles's Art Deco architecture has come to be appreciated, preserved, and restored. Exemplary buildings like the El Rey Theater (5519 Wilshire) stand out as examples of period design (in spite of the fact that it now houses a restaurant). In the Callender's Restaurant (corner of Wilshire and Curson), there are recent murals and old photographs that effectively depict life on the Miracle Mile during its heyday.

Across Curson Avenue is Hancock Park, an actual park, and not to be confused with Hancock Park, the residential neighborhood. This park is home to two of the city's best museums, as well as the city's world-famous fossil source, the **La Brea Tar Pits.** Despite the fact that *la brea* already means "tar" in Spanish and to say "La Brea Tar Pits" is redundant, the name remains firm in local minds. These tar pits were known to the earliest inhabitants of the area and the tar from them was long used to seal leaky boats and roofs. In the early 20th century, geologists discovered that the sticky goo contained the largest collection of Pleistocene fossils ever found at one location. More than 200 varieties of birds, mammals, plants, reptiles, and insects have been discovered here. The statues of mammoths in the big pit near the corner of Wilshire and Curson depict how many of them were entombed: Edging down to a pond of water to drink, animals were caught in the tar and unable to extricate themselves.

The pits were formed about 35,000 years ago when deposits of oil rose to the Earth's surface, collected in shallow pools, and coagulated into sticky asphalt. Over 100 tons of fossil bones have been removed in the 70 years since excavations began here. There are several pits scattered around Hancock Park; they serve as a reminder of nature's superiority over man. Construction in the area has often had to accommodate these oozing pits, and in nearby streets and along sidewalks, little bits of tar occasionally ooze up, unstoppable.

Also in Hancock Park, the **George C. Page Museum of La Brea Discoveries** is a satellite of the Los Angeles County Museum of Natural History. The museum is situated at the tar pits and set, bunkerlike, half underground. A bas-relief around four sides depicts life in the Pleistocene era, and the museum has over one million Ice Age fossils. Exhibits include reconstructed, life-size skeletons of mammals and birds whose fossils were recovered from the pits: saber-tooth cats, mammoths, wolves, sloths, eagles, and condors. Several large murals and colorful dioramas depict the history of the Pleistocene period. The glass-enclosed Paleontological Laboratory permits observation of the ongoing cleaning, identification, and cataloguing of fossils excavated from the nearby asphalt deposits. *The La Brea Story* and *Dinosaurs, the Terrible Lizards*, are short documentary films shown every 15–30 minutes as museum traffic requires. A hologram magically puts flesh on "La Brea Woman," and a tar contraption shows visitors just how hard it would be to free oneself from the sticky mess. An excellent gift shop offers nature-oriented books and trinkets. *5801 Wilshire Blvd., tel. 213/936–2230. Admission: $3 adults, 75¢ children; free the second Tues. of the month. Open Tues.–Sun. 10–5.*

The **Los Angeles County Museum of Art,** also in Hancock Park, is the largest museum complex in Los Angeles, comprising five buildings surrounding a grand central court. The Times Mirror Central Court provides both a visual and symbolic focus for the museum complex. The Ahmanson Building, set around a central atrium, houses the museum's collection of paintings, sculpture, costumes and textiles, and decorative arts from a wide range of cultures and periods. These include Chinese and Korean art; pre-Columbian Mexican art; American paintings, sculpture, and decorative arts from colonial times to the mid-20th century; European paintings, sculpture, and decorative arts from the Middle Ages through early 1900s; Greek and Roman sculpture; Islamic art; a unique assemblage of glass from Roman times to the 19th century; the renowned Gilbert collection of mosaics and monumental silver; one of the nation's largest holdings of costumes and textiles; and an Indian and Southeast Asian art collection considered to be one of the most comprehensive in the world.

The Hammer Building features major special-loan exhibitions as well as galleries of prints, drawings, and photographs. The Anderson Building features 20th-century painting and sculpture as well as special exhibitions. Lectures, films, and concerts are held in the Leo S. Bing Center's 600-seat theater and 100-seat auditorium. The museum's collection of Japanese sculpture, paintings, ceramics, lacquerware and extraordinary netsuke, including the internationally renowned Shin'enkan collection of Japanese paintings, is on view in the Pavillion for Japanese Art.

The Contemporary Sculpture Garden comprises nine large-scale outdoor sculptures. The B. Gerald Cantor Sculpture Garden features bronzes by Auguste Rodin, Émile-Antoine Bourdelle, and George Kolbe. The museum offers a continuing program of outstanding special exhibitions, film series, lectures, concerts, and educational events.

The museum, as well as the adjoining Page Museum and Hancock Park itself, brims with visitors on warm weekends. Although crowded, it can be the most exciting time to visit the area. Mimes and itinerant musicians ply their trades. Street vendors sell fast-food treats and there are impromptu soccer games on the lawns. To really study the art, though, a quieter weekday visit is recommended. *5905 Wilshire Blvd., tel. 213/857–6111 or tel. 213/857–6010 for ticket information. Times Mirror Central Court Cafe, tel. 213/857–6190. Museum Shop Plaza, tel. 213/857–6144. Museum Shop, Japanese Pavilion, tel. 213/857–6520. Admission: $5 adults, $3 children ($2 for special exhibits). A variety of tours are offered free with admission price. Open Tues.– Thurs. 10–5, Fri. 10–9, Sat.–Sun. 11–6.*

The **Craft and Folk Art Museum,** across Wilshire Boulevard from Hancock Park, offers consistently fascinating exhibits of both contemporary crafts and folk crafts from around the world. The museum's collections include Japanese, Mexican, American, and east Indian folk art, textiles, and masks. Six to eight major exhibitions are held each year. The International Festival of Masks, one of the more popular, is held annually the last week in October. In late 1994, the museum is scheduled to move into its permanent home in a 22-story tower on Wilshire Boulevard and Curson Street. Until then, it will continue to occupy this 10,000-square-foot location donated by May Company's Wilshire/Fairfax store, adjacent to the Los Angeles County Museum of Art. The museum library, open by appointment, is on the mezzanine. *Mailing address: 6067 Wilshire Blvd., Los Angeles, CA. 90036; tel. 213/937–5544. Admission free, 2-hour validated parking available. Open Tues.–Sat. 10–5, Sun. 11–5. Museum Shop, 5800 Wilshire Blvd., open Tues.–Sat. 10–5. Museum offices on 5th floor.*

Continue west on Wilshire a few blocks to the corner of Fairfax Avenue. On the northeast corner is the May Co. department store, another 1930s landmark with a distinctive curved corner.

Head north on Fairfax a few blocks to the **Farmer's Market,** a favorite L.A. attraction since it opened in 1934. Along with the 120 shops, salons, stores, and produce stalls, there are 21 restaurants (some of which offer alfresco dining under umbrellas) serving an interesting variety of international and domestic fare. Although originally exactly what the name implies—a farmer's market—these days you will find not only food and produce, but gifts, clothing, beauty salons, and even a shoe repair shop. Because it is next door to the CBS Television Studios, you never know whom you will run into, as TV celebrities shop and dine here often. *6333 W. 3rd St., tel. 213/933–9211. Open Mon.–Sat. 9–6:30, Sun. 10–5. Open later during summer.*

Time Out **Kokomo** is not only the best eatery inside the Farmer's Market, it also has some of the best new-wave diner food anywhere in L.A. Lively, entertaining service is almost always included in the reasonable prices. For those in a hurry, Kokomo A Go Go, its takeout store, is adjacent. *Located on the Third St. side of the market, tel. 213/933–0773. No credit cards. Open Mon.–Sat. 8 AM–7 PM, Sun. 8AM–6 PM during summer.*

North of the market, Fairfax is the center of Los Angeles's Jewish life. The shops and stands from Beverly Boulevard north are enlivened with friendly conversations between shopkeepers and regular customers. Canter's Restaurant, Deli, and Bakery (419 N. Fairfax, tel. 213/651–2030) is a traditional hangout.

The Westside

Numbers in the margin correspond to points of interest on the Westside map.

The Westside of Los Angeles, which to residents means from La Brea Avenue westward to the ocean, is where the rents are the most expensive, the real-estate prices sky high, the restaurants (and the restaurateurs) the most famous, and the shops the most chic. It's the best of the good life, Southern California style, and to really savor (and understand) it, spend a few leisurely days or half days exploring this area. Short on such traditional tourist attractions as amusement parks, historic sites, and museums, it more than makes up for those gaps with great shopping districts, exciting streets, outdoor cafés, and a lively nightlife.

The Westside can be best enjoyed in at least three separate outings, allowing plenty of time for browsing and dining. Attractions 1 through 4 are in the West Hollywood area; 5 through 8 in Beverly Hills; and 9 through 11 in Westwood. But the Westside is also small enough that you can pick four or five of these sites to visit in a single day, depending on your interests.

West Hollywood is a fairly glitzy section of Los Angeles. Once an almost forgotten parcel of county land surrounded by the city of L.A. and Beverly Hills, it became an official city in 1984. The West Hollywood attitude—trendy, stylish, and with plenty of disposable income—spills over beyond the official city borders.

❶ Melrose Avenue, which isn't exactly in West Hollywood, nevertheless remains firmly fixed in residents' minds as *very* West Hollywood. If you're entertained by post-punk fashion plates, people in spiked hairdos, and just about the most outlandish ensembles imaginable, then Melrose is the place for you. It's where panache meets paparazzi, and Beverly Hills chic meets Hollywood hip. The busiest stretch of Melrose is between Fairfax and La Brea avenues. Here you'll find one-of-a-kind boutiques and small, chic restaurants for more than a dozen blocks. Park on a side street (and read the parking signs carefully: Parking regulations around here are vigorously enforced and a rich vein for the city's coffers) and begin walking. On the 7400 block are Tempest and Notorious, boutiques with the latest of California's trend-setting designers' clothes for women, along with Mondial, for men. Mark Fox in the same block supplies the sought-after Western look. On the next block over, Cocobianca (8443) and Maxfield (8825) provide excellent special-occasion designs. In the other direction—and in more ways than one—A Star Is Worn (7303) is a resale boutique for celebrity and designer clothing. A list at the entrance notes the celebrities whose clothes are on the racks. Creations for Cher and Liza Minnelli are usually found there. Melrose Place Antique Market (7002 Melrose) is a collection of small items, vintage in nature, high in appeal.

Time Out Melrose has no shortage of great eateries. Part of any visit here consists of trying to pick from the dozens of choices: Thai, Mexican, sausages, yogurt, Italian, and more. The ultimate Melrose "joint" is **Johnny Rocket's** (7507 Melrose Ave., tel. 213/651–3361), a very hip '50s-style diner near the corner of Gardner Street. It's just stools at a counter, the best of old-time rock and roll on tape, and great hamburgers, shakes, and fries—and almost always crowded, with people lined up behind the stools to slip in the moment they are vacated. A patio offers outdoor dining also.

❷ That hulking monolith dominating the corner of La Cienega and Beverly boulevards is none other than the **Beverly Center** (8500 Beverly Blvd. at La Cienega, Los Angeles, tel. 310/854–0070). Designed as an all-in-one stop for shopping, dining, and movies, it has been a boon to Westsiders—except for those who live so close as to suffer the consequences of the heavy traffic. Parking is on the second through fifth floors, shops on the sixth, seventh, and eighth floors, and movies and restaurants on the eighth floor. The street level features Irvine Ranch Market, a gourmet's grocery haven; Conran's Habitat for home furnishings; and Hard Rock Cafe (look for the vintage green Cadillac on the roof). In the center are two major department stores, Bullocks and The Broadway; dozens of upscale clothing boutiques; 13 movie theaters; and a wide variety of restaurants (California Pizza Kitchen, Siam Orchid, La Rotisserie, plus Mrs. Field's Cookies and Haägen Dazs ice-cream outlets). Sam Goody's, whose 15,000 square feet make it the world's largest enclosed music store, features a glass-walled, and spectacular, view of Hollywood. A uniquely L.A. shop here is the Warner Bros. Studio Store. Popular with both adults and kids, it's crammed with movie and cartoon memorabilia and apparel.

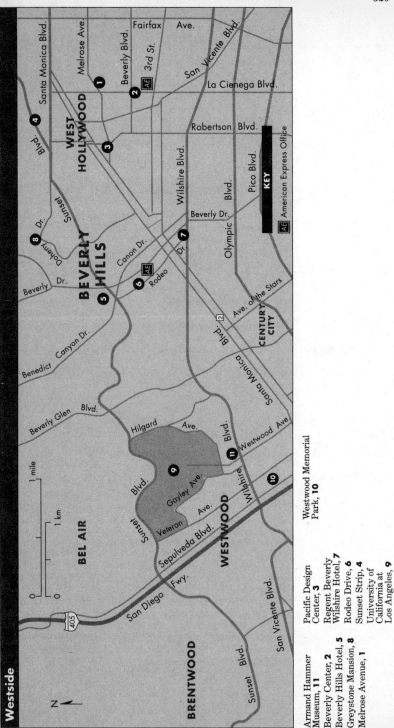

Westside

N

BRENTWOOD

BEL AIR

WEST HOLLYWOOD

BEVERLY HILLS

CENTURY CITY

WESTWOOD

Santa Monica Blvd.
Melrose Ave.
Beverly Blvd.
Fairfax Ave.
3rd St.
San Vicente Blvd.
La Cienega Blvd.
Robertson Blvd.
Wilshire Blvd.
Pico Blvd.
Beverly Dr.
Olympic Blvd.
Ave. of the Stars
Century Park Blvd.
Canon Dr.
Rodeo Dr.
Doheny Dr.
Sunset Blvd.
Benedict Canyon Dr.
Beverly Glen Blvd.
Hilgard Ave.
Gayley Ave.
Veteran Ave.
Westwood Ave.
Westwood Blvd.
Sepulveda Blvd.
San Diego Fwy.
San Vicente Blvd.
Sunset Blvd.
405

0   1 km
0   1 mile

KEY
AE American Express Office

Armand Hammer
Museum, 11
Beverly Center, 2
Beverly Hills Hotel, 5
Greystone Mansion, 8
Melrose Avenue, 1

Pacific Design
Center, 3
Regent Beverly
Wilshire Hotel, 7
Rodeo Drive, 6
Sunset Strip, 4
University of
California at
Los Angeles, 9

Westwood Memorial
Park, 10

❸ West Hollywood is the center of Los Angeles's thriving interior-decorating business. **The Pacific Design Center** (8687 Melrose Ave., West Hollywood, tel. 310/657–0800) is known to residents as the "Blue Whale." The blue-glass structure, designed by Cesar Pelli and built in 1975, houses to-the-trade-only showrooms filled with the most tempting furnishings, wall coverings, and accessories. In 1988 the center added a second building by Pelli, this one clad in green glass. The building is open to the public (Mon.–Fri. 9–5), who are allowed to browse in many of the more than 200 showrooms. Purchases, however, can be made only through design professionals. A referral system is available. The Murray Feldman Gallery, featuring various art, design, and cultural exhibitions, sits on the adjacent 2-acre landscaped public plaza. *Open Tues.–Sat. noon–6.*

Along the "Robertson Boulevard," the area that surrounds the Blue Whale, are more to-the-trade showrooms. These are not confined to Robertson Boulevard and are well represented along Beverly Boulevard and Melrose Avenue. This area is exceptionally strollable, and residents often walk their dogs here in the evening (even driving them here to then do their walking) so they can browse the well-lit windows. A few of the showrooms will accommodate an occasional retail buyer, so if you see something to die for, it's worth an inquiry inside.

❹ **Sunset Strip,** as in "77 Sunset Strip," was famous in the '50s, but it was popular as far back as the 1930s, when nightclubs like Ciro's and Mocambo were in their heyday, and movie stars frequented the area as an after-work gathering spot. This winding, hilly stretch is a visual delight, enjoyed both by car (a convertible would be divine) or on foot. Drive it once to enjoy the hustle-bustle, the vanity boards (huge billboards touting new movies, new records, new stars), and the dazzling shops. Then pick a section and explore a few blocks on foot. The Sunset Plaza section is especially nice for walking. The stretch is a cluster of expensive shops and outdoor cafés (Tutto Italia, Chin Chin) that are packed for lunch and on warm evenings. At Horn Street, Tower Records (a behemoth of a record store with two satellite shops across the street), Book Soup (L.A.'s literary bookstore), and Spago (tucked a half block up the hill on Horn) make for a satisfying browse, especially in the evening.

The glitz of the Strip ends abruptly at Doheny Drive, where Sunset Boulevard enters the world-famous and glamorous city of Beverly Hills. Suddenly the sidewalk life gives way to expansive, perfectly manicured lawns and palatial homes.

❺ West of the Strip a mile or so is the **Beverly Hills Hotel** (9641 Sunset Blvd.). Dubbed the "Pink Palace," its quiet Spanish Colonial Revival architecture and soft pastel exterior belie the excitement inside, where Hollywood wheelers and dealers have meetings over margaritas in the Polo Lounge and where many stars keep permanent bungalows as second homes. The venerable hotel is shutting down for renovations in early 1993, but you can still look at the outside.

It is on this stretch of Sunset, especially during the daytime, that you'll see hawkers peddling maps to stars' homes. Are the maps reliable? Well, that's a matter of debate. Stars do move around, so it's difficult to keep any map up to date. But the fun of looking at some of these magnificent homes, regardless of whether they're owned by a star at the moment, makes many people buy such maps and embark on tours.

Beverly Hills was incorporated as a city early in the century and has been thriving ever since. As a vibrant city within the larger city, it has retained and enhanced its reputation for wealth and luxury, an assessment with which you will surely agree as you drive along any of its main thoroughfares: Sunset, Wilshire, and Santa Monica boulevards (which is actually two parallel streets at this point: "Big Santa Monica" is the northern street; "Little Santa Monica," the southern one).

Within a few square blocks in the center of Beverly Hills are some of the most exotic, to say nothing of high-priced, stores in Southern California. Here you can find such items as a $200 pair of socks wrapped in gold leaf and stores that cater to customers only by appointment. A fun way to spend an afternoon is to **6** stroll famed **Rodeo Drive** between Santa Monica and Wilshire boulevards. Some of the Rodeo (pronounced ro-DAY-o) shops may be familiar to you since they supply clothing for major network television shows and their names often appear among the credits. Others, such as Gucci, have worldwide reputations. Fortunately, browsing is free (and fun), no matter how expensive the store's wares are. Several nearby restaurants have patios where you can sit and sip a drink while watching the fashionable shoppers stroll by.

7 The **Regent Beverly Wilshire Hotel** (9500 Wilshire Blvd., tel. 310/275–5200) anchors the south end of Rodeo Drive, at Wilshire. Opened in 1928, and vigorously expanded and renovated since, the hotel is often home to visiting royalty and celebrities, who arrive amid much fanfare at the porte cochere in the rear of the old structure. The lobby is quite small for a hotel of this size and offers little opportunity to meander; you might stop for a drink or a meal in one of the hotel's restaurants.

8 The **Greystone Mansion** was built by oilman Edward Doheny in 1927. This Tudor-style mansion, now owned by the city of Beverly Hills, sits on 18½ landscaped acres and has been used in such films as *The Witches of Eastwick* and *All of Me*. The gardens are open for self-guided tours and peeking (only) through the windows is permitted. The courtyard and garden areas can be booked for private receptions and weddings. Picnics are permitted in specified areas during its hours of operation. *905 Loma Vista Dr., Beverly Hills, tel. 310/550–4796. Admission free. Open daily 10–5.*

One of Beverly Hills' mansions opens its grounds to visitors. The **Virginia Robinson Gardens** are 6.2 terraced acres on the former estate of the heir to the Robinson Department Store chain. A guide will take you on an hour tour of the gardens and the exquisite exteriors of the main house, guest house, servants' quarters, swimming pool, and tennis court. A highlight of the tour is the collection of rare and exotic palms. Since the gardens' administration is trying to avoid congestion in the cul-de-sac where the gardens are situated, visitors must call for reservations and information. *Tel. 310/276–5367. Admission: $3. Tours Tues.–Thurs. 10 AM and 1 PM, Fri. 10 AM.*

Westward from Beverly Hills, Sunset continues to wind past **9** palatial estates and passes by the **University of California at Los Angeles.** Nestled in the Westwood section of the city and bound by LeConte Street, Sunset Boulevard, and Hilgard Avenue, the parklike UCLA campus is an inviting place for visitors to stroll. The most spectacular buildings are the original ones, Royce Hall and the library, both in Romanesque style. In the heart of the north campus is the Franklin Murphy Sculpture Garden, with works by Henry Moore and Gaston Lachaise enhancing the landscape. For a gardening buff, UCLA is a treasure of unusual and well-labeled plants. The Mildred Mathias Botanic Garden is located in the southeast section of the campus and is accessible from Tiverton Avenue. Sports fans will enjoy the Morgan Center Hall of Fame (west of Campus bookstore). Memorabilia and trophies of the athletic departments are on display. Maps and information are available at drive-by kiosks at major entrances, even on weekends, and free 90-minute, guided walking tours of the campus are offered on weekdays. The campus has several indoor and outdoor cafés, plus bookstores that sell the very popular UCLA Bruins paraphernalia. *Tel. 310/825–4574. Tours weekdays at 10:30 AM and 1:30 PM. Meet at 10945 LeConte St., room 1417, on the south edge of the campus, facing Westwood.*

The **Hannah Carter Japanese Garden,** located in Bel Air just north of the campus, is owned by UCLA and may be visited by making phone reservations two weeks in advance (tel. 310/825–4574).

Directly south of the campus is Westwood, once a quiet college town and now one of the busiest places in the city on weekend evenings—so busy that during the summer, many streets are closed to car traffic and visitors must park by Federal Building (Wilshire and Veteran Blvds.) and shuttle over. However you arrive, Westwood remains a delightful village filled with clever boutiques, trendy restaurants, movie theaters, and colorful street life.

The village proper is delineated on the south by Wilshire Boulevard, which is now a corridor of cheek-by-jowl office buildings whose varying architectural styles can be jarring, to say the ❿ least. Tucked behind one of these behemoths is **Westwood Memorial Park** (1218 Glendon Ave.). In this very unlikely place for a cemetery is one of the most famous graves in the city. Marilyn Monroe is buried in a simply marked wall crypt. For 25 years after her death, her former husband Joe DiMaggio had six red roses placed on her crypt three times a week. Also buried here is Natalie Wood.

⓫ **Armand Hammer Museum of Art and Cultural Center** is one of the city's newest museums. Although small compared with other museums in Los Angeles, the permanent collection here includes thousands of works by Honoré Daumier, and a rare portfolio of Leonardo da Vinci's technical drawings. However, the Hammer regularly features special blockbuster displays that cannot be seen elsewhere, such as the 1992 exhibit "Catherine the Great: Treasures of Imperial Russia." *10899 Wilshire Blvd., tel. 310/443–7000. Admission: $4.50 adults, $3 senior citizens and students, free to 17 and under. Open Tues.–Sun. 10–6 (extended hours during special exhibitions).*

Santa Monica, Venice, Pacific Palisades, and Malibu

Numbers in the margin correspond to points of interest on the Santa Monica and Venice map.

The towns that hug the coastline of Santa Monica Bay reflect the wide diversity of Los Angeles, from the rich-as-can-be Malibu to the cheek-by-jowl Yuppie/seedy mix of Venice. The emphasis is on being out in the sunshine, always within sight of the Pacific. You would do well to visit the area in two excursions: Santa Monica to Venice in one day and Pacific Palisades to Malibu in another.

From Santa Monica to Venice Santa Monica is a sensible place. It's a tidy little city, 2 miles square, whose ethnic population is largely British (there's an English music hall and several pubs here), attracted perhaps by the cool and foggy climate. The sense of order is reflected in the economic/geographic stratification: The northernmost section has broad streets lined with superb, older homes. Farther south, real-estate prices drop $50,000 or so every block or two. The middle class lives in the middle and the working class, to the south, along the Venice border.

❶ Begin exploring at **Santa Monica Pier,** located at the foot of Colorado Avenue and easily accessible to beach goers as well as sightseers in cars. Cafés, gift shops, a psychic adviser, bumper cars, and arcades line the truncated pier, which was severely damaged in a storm a few years ago. The 46-horse carousel, built in 1922, has seen action in many movie and television shows, most notably the *Paul Newman/Robert Redford film* The Sting. *Tel. 310/394–7554. Rides: 50¢ adults, 25¢ children. Carousel open in summer, Tues.–Sun. 10–9; in winter, weekends 10–5.*

❷ **Palisades Park** is a ribbon of green that runs along the top of the cliffs from Colorado Avenue to just north of San Vicente Boulevard. The flat walkways are usually filled with casual strollers as well as joggers who like to work out with a spectacular view of the Pacific as company. It is especially enjoyable at sunset.

The Visitor Information Center is located in the park, at Santa Monica Boulevard. It offers bus schedules, directions, and information on Santa Monica–area attractions. *Tel. 310/393–7593. Open daily 10–4.*

❸ Santa Monica has grown into a major center for the L.A. art community, and the **Santa Monica Museum of Art** is poised to boost that reputation. Designed by local architect Frank Gehry, the museum presents the works of performance and video artists and exhibits works of lesser-known painters and sculptors. *2437 Main St., Santa Monica, tel. 310/399–0433. Admission: $3 adults, $1 artists, senior citizens, and students. Open Wed. and Thurs. 11–6, Fri.–Sat. 11–10, Sun. 11–6.*

❹ The **Santa Monica Heritage Museum,** housed in an 1894-vintage, late-Victorian home once owned by the founder of the city, was moved to its present site on trendy Main Street in the mid-1980s. Three rooms have been fully restored: the dining room in the style of 1890–1910; the living room, 1910–1920; and the kitchen, 1920–1930. The second-floor galleries feature photography and historical exhibits as well as shows by contemporary Santa Monica artists. *2612 Main St., Santa Monica, tel. 310/392–8537. Open Thurs.–Sat. 11–4, Sun. noon–4.*

The museum faces a companion home, another Victorian delight moved to the site that is now Monica's restaurant. These two dowagers anchor the northwest corner of the funky Main Street area of Santa Monica. Several blocks of old brick build-

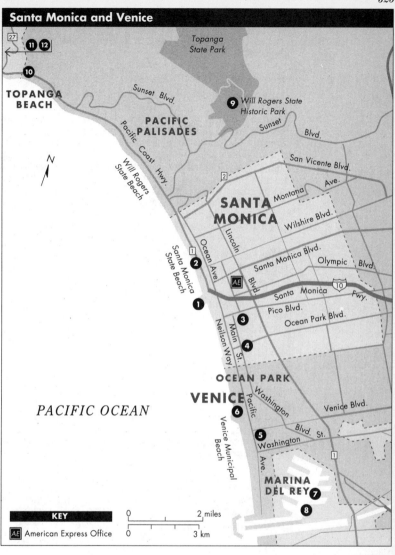

Santa Monica and Venice

27

11 12

10

TOPANGA BEACH

Sunset Blvd.

Pacific Coast Hwy.

Will Rogers State Beach

PACIFIC PALISADES

9 Will Rogers State Historic Park

Sunset Blvd.

San Vicente Blvd.

Ave.

2

SANTA MONICA

Montana Ave.

Wilshire Blvd.

Lincoln

Ocean Ave.

1

2

AE

Santa Monica Blvd.

Olympic Blvd.

Blvd.

Santa Monica State Beach

Santa Monica Fwy.

10

1

Pico Blvd.

3

Ocean Park Blvd.

Neilson Way

4

Main St.

OCEAN PARK

VENICE

6

Pacific

Washington

Venice Blvd.

PACIFIC OCEAN

5

Blvd. St.

Washington

Venice Municipal Beach

Ave.

1

MARINA DEL REY 7

8

KEY	0		2 miles
AE American Express Office	0		3 km

Adamson House, **11**
Burton Chase Park, **7**
Fisherman's Village, **8**
J. Paul Getty Museum, **10**
Malibu Lagoon State Park, **12**
Palisades Park, **2**

Santa Monica Heritage Museum, **4**
Santa Monica Museum of Art, **3**
Santa Monica Pier, **1**
Venice Boardwalk, **6**
Venice Canals, **5**
Will Rogers State Park, **9**

ings here have undergone recent rejuvenation (and considerable rent increases) and now house galleries, bars, cafés, omelet parlors, and boutiques. With Main Street's proximity to the beach, parking here can be tight on summer weekends; best bets are the city pay lots behind the Main Street shops, between Main and Neilsen Way.

Venice was a turn-of-the-century fantasy that never quite came true. Abbot Kinney, a wealthy Los Angeles businessman, envisioned this little piece of real estate, which then seemed so far from downtown, as a romantic replica of Venice, Italy. He developed an incredible 16 miles of canals, floated gondolas on them, and built scaled-down versions of St. Marks palace and other Venetian landmarks. The name remains but the connection with Old World Venice is as flimsy as ever. Kinney's project was plagued by ongoing engineering problems and disasters **5** and drifted into disrepair. Three small **canals** and bridges remain and can be viewed from the southeast corner of Pacific Avenue and Venice Boulevard, but long gone are the amusement park, swank seaside hotels, and the gondoliers.

Venice today is a colorful mishmash of street life: here can be found the liveliest waterfront walkway in Los Angeles, known **6** as Ocean Front Walk or **Venice Boardwalk.** It begins at Washington Street and runs north. Save this visit for a weekend. There is plenty of action year-round: Bicyclists and bikini-clad roller skaters gather crowds as they put on impromptu demonstrations, vying for attention with the unusual breeds of dogs that locals love to prance along the walkway. A local bodybuilding club works out on the adjacent beach, and it's nearly impossible not to stop to ogle at the pecs as these strong men lift weights.

At the south end of the boardwalk, along Washington Street, near the Venice Pier, in-line skates, roller skates, and bicycles (some with baby seats) are available for rent.

Time Out The boardwalk is lined with fast-food stands, and food can be brought a few feet away to be enjoyed as a picnic on the beach. But for a somewhat more relaxing meal, stand in line for a table at **Sidewalk Cafe** (1401 Ocean Front Walk, tel. 310/399–5547). Wait for a patio table, where you can watch the free spirits on parade. Despite their flamboyant attire, they seem like weekend wild ones, and it's amusing to imagine them in their sedate Monday-go-to-work suits. A recently enlarged bar accommodates the bands that play Thursday–Saturday evenings. A guitarist entertains other evenings.

Just south of Venice is a quick shift of the time frame. Forget about Venice—Italy or California—Marina del Rey is a modern and more successful, if less romantic, dream. It is the largest man-made boat harbor in the world, with a commercial area catering to the whims of boat owners and boat groupies. The stretch between Admiralty Way and Mindinao Way has some of the area's best restaurants, expensive but worth it. Most of the better hotel chains, such as the Ritz-Carlton, also have properties here.

For boatless visitors, the best place from which to view the **7** marina is **Burton Chase Park,** at the end of Mindinao Way. Situated at the tip of a jetty and surrounded on three sides by water and moored boats, this small, 6-acre patch of green offers a

This trip we found a road less traveled. And the perfect way to see it.

©1992 Budget Rent a Car Corporation

Vacation Cars. Vacation Prices. Wherever you travel, Budget offers you a wide selection of quality cars – from economy models to roomy minivans and even convertibles. You'll find them all at competitively low rates that include unlimited mileage. At over 1500 locations in the U.S. and Canada. For information and reservations, call your travel consultant or Budget at **800-527-0700**. In Canada, call **800-268-8900**.

THE SMART MONEY IS ON BUDGET.®

We feature Lincoln-Mercury and other fine cars.   *A system of corporate and licensee owned locations.*

No matter what your travel style, the best trips start with **Fodor's**

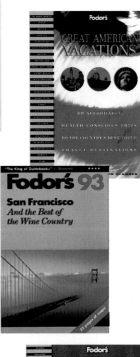

cool and breezy spot from which to watch boats move in and out of the channel, and it's great for picnicking.

8 **Fisherman's Village** is a collection of cute Cape Cod clapboards housing shops and restaurants. It's not much of a draw unless you include a meal or a snack or take one of the 45-minute marina cruises offered by Hornblower Dining Outs that depart from the village dock. *13755 Fiji Way, tel. 310/301–6000. Tickets: $5 adults, $3.50 senior citizens, $4 children. Open in summer, daily 11 AM–4 PM, in winter, weekends 11–4. Cruises leave every hour, weekdays 12–3, weekends 11–5.*

A Tour of Pacific Palisades and Malibu
The drive on Pacific Coast Highway north of Santa Monica toward Malibu is one of the most pleasant in Southern California, day or evening. The narrow-but-expensive beachfront houses were home to movie stars in the 1930s.

9 Spend a few hours at **Will Rogers State Historic Park** in Pacific Palisades and you may understand what endeared America to this cowboy/humorist in the 1920s and 1930s. The two-story ranch house on Rogers's 187-acre estate is a folksy blend of Navajo rugs and Mission-style furniture. Rogers's only extravagance was raising the roof several feet (he waited till his wife was in Europe to do it) to accommodate his penchant for practicing his lasso technique indoors. The nearby museum features Rogers memorabilia. The short films showing his roping technique will leave even sophisticated city slickers breathless, and hearing his homey words of wisdom can be a real mood elevator.

Rogers was a polo enthusiast, and in the 1930s, his front-yard polo field attracted such friends as Douglas Fairbanks for weekend games. The tradition continues, with free games scheduled most summer weekends. The park's broad lawns are excellent for picnicking. For postprandial exercise, there's hiking on miles of eucalyptus-lined trails. Those who make it to the top will be rewarded with a panoramic view of the mountains and ocean. Neighborhood riders house their horses at the stable up the hill and are usually agreeable to some friendly chatter (no rental horses, alas). *14253 Sunset Blvd., Pacific Palisades, tel. 310/454–8212. Call for polo schedule.*

10 The **J. Paul Getty Museum** contains one of the country's finest collections of Greek and Roman antiquities (also a few items of uncertain provenance). The building is a re-creation of a 1st-century Roman villa. The main level houses sculpture, mosaics, and vases. Of particular interest are the 4th-century Attic stelae (funerary monuments) and Greek and Roman portraits. The newly expanded decorative-arts collection on the upper level features furniture, carpets, tapestries, clocks, chandeliers, and small decorative items made for the French, German, and Italian nobility, with a wealth of royal French treasures (Louis XIV to Napoleon). Richly colored brocaded walls set off the paintings and furniture to great advantage.

All major schools of Western art from the late-13th century to the late-19th century are represented in the painting collection, which emphasizes Renaissance and Baroque art and includes works by Rembrandt, Rubens, de la Tour, Van Dyck, Gainsborough, and Boucher. Recent acquisitions include Old Master drawings, and medieval and Renaissance illuminated manuscripts, works by Picasso, Van Gogh's *Irises*, and a select collection of Impressionist paintings including some by Claude Monet.

The museum itself has a fascinating history. The oil millionaire began collecting art in the 1930s, concentrating on the three distinct areas that are represented in the museum today: Greek and Roman antiquities, Baroque and Renaissance paintings, and 18th-century decorative arts. In 1946 he purchased a large Spanish-style home on 65 acres of land in a canyon just north of Santa Monica to house the collection. By the late 1960s, the museum could no longer accommodate the rapidly expanding collection and Getty decided to build an entirely new museum, which was completed in 1974. The museum building is a re-creation of a luxurious 1st-century Roman villa surrounded by extensive gardens.

The museum's bookstore carries art books, reproductions, calendars, and a variety of scholarly and general-interest publications. A self-service lunch is available in the indoor/outdoor Garden Tea Room. There are no tours, but docents give 15-minute orientation talks. Summer evening concerts (reservations are required) are given on an irregular basis, with the lower galleries open at intermission. Parking reservations are necessary, and there is no way to visit the museum without using the parking lot unless you are dropped off or take a tour bus. They should be made one week in advance by telephoning or writing to the museum's Reservations Office. *17985 Pacific Coast Hwy., Malibu, tel. 310/458-2003. Admission free. Open Tues.-Sun. 10-5.*

⓫ Adamson House is the former home of the Rindge family, which owned much of the Malibu Rancho in the early part of the 20th century. Malibu was quite isolated then, with all visitors and supplies arriving by boat at the nearby Malibu Pier (and it can still be isolated these days when rock slides close the highway). The Moorish-Spanish home, built in 1928, has been opened to the public and may be the only chance most visitors get to be inside a grand Malibu home. The Rindges led an enviable Malibu lifestyle, decades before it was trendy. The house is right on the beach (high chain-link fences keep out curious beach goers). The family owned the famous Malibu Tile Company and their home is predictably encrusted with some of the most magnificent tilework in rich blues, greens, yellows, and oranges. Even an outside dog shower, near the servants' entrance, is a tiled delight. Docent-led tours help visitors to envision family life here as well as to learn about the history of Malibu and its real estate (you can't have one without the other). *23200 Pacific Coast Hwy., Malibu, tel. 310/456-8432. Admission: $2 adults, $1 children. Open Wed.-Sun. 11-3.*

⓬ Adjacent to Adamson House is **Malibu Lagoon State Park** (23200 Pacific Coast Hwy., Malibu), a haven for native and migratory birds. Visitors must stay on the boardwalks so that the egrets, blue herons, avocets, and gulls can enjoy the marshy area. The signs that give opening and closing hours refer only to the parking lot; the lagoon itself is open 24 hours and is particularly enjoyable in the early morning and at sunset. Luckily, street-side parking is available then (but not at midday).

Palos Verdes, San Pedro, and Long Beach

Numbers in the margin correspond to points of interest on the Palos Verdes, San Pedro, and Long Beach map.

Few local residents take advantage of Long Beach's attractions. If they should take a day to see the *Queen Mary* when their in-laws visit from back east, they are astounded to discover Long Beach's impressive skyline, the string of hotels along Ocean Boulevard, the revitalized downtown area, and the city's proximity to the rest of L.A. and Orange County. How could this entire city, the fifth largest in the state, be right here and they never really knew about it?

The drive on Pacific Coast Highway around the water's edge takes you soaring high above the cliffs. An aerial shot of this area was used in the original opening of television's "Knot's Landing." The real estate in these small peninsula towns, ranging from expensive to very expensive, are zoned for stables and you'll often see riders along the streets (they have the right of way).

① **Wayfarers Chapel** (5755 Palos Verdes Dr. S, Rancho Palos Verdes, tel. 310/377-1650), designed by architect Frank Lloyd Wright, was built in 1949. He planned this modern glass church to blend in with an encircling redwood forest. The redwoods are gone (they couldn't stand the rigors of urban encroachment), but another forest has taken their place and the breathtaking combination of ocean, trees, and man-made structure remains. This "natural church" is a popular wedding site.

San Pedro shares the peninsula with the Palos Verdes towns, but little else. Here, the cliffs give way to a hospitable harbor. The 1950s-vintage executive homes give way to tidy 1920s-era white clapboards, and horses give way to boats. San Pedro (locals steadfastly ignore the correct Spanish pronunciation—it's "San Peedro" to them) is an old seaport community with a strong Mediterranean and Eastern European flavor. There are enticing Greek and Yugoslavian markets and restaurants throughout the town.

② **Cabrillo Marine Museum** is a gem of a small museum dedicated to the marine life that flourishes off the Southern California coast. Recently installed in its new home in a modern Frank Gehry–designed building right on the beach, the museum is popular with school groups because its exhibits are especially instructive as well as fun. The 35 saltwater aquariums include a shark tank, and a see-through tidal tank gives visitors a chance to see the long view of a wave. On the back patio, docents supervise as visitors reach into a shallow tank to touch starfish and sea anemones. *3720 Stephen White Dr., San Pedro, tel. 310/548-7546. Admission free. Parking $5.50. Open Tues.–Fri. noon–5, weekends 10–5.*

If you're lucky enough to visit at low tide, take time to explore the tide pool on nearby Cabrillo Beach (museum staff can direct you).

③ **Ports O' Call Village** is a commercial rendition of a New England shipping village, an older version of Fisherman's Village

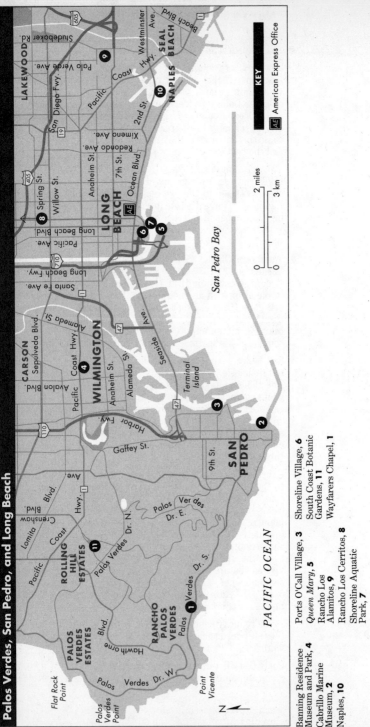

Palos Verdes, San Pedro, and Long Beach

PACIFIC OCEAN

San Pedro Bay

Banning Residence
Museum and Park, **4**
Cabrillo Marine
Museum, **2**
Naples, **10**

Ports O'Call Village, **3**
Queen Mary, **5**
Rancho Los
Alamitos, **9**
Rancho Los Cerritos, **8**
Shoreline Aquatic
Park, **7**

Shoreline Village, **6**
South Coast Botanic
Gardens, **11**
Wayfarers Chapel, **1**

KEY

AE American Express Office

0   2 miles

0   3 km

in Marina del Rey, with shops, restaurants, and fast-food windows. *Berth 77, San Pedro, tel. 310/547–9977. Two companies run harbor cruises. Fares: $10 adults, $5 children. 1- to 1½-hr cruises depart from the village dock. Whale-watching cruises, $12–$15 adults, $5–$8 children. Call for schedules.*

❹ **Banning Residence Museum and Park,** in Wilmington, is a pleasant, low-keyed stop. In order to preserve transportation and shipping interests for the city of Los Angeles, Wilmington was annexed in the late-19th century. A narrow strip of land, mostly less than ½-mile wide, it follows the Harbor Freeway from downtown south to the port.

General Phineas Banning was an early entrepreneur in Los Angeles and is credited with developing the harbor into a viable economic entity and naming the area Wilmington (he was from Delaware). Part of his estate has been preserved in a 20-acre park that offers excellent picnicking possibilities. A 100-year-old wisteria, near the arbor, blooms in the spring. *401 E. M St., Wilmington, tel. 310/548–7777. Admission: $2. The interior of the house can be seen only on docent-led tours, Tues.–Thurs. 12:30–2:30, Sat. and Sun. 12:30–3:30, on the half hour.*

Long Beach began as a seaside resort in the 19th century and during the early part of the 20th century was a popular destination for midwesterners and Dust Bowlers in search of a better life. They built street after street of modest wood homes.

At the corner of 1st Street and Long Beach Avenue is the terminus of the new Metro Rail system's Blue Line trains that run between Long Beach and downtown Los Angeles.

❺ The first glimpse of the *Queen Mary,* the largest passenger ship ever built, as she sits so smugly in Long Beach Harbor is disarming. What seemed like sure folly when Long Beach officials bought her in 1964 has turned out to be a crowd pleaser that put the city on the proverbial map. She stands permanently moored at Pier J.

The 50,000-ton *Queen Mary* was launched in 1934, a floating treasure of Art Deco splendor. It took a crew of 1,100 to minister to the needs of 1,900 demanding passengers. This most luxurious of luxury liners is completely intact, from the extensive wood paneling to the gleaming nickel- and silver-plated handrails and the hand-cut glass. Tours through the ship are available, and guests are invited to browse the 12 decks and witness at close range the bridge, staterooms, officers' quarters, and engine rooms. There are several restaurants and shops on board. *Pier J, Long Beach, tel. 310/435–3511. Admission: $17.95 adults, $9.50 children for all-day combination ticket to the* Queen Mary *and* Spruce Goose. *Guided 45-min. tour, included in admission, leaves every ½ hour beginning at 10:30. Open July 4–Labor Day, daily 9–9, rest of year, daily 10–6. At press time, it was not known what changes would be made when and if new management takes over the* Queen Mary's *operations in late 1992. Call for information.*

❻ **Shoreline Village** is the most successful of the pseudo–New England harbors here. Its setting, between the downtown Long Beach and the *Queen Mary,* is reason enough to stroll here, day or evening (when visitors can enjoy the lights of the ship twinkling in the distance). In addition to gift shops and restaurants there's a 1906 carousel with bobbing giraffes, camels, and horses. *Corner of Shoreline Dr. and Pine Ave., tel. 310/590–8427. Rides: $1. The carousel is open daily 10–10 in summer, 10–9 the rest of the year.*

❼ Shoreline Aquatic Park (205 Marina Dr.) is literally set in the middle of Long Beach Harbor (another inspired landfill project) and is a much-sought-after resting place for RVers. Kite-flyers also love it, because the winds are wonderful here. Casual passersby can enjoy a short walk, where the modern skyline, the quaint Shoreline Village, the *Queen Mary*, and the ocean all vie for attention. The park's lagoon is off-limits to swimming, but aquacycles and kayaks can be rented during the summer months. Contact **Long Beach Water Sports** (730 E. 4th St., Long Beach, tel. 310/432–0187) for information on sea-kayaking lessons, rentals, and outings.

❽ Rancho Los Cerritos is a charming Monterey-style adobe built by the Don Juan Temple family in 1844. Monterey-style homes can be easily recognized by two features: They are always two-storied and have a narrow balcony across the front. Seen from the outside, it's easy to imagine Zorro, that swashbuckling fictional hero of the rancho era, jumping from the balcony onto a waiting horse and making his escape. The 10 rooms have been furnished in the style of the period and are open for viewing. But don't expect an Old California–style Southwest fantasy with primitive Mexican furniture, and cactus in the garden. The Temple family shared the prevalent taste of the period, in which the American East Coast and Europe still set the style, emphasizing fancy, dark woods and frou-frou Victorian bric-a-brac. The gardens here, designed by well-known landscape architect Ralph Cornell and completed in the 1930s, have been recently restored. *4600 Virginia Rd., Long Beach, tel. 310/424–9423. Open Wed.–Sun. 1–5. Self-guided tours on weekdays. Free 50-min guided tours on weekends hourly 1–4.*

❾ Rancho Los Alamitos is said to be the oldest one-story domestic building still standing in the county. It was built in 1806 when the Spanish flag still flew over California. There's a blacksmith shop in the barn. *6400 E. Bixby Hill Rd., Long Beach, tel. 310/431–3541. Open Wed.–Sun. 1–5. 90–min. Free tours leave every half hour until 4 PM.*

❿ The **Naples** section of Long Beach is known for its pleasant and well-maintained canals. Canals in *Naples*, you ask? Yes, this is a misnomer. But better misnamed and successful than aptly named and a bust. The developer who came up with the Naples canal idea learned from the mistakes and bad luck that did in Venice, just up the coast, and built the canals to take full advantage of the tidal flow that would keep them clean. Naples is actually three small islands in man-made Alamitos Bay. It is best experienced on foot. Park near Bayshore Drive and Second Street and walk across the bridge, where you can begin meandering the quaint streets with very Italian names. This well-restored neighborhood boasts eclectic architecture—vintage Victorians, Craftsman bungalows, and Mission Revivals. You may spy a real gondola or two on the canals. You can hire them for a ride but not on the spur of the moment. Gondola Getaway offers one-hour rides, usually touted for romantic couples, although the gondolas can accommodate up to four people. *5437*

E. Ocean Blvd., Naples, tel. 310/433–9595. Rides: $50 a couple, $10 for each additional person. Reservations essential, at least 1 to 2 wks. in advance. Open 11 AM–midnight.

⑪ South Coast Botanic Gardens began life ignominiously—as a garbage dump–cum-landfill. It's hard to believe that as recently as 1960, truckloads of waste (3.5 million tons) were being deposited here. With the intensive ministerings of the experts from the L.A. County Arboreta department, the dump soon boasted lush gardens with plants from every continent except Antarctica. The gardens are undergoing an ambitious five-year reorganization at the end of which all the plants will be organized into color groups. Self-guided walking tours take visitors past flower and herb gardens, rare cacti, and a lake with ducks. Picnicking is limited to a lawn area outside the gates. *26300 S. Crenshaw Blvd., Rancho Palos Verdes, tel. 310/544–6815. Admission: $3 adults, $1.50 children and senior citizens. Open daily 9–5.*

Highland Park

Numbers in the margin correspond to points of interest on the Highland Park, Pasadena, San Marino map.

The suburbs north of downtown Los Angeles have much of the richest architectural heritage in Southern California as well as several fine museums. The Highland Park area can be explored in a leisurely afternoon. Pasadena could take a full day, more if you want to savor the museums' collections.

A Tour of Highland Park To take advantage of the afternoon-only hours of several sites here, and to enjoy a relaxed Old California patio lunch or dinner, this tour is best scheduled in the afternoon.

Once past Chinatown, the Pasadena Freeway (110) follows the curves of the arroyo (creek bed) that leads north from downtown. It was the main road north during the early days of Los Angeles where horses-and-buggies made their way through the chaparral-covered countryside to the small town of Pasadena. In 1942, the road became the Arroyo Seco Parkway, the first freeway in Los Angeles, later renamed the Pasadena Freeway. It remains a pleasant drive in non-rush-hour traffic, with the freeway, lined with old sycamores, winding up the arroyo like a New York parkway.

Highland Park, midway between downtown Los Angeles and Pasadena, was a genteel suburb in the late 1800s, where the Anglo population tried to keep an Eastern feeling alive in their architecture in spite of the decidedly Southwest landscape. The streets on both sides of the freeway are lined with faded beauties, classic old clapboards that have gone into decline in the past half century.

❶ Heritage Square is the ambitious attempt by the Los Angeles Cultural Heritage Board to preserve some of the city's architectural gems of the 1865–1914 period from the wrecking ball. During the past 20 years four residences, a depot, a church, and a carriage barn have been moved to this small park from all over the city. The most breathtaking building here is Hale House, built in 1885. The almost-garish colors of both the interior and exterior are not the whim of some aging hippie painter, but rather a faithful re-creation of the palette that was actually in fashion in the late 1800s. The pristine whitewashing we associate with these old Victorians was the result of a later vogue. The Palms Depot, built in 1886, was moved to the site from the Westside of L.A. The night the building was moved down city streets and up freeways is documented in photomurals on the depot's walls. *3800 Homer St., Highland Park, off Ave. 43 exit, tel. 818/449-0193. Admission: $5 adults, $3 children 12-17 and senior citizens. Open Fri., Sat, Sun., most holidays noon-4 PM. Tours every 45 minutes or so.*

2 **El Alisal** was the home of eccentric easterner-turned-westerner-with-a-vengeance Charles Lummis. This Harvard graduate was captivated by Indian culture (he founded the Southwest Museum), often living the lifestyle of the natives, much to the shock of the staid Angelenos of the time. His home, built from 1898 to 1910, is constructed of boulders from the arroyo itself, a romantic notion until recent earthquakes made the safety of such homes questionable. The Art Nouveau fireplace was designed by Gutzon Borglum, the sculptor of Mt. Rushmore. *200 E. Ave. 43, Highland Park, tel. 213/222-0546. Admission free. Open weekends 1-4.*

3 **The Southwest Museum** is the huge Mission Revival building that stands halfway up Mt. Washington and can be seen from the freeway. It contains an extensive collection of Native American art and artifacts, with special emphasis on the people of the Plains, Northwest Coast, Southwest U.S., and northern Mexico. The basketry collection is outstanding. *234 Museum Dr., Highland Park, off the Ave. 43 exit, tel. 213/221-2163. Admission: $5 adults, $3 senior citizens and students, $2 children 7-18. Open Tues.-Sun. 11-5.*

4 **Casa de Adobe** is a satellite of the Southwest Museum and is located directly below it at the bottom of the hill. What appears to be the well-preserved, authentically furnished hacienda of an Old California don is actually a 1917 re-creation of a 19th-century ranch. The central-courtyard plan is characteristic of the style. *4605 Figueroa St., Highland Park, tel. 213/221-2163. Admission free. Open Tues.-Sun. 11-5.*

Time Out **Lawry's California Center** is a more recent attempt to capture
5 the romance of Old Mexico—Zorro and Ramona all rolled up in one—but this one leaves no doubt that it is a recent construction. This is *Sunset* magazine come to life, with bougainvillea-covered patios and flowers in pots at every turn, winter and summer. A spice-blending company, Lawry's offers free tours of its plant on weekdays, but the best reason to come here is to enjoy a meal on the patio. Lunches, both cafeteria style and full service, are served year-round 11-3. Fiesta dinners are served (May-Oct.) nightly under the stars to the accompaniment of strolling mariachis. Wine and gourmet shops stay open late for after-dinner browsing. *570 W. Ave. 26, Los Angeles, tel. 213/225-2491. Open daily.*

Pasadena and San Marino

Although now fully absorbed into the general Los Angeles sprawl, Pasadena was once a separate and distinctly defined, and refined, city. Its varied architecture, augmented by lush landscaping, is the most spectacular in Southern California.

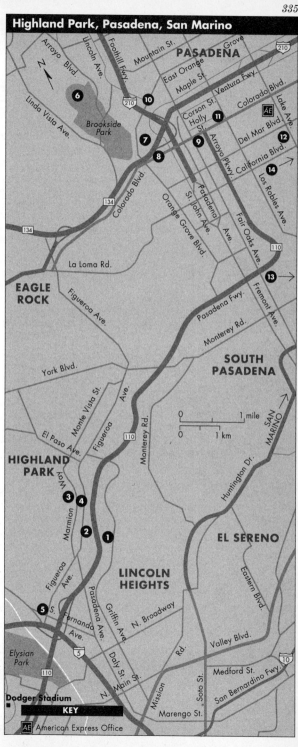

Highland Park, Pasadena, San Marino

Casa de Adobe, **4**

El Alisal, **2**

Gamble House, **7**

Heritage Square, **1**

Huntington Library, Art Gallery, and Botanical Gardens, **14**

Kidspace, **12**

Lawry's California Center, **5**

Norton Simon Museum, **8**

Old Town Pasadena, **9**

Pacific Asia Museum, **11**

Pasadena Historical Society, **10**

Ritz-Carlton, Huntington Hotel, **13**

Rose Bowl, **6**

Southwest Museum, **3**

With only a few hours to spend, visitors should consider at least driving past the Gamble House, through Old Town, and then on to the grand old neighborhood of the Huntington Library, spending most of their time there.

❻ The Rose Bowl (991 Rosemont Ave., Pasadena) is set at the bottom of a wide area of the arroyo in an older wealthy neighborhood that must endure the periodic onslaught of thousands of cars and party-minded football fans. The stadium is closed except for games and special events such as the monthly Rose Bowl Swap Meet. Held the second Sunday of the month, it is considered the granddaddy of West Coast swap meets.

❼ Gamble House, built by Charles and Henry Greene in 1908, is the most spectacular example of Craftsman-style bungalow architecture. The term "bungalow" can be misleading, since the Gamble House is a huge two-story home. To wealthy easterners such as the Gambles, who commissioned the Greenes to build a vacation house for them, this type of home seemed informal compared with their accustomed mansions. What makes visitors swoon here is the incredible amount of hand-craftsmanship: the hand-shaped teak interiors, the Greene-designed furniture, the Louis Tiffany glass door. The dark exterior has broad eaves, with many sleeping porches on the second floor. *4 Westmoreland Pl., Pasadena, tel. 818/793–3334. Admission: $4 adults, $3 senior citizens, $2 students, children 12 and under free. Open Thurs.–Sun. noon–3. 1-hr. tours every 15–20 min.*

❽ The Norton Simon Museum will be familiar to television viewers of the Rose Parade. The TV cameras position themselves to take full advantage of the sleek, modern building as a background for the passing floats. Like the more famous Getty Museum, the Norton Simon is a tribute to the art acumen of an extremely wealthy businessman. In 1974, Simon reorganized the failing Pasadena Museum of Modern Art and assembled one of the world's finest collections, richest in its Rembrandts, Goyas, Degas, and Picassos, and dotted with Rodin sculptures throughout.

The museum's collections of Impressionist (van Gogh, Matisse, Cézanne, Monet, Renoir, et al.) and Cubist (Braque, Gris) work are extensive. Older works range from Southeast Asian art from 100 BC, and bronze, stone, and ivory sculptures from India, Cambodia, Thailand, and Nepal.

The museum's wealth of Early Renaissance, Baroque, and Rococo artworks could fill an art-history book. Church works by Raphael, Guariento, de Paolo, Filippino Lippi, and Lucas Cranach give way to robust Rubens maidens and Dutch landscapes, still lifes, and portraits by Frans Hals, Jacob van Ruisdael, and Jan Steen. A magical Tiepolo ceiling highlights the Rococo period. The most recent additions to the collection are seven 19th-century Russian paintings.

The museum bookstore has posters, prints, and postcards. There are no dining facilities. *411 W. Colorado Blvd., Pasadena, tel. 818/449–6840. Admission: $4 adults, $2 senior citizens and students. Open Thurs.–Sun. noon–6.*

❾ Half a mile east of the museum, **Old Town Pasadena** is an ambitious, ongoing restoration. Having fallen into decay in the past 50 years, the area is being revitalized as a blend of restored brick buildings with a Yuppie overlay. Rejuvenated buildings include bistros, elegant restaurants, and boutiques. On Raymond Street, the Hotel Green, now the Castle Apartments, dominates the area. Once a posh resort hotel, the Green is now a faded Moorish fantasy of domes, turrets, and balconies reminiscent of the Alhambra but with, true to its name, a greenish tint. Holly Street, between Fair Oaks Avenue and Arroyo Parkway, is home to several shops offering an excellent selection of vintage '50s objects, jewelry, and clothes. This area is best explored on foot. Old Town is bisected by Colorado Boulevard, where on New Year's Day throngs of people line the street for the Rose Parade.

Time Out If browsing the Holly Street shops leaves you both nostalgic and hungry, walk down Fair Oaks Avenue to the **Rose City Diner.** Classic diner fare, from chicken-fried steak and eggs to macaroni and cheese, is served in an *American Graffiti* setting. Bebop singers roam the joint from 11 AM to 3 PM every Sunday for added '50s flavor. *45 S. Fair Oaks Ave., tel. 818/793–8282. Open daily 6 AM–2:30 AM.*

⑩ The **Pasadena Historical Society** is housed in Fenyes Mansion. The 1905 building still holds the original furniture and paintings on the main and second floors; in the basement, the focus is on Pasadena's history. There are also 4 acres of well-landscaped gardens. *170 N. Orange Grove Blvd., Pasadena, tel. 818/795–3002. Historical Society Museum, 470 W. Walnut St., tel. 818/577–1660. Admission: $4 adults, $3 students and senior citizens, children under 12 free. Open Tues., Thurs., and Sun. 1–4.*

⑪ The **Pacific Asia Museum** is the gaudiest Chinese-style building in Los Angeles outside Chinatown. Designed in the style of a northern Chinese imperial palace with a central courtyard, it is devoted entirely to the arts and crafts of Asia and the Pacific Islands. Most of the objects are on loan from private collections and other museums, and there are usually changing special exhibits that focus on the objects of one country. A bookstore and the Collectors Gallery shop sell fine art items from members' collections. The extensive research library can be used by appointment only. *46 N. Los Robles Dr., Pasadena, tel. 818/449–2742. Admission: $3 adults, $1.50 senior citizens, and students children free. Open Wed.–Sun. noon–5.*

⑫ **Kidspace** is a children's museum housed in the gymnasium of an elementary school. Here kids can talk to a robot, direct a television or radio station, dress up in the real (and very heavy) uniforms of a fire fighter, an astronaut, a football player, and more. A special "Human Habitrail" challenges children by changing architectural environments, and "Illusions" teases one's ability to perceive what is real and what is illusion. *390 S. El Molino Ave., Pasadena, tel. 818/449–9144. Admission: $4 adults, $5 children 2 and over, $2.50 children 1–2, $3.50 senior citizens. Open during the school year, Wed. 2–5, weekends 12:30–5, school vacations Mon.–Fri. 1–5, summer Tues.–Fri. 1–5.*

⑬ The **Ritz-Carlton, Huntington Hotel** (1401 S. Oak Knoll Ave., Pasadena, tel. 818/568–3900), is situated in Pasadena's most genteel neighborhood of Oak Knoll, close to San Marino. The hotel, built in 1906, reopened in March 1991, after five years of renovations necessary to bring it up to earthquake code standards, while still preserving its original design, including the Japanese and Horseshoe Gardens. Don't miss the historic Picture Bridge with its murals depicting scenes of California along its 20 gables. You can still make reservations here, but only for the 106 newer rooms.

⑭ The **Huntington Library, Art Gallery, and Botanical Gardens** is the area's most important site. If you only have time for a quick drive through the area and one stop, this should be it. Railroad tycoon Henry E. Huntington built his hilltop home in the early 1900s. It has established a reputation as one of the most extraordinary cultural complexes in the world, annually receiving more than a half-million visitors. The library contains 6 million items, including such treasures as a Gutenberg Bible, the earliest known edition of Chaucer's *Canterbury Tales*, George Washington's genealogy in his own handwriting, and first editions by Ben Franklin and Shakespeare. In the library's hallway are five tall hexagonal towers displaying important books and manuscripts.

The art gallery, devoted to British art from the 18th and 19th centuries, contains the original "Blue Boy" by Gainsborough, "Pinkie," a companion piece by Lawrence, and the monumental *Sarah Siddons as the Tragic Muse* by Reynolds.

The Huntington's awesome 130-acre garden, formerly the grounds of the estate, now includes a 12-acre Desert Garden featuring the largest group of mature cacti and other succulents in the world, all arranged by continent. The Japanese Garden offers traditional Japanese plants, stone ornaments, a moon bridge, a Japanese house, a bonsai court, and a Zen rock garden. Besides these gardens, there are collections of azaleas and 1,500 varieties of camellias, the world's largest public collection. The 1,000-variety rose garden displays its collection historically so that the development leading to today's strains of roses can be observed. There are also herb, palm, and jungle gardens plus a Shakespeare garden, where plants mentioned in Shakespeare's works are grown.

Because of the Huntington's vastness, a variety of orientation options is available for visitors. They include a 12-minute slide show introducing the Huntington; an hour-and-a-quarter guided tour of the gardens; a 45-minute audio tape about the art gallery (which can be rented for a nominal fee); a 15-minute introductory talk about the library; and inexpensive, self-guided tour leaflets.

In 1980, the first major facility constructed on the Huntington grounds in more than 60 years opened. The $5 million Huntington Pavilion offers visitors unmatched views of the surrounding mountains and valleys and houses a bookstore, displays, and information kiosks as well. Both the east and west wings of the pavilion display paintings on public exhibition for the first time. The Ralph M. Parsons Botanical Center at the pavilion includes a botanical library, an herbarium, and a laboratory for research on plants. No picnicking or pets. A refreshment room is open to the public. *Oxford Rd., San Marino, tel. 818/405-2100. Reservations required Sun. Donation requested. Open Tues.–Fri. 1–4:30, weekends 10:30–4:30.*

Other Places of Interest

Burbank Studios. Warner Brothers and Columbia Studios share this lot, where a two-hour guided walking tour is available. Because the tours involve a lot of walking, you should dress comfortably and casually. This tour is somewhat technically oriented and centered more on the actual workings of filmmaking than the one at Universal. It also varies from day to day to take advantage of goings-on on the lot. Most tours see the backlot sets, prop-construction department, and sound complex. *400 Warner Blvd., Burbank, tel. 818/954–1008. Tours given weekdays at 10 and 2. Admission: $25. No children under 10 permitted. Reservations essential, 1 wk in advance.*

Exposition Park (Figueroa St. at Exposition Blvd., Los Angeles). This beautiful park was the site of the 1932 Olympics and the impressive architecture still stands. Adjoining the University of Southern California, Exposition Park is the location of two major museums: the California Museum of Science and Industry and the Natural History Museum (*see* Museums, above). Also included in the 114-acre park is the Los Angeles Swimming Stadium (home of Los Angeles aquatic competitions), which is open to the public in summer, and the Memorial Coliseum, the site of college football games. There are plenty of picnic areas on the grounds as well as a sunken rose garden.

Forest Lawn Memorial Park–Hollywood Hills. Just west of Griffith Park on the north slope of the Hollywood Hills, this 340-acre sister park to Forest Lawn Glendale is dedicated to the ideal of American liberty. Featured are bronze and marble statuary, including Thomas Ball's 60-foot Washington Memorial and a replica of the Liberty Bell. There are also reproductions of Boston's Old North Church and Longfellow's Church of the Hills. The film *The Many Voices of Freedom* is shown daily and Revolutionary War documents are on permanent display. Among the famous people buried here are Buster Keaton, Stan Laurel, Liberace, Charles Laughton, and Freddie Prinze. *6300 Forest Lawn Dr., Hollywood, tel. 213/254–7251. Open daily 8–5.*

Gene Autry Western Heritage Museum. The American West, both the movie and real-life versions, is celebrated via memorabilia, artifacts, and art in a structure that draws on Spanish Mission and early western architecture. The collection includes Teddy Roosevelt's Colt revolver, Buffalo Bill Cody's saddle, and Annie Oakley's gold-plated Smith and Wesson guns, alongside video screens showing clips from old westerns. *4700 W. Heritage Way, Los Angeles, tel. 213/667–2000. Admission $6 adults, $4.50 senior citizens, $2.50 children 2–12. Open Tues.– Sun. 10–5.*

Griffith Park Observatory and Planetarium. Located on the south side of Mt. Hollywood in the heart of Griffith Park, the planetarium offers dazzling daily shows that duplicate the starry sky. A guide narrates the show and points out constellations. One of the largest telescopes in the world is open to the public for free viewing every clear night. Exhibits display models of the planets with photographs from satellites and spacecraft. A Laserium show is featured nightly, and other special astronomy shows are offered frequently. The Observatory sits high above Los Angeles and from the outside decks and walkways offers a spectacular view of the city, very popular on warm evenings. *Griffith Park, tel. 213/664–1191. Enter at the Los Feliz Blvd. and Vermont Ave. entrance. Hall of Science and telescope are free. Planetarium shows: $3.50 adults, $2 children. Laserium show: $6.50 adults, $5.50 children. Call for schedule. Open Tues.–Fri. 2–10, weekends 12:30–10.*

Hollyhock House. Frank Lloyd Wright designed a number of homes in the Los Angeles area. Hollyhock House was his first, commissioned by heiress Aline Barnsdall and built in 1921. It was done in the pre-Columbian style Wright was fond of at that time. As a unifying theme, he used a stylized hollyhock flower, which appears in a broad band around the exterior of the house and even on the dining-room chairs. Now owned by the city, as is Barnsdall Park, where it is located, Hollyhock House has been restored and furnished with original furniture designed by Wright and reproductions. His furniture may not be the comfiest in the world, but it sure looks perfect in his homes. *4800 Hollywood Blvd., Hollywood, tel. 213/662–7272. Admission: $1.50 adults, children free. Tours conducted Tues.–Sun., noon, 1, 2, and 3.*

Mulholland Drive. One of the most famous thoroughfares in Los Angeles, Mulholland makes its very winding way from the Hollywood Hills across the spine of the Santa Monica mountains west almost to the Pacific Ocean. Driving its length is slow, but the reward is sensational views of the city, the San Fernando Valley, and the expensive homes along the way. For a quick shot, take Benedict Canyon north from Sunset Boulevard, just west of the Beverly Hills Hotel, all the way to the top, and turn right at the crest, which is Mulholland. There's a turnout within a few feet of the intersection, and at night, the view of the valley side is incredible.

NBC Television Studios is also in Burbank, as any regular viewer of "The Tonight Show" can't help knowing. For those who wish to be part of a live studio audience, free tickets are still being made available for tapings of the various NBC shows done here, like "Cheers" and "Wheel of Fortune." *3000 W. Alameda Ave., Burbank, tel. 818/840–3537.*

Universal Studios Hollywood is the best place in Los Angeles for seeing behind the scenes of the movie industry. The five- to seven-hour Universal tour is an enlightening and amusing (if a bit sensational) day at the world's largest television and movie studio. The complex stretches across more than 420 acres, many of which are traversed during the course of the tour by trams featuring usually witty running commentary provided by enthusiastic guides. You can experience the parting of the Red Sea, an avalanche, and a flood; meet a 30-foot-tall version of the legendary King Kong; live through an encounter with a runaway train and an attack by the ravenous killer shark of *Jaws* fame; and endure a confrontation by aliens armed with death rays—all without ever leaving the safety of the tram. And now, thanks to the magic of Hollywood, you can also experience the perils of The Big One—an all-too-real simulation of an 8.3 earthquake, complete with collapsing earth, deafening train wrecks, floods, and other life-threatening amusements. There is a New England village, an aged European town, and a replica of an archetypal New York street. The newest exhibits are *Back To the Future*, a show showing off state-of-the-art special effects, and *Lucy: A Tribute to Lucille Ball*, housed in a 2,200-square-foot heart-shaped museum containing a re-creation of the "I Love Lucy" set, plus television film clips, costumes, and bound scripts from the beloved redhead's television show, which aired from 1951 to 1957. *100 Universal Pl., Universal City, tel. 818/508–9600. Box office open daily 8:30–4. Admission: $26 adults, $19 senior citizens and children 3–11.*

Watts Towers (1765 E. 107th St.). This is the folk-art legacy of an Italian immigrant tile-setter, Simon Rodia, and one of the great folk-art structures in the world. From 1920 until 1945, without helpers, this eccentric and driven man erected three cement towers, using pipes, bed frames, and anything else he could find, and embellished them with bits of colored glass, broken pottery, seashells, and assorted discards. The tallest tower is 107 feet. Plans are under way to stabilize and protect this unique monument, often compared to the 20th-century architectural wonders created by Barcelona's Antonio Gaudí. It is worth a pilgrimage for art and architecture buffs (or anyone else, for that matter).

Los Angeles for Free

In Los Angeles, every day is a free event in terms of nature; the sun, sand, and ocean alone can fill a vacation. But there are plenty of other free activities, events, and cultural attractions to keep even those with limited budgets busy.

Christmas Boat Parades. During December, many local marinas celebrate Christmas in a special way. Boat owners decorate their boats with strings of lights and holiday displays and then cruise in a line for dockside visitors to see. Call for specific dates (Marina del Rey, tel. 310/821–0555; Port of Los Angeles, tel. 213/519–3508).

Rose Parade. Seen from the streets (rather than the bleachers), the Rose Parade is as free as it is on television. Arrive before dawn and dress warmly. Thousands of residents prefer to watch on television and then go out to East Pasadena a day or two later to view the floats, which are parked there for a few days for observation. *Corner of Sierra Madre Blvd. and Washington St., Pasadena. Call for viewing hours, tel. 818/449–7673.*

Santa Monica Mountains Nature Walks. The rangers and docents of the many parks in the Santa Monica mountains offer an ambitious schedule of walks for all interests, ages, and levels of exertion. These include wildflower walks, moonlight hikes, tide-pool explorations, and much more. Several outings are held every day. For updated information, call the National Park Service (tel. 818/597–9192).

What to See and Do with Children

The youngsters of Los Angeles have plenty going for them: their own museums, our museums, a world-class zoo, children's theater every weekend, nature walks, pony rides, art classes, and much more.

In addition to the attractions listed here, check the Parks and Gardens section, below, for more places to take children. Also, the Los Angeles *Times* provides ideas for the coming week in two regular columns: "54 Hours," which runs on Thursdays in the View section, and "Family Spots," which runs on Saturdays in View. *L.A. Parent,* a monthly tabloid devoted to family life, has a monthly calendar.

Children's Museum at La Habra. Housed in a 1923-vintage Union Pacific Railroad depot, with old railroad cars resting nearby, this museum combines permanent and special exhibitions all designed to stimulate young minds—the painless way. In Grandma's Attic, children can try on old clothes and parade in front of a mirror. There's a real beehive (behind glass) and dozens of stuffed animals. A recent special exhibit focused on the world of handicapped children and allowed visitors to try out crutches and wheelchairs and learn a bit of sign language. *301 S. Euclid St., La Habra, tel. 310/905–9793. Admission: $2 adults, $1.50 children. Open Mon.–Sat. 10–4.*

Long Beach Children's Museum. Recently moved to expanded quarters in a Long Beach mall, the museum features the regulation-issue children's-museum exhibits such as The Art Cafe and Granny's Attic. All exhibits welcome curious minds and eager hands. *445 Long Beach Blvd. at Long Beach Plaza, Long Beach, tel. 310/495–1163. Admission: $2.95. Open Thurs.–Sat. 10–4, Sun. noon–4.*

Magic Mountain. The only real amusement park actually in Los Angeles County, Magic Mountain offers 260 acres of rides, shows, and entertainments. There are enough rides to satisfy any thrill-seeker, as well as numerous other attractions, including a puppet theater, celebrity musical revues, Dixieland jazz, rock concerts, and the Aqua Theater high-diving shows. Spillikin's Handcrafters Junction is a 4-acre compound in which craftspeople exhibit skills and wares from blacksmithing to glassblowing. *26101 Magic Mountain Pkwy., off I–5, Valencia, tel. 818/992–0884. Admission: $23 adults, $11 senior citizens, $14 children 4 ft. tall and under. Open May 19–Labor Day, daily 10–10 (later on weekends), rest of the year, weekends and holidays.*

Los Angeles Zoo. The zoo, one of the major zoos in the United States, is noted for its breeding of endangered species. Koalas and white tigers are the latest additions. The 113-acre compound holds more than 2,000 mammals, birds, amphibians, and reptiles. *Junction of the Ventura and Golden State freeways, Griffith Park, tel. 213/666–4090. Admission: $6 adults, $5 senior citizens, $2.75 children under 12. Open daily 10–5.*

Merry-Go-Round in Griffith Park. Just up the road from the real pony rides, this 1926-vintage carousel offers safe and melodic rides for families. The broad lawn nearby was the scene of some of the most colorful love-ins of the 1960s.

Pony Rides. Most youngsters in Los Angeles (and their parents before them) had their first pony ride at the track in Griffith Park. Two-year-olds are routinely strapped on and paraded around on the slowest of old nags, and these days, the event is dutifully recorded on video camera. The ponies come in three versions: slow, medium, and fast. To round out an eventful morning (the lines are long in late afternoon), there are stagecoach rides and a miniature-train ride that makes a figure eight near the pony rides. *Crystal Springs Dr., Griffith Park, tel. 213/664–3266. Use entrance near Golden State Freeway (I–5)* *and Los Feliz Blvd. Pony rides $1 for two rounds; stagecoach rides $1; miniature-train rides $1.50 adults, $1.25 children. Open in summer, weekdays 10–5:30, weekends 10–6:30, rest of year, Tues.–Fri. 10–4:30, weekends 10–5.*

Travel Town. Fifteen vintage railroad cars are resting here, all welcoming the onslaught of climbing and screaming children, who love to run from car to car, jump in the cab, run through the cars, and jump off the high steps. The collection includes a narrow-gauge sugar train from Hawaii, a steam engine, and an old L.A. trolley. Travel Town goes beyond just trains with a collection of old planes such as World War II bombers. There are also an old fire engine, milk wagon, buggies, and classic cars. A miniature train takes visitors on a ride around the area. *5200 Zoo Dr., Griffith Park, tel. 213/662–5874. Admission free. Open weekdays 10–4, weekends 10–6.*

Off the Beaten Track

The Flower Market. Just east of the downtown high rises, in the 700 block of Wall Street, is a block-long series of stores and stalls that open up in the middle of the night to sell wholesale flowers and houseplants to the city's florists, who rush them to their shops to sell that day. Many of the stalls stay open until late morning to sell leftovers to the public at the same bargain prices. And what glorious leftovers they are: Hawaiian ginger, Dutch tulips, Chilean freesia. The public is welcome after 9 AM and the stock is quickly depleted by 11 AM. Even if you don't buy, it's a heady experience to be surrounded by so much fragile beauty.

Laurel and Hardy's Piano Stairway. One of the most famous scenes in the history of movies is one in *The Music Box* where Laurel and Hardy try to get a piano up an outdoor stairway. This Sisyphean tale was filmed in 1932 at 923–927 Vendome Street (where the stairway remains today much as it was then), in the Silverlake section of Los Angeles, a few miles northeast of downtown.

Pig Murals (3049 E. Vernon Ave., Vernon). Vernon Avenue is the heart of Los Angeles's meat-packing industry and to be stuck in traffic on Vernon Avenue on a hot summer afternoon is an odorific experience not soon forgotten. Nevertheless, for aficionados of offbeat sites and/or street murals, the Pig Murals on the outside walls of the Farmer John Company are great fun. Probably the first public murals in Los Angeles, they were originally painted by Leslie Grimes, who was killed in a fall from the scaffolding while painting. They depict bucolic scenes of farms and contented pigs, rather an odd juxtaposition to what goes on inside the packing plant.

Beaches

The beach scene is an integral part of the Southern California lifestyle. There is no public attraction more popular in L.A. than the white, sandy playgrounds that line the deep blue Pacific.

From the L.A. Civic Center, the easiest way to hit the coast is by taking the Santa Monica Freeway (I–10) due west. Once you reach the end of the freeway, I–10 turns into the famous Highway 1, better known as the Pacific Coast Highway, or PCH, and continues up to Oregon. Other basic routes from the downtown area include Pico, Olympic, Santa Monica, or Wilshire boulevards, which all run east–west through the city. Sunset Boulevard offers a less direct but more scenic drive to the beaches. Starting near Dodger Stadium, it passes through Hollywood, Beverly Hills, and Pacific Palisades, and eventually reaches the Pacific Ocean 1 mile south of Malibu. The RTD bus lines, L.A.'s main form of public transportation (at least until the new Metro Rail is completed), runs every 20 minutes to and from the beaches along each of these streets.

Los Angeles County beaches (and state beaches operated by the county) have lifeguards, and public parking (for a fee) is available at most. The following beaches are listed in north–south order. Some are excellent for swimming, some for surfing (check with lifeguards for current conditions for either activity), others better for exploring.

Leo Carillo State Beach. This beach along a rough and mountainous stretch of coastline is the most fun at low tide, when a spectacular array of tide pools blossom for all to see. Rock formations on the beach have created some great secret coves for picnickers looking for solitude. There are hiking trails, sea caves, and tunnels, and whales, dolphins, and sea lions are often seen swimming in the offshore kelp beds. The waters here are rocky and best for experienced surfers and scuba divers; fishing is good. Picturesque campgrounds are set back from the beach. Camping fee is $14 per night. *35000 block of PCH, Malibu, tel. 310/706–1310. Facilities: parking, lifeguard, rest rooms, showers, fire pits.*

Zuma Beach County Park. This is Malibu's largest and sandiest beach, and a favorite spot of surfers. It's also a haven for high-school students who've discovered Nautilus Plus. *30050 PCH, Malibu, tel. 310/457–9891. Facilities: parking, lifeguard, rest rooms, showers, food, playground, volleyball.*

Westward Beach/Point Dume State Beach. Another favorite spot for surfing, this ½-mile-long sandy beach has tide pools and sandstone cliffs. *South end of Westward Beach Rd., Malibu, tel. 310/457–9891. Facilities: parking, lifeguard, rest rooms, food.*

Paradise Cove. With its pier and equipment rentals, this sandy beach is a mecca for sportfishing boats. Though swimming is allowed, there are lifeguards during the summer only. *28128 PCH, Malibu, tel. 310/457–2511. Facilities: parking, rest rooms, showers, food (concessions open during the summer only).*

Surfrider Beach/Malibu Lagoon State Beach. The steady 3- to 5-foot waves make this beach, just north of Malibu Pier, a great long-board surfing beach. The International Surfing Contest is held here in September. Water runoff from Malibu Canyon forms a natural lagoon, which is a sanctuary for many birds. There are also nature trails perfect for romantic sunset strolls. *23200 block of PCH, Malibu, tel. 310/706–1310. Facilities: parking, lifeguard, rest rooms, picnicking, visitor center.*

Las Tunas State Beach. Las Tunas is small (1,300 ft. long, covering a total of only 2 acres), narrow, and sandy, with some rocky areas, and set beneath a bluff. Surf fishing is the biggest attraction here. There is no lifeguard, and swimming is not encouraged because of steel groins set offshore to prevent erosion. *19400 block of PCH, Malibu, tel. 310/457–9891. Facilities: parking, rest rooms.*

Topanga Canyon State Beach. This rocky beach stretches from the mouth of the Topanga Canyon down to Coastline Drive. Catamarans dance in these waves and skid onto the sands of this popular beach, where dolphins sometimes come close enough to shore to startle sunbathers. The area near the canyon is a great surfing spot. *18700 block of PCH, Malibu, tel. 310/394–3266. Facilities: parking, lifeguard, rest rooms, food.*

Will Rogers State Beach. This wide, sandy beach is several miles long and has even surf. Parking in the lot here is limited, but there is plenty of beach, volleyball, and body surfing. *15800 PCH, Pacific Palisades, tel. 310/394–3266. Facilities: parking, lifeguard, rest rooms.*

Santa Monica Beach. This is one of L.A.'s most popular beaches. It has a pier and a promenade, and a man-made breakwater just offshore that has caused the sand to collect and form the widest stretch of beach on the entire Pacific coast. And wider beaches mean more bodies. If you're up for some sightseeing on land, this is one of the more popular gathering places for L.A.'s young, toned, and bronzed. All in all, the 2-mile-long beach is well equipped with bike paths, facilities for the disabled, playgrounds, and volleyball. In summer, free rock and jazz concerts are held at the pier on Thursday nights. *West of PCH, Santa Monica, tel. 310/394–3266. Facilities: parking, lifeguard, rest rooms, showers.*

Venice Municipal Beach. While the surf and sands of Venice are fine, the main attraction here is the boardwalk scene. Venice combines the beefcake of some of L.A.'s most serious bodybuilders with the productions of lively crafts merchants and street musicians. There are roller skaters and break-dancers to entertain you, and cafés to feed you. You can rent bikes at Venice Pier Bike Shop (21 Washington St.) and skates at Skatey's (102 Washington St.). *1531 Ocean Front Walk, Venice, tel. 310/ 394–3266. Facilities: parking, rest rooms, showers, food, picnicking.*

Playa del Rey. South of Marina del Rey lies a beach not quite as famous as its neighbors, but known to residents as one of the more underrated beaches in Southern California. Its sprawling white sands stretch from the southern tip of Marina del Rey almost 2 miles down to Dockweiler Beach. The majority of the crowds that frequent these sands are young.

One of the more attractive features of this beach is an area called Del Rey Lagoon. Located right in the heart of Playa del Rey, this grassy oasis surrounds a lovely pond inhabited by dozens of ducks, and it offers picnickers barbecue pits and tables to help fend off starvation on afternoon outings. *6660 Esplanade, Playa del Rey. Facilities: parking, lifeguard, rest rooms, food.*

Dockweiler State Beach. There are consistent waves for surfing here, and it is not crowded, due to an unsightly power plant with towering smokestacks parked right on the beach. While the plant presents no danger to swimmers in the area, its mere presence, combined with the jumbo jets taking off overhead from L.A.'s International Airport, makes this beach a better place for surfing or working out than for lying out. There is firewood for sale for barbecues on the beach; beach fires are legal in this area as long as they are contained within the special pits that are already set up along the beach. *Harbor Channel to Vista del Mar and Grand Ave., Playa del Rey, tel. 310/322–5008. Facilities: parking, lifeguard, rest rooms, showers.*

Manhattan State Beach. Here are 44 acres of sandy beach for swimming, diving, surfing, and fishing. Polliwog Park is a charming, grassy landscape a few yards back from the beach that parents with young children may appreciate. Ducks waddle around a small pond, and picnickers enjoy a full range of facilities including grills and rest rooms. *West of Strand, Manhattan Beach, tel. 310/372–2166. Facilities: volleyball, parking, lifeguard, rest rooms, showers, food.*

Redondo State Beach. The beach is wide, sandy, and usually packed in summer, and parking is limited. The Redondo Pier marks the starting point of the beach area, which continues south for more than 2 miles along a heavily developed shoreline community. Storms have damaged some of the restaurants and shops along the pier, but plenty of others are still functioning. Excursion boats, boat-launching ramps, and fishing are other attractions. There is a series of rock and jazz concerts held at the pier during the summer. *Foot of Torrance Blvd., Redondo Beach, tel. 310/372–2166. Facilities: volleyball, parking, lifeguard, rest rooms, showers, food.*

Shopping

By Jane E. Lasky

Most Los Angeles shops are open from 10 to 6 although many remain open until 9 or later, particularly at the shopping centers, on Melrose Avenue, and in Westwood Village during the summer. Melrose shops, on the whole, don't get moving until 11 AM but are often open on Sundays, too. At most stores around town, credit cards are almost universally accepted, as are traveler's checks when presented with proper identification. If you're looking for sales, check the *Los Angeles Times.*

Shopping Districts

When asked where they want to shop, visitors to Los Angeles inevitably answer, "Rodeo Drive." This famous thoroughfare is not only high-high-end—and therefore somewhat limited—it is also only one of many enticing shopping streets Los Angeles has to offer. Consequently, visitors should also consider other shopping districts within this huge metropolitan area. Remember, though, that distances between each can be vast, so don't choose too many different stops in one day. If you do, you'll spend more time driving than shopping.

Downtown

Although downtown Los Angeles has many enclaves to explore, we suggest that the bargain hunter head straight for the **Cooper Building** (860 S. Los Angeles St., tel. 213/622–1139). Eight floors of small clothing and shoe shops (mostly for women) offer some of the most fantastic discounts in the city. Grab a free map in the lobby, and seek out as many of the 82 shops as you can handle. Nearby are myriad discount outlets selling everything from shoes to suits to linens.

Near the Hilton Hotel, **Seventh Street Marketplace** (735 S. Figueroa St., tel. 213/955–7150) was erected in 1986 and is worth a visit. It's an indoor/outdoor multilevel shopping center with an extensive courtyard that boasts many busy cafés and lively music. The stores surrounding this courtyard include **G. B. Harb** (tel. 213/624–4785), a fine menswear shop, and **Bullocks** (tel. 213/624–9494), a small version of the big department store geared to the businessperson.

Melrose Avenue   West Hollywood, especially Melrose Avenue, is where young shoppers should try their luck, as should those who appreciate vintage styles in clothing and furnishings. The 1½ miles of intriguing, one-of-a-kind shops and bistros stretch from La Brea to a few blocks west of Crescent Heights; it is definitely one of Los Angeles's hottest shopping areas. A sampling of the stores that operate there: **Betsey Johnson** (7311 Melrose Ave., tel. 213/931–4490) offers the designer's vivid, hip women's fashions; **Cottura** (7215 Melrose Ave., tel. 213/933–1928) offers brightly colored Italian ceramics; **Comme des Fous** (7384 Melrose Ave., tel. 2l3/653–5330) is an avant-garde (and pricey) clothing shop packed with innovative European designs; **Emphasis** (7361 Melrose Ave., tel. 213/653–7174) offers a pristine collection of fashion-forward clothes for women; **Modern Living** (8125 Melrose Ave., tel. 213/655–3898) is a gallery of 20th-century design, representing renowned international furniture designers, including Philippe Starck, Ettore Sottsass, and Massino Isosaghini; **A Star Is Worn** (7303 Melrose Ave., tel. 213/939–4922) sells secondhand clothing once worn by celebrities; **Wacko** (7416 Melrose Ave., tel. 213/651–3811) is a wild space crammed with all manner of blow-up toys, cards, and other semi-useless items that make good Los Angeles keepsakes.

The Beverly Center   The **Beverly Center** (tel. 310/854–0070), bound by Beverly Boul-
and Environs   evard, La Cienega Boulevard, San Vicente Boulevard, and Third Street, covers more than 7 acres and contains some 200 stores, including **By Design** and **Conran's** for home furnishings, **By Oliver** for fashionable women's clothes, and **Alexio** for fashionable men's clothes. The shopping center is anchored by the **Broadway** department store on one end and **Bullocks** on the other. Inside, there are also some interesting restaurants (like the **Kisho-an**, a Japanese restaurant known for its fine sushi, and **The Hard Rock Cafe**, known for its bargain cuisine and fascinating decor, including a 1959 Caddy that dives into the roof of the building above the restaurant) and one of Los Angeles's finest cineplexes with 14 individual movie theaters. It's worthwhile to venture outside the confines of the Beverly Center to discover some very interesting shops.

The **Pacific Design Center** (corner of Melrose Ave. and San Vicente Blvd., tel. 310/657–0800) is where leading interior designers find the best in home furnishings and accessories for clients who aim to impress. Set in two startlingly big colored-glass buildings—known to locals as the Blue Whale and the Green Giant—the PDC's exclusive showrooms sell only to the trade. If you would like to do more than look here, contact LA Design Concepts, an interior-design shopping service (8811 Alden Dr., tel. 310/276–2109). A design professional will guide you through the PDC for an hourly fee, offer advice, and order items for you at less than half the standard industry markup of 33%.

Century City **Century City Shopping Center & Marketplace** (tel. 310/277–3898) is set among gleaming steel office buildings. Here, in the center of a thriving business atmosphere, is a city kind of mall—open-air. Besides The Broadway and Bullocks, both department stores, you'll find **Sasha of London** for trendy shoes and bags; **Ann Taylor** for stylish but not outlandish clothing and **Joan & David** shoes; and **The Pottery Barn** for contemporary furnishings at reasonable prices. **Card Fever** is a whimsical boutique with fun and funky messages to send. **Go Sport** is a gigantic European sporting-goods store. **Brentano's** is one of the city's largest bookstores. You'll find California wines, a great gift to take home, at **Gelson's,** a gourmet food market.

West Los Angeles The **Westside Pavilion** (tel. 310/474–6255) is a pastel postmodern mall on Pico and Overland boulevards. The three levels of shops and restaurants run the gamut from high-fashion boutiques for men and women to a store devoted solely to travelers' needs, large and small. Among them are **Muppet Stuff,** filled with novelties commemorating these familiar characters; **The May Company** and **Nordstrom,** two full-scale department stores; **Mr Gs for Kids,** a good place for children's gifts; **Chanin's,** filled with women's designer clothing; and **Victoria's Secret,** a lingerie boutique. Worth visiting even if you're not here to shop—and a welcome stop, if you are—is **Sisley Italian Kitchen,** which serves California-Italian dishes, pizzas, and terrific salads.

Santa Monica Another worthwhile and multifaceted area, farther west and next to the ocean, offers both malls and street shopping. **Santa Monica Place Mall** (315 Broadway, tel. 310/394–5451) is a three-story enclosed mall that's nothing special. Next door, **Santa Monica Promenade** (tel. 310/393–8355) is an open-air arena of shops with pedestrian walkways and a landscaped island. A light, airy atrium views all three floors of the mall at once, and from particular points you can see the Pacific in the background. **Robinson's** and **The Broadway** are department stores in this complex.

Along **Montana Avenue** is a stretch of a dozen or so blocks that has evolved into an L.A. version of New York City's Columbus Avenue. Boutique after boutique of quality goods can be found along Montana from Seventh to 17th streets. The stretch of **Main Street** leading from Santa Monica to Venice (Pico Blvd. to Rose Ave.) makes for a pleasant walk, with a collection of quite good restaurants, unusual shops and galleries, and an ever-present ocean breeze.

Beverly Hills We've saved the most famous section of town for last. **Rodeo Drive** is often compared to such famous streets as Fifth Avenue in New York and the Via Condotti in Rome. Along the several blocks between Wilshire and Santa Monica boulevards, you'll find an abundance of big-name retailers—but don't shop Beverly Hills without shopping the streets that surround illustrious Rodeo Drive. There are plenty of treasures to be purchased on those other thoroughfares as well.

Some of the many shops, boutiques, and department stores in Beverly Hills: **Polo/Ralph Lauren** (444 N. Rodeo Dr., tel. 310/281–7200) serves up a complete presentation of Lauren's all-encompassing lifestyle philosophy; **Ann Taylor** (357 N. Camden Dr., tel. 310/858–7840) is the flagship shop of this chain of women's clothing stores, offering the epitome of the young executive look; **Celine** (460 N. Rodeo Dr., tel. 310/273–1243) is for luggage, shoes, and accessories as well as traditionally tailored clothing; **Jaeger International Shop** (9699 Wilshire Blvd., tel. 310/276–1062) is one of Britain's best-known clothiers, with a complete line of cashmere and woolen separates available in traditionally designed fashions; **Alfred Dunhill of London** (201 N. Rodeo Dr., tel. 310/274–5351) is an elegant shop selling British-made suits, shirts, sweaters, and slacks, although pipes, tobacco, and cigars are this store's claim to fame; **Bijan** (420 N. Rodeo Dr., tel. 310/273–6544) is a store where it helps to make an appointment—Bijan claims that many Arabian sheiks and other royalty shop here, along with some of the wealthiest men in the United States; **Cartier** (370 N. Rodeo Dr., tel. 310/275–4272), **Tiffany and Company** (210 Rodeo Dr., tel. 310/273–8880), and **Van Cleef and Arpels** (300 N. Rodeo Dr., tel. 310/276–1161) are just the places for expensive baubles and fine jewelry; and **Hammacher-Schlemmer** (309 N. Rodeo Dr., tel. 310/859–7255) is a fabulous place to unearth those hard-to-find presents for adults who never grew up.

Even Beverly Hills has a couple of shopping centers, although owners wouldn't dare call their collection of stores and cafés "malls." The **Rodeo Collection** (tel. 310/276–9600) is located at 421 North Rodeo Drive between Brighton Way and Santa Monica Boulevard, and is nothing less than the epitome of opulence and high fashion. Many famous upscale European designers opened their doors in this piazzalike area of marble and brass.

Department Stores **The Broadway** (The Beverly Center, 8500 Beverly Blvd., tel. 213/854–7200). This complete department store offers merchandise in the moderate price range, from cosmetics, to housewares, to linens, to clothing for men and women. There are stores throughout Los Angeles.

Bullocks (Citicorp Plaza, 925 W. 8th St., downtown, tel. 213/624–9494). More upscale than The Broadway, Bullocks carries an extensive collection of clothing for men and women, as well as housewares and cosmetics. Stores are throughout Southern California, with the flagship store at the Beverly Center (8500 Beverly Blvd., tel. 213/854–6655).

I. Magnin (Wilshire district, 3050 Wilshire Blvd., tel. 213/382–6161). This large store with many designer items for men and women and a good handbag and luggage department has stores throughout Southern California. The flagship store (I. Magnin Wilshire) is an Art Deco landmark.

The May Company (Downtown at 6067 Wilshire Blvd., tel. 213/938–4211). Modestly priced clothing and furniture without glitz or glitter are offered in these stores throughout Southern California.

Nordstrom (Westside Pavilion at 500 N. Pico Blvd., in West Los Angeles, tel. 213/470–6155). This Seattle-based department store infiltrated Southern California within the past decade and has brought with it a wide selection of clothing for men and women as well as a reputation for fine customer service, a huge shoe department, and the entertainment of popular music played on the store's grand piano.

Robinson's (9900 Wilshire Blvd., Beverly Hills, tel. 213/275–5464). This high-end department store has many women's selections, a few men's selections, and a good housewares department. Its stores can be found throughout Southern California.

Saks Fifth Avenue (9600 Wilshire Blvd., Beverly Hills, tel. 213/275–4211). The Los Angeles version of this New York store isn't as impressive as the one you'll find next to St. Patrick's Cathedral in Manhattan. Still, the buyers have good taste.

Participant Sports

If you're looking for a good workout, you've come to the right city. Los Angeles is one of the major sports capitals in the United States. Whether your game is basketball, golf, billiards, or bowling, L.A. is a dream town for athletes of all kinds. Not only does the near-perfect climate allow sports enthusiasts to play outdoors almost year-round, but during some seasons it's not impossible to surf in the morning and snow-ski in the afternoon . . . all in the same county.

Bicycling and Roller Skating In the last few years, Los Angeles has made a concerted effort to upgrade existing bike paths and to designate new lanes along many major boulevards for cyclists' use. Perhaps the most famous bike path in the city, and definitely the most beautiful, can be found on the beach. The path starts at Temescal Canyon, and works its way down to Redondo Beach. San Vicente Boulevard in Santa Monica has a nice wide lane next to the sidewalk for cyclists. The path continues for about a 5-mile stretch. Balboa Park in the San Fernando Valley is another haven for two-wheelers. A map of bike trails throughout the county can be obtained from the **L.A. County Parks and Recreation Department** (tel. 213/738–2961). All of the cycling areas mentioned above are also excellent for roller skating, even though cyclists still have the right of way. Venice Beach is the skating capital of the city—maybe the world.

Fishing **Saltwater fishing** in L.A. offers the angler a number of different ways to get hold of a fresh catch from the Pacific. Shore fishing and surf casting are excellent on many of the beaches (*see* Beaches, above). Pier fishing is another popular method of hooking your dinner. The Malibu, Santa Monica, and Redondo Beach piers each offer nearby bait-and-tackle shops, and you can generally pull in a healthy catch. If you want to break away from the piers, however, the **Malibu Pier Sport Fishing Company** (23000 Pacific Coast Hwy., tel. 310/456–8030) offers boat excursions for $20 per half day. The **Redondo Sport Fishing Company** (233 N. Harbor Dr., tel. 310/372–2111) have half-day and full-day charters. Half-day charters, 7:30 AM–12:30 PM or 1 PM–6 PM, run about $18 per person; a three-quarter day costs $27, and a full day goes for about $65. You can rent a pole for $6.50. Sea bass, halibut, bonito, yellowtail, and barracuda are the usual catch.

For something with a little more bite, there are a number of fishing charters out of Marina del Rey, like **Twenty Second Street Landing** (141 W. 22nd St., San Pedro, tel. 310/832–8304). Since you can't see the fish anyway, this overnight charter is perfect because at least it affords you a look at the stars while waiting for a bite. Complete with bunk beds and full galley, these boats leave at 10 PM and 10:30 PM and dock between 5 PM and 9 PM the next night. Per-person price is $55 for the 10 PM excursion and $50 for the 10:30 PM charter. Day charters are available as well, at $25–$40, with half-day excursions on weekends for $20.

The most popular and unquestionably the most unusual form of fishing in the L.A. area involves no hooks, bait, or poles. The great **grunion runs,** which take place March–August, are a spectacular natural phenomenon in which hundreds of thousands of small silver fish, called grunion, wash up on Southern California beaches to spawn and lay their eggs in the sand. The Cabrillo Marine Museum in San Pedro (tel. 310/548–7562) has entertaining and educational programs about grunion during most of the runs. In certain seasons, however, touching grunion is prohibited, so it's advisable to check with the Fish and Game Department (tel. 310/590–5132) before going to see them wash ashore.

Golf The Department of Parks and Recreation lists seven public 18-hole courses in Los Angeles. **Rancho Park Golf Course** (10460 W. Pico Blvd., tel. 310/838–7373) is one of the most heavily played links in the entire country. There are also several good public courses located in the San Fernando Valley. The **Balboa and Encino Golf Courses** are located right next to each other at 16821 Burbank Boulevard in Encino, tel. 818/995–1170. The **Woodley Golf Course** (6331 Woodley Ave. in Van Nuys, tel. 818/780–6886) is a carpenter's dream . . . flat as a board, and with no trees!

Perhaps the most concentrated area of golf courses in the city can be found in **Griffith Park.** Here you'll find two splendid 18-hole courses along with a challenging nine-hole course. **Harding Golf Course** and **Wilson Golf Course** (both at 4730 Crystal Springs Dr., tel. 213/663–2555) are located about a mile and a half inside the Griffith Park entrance at Riverside Drive and Los Feliz Boulevard. Bridle paths surround the outer fairways, and the San Gabriel mountains make up the rest of the gallery in a scenic background. The nine-hole **Roosevelt Course** (2650 N. Vermont Ave., tel. 213/665–2011) can be reached through the Hillhurst Street entrance to Griffith Park.

Yet another course in the Griffith Park vicinity, and one at which there's usually no waiting, is the nine-hole **Los Feliz Pitch 'n' Putt** (3207 Los Feliz Blvd., tel. 213/663–7758). Other pitch 'n' putt courses in Los Angeles include **Holmby Hills** (601 Club View Dr., West L.A., tel. 310/276–1604) and **Penmar** (1233 Rose Ave., Venice, tel. 310/396–6228).

Health Clubs Many movies, TV shows, and songs have depicted Angelenos as mythological creatures possessing the secret of the three Ts: tanning, toning, and tightening. Well, that sort of definition doesn't just grow on you when you get off the plane at LAX . . . it takes hard work.

There are dozens of health-club chains in the city that offer monthly and yearly memberships. **Nautilus Aerobics Plus** and **Holiday Spa Health Clubs** are the most popular local chains. The Holiday Club located between Hollywood and Sunset boulevards (1628 El Centro, tel. 213/461–0227) is the flagship operation. To find the Holiday Spa nearest you, call 800/695–8111. **Sports Club L.A.** (1835 Sepulveda Blvd., West L.A., tel. 310/473–1447) is a hot spot, attracting a diverse group of celebrities, such as James Woods, and Princess Stephanie of Monaco. Probably the most famous body-pumping facility of this nature in the city is **Gold's Gym** (360 Hampton Dr., Venice, tel. 310/392–6004). This is where all the incredible hulks turn themselves into modern art. For $15 a day or $50 a week, several tons of weights and Nautilus machines can be yours.

Horseback Riding Although horseback riding in Los Angeles is extremely popular, stables that rent horses are becoming an endangered species. Of the survivors, **Bar "S" Stables** (1850 Riverside Dr., in Glendale, tel. 818/242–8443) will rent you a horse for $13 an hour (plus a $10 deposit). Riders who come here can take advantage of over 50 miles of beautiful bridle trails in the Griffith Park area. **Sunset River Trails** (Rush St., at end of Peck Rd., El Monte, tel. 818/444–2128) offers riders the nearby banks of the San Gabriel River to explore at $15 an hour. **Los Angeles Equestrian Center** (480 Riverside Dr., Burbank, tel. 818/840–8401) rents pleasure horses—English and western—for riding along bridle paths throughout the Griffith Park hills. Horses cost $13 per hour. **Sunset Stables** (3400 Beachwood Dr., Hollywood, tel. 213/469–5450) offers a "dinner cruise" at $30, not including cost of the dinner. Riders take a trail over the hill into Burbank at sunset where they tie up their horses and have a feast at a Mexican restaurant.

Jogging Most true joggers don't care where they run, but if you've got the time to drive to a choice location to commence your leg-pumping exercises, here are a few suggestions: First of all, just about every local high school and college in the city has a track. Most are public and welcome runners, and the private schools usually don't give a hoot who jogs on their tracks between 5 AM and 8 AM. A popular scenic course for students and downtown workers can be found at Exposition Park. Circling the Coliseum and Sports Arena is a jogging/workout trail with pull-up bars and other simple equipment spread out every several hundred yards. San Vicente Boulevard in Santa Monica has a wide grassy median that splits the street for several picturesque miles. The Hollywood Reservoir, just east of Cahuenga Boulevard in the Hollywood Hills, is encircled by a 3.2-mile asphalt path and has a view of the Hollywood sign. Within hilly Griffith Park are thousands of acres' worth of hilly paths and challenging terrain, although Crystal Springs Drive from the main entrance at Los Feliz to the zoo is a relatively flat 5 miles. Circle Drive, around the perimeter of UCLA in Westwood, provides a 2.5-mile run through academia, L.A. style. Of course, the premium spot in Los Angeles for any kind of exercise can be found along any of the beaches.

Tennis And on the eighth day, God created the tennis court. At least, it can seem that way when you drive around most L.A. neighborhoods. If you want to play tennis, you'll have no problem finding a court in this town—although you might have to wait a while for it once you get there. Many public parks have courts that require an hourly fee. **Lincoln Park** (Lincoln and Wilshire Blvd., Santa Monica), **Griffith Park** (Riverside Dr. and Los Feliz Blvd.), and **Barrington Park** (Barrington Ave. just south of Sunset Blvd. in L.A.), all have well-maintained courts with lights.

For a complete list of the public tennis courts in Los Angeles, contact the L.A. Department of Recreation and Parks (tel. 213/485–5515) or the **Southern California Tennis Association,** Los Angeles Tennis Center, UCLA Campus (420 Circle Dr., Los Angeles 90024, tel. 310/208–3838).

Hotels with If you're in town for just a few days and you don't have time to
Tennis Courts shop around for a court, you may already be staying at a hotel
that has facilities. The **Ritz-Carlton Marina del Rey** (4375 Admiralty Way, tel. 310/823–1700) has three lighted courts. Per-person, hourly rates are $10 for hotel guests and $15 for the public. The **Sheraton Town House** (2961 Wilshire Blvd., tel. 213/382–7171) has four courts available at $10 an hour. *See* Lodging, below, for other details on these hotels.

Spectator Sports

If you enjoy watching professional sports, you'll never hunger for action in this town. Los Angeles is the home of some of the greatest franchises in pro basketball, football, and baseball. And while most cities would be content to simply have one team in each of those categories, L.A. fans can root for two.

Baseball The **Dodgers** will take on all of their National League rivals in another eventful season at the ever-popular Dodger Stadium. For ticket information, call 213/224–1400. Down the freeway a bit in Anaheim, the **California Angels** continue their quest for the pennant in the American League West. For Angels ticket information, contact Angel Stadium: tel. 213/625–1123.

Basketball While the great American pastime may be baseball, in the town where the perennial world champion **Los Angeles Lakers** display what they call "showtime," basketball is king. The Lakers' home court is the Great Western Forum in Inglewood. Ticket information: tel. 310/419–3182. L.A.'s "other" team, the **Clippers,** make their home at the L.A. Sports Arena downtown next to the Coliseum. Ticket information: tel. 213/748–6131.

Football The L.A. Coliseum (3911 S. Figueroa St., downtown, tel. 213/747–7111) continues to be refurbished to its home-team L.A. Raiders' specifications. For tickets, call Ticket Master at 213/480–3232. The **Los Angeles Rams** will continue their struggle to get back to the Super Bowl this year. The team plays out of Anaheim Stadium. Ticket information: tel. 213/625–1123. From within California, call 800/6–ANGELS.

Hockey The **L.A. Kings** put their show on ice at the Forum, November–April. Ticket information: tel. 310/419–3182.

Horse Racing **Santa Anita Race Track** (Huntington Dr. and Colorado Pl., Arcadia, tel. 818/574–7223) is still the dominant site for exciting Thoroughbred racing. You can always expect the best racing in the world at this beautiful facility. **Hollywood Park** is another favorite racing venue. Since the completion of the Cary Grant Pavilion, a sense of class and style that has been lacking from this once-great park for some time has been restored. The track is next to the Forum in Inglewood, at Century Boulevard and Prairie Ave., tel. 310/419–1500. It's open late April–mid-July. For harness racing, **Los Alamitos** (4961 Katella Ave.) has both day and night racing. For track information, call 714/236–4400 or 310/431–1361.

Dining

By Bruce David Colen

Since 1974, Bruce David Colen has been the restaurant and food critic for Los Angeles magazine. He has also written on food and travel for Town & Country, Architectural Digest, Bon Appétit, Travel and Leisure, and Endless Vacations.

The high-living '80s saw Los Angeles emerge as a top gastronomic capital of the world. It was an amazing and delicious transformation. Where once the city was known only for its chopped Cobb salad, Green Goddess dressing, drive-in hamburger stands, and outdoor barbecues, today it is home to many of the best French and Italian restaurants in the United States, and so many places featuring international cuisines that listing them would be like roll call at the United Nations. There are so many new—and good—dining establishments opening every week that, currently, there are more chairs, booths, and banquettes than there are bodies to fill them. The result is a fierce competition among upscale restaurateurs that has made L.A. one of the least expensive big cities—here or abroad—in which to eat well.

Locals tend to dine early, between 7:30 and 9 PM, which is, in part, a holdover from when this was a "studio" town and the filmmaking day started at 6 AM, but these days mealtimes are scheduled earlier more to allow for early morning exercise. Advance reservations are essential at the "starred" restaurants, and at almost all restaurants on weekend evenings.

Highly recommended restaurants are indicated by a star ★.

Category	Cost*
Very Expensive	over $60
Expensive	$40–$60
Moderate	$20–$40
Inexpensive	under $20

per person, without tax (8.25%), service, or drinks

American
Beverly Hills
★

The Grill. This eatery is the closest Los Angeles comes in looks and atmosphere to one of San Francisco's venerable bar and grills, with their dark wood paneling and brass trim. The food is basic American, cleanly and simply prepared, and includes fine steaks and chops, grilled fresh salmon, corned beef hash, braised beef ribs, and a creamy version of the Cobb salad. *9560 Dayton Way, tel. 310/276–0615. Reservations required. Dress: casual. Valet parking in evening. AE, DC, MC, V. Closed Sun. Moderate.*

Ed Debevic's. This is a good place to take the kids and yourself, if you are yearning for the nostalgia of youth. Old Coca-Cola signs, a blaring jukebox, gum-chewing waitresses in bobby sox, and meat loaf and mashed potatoes will take you back to the diners of the '50s. *134 N. La Cienega Blvd., tel. 310/659–1952. No weekend reservations, weekday reservations advised. Dress: casual. Valet parking. No credit cards. Inexpensive.*

RJ'S the Rib Joint. There is a large barrel of free peanuts at the door, sawdust on the floor, and atmosphere to match. The outstanding salad bar has dozens of fresh choices and return privileges, and there are big portions of everything—from ribs, chili, and barbecued chicken, to mile-high layer cakes—all at very reasonable prices. *252 N. Beverly Dr., tel. 310/274–RIBS. Reservations advised. Dress: casual. Valet parking in evening. AE, DC, MC, V. Inexpensive.*

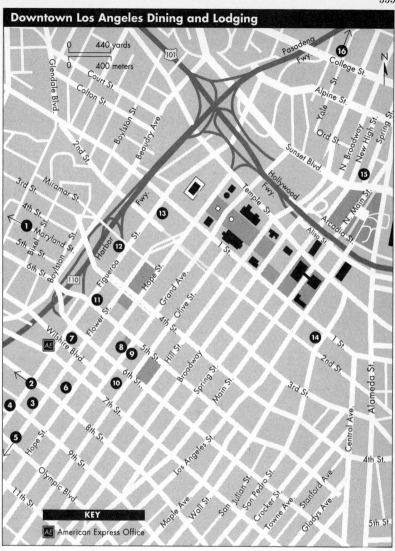

Downtown Los Angeles Dining and Lodging

Dining

The Chronicle, **16**

Engine Co. #28, **7**

Mon Kee's Seafood Restaurant, **15**

Pacific Dining Car, **1**

Restaurant Horikawa, **14**

Rex Il Ristorante, **10**

Lodging

The Biltmore Hotel, **9**

Checkers Kempinski Hotel, **8**

Figueroa Hotel, **4**

Holiday Inn L.A. Downtown, **2**

Hyatt Regency L.A., **6**

The New Otani Hotel and Garden, **13**

Orchid Hotel, **3**

Sheraton Grande Hotel, **12**

The Westin Bonaventure, **11**

University Hilton Los Angeles, **5**

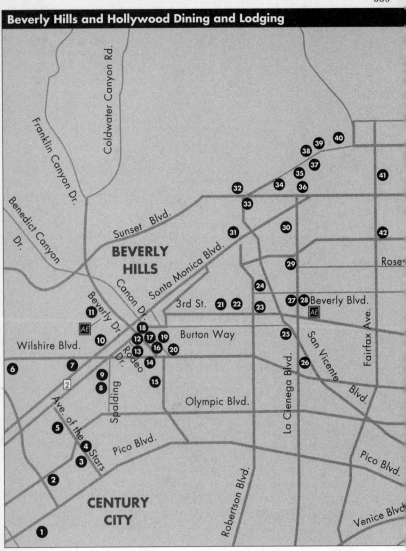

Dining

Antonio's Restaurant, **44**
The Bistro, **16**
The Bistro Garden, **20**
Border Grill, **42**
California Pizza Kitchen, **15**
Carnegie Deli, **18**
Cha Cha Cha, **53**

Chan Dara, **46**
Chasen's, **24**
Chopstix, **45**
Citrus, **47**
Columbia Bar & Grill, **49**
The Dining Room, **14**
Ed Debevic's, **26**
El Cholo, **56**
The Grill, **13**

Hard Rock Cafe, **27**
Harry's Bar & American Grill, **4**
Jimmy's, **8**
L.A. Nicola, **52**
La Toque, **40**
Le Dome, **34**
Locanda Veneta, **23**
L'Orangerie, **30**
The Mandarin, **12**

Nate 'n Al's, **17**
The Palm, **31**
Prego, **11**
Primi, **1**
Restaurant Katsu, **51**
RJ's the Rib Joint, **19**
Spago, **32**
Tommy Tang's, **43**
Trader Vic's, **9**
Trumps, **29**
Tuttobene, **41**

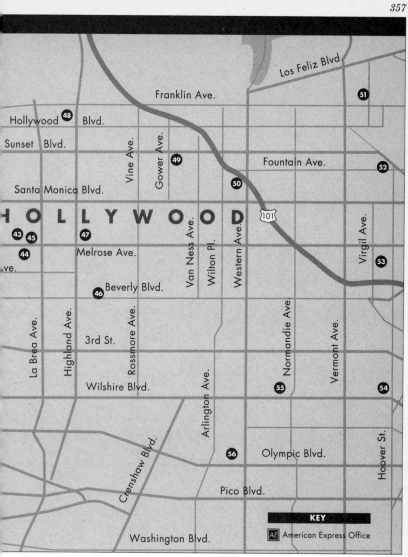

Lodging

Beverly Hills Comstock, **6**

Beverly House Hotel, **9**

Beverly Rodeo, **10**

Century City Inn, **2**

Century Plaza Hotel, **5**

Château Marmont Hotel, **39**

Four Seasons Los Angeles, **22**

Hollywood Holiday Inn, **48**

Hotel Nikko, **25**

Hyatt on Sunset, **38**

Hyatt Wilshire, **55**

J W Marriott Hotel at Century City, **3**

L'Ermitage Hotel, **21**

Le Bel Age Hotel, **33**

Le Dufy Hotel, **36**

Le Mondrian Hotel, **35**

Ma Maison Sofitel Hotel, **28**

Peninsula Beverly Hills, **7**

Regent Beverly Wilshire, **14**

Saint James's Club, **37**

Sheraton Towne House, **54**

Sunset Dunes Motel, **50**

Dining

Babettes, **19**
Beaurivage, **1**
Chinois on Main, **12**
Dynasty Room, **17**
Gillilands, **11**
Gladstone's 4 Fish, **6**
The Good Earth, **25**
Granita, **3**
The Hotel Bel-Air, **4**
La Scala-Malibu, **2**
Orleans, **13**
Valentino, **23**
West Beach Cafe, **14**

Lodging

Barnaby's Hotel, **21**
The Hotel Bel-Air, **4**
Best Western Royal
Palace Hotel, **24**
Carmel Hotel, **5**
Century Wilshire, **26**
Doubletree Inn, **15**
Holiday Inn Santa
Monica Pier, **10**
Loews Santa Monica
Beach Hotel, **8**
Marina del Rey
Hotel, **20**
Marina International
Hotel, **18**
Marina Pacific Hotel &
Suites, **17**
Miramar Sheraton, **7**
Pacific Shore, **9**
The Ritz-Carlton,
Marina del Rey, **16**
Sheraton at Redondo
Beach, **22**
Westwood Marquis, **27**

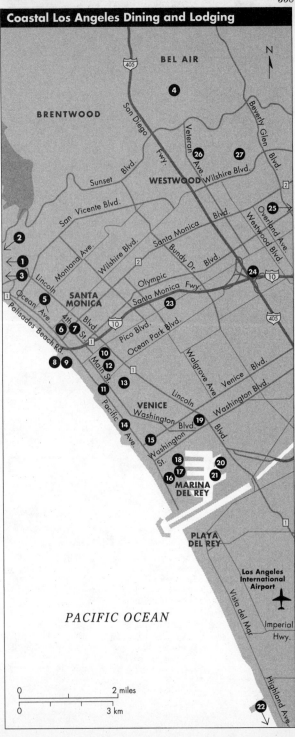

Coastal Los Angeles Dining and Lodging

Downtown **Pacific Dining Car.** This is one of L.A.'s oldest restaurants, located in a 1920s railroad car and expanded over the years. Best-known for well-aged steaks, rack of lamb, and an extensive California wine list at fair prices, it's a favorite haunt of politicians and lawyers around City Hall and of sports fans after Dodger games. *1310 W. 6th St., tel. 213/483–6000. Reservations advised. Dress: casual. Valet parking. MC, V. Moderate–Expensive.*

Engine Co. #28. The ground floor of this National Historic Site building was refurbished and refitted to become a very polished, "uptown" downtown bar and grill, and it's been crowded from day one. The reason? All-American food carefully prepared and served with obvious pride. Don't miss the corn chowder, "Firehouse" chili, grilled pork chop, smoked rare tenderloin, and grilled ahi tuna. And there's a great lemon meringue pie. *Figueroa St. and Wilshire Blvd., tel. 213/624–6966. Reservations required. Jacket and tie suggested at lunch, dress casual at dinner. Valet parking. AE, MC, V. No lunch weekends. Moderate.*

Eastside **The Chronicle.** You'll think you're in San Francisco's Sam's or the Tadich Grill, both very good places to be. The Chronicle's steaks, chops, prime rib, oysters and other shellfish are excellent, and it has one of the best California wine lists south of the Napa Valley. *897 Granite Dr., tel. 818/792–1179. Reservations advised. Jacket and tie required. Valet parking. AE, D, DC, MC, V. Moderate.*

Hollywood **Columbia Bar & Grill.** Located front and center in the heart of Tinsel Town, this comfortably contemporary restaurant, with Jasper Johns and David Hockney artwork on the walls, is the daytime mecca for people from the surrounding television and film studios. The food is definitely above par. Don't pass up the crab cakes; Caesar salad; or the fish, fowl, and meats grilled over a variety of flavor-filled woods. *1448 N. Gower St., tel. 213/461–8800. Reservations required. Dress: casual. Valet parking. AE, DC, MC, V. Closed Sun. Moderate–Expensive.*

L.A. Nicola. Owner/chef Larry Nicola spent his early years in his family's produce market. His appreciation for fresh vegetables, seafood, and meats is evident in all his offerings, as is his penchant for offbeat American cooking, utilizing the bounty of California's farms and waters. Nicola raises the lowly hamburger to a place of eminence. And don't miss the grilled shark, veal chop with capers, or the appetizer of fried artichoke hearts. Perhaps the nicest thing about this California-style bistro, with its white walls and huge pails of fresh flowers, is its hideaway atmosphere. It is a place with style but no pretensions. *4326 Sunset Blvd., tel. 213/660–7217. Reservations advised. Dress: casual. Valet parking. AE, DC, MC, V. Closed Sun. Moderate.*

San Fernando Valley **Paty's.** Located near NBC, Warner Brothers, and the Disney Studio, Paty's is a good place for stargazing without having to mortgage your home to pay for the meal. This is an all-American–style upgraded coffee shop with a comfortable, eclectic decor. Breakfasts are charming; the omelets are plump, and the biscuits are homemade and served with high-quality jam. Lunches and dinners include Swiss steak and a hearty beef stew that is served in a hollowed-out loaf of home-baked bread. All desserts are worth saving room for: New Orleans bread pudding with a hot brandy sauce is popular, and the Danishes are gigantic. *10001 Riverside Dr., Toluca Lake, tel. 818/760–9164. No reservations. Dress: casual. No credit cards. Inexpensive.*

West Hollywood **Chasen's.** It may no longer be Hollywood's "in" spot (and it hasn't been for a very long time), but the clublike rooms are full of nostalgia and have a quaintly formal charm, two qualities that are making a comeback in the low-profile '90s. The dishes that Alfred Hitchcock, Gary Cooper, and Henry Fonda loved—and George Burns still does—are as good as ever: hobo steak, double-rib lamb chops, boiled beef with matzo dumplings, and the late Dave Chasen's famous chili. For the finales, try the sensational banana shortcake or frozen éclair. This is a place for special celebrations and great old-time service. *9039 Beverly Blvd., tel. 310/271–2168. Weekend reservations advised. Jacket and tie required. Valet parking. AE, MC, V. No lunch weekends. Closed Mon. Expensive.*

The Palm. If you don't mind the roar of the jocks, or having the New York–style waiters rush you through your Bronx cheesecake, this is where you'll find the biggest and best steamed Maine lobster, good steaks and chops, great french-fried onion rings, and paper-thin potato slices. Have the roast beef hash for lunch, and you can skip dinner. A three-person-deep bar adds to the noise. *9001 Santa Monica Blvd., tel. 310/550–8811. Reservations advised. Dress: casual. Valet parking. AE, DC, MC, V. No lunch weekends. Expensive.*

The Hard Rock Cafe. Big burgers, rich milkshakes, banana splits, BLTs, and other pre-nouvelle food delights, along with loud music, and rock-and-roll memorabilia have made this '50s-era barn of a café the favorite of local teenagers. There is a large and busy bar for curious adults, many of whom are parents watching the kids. The place drew national attention—and spawned other Hard Rocks—for its fish-tail Cadillac jutting out of the roof, Fonzie's leather jacket on the wall, and Elvis's motorcycle. *8600 Beverly Blvd., tel. 310/276–7605. No reservations. Dress: casual. Valet parking. AE, DC, MC, V. Inexpensive.*

Westside **West Beach Cafe.** It seems that Bruce Madder can do no wrong. ★ More than 10 years ago, he opened this upscale restaurant within a Frisbee toss of the action on the Venice Beach strand. Next came Rebecca's, just across the street, where Mexican food is treated as semi-haute cuisine and idolized by the upscale. Then came his most recent hit, the Broadway Deli in Santa Monica. Best bets at the West Beach are: Caesar salad, filet mignon taco, braised lamb shank, ravioli with port and radicchio, fisherman's soup, and what many consider the best hamburger and fries in all of Los Angeles. There's also a fabulous selection of French wines and after-dinner liqueurs. *60 N. Venice Blvd., tel. 310/823–5396. Reservations advised. Dress: casual. Valet parking. AE, DC, MC, V. Moderate–Expensive.*

Gilliland's. Gerri Gilliland was teaching cooking in her native Ireland, took a vacation in Southern California, and never went back. Instead, she stayed and created this charming restaurant, which offers the best of both culinary worlds and showcases her fascination with Mediterranean dishes. The soda bread, Irish stew, and corned beef and cabbage are wonderful; and marvelous is the only word for her bitter lemon tart. The place is warm and friendly, just like its owner. *2424 Main*

St., Santa Monica, tel. 310/392–3901. Reservations advised. Dress: casual. AE, MC, V. Moderate.

Gladstone's 4 Fish. This is undoubtedly the most popular restaurant along the Southern California coast, serving well over a million beach goers a year. Perhaps the food is not the greatest in the world, but familiar seashore fare is prepared adequately and in large portions, and the prices are certainly right. Best bets: crab chowder, steamed clams, three-egg omelets, hamburgers, barbecued ribs, and chili. And then there's the wonderful view, especially from the beach-side terrace—ideal for whale-, porpoise-, and people-watching. *17300 Pacific Coast Hwy. at Sunset Blvd., Pacific Palisades, tel. 310/GL4–FISH. Dress: casual. Reservations advised. Valet parking. AE, DC, MC, V. Inexpensive.*

Cajun
Westside

Orleans. The jambalaya and gumbo dishes are hot—in more ways than one—at this spacious eatery, where the cuisine was created with the help of New Orleans celebrity-chef Paul Prudhomme. The blackened redfish is probably the best catch on the menu. *11705 National Blvd., W. Los Angeles, tel. 310/479–4187. Reservations advised. Dress: casual. AE, DC, MC, V. Moderate.*

California
Beverly Hills

The Bistro Garden. The flower-banked outdoor dining terrace makes this the quintessential Southern California luncheon experience. It's chic and lively without being pretentious or too "Hollywood." There's excellent smoked salmon, fresh cracked crab, steak tartare, calves' liver with bacon, and a unique apple pancake. *176 N. Canon Dr., tel. 310/550–3900. Reservations required. Jacket and tie required at dinner. Valet parking. AE, DC, MC, V. Closed Sun. Moderate–Expensive.*

★ **The Dining Room.** Located in the remodeled Regent Beverly Wilshire, this elegant, European-looking salon is the best thing to happen to L.A. hotel dining in decades: wonderful California cuisine, plus splendid service at surprisingly non-posh prices. Adjoining is an equally attractive, sophisticated cocktail lounge, with romantic lighting and a pianist playing show tunes. *9500 Wilshire Blvd., tel. 310/275–5200. Reservations advised. Jacket and tie required. Valet parking. AE, DC, MC, V. Moderate.*

California Pizza Kitchen. This is the place to go if you hanker for a good pizza at a fair price but don't feel like the usual pizza-parlor surroundings. There's an immaculate, pleasingly modern dining room, plus counter service by the open kitchen, and a wide, rather esoteric choice of pizza toppings. The pastas are equally interesting and carefully prepared. The few sidewalk tables are in great demand. *207 S. Beverly Dr., tel. 310/272–7878. No reservations. Dress: casual. AE, MC, V. Inexpensive.*

West Hollywood
★

Citrus. Tired of being known only as one of the country's greatest pastry chefs, Michel Richard opened this contemporary restaurant to display the breadth of his talent. He creates superb dishes by blending French and American cuisines. You can't miss with the delectable tuna burger, the thinnest-possible angel-hair pasta, or the deep-fried potatoes, sautéed foie gras, rare duck, or sweetbread salads. Get your doctor's permission before even looking at Richard's irresistible desserts. *6703 Melrose Ave., tel. 310/857–0034. Reservations advised. Jacket required. Valet parking. AE, MC, V. Closed Sun. Moderate–Expensive.*

★ **Spago.** This is the restaurant that propelled owner/chef Wolfgang Puck into the national and international culinary spotlights. He deserves every one of his accolades for raising California cuisine to an imaginative and joyous gastronomic level, using only the finest West Coast produce. The proof is in the tasting: grilled baby Sonoma lamb, pizza with Santa Barbara shrimp, thumbnail-size Washington oysters topped with golden caviar, grilled free-range chickens, and, from the North Pacific, baby salmon. As for Puck's incredible desserts, he's on Weight Watchers' Most Wanted List. This is the place to see *People* magazine live, but you'll have to put up with the noise in exchange. Play it safe: Make reservations at least two weeks in advance. *1114 Horn Ave., tel. 310/652–4025. Reservations required. Jacket required. Valet parking. AE, DC, MC, V. No lunch. Moderate–Expensive.*

Trumps. In this smartly designed contemporary adobe building, with striking abstract art on the pure-white walls, the best artist in the house is chef/co-owner Michael Roberts. This imaginative young American takes special pleasure in combining offbeat flavors that result in a delectable whole: brie-and-apple bisque, salmon tartare with tomatillo, corn pancakes with mussels, duck breast and pickled pumpkin, and gingersnap cheesecake. This place is the perfect cure for jaded appetites and a popular rendezvous for L.A.'s tastemakers. It also serves the best afternoon tea in town. *8764 Melrose Ave., tel. 310/855–1480. Reservations advised. Jacket required. AE, DC, MC, V. No lunch weekends. Moderate–Expensive.*

Westside **Hotel Bel-Air.** Even if the food were terrible, you wouldn't care,
★ since the romantic, country-garden setting is, by itself, so satisfying. But the California-Continental cooking is very good indeed, be it breakfast, lunch, or dinner. A meal at the Bel-Air is a not-to-be-missed experience. *701 Stone Canyon Rd., Bel Air, tel. 310/472–1211. Reservations advised. Jacket and tie advised for dinner. Valet parking. AE, DC, MC, V. Expensive.*

Granita. At Wolfgang Puck's latest triumph, close to $3 million was spent on construction, and the interior detail work includes handmade tiles embedded with seashells, blown-glass lighting fixtures, and etched-glass panels with wavey edges. It's as close as you'll come to the beach without getting sand in your shoes. Even the blasé Malibu film colony is impressed. While Puck's menu favors seafood items such as grilled John Dory with a Thai curry sauce, Mediterranean fish soup with half a lobster, seared Nantucket scallops on black pepper fettuccini, there are also some of his standard favorites like spicy shrimp pizza, ginger duck stir-fry in a scallion pancake, grilled quail on pumpkin ravioli, and wild mushroom risotto. *23725 W. Malibu Rd., Malibu, tel. 310/456–0488. Reservations required 1 wk. in advance. Dress: casual chic. AE, DC, MC, V. No lunch Mon.–Tues. Moderate–Expensive.*

Caribbean **Cha Cha Cha.** When the Cajun cuisine craze cooled off among
Hollywood L.A. foodies, Caribbean cooking became the trend, and this small shack of a place was, for a while, the hottest spot in town. There's cornmeal chicken, spicy swordfish, fried banana chips, and assorted flans. This is a hangout for celebrities gone slumming. A "Valley" branch (17499 Ventura Blvd., Encino, tel. 818/789–3600) of Cha Cha Cha has recently opened, in much more stylish quarters. *656 N. Virgil Ave., tel. 310/664–7723.*

Reservations required, but expect to wait. Dress: casual. Valet parking. AE, DC, MC, V. Moderate.

Chinese
Beverly Hills
★

The Mandarin. Who said you only find great Chinese food in hole-in-the-wall places with oilcloth-topped tables? Here is a good- looking restaurant with the best crystal and linens, serving an equally bright mixture of Szechuan and Chinese country cooking. Minced squab in lettuce-leaf tacos, Peking duck, a superb beggar's chicken, scallion pancakes, and any of the noodle dishes are recommended. *430 N. Camden Dr., tel. 310/272–0267. Reservations required. Jacket required. Valet parking. AE, DC, MC, V. No lunch weekends. Moderate.*

Downtown
★

Mon Kee Seafood Restaurant. The name pretty much spells it out—except how good the cooking is and how morning-fresh the fish are. The delicious garlic crab is addictive; the steamed catfish is a masterpiece of gentle flavors. In fact, almost everything on the menu is excellent. This is a crowded, messy place; be prepared to wait for a table. *679 N. Spring St., tel. 213/628–6717. No reservations. Dress: casual. Pay-parking lot. MC, V. Inexpensive–Moderate.*

Pasadena
★

Yujean Kang's Gourmet Chinese Cuisine. Despite its length, this name doesn't say it all. Mr. Kang, formerly of San Francisco, is well on his way to becoming the finest nouvelle-Chinese chef in the nation. Forget any and all preconceived notions of what Chinese food should look and taste like. Start with the tender slices of veal on a bed of enoki and black mushrooms, topped with a tangle of quick-fried shoestring yams, or the catfish with kumquats and a passion fruit sauce, and finish with poached plums, or watermelon ice under a mantle of white chocolate, and you will appreciate that this is no chop-suey joint. *69 N. Raymond Ave., tel. 818/585–0855. Dress: casual. AE, MC, V. No lunch Thurs.–Sun. Closed Tues. Moderate–Expensive.*

West Hollywood

Chopstix. Never underestimate the ability of Californians to adopt—and adapt—an ethnic-food vogue. In this case, dim sum, subtly doctored for non-Oriental tastes. The result is nouvelle-Chinese junk food served in a mod setting, at high-stool tables or at a dinerlike counter. The dishes are appetizing, but don't expect a native Chinese to agree. Nonetheless, branches are springing up all over the Southland, faster than you can say "I'd like one of those . . ." The latest addition is in Malibu. *729 Melrose Ave., West Hollywood, tel. 310/935–2944. 22917 Pacific Coast Hwy., Malibu, tel. 310/456–7774. No reservations. Dress: casual. AE, DC, MC, V. Inexpensive.*

Continental
Beverly Hills

The Bistro. The kitchen is not quite as good as Jimmy's (see below), but nobody has ever questioned that this replica of a Parisian boîte is one of the most stylish dining rooms west of Europe. The original owner, director Billy Wilder, was responsible for the interior design: mirrored walls, etched-glass partitions, giant bouquets of fresh flowers, and soft lighting. The food is more American bistro than French. There is a delicious, juicy chopped steak, good veal medallions, Eastern lobster on tagliatelli (flat, ribbon pasta), and, most likely, the greatest chocolate soufflé you've ever tasted. *246 N. Canon Dr., tel. 310/273–5633. Reservations required. Jacket and tie required. Valet parking. AE, DC, MC, V. No lunch Sat. Closed Sun. Expensive.*

Century City **Jimmy's.** When the Beverly Hills CEOs are not entertaining, they head here or to the Bistro (*see* above). Owner Jimmy Murphy provides the warmth in this expensive, decorator-elegant restaurant. The best dishes on the broad menu include smoked Scottish salmon, prawns with herbs and garlic, saddle of lamb, chateaubriand, and pheasant breast with wild blueberry sauce. There's steak tartare at lunch. *201 Moreno Dr., tel. 310/ 879–2394. Reservations required. Jacket and tie required. Valet parking. AE, DC, MC, V. Expensive.*

San Fernando Valley **Europa.** The menu here roams the world: great goulash, terrific teriyaki—even matzo-ball soup. The dining room is tiny and casual; reservations are a must, as this is a community favorite. *14929 Magnolia Blvd., Sherman Oaks, tel. 818/501–9175. Reservations advised. Dress: casual. MC, V. No lunch. Closed Mon. Inexpensive–Moderate.*

Westwood **Dynasty Room.** This peaceful, elegant room in the Westwood Marquis Hotel has a European flair and tables set far enough apart for privacy. Besides well-handled Continental fare, there is a *cuisine minceur* menu for calorie counters. Best of all is an especially lavish, excellent Sunday brunch. *930 Hilgard Ave., tel. 310/208–8765. Reservations required. Jacket and tie required. Valet parking. AE, DC, MC, V. No lunch. Moderate.*

Deli **Carnegie Deli.** Oil millionaire Marvin Davis got tired of jetting *Beverly Hills* cheesecake, pastrami, and lox back from the parent Carnegie in New York City, so he financed a Beverly Hills taste-alike to challenge Nate 'n Al's preeminence. His big guns are corned beef and pastrami sandwiches that are 4½ inches high, cheese blintzes under a snowcap of sour cream, and wonderfully creamy cole slaw. *300 N. Beverly Dr., tel. 310/275–3354. No reservations. Dress: casual. AE, MC, V. Inexpensive.*

Nate 'n Al's. A famous gathering place for Hollywood comedians, gag writers, and their agents. Nate 'n Al's serves first-rate matzo-ball soup, lox and scrambled eggs, cheese blintzes, potato pancakes, and the best deli sandwiches west of Manhattan. *414 N. Beverly Dr., tel. 310/274–0101. No reservations. Dress: casual. AE, V. Free parking. Inexpensive.*

San Fernando Valley **Art's Delicatessen.** One of the best Jewish-style delicatessens in the city serves breakfast, lunch, and dinner daily. The sandwiches are mammoth and are made from some of the best corned beef, pastrami, and other cold cuts around. Matzo-ball soup and sweet-and-sour cabbage soup are specialties, and there is good chopped chicken liver. *12224 Ventura Blvd., Studio City, tel. 818/762–1221. No reservations. Dress: casual. D, DC, MC, V. Inexpensive.*

French **L'Orangerie.** For sheer elegance and classic good taste, it would *West Hollywood* be hard to find a lovelier restaurant in this country. And the ★ cuisine, albeit nouvelle-light, is as French as the l'Orangerie at Versailles. Specialties include coddled eggs served in the shell and topped with caviar, squab with foie gras, pot-au-feu, rack of lamb for two, and an unbeatable apple tart served with a jug of double cream. *903 N. La Cienega Blvd., tel. 213/652–9770. Reservations required. Jacket and tie required. Valet parking. AE, DC, MC, V. No lunch. Expensive.*

★ **La Toque.** Amid the hurly-burly of the Sunset Strip is this small, unassuming, one-story building. But step through the door, and you've entered a French country inn. This charming hideaway is the province of Ken Frank, one of the nation's best

American, French-cooking chefs. Each day some new delight graces the menu: raviolis stuffed with foie gras and pheasant, fettuccine with egg and black truffle, venison seared with Armagnac, or grilled duck breast in a Calvados sauce. Be sure to order the roasted, shredded potato pancake with golden caviar and crème fraîche. *8171 Sunset Blvd., tel. 213/656–7515. Reservations required. Jacket required. Valet parking. AE, DC, MC, V. No lunch Sat. Closed Sun. Moderate–Expensive.*

Le Dome. For some reason, local food critics have never given this brasserie the attention it deserves. Perhaps they are intimidated by the hordes of show- and music-biz celebrities who keep the place humming. By and large the food is wonderful, honest, down-to-earth French: cockles in white wine and shallots, veal ragout, marvelous veal sausage with red cabbage, and a genuine, stick-to-the-ribs cassoulet. *8720 Sunset Blvd., tel. 213/659–6919. Reservations required. Dress: casual. Valet parking. AE, DC, MC, V. Closed Sun. Moderate.*

Westside ★ **Chinois on Main.** The second of the Wolfgang Puck pack of restaurants, this one is designed in tongue-in-cheek kitsch by his wife, Barbara Lazaroff. Both the look of the place and Puck's merging of Chinese and French cuisines for contemporary tastes are great good fun. A few of the least resistible dishes on an irresistible menu include Mongolian lamb with eggplant, poach-curried oysters, whole catfish garnished with ginger and green onions, and rare duck with a wondrous plum sauce. The best desserts are three differently flavored crèmes brûlées. This is one of L.A.'s most crowded spots—and one of the noisiest. Bring earplugs. *2709 Main St., Santa Monica, tel. 310/392–9025. Reservations required for dinner. Dress: casual. Valet parking in evening. AE, DC, MC, V. No lunch Sat.–Tues. Moderate–Expensive.*

Beaurivage. A charming, romantic restaurant designed in the fashion of an *auberge* (an inn) on the Côte D'Azur, this is the best of the Malibu dining places with a view of the beach and ocean. The menu complements the Provençal atmosphere: roast duckling Mirabelle, pasta with shellfish, mussel soup, filet mignon with a three-mustard sauce and, in season, wild game specials. It's a satisfying getaway. *26025 Pacific Coast Hwy., tel. 310/456–5733. Reservations required. Dress: casual. Parking lot. AE, D, MC, V. No lunch weekday or Sat. Moderate–Expensive.*

Babette's. It may not be in the most attractive area of Marina del Rey, but this small French restaurant with its delightful outdoor dining gazebo deserves a star for the superiority of chef/owner Christian Royere's cuisine and his wife, Babette's gracious hostessing. Add to that the low menu prices and Babette's becomes a rare find in Los Angeles. You'll be pleased by anything you order, but a few of Royere's best offerings include Niçoise salad, the best pâtés in town, house-cured salmon, grilled quail wrapped in spinach leaves, grilled tiger shrimp and mussels, and pear tart. *3100 Washington Blvd., tel. 310/822–2020. Reservations advised. Dress: casual. AE, DC, V. No lunch weekends. Closed Sun. Moderate.*

Greek
San Fernando
Valley
Great Greek. This joint jumps with Greek music and everyone joins in for Old World dancing. The food is a delight: loukaniki; Greek sausages; butter-fried calamari; and two kinds of shish kebab. *13362 Ventura Blvd., Sherman Oaks, tel. 818/905–5250. Reservations advised. Dress: casual. Valet parking. AE, DC, MC, V. Moderate.*

Health Food   **The Good Earth.** Eating healthfully doesn't have to mean a
Westside   strict diet of alfalfa sprouts and wheat germ. The menus of this
health-oriented chain feature whole-grain breads, desserts
baked with honey, and entrées heavy on fruit and vegetables
rather than on meat. Even the decor, with earth-tone walls and
furnishings and macramé and wicker baskets on the walls, is
earthy. Breakfast items include turkey sausages, 10-grain
sourdough pancakes, and a choice of omelets. Vegetarian burgers, curried chicken, and Zhivago's beef Stroganoff are superi-
or lunch and dinner specialties. *10700 W. Pico Blvd., tel. 310/
475–7557. Reservations accepted. Dress: casual. MC, V. Inexpensive–Moderate.*

Italian   **Primi.** Valentino's younger, less expensive brother has a menu
Beverly Hills   that features a wide variety of appetizer-size portions of northern Italian treats, including pasta and salad selections. This is a
cheerful, contemporary setting, with a pleasant outside terrace. *10543 W. Pico Blvd., tel. 310/475–9235. Reservations advised. Jacket required. Valet parking. AE, DC, MC, V. Closed
Sun. Moderate.*

Prego. This is a super bargain in the highest of high-rent districts. The baby lamb chops, large broiled veal chop, and Florentine rib steak are among the best, dollar for dollar, in town.
The house-baked bread sticks are great. *362 N. Camden Dr.,
tel. 310/277–7346. Reservations advised. Dress: casual. Valet
parking in evening. AE, DC, MC, V. No lunch Sun. Inexpensive–Moderate.*

Century City   **Harry's Bar & American Grill.** A more posh, private, and uptown version of Prego, this is run by the same management.
The decor and selection of dishes are acknowledged copies of
Harry's Bar in Florence, but you'll find that for first-rate
food—paper-thin carpaccio, excellent pastas, grilled fish and
steaks, along with fine hamburgers—the check will be far lower than it would be in Italy. This is the best place to dine before
or after seeing a movie in the area. *2020 Ave. of the Stars, tel.
310/277–2333. Reservations advised. Jacket required. Valet
parking. AE, DC, MC, V. No lunch Sun. Moderate.*

Downtown   **Rex Il Ristorante.** Owner Mauro Vincenti probably knows more
★   about Italian cuisine than any other restaurateur in this country. The Rex is the ideal showcase for his talents: Two ground
floors of a historic Art Deco building were remodeled to resemble the main dining salon of the circa-1930 Italian luxury liner
Rex. The cuisine, the lightest of *nuova cucina*, is equally special. Be prepared for small and costly portions. *617 S. Olive St.,
tel. 213/627–2300. Reservations required. Jacket and tie required. Valet parking. AE, DC, MC, V. No lunch Sat.–Wed.
Closed Sun. Very Expensive.*

West Hollywood   **Locanda Veneta.** The food may be more finely wrought at one or
★   two other spots, but the combination of a splendid Venetian
chef, Antonio Tomassi, and a simpatico co-owner, Jean Louis de
Mori, has re-created the atmospheric equivalent of a genuine
Italian trattoria, at reasonable prices. Specialties include fried
whitebait, risotto with porcini mushrooms, veal chop, ricotta
and potato dumplings, linguini with clams, lobster ravioli with
saffron sauce, and pear tart. *8638 W. 3rd St., tel. 310/274–1893.
Reservations required. Jacket required. Valet parking. AE,
DC, MC, V. No lunch Sat. Closed Sun. Moderate.*

Tuttobene. If Silvio de Mori, Jean Louis's older brother, served
nothing more than peanut-butter sandwiches, his place would

still be doing SRO business. But this best-loved restaurateur, a genuinely gracious, caring host, also happens to provide some of the most delectable trattoria dishes west of Tuscany. There are different, freshly baked breads every day, superb down-to-earth pastas and *gnocchi* (dumplings), luscious risotto with wild mushrooms, picked-that-morning arugula salad—all at very fair prices. *945 N. Fairfax Ave., tel. 310/655–7051. Reservations required. Dress: casual. Valet parking. AE, MC, V. Moderate.*

Westside **Valentino.** Rated among the best Italian restaurants in the na-
★ tion, Valentino is generally considered to have the best wine list outside Italy. Owner Piero Selvaggio is the man who introduced Los Angeles to the best and lightest of modern-day Italian cuisine, and the grateful natives have loved him ever since. There's superb prosciutto, bresola, fried calamari, lobster cannelloni, fresh broiled porcini mushrooms, and osso buco. *3115 Pico Blvd., Santa Monica, tel. 213/829–4313. Reservations required. Jacket required. Valet parking. AE, DC, MC, V. No lunch Sat.–Thurs. Closed Sun. Expensive.*

La Scala Malibu. Malibu's most celebrity-crowded hangout has moved to brand-new, cheerful quarters, and, in the process, the northern Italian food has improved, and the prices have come down a notch. You can't quite see the ocean, but you can see stars, as in "There's Cher over there talking to Olivia Newton-John and Jack Lemmon, next to the table with Larry Hagman and Walter Matthau." *3874 Cross Creek Rd., tel. 310/456–1979. Reservations advised. Dress: casual. AE, MC, V. No lunch weekends. Closed Mon. Moderate.*

Japanese **Restaurant Horikawa.** This department store of Japanese cui-
Downtown sines offers sushi, teppan steak, tempura, sashimi, shabu-shabu (meat and vegetables boiled briefly at your tableside), teriyaki, and a $50-per-person kaiseki (set) dinner. All are good or excellent, but the sushi bar is the best. The decor is traditional Japanese, with private sit-on-the-floor dining rooms for two to 24 people. *111 S. San Pedro St., tel. 213/680–9355. Reservations advised. Jacket and tie required. Valet parking. AE, DC, MC, V. No lunch weekends. Moderate–Expensive.*

Los Feliz **Restaurant Katsu.** A stark, simple, perfectly designed sushi
★ bar with a small table area, Katsu serves the most exquisite and delicious delicacies in all of Southern California. This is a treat for eye and palate. *1972 N. Hillhurst Ave., tel. 213/665–1891. No lunch reservations, dinner reservations advised. Dress: casual. Valet parking. AE, MC, V. No lunch Sat. Moderate.*

Mexican **El Cholo.** This progenitor of the present-day, upscale South-
Hollywood land chain has been packing them in since the '20s. It serves good bathtub-size margaritas, a zesty assortment of tacos, make-your-own tortillas, and, from June to September, green-corn tamales. It's friendly and fun, with large portions for only a few pesos. *1121 S. Western Ave., tel. 213/734–2773. Reservations advised. Dress: casual. Parking lot. AE, MC, V. Inexpensive.*

West Hollywood **Border Grill.** This is a very trendy, very loud storefront place, owned by two female chefs with the most eclectic tastes in town. The menu ranges from crab tacos to vinegared-and-peppered grilled turkey to pickled pork sirloin. It's worth dropping by, if you don't mind the noise while you're there. A much larger, wilder Border Grill (tel. 310/451–1655) has opened across town, in Santa Monica. *7407½ Melrose Ave., tel. 310/ 658–7495. Reservations advised. Dress: casual. AE, MC, V. Moderate.*

Antonio's Restaurant. Don't let the strolling mariachis keep you from hearing the daily specials: authentic Mexico City dishes that put this unpretentious favorite several cuts above the ubiquitous taco-enchilada cantinas. The chayote (squash) stuffed with ground beef; ricotta in a spicy tomato sauce; pork ribs in a sauce of pickled chipotle peppers; veal shank with garlic, cumin, and red pepper; and chicken stuffed with apples, bananas and raisins are definitely worth trying. Have the flan for dessert. *7472 Melrose Ave., tel. 310/655–0480. Dinner reservations advised. Dress: casual. Valet parking. AE, MC, V. Inexpensive–Moderate.*

Polynesian **Trader Vic's.** Sure, it's corny, but this is the most restrained
Beverly Hills and elegant of the late Victor Bergeron's South Sea extravaganzas. Besides, who says corn can't be fun—and tasty, too. The crab Rangoon, grilled cheese wafers, skewered shrimp, grilled pork ribs, and the steaks, chops, and peanut-butter–coated lamb cooked in the huge clay ovens are just fine. As for the array of exotic rum drinks, watch your sips. *9876 Wilshire Blvd., tel. 310/274–7777. Reservations required. Jacket and tie required. Valet parking. AE, DC, MC, V. No lunch. Moderate–Expensive.*

Thai **Chan Dara.** Here you'll find excellent Thai food in a bright and
Hollywood shiny Swiss chalet! Try any of the noodle dishes, especially those with crab and shrimp. There is noise here, but it's bearable. *310 N. Larchmont Blvd., tel. 213/467–1052. Reservations advised for parties of more than 4. Dress: casual. AE, MC, V. Inexpensive.*

West Hollywood **Tommy Tang's.** This place is a very "in" grazing ground for yuppies and celebs alike. So much people-watching goes on, that nobody seems to notice the small portions on the plates. The kitchen features crisp duck marinated in ginger and plum sauce, blackened sea scallops, and a spinach salad tossed with marinated beef. There is also a sushi bar. *7473 Melrose Ave., tel. 213/651–1810. Reservations advised. Dress: casual. Valet parking. AE, DC, MC, V. No lunch. Moderate.*

Lodging

By Jane E. Lasky

You can find almost any kind of accommodations in Los Angeles, from a simple motel room that allows you to park right in front of your room to a posh hotel where an attendant will park your car and whisk you off to a spacious room or to your own bungalow.

Because L.A. is so spread out—it's actually a series of suburbs connected by freeways—it's a good idea to select a hotel room not only for its ambience, amenities, and price but also for a location that is convenient to where you plan to spend most of your time. West Hollywood and Beverly Hills are at the heart of the city, equidistant from the beaches and downtown. Downtown is attractive if you are interested in Los Angeles's cultural offerings since this is where the Music Center and the Museum of Contemporary Art are located. The more recently developed Century City, located between Westwood and Beverly Hills, and built around the back lot of Twentieth Century Fox, offers quick access to Rodeo Drive shopping. If it's the Pacific that lures you with its miles of sandy beach, be sure to book a hotel on the Westside. To be as close as possible to the beach, check-in in Santa Monica, Marina del Rey, or Malibu.

It's best to plan ahead and reserve a room; many hotels offer special prices for weekend visits and offer tickets to amusement parks or plays. A travel agent can help in making your arrangements.

Hotels are listed in categories determined first by location: Downtown, Mid-Wilshire, Hollywood/West Hollywood, Beverly Hills/Bel Air, West Los Angeles, Santa Monica, Marina del Rey, South Bay Beach Cities, the Airport, and the San Fernando Valley. They are further divided, under location, into categories determined (roughly) by the price of a room for two people, on the European plan.

The most highly recommended accommodations are indicated by a star ★.

Category	Cost*
Very Expensive	over $155
Expensive	$110–$155
Moderate	$70–$110
Inexpensive	under $70

for a double room

Downtown
Very Expensive

Biltmore Hotel. Since its 1923 opening, the Biltmore has hosted such notables as Mary Pickford, J. Paul Getty, Eleanor Roosevelt, Princess Margaret, and several U.S. presidents. Now a historic landmark, it was renovated in 1986 for $35 million, with modern, updated guest rooms decorated in pastels. The lobby ceiling was painted by Italian artist Giovanni Smeraldi; imported Italian marble and plum-color velvet grace the Grand Avenue Bar, which features excellent jazz nightly. *506 S. Grand Ave., 90071, tel. 213/624–1011 or 800/245–8673. 704 rooms. Facilities: restaurants, lounge, entertainment, health club. AE, DC, MC, V.*

Checkers Kempinski Hotel. With its excellent pedigree and smaller scale, Checkers is a sophisticated, welcome addition to the downtown hotel scene. Set in one of this neighborhood's few remaining historic buildings, this property opened as the Mayflower Hotel in 1927. Rooms are furnished with oversize beds, upholstered easy chairs, writing tables, and minibars. A library is available for small meetings or tea. *535 S. Grand Ave., 90071, tel. 213/624–0000. 190 rooms. Facilities: restaurant, rooftop spa and lap pool, exercise studio. AE, DC, MC, V.*

Hyatt Regency, Los Angeles. The Hyatt is located in the heart of the "new" downtown financial district, minutes away from the Convention Center, Dodger Stadium, and the Music Center. Each room has a wall of windows with city views. The Regency Club has a private lounge. The hotel is part of the Broadway Plaza, which comprises 35 shops. Nearby tennis and health-club facilities are available at an extra cost. *711 S. Hope St., 90017, tel. 213/683–1234 or 800/233–1234. 485 rooms. Facilities: restaurant, coffee shop, lounge, entertainment. AE, DC, MC, V.*

★ **Sheraton Grande Hotel.** Opened in 1983, this 14-story, mirrored hotel is near Dodger Stadium, the Music Center, and downtown's Bunker Hill district. Rooms have dark wood furniture, sofas, minibars; colors are aqua or copper; baths are marble. Butler service on each floor is provided. Stay in the penthouse suite if you can afford it. Limousine service is available, and there are privileges at a local health club. *333 S. Figueroa St., 90071, tel. 213/617–1133 or 800/325–3535. 469 rooms. Facilities: restaurants, nightclub, outdoor pool, 23 meeting rooms, 4 movie theaters. AE, DC, MC, V.*

Westin Bonaventure. This is architect John Portman's striking masterpiece: a 35-story, circular-towered, mirrored-glass high rise in the center of downtown. Rooms have a wall of glass, streamlined pale furnishings, and comfortable appointments. The outside elevators provide stunning city views and there are 5 acres of ponds and waterfalls in the lobby. *404 S. Figueroa St., 90071, tel. 213/624–1000 or 800/228–3000. 1,474 rooms. Facilities: restaurant, lounge, entertainment, pool, 5-level shopping arcade. AE, DC, MC, V.*

Expensive–
Very Expensive
★
New Otani Hotel and Garden. East meets West in L.A., and the exotic epicenter downtown is this 21-story, ultramodern hotel surrounded by Japanese gardens and waterfalls. The decor combines a serene blend of westernized luxury and Japanese simplicity. Each room has a refrigerator, an alarm clock, color TV, and phone in the bathroom, and most provide a yukata (robe). For the ultimate Little Tokyo experience, book a Japanese suite. These suites are so authentic that guests sleep on futons on mats on the floor. *120 S. Los Angeles St., 90012, tel. 213/629–1200; 800/421–8795; in CA, 800/273-2294. 440 rooms. Facilities: restaurants, nightclubs, sauna and massage (fee), parking (fee). AE, DC, MC, V.*

University Hilton Los Angeles. If you're doing business at USC, the Coliseum, or the Sports Arena, this is the best hotel in the area. All the modern-style rooms have a view of the pool area, the lush gardens, or the nearby USC campus. It's well equipped to handle banquets and conventions. *3540 S. Figueroa St., 90007, tel. 213/748–4141; 800/445–8667; in CA, 800/872–1104. 241 rooms. Facilities: restaurant, coffee shop, lounge, pool, parking (fee). AE, DC, MC, V.*

Moderate
Figueroa Hotel. This hotel has managed to keep its charming Spanish style intact as it enters its second half-century. There's a poolside bar. The hotel is on the Gray Line sightseeing tour route and there is airport service every hour to LAX. *939 S. Figueroa St., 90015, tel. 213/627–8971; 800/421–9092; in CA, 800/331–5151. 285 rooms. Facilities: restaurants, coffee shop, lounge, pool, free parking. AE, DC, MC, V.*

Holiday Inn L.A. Downtown. This offers Holiday Inn's usual professional staff and services, and standard room decor. Pets are allowed, and there is plenty of free parking. It's also close to the Museum of Contemporary Art and Dodger Stadium. *750 Garland Ave., 90017, tel. 213/628–5242 or 800/465–4329. 204 rooms. Facilities: restaurant, lounge, pool, parking. AE, DC, MC, V.*

Inexpensive
Orchid Hotel. One of the smaller downtown hotels, this is very reasonably priced. There are no frills, but the standard rooms are clean. Note that there is no parking at the hotel, but public lots are close by. *819 S. Flower St., 90017, tel. 213/624–5855. 66*

rooms. *Facilities: color TV, coin-operated laundry. AE, DC, MC, V.*

Mid-Wilshire **Sheraton Towne House.** Howard Hughes slept (and lived) here.
Expensive– A great example of L.A.'s best Art Deco architecture, this ho-
Very Expensive tel, built in the 1920s, retains its original charm and elegance.
Marble fireplaces, antiques, and cedar-lined closets enhance
the country-estate tone. It's convenient to I. Magnin department store. *2961 Wilshire Blvd., 90010, tel. 213/382–7171 or
800/325–3535. 300 rooms. Facilities: restaurants, coffee shop,
pool, tennis, parking (fee). AE, DC, MC, V.*

Hollywood/West **Le Bel Age Hotel.** This all-suite, European-style hotel has a dis-
Hollywood tinctive restaurant, which features fine Russian meals with an
Very Expensive elegant French flair. There are many extravagant touches, like
★ three telephones with five lines in each suite, original art, private terraces, and courtesy limousine service. Suites that face
south have terrific views looking out over the L.A. skyline as
far as the Pacific. The decor is French-country style. *1020 N.
San Vicente Blvd., West Hollywood 90069, tel. 310/854–1111 or
800/424–4443. 190 suites. Facilities: 2 restaurants, lounge,
pool. AE, DC, MC, V.*
Le Dufy Hotel. This luxury hotel features all suites that are
decorated in a modern style and shades of blue, pink, and salmon. All have private balconies. It's great for business travelers,
near Restaurant Row, and not as expensive as other hotels in
this price category. *1000 Westmont Dr., West Hollywood 90069,
tel. 310/657–7400. 103 suites. Facilities: restaurant, bar, pool,
whirlpool, spa, sauna, sundeck. AE, DC, MC, V.*
Le Mondrian Hotel. Accommodations here are spacious, with
pale wood furniture and curved sofas in the seating area. Ask
for south-corner suites; they tend to be quieter than the rest. A
chauffeured limo is placed at each guest's disposal. The hotel is
convenient to major recording, film, and TV studios. *8440 Sunset Blvd., West Hollywood 90069, tel. 213/650–8999 or 800/424–
4443. 243 suites. Facilities: restaurant, pool, health club, parking. AE, DC, MC, V.*
★ **Saint James's Club/Los Angeles.** Located on the Sunset Strip,
this building has been around since the 1930s; today all the furnishings are exact replicas of Art Deco masterpieces, the originals of which are in New York's Metropolitan Museum of Art.
Ask for a city or mountain view. Both are great, but the cityside accommodations are more expensive. *8358 Sunset Blvd.,
West Hollywood 90069, tel. 213/654–7100 or 800/225–2637. 63
rooms. Facilities: restaurant, health center, sauna, pool, sec-
retarial services, small meeting facilities. AE, DC, MC, V.*

Expensive **Chateau Marmont Hotel.** Although planted on the Sunset Strip
amid giant billboards and much sun-bleached Hollywood glitz,
this castle of Old World charm and French Normandy design
still promises its guests a secluded hideaway close to Hollywood's hot spots. A haunt for many show-biz personalities and
discriminating world travelers since it opened in 1927, this is
the ultimate in privacy. All kinds of accommodations are available, including fully equipped cottages, bungalows, and a penthouse. *8221 Sunset Blvd., Hollywood 90046, tel. 213/656–1010
or 800/CHATEAU. 63 rooms. Facilities: dining room, gardens,
pool, patios. AE, DC, V.*
Hyatt on Sunset. In the heart of the Sunset Strip, this Hyatt is a
favorite of music-biz execs and rock stars. There are penthouse
suites, some rooms with private patios, and a rooftop pool. The

rooms are decorated in peach colors and modern furniture; some have aquariums. *8401 W. Sunset Blvd., West Hollywood 90069, tel. 213/656–4101 or 800/233–1234. 262 rooms. Facilities: restaurant, lounge, entertainment, pool, parking (fee). AE, DC, MC, V.*

Moderate **Hollywood Holiday Inn.** You can't miss this hotel, one of the tallest buildings in Hollywood. It's 23 stories high, topped by Windows, a revolving restaurant-lounge. The rooms are decorated in light gray and rose in standard-issue Holiday Inn fashion. There is a safekeeping box in each room. The hotel is only minutes from the Hollywood Bowl, Universal Studios, and Mann's Chinese Theater, and it's a Gray Line Tour Stop. *1755 N. Highland Ave., Hollywood 90028, tel. 213/462–7181 or 800/465–4329. 468 rooms. Facilities: restaurant, coffee shop, pool, coin laundry, parking (fee). AE, DC, MC, V.*

Inexpensive **Sunset Dunes Motel.** Across the street from two TV stations, this hotel with modern rooms is a popular stop for studio folk. *5625 Sunset Blvd., Hollywood 90028, tel. 213/467–5171; 800/452–3863; in CA, 800/443–8637. 54 rooms. Facilities: restaurant, lounge, free parking. AE, DC, MC, V.*

Beverly Hills **Four Seasons Los Angeles.** This hotel combines the best in East
Very Expensive and West Coast luxury, one of L.A.'s only Mobil Five Star
★ Award–winning properties. Formal European decorative details are complemented by outpourings of flora from the porte cochere to the rooftop pool deck. There is an outstanding restaurant on the premises and great shopping only five minutes away on Rodeo Drive and Melrose Avenue. Many of the suites have French doors and a balcony. *300 S. Doheny Dr., Los Angeles 90048, tel. 310/273–2222 or 800/332–3442. 285 rooms. Facilities: restaurant, 1-hr. pressing service, pool, exercise equipment. AE, DC, MC, V.*

Hotel Nikko. Distinctive Japanese accents distinguish this contemporary hotel located near Restaurant Row. Guest rooms cater to the business traveler with its oversize desks, work areas with computer, and fax hook-up capabilities. Traditional Japanese soaking tubs dominate luxurious bathrooms, and a bedside remote-control conveniently operates in-room lighting, temperature, TV, and stereo. Matrixx, the hotel restaurant, features California cuisine. *465 La Cienega Blvd., Los Angeles 90035 (on fringe of Beverly Hills), tel. 310/247–0400 or 800/NIKKO–US. 304 rooms. Facilities: restaurants, pool, Japanese garden, fitness center, business center, lobby lounge. AE, DC, MC, V.*

★ **L'Ermitage Hotel.** L'Ermitage features Old World charm with modern conveniences, and is one of the few hotels on the West Coast to garner a Mobil Four Star Award. The property is near Beverly Hills' elegant shopping, and Twentieth Century Fox. The suites have balconies and sunken living rooms with fireplaces. The best is the split-level town-house suite. The fine Le Club restaurant is reserved exclusively for hotel guests. Amenities include complimentary Continental breakfast; chauffeured limo within Beverly Hills. *9291 Burton Way, Beverly Hills 90210, tel. 310/278–3344 or 800/424–4443. 114 rooms. Facilities: restaurant, pool, whirlpool, spa, private solarium, parking. AE, DC, MC, V.*

The Peninsula Beverly Hills. The hotel's appearance is classic, done in French Renaissance architecture with contemporary overtones. Rooms are decorated in a residential motif, with antiques, rich fabrics, and marble floors. Minibars and refrigerators can be found behind French doors in all rooms, and all suites are equipped with compact disc players, fax machines, and individual security systems. *9882 Santa Monica Blvd., Beverly Hills 90212, tel. 310/273–4888 or 800/462–7899. 200 rooms. Facilities: restaurants, bars, business center, rooftop gardens, lap pool, health club, poolside cabanas, 24-hr. valet parking, voice mail. AE, DC, MC, V.*

Regent Beverly Wilshire. This famous hotel facing Rodeo Drive and the Hollywood Hills is fittingly stylish, with personal service and extras to match. There are great restaurants on the premises, limo service to the airport, and a multilingual staff. *9500 Wilshire Blvd., Beverly Hills 90212, tel. 310/275–5200 or 800/427–4354. 301 rooms. Facilities: restaurants, pool, health spas, parking (fee). AE, DC, MC, V.*

Expensive **Beverly Hills Comstock.** Because this is a low-rise hotel (only three floors), guests need not walk through long corridors to reach their rooms. All the suites are situated off the pool. Furnishings are smart and contemporary; all feature kitchen/ living room, one bedroom, and bath. *10300 Wilshire Blvd., Beverly Hills 90024, tel. 310/275–5575 or 800/800–1234. 116 rooms. Facilities: restaurant, pool, Jacuzzi, garage. AE, DC, MC, V.*

Beverly Rodeo. Modern elegance characterizes the rooms of this small European-style hotel. Cafe Rodeo, an outdoor eatery popular with locals, is an added feature. Renovated in 1992, the understated rooms are decorated in floral prints, which enhance the homey atmosphere. A plus is its proximity to shopping. *360 Rodeo Dr., Beverly Hills 90210, tel. 310/273–0300. 86 rooms. Facilities: restaurant, bar, lounge, sundeck, garage. AE, DC, MC, V.*

Moderate **Beverly House Hotel.** This is a small, elegantly furnished, European-style bed-and-breakfast hotel. Even though it's near busy
★ areas of L.A. (Century City and Beverly Hills shopping), this hotel is quiet and actually quaint. *140 S. Lasky Dr., Beverly Hills 90212, tel. 310/271–2145 or 800/432–5444. 50 rooms. Facilities: laundry, free parking. AE, DC, MC, V.*

West Los Angeles **Century Plaza Hotel.** This 20-story hotel, on 14 acres of tropical
Very Expensive plants and reflecting pools, is furnished like a mansion, with a
★ mix of classic and contemporary appointments. Each room has a refrigerator and balcony with ocean or city view. Complimentary car service is provided to Beverly Hills. *2025 Ave. of the Stars, Century City 90067, tel. 310/277–2000 or 800/228–3000. 1,072 rooms. Facilities: restaurants, 2 pools, whirlpools, parking. AE, DC, MC, V.*

★ **J. W. Marriott Hotel at Century City.** This hotel is the West Coast flagship of the multifaceted Marriott chain. Its elegant, modern rooms are decorated in soft pastels and equipped with minibars, lavish marble baths, and facilities for the handicapped. Ask for accommodations that overlook Twentieth Century Fox's back lot. The hotel offers complimentary limo service to Beverly Hills and boasts the 2,000-square-foot Presidential Suite and excellent service. *2151 Ave. of the Stars, Century City 90067, tel. 310/277–2777 or 800/228–9290. 375 rooms. Facilities: restaurant, indoor and outdoor pools, whirlpools, fitness center. AE, DC, MC, V.*

Moderate **Century City Inn.** This hotel is small but designed for comfort. Rooms have a refrigerator, microwave oven, remote-control TV, and VCR, as well as a 10-cup coffee unit with fresh gourmet-blend coffee and tea. Baths have whirlpool tubs and a phone. Complimentary Continental breakfast is also served. *10330 W. Olympic Blvd., Los Angeles 90064, tel. 310/553–1000 or 800/553–1005. 46 rooms. Facilities: rental cars, parking. AE, DC, MC, V.*

Coastal Los Angeles
Very Expensive

Hotel Bel-Air. This is a charming, secluded hotel (and celebrity mecca) with lovely gardens and a creek complete with swans. The rooms and suites are decorated individually in peach and earth tones. All are villa/bungalow style with Mediterranean decor. For their quietest accommodations, ask for a room near the former stable area. The Bel-Air has a five-star rating from the Mobil Guide, and five diamonds from AAA. *701 Stone Canyon Rd., Bel Air 90077, tel. 310/472–1211 or, outside CA, 800/ 648–4097. 60 rooms, 32 suites. Facilities: restaurant, lounge, pool, parking. AE, DC, MC, V.*

Westwood Marquis. This hotel near UCLA is a favorite of corporate and entertainment types. Each individualized suite in its 15 stories has a view of Bel Air, the Pacific Ocean, or Century City. South-facing suites overlooking the pool also offer expansive views of the city and sea. *930 Hilgard Ave., Los Angeles 90024, tel. 310/208–8765 or 800/692–2140. 258 suites. Facilities: 2 pools, sauna, phones in bathrooms, banquet and meeting rooms, parking (fee). AE, DC, MC, V.*

Moderate– Expensive

Century Wilshire. Most units in this European-style hotel are suites featuring kitchenettes. There are tiled baths and homey English-style pastel decor. Within walking distance of UCLA and Westwood Village, this simple hotel has views of Wilshire and the courtyard. The clientele here is mostly European. *10776 Wilshire Blvd., West Los Angeles 90024, tel. 310/474– 4506 or 800/421–7223. 100 rooms. Facilities: heated swimming pool, complimentary Continental breakfast, free parking. AE, DC, MC, V.*

Inexpensive

Best Western Royal Palace Hotel. This small hotel located just off I–405 (San Diego Freeway) has all suites, decorated with modern touches, lots of wood and mirrors. In-room morning coffee and tea are complimentary, as is parking to hotel guests. Suites have kitchenettes. *2528 S. Sepulveda Blvd., West Los Angeles 90064, tel. 310/477–9066 or 800/528–1234. 55 rooms. Facilities: pool, Jacuzzi, exercise room and billiard room, laundry facilities. AE, DC, MC, V.*

Santa Monica
Very Expensive

Loews Santa Monica Beach Hotel. Set on the most precious of L.A. real estate—beachfront—just south of the Santa Monica Pier, most of the contemporary rooms here have ocean views and private balconies, and all guests have direct access to the beach. Its restaurant, Riva, serves northern Italian cuisine with an emphasis on seafood. *1700 Ocean Ave., 90401, tel. 310/ 458–6700 or 800/223–0888. 350 rooms, including 31 suites. Facilities: restaurant, café, fitness center, indoor/outdoor pool, valet parking. AE, DC, MC, V.*

Miramar Sheraton. This hotel, "where Wilshire meets the sea," is close to all area beaches, across the street from Pacific Palisades Park, and near deluxe shopping areas and many quaint eateries. The landscaping incorporates the area's second-largest rubber tree. Many rooms have balconies overlooking the ocean. The decor in some rooms is up-to-the-minute contemporary, with bleached wood, marble, granite, glass, and brick. *101 Wilshire Blvd., 90403, tel. 310/576–7777 or 800/325–*

3535. 305 rooms. Facilities: 3 restaurants, lounge, entertainment, pool. AE, DC, MC, V.

Moderate **Holiday Inn Santa Monica Pier.** Close to many restaurants, major shopping centers, the beach, and Santa Monica Pier, this inn features standard Holiday Inn rooms and amenities. *120 Colorado Ave., 90401, tel. 310/451-0676. 132 rooms. Facilities: restaurant, lounge, pool, laundry facilities, meeting and banquet rooms, room service, free parking. AE, DC, MC, V.*

Pacific Shore. Formerly the Royal Inn of Santa Monica, this modern building is a half block from the beach and many restaurants. The attractive rooms are decorated with contemporary fabrics and modern furniture; some have ocean views. *1819 Ocean Ave., 90401, tel. 310/451-8711 or 800/622-8711. 169 rooms. Facilities: restaurant, lounge, pool, sauna, therapy pool, Jacuzzi, laundry facilities, rental cars, gift shop, free parking. AE, DC, MC, V.*

Inexpensive **Carmel Hotel.** This charming hotel from the 1920s is one block from the beach and the new Santa Monica Shopping Plaza, as well as from movie theaters and many fine restaurants. Electric ceiling fans add to the room decor. There is a Mexican-American restaurant on the premises. *201 Broadway, 90401, tel. 310/451-2469. 110 rooms. Facilities: restaurant, parking. AE, DC, MC, V.*

Marina del Rey **Doubletree Inn.** This luxurious nine-story high-rise hotel has
Very Expensive high-tech design softened by a pastel-toned decor accented in
★ brass and marble. Ask for upper-floor rooms that face the marina. There are lovely touches, such as a gazebo in the patio and rooms with water views. The restaurant Stones is known for its fresh seafood. The hotel offers 24-hour free transportation to and from LAX. All of the rooms are decorated in pastels and have a safe for valuables. *4100 Admiralty Way, 90292, tel. 310/301-3000; 800/862-7462; in CA, 800/862-7462. 386 rooms. Facilities: restaurant, lounges, pool, pay parking. AE, DC, MC, V.*

Marina del Rey Hotel. Completely surrounded by water, this deluxe waterfront hotel is on the marina's main channel, making cruises and charters easily accessible. Guest rooms (contemporary with a nautical touch) offer balconies, patios, and harbor views. For splendid views, book a room that faces the water. The hotel is within walking distance of shopping and only a bike ride away from Fisherman's Village. There are meeting rooms and a beautiful gazebo area for parties. *13534 Bali Way, 90292, tel. 310/301-1000, 800/8-MARINA, or 800/882-4000. 160 rooms. Facilities: 2 restaurants, lounge, pool, putting green, airport transportation, free parking. AE, DC, MC, V.*

Expensive– **Marina International Hotel.** Across from a sandy beach within
Very Expensive the marina, this hotel is unique for its village-style decor. The rooms are done in earth tones with California-style furniture. Each of the very private rooms offers a balcony or patio that faces the garden or the courtyard. Ask for a bungalow—they're huge. The Crystal Fountain restaurant has Continental cuisine. Boat charters are available for as many as 200 people. *4200 Admiralty Way, 90292, tel. 310/301-2000, 800/8-MARINA, or 800/882-4000. 110 rooms, 25 bungalows. Facilities: restaurant, lounge, pool, airport transportation, free parking. AE, DC, MC, V.*

The Ritz-Carlton, Marina del Rey. This sumptuous property sits on some prime real estate at the northern end of a basin, offering a panoramic view of the Pacific. The attractive rooms have marble baths, honor bars, and plenty of amenities—from maid service twice a day to plush terry robes. *4375 Admiralty Way, Marina del Rey 90292, tel. 310/823–3656. 306 rooms. Facilities: pool, sundeck, fitness center, tennis courts, boutiques, complimentary transportation to LAX. AE, DC, MC, V.*

Moderate **Marina Pacific Hotel & Suites.** This hotel faces the Pacific and one of the world's most vibrant boardwalks; it's nestled among Venice's art galleries, shops, and elegant, offbeat restaurants. The marina is just a stroll away. The Spanish-style rooms are decorated in light beige tones. Comfortable accommodations include suites, conference facilities, full-service amenities, and a delightful sidewalk café. For the active traveler, there are ocean swimming, roller skating along the strand, racquetball, and tennis nearby. *1697 Pacific Ave., Venice 90291, tel. 310/ 399–7770 or 800/421–8151. 125 rooms. 1-bedroom apartments available. Facilities: restaurant, laundry. AE, DC, MC, V.*

South Bay Beach **Sheraton at Redondo Beach.** Located across the street from the
Cities Redondo Beach Pier, this swank five-story hotel overlooks the
Expensive– Pacific. There are plenty of amenities, including indoor and
Very Expensive outdoor dining and a nightclub. The rooms are decorated in a seaside theme of light woods and soft colors. *300 N. Harbor Dr., Redondo Beach 90277, tel. 310/318–8888 or 800/HOLI-DAY. 339 rooms. Facilities: restaurant, lounge, entertainment, pool, exercise room, game room, sauna, whirlpool, tennis, pay parking. AE, DC, MC, V.*

Moderate **Barnaby's Hotel.** Modeled after a 19th-century English inn,
★ with four-poster beds, lace curtains, and antique decorations, Barnaby's also has an enclosed greenhouse pool. The London Pub resembles a cozy English hangout, with live entertainment; Barnaby's Restaurant features Continental cuisine and curtained private booths. Complimentary English buffet breakfast is served. Weekend packages are available. *3501 Sepulveda Blvd., at Rosecrans Blvd., Manhattan Beach, tel. 310/545–8466 or 800/552–5285. 128 rooms. Facilities: restaurants, lounge, pool. AE, DC, MC, V.*

Airport **Sheraton Los Angeles Airport Hotel.** A luxurious 15-story ho-
Expensive– tel, this is in a perfect setting for business and leisure travelers
Very Expensive alike. The contemporary rooms are decorated in muted shades of mauve, brown, green, and purple. *6101 W. Century Blvd., Los Angeles 90045, tel. 310/642–1111. 807 rooms. Facilities: restaurants, lounges, multilingual concierge, room service, currency exchange. AE, DC, MC, V.*

Expensive **Hyatt Hotel–LAX.** Rich brown marble in the lobby entrance, and dark wood columns, wall coverings, and furniture upholstered in green or black leather punctuate the decor in this contemporary 12-story building. Close to LAX, Hollywood Park, the Forum, and Marina del Rey, the Hyatt keeps business travelers in mind, and offers large meeting rooms with ample banquet space. The hotel's staff is multilingual, and a concierge is on duty 24 hours a day. *6225 W. Century Blvd., 90045, tel. 310/670–9000 or 800/233–1234. 596 rooms. Facilities: restaurant, coffee shop, lounge, entertainment, pool, sauna, exercise room, pay parking. AE, DC, MC, V.*

★ **Stouffer Concourse Hotel.** This is a good place to stay if you're looking to be pampered but also need to be the airport. Rooms and suites are decorated in muted earth tones to complement the contemporary decor; many suites have private outdoor spas. The expansive, luxurious lobby is decorated in marble and brass. The Trattoria Grande restaurant features pasta and seafood specialties. *5400 W. Century Blvd., Los Angeles 90045, tel. 310/216–5858 or 800/468–3571. 750 rooms. Facilities: 2 restaurants, lounge, entertainment, pool, sauna, fitness center, parking (fee). AE, DC, MC, V.*

Moderate **Holiday Inn–LAX.** This recently decorated, international-style hotel is ideal for families and business types. The hotel features standard Holiday Inn rooms in such colors as beige, burgundy, orange, or green. Other amenities include a California-cuisine restaurant and cocktail lounge, multilingual telephone operators, and tour information. *9901 La Cienega Blvd., 90045, tel. 310/649–5151 or 800/238–8000. 403 rooms. Facilities: restaurant, pool, free parking. AE, DC, MC, V.*

Pacifica Hotel. Just 3 miles north of LAX and a few minutes from Marina del Rey, this deluxe Spanish American–style hotel is convenient for business types. There is both elegant and casual dining. The Culver's Club Lounge has lively entertainment and dancing. Extra special is the Shalamar Suite, with beautiful decorations and its own indoor pool. Package rates are available. *6161 Centinela Ave., Culver City 90230, tel. 310/649–1776 or 800/541–7888. 368 rooms. Facilities: restaurant, lounge, entertainment, pool, sauna, health club, free parking. AE, DC, MC, V.*

San Fernando Valley **Sheraton Universal.** You're apt to see movie and TV stars in this large, 23-story hotel. The hotel is on the grounds of Universal
Very Expensive Studios, where you experience the Universal Amphitheater and can tour the largest movie studio in the world. The hotel overlooks Hollywood. The rooms have been decorated in muted shades of blue, beige, and gray. *333 Universal Terrace Pkwy., Universal City 91608, tel. 818/980–1212. 446 rooms. Facilities: restaurant, pool, whirlpool spa. AE, DC, MC, V.*

Moderate **Sportsman's Lodge Hotel.** An English country–style building with a resort atmosphere, this hotel features beautiful grounds with waterfalls. Guest rooms are large, with country decor in such colors as mauve and blue. Studio suites with private patios are available, and there's an Olympic-size swimming pool and a restaurant with American and Continental cuisines. The hotel is close to the Universal Studios Tour and Universal Amphitheater. *12825 Ventura Blvd., Studio City 91604, tel. 818/769–4700. 196 rooms. Facilities: restaurant, coffee shop, room service, pool, free parking. AE, DC, MC, V.*

Inexpensive **St. George Motor Inn.** This English Tudor–style hotel, near Warner Center, business hub of the west San Fernando Valley, features crisp, contemporary decor, redone in 1992. It's convenient for its proximity to such restaurants as Victoria Station and Charlie Brown's. *19454 Ventura Blvd., Tarzana 91356, tel. 818/345–6911 or 800/445–6911. 57 rooms. Facilities: heated pool, Jacuzzi, kitchenettes, free parking. AE, DC, MC, V.*

The Arts

For the most complete listing of weekly events, get the current issue of *Los Angeles* magazine. The Calendar section of the *Los Angeles Times* also offers a wide survey of Los Angeles arts events, as do the more irreverent free publications the *L.A. Weekly* and the *L.A. Reader*.

Most tickets can be purchased by phone (with a credit card) from **Ticketmaster** (tel. 213/480–3232), **TeleCharge** (tel. 800/762–7666), **Good Time Tickets** (tel. 213/464–7383), or **Murray's Tickets** (tel. 213/234–0123).

Theater   Even small productions might boast big names from "the Business" (the Los Angeles entertainment empire). Many film and television actors love to work on the stage between "big" projects or while on hiatus from a TV series as a way to refresh their talents or regenerate their creativity in this demanding medium. Doing theater is also an excellent way to be seen by those who matter in the glitzier end of show biz. Hence there is a need for both large houses—which usually mount productions that are road-company imports of Broadway hits or, on occasion, where Broadway-bound material gets a tryout—and a host of small, intimate theaters to showcase the talent that abounds in this city.

The sampling below includes some of the major houses in the area. All are located in Los Angeles unless otherwise noted.

Ahmanson Theater. With 2,071 seats, this is the second largest of the three-theater Music Center complex (with the Dorothy Chandler Pavilion and the Mark Taper Forum), and productions include both classics and new plays. The list of artists who have worked at this theater reads like a Who's Who of stage and screen, including Neil Simon, who has premiered five of his plays here. *135 N. Grand Ave., tel. 213/972–7211. Tickets: $37–$50. AE, DC, MC, V.*

Mark Taper Forum. Also part of the Music Center, and the smallest, this house's 760 seats provide an intimate setting with excellent acoustics. The theater, under the direction of Gordon Davidson, is committed to presenting new works, and to the development of a community of artists. Many of its plays, including *Children of a Lesser God*, have gone on to Broadway. *135 N. Grand Ave., tel. 213/972–7373. Tickets: $26–$32. AE, DC, MC, V.*

Westwood Playhouse. An acoustically superior theater with great sightlines, the 498-seat playhouse showcases new plays in the summer, primarily musicals and comedies. Many of the productions here are on their way to or from Broadway. This is also where Jason Robards and Nick Nolte got their starts. *10886 Le Conte Ave., Westwood, tel. 310/208–6500 or 310/208–5454. Tickets: $17.50–$30. AE, MC, V.*

Wilshire Theater. The interior of this 1,900-seat house is Art Deco style; musicals from Broadway are the usual fare. *8440 Wilshire Blvd., Beverly Hills, tel. 310/480–3232. Tickets: $6–$30. MC, V.*

Concerts   Los Angeles is not only the focus of America's pop/rock music recording scene, but now, after years of being denigrated as a cultural invalid, is also a center for classical music and opera.

The following is a list of Los Angeles's major concert halls:

Dorothy Chandler Pavilion (135 N. Grand Ave., tel. 213/972–7211). Part of the Los Angeles Music Center and—with the Hollywood Bowl—the center of L.A.'s classical music scene, the 3,200-seat pavilion is the home of the Los Angeles Philharmonic. The L.A. Opera presents classics from September through June. *AE*, *MC*, *V*.

The Greek Theater (2700 N. Vermont Ave., tel. 213/410–1062). This open-air auditorium near Griffith Park offers some classical performances in its mainly pop/rock/jazz schedule from June to October. Its Doric columns evoke the amphitheaters of ancient Greece. *AE*, *MC*, *V*.

The Hollywood Bowl (2301 Highland Ave., tel. 213/850–2000). Open since 1920, the bowl is one of the world's largest outdoor amphitheaters, and located in a park surrounded by mountains, trees, and gardens. The L.A. Philharmonic spends its summer season here. Concert goers usually arrive early, bringing or buying picnic suppers. There are plenty of picnic tables, and box-seat subscribers can reserve a table right in their own box. Restaurant dining is available on the grounds (reservations recommended, tel. 213/851–3588). The seats are wood, so you might bring or rent a cushion—and bring a sweater; it gets chilly here in the evening. A convenient way to enjoy the Hollywood Bowl experience without the hassle of parking is to take one of the Park-and-Ride buses, which leave from various locations around town; call the bowl for information. *MC*, *V*.

Royce Hall (405 N. Hilgard, tel. 310/825–9261). Internationally acclaimed performers are featured in this 1,800-seat auditorium at UCLA. The university's **Schoenberg Hall,** smaller but with wonderful acoustics, also hosts a variety of concerts. *AE*, *MC*, *V*.

The Shrine Auditorium (665 W. Jefferson Blvd., tel. 213/749–5123). Built in 1926 by the Al Malaikah Temple, the auditorium's decor could be called Baghdad and Beyond. Touring companies from all over the world, along with assorted gospel and choral groups, appear in this one-of-a-kind, 6,200-seat theater. *AE*, *MC*, *V*.

Wiltern Theater (Wilshire Blvd. and Western Ave., tel. 213/380–5005 or 213/380–5031). Reopened in 1985 as a venue for the Los Angeles Opera Theater, the building was constructed in 1930, is listed in the National Register of Historic Places, and is a magnificent example of Art Deco in its green terra-cotta glory. *MC*, *V*.

Dance   Due to lack of Music Center funding, Los Angeles lost the Joffrey Ballet in 1991, and Angelenos have since turned to local dance companies. You can find talented companies dancing around town at various performance spaces. Check the *L.A. Weekly* free newspaper under "dance" to see who is dancing where, including L.A.'s own **Bella Lewistsky Dance Co.** (tel. 213/627–5555), or call **The Dance Resource Center of Greater L.A.'s** hot line—tel. 213/281–1918).

Visiting companies such as Martha Graham, Paul Taylor, and Hubbard Street Dance Company perform in UCLA Dance Company's home space at **UCLA Center for the Arts** (405 N. Hilgard, tel. 310/825–9261. AE, MC, V.).

Larger companies such as the Kirov, the Bolshoi, and the American Ballet Theatre (ABT) perform at various times during the year at the Shrine Auditorium (665 W. Jefferson Blvd., tel. 213/749–5123. AE, MC, V.).

Also, two prominent dance events occur annually: The Dance Fair in March and Dance Kaleidoscope in July. Both events take place at **Cal State L.A.'s Dance Department** (5151 State University Dr.; tel. 213/343–5124).

Nightlife

Nightlife in Los Angeles can mean anything from catching a stand-up routine at the Comedy Store to frenetic disco dancing at Chippendale's. There is a potpourri of specialized entertainment, not only in the hub of the city but also in the outlying suburbs.

Despite the high energy level of the nightlife crowd, Los Angeles nightclubs aren't known for keeping their doors open until the wee hours. This is still an early-to-bed city, and it's safe to say that by 2 AM, most jazz, rock, and disco clubs have closed for the night. Perhaps it's the temperate climate and the daytime sports orientation of the city: Most Angelenos want to be on the tennis court or out jogging first thing in the AM, making a late-night social life out of the question.

Dress codes vary depending on the place you visit. Jackets are expected at cabarets and hotels. Discos are generally casual, although some will turn away the denim-clad. The rule of thumb is to phone ahead and check the dress code, but on the whole, Los Angeles is oriented toward casual wear.

The following night spots are divided according to their orientation: jazz, folk/pop/rock, cabaret, disco/dancing, country, hotel rooms and piano bars, and comedy and magic. Consult *Los Angeles* magazine for current listings. The Sunday *Los Angeles Times* Calendar section, and the free *L.A. Weekly* and *L.A. Reader* also provide listings.

Jazz **The Baked Potato.** In this tiny club they pack you in like sardines to hear a powerhouse of jazz. The featured item on the menu is, of course, baked potatoes; they're jumbo and stuffed with everything from steak to vegetables. *3787 Cahuenga Blvd. W, North Hollywood, tel. 818/980–1615. AE, MC, V.*

Birdland West. This is the place to come for contemporary jazz, Art Deco decor, and great happy hours. *105 W. Broadway, Long Beach, tel. 310/436–9341. Open daily. AE, MC, V.*

Jax. This intimate club serves a wide variety of food, from sandwiches to steak and seafood; live music is an added draw. *339 N. Brand Blvd., Glendale, tel. 818/500–1604. AE, MC, V. No cover.*

The Lighthouse. One of Los Angeles's finest, this club offers a broad spectrum of music, from reggae to big band. Jam sessions are often held on weekends. Freddie Hubbard, Woody Herman, and Jimmy Witherspoon all have played here. The decor is wood, brass, and brick, with a lot of plants. Dine on fettuccine, appetizers, or steaks while listening to the sounds. *30 Pier Ave., Hermosa Beach, tel. 310/372–6911 or 213/376–9833. MC, V with a $5 minimum. No cover.*

Nucleus Nuance. This Art Deco restaurant features vintage jazz every night. *7267 Melrose Ave., West Hollywood, tel. 213/939–8666. AE, DC, MC, V.*

Vine Street Bar and Grill. This elegant club in the heart of Hollywood (across the street from the James Doolittle Theater) features two shows nightly. Past performers have included Eartha Kitt, Cab Calloway, and Carmen McRae. Italian food is served. *1610 N. Vine St., Hollywood, tel. 213/463–4375. AE, MC, V.*

Folk/Pop/Rock

Blue Saloon. For rock and roll, this is the place to go. (You'll catch a smattering of country and blues at times, too.) If your rear gets tired while sitting and listening to the music, rustle up a game of billiards or darts. This is the friendliest club around. *4657 Lankershim Blvd., North Hollywood, tel. 818/ 766-4644. Open noon-2 AM. No credit cards.*

Club Lingerie. One local describes this place as "clean enough for the timid, yet seasoned quite nicely for the tenured scenester." Best of all is its mix of really hot bands. *6507 Sunset Blvd., Hollywood, tel. 213/466-8557. No credit cards.*

Gazzarri's. A Sunset Strip landmark offers pure rock and roll aimed at the 19–early 20s age group. *9039 Sunset Blvd., West Hollywood, tel. 310/273-6606. No credit cards. Open Sun.- Thurs.*

The Palace. The "in" spot for the upwardly mobile is plush Art Deco—truly a palace—and boasts live entertainment, a fabulous sound system, full bar, and dining upstairs. The patrons here dress to kill. *1735 N. Vine St., Hollywood, tel. 213/462- 3000. AE, MC, V.*

Pier 52. From Wednesday through Sunday there are live dance bands here playing pure rock and roll. *52 Pier Ave., Hermosa Beach, tel. 310/376-1629. MC, V.*

The Roxy. The premier Los Angeles rock club, classy and comfortable, offers performance art as well as theatrical productions. Many famous Los Angeles groups got their start here as opening acts. *9009 Sunset Blvd., West Hollywood, tel. 310/ 276-2222. AE, DC, MC, V.*

The Strand. This major concert venue covers a lot of ground, hosting hot new acts, or such old favorites as Asleep at the Wheel, bluesman Albert King, rock vet Robin Trower, and Billy Vera, all in the same week. Who says you can't have it all? *1700 S. Pacific Coast Hwy., Redondo Beach, tel. 310/316-1700. AE, MC, V.*

The Troubador. In the early '70s this was one of the hottest clubs in town for major talent. Then business entered a shaky phase while the music industry changed its focus, but now it's rolling again, this time with up-and-coming talent. The adjoining bar is a great place in which to see and be seen. *9081 Santa Monica Blvd., West Hollywood, tel. 310/276-6168. No credit cards.*

Whiskey A Go Go. This, the most famous rock-and-roll club on Sunset Strip, has hosted everyone from Otis Redding to AC/DC and now presents up-and-coming heavy-metal and very hard rock bands. *8901 Sunset Blvd., West Hollywood, tel. 310/652- 4202.*

Cabaret

Black and Blue. This place is a load of fun. Stop by to listen to live rock bands—the best in the city—or for a session of dancing every night. The adjoining restaurant specializes in Continental/Italian cuisine. *7574 Sunset Blvd., Hollywood, tel. 213/ 876-1120. AE, DC, MC, V.*

Studio One Backlot. This elegant, classy night spot features excellent musical acts, singers, comedians, and dancers. *652 N. La Peer, West Hollywood, tel. 310/659-0472. AE, MC, V.*

Disco/Dancing

Bar One. Celebrities such as Warren Beatty and Charlie Sheen enjoy this restaurant and bar. A hot, hip place for dancing, this is L.A.'s club of the moment. There's also a pool table and comfortable lounging areas. *9229 Sunset Blvd., Beverly Hills, tel. 310/271-8355. AE, MC, V.*

Excess. If you're looking for rap music, or you simply want to salsa, catch the action at this out-of-the-way club. The dance floor is one of the largest around and is convenient to downtown. *223 N. Glendale Ave., Glendale, tel. 818/500–1665. AE, MC, V.*

Coconut Teaszer. Disco dancing, a great barbecue menu, and killer drinks make for lively fun. *8177 Sunset Blvd., Los Angeles, tel. 213/654–4773. AE, MC, V.*

Crush Bar Continental Club. If the 1960s is a decade that appeals to you, stop by this happening dance club. After all, there's nothing like some golden Motown to get you moving. *1743 Cahuenga Ave., Hollywood, tel. 213/461–9017. Open Thurs.–Sat. 9 PM–2 AM. $5–$7 cover. MC, V.*

DC3. Hip and uptown, this club/restaurant in the Santa Monica Airport plays pop music until 2 AM. Look for an older, upscale crowd and sophisticated lighting effects. *2800 Donald Douglas Loop N, Santa Monica, tel. 310/399–2323. AE, DC, MC, V.*

Florentine Gardens. One of Los Angeles's largest dance areas has spectacular lighting to match. *5951 Hollywood Blvd., Hollywood, tel. 213/464–0706. Open Fri. and Sat. until 4 AM. No credit cards.*

Vertigo. This New York–style club with restricted entrance policy has a large dance floor, balcony bar, and restaurant. It is open Friday and Saturday until 4 AM, which is unusual for this city. There's a large celebrity clientele, and everybody's dressed to kill. *333 S. Boylston, Los Angeles, tel. 213/747–4849. $15 cover. MC, V.*

Country **The Palomino.** There's occasionally a wild crowd at this premier country showcase in Los Angeles. Good old boys and urban cowboys meet here, and everybody has a good time. *6907 Lankershim Blvd., North Hollywood, tel. 818/764–4010. AE, DC, MC, V.*

Comedy and Magic **Comedy and Magic Club.** This beachfront club features many magicians and comedians seen on TV and in Las Vegas. The Unknown Comic, Elayne Boosler, and Pat Paulsen have all played here. The menu features light American fare and many appetizers. *1018 Hermosa Ave., Hermosa Beach, tel. 310/372–1193. Reservations advised. AE, MC, V.*

Comedy Store. In Los Angeles's premier comedy showcase for over a decade, many famous comedians, including Robin Williams and Steve Martin, occasionally make unannounced appearances. The cover varies. *8433 Sunset Blvd., Hollywood, tel. 213/656–6225. AE, MC, V.*

Igby's Comedy Cabaret. You'll see familiar television faces here as well as up-and-coming comedians Tuesday through Saturday. Cabaret fare includes cocktails and dining in a friendly ambience. Reservations are necessary. *11637 Tennessee Pl., Los Angeles, tel. 310/477–3553. AE, DC, MC, V.*

The Improvisation. The Improv is a transplanted New York establishment. Comedy is showcased, with some vocalists. This place was the proving ground for Liza Minnelli and Richard Pryor, among others. Reservations are recommended. *8162 Melrose Ave., West Hollywood, tel. 213/651–2583 and 321 Santa Monica Blvd., Santa Monica, tel. 310/394–8664. MC, V. (for food and drinks only).*

Merlin McFly Magical Bar and Grill. If you're seeing double here, it might not be the drinks: Magical illusions are featured nightly until midnight. Ladies, watch out for the powder room; lights will dim there, and you'll see a Houdini-like figure with a crystal ball appear in the mirror. *2702 Main St., Santa Monica, tel. 310/392–8468. AE, DC, MC, V.*

Excursion to Catalina Island

When you approach Catalina Island through the typical early morning ocean fog, it's easy to wonder if perhaps there has been some mistake. What is a Mediterranean island doing 22 miles off the coast of California? Don't worry, you haven't left the Pacific—you've arrived at one of the Los Angeles area's most popular resorts.

Though lacking the sophistication of some European pleasure islands, Catalina does offer virtually unspoiled mountains, canyons, coves, and beaches. It is Southern California without the freeways, a place to relax and play golf or tennis, go boating, hiking, diving, or fishing, or just lie on the beach. The island's only "city" is Avalon, a charming, old-fashioned beach town, in some ways resembling an overgrown marina. Yachts are tied up in neat rows in the crescent-shape bay, palm trees rim the main street, and there are plenty of restaurants and shops to attract the attention of day-trippers out strolling in the sunshine.

Of course, life was not always this leisurely on Catalina. Discovered by Juan Rodríguez Cabrillo in 1542, the island has sheltered many dubious characters, from sun-worshiping Indians, Russian fur trappers (seeking sea-otter skins), slave traders, pirates, and gold miners, to bootleggers, filmmakers, and movie stars. Avalon was named in 1888 after the island of Avalon in Tennyson's *Idylls of the King*. In 1919, William Wrigley, Jr., the chewing-gum magnate, purchased controlling interest in the company developing the island. Wrigley had the island's most famous landmark, the Casino, built in 1929, and he made Catalina the site of spring training for his Chicago Cubs baseball team. The Santa Catalina Island Conservancy, a nonprofit foundation, acquired about 86% of the island in 1974 to help preserve Catalina's natural resources.

A wide variety of tours offers samples of those resources, either by boat along the island's coast or by bus or van into Catalina's rugged interior country. Depending on which route you take, you can expect to see roving bands of buffalo, deer, goats, and boar, or unusual species of sea life, including such oddities as electric perch, saltwater goldfish, and flying fish. The buffalo were brought to the island in 1924 for the filming of *The Vanishing American;* apparently, they liked it well enough to stay.

Although Catalina can certainly be seen in a day, there are several inviting romantic hotels that promise to make it worth extending your stay for one or more nights. Between Memorial Day and Labor Day we strongly suggest you make reservations *before* heading out to the island. After Labor Day, rooms are much easier to find on shorter notice, and rates drop dramatically.

Arriving and Departing

By Boat Boats to Catalina run from San Pedro and Long Beach. **Catalina Express** (tel. 310/519–1212) makes the hour-long run from Long Beach or San Pedro to Avalon; round-trip fare from Long Beach is $34 for adults, $25 for children 2–11; from San Pedro, $29.20 for adults and $21.70 for children. **Catalina Cruises** (tel. 800/888–5939), also leaving from Long Beach, is a bit slower, taking two hours, but cheaper, charging $28. Service is also available from Newport Beach through **Catalina Passenger Service** (tel. 714/673–5245), which leaves from Balboa Pavilion at 9 AM, takes 75 minutes to reach the island, and costs $28 round-trip. The return boat leaves Catalina at 4:30 PM. Advance reservations for all lines are strongly recommended.

By Plane **Helitrans** (tel. 310/548–1314 or 800/262–1472) offers helicopter service from San Pedro's Catalina Island Terminal to Pebbly Beach, five minutes by van from Avalon. **Island Express** (tel. 310/491–5550) flies from San Pedro and Long Beach. The trip takes about 15 minutes and costs $55 one way, $95 round-trip. Commuter air service is available from Long Beach Airport and John Wayne/Orange County Airport to Catalina's Airport in the Sky. Call **Allied Air Charter** (tel. 310/510–1163) for schedules and fares.

Guided Tours

The major tour operators on the island are the **Santa Catalina Island Co.** (tel. 310/510–2000 or 800/428–2566). Tours include coastal cruise to Seal Rocks (summer only), the Flying Fish boat trip (evenings, summer only), inland motor tour, Skyline Drive, casino tour, Avalon scenic tour, and the glass-bottom-boat tour. Advance reservations are highly recommended for the inland tours; the others are offered several times daily. Costs range from $6 to $22 (adults); discounts are available for senior citizens over 55 and children under 12 years. Catalina Adventure Tours also offers parasailing, fishing, and diving options.

The Catalina Conservancy (tel. 310/510–1421) offers walks led by knowledgeable docents.

Exploring

Catalina Island is one of the few places in the L.A. environs where walking is considered quite acceptable; it is, in fact, virtually unavoidable. You cannot bring a car onto the island or rent one once you get there. If you are determined to have a set of wheels, rent a bicycle or golf cart along Crescent Avenue as you walk in from the docks. To hike into the interior of the island you will need a permit, available free from the L.A. County Department of Parks and Recreation (Island Plaza, Avalon, tel. 310/510–0688).

The **Santa Catalina Island Company's Visitors Center** and the **Chamber of Commerce Visitors Bureau** are good places to get your bearings, check into special events, and plan your itinerary. The Visitors Center (tel. 310/510–2500) is located on the corner of Crescent Avenue and Catalina Avenue, across from the Green Pier; the chamber's Visitors Bureau is on the pier.

Housed on the northwest point of Crescent Bay is the **Casino**. The round structure is an odd mixture of Spanish, Moorish, and Art Deco–modern style, with Art Deco murals on the porch as you enter. "Casino" is the Italian word for "gathering place," and has nothing to do with gambling. At least not here. Inside the Casino are an art gallery, museum, movie theater (tel. 310/510–0179), and ballroom. Guided tours are available.

The Wrigley Memorial and Botanical Garden is 2 miles south of Avalon via Avalon Canyon Road. The Wrigley family commissioned this monument, replete with grand staircase and Spanish mausoleum with Art Deco touches. Despite the fact that the mausoleum was never used by the Wrigleys, who are instead buried in Los Angeles, the structure is worth a look, and the view from the mausoleum is all the more so. The garden is small but exceptionally well planted. Tram service between the memorial and Avalon is available daily between 8 AM and 5 PM. There is a nominal entry fee of $1.

If modern architecture interests you, be sure to stop by the **Wolfe House** (124 Chimes Rd.). Built in 1928 by noted architect Rudolph Schindler, its terraced frame is carefully set into a steep site, affording extraordinary views. The house is a private residence, rarely open for public tours, but you can get a good view of it from the path below it and from the street.

El Rancho Escondido is a ranch in Catalina's interior, home to some of the country's finest Arabian horses. The ranch can be visited on the Inland motor tour *(see* Guided Tours, above).

Dining

American **The Sand Trap.** Omelets are the specialty at this local favorite located on the way to Wrigley Botanical Garden. *Falls Canyon, tel. 310/510–1349. No credit cards. Closed for dinner. Inexpensive (under $10).*

Italian **Cafe Prego.** This restaurant features an intimate setting on the waterfront, several good pasta dishes, and a hearty minestrone. *603 Crescent Ave., tel. 310/510–1218. AE, D, DC, MC, V. Closed for lunch. Moderate ($10–$20).*
Antonio's Pizzeria. You'll find spirited atmosphere, decent pizza, and appropriately messy Italian sandwiches. *2 locations: 230 Crescent Ave., tel. 310/510–0008, and 114 Sumner Ave., tel. 310/510–0060. MC, V. Moderate ($10–$20).*

Seafood **Pirrone's.** This restaurant has a bird's-eye view of the bay and serves fresh seafood. *417 Crescent Ave., tel. 310/510–0333. MC, V. Closed for lunch and Sun. dinner in winter. Moderate ($10–$20).*

Lodging

Inn on Mt. Ada. The former Wrigley Mansion is now the island's most exclusive hotel. The views are spectacular, and the grounds superbly planted. All meals and the use of a golf cart are complimentary. *Box 2560, Avalon 90704, tel. 310/510–2030. 6 rooms. MC, V. Very Expensive ($290–$580).*
Glenmore Plaza Hotel. This striking Victorian hotel dating from 1891 has hosted the likes of Clark Gable, Teddy Roosevelt, and Amelia Earhart. Located near the beach, the hotel offers complimentary breakfast and suites with whirlpool or Jacuzzi.

120 Sumner Ave., Avalon 90704, tel. 310/510–0017. 45 rooms. AE, D, DC, MC, V. Moderate–Very Expensive ($100–$325).

Hotel Villa Portofino. This is a Mediterranean-style waterfront hotel with a sundeck, an art gallery, and an ambitious Italian restaurant. *111 Crescent Ave., Avalon 90704, tel. 310/510–0555. 34 rooms. AE, D, DC, MC, V. Moderate–Expensive ($82–$225).*

Hotel Catalina. A renovated Victorian, half a block from the beach, the Catalina offers a choice of rooms and cottages. Extra touches include an attractive sundeck with Jacuzzi and free movies every afternoon. *129 Whittley Ave., Avalon 90704, tel. 310/510–0027. 32 rooms, 4 cottages. AE, D, MC, V. Moderate ($85–$110).*

Zane Grey Pueblo Hotel. The former home of the famous American novelist, this hotel offers a stunning harbor view from its hilltop perch. Built in 1926 in Hopi Indian pueblo style, the Zane Grey offers such amenities as eccentric decor, a swimming pool, and a courtesy bus. No phones or TVs in rooms. *199 Chimes Tower Rd., Avalon 90704, tel. 310/510–0966. 18 rooms. AE, MC, V. Moderate ($95–$110).*

Atwater Hotel. This family-oriented hotel is a half block from the beach. *Box 737, Avalon 90704, tel. 310/510–1788. 84 rooms. AE, D, DC, MC, V. Moderate–Inexpensive ($65–$140).*

Excursion to Antelope Valley

The most memorable parts of a trip are often its surprises— the places and people you stumble onto where and when you least expect to. Antelope Valley, which makes up the western corner of the Mojave Desert, holds several unexpected pleasures. A sudden turn along a desert road reveals a riot of flaming orange poppies on acres of rolling hills nestled between barren rises and desolate flatlands. In the late summer and fall, after the flowers have faded, you can pick your own cherries, peaches, and pears at nearby orchards incongruously set in the desert. Head east and you can hike to the top of Saddleback Butte for a spectacular view of where the desert ends and the San Gabriel mountains begin, their snowcapped peaks a beautiful contrast to the arid valley.

Another surprise is the valley's wildlife. No, don't look for the hoary antlers of the antelope that lent their name to the area. Once practically overrunning the region, the antelope went into decline with the arrival of the railroad in 1876. They apparently refused to cross the tracks that blocked the route to their traditional grazing grounds and many starved to death. A severe winter in the 1880s and the growth of ranching and farming in the early 1900s spelled the end for the few that had survived.

What you can see on an Antelope Valley safari are the eminently amusing and increasingly rare desert tortoises. Thanks to preservationists, a safe haven has been created for California's official state reptile. Visiting the tortoise in its natural habitat is a great opportunity for budding photographers—not noted for their speed, the tortoises make willing subjects. If birds are more your fancy, there is also a 40-acre wildlife sanctuary in the valley noted for its winged inhabitants.

Man, of course, has also made his mark in Antelope Valley. You'll find gold mines and historic railroad towns that evoke the spirit of the Old West. Some $40 million in gold and silver was taken out of the hills between Rosemond and Mojave after a Mr. Hamilton hit pay dirt in the 1890s on what is now called Tropico Hill. The Burton Mining Company believes there is still some gold to be found in Tropico and is today excavating the same hill Hamilton made his fortune on.

Arriving and Departing

By Car Heading north from Los Angeles, I–5 will lead you to Highway 14, which runs north through Palmdale, Lancaster, Rosemond, and Mojave. It should take about 90 minutes to reach Palmdale and another hour between Palmdale and Mojave. To reach the Antelope Valley California Poppy Reserve, take the Avenue I exit in Lancaster off Highway 14 and head west about 10 miles. For the Desert Tortoise Natural Area, take Highway 14 about 4 miles past Mojave and then turn east on California City Boulevard through California City; turn left on Randsburg-Mojave Road and follow signs for about 5 miles to the preserve. Take Avenue J (Rte. N5) east from Lancaster for about 19 miles to get to Saddleback Butte State Park. To reach the Devil's Punchbowl Natural Area Park and nearby Hamilton Preserve, take Highway 138 southwest from Palmdale; just past Pearblossom turn south on Route N6 (Longview Rd.) and go about 8 miles. On Highway 138, you can continue southeast along the San Gabriel mountains, pick up I–15 south through Cajon Pass, and return to Los Angeles via I–10 heading west.

Exploring

You can't miss the **Antelope Valley California Poppy Reserve**— its orange glow with dots of purple lupine and yellow goldfields and fiddleneck can be seen long before you reach the reserve itself. The peak flower time is between March and May. There are four short (between a mile and 2 mi) walking trails leading through the fields, some reaching wonderful viewpoints. While there is a perfectly serviceable picnic area by the parking lot, a snack on the bench atop Kitanemuk Vista (an easy 5-min. stroll up a well-marked trail) offers much finer scenery. Take a few minutes to walk through the visitor center. The uniquely designed building is burrowed into a hill to keep the building cooler during the summer and warmer during the winter. You can pick up trail maps and other useful information. *Visitor Center open Mar.–May, daily 9–3. State Park day-use fee: $5 per car. For more information and schedules of guided tours, call the California Dept. of Parks and Recreation, tel. 805/942–0662 or 619/724–1180 during flower season for information on where to find the best blooms.*

You will find the area's fruit orchards along State Highway 138 in the communities of **Littlerock** and **Pearblossom,** and in **Leonia,** just to the southwest of Lancaster. Harvesting season starts in June. The Lancaster Chamber of Commerce and Visitors Center (44335 Lowtree, Lancaster 93534, tel. 805/948–4518) has a map showing where to find peaches, apricots, plums, and pears.

Antelope Valley Indian Museum contains an interesting collection of pottery and baskets made by Acoma, Papago, Pima,

Apache, and Hopi tribes. There's a kachina collection, and artifacts from coastal cultures. *15701 E. Ave. M, Lancaster, tel. 619/942–0662. Admission: $2 adults, $1 children. Open Oct.– June, weekends.*

The **Desert Tortoise Natural Area**, northeast of Mojave at California City, is a good place in which to commune with nature. Cars must be left behind as you stroll along the preserve's interpretive nature trails. The best time of the year for viewing the tortoises is generally March through June, when naturalist-guided tours are available. Avoid the mid-afternoon, however, when it can get quite hot out here. The tortoises sensibly stay cool during the heat of the day by retiring to their shallow burrows. Two warnings about the natural area: The road into the area is wide and flat, but not paved, so your car is bound to get dusty; also, there is no drinking or other water available at the preserve. The preserve is open land, there is no admission, and you may feel free to roam about whenever you like.

East of Lancaster, along Highway N5, is **Saddleback Butte State Park,** a favorite of hikers and campers. A 2½-mile trail leads to the 3,651-foot summit of the butte the park is named for, which offers some grand views. Throughout the park there is plenty of typical high-desert plant and animal life—stands of Joshua trees, desert tortoises, golden eagles, and many other species of reptiles, mammals, and birds. Near the park headquarters is a picnic area with tables, stoves, and rest rooms. Information on camping at Saddleback Butte is available from the State Department of Parks (tel. 805/942–0662); admission is $5 per car.

Farther south is another popular spot for hikers—**Devils Punchbowl Natural Area Park.** At the bottom of an ocean millions of years ago, and currently nestled between the active San Andreas and San Jacinto faults, the park offers a network of well-planned trails. The nearby **Hamilton Preserve** consists of 40 acres of piñon-juniper woodland sheltering numerous bird species.

Antelope Valley is also home to **Edwards Air Force Base** and the **NASA Ames-Dryden Flight Research Facility** (off State Hwy. 14, northeast of Lancaster). Tours of the facility are available, with a film describing the history of test-flight programs, a walk through a hangar, and a look at experimental aircraft. This is where Chuck Yeager and other fighter-jocks with the right stuff chased down the sound barrier in the late 1940s. This is also the place to see the space shuttle land. *Free tours weekdays 10:15 AM and 1:15 PM. Call ahead (tel. 805/258–3446), as the base is occasionally closed for security reasons.*

Dining

Antelope Valley is not known for its fine dining. There are several fast-food and very average roadside restaurants in Lancaster, Palmdale, and Mojave. You might be better off packing a gourmet picnic basket before you leave Los Angeles and dining alfresco at one of the many scenic spots you will come across throughout the valley.

13 Orange County

Orange County is one of the top tourist destinations in California, and once you've arrived here it doesn't take long to see why. The county has made tourism its number one industry, attracting nearly 40 million visitors annually. Two theme parks, Disneyland and Knott's Berry Farm, attract millions. Orange County is the home of the California Angels baseball team and Los Angeles Rams football team. The enormous Anaheim Convention Center hosts an average of one meeting per day. Accommodations for visitors are plentiful and generally of high quality.

People actually live in Orange County, too, many of them in high-priced pink, Mediterranean-style suburbs that are strung along the 24-mile-long coastline. Orange County residents actually shop in the classy malls that lure visitors as well. Like visitors, locals can be found at the beach sunning themselves or waiting for the big wave. Locals even dine and stay at the luxurious oceanfront resorts that perch on the edge of the Pacific.

Indeed, Orange County people believe that they've discovered the perfect place to live. They're eager to share the pleasures of life in the Big Orange with visitors.

Served by convenient airports and only an hour's drive from Los Angeles, Orange County is both a destination on its own and a very popular excursion from Los Angeles.

Getting Around

By Plane Several airports are accessible to Orange County. **John Wayne Orange County Airport** (tel. 714/252–5252), in Santa Ana, is centrally located, and the county's main facility. It is serviced by Alaska Airlines (tel. 800/426–0333), America West Airlines (tel. 800/247–5692), American/American Eagle (tel. 800/433–7300), Continental (tel. 800/525–0280), Delta (tel. 800/221–1212), Northwest (tel. 800/225–2525), Skywest (tel. 800/453–9417), TWA (tel. 800/221–2000), and United/United Express (tel. 800/251–6522).

Los Angeles International Airport is only 35 miles west of Anaheim, and still the destination of most nonstop transcontinental flights. **Ontario Airport**, just northwest of Riverside, is 30 miles north of Anaheim, and a growing alternative to LAX.

Long Beach Airport (tel. 310/421–8295), at the southern tip of Los Angeles County, is another good choice for Orange County visits. It is about 20 minutes by coach from Anaheim. Airlines flying into Long Beach include Alaska, America West, American Airlines, and United.

Airport Coach (tel. 800/491–3500 nationwide or 800/772–5299 in CA) services LAX to Anaheim, Buena Park, and Pasadena. Fare from the airport to Anaheim is $14 one way, $20 roundtrip.

Prime Time Airport Shuttle (tel. 213/558–1606 or 818/901–9901) offers door-to-door service to LAX and John Wayne airports, hotels near John Wayne, and the San Pedro cruise terminal. The fare is $12 from Anaheim hotels to LAX. Children under 2 ride free.

SuperShuttle (tel. 714/973–1100 or 800/554–6458) provides 24-hour door-to-door service from all the airports to all points in Orange County. Fare to the Disneyland area is $10 a person from John Wayne, $36 from Ontario, $13 from LAX. Phone for other fares and reservations.

By Car Two major freeways, I–405 (San Diego Freeway) and I–5 (Santa Ana Freeway), run north and south through Orange County. South of Laguna they merge into I–5. Avoid these during rush hours (6–9 AM and 3:30–6 PM), when they can slow to a crawl and back up for miles. Highways 22, 55, and 91 go west to the ocean and east to the mountains: Take Highway 91 or Highway 22 to inland points (Buena Park, Anaheim) and take Highway 55 to Newport Beach. Caution: Orange County freeways are undergoing major construction; expect delays at unexpected times.

Pacific Coast Highway (Highway 1) allows easy access to beach communities and is the most scenic route. It follows the entire Orange County coast, from Huntington Beach to San Clemente.

By Train **Amtrak** (tel. 800/USA–RAIL) has several stops in Orange County: Fullerton, Santa Ana, Anaheim, San Juan Capistrano, and San Clemente. There are eight departures daily. A special motorcoach also takes people to Disneyland from the Fullerton station.

By Bus Anywhere in Southern California, relying on public transportation is usually a mistake, unless you have plenty of time and patience. The **Los Angeles RTD** has limited service to Orange County. You can get the No. 460 to Anaheim; it goes to Knott's Berry Farm and Disneyland.

The **Orange County Transit District** (tel. 714/636–7433) will take you virtually anywhere in the county, but, again, it will take time; OCTD buses go from Knott's Berry Farm and Disneyland to Huntington and Newport beaches. The No. 1 bus travels along the coast.

Greyhound-Trailways (tel. 213/394–5433) has scheduled bus service to Orange County.

Scenic Drives Winding along the seaside edge of Orange County on the **Pacific Coast Highway** is an eye-opening experience. Here, surely, are the contradictions of Southern California revealed—the powerful, healing ocean vistas and the scars of commercial exploitation; the appealingly laid-back, simple beach life and the tacky bric-a-brac of the tourist trail. Oil rigs line the road from Long Beach south to Huntington Beach, and then suddenly give way to pristine stretches of water and dramatic hillsides. Prototypical beach towns like Laguna Beach, Dana Point, and Corona del Mar serve as casual stopping points irregularly arrayed along the route. This is a classic coastline drive.

For a scenic mountain drive, try **Santiago Canyon Road,** which winds through the Cleveland National Forest in the Santa Ana mountains. Tucked away in these mountains are Modjeska Canyon, Irvine Lake, and Silverado Canyon, of silver-mining lore. The terrain is so rugged that you'll forget that you're so near urban civilization.

Guided Tours

General-Interest Tours **Pacific Coast Sightseeing Tours** (tel. 714/978–8855) provides guided tours from Orange County hotels to Disneyland, Knott's Berry Farm, Universal, and the San Diego Zoo.

Boat Tours At the **Cannery** in Newport Beach, you can hop a boat and go for a weekend brunch cruise around the harbor. Cruises last two hours and depart at 10 AM and 1:30 PM. Champagne brunches cost $25 per person. For more information call 714/675–5777.

Catalina Passenger Service (tel. 714/673–5245) at the Balboa Pavilion offers a full selection of sightseeing tours and fishing excursions to Catalina and around Newport Harbor. The 45-minute narrated tour of Newport Harbor, at $6, is the least expensive. Whale-watching cruises (Dec.–Mar.) are especially enjoyable. Narrated by a speaker from the American Cetacean Society, the tours follow the migration pattern of the giant gray whales.

Hornblower Yachts (tel. 714/646–0155) offers a number of special sightseeing brunch cruises. Whale-watching brunches (Jan.–Apr.) are scheduled each Saturday and Sunday; special cruises take place on such holidays as Valentine's Day, Easter, Halloween, Thanksgiving, and Christmas.

Walking Tours If you want to walk in Orange County, you have to drive somewhere first. For a respite from suburban sprawl and urban smog, the **Tucker Wildlife Preserve** in Modjeska Canyon (tel. 714/649–2760), 17 miles southeast of the city of Orange via Chapman Avenue, is worth the effort. The preserve is a haven for more than 140 bird species, including seven varieties of hummingbird, and a variety of mammals and reptiles.

Free walking tours of **Mission San Juan Capistrano** are offered every Sunday at 1 PM, whether the swallows are in town or not. The tours take in the ruins of the Great Stone Church, destroyed by an earthquake in 1812, the Serra Chapel, the mission's courtyards and fountains, and other historical sights.

Shopping Tours Several shopping shuttles transport visitors staying at Anaheim-area hotels to shopping malls. **South Coast Plaza's Shuttle Service** (tel. 714/978–8855) furnishes round-trip transportation to this ritzy shopping area. Santa Ana's **Main Place** (tel. 714/547–7000) offers several shuttles a day from Anaheim hotels. One-way fare is $2 for adults. **The City Shopper** (tel. 714/535–2211) offers hourly transportation to the Crystal Cathedral, the City Shopping Center in Orange, and local hotels for $2 one way. Information on all these services is available at hotels.

Important Addresses and Numbers

Tourist Information The main source of tourist information is the **Anaheim Area Convention and Visitors Bureau,** located at the Anaheim Convention Center (800 W. Katella Ave., 92802, tel. 714/999–8999). The **Visitor Information Hot Line** (tel. 714/635–8900) offers recorded information on entertainment, special events, attractions, and amusement parks; information about special events may be outdated.

Other area chambers of commerce and visitors bureaus are generally open Monday–Friday 9–5 and will help with information. These include the following:

Buena Park Visitors Bureau (6280 Manchester Blvd., 90261, tel. 714/994–1511).

Huntington Beach Conference and Visitors Bureau, 2100 Main St., Suite 190, 92648, tel. 800/SAY–OCEAN.

Newport Harbor Chamber of Commerce (1470 Jamboree Rd., 92660, tel. 714/644–8211).

Laguna Beach Chamber of Commerce (357 Glenneyre, 92651, tel. 714/494–1018).

Dana Point Chamber of Commerce (Box 12, 92629, tel. 714/496–1555).

San Clemente Tourism Bureau (1100 N. El Camino Real, 92672, tel. 714/492–1131).

San Juan Capistrano Chamber of Commerce and Visitors Center (31682 El Camino Real, 92675, tel. 714/493–4700).

Emergencies   Dial 911 for **police** and **ambulance** in an emergency.

Doctor   Orange County is so spread out and comprises so many different communities that it is best to ask at your hotel for the closest emergency room. Here are a few: **Anaheim Memorial Hospital** (1111 W. La Palma, tel. 714/774–1450), **Western Medical Center** (1025 S. Anaheim Blvd., Anaheim, tel. 714/533–6220), **Hoag Memorial Hospital** (301 Newport Blvd., Newport Beach, tel. 714/645–8600), **South Coast Medical Center** (31872 Coast Hwy., South Laguna, tel. 714/499–1311).

Exploring Orange County

Without its tourist attractions—Disneyland, Knott's Berry Farm, the beaches—Orange County might have grown into just another tentacle of the urban sprawl surrounding Los Angeles. With its attractions, Orange County is a destination all by itself, and, according to a survey reported in the *Los Angeles Times*, the attractions give life here a unique quality.

Consider, for example, the elderly couples who long for the simplicity of Main Street; many regularly experience it on a park bench just inside the entrance to Disneyland. Likewise Knott's Berry Farm has always been an integral part of the community in which it's located; residents dine at the Chicken Dinner Restaurant and shop in the boutiques outside the park gates.

But experiencing Orange County is more than visiting Disneyland and Knott's. There are real communities here, many with distinctive character and now quite a few urban problems. Seaside communities, in particular, attract the creative, artistic, and upscale as well as the young and athletic. Meanwhile, the central part of the county has a tiredness about it and faces an uphill battle against crime and congestion.

In planning your trip to Orange County, first select a destination, based on the main purpose of your trip. If Disneyland is the highlight, you'll probably want to organize your activities around the tourist attractions that fill the central county and take excursions to selected coastal spots. The reverse is true, of course, if you're planning to hang out on the beach. In that case, select a coastal headquarters and make forays to the Magic Kingdom.

If you're traveling with children, you could easily devote several full days to the theme parks: a day or two for Disneyland, a day for Knott's Berry Farm, and perhaps a day driving between some of the area's lesser-known attractions. To rent a sailboard or other water-sports paraphernalia, you'll have to head to the beach towns. Beach days can be a mix of sunning, studying surf culture, and browsing the small shops native to the beach communities.

Inland Orange County

Numbers in the margin correspond to points of interest on the Orange County map.

With Disneyland as its centerpiece, Anaheim is indisputably the West's capital of family entertainment. Now at the center of a vast tourism complex that also includes the Anaheim Convention Center, Anaheim Stadium, and the soon-to-open Anaheim Arena, Disneyland still dominates the city. The Anaheim Convention Center lures almost as many conventioneers as Disneyland attracts children, and for many visitors, a trip to the Magic Kingdom may be a bonus extra of an Anaheim meeting.

① Perhaps more than any other place in the world, **Disneyland,** the first Disney theme park and the lasting physical evidence of Walt Disney's dream, is a symbol of the enduring child in all of us, a place of wonder and enchantment—also an exceptionally clean and imaginatively developed wonder.

When Disney carved the park out of the orange groves in 1955, it consisted of four lands and fewer than 20 major attractions radiating from his idealized American Main Street. Much has changed in the intervening years, including the massive expansion of the park to include two more lands and some 40 more attractions. But Main Street retains its turn-of-the-century charm, and in ever sharper contrast with the world just outside the gates of the park. Disney's vision of the Magic Kingdom was one of a never-ending fantasy. Thus designers and engineers continue to come up with new ways to tantalize and treat guests.

Disney's technological wizards have consistently done just that. New Orleans Square with its small-scale, twisting cobblestone streets captures the look and charm of the Crescent City so well that it's hard to believe you're in California, not Louisiana. While the audio-animatronic bears who inhabit Critter Country don't look *real*, it's hard to believe that they aren't alive. Repeat visitors will be amazed at the nighttime extravaganza that emerges from Tom Sawyer's Island. Fantasmic! opened in 1992 and stretches the art of illusion about as far as it can go in a live show. Starring Mickey Mouse, this show employs pyrotechnics, lasers, fog, fiber optics, and giant mist screens, and involves about 50 performers.

Disneyland is big, and, during the busy summer season, crowded. Strategizing your visit, as the locals do, will help you get the most out of it. If you can, pick a rainy midweek day; surprisingly most Disney attractions are indoors. Arrive early; the box office opens a half hour before the park's scheduled opening time. Go immediately to the most popular attractions: Space Mountain, Star Tours, Pirates of the Caribbean, Haunted Mansion, It's a Small World, and Splash Mountain. Lines for rides will also be shorter during parades and the evening fireworks display (usually around 9:30 PM), as well as near opening or closing times. Just the same, even on a slow day expect to wait in line for 15 minutes or so. As with the rides, strategize your eating as well. Restaurants are less crowded toward the beginning and end of meal periods. Also, fast-food spots abound, and you can now get healthy fare such as fruit, pasta, and frozen yogurt at various locations throughout the park. Whatever you wind up eating, food prices will be higher than on the outside. When shopping, remember that there are lockers just off Main Street in which you can store purchases and thereby avoid lugging bundles around all day or putting off shopping just before the park's closing time when stores are crowded. If your feet get tired, you can move from one area of the park to another on the train or monorail, or even in a horse-drawn carriage.

Each of Disney's lands has its own themed rides. Stepping through the doors of Sleeping Beauty's castle into **Fantasyland** can be a dream come true for children. Mickey Mouse may even be there to greet them. Once inside they can join Peter Pan on his magic flight; take a Wild Ride with Mr. Toad; follow Alice and the White Rabbit down the hole; spin around in giant cups at the Mad Tea Party; swoosh through the Matterhorn; or visit It's a Small World where figures of children from 100 countries sing of unity and peace.

In **Frontierland** you can take a cruise on the steamboat *Mark Twain* or sailing ship *Columbia* and experience the sight and sound of spectacular Rivers of America. Kids of every age enjoy rafting to Tom Sawyer's Island for an hour or so of tracking and exploring.

Some visitors to **Adventureland** have taken the Jungle Cruise so many times that they know the patter offered up by the operators by heart. Other attractions here include shops with African and South Seas wares.

Time Out   **Blue Bayou,** featuring Creole food, is a great place to eat. It is located in the entrance to the Pirates of the Caribbean, so you can hear the antics in the background.

The twisting streets of **New Orleans Square** offer interesting browsing and shopping, strolling Dixieland musicians, and the ever-popular Pirates of the Caribbean ride. The Haunted Mansion, populated by 999 holographic ghosts, is nearby. Theme shops purvey hats, perfume, Mardi Gras merchandise, and gourmet items. The Disney Gallery here has now-trendy (and expensive) original Disney art.

The animated bears in **Critter Country** may charm kids of all ages, but it's Splash Mountain, the steepest, wettest Disney adventure, that keeps them coming back for more.

Disney's vision of the future in **Tomorrowland** has undergone the most changes over the years, reflecting advances in technology. You can still take a Submarine Voyage or ride the Monorail, but you can also be hurled into outer space on Space Mountain, take Star Tours, or watch Michael Jackson perform in *Captain EO.*

A stroll along **Main Street** reveals a bit of treasured nostalgia, that of small-town America, circa 1900, that never existed except in the popular imagination and fiction and films. Interconnected shops and restaurants line both sides of the street. The Emporium is the largest and most comprehensive of the shops offering a full line of Disney products. But you'll also find magic items, crystal, hobby and sports memorabilia, clothing, and

Orange County

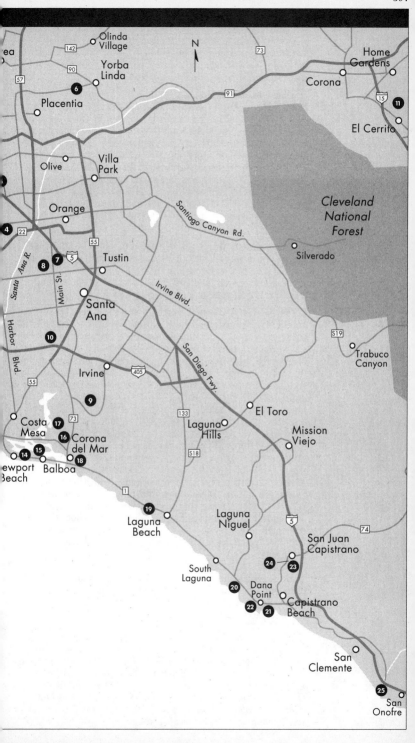

photo supplies here. *1313 Harbor Blvd., Anaheim, tel. 714/ 999–4565. Admission: $28.75 adults, $23 children 3–11; this allows entrance to all the rides and attractions. Guided tours available. In summer, open Sun.–Fri. 9 AM–midnight, Sat. 9 AM–1 AM, in fall, winter, and spring, open Mon.–Fri. 10–6, weekends 9–midnight. Hours subject to change.*

If Disneyland specializes in a high-tech brand of fantasy, **Knott's Berry Farm,** located nearby in Buena Park, offers a dose of reality. The farm has been rooted in the community since 1934, when Cordelia Knott began serving chicken dinners on her wedding china to supplement the family's meager income. The dinners and the boysenberry pies proved more profitable than husband Walt's berry farm, so the family moved first into the restaurant business, and then into the entertainment business. The park with its Old West theme is now a 150-acre complex with 100-plus rides and attractions, 60 eating places, and 60 shops, including several that have been here for decades.

There are attractions both inside and outside the gates of the park. Mrs. Knott's Chicken Dinner Restaurant is the centerpiece of Knott's **California MarketPlace,** a collection of 32 shops and restaurants outside the gates. The rides, shows, and attractions are, of course, located inside the gates.

Like Disneyland, the park has themed areas. **Ghost Town** offers a delightful human-scale visit to the Old West. Many of the buildings were relocated here from their original mining-town sites. You can stroll down the street, stop and chat with the blacksmith, pan for gold, crack open a geode, ride in an authentic 1880s passenger train, or take the Gold Mine ride and descend into a replica of a working gold mine. A real treasure here is the antique Dentzel carousel with a menagerie of animals. **Camp Snoopy** is a kid-sized High Sierra wonderland where Snoopy and his "Peanuts" friends hang out. Tall trees frame **Wild Water Wilderness,** where you can really ride white water in an inner tube in Big Foot Rapids. Themes aside, thrill rides are placed throughout the park. Teenagers, especially, love the rides found in **Roaring '20s:** the Boomerang roller coaster; X-K-1, a living version of a video game; and Kingdom of the Dinosaurs. More thrill rides including Montezooma's Revenge, a roller coaster that goes from 0 to 55 mph in less than 5 seconds, can be found in **Fiesta Village.** Throughout the park, costumed interpreters offer insight into the natural and human history of the attraction; visitors are encouraged to ask questions.

Time Out   Don't forget what made Knott's famous: Mrs. Knott's fried-chicken dinners and boysenberry pies at **Mrs. Knott's Chicken Dinner Restaurant,** just outside the park in Knott's California MarketPlace.

Knott's also offers entertainment throughout the day with shows scheduled in Ghost Town, the Bird Cage Theater, and the Good Time Theater; occasionally name stars appear here. *8039 Beach Blvd., Buena Park, tel. 714/220–5200. Admission: $22.95 adults, $15.95 senior citizens, $9.95 children 3–11. Open in summer, Sun.–Fri. 9 AM–midnight, Sat. 9 AM–1 AM, in winter, weekdays 10 AM–6 PM, Sat. 10 AM–10 PM, Sun. 10 AM–7 PM. Times and prices subject to change.*

Visitors will find 70 years of movie magic immortalized at
❸ **Movieland Wax Museum** in 250 wax sculptures of Hollywood's
greatest stars including Michael Jackson, Dudley Moore, John
Wayne, Marilyn Monroe, and George Burns. Figures are dis-
played in realistic sets from movies such as *Gone with the Wind,*
Star Trek, The Wizard of Oz, and *Rocky IV.* The Chamber of
Horrors is designed to scare the daylights out of you. *7711*
Beach Blvd., one block north of Knott's, tel. 714/522–1155. Ad-
mission: $11.95 adults, $6.95 children; combination tickets in-
cluding admission to Ripley's Believe It or Not across the street
are also available. Open daily in summer 9 AM–8 PM; daily in
winter 10 AM–8 PM.

Garden Grove, a community just south of Anaheim and Buena
Park, is the home of one of the most impressive churches in the
❹ country, the **Crystal Cathedral.** The domain of television evan-
gelist Robert Schuller, this sparkling glass structure resembles a four-pointed star with more than 10,000 panes of glass
covering a weblike steel truss to form translucent walls. The
feeling as you enter is nothing less than mystical. In addition to
tours of the cathedral, two pageants are offered yearly—"The
Glory of Christmas" and "The Glory of Easter" –featuring live
animals in the cast, flying angels, and other special effects.
12141 Lewis St., Garden Grove, tel. 714/971–4013. $2 donation.
Guided tours Mon.–Sat. 9–3:30, Sun. 1:30–3:30. Call for
schedule. For reservations for the Easter and Christmas pro-
ductions, call 714/54–GLORY.

❺ Several unique museums fill the inland area. The **Anaheim Mu-**
seum, housed in a 1908 Carnegie Library building, illustrates
the history of Anaheim, including the original wine-producing
colony. Changing exhibits include art collections, women's history, and hobbies. *241 S. Anaheim Blvd., tel. 714/778–3301.*
Suggested admission: $1.50; children free. Open Wed.–Fri.
10–4, Sat. noon–4. Closed Sun.

About 7 miles north of Anaheim, off Highway 57 (Yorba Linda
❻ Blvd. exit), **The Richard Nixon Library and Birthplace** is more
museum than library. Displays illustrate the checkered career
of the 37th president, the only one to resign from office. Interactive exhibits give visitors a chance to interview Nixon, press-
conference style, and get pre-recorded replies on 300 topics.
One room contains impressive life-size sculptures of world leaders and an array of gifts received from international heads of
state. Visitors can listen to Nixon's Checkers speech or to the
so-called smoking-gun tape from the Watergate days, among
other recorded material. In contrast to the high-tech exhibits
across the lawn and palm tree–lined reflecting pond is the small
farmhouse where Nixon was born in 1913. The restored structure contains the original furnishings, including a cast-iron
stove, piano, Bible, and family photos. Within the main building is a small but interesting gift shop containing presidential
souvenir items. *18001 Yorba Linda Blvd., Yorba Linda, tel.*
714/993–3393. Admission: $4.95 adults, $2.95 senior citizens
62 and older, children 11 and under free. Open Mon.–Sat.
10–5, Sun. 11–5.

❼ The **Bowers Museum** focuses on arts of pre-Columbian American, Oceanic, Native American, and Pacific Rim cultures.
Shows scheduled for 1993 include "Thailand," "Bird Costumes
of pre-Columbian Mexico," and "Spirits of the Borneo Rain

Forest." *2002 N. Main St., Santa Ana, tel. 714/972–1900. Admission free. Open Tues.–Sun. 10–5.*

⑧ Santa Ana, the county seat, is undergoing a dramatic restoration in its downtown area. Gleaming new government buildings meld with turn-of-the-century structures to give a sense of where the county came from and where it is going. The **Fiesta Marketplace** is a new downtown development, notable as a grass-roots effort involving businessmen and government. The Spanish-style, four-block project brings life to one of the traditionally most successful Hispanic marketplaces in Southern California.

⑨ Known for its forward-looking concept of community planning, Irvine is also a center for higher education. The **University of California at Irvine** was established on 1,000 acres of rolling ranchland donated by the Irvine family (who had once owned one fourth of what is now Orange County) in the mid-1950s. The Bren Events Center Fine Art Gallery on campus sponsors exhibitions of 20th-century art (tel. 714/856–5000; admission free; open Tues.–Sat. 10–5). Tree lovers will be enthralled by the campus; it's an arboretum with more than 11,000 trees from all over the world. *Take the San Diego Fwy. (I–405) to Jamboree Rd. Go west to Campus Dr. S.*

⑩ It is no small irony that the Costa Mesa/South Coast Metro area is known first for its posh shopping mall and second for its performing-arts center. **South Coast Plaza** (3333 S. Bristol St., Costa Mesa) attracts more than 20 million visitors a year, making it the busiest mall in Southern California. This is Adventureland for the Gold Card set, built around attractions with names like Polo/Ralph Lauren, Charles Jourdan, Godiva Chocolates, and Courrèges. The adjacent **Orange County Performing Arts Center** (600 Town Center Dr., tel. 714/556–2787) is a world-class complex, hosting such notables as the Los Angeles Philharmonic, the Pacific Symphony, and the New York City Opera. *California Scenario*, a 1.6-acre sculpture garden designed by artist Isamu Noguchi, connects the arts center and the mall, completing this unusual union of art and upscale consumerism. Noguchi uses sandstone, running water, concrete, and native plants to evoke different aspects of the California environment.

Time Out For a quick, healthful meal during a South Coast Plaza visit, try **Forty Carats** on the lower level between Saks and Bullocks. This spin-off of a restaurant in Bloomingdale's has a selection of tasty natural muffins, carrot and pumpkin among them.

⑪ After you've sightseen yourself to exhaustion, pamper yourself at **Glen Ivy Hot Springs.** Thirty-five miles east of Anaheim, the spa is a day-use-only resort. It features an Olympic-size mineral-water pool, seven outdoor whirlpool baths, a pool designed for tanning, champagne pools, and full-service salon on 15 tropically landscaped acres. The highlight is California's only European-style clay bath. Certified massage therapists are on duty. *Take Hwy. 91 east to I–15 south. Continue 8 mi to Temescal Canyon Rd. exit, turn right and go 1 mi to Glen Ivy Rd. to its end. Tel. 714/277–3529. Admission: $14.75 Sat., Sun., and holidays; $12.50 weekdays. Open daily 10–6.*

The Coast

Coastal Orange County, dotted with charming beach towns, and punctuated with world-class resorts, offers the quintessential laid-back Southern California experience. You can catch a monster wave with the bronzed local kids, get a glimpse of some rich and famous lifestyles, and take a walk through this stretch of shoreline's natural treasures. Sites and stops on this tour are strung out along some 30 miles of the Pacific Coast Highway (known locally as PCH), and we'll take this route north to south. While there is bus service along the coast road, by car is really the best way to explore it.

⓬ If you're interested in wildlife, a walk through **Bolsa Chica Ecological Reserve** (tel. 714/842–1312) will reward you with a chance to see an amazingly restored 300-acre salt marsh, which is home to 315 species of birds, plus other animals and plants. You can see many of them by exploring the 1.5-mile loop trail that meanders through the reserve. The walk is especially delightful in winter months, when you're likely to see great blue heron, snowy and great egrets, common loons, and other migrating birds. The salt marsh, located off PCH between Warner Avenue and Golden West Street, can be visited at any time, but a local support group, Amigos de Bolsa Chica, offers free guided tours from 9 to 10:30 AM on the first Saturday of the month, September through April.

⓭ **Huntington Beach**, with its 9 miles of white sand and sometimes towering waves, has long been home to the hang-10 set. This beach is a favorite of Orange County residents and has ample parking, food concessions, fire pits, and lifeguards. For years, the town itself was little more than a string of small, tacky buildings across PCH from the beach containing surf shops, T-shirt emporiums, and hot-dog stands. In the early '90s, however, work began on a face-lift aimed at transforming the town into a shining resort area, with the newly reconstructed 1,800-foot-long **Huntington Pier** as its centerpiece. The new Pierside Pavilion, across PCH from the pier, contains shops, a restaurant, nightclub, and theater complex. The Waterfront Hilton Hotel is the first of four hotels scheduled to go up along the coast in the coming years. The **Museum of Surfing** (411 Olive St., tel. 714/960-3483; call for schedule) contains an extensive collection of surfing memorabilia.

Newport Beach has a dual personality: It's best-known as the quintessential (upscale) beach town, with its island-dotted yacht harbor and a history of such illustrious residents as John Wayne, author Joseph Wambaugh, and Watergate scandal figure Bob Haldeman; and then there's inland Newport Beach, just southwest of John Wayne airport, a business and commercial hub of the county with a major shopping center and a clutch of high-rise office buildings and hotels.

Even if you're not a boat captain, and you don't qualify as seaside high society, you can explore the charming avenues and al-
⓮ leys surrounding the famed **Newport Harbor**, which shelters nearly 10,000 small boats. If you're here during the Christmas holidays, don't miss the Christmas boat parade—one of the best on the West Coast—with hundreds of brightly lit and decorated yachts cruising through the channels. You can see the parade from various restaurants overlooking the marina, but reserve a table early.

⑮ The waterside portion of Newport Beach consists of a U-shaped harbor with the mainland along one leg and the **Balboa Peninsula** separating the marina from the ocean along the other. Set within the harbor are eight small islands, including Balboa and Lido, both well known for their famous residents. The homes lining the shore may seem modest, but remember that this is some of the most expensive real estate in the world.

You can reach the peninsula from PCH at Newport Boulevard, which will take you to Balboa Boulevard. Begin your exploration of the peninsula at the **Newport Pier**, which juts out into the ocean near 20th Street. Street parking is difficult here, so grab the first space you find and be prepared to walk. A stroll along Ocean Front reveals much of the character of this place. On weekday mornings you're likely to encounter the historic fleet of dory fishermen on the beach near the pier, hawking their predawn catches. On weekends the walk is alive with kids (of all ages) on skates, Roller Blades, skateboards, and bikes weaving among the strolling pedestrians and whizzing past fast-food joints, swimsuit shops, and seedy bars.

Continue your drive along Balboa Boulevard nearly to the end of the peninsula, where the charm is of quite a different character. On the bay side is the very Victorian **Balboa Pavilion**, perched on the water's edge. Built in 1902 as a bath and boat house, it hosted big-band dances in the 1940s. Today it houses a restaurant and shops and is a departure point for harbor and whale-watching cruises. Adjacent to the pavilion is the three-car ferry, which connects the peninsula to Balboa Island. Several blocks surrounding the pavilion support shops that are a little nicer than those at Newport Pier, restaurants, and a small Fun Zone with a Ferris wheel and arcade. On the ocean side of the peninsula the Balboa Pier juts into the surf, backed by a long, wide beach that seems to stretch to forever.

⑯ The attractions of inland Newport Beach are in striking contrast to the beach scene. **Fashion Island** is a trendy shopping mall centered in a circle of office and hotel buildings. Anchored by department stores such as Robinson's and Broadway, it holds an array of shops and boutiques. **Atrium Court**, a Mediterranean-style complex, is popular with upscale shoppers, featuring shops such as Splash and Flash, with trendy swimwear; Amen Wardy, with the most haughty of women's fashions; and Posh, a men's store. *On Newport Center Dr. between Jamboree and MacArthur Blvds., just off PCH.*

Time Out   **Farmer's Market at Atrium Court** (tel. 714/760–0403) is a grocery store and more, selling a vast array of exotic foods, prime meats, and glorious fresh produce arranged in color-coordinated patterns. Also on the ground floor of the Atrium Court is a gourmet food fair, with stands offering sushi, exotic coffees, a salsa bar, a Johnny Rocket's hamburger stand, plus the usual deli selections.

⑰ The **Newport Harbor Art Museum** is internationally known for its impressive collection of abstract expressionist works and cutting-edge contemporary works by California artists. Snacks are available in the Sculpture Garden Cafe. *850 San Clemente Dr., tel. 714/759–1122. Admission: $3 adults, $1 children. Open Tues.–Sun. 10–5.*

Just south of Newport Beach, **Corona del Mar** is a small jewel of a town with an exceptional beach. You can walk clear out onto the bay on a rough-and-tumble rock jetty. Much of the beach around here is backed by short cliffs that resemble scaled-down versions of the Northern California coastline. The town itself stretches only a few blocks along the PCH, but some of the fanciest stores and ritziest restaurants in the county are located here. **Sherman Library and Gardens,** a lush botanical garden and library specializing in southwest flora and fauna, offers diversion from sun and sand. You can wander among cactus gardens, rose gardens, a wheelchair-height touch-and-smell garden, and a tropical conservatory. *2647 E. Coast Hwy., Corona del Mar, tel. 714/673-2261. Admission: $2. Gardens open daily 10:30-4.*

The drive south to Laguna Beach passes some of Southern California's most beautiful oceanfront; Crystal Cove State Beach stretches from Corona del Mar to Laguna, and its undersea park lures swimmers and divers. Each curve in the highway along here turns up a sparkling vista of crashing surf to one side and gently rolling golden brown hills sweeping inland to the other.

Laguna Beach has been called SoHo by the Sea, which is at least partly right. It is an artists' colony, which during the 1950s and 1960s attracted the beat, hip and far-out, but it is also a colony of conservative wealth. The two camps coexist in relative harmony, with Art prevailing in the congested village, and Wealth entrenched in the canyons and on the hillsides surrounding the town.

Walk along PCH in town or side streets such as Forest or Ocean and you'll pass gallery after gallery filled with art ranging from billowy seascapes to neon sculpture and kinetic structures. In addition, you'll find a wide selection of crafts, high fashion, beachwear and jewelry shops. To get a sense of Laguna's beat-generation past, stop at **Fahrenheit 451** (540 S. PCH, tel. 714/494-5151) for a cup of coffee and stimulating conversation; this alternative bookstore, established in 1968, presents live music every night and carries an eclectic selection of volumes not found in your everyday mall bookshop.

The **Laguna Beach Museum of Art,** right near Heisler Park, has exhibits of historical and contemporary California art. *307 Cliff Dr., tel. 714/494-6531. Admission: $3. Open Tues. through Sun. 11 AM-5 PM.*

Time Out The patio at **Las Brisas** (tel. 714/494-5434) restaurant right next door to the museum offers one of the loveliest views of the coastline available in Laguna Beach. Stop here for a snack and drink in the scene.

In front of the Pottery Shack on PCH is a bit of local nostalgia—a life-size statue of Eiler Larson, the town greeter, who for years stood at the edge of town saying hello and goodbye to visitors.

Laguna's many festivals are what give it a worldwide reputation in the arts community. During July and August, the Sawdust Festival and Art-a-Fair, the Laguna Festival of the Arts, and the **Pageant of the Masters** take place. The Pageant of the Masters (tel. 714/494-1147) is Laguna's most impressive event, a blending of life and art. Live models and carefully orchestrated backgrounds are arranged in striking mimicry of famous paintings. Participants must hold a perfectly still pose for the length of their stay onstage. It is an impressive effort, requiring hours of training and rehearsal by the 400 or so residents who volunteer each year.

Going to Laguna without exploring its beaches would be a shame. To get away from the hubbub of Main Beach, go north to Woods Cove, off the Coast Highway at Diamond Street; it's especially quiet during the week. Big rock formations hide lurking crabs. As you climb the steps to leave, you'll see a stunning English-style mansion that was once the home of Bette Davis. At the end of almost every street in Laguna, there is a little cove with its own beach.

20 **The Ritz Carlton** in Dana Point is the classiest hotel for miles and has developed a worldwide following for its oceanside location, gleaming marble, and stunning antiques. Even if you're not a registered guest, you can enjoy the view and the elegant service by taking English tea, which is served each afternoon in the Library. *33533 Ritz Carlton Dr., Dana Point, tel. 714/ 240–2000.*

21 **Dana Point** is Orange County's newest aquatic playground, a small-boat marina tucked into a dramatic natural harbor surrounded by high bluffs. The harbor was first described more than 100 years ago by its namesake Richard Henry Dana in his book, *Two Years before the Mast.* The marina has docks for small boats and marine-oriented shops and restaurants. Recent development includes a hillside park with bike and walking trails, hotels, small shopping centers, and a collection of eateries. A monument to Dana stands in a gazebo at the top of the bluffs in front of the Blue Lantern Inn. There's a pleasant sheltered beach and park at the west end of the marina. Boating is the big thing here. Dana Wharf Sportfishing (tel. 714/ 496–5794) has charters year-round and runs whale-watching excursions in winter, and the community sponsors an annual whale festival in late February.

22 The **Orange County Marine Institute** offers a number of programs and excursions designed to entertain and educate about the ocean. Three tanks containing touchable sea creatures are available on weekends. Anchored near the institute is *The Pilgrim,* a full-size replica of the square-rigged vessel on which Richard Henry Dana sailed. Tours of *The Pilgrim* are offered Sunday from 11 to 2:30. A gallery and gift shop are open daily. *24200 Dana Point Harbor Dr., tel. 714/496–2274. Admission free. Open daily 10 AM–3:30 PM.*

San Juan Capistrano is best-known for its mission, and, of course, for the swallows that migrate here each year from their winter haven in Argentina. The arrival of the birds on St. Joseph's Day, March 19, launches a week of festivities. After summering in the arches of the old stone church, the swallows head home on St. John's Day, October 23.

23 Founded in 1776 by Father Junípero Serra, **Mission San Juan Capistrano** was the major Roman Catholic outpost between Los Angeles and San Diego. Although the original Great Stone Church lies in ruins, the victim of an 1812 earthquake, many of the mission's adobe buildings have been restored and illustrate life during the mission period. Exhibits include an olive millstone, tallow ovens, tanning vats, metalworking furnaces, and padres' living quarters. The impressive Serra Chapel is believed to be the oldest building still in use in California. The knowledgeable staff in the mission's visitors center can help you with a self-guided tour. *Camino Capistrano and Ortega Hwy., tel. 714/493–1111. Admission: $3 adults, $2 children 11 and under. Open daily 8:30–5.*

㉔ Near the mission is the postmodern **San Juan Capistrano Library,** built in 1983. Architect Michael Graves mixed classical design with the style of the mission to striking effect. Its courtyard has secluded places for reading, as well as a running water fountain. *31495 El Camino Real, tel. 714/493–3984. Open Mon.–Thurs. 10–9, Fri.–Sat. 10–5.*

The **Decorative Arts Study Center,** just up the street from the mission, presents exhibits and lectures on interior design and decorating, gardens, plus an annual antiques show and storytelling festival in October. *31431 Camino Capistrano, tel. 714/ 496–2132. Open Tues.–Sat. 10–3.*

Galleria Capistrano is one of Southern California's leading galleries devoted to the art of Native Americans. Exhibits include first-rate paintings, prints, jewelry, and sculpture from Southwest and Northwest artists. *31892 Camino Capistrano, tel. 714/661–1781. Open Tues.–Sun. 11–6, Mon. noon–5.*

Time Out The **Capistrano Depot** (26701 Verdugo St., tel. 714/496–8181) is not only the local Amtrak train station but also a restaurant. The eclectic menu runs from rack of lamb to southwestern fare to pasta. There's entertainment nightly and Dixieland jazz on Sunday. It's a perfect way to see San Juan if you are based in Los Angeles—a train ride, a meal, and then a little sightseeing.

The southernmost city in Orange County, San Clemente, is probably best-remembered as the site of Richard Nixon's Western White House. Casa Pacifica was often in the news during Nixon's presidency. Situated on a massive 25-acre estate, the house, now a private residence, is visible from the beach; just look up to the cliffs.

Perhaps even more infamous than Nixon's house—and a good **㉕** deal more sinister as far as locals are concerned—is the **San Onofre Nuclear Power Plant,** a controversial installation lending an eerie feeling to the nearby beach, where surfers ride the waves undaunted. Off the Coast Highway, the San Onofre Nuclear Information Center is a must for those who want to know more about the mechanics of nuclear energy.

San Clemente State Beach is one of the least crowded and most beautiful of the state beaches. The area around San Clemente also offers a wide selection of activities that make Southern California the playground that it is: swimming, surfing, sailing, fishing, and picnicking.

For avid bicycle riders, the next 20 miles south of San Clemente is prime terrain. Camp Pendleton welcomes cyclists to use some of its roads—just don't be surprised to see a troop helicopter taking off right beside you. Pendleton is the country's largest Marine Corps base. Training involves offshore landings; overland treks are also conducted on the installation's three mountain ranges, five lakes, and 250 miles of roads.

What to See and Do with Children

Disneyland and Knott's Berry Farm are the prime attractions (*see* Inland Orange County, above), but there are many other amusements designed for children and families.

Raging Waters is a water theme park sure to please the whole family. It's actually in southeast Los Angeles County, but not far from Anaheim. Clean beaches and river rapids (man-made), water slides, and safe water fun for the smallest of children are found here. *111 Via Verde, San Dimas, where I–10 and I–210 meet (take the Raging Waters Blvd. exit), tel. 714/592–6453. Admission: $18.50 adults, $9.95 children 42–48 inches tall, children under 42 inches free, reduced rates for senior citizens and nonsliders. Open Apr.–May, weekends 10–7, from end of June, weekdays 10–9, weekends 9–10.*

Wild Rivers is Orange County's newest water theme park. It has more than 40 rides and attractions. Among them: a wave pool, several daring slides, a river inner-tube ride, and several places at which to eat and shop. *8800 Irvine Center Dr., Laguna Hills (just off I–405 at Irvine Center Dr.), tel. 714/768–WILD. Admission: $15.95 adults, $11.95 children 3–9; discounts after 4 PM. Open mid-May–Sept. Call for hours.*

Golf-n-Stuff offers unusual family golfing fun. This miniature-golf and arcade center is near Disneyland. Colored lights sparkle on geyser fountains amid windmills, castles, and waterfalls. *1656 S. Harbor Blvd., 714/994–2110. Admission: $5 adults and children 6 and up; special family rates. Open Sun.–Thurs. 10 AM–10 PM, Fri. and Sat. 10 AM–midnight.*

Hobby City Doll and Toy Museum houses antique dolls and toys from around the world in a replica of the White House. It is one of the world's largest hobby, crafts, and collector centers. *1238 S. Beach Blvd., Anaheim, tel. 714/527–2323. Open daily 10 AM–6 PM.*

The **Children's Museum at La Habra** features all kinds of diversions for children. The restored 1923 railroad depot has a beehive, railroad cars, and several touchable displays. *301 S. Euclid St., tel. 213/905–9793. Admission: $3 adults, $2.50 children 2–16 and senior citizens. Open Mon.–Sat. 10 AM–4 PM.*

Laguna Moulton Playhouse has a special children's theater with changing fare. *606 Laguna Canyon Rd., tel. 714/494–0743.*

Off the Beaten Track

If you find time to visit any of these spots during your trip to Orange County, you can term yourself local. These are some of the "in" spots that natives know well.

Lido Isle. This island in Newport Harbor, the location of many elegant homes, provides some insight into the upper-crust Orange County mind-set. A number of grassy areas offer great harbor views; each is marked "Private Community Park." *Take Hwy. 55 to PCH in Newport Beach. Turn left at the signal onto Via Lido and follow this street onto the island.*

Old Towne Orange contains at least 1,200 buildings documented as historically relevant. A walking tour explores some of the most interesting of these, including the Ainsworth House, a museum dedicated to the city's early lifestyle; the 1901 Finley Home, location of the 1945 film *Fallen Angels;* and O'Hara's Irish Pub, a hangout for local reporters. A brochure describing all the stops is available. *City of Orange, 300 E. Chapman Ave., Room 12, Orange 92666, tel. 714/744-7220.*

Little Saigon, an area of the city of Westminster, north and south of Bolsa Avenue, is home to Orange County's sizable Vietnamese community, the largest concentration outside Vietnam. Offering a view into another world, Little Saigon is dominated by Asian architecture and Oriental symbols. Restaurants serving Asian delicacies are plentiful along here; among the most popular are the Dragon and Phoenix Palace at 9211 Bolsa Avenue, which is said to have the best dim sum in town.

C'est Si Bon. This little shopping-mall café lures locals for its great selection of coffees, pastries, cheeses, and pâtés. Soups and sandwiches are available to eat here or take out. *149 Riverside Ave., off PCH in Newport Beach, tel. 714/645-0447. Open Mon.-Fri. 6:30-6, Sat. 7:30-5, Sun. 8 AM-1:30 PM.*

Shopping

"When the going gets tough, Orange County goes shopping," says the inscription on totes carried by many residents as they navigate the aisles of their local malls. Shopping is Orange County's favorite indoor sport, and it's got the shopping malls to prove it. Indeed, Orange County is home to some of the biggest, most varied, classiest malls in the world. Even if the merchandise offered by Tiffany, Chanel, and Brooks Brothers is beyond your budget, you can always window-shop. The following is just a small selection of the shopping possibilities in the county.

South Coast Plaza (Bristol and Sunflower Sts., Costa Mesa), the most amazing of all the malls and the largest in Orange County, is actually two enclosed shopping centers, complete with greenery and tumbling waterfalls bisecting the wide aisles. The older section is anchored by Nordstrom and May Company, and the newer Crystal Court across the street has Robinson's and the Broadway department stores at its ends. However, it's the variety of stores that makes this mall special. You'll find Gucci, Charles Jourdan, FAO Schwarz, Sak's Fifth Avenue, and Mark Cross just up the aisle from Sears. There's even an outpost of the Laguna Beach Museum of Art here; it's located near the Carousel Court, just a few steps from MacDonald's and Eddie Bauer. For literary buffs, there is a branch of the famous Rizzoli's International Bookstore.

Fashion Island on Newport Center Drive in Newport Beach sits on the top of a hill, and shoppers can enjoy the ocean breeze. It is an open-air, single-level mall of more than 120 stores. The recently constructed Atrium Court is an enclosed section containing five stories of boutiques and stores such as Sharper Image, Benetton, and Caswell & Massey.

Main Place, just off I-5 in Santa Ana, opened recently with major department stores such as Robinson's, Bullocks, and Nordstrom as its anchors. While many of the shops are upscale, the mall itself resembles a warehouse. It's busy and noisy.

If you can look past the inflatable palm trees, unimaginative T-shirts and other tourist novelties, there is some good browsing to be done in Laguna Beach. There are dozens of art galleries, antiques shops, one-of-a-kind craft boutiques, and custom jewelry stores. **Thee Foxes Trot,** 264 Forest Avenue, features a delightful selection of handcrafted items from around the world; **George's Art Glass and Jewelry,** 269 Forest Avenue, contains a large selection of etched- and blown-glass bowls, vases, glassware, and jewelry; **From Laguna,** 241 Forest Avenue, carries casual fashions for women and men; and **Toni's Kids Closet,** Coast Highway, sells designer children's clothing and hand-crafted wooden toys.

Participant Sports

Orange County is a sportsperson's playground; from surfing to walking, from sailing to biking, there is something for everyone who wants to be active.

Bicycling   Bicycles and roller skates are some of the most popular means of transportation along the beaches. A bike path spans the whole distance from Marina del Rey all the way to San Diego, with only some minor breaks. Most beaches have rental stands. In Laguna, try the **Laguna Cyclery** (tel. 800/400–2453); in Huntington Beach, **Team Bicycle Rentals** (tel. 714/969–5480).

Golf   Golf is one of the most popular sports in Orange County, and owing to the climate, almost 365 days out of the year are perfect golf days. Here is a selection of golf courses:

Anaheim Hills Public Country Club (tel. 714/637–7311); **Costa Mesa Public Golf and Country Club** (tel. 714/540–7500); **Mile Square Golf Course,** Fountain Valley (tel. 714/545–3726); **Meadowlark Golf Course,** Huntington Beach (tel. 714/846–1364); **Rancho San Joaquin Golf Course,** Irvine (tel. 714/786–5522); **Costa del Sol Golf Course,** Mission Viejo (tel. 714/581–0940); **Newport Beach Golf Course** (tel. 714/852–8681); **San Clemente Municipal Golf Course** (tel. 714/492–3943); **San Juan Hills Country Club,** San Juan Capistrano (tel. 714/837–0361); **Aliso Creek Golf Course,** South Laguna (tel. 714/499–1919).

Snorkeling   The fact that Corona del Mar—along with its two colorful reefs—is off-limits to boats makes it a great place for snorkeling. Laguna Beach is also a good spot for snorkeling and diving; the whole beach area of the city is a marine preserve.

Surfing   Orange County's signature sport may be too rough-and-tumble for some; you can get the same feel with a boogie board. Rental stands are found at all beaches. Body surfing is also a good way to start. Huntington Beach is popular with surfers and spectators. "The Wedge" at Newport Beach is one of the most famous surfing spots in the world. Don't miss the spectacle of surfers, who appear to be tiny in the middle of the waves, flying through this treacherous place. San Clemente surfers are usually positioned in a primo spot right across from the San Onofre Nuclear Reactor.

Swimming   All of the state, county, and city beaches in Orange County allow swimming. Make sure there is a manned lifeguard stand nearby and you will be pretty safe. Also keep on the lookout for posted signs about undertow: It can be mighty nasty in certain places around here.

Tennis Most of the larger hotels have tennis courts. Here are some other choices; try the local Yellow Pages for further listings.

Huntington Beach **Edison Community Center** (21377 Magnolia St., tel. 714/960–8870) has two courts available on a first-come, first-served basis, or reservations can be made. The **Murdy Community Center** (7000 Norma Dr., tel. 714/960–8895) has four courts, either first come, first served or by reservations. Cost for each facility is $2 an hour.

Laguna Beach Eight metered courts can be found at **Laguna Beach High School,** on Park Avenue. Two courts are available at the **Irvine Bowl,** Laguna Canyon Road, and six new courts are available at **Alta Laguna Park,** at the end of Alta Laguna Blvd., off Park Ave., on a first-come, first-served basis. For more information, call the City of Laguna Beach Recreation Department at 714/497–0716.

Newport Beach Call the recreation department at 714/644–3151 for information about court use at **Corona del Mar High School** (2101 E. Bluff Dr.). There are eight courts for public use.

San Clemente There are four courts at **San Luis Rey Park,** on Avenue San Luis Rey. They are offered on a first-come, first-served basis. Call the recreation department at 714/361–8200 for further information.

Water Sports Rental stands for surfboards, Windsurfers, small powerboats, and sailboats can be found near most of the piers. **Hobie Sports** has three locations for surfboard and boogie-board rentals—two in Dana Point (tel. 714/496–2366 or 714/496–1251) and one in Laguna (tel. 714/497–3304).

In the biggest boating town of all, Newport Beach, you can rent sailboats and small motorboats at **Balboa Boat Rentals** in the harbor (tel. 714/673–1320; open Fri.–Sun. 10 AM–4 PM). Sailboats rent for $25 an hour, and motorboats for $26 an hour, half price for each subsequent hour. You must have a driver's license, and some knowledge of boating is helpful; rented boats are not allowed out of the bay.

Parasailing is also rising as a water sport. At **Davey's Locker** in the Balboa Pavilion (tel. 714/673–1434; open daily 9 AM–5:30 PM during the summer), you can parasail for 10 to 15 minutes during a 90–minute boat ride. Cost is $40 per person, with up to six persons per boat. The last excursion leaves at 4 PM.

In Dana Point, power and sailboats can be rented at **Embarcadero Marina** (tel. 714/496–6177, open Mon.–Fri. 8 AM–5 PM, Sat. and Sun. 7 AM–5:30 PM), near the launching ramp at Dana Point Harbor. Boat sizes vary—sailboats range from $12 to $20 an hour, motorboats are $18 an hour. Cash only is accepted. Parasailing is available from **Dana Wharf Sports Fishing** (tel. 714/496–5794) during the spring and summer. Call for hours and prices.

Spectator Sports

Orange County has some of the best, unplanned, casual spectator sports; besides the surfers, you are bound to catch a vigorous volleyball or basketball game at any beach on any given weekend. Professional sports in Orange County include the following:

Baseball	The **California Angels** (tel. 714/634–2000) play at the Anaheim Stadium from April through October.
Football	The **Los Angeles Rams** (tel. 714/937–6767) have called Anaheim Stadium their home since 1980. The season runs from August through December.
Horse Racing	The **Los Alamitos Race Course** (tel. 714/995–1234) has quarter horse racing and harness racing on a ⅝-mile track. Thoroughbred racing is part of the fare here as well.
Horse Shows	Twice monthly at the **Orange County Fair Equestrian Center** (tel. 714/641–1328) show jumping is featured. Admission is free.

Beaches

Huntington Beach State Beach (tel. 714/536–1454) runs for 9 miles along the Pacific Coast Highway (take Beach Blvd. [Hwy. 39] if you are coming from inland). There are changing rooms, concessions, barbecue pits, and vigilant lifeguards on the premises, and there is parking. **Bolsa Chica State Beach** (tel. 714/536–1454), just north of Huntington and across from the Bolsa Chica Ecological Reserve, has barbecue pits and is usually less crowded than its neighbor.

Lower Newport Bay provides an enclave sheltered from the ocean. This area, off Coast Highway on Jamboree, is a 740-acre preserve for ducks and geese. **Newport Dunes Resort** (tel. 714/729–3863), nearby, offers RV spaces, picnic facilities, changing rooms, water-sports rentals, and a place to launch boats.

Just south of Newport Beach, **Corona del Mar State Beach** (tel. 714/644–3044) has a tide pool and caves waiting to be explored. It also boasts one of the best walks in the county—a beautiful rock pier jutting into the ocean. Facilities include barbecue pits, volleyball poles, food, rest rooms, and parking.

Located at the end of Broadway at Pacific Coast Highway, **Laguna Beach**'s Main Beach Park has sand volleyball, two half-basketball courts, children's play equipment, picnic areas, rest rooms, showers, and road parking.

The county's best spot for scuba diving is in the **Marine Life Refuge** (tel. 714/494–6571), which runs from Seal Rock to Diver's Cove in Laguna. Farther south, in South Laguna, **Aliso County Park** (tel. 714/661–7013) is a recreation area with a pier for fishing, barbecue pits, parking, food, and rest rooms. Swim Beach, near Dana Point Harbor (tel. 714/661–7013), also has a fishing pier, barbecues, food, parking, and rest rooms, as well as a shower.

Doheny State Park (tel. 714/496–6171), near Dana Point Harbor, has food stands and shops nearby. Camping is permitted here; there are also picnic facilities and a pier for fishing. **San Clemente State Beach** (tel. 714/492–3156) is one of the least crowded and a favorite of locals and surfers. It has ample camping facilities, RV hook–ups, and food stands.

Dining

By Bruce David Colen

Orange County seems to prove that nothing raises the quality of restaurants quite so much as being in a high-rent district. Since the region became one of the most costly places to buy a home, the dining scene has vastly improved. Restaurant prices, however, are still not as high as in upscale neighborhoods of Los Angeles and San Francisco (perhaps high mortgage payments have made the natives dining-dollar wary). The growing number of luxury hotels, with dining rooms to match, has also broadened gastronomic choices. The French cuisine at Le Meridien, in Newport, for example, is among the best of any Southern California hotel. You'll need a reservation there as well as at the pricier places.

The most highly recommended restaurants are indicated by a star ★.

Category	Cost*
Very Expensive	over $40
Expensive	$30–$40
Moderate	$15–$30
Inexpensive	under $15

per person, without tax (8.25%), service, or drinks

Anaheim
Expensive

JW's. You would never guess you were in a hotel—the dining room looks like a French country inn, complete with a fireplace. The food is well-prepared classic French, featuring roasted saddle of lamb, venison, and wild boar. *Marriott Hotel, 700 W. Convention Way, tel. 714/750–8000. Reservations required. Jacket required. AE, D, DC, MC, V. Valet parking. Dinner only. Closed Sun.*

Moderate

Bessie Wall's. Citrus rancher John Wall built this house for his bride-to-be in 1927. It has been restored and the rooms converted into dining areas decorated with Wall memorabilia. Bessie's favorite chicken-and-dumplings recipe is on the menu, which also features Southern California–Mexican dishes. *1074 N. Tustin Blvd., tel. 714/630– 2812. Reservations advised. Jacket advised. AE, D, DC, MC, V. Closed Sat. lunch.*

Overland Stage. A dining Disneyland of sorts, this restaurant's theme is California's Wild West days. There's a stagecoach over the entrance and all sorts of Western bric-a-brac within. The daily specials are intriguing: wild boar, buffalo, rattlesnake, bear, and elk. *1855 S. Harbor Blvd., tel. 714/750–1811. Reservations advised. Jacket advised. AE, D, DC, MC, V. Closed for lunch weekends.*

Corona del Mar
Expensive

Trees. The contemporary look, atmosphere, and menu of this upscale restaurant are among the most appealing in the county. The three dining rooms, with walls and table appointments done in shades of pink, surround a glassed-in atrium planted with towering ficus trees. Each room has its own fireplace. Satisfying cooking matches the setting: Maryland crab cakes, roast turkey dinners on Sunday; Chinese chicken salad, pot stickers and spring rolls; veal sweetbreads in puff pastry. Don't pass up the apricot mousse dessert. There's also a piano bar. *440 Heliotrope Ave., tel. 714/673–0910. Reservations required. Jacket required. AE, D, DC, MC, V. Closed for lunch.*

Moderate
★

The Five Crowns. This surprisingly faithful replica of Ye Old Bell, England's oldest inn, has its barmaids and waitresses costumed in Elizabethan dress. There's a wide array of British ales and, of course, Guinness stout. The roast beef with Yorkshire pudding and the rack of lamb are very good, as are the fish dishes, and all at reasonable prices. *3801 E. Pacific Coast Hwy., tel. 714/760–0331. Reservations required. Jacket advised. AE, D, DC, MC, V. Closed for lunch; open for Sun. brunch.*

Costa Mesa
Inexpensive

Mandarin Gourmet. Dollar for bite, owner Michael Chang provides what the critics and locals consider the best Chinese cuisine in the area. His specialties include a crisp-yet-juicy Peking duck, cashew chicken, and, seemingly everyone's favorite, mushu pork. There is also a very good wine list. *1500 Adams Ave., tel. 714/540–1937. Reservations accepted. Dress: casual. AE, DC, MC, V.*

Ruby's. This is one in a chain of five lunch spots in Orange County that recall 1940s diners. Everyone seems to order Ruby's hamburger "with the works." Following in popularity: smothered steak and satay chicken. The location at the Balboa Pier has a great view. *Crystal Court, 3333 Bear St., tel. 714/662–7829. Dress: casual. AE, MC, V.*

Dana Point
Expensive

Watercolors. This light, cheerful dining room provides a clifftop view of the harbor and an equally enjoyable Continental-California menu, along with low-calorie choices. Try the baked breast of pheasant, roast rabbit, grilled swordfish, and either the Caesar or poached spinach salad. *Dana Point Resort, tel. 714/661–5000. Reservations suggested. Dress: resort casual. AE, D, DC, MC, V. Valet parking.*

Moderate

Chart House. This is one of the most popular of the small chain of steak-and-seafood houses in Southern California. Mud pie is the dessert everyone asks for. This particular location has a sensational view of the harbor from most of the tables and booths. *34442 Green Lantern, tel. 714/493–1183. Reservations advised. Jacket advised. AE, DC, MC, V. Closed for lunch weekends.*

Delaney's Restaurant. Fresh seafood from nearby San Diego's fishing fleet is what this place is all about. Your choice is prepared as simply as possible. If you have to wait for a table, pass the time at the clam and oyster bar. *25001 Dana Dr., tel. 714/496–6196. Reservations advised. Dress: casual. AE, D, DC, MC, V.*

Fullerton
Expensive
★

The Cellar. The name tells the story here: a subterranean dining room with beamed ceiling and stone walls, wine racks, and casks. Appropriately, the list of wines from Europe and California is among the best in the nation. The bill of fare is classic French cuisine that has been lightened for the California palate. *305 N. Harbor Blvd., tel. 714/525–5682. Reservations required. Jacket and tie advised. AE, DC, MC, V. Closed for lunch and Sun. and Mon.*

Huntington Beach
Inexpensive

Texas Loosey's Chili Parlor & Saloon. This place serves up Tex-Mex cooking with the fixin's to make it even hotter, plus steaks, ribs, and burgers. Country-and-western music is played in the evenings. *14160 Beach Blvd., tel. 714/898–9797. No reservations. Dress: informal. AE, MC, V.*

Irvine
Moderate–Expensive

Chanteclair. This Franco-Italian country house is a lovely, tasteful retreat amid an island of modern high-rise office buildings. French Riviera–type cuisine is served, and the Chateaubriand for two and rack of lamb are recommended. *18912 MacArthur Blvd., tel. 714/752–8001. Reservations advised.*

Jacket required. AE, D, DC, MC, V. Closed for lunch Sat.; open for Sun. brunch.

Moderate **Gulliver's.** Jolly old England is the theme of this groaning board. Waitresses are addressed as "wenches" and busboys as "squires." Prime rib is the specialty. *18482 MacArthur Blvd., tel. 714/833–8411. Reservations advised. Jacket advised. AE, DC, MC, V. Closed for lunch weekends.*

Pavilion. Excellent Chinese food is offered in what resembles a formal eating hall of Chef Hu's native Taiwan. Specialties include steamed whole fish, ginger duck, and Hunan lamb. *14110 Culver Dr., tel. 714/551–1688. Reservations advised. Dress: casual. AE, MC, V.*

Prego. A much larger version of the Beverly Hills Prego, this one is located in an attractive approximation of a Tuscan villa and has a patio: a favorite of Orange County Yuppies, who rave about the watch-the-cooks-at-work open kitchen and the oak-burning pizza oven. Try the spit-roasted meats and chicken, or the charcoal-grilled fresh fish. Also try one of the reasonably priced California or Italian wines. *18420 Von Karman Ave., tel. 714/553–1333. Reservations recommended. Dress: casual. AE, DC, MC, V. Valet parking. Closed for lunch weekends.*

Laguna Beach **The Ritz-Carlton.** The Dining Room in this oceanside resort ho-
Expensive tel serves rather pretentious pseudo-nouvelle cuisine, but its Cafe's lavish Sunday brunch is considered the best in Southern California. Be sure to make reservations several days in advance and ask for a table on the terrace, overlooking the swimming pool. *33533 Ritz-Carlton Dr., Niguel, tel. 714/240–2000. Reservations required. Dress: casual but neat. AE, DC, MC, V.*

Moderate **Las Brisas.** From its clifftop terrace, this longtime coastal favorite has a spectacular view of the rugged coastline, wonderful margaritas, addictive guacamole, and nouvelle-Mexican dishes. The first three compensate for the last. *361 Cliff Dr., tel. 714/497–5434. Reservations advised. Dress: casual. AE, DC, MC, V.*

Partners Bistro. Beveled glass, antiques, and lace curtains adorn this neighborhood hangout. The menu features Continental fare such as fresh fish and tournedos of beef. *448 S. Coast Hwy., tel. 714/497–4441. Reservations advised. Dress: casual. AE, MC, V.*

The White House. Bing Crosby and Cecil B. DeMille dined at this local hangout. The broad, mostly American menu has everything from bagels and lox to Mexican favorites. There's also a salad bar, for while you're making up your mind. *340 S. Coast Hwy., tel. 714/494–8088. No reservations. Dress: casual. AE, DC, MC, V.*

Inexpensive **The Beach House.** A Laguna tradition, the Beach House has a white-water view from every table. Fresh fish, lobster, and steamed clams are the drawing cards. *619 Sleepy Hollow La., tel. 714/494–9707. Reservations advised. Jacket advised. AE, MC, V.*

The Cottage. The menu is heavy on vegetarian dishes, and the price is right. Specialties include fresh fish, Victoria Beach scallops, and chicken Alfredo. *308 N. Pacific Coast Hwy., tel. 714/494–3023. Weekend reservations advised. Dress: casual. AE, D, DC, MC, V.*

Tortilla Flats. This hacienda-style restaurant specializes in first-rate chile rellenos, carne Tampiqueña, soft-shell tacos, and beef or chicken fajitas. There's also a wide selection of Mexican tequilas and beers. *1740 S. Coast Hwy., tel. 714/494–6588. Dinner reservations advised. Dress: casual. AE, MC, V. Sun. brunch.*

La Habra **Café El Cholo/Burro Alley.** This is a sibling of the ever-popular
Inexpensive El Cholo in Los Angeles, where people have been going for decades to enjoy the very best in Mexican cooking geared to American tastes. Green corn tamales served in season, Sonora-style enchilada, fajitas, and grilled chicken and beef are among the specialties. There is a cheery outdoor patio and maybe the best margaritas north of the border. *840 E. Whittier Blvd., tel. 714/ 525–1320. Dress: informal. AE, D, MC, V.*

Newport Beach **Antoine's.** This lovely, candle-lit dining room is made for ro-
Expensive mance and quiet conversation. It serves the best French cui-
★ sine of any hotel in Southern California; the fare is nouvelle, but is neither skimpy nor gimmicky. *4500 MacArthur Blvd., tel. 714/ 476–2001. Reservations advised. Jacket and tie required. Closed for lunch; open for brunch Sun.*

★ **The Ritz.** One of the most comfortable Southern California restaurants—the bar area has red leather booths, etched-glass mirrors, and polished brass trim. Don't pass up the smorgasbord appetizer, the roast Bavarian duck, or the rack of lamb from the spit. This is one of those rare places that seems to please everyone. *880 Newport Center Dr., tel. 714/720–1800. Reservations advised. Jacket required. AE, DC, MC, V. Closed for lunch weekends, closed for dinner Tues.–Fri.*

★ **Pascal.** Although it's in a shopping center, you'll think that you're in St-Tropez once you step inside this bright and cheerful bistro. And, after one taste of Pascal Olhat's light Provençal cuisine, the best in Orange County, you'll swear you're in the south of France. Try the sea bass with thyme, the rack of lamb, and the lemon tart. *1000 Bristol St., tel. 714/752–0107. Reservations suggested. Jacket advised. AE, DC, MC, V.*

Moderate **Le Biarritz.** Newport Beach natives have a deep affection for this restaurant, with its country French decor, hanging greenery, and skylit garden room. There's food to match the mood: a veal-and-pheasant pâté, seafood crepes, boned duckling and wild rice, sautéed pheasant with raspberries, and warm apple tart for dessert. *414 N. Newport Blvd., tel. 714/645–6700. Reservations advised. Dress: casual. AE, D, DC, MC, V. Closed for lunch weekends.*

Cannery. The building once was a cannery, and it has wonderful wharf-side views. The seafood entrées are good, and the sandwiches at lunch are satisfying, but the location and lazy atmosphere are the real draw. *3010 Lafayette Ave., tel. 714/ 675– 5777. Reservations advised. Dress: casual. AE, D, DC, MC, V.*

Marrakesh. In a casbah setting straight out of a Hope-and-Crosby road movie, diners become part of the scene—you eat with your fingers while sitting on the floor or lolling on a hassock. Chicken b'stilla, rabbit couscous, and skewered pieces of marinated lamb are the best of the Moroccan dishes. It's fun. *1100 Pacific Coast Hwy., tel. 714/645–8384. Reservations advised. Dress: casual. AE, DC, MC, V. Closed for lunch. (Also in La Jolla, tel. 619/454–2500, and La Mesa, tel. 619/462– 3663.)*

Inexpensive **Crab Cooker.** If you don't mind waiting in line, this shanty of a place serves fresh fish grilled over mesquite at low-low prices. The clam chowder and cole slaw are quite good, too. *2200 New-*

port Blvd., tel. 714/673–0100. No reservations. Dress: casual. No credit cards.

★ **El Torito Grill.** Southwestern cooking incorporating south-of-the-border specialties is the attraction here. The just-baked tortillas with a green pepper salsa, the turkey molé enchilada, and the blue-corn duck tamalitos are good choices. The bar serves 20 different tequila brands and hand-shaken margaritas. *951 Newport Center Dr., tel. 714/640–2875. Reservations advised. Dress: casual. AE, D, DC, MC, V.*

Orange
Expensive

The Hobbit. This is the place for a feast, if you make reservations two to three months in advance. The six- to eight-course French-Continental meal starts in the wine cellar at 7:30 and ends about three hours later. *2932 E. Chapman Ave., tel. 714/997–1972. Reservations required far in advance. Jacket and tie required. MC, V. One seating only. Closed Mon.*

Moderate

La Brasserie. It doesn't *look* like a typical brasserie, but the varied French cuisine befits the name over the door. One dining room in the multilevel house is done as an attractive, cozy library. There's also an inviting bar-lounge. *202 S. Main St., tel. 714/978–6161. Reservations advised. Dress: casual. AE, DC, MC, V. Closed for lunch weekends, closed for dinner Tues.–Fri.*

San Clemente
Moderate

Andreino's. Pasta is the key word at this Italian restaurant decorated with antiques, flowers, and lace curtains. *1925 S. El Camino Real, tel. 714/492–9955. Reservations advised. Jacket advised. AE, MC, V. Closed for lunch, and Sun. and Mon.*

Etienne's. Smack-dab in the center of town, this restaurant is housed in a white stucco historical landmark. There is outdoor seating on a terra-cotta patio with fountains. Indoors, the decor is French château. Only the freshest fish is served; Chateaubriand, frogs' legs, and other French favorites are on the menu, along with flaming desserts. *215 S. El Camino Real, tel. 714/492–7263. Reservations advised. Jacket advised. AE, D, DC, MC, V. Closed for lunch and Sun.*

San Juan Capistrano
Moderate

El Adobe. President Nixon memorabilia fills the walls in this early American–style eatery serving Mexican-American food. Mariachi bands play Wednesday–Sunday. *31891 Camino Capistrano, tel. 714/830–8620. AE, D, MC, V.*

L'Hirondelle. There are only 12 tables at this charming French inn. Duckling is the specialty and is prepared three different ways. *31631 Camino Capistrano, tel. 714/661–0425. Reservations necessary. MC, V. Sun. brunch. Closed for lunch, and Mon. and Tues.*

Santa Ana
Inexpensive

Saddleback Inn. The decor here harks back to Orange County's hacienda days, blending Old Spain and California Mission styles. Slow-cooked barbecued roast beef is the house specialty; filet of sole amandine, barbecued baked chicken, and filet mignon with bordelaise sauce are other choices. *1660 E. First St., tel. 714/835–3311. AE, MC, V.*

Lodging

Lodging to suit every budget and taste is available in Orange County; offerings range from the very expensive four-star Ritz-Carlton on the coast to the comfortable-but-plain chain motels around Disneyland. Those who haven't been to Orange County for a while will be pleasantly suprised to see that many hotels near Disneyland have recently undergone renovation and now have a bright new look. In addition to the choices listed here for the Anaheim area, there are a number of motels; but visitors should be careful to pick only familiar chain names. Central Orange County also supports a number of lodgings that normally cater to business travelers but offer substantial discounts on weekends.

Prices listed here are based on summer rates. Winter rates, especially near Disneyland, tend to be somewhat less. It pays to shop around for promotional and weekend rates.

The most highly recommended lodgings in each price category are indicated by a star ★.

Category	Cost*
Very Expensive	over $130
Expensive	$90–$130
Moderate	$70–$90
Inexpensive	under $70

for a double room

Anaheim
Very Expensive

Anaheim Hilton and Towers. This hotel is a good choice for anyone attending functions at the Anaheim Convention Center, which is just a few steps from the front door. It is virtually a self-contained city—complete with its own post office. The lobby is dominated by a bright, airy atrium, and guest rooms are decorated in pinks and greens with light-wood furniture. *777 Convention Way, 92802, tel. 714/750–4321 or 800/222–9923. 1,600 rooms. Concierge floor. Facilities: 4 restaurants, lounges, shops, outdoor pool, Jacuzzis, golfing center, fitness center ($10 charge), sundeck, concierge. AE, D, DC, MC, V.*

Anaheim Marriott. This hotel, comprising two towers of 16 and 18 floors, is another good headquarters for Convention Center attendees and was recently renovated under a more contemporary look. The expanded lobby's huge windows allow sunlight to stream in, highlighting the gleaming marble. Rooms, decorated with pastels, have balconies. Discounted weekend packages are available. *700 W. Convention Way, 92802, tel. 714/750–8000. 1,039 rooms. Concierge level. Facilities: 2 restaurants, 2 heated swimming pools, Jacuzzi, fitness center, video games, lounge, entertainment, gift shops, beauty salon. AE, D, DC, MC, V.*

★ **Disneyland Hotel.** This hotel, which is connected to the Magic Kingdom by monorail, offers an extension of the Disneyland experience, right down to the marina around which the three hotel towers are built. There are lakes, streams, tumbling waterfalls, and lush landscaping. One section has remote-controlled boats, another pedalboats; Fantasy Waters offer a nighttime lighted fountain and music display. Renovation of the hotel was completed in 1991, and the lobby's walls and floors are now covered in marble. Nearly all of the rooms have a view of the marina or the city and are decorated in soft green, peach, or pink colors. *1150 W. Cerritos Ave., 92802, tel. 714/778–6600 or 800/MICKEY-1. 1,131 rooms. Facilities: 6 restaurants, 3 swimming pools, spa, white sand beach, 10 tennis courts, beauty/barber shop, 5 lounges, 20 shops, entertainment, concierge floor. AE, DC, MC, V.*

Hyatt Regency Alicante. This hotel, located a few blocks south of Disneyland and Convention Center, is a good choice for those seeking some distance from the park. Set beneath a 17-story high steel and glass atrium, the lobby has an indoor/outdoor feel, and abounds with tropical greenery, 60-foot-high palm trees and fountains. The guest rooms are standard issue, but on a clear day those on the upper floors have mountain and city views. *Harbor at Chapman, Box 4669, 92803, tel. 714/750–1234, 800/972–2929. 380 rooms. Concierge floor. Facilities: 2 restaurants, swimming pool, spa, fitness area, 2 lighted tennis courts, lounge, suites, Camp Hyatt, shuttle service to area attractions. AE, D, DC, MC, V.*

Expensive **Anaheim Plaza Hotel.** Soft pastels and plants fill the lobby of this low-rise hotel on 10 acres of tropical gardens near Disneyland. Wheelchair units and suites are available. *1700 S. Harbor Blvd., 92802, tel. 714/772–5900 or 800/228–1357. 298 rooms, 6 suites. Facilities: heated pool, whirlpool, restaurant. AE, DC, MC, V.*

Grand Hotel. Lobby and rooms are decorated in a pleasant plum-teal combination. The property is adjacent to Disneyland and offers a free shuttle. Each room in the nine-story high rise has a balcony. *7 Freedman Way, 92802, tel. 714/772–7777. 242 rooms. Facilities: pool, Jacuzzi, fitness facilities, video games, gift shop, dining room, coffee shop, corporate lounge. AE, DC, MC, V.*

Inn at the Park. Mountains of all kinds—the Matterhorn at Disneyland and the Santa Ana Mountains—can be seen from the rooms' private balconies. Rooms are decorated in standard-issue modern hotel style using subdued and inoffensive colors. *1855 S. Harbor Blvd., 92802, tel. 714/750–1811. 497 rooms. Facilities: restaurant, coffee shop, lounge, heated pool, spa, exercise room. AE, D, DC, MC, V.*

Pan Pacific Anaheim. This hotel is geared toward business travelers. Its distinctive atrium lobby has glass-enclosed elevators. Contemporary graphics fill the rooms. Nonsmoking rooms are available. *1717 S. West St., 92802, tel. 714/999–0990 or 800/663–1515. 502 rooms. Facilities: 2 restaurants, pool, sun deck, Jacuzzi, and video games. AE, DC, MC, V.*

Sheraton-Anaheim Motor Hotel. This Tudor-style hotel was recently renovated and now has a contemporary, bright look while retaining its castle theme in large tapestries, faux stone walls, and frescoes in the public areas. The large guest rooms open onto interior gardens. A Disneyland shuttle, and multi-language services are available. *1015 W. Ball Rd., 92802, tel. 714/778–1700 or 800/325–3535. 500 rooms. Facilities: dining room, deli, heated pool, suites, game room, and bar. Wheelchair units available. AE, D, DC, MC, V.*

Moderate **Holiday Inn Anaheim Center.** This is a big pink Mediterranean-style building set at the edge of Disneyland at the Santa Ana Freeway. Designed for families visiting the Magic Kingdom, it has pleasant, if functional, rooms including some with separate sitting areas. Shuttle service is available to nearby attractions including Knott's Berry Farm, Movieland Wax Museum, and Medieval Times. *1221 S. Harbor Blvd., 92805. tel. 714/758–0900 or 800/545–7275. 252 rooms. Facilities: pool, spa, sauna, restaurant, lounge, video games, gift shop, handicapped access. AE, D, DC, MC, V.*

Holiday Inn Maingate Anaheim. Large glass chandeliers in the lobby set the tone at this establishment one block south of Disneyland. *1850 S. Harbor Blvd., 92802, tel. 714/750–2801 or 800/624-6855. 312 rooms. Facilities: heated pool, suites, dining room, lounge, gift shop, video games. AE, D, DC, MC, V.*

Quality Hotel and Conference Center. A large, open, red-tile lobby is filled with mirrors, plants, and flowers; guest rooms are decorated in greens and yellows. The hotel is close to Disneyland and the Convention Center. *616 Convention Way, 92802, tel. 714/750–3131 or 800/231-6215. 284 rooms. Facilities: suites, heated pool, gift shop, lounge, 2 restaurants, game room, beauty parlor. AE, DC, MC, V.*

Ramada Maingate/Anaheim. This clean, reliable, new member of the worldwide chain is located across the street from Disneyland, with free shuttle service to the park. *1460 S. Harbor Blvd., 92802, tel. 714/772–6777 or 800/447-4048. 465 rooms. Facilities: pool, Jacuzzi, restaurant, game room, room service provided by McDonald's. AE, MC, V.*

Inexpensive **Hampton Inn.** Here's basic lodging at a basic price. *300 E. Katella Way, 92802, tel. 714/772–8713. 136 rooms. Facilities: pool, cable TV, complimentary breakfast. AE, DC, MC, V.*

Buena Park
Expensive **Buena Park Hotel and Convention Center.** A spiral staircase leads to the mezzanine from the ground-floor lobby of marble, brass, and glass. Rooms are done in greens and peach tones. *7675 Crescent Ave., 90620, tel. 714/995–1111, 800/854-8792. 350 rooms. Facilities: heated pool, Jacuzzi, dining rooms, lounge, nightclub, coffee shop. AE, DC, MC, V.*

Costa Mesa
Very Expensive **Westin South Coast Plaza.** This hotel, which caters to business travelers, was recently renovated. Ambience is soothing with soft mauve and teal colors and plenty of marble surfaces. The hotel is convenient to the Orange County Performing Arts Center, theaters, and South Coast Plaza shopping mall. *686 Anton Blvd., 92626, tel. 714/540–2500 or 800/228-3000. 394 rooms. Facilities: shuffleboard, 4 lighted tennis courts, café, 2 lounges, live entertainment, gift shop, handicapped access. AE, D, DC, MC, V.*

Dana Point
Very Expensive **Blue Lantern Inn.** This brand new Cape Cod-style bed-and-breakfast is perched on top of the bluffs, and has stunning harbor and ocean views. Rooms are individually decorated with period furnishings, fireplaces, stocked refrigerators, and private Jacuzzis. Breakfast and afternoon refreshments are included in the price. *34343 Street of the Blue Lantern, 92629, tel. 714/661–1304. 29 rooms. Facilities: library, concierge service, fitness facilities. AE, MC, V.*

★ **Dana Point Resort.** This Cape Cod–style hillside resort is done in shades of sea-foam green and peach. The lobby is filled with large palm trees and original artwork. Most rooms have ocean views. The ambience here is casual yet elegant. The Capistrano Valley Symphony performs here in the summer. The grounds are attractively landscaped. *25135 Park Lantern, 92629, tel. 714/661–5000 or 800/533-9748. 350 rooms. Concierge level. Facilities: 3 pools, 3 spas, health club, restaurant, lounge with jazz entertainment, gift shop, croquet, volleyball, basketball. AE, D, DC, MC, V.*

★ **The Ritz-Carlton Laguna Niguel.** This acclaimed hotel has earned itself world-class status for its gorgeous setting right on the edge of the Pacific, its sumptuous Mediterranean architecture and decor, and its reputation for flawless service. With colorful landscaping outside and an imposing marble columned and antiques-filled entry, it feels like an Italian country villa.

Every possible amenity, and then some, is available to guests. Reduced-rate packages are sometimes available. *33533 Ritz Carlton Dr., 92677, tel. 714/240–2000. 393 rooms. Facilities: beach access, health club with steam room and massage service, 4 tennis courts, 2 pools, Jacuzzis, saunas, 3 restaurants, 3 lounges and a club with entertainment, concierge. Adjacent to an ocean-view 18-hole golf course with guaranteed tee times. AE, D, DC, MC, V.*

Moderate **Marina Best Western.** Set right in the marina, this hotel is convenient to docks, restaurants, and shops. Rooms vary in size from basic to family units with kitchens and fireplaces. Many rooms in this three-level motel have balconies and harbor views. *24800 Dana Point Harbor Dr., 92629, tel. 714/496–1203 or 800/255–6843. 136 rooms. Facilities: pool, fitness facilities. AE, D, DC, MC, V.*

Huntington Beach **The Waterfront Hilton.** This new oceanfront hotel rises 12 stories above the surf. The Mediterranean-style resort is decorated in soft mauves, beiges, and greens, and offers a panoramic ocean view from every guest room. *21100 Pacific Coast Hwy., 92648, tel. 714/960–SURF or 800/822–7873. 293 rooms. Facilities: concierge level, 2 restaurants, lounge, 2 lighted tennis courts, pool, Jacuzzi, fitness center, gift shop, bike-, beach-equipment rentals. AE, DC, MC, V.*
Very Expensive

Expensive **Best Western Huntington Beach Inn.** This inn, decorated in light green and mauve, is right across from the ocean. *21112 Pacific Coast Hwy., 92648, tel. 714/962–4244. 94 rooms. Facilities: restaurant, pool, coffee shop, lounge, gift shop, 3-par golf course. AE, DC, MC, V.*

Moderate **Huntington Shore Motor Hotel.** Just across from the ocean, ★ some rooms at this small hotel have balconies and ocean views. The lobby is made cozy by a fireplace. The rooms are extra large, decorated in earth tones. Complimentary Continental breakfast is offered. *21002 Pacific Coast Hwy., 92648, tel. 714/536–8861 or 800/554–6799. 50 rooms. Facilities: heated pool, children's pool, restaurant, some kitchens. AE, DC, MC, V.*

Irvine **Hyatt Regency Irvine.** This beautiful hotel has all the amenities of a first-class resort. It is elegantly decorated in soft contemporary tones, and the marble lobby is flanked by glass-enclosed elevators. The lower weekend rates are a great deal. *17900 Jamboree Rd., 92714, tel. 714/863–3111. 536 rooms. Facilities: pool, Jacuzzi, sauna, tennis, tennis pro, workout room, entertainment, 2 restaurants, 2 cocktail lounges, concierge, bike rentals, handicapped access. AE, D, DC, MC, V.*
Very Expensive

Expensive **Irvine Marriott.** This contemporary looking hotel towers over Koll Business Center, making it a convenient spot for business travelers. Ask about special reduced-rate weekend packages. *1800 Von Karman, 92715, tel. 714/553–0100. 485 rooms. Facilities: restaurant, indoor-outdoor pool, spa, tennis courts, tennis pro, health club, sports-oriented bar, massage room, concierge floors, beauty salon, American Airlines and Hertz Rental Car desks. AE, D, DC, MC, V.*

Moderate **Airporter Inn Hotel.** To cater to businesspeople, all rooms here have a work area and are decorated in soft colors. One deluxe suite even has its own private pool. *18700 MacArthur Blvd., 92715, tel. 714/833–2770 or 800/854–3012. 211 rooms. Facili-*

ties: heated pool, fitness center, beauty salon, dining room, coffee shop, cocktail lounge, suites. AE, D, DC, MC, V.

Laguna Beach
Very Expensive

Surf and Sand Hotel. This is the largest hotel in Laguna and is right on the beach. The rooms are decorated in soft sand colors, have wooden shutters, and have private balconies. Weekend packages are available. *1555 S. Coast Hwy., 92651, tel. 714/497–4477 or 800/524–8621. 157 rooms. Facilities: private beach, pool, lounge, 2 restaurants, suites, concierge, gift shop. AE, DC, MC, V.*

Expensive–
Very Expensive

The Carriage House. This bed-and-breakfast has one- and two-bedroom suites surrounding a lushly landscaped courtyard, New Orleans style. Complimentary family-style breakfast is offered daily. Fresh fruit and wine gifts welcome guests. *1322 Catalina St., 92651, tel. 714/494–8945. 6 suites. No credit cards. 2-night minimum on weekends.*

★ **Inn at Laguna.** This new southwest-style inn has one of the best locations in town. It's close to Main Beach and Las Brisas restaurant and bar, one of Laguna's most popular watering holes, yet far enough away to be secluded. Set on a bluff overlooking the ocean, the inn has luxurious amenities, and many rooms with views. *211 N. Coast Hwy., 92651, tel. 714/497–9722. 70 rooms, Facilities: VCRs in the rooms, heated pool, Jacuzzi, complimentary Continental breakfast in the rooms, complimentary parking. AE, DC, MC, V.*

Expensive

Eiler's Inn. A light-filled courtyard centers this European-style B&B. Rooms are on the small side, but each is unique and decorated with antiques. Breakfast is served outdoors, and in the afternoon there's wine and cheese, often to the accompaniment of live music. A sun deck in back has an ocean view. *741 S. Coast Hwy., 92651, tel. 714/494–3004. 12 rooms. AE, MC, V.*

Hotel Laguna. This downtown landmark, the oldest hotel in Laguna, has recently been redone with four rooms now featuring canopy beds and reproduction Victorian furnishings. Lobby windows look out onto manicured gardens, and a patio restaurant overlooks the ocean. *425 S. Coast Hwy., 92651, tel. 714/494–1151. 65 rooms. Facilities: restaurant, private beach, lounge, entertainment. AE, DC, MC, V.*

Newport Beach
Very Expensive
★

Four Seasons Hotel. This hotel lives up to the quality of its chain's reputation. Marble and antiques fill the airy lobby; all rooms—decorated with beiges, peaches, and southwestern tones—have spectacular views, private bars, original art on walls. Weekend golf packages are available in conjunction with the nearby Pelican Hill golf course, as well as fitness weekend packages. *690 Newport Center Dr., 92660, tel. 714/759–0808 or 800/775–0690. 285 rooms. Facilities: pool, whirlpool, sauna, 2 lighted tennis courts, health club with steam room and massage service, 2 restaurants, lounge, concierge, handicapped access. AE, D, DC, MC, V.*

Hotel Meridien Newport Beach. The eye-catching cantilevered design is the trademark of this ultramodern hotel in Koll Center. The decor is Southern Californian, with striking pastel accents. Luxuriously appointed rooms have minibars and built-in hair dryers. This is also the home of Antoine, one of the best restaurants in Orange County. Special weekend theater and Pageant of the Masters packages are available. *4500 MacArthur Blvd., 92660, tel. 714/476–2001. 435 rooms. Facilities: pool, tennis courts, 2 restaurants, lounge, health club with*

Jacuzzi, complimentary bicycles, concierge. AE, D, DC, MC, V.

The Hyatt Newporter Resort. The garden setting of this recently redecorated and expanded resort imparts a get-away-from-it-all feeling that's quite unexpected given its proximity to Newport Center and Fashion Island. There's plenty here to lure you outdoors: landscaped grounds, Upper Newport Bay, or a challenging tennis match at John Wayne Tennis Club next door. *1107 Jamboree Rd., 92660, tel. 714/644–1700. 410 rooms. Facilities: par-3, 9-hole golf course, jogging paths, exercise room, 3 pools, 2 restaurants, lounge, entertainment, concierge. AE, DC, MC, V.*

Expensive **Newport Beach Marriott Hotel and Tennis Club.** Arriving guests' first view of the hotel's interior is the distinctive fountain surrounded by a high, plant-filled atrium. Rooms in two towers have balconies or patios, overlook lush gardens; many have a stunning Pacific view. The hotel is located directly across the street from Fashion Island shopping center. *900 Newport Center Dr., 92660, tel. 714/640–4000 or 800/228–9290. 585 rooms. Facilities: pools, health club, sauna, 8 lighted tennis courts, Jacuzzi, adjacent golf course, 2 restaurants, lounge, entertainment, concierge. AE, D, DC, MC, V.*

Sheraton Newport Beach. Bamboos and palms decorate the lobby in this Southern California beach-style hotel. Vibrant teals, mauves, and peaches make up the color scheme. Complimentary morning paper, buffet breakfast, and cocktail parties are offered daily. *4545 MacArthur Blvd., 92660, tel. 714/833–0570. 338 rooms. Facilities: pool, Jacuzzi, 2 tennis courts, 3 restaurants, lounge, entertainment. AE, D, DC, MC, V.*

Orange **Doubletree Inn.** This hotel has a dramatic lobby of marble and
Expensive–Very granite and silent waterfalls cascading down the walls. The re-
Expensive cently renovated guest rooms are large and come equipped with a small conference table. It is located near the shopping center called The City, UCI Medical Center, and Anaheim Stadium. *100 The City Dr., 92668, tel. 714/634–4500 or 800/ 528–0444. 441 rooms. Facilities: swimming pool, spa, 2 tennis courts, 2 restaurants, concierge floor, access for the handicapped. AE, D, DC, MC, V.*

Inexpensive **Best Western El Camino.** This motel is convenient to Knott's Berry Farm and Disneyland. The large lobby is comfortably decorated with overstuffed sofas. Complimentary Continental breakfast is offered. *3191 N. Tustin Ave., 92665, tel. 714/998–0360. 56 rooms. Facilities: heated pool. AE, D, DC, MC, V.*

San Clemente **San Clemente Inn.** This time-share condo resort is located in
Expensive the secluded southern part of San Clemente, adjacent to Calafia State Beach. Studio and one-bedroom units (accommodating up to six) are equipped with kitchens, and bars are available. *2600 Avenida del Presidente, 92672, tel. 714/492–6103. 95 units. Facilities: pool, Jacuzzi, sauna, tennis, exercise equipment, children's playground, barbecue pits. MC, V.*

Moderate **Ramada Inn San Clemente.** This Mission-style hotel is beautifully set on a lush hillside. The lobby has a dramatic vaulted ceiling. Rooms have private balconies or patios; many also have refrigerators. *35 Calle de Industrias, 92672, tel. 714/498–8800 or 800/2–RAMADA. 110 rooms. Facilities: pool, restaurant, lounge, access for the handicapped. AE, D, DC, MC, V.*

The Arts

The **Orange County Performing Arts Center** (600 Town Center Dr., tel. 714/556–ARTS), in Costa Mesa, is the hub of the arts circle, hosting a variety of touring companies year-round. Groups that regularly schedule performances here include New York City Opera, American Ballet Theater, Los Angeles Philharmonic Orchestra, as well as touring companies of popular musicals such as *Les Misérables.* Information about current offerings can be found in the Calendar section of the *Los Angeles Times.*

Concerts   The **Irvine Meadows Amphitheater** (8808 Irvine Center Dr., tel. 714/855–4515) is a 15,000-seat open-air venue offering a variety of musical events from May through October.
The **Pacific Amphitheater** (Orange County Fairgrounds, Costa Mesa, tel. 714/634–1300) offers musical entertainment and stages plays from April through October.

Theater   **South Coast Repertory Theater** (655 Town Center Dr., tel. 714/957–4033), near the Orange County Performing Arts Center in Costa Mesa, is an acclaimed regional theater complex with two stages presenting both traditional and innovative new works. A resident group of actors forms the nucleus for this facility's innovative productions.
La Mirada Theater for the Performing Arts (14900 La Mirada Blvd., tel. 714/994–6150) presents a wide selection of Broadway shows, concerts, and film series.

Nightlife

Bars   The **Cannery** (3010 Lafayette Ave., tel. 714/675–5757) and the **Warehouse** (3450 Via Oporto, tel. 714/673–4700) are two crowded Newport Beach bars that offer live entertainment. The **Studio Cafe** (100 Main St., on the Balboa Peninsula, tel. 714/675–7760) presents jazz musicians every night.

In Laguna Beach, the **Sandpiper** (1183 S. Pacific Coast Hwy., tel. 714/494–4694) is a tiny dancing joint that attracts an eclectic crowd. And **Laguna's White House** (340 S. Pacific Coast Hwy., tel. 714/494–8088) has nightly entertainment that runs the gamut from rock to motown, reggae to pop.

Comedy   **Irvine Improv** (4255 Campus Dr., Irvine, tel. 714/854–5455) is probably the funniest place in the county. Well- and lesser-known comedians try out their acts nightly.

Country   **Cowboy Boogie Co.** (1721 S. Manchester, Anaheim, tel. 714/956–1410) offers live country music Tuesday through Sunday night. The complex comprises three dance floors and four bars.

Dinner Theater   Several night spots in Orange County serve up entertainment with dinner. **Tibbie's Music Hall** (16360 Coast Hwy., Huntington Beach, tel. 714/840–5661) offers comedy show along with prime rib, fish, or chicken.

Medieval Times Dinner and Tournament (7662 Beach Blvd., Buena Park, tel. 714/521–4740 or 800/899–6600) takes guests back to the days of knights and ladies. Knights on horseback compete in medieval games, swordfighting, and jousting. Dinner, all of which is eaten with your hands, includes appetizers, whole roasted chicken or spareribs, soup, pastry, and beverages such as mead.

Wild Bill's Wild West Extravaganza (7600 Beach Blvd., Buena Park, tel. 714/522–6414) is a two-hour action-packed Old West show featuring foot-stomping musical numbers, cowboys, Indians, dancing girls, specialty acts, and audience participation in sing-alongs.

Elizabeth Howard's Curtain Call Theater (690 El Camino Real, Tustin, tel. 714/838–1540) presents a regular schedule of Broadway musicals.

Nightclubs
Crackers (710 Katella Ave., Anaheim, tel. 714/978–1828), is a zany restaurant and nightclub where waiters and waitresses double as onstage musical performers. There's live entertainment seven days a week which varies from music of the '40s to the '90s. It's a casual place, but don't come in your beachwear.
The Righteous Brothers' Hop (18774 Brookhurst St., Fountain Valley, tel. 714/963–2366) is a 1950s–1960s-style diner/nightclub owned by—you guessed it—the Righteous Brothers. Nostalgia fills this fun place, which has a basketball court–dance floor and a '56 Chevy attached to the front of the DJ booth. Dress casually, but not for the beach.

14 San Diego

*By Maribeth
Mellin*

Each year, San Diego absorbs thousands of visitors who are drawn by the climate: sunny, dry, and warm nearly year-round. They swim, surf, and sunbathe on long beaches facing the turquoise Pacific, where whales, seals, and dolphins swim offshore. They tour oases of tropical palms, sheltered bays fringed by golden pampas grass, and far-ranging parklands blossoming with brilliant bougainvillea, jasmine, ice plant, and birds of paradise. They run and bike and walk for hours down wide streets and paths planned for recreation among the natives, who thrive on San Diego's varied health, fitness, and sports scenes.

San Diego County is the nation's sixth largest—larger than nearly a dozen U.S. states—with a population of more than 2.5 million. It sprawls east from the Pacific Ocean through dense urban neighborhoods to outlying suburban communities that seem to sprout on canyons and cliffs overnight. The city of San Diego is the state's second largest, after Los Angeles. It serves as a base for the U.S. Navy's 11th Naval District and a port for ships from many nations. A considerable number of its residents were stationed here in the service and decided to stay put. Others either passed through on vacation or saw the city in movies and TV shows and became enamored of the city and its reputation as a prosperous Sunbelt playground. From its founding San Diego has attracted a steady stream of prospectors, drawn to the nation's farthest southwest frontier.

Tourism is San Diego's third largest industry, after manufacturing and the military. San Diego's politicians, business leaders, and developers have set the city's course toward a steadily increasing influx of visitors—which gives residents pleasant attractions as well as not-so-enjoyable distractions. With growth comes congestion, even in San Diego's vast expanse.

Arriving and Departing

By Plane

There are regularly scheduled nonstop flights to San Diego from many U.S. and Mexican cities. San Diego is served by **Aero California** (tel. 800/258–3311), **AeroMexico** (tel. 800/237–6639), **Alaska Airlines** (tel. 800/426–0333), **America West** (tel. 619/560–0727), **American** (tel. 800/433–7300), **Continental** (tel. 800/525–0280), **Delta** (tel. 800/323–2323), **Northwest** (tel. 800/225–2525), **Skywest** (tel. 800/453–9417), **Southwest** (tel. 619/232–1221), **Trans World Airlines** (tel. 619/295–7009), **United** (tel. 619/234–7171), and **USAir** (tel. 800/428–4322).

*From the Airport
to Center City*

All flights arrive at Lindbergh Field, just 3 miles northwest of downtown. **San Diego Transit** Route 2 buses leave every 30 minutes, from 5 AM to 11:45 PM, from the center traffic aisle at the East Terminal and at the traffic island at the far west end of the West Terminal. The buses go to Fourth Street and Broadway, downtown. The fare is $1.25 per person. Taxi fare is $5–$6, plus tip, to most center-city hotels. **The Super Shuttle Airport Limousine** (tel. 619/278–5700; in San Diego, 800/948–8853) will take you directly to your destination, often for less than a cab would cost. Numerous hotels and motels offer their guests complimentary transportation. If you have rented a car at the airport, follow the signs to I–5 and go south for about 3 miles to the downtown area.

Exploring San Diego *(Boxes Refer to Detail Maps)*

N

Torrey Pines
State Beach

Mira Mesa Blvd.

N. Torrey Pines Rd. S21

Genesee Ave.

805

Miramar Rd.

MIRAM

MIRAMAR
NAVAL AIR
STATION

Gilman Dr.

Torrey Pines Rd.

Ardath Rd.

La Jolla

52

Clairemont Mesa Blvd.

163

5

Clairmont Dr.

Balboa Ave.

Genesee Ave.

Aero Dr.

La Jolla Blvd.

San Diego Fwy.

Cabrillo Fwy.

805

PACIFIC BEACH

Grand Ave.

Mission Bay

LINDA VISTA

Ingraham St.

Mission Blvd.

Mission Bay

MISSION BEACH

Mission Bay Dr.

Linda Vista Rd.

Friars Rd.

San Diego R

■ Sea World

Old Town

Adams A

8

163

OCEAN BEACH

Nimitz Blvd.

Sunset Cliffs Blvd.

Catalina Blvd.

Rosecrans

209

Pacific Hwy.

Harbor Dr.

Universi

Balboa Park

POINT LOMA

Cabrillo Memorial Dr.

North Island

**U.S. NAVAL
AIR STATION**

DOWNTOWN

Imper

Harbor Dr.

75

San Diego Bay

*Coronado
Beach*

Silver

Central San Diego

Strand Blvd.

PACIFIC OCEAN

*Silver Strand
State Beach*

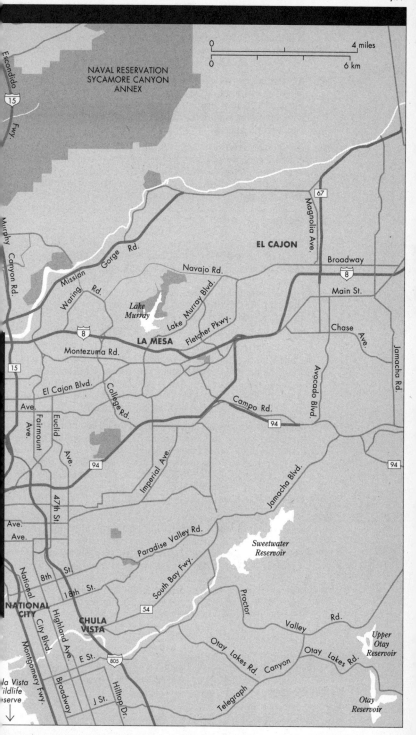

NAVAL RESERVATION
SYCAMORE CANYON
ANNEX

0   4 miles
0   6 km

Escondido Fwy.

15

Murphy Canyon Rd.

Mission Gorge Rd.

Waring Rd.

Navajo Rd.

Lake Murray Blvd.

EL CAJON

Magnolia Ave.

67

Broadway

8

Main St.

Lake Murray

Fletcher Pkwy.

LA MESA

Montezuma Rd.

8

Chase Ave.

15

El Cajon Blvd.

College Rd.

Campo Rd.

94

Avocado Blvd.

Jamacha Rd.

Ave.

Fairmount Ave.

Euclid Ave.

94

Imperial Ave.

94

47th St.

Ave.
Ave.

Paradise Valley Rd.

Sweetwater Reservoir

Jamacha Blvd.

National Ave.

8th St.

18th St.

South Bay Fwy.

54

NATIONAL CITY

City Blvd.

Highland Ave.

CHULA VISTA

E St.

805

Proctor

Valley

Rd.

Upper Otay Reservoir

94

la Vista
ildlife
serve

Montgomery Fwy.

Broadway

J St.

Hilltop Dr.

Otay Lakes Rd.

Canyon

Otay Lakes Rd.

Telegraph

Otay Reservoir

↓

By Car I–5 stretches from Canada to the Mexican border and bisects San Diego. I–8 provides access from Yuma, Arizona, and points east. Drivers coming from Nevada and the mountain regions beyond can reach San Diego on I–15. Avoid rush-hour periods, when the traffic can be jammed for miles.

By Train **Amtrak** trains (tel. 800/USA–RAIL) from Los Angeles arrive at Santa Fe Depot, at Kettner Boulevard and Broadway, near the heart of downtown. There are additional stations in Del Mar and Oceanside, both located in north San Diego County. Eight trains operate daily in either direction.

By Bus **Greyhound/Trailways** (tel. 619/239–9171 or 800/752–4841) operates frequent daily service between the downtown terminal at 120 West Broadway and Los Angeles, connecting with buses to all major U.S. cities. Many buses are express or nonstop; others make stops at coastal towns en route.

Getting Around

Many attractions, such as the Gaslamp Quarter, Balboa Park, and La Jolla, are best seen on foot. A variety of public transportation can be incorporated to reach any major tourist and shopping area, but it is best to have a car for exploring more remote coastal and inland regions. The International Visitor Information Center in Horton Plaza, at the corner of 1st Avenue and F Street, provides maps of the city.

By Bus Fares on **San Diego Transit** buses are $1.25, $1.50 on express buses; senior citizens pay 60¢ on all buses. A free transfer is included in the fare, but it must be requested upon boarding. Buses to most major attractions leave from 4th Avenue or 5th Avenue and Broadway. San Diego Transit Information Line (tel. 619/233–3004) is open daily 5:30 AM–8:30 PM. Call for precise details on getting to and from any location.

By Taxi Taxi fares are regulated at the airport—all companies charge the same rate. Fares vary among companies on other routes, however, including the ride back to the airport. Cab companies that serve most areas of the city are **Yellow Cab** (tel. 619/234–6161), **Orange Cab** (tel. 619/291–3333), **La Jolla Cab** (tel. 619/453–4222), **Co-op Silver Cabs** (tel. 619/280–5555), **Coast Cab** (tel. 619/226–8294), and **Coronado Cab** (tel. 619/435–6211).

By Trolley The **San Diego Trolley** (tel. 619/233–3004) travels from downtown to within 100 feet of the United States–Mexican border, stopping at 21 suburban stations en route. The basic fare is 50¢–$2.25 one way. The trolley also travels from downtown to La Mesa, El Cajon, and Lemon Grove in East County. Ticket vending machines, located at each station, require exact change. Tickets must be purchased before boarding. Trolleys operate daily, approximately every 15 minutes, 5 AM–1 AM. The Bayside line serves the Convention Center and Seaport Village; lines to Old Town, Mission Valley, and North County are under construction.

By Ferry The San Diego–Coronado Ferry (tel. 619/234–4111) leaves from the Broadway Pier daily, every hour on the hour, 9 AM–10:30 PM. The fare is $1.60 each way. **The Harbor Hopper** (tel. 619/229–8294) is a water-taxi service that shuttles passengers from one side of San Diego Harbor to the other, with 87 possible pickup points. The fare is $3 each way, $5 round-trip.

By Limousine Limousine companies provide chauffeured service for business or pleasure. Some offer airport shuttles and customized tours. Rates vary and are per hour, per mile, or both, with some minimums established. Companies that offer a range of services include **A Touch of Class** (tel. 619/698–6301), **Olde English Limousines** (tel. 619/232–6533), **La Jolla Limousines** (tel. 619/459–5891), and **Presidential Limousine** (619/291–2820).

Important Addresses and Numbers

Tourist Information **International Visitor Information Center** is in Horton Plaza, at the corner of 1st Avenue and F Street, tel. 619/236–1212. *Open daily 8:30–5; closed Thanksgiving and Christmas.*

Recorded visitor information (tel. 619/236–1212).

The **Visitor Information Center** is located at 2688 East Mission Bay Drive, off I–5 at the Mission Bay side of the Clairemont Drive exit, tel. 619/276–8200. *Open daily 9–5:30.*

Balboa Park Information Center is at 1549 El Prado, in Balboa Park, tel. 619/239–0512. *Open daily 9–4:30.*

San Diego City Beach and Weather Conditions Information Line (tel. 619/221–8884).

Weather Forecast (tel. 619/289–1212).

Emergencies **Police, ambulance,** and **fire** departments can all be reached by dialing 911. For the **Poison Control Center,** call 619/543–6000.

Doctors Hospital emergency rooms, with physicians on duty, are open 24 hours. Major hospitals are **UCSD Medical Center** (225 Dickinson St., tel. 619/543–6400), **Mercy Hospital and Medical Center** (4077 5th Ave., tel. 619/260–7000), **Scripps Memorial Hospital** (9888 Genesee Ave., La Jolla, tel. 619/457–6150), **Veterans Administration Hospital** (3350 La Jolla Village Dr., La Jolla, tel. 619/552–8585).

Guided Tours

Orientation Tours Both **Gray Line Tours** (tel. 619/491–0011 or 800/331–5077) and **San Diego Mini Tours** (tel. 619/477–8687) offer daily four-hour sightseeing excursions. Gray Line uses 45-passenger buses; San Diego Mini Tours uses 25-passenger tour buses. Cost: $25–$65, depending on the length of the tour and the attractions visited. **Old Town Trolley** (tel. 619/298–8687 or 619/298–8752) travels to almost every attraction and shopping area on open-air trackless trolleys. Drivers double as tour guides. You can take the full 90-minute, narrated city tour or get on and off as you please at any of the 10 stops. An all-day pass costs only $14 for adults, and $7 for children 5–12. The trolley carries 34 passengers and operates daily 9–5. Free two-hour bus tours of the downtown redevelopment area, including the Gaslamp Quarter, are hosted by **Centre City Development Corporation** (tel. 619/235–2222). Groups of 43 passengers leave from 119 West F Street, downtown, every Saturday at 10 AM. Reservations are necessary. The tour may be canceled if there aren't enough passengers.

Special-Interest Tours **Flight Trails Helicopters,** also known as Civic Helicopters (tel. 619/438–8424), has helicopter tours starting at $65 per person per half-hour.

Holidays on Horseback (tel. 619/445–3997) offers horseback-riding excursions in the backcountry.

National Air (tel. 619/440–7752) has round-trip flights to Catalina Island, the Grand Canyon, and other destinations.

Pied Piper Tours (tel. 619/224–7455) customizes shopping trips for individuals or groups, specializing in excursions to the Los Angeles garment district.

San Diego Harbor Excursion (tel. 619/234–4111) and **Invader Cruises** (tel. 619/234–8687) sail with more than 100 passengers on narrated cruises of San Diego Harbor. Both vessels have snack bars. One-hour cruises depart from the Broadway Pier several times daily. San Diego Harbor Excursion offers a two-hour tour each day at 2 PM. No reservations are necessary for any of the tours. Cost: $10 for a one-hour tour; $15 for a two-hour tour. **Mariposa Sailing Cruises** (tel. 619/542–0646) has morning and afternoon sailing tours of the harbor and San Diego Bay as well as whale-watching expeditions on the 35-foot cutter *Mariposa*.

Walkabout (tel. 619/223–9255) offers several different walking tours throughout the city each week.

Balloon Tours Six-passenger hot-air balloons lift off from San Diego's north country. Most flights are at sunrise or sunset and are followed by a traditional champagne celebration. Companies that offer daily service, weather permitting, are **A Beautiful Morning Balloon Co.** (tel. 619/481–6225), **California Dreamin'** (tel. 619/438–3344), and **Pacific Horizon Balloon Tours** (tel. 619/756–1790). Balloon-flight costs start at $110 weekdays and $125 weekends for an hour-long ride.

Whale-Watching Tours Gray whales migrate south to Mexico and back north from mid-December to mid-March. As many as 200 whales pass the San Diego coast each day, coming within yards of tour boats.

The Avanti (tel. 619/222–0391), a 70-foot, luxury motor yacht, offers 2½-hour narrated tours twice a day during the week, three times a day on weekends. Mariposa Sailing Cruises (tel. 619/542–0646) tailors whale-watching expeditions for up to six people. H&M Landing (tel. 619/222–1144) and Seaforth Sportfishing (tel. 619/224–3383) have daily whale-watching trips in large party boats.

Walking Tours **The Gaslamp Foundation** (410 Island Ave., tel. 619/233–5227) leads 1½-hour guided walks of the restored downtown historic district, highlighting the Victorian architecture. Groups meet at the foundation office, near Horton Plaza, Saturday at 11 AM. A donation is requested. Self-guided tour brochures are available at the office weekdays 8:30–5.

On weekends, the State Park Department (tel. 619/237–6770) gives free walking tours of Old Town. Groups leave from 4002 Wallace Street at 2 PM every Saturday and Sunday.

Exploring San Diego

Exploring San Diego is an endless adventure, limited only by time and transportation constraints, which, if you don't have a car, can be considerable. San Diego is more a chain of separate communities than a cohesive city. Many of the major attractions are at least 5 miles away from one another and are most easily reached by traveling on the freeways. The streets are fun for getting an up-close look at how San Diegans live, and if you've got a car, be sure to drive through Mission and Pacific beaches along Mission Boulevard for a good view of the vibrant beach scene. But true Southern Californians use the freeways, which crisscross the county in a sensible fashion. I–5 runs a direct north–south route through the county's coastal communities to the Mexican border. I–805 and I–15 do much the same inland, with I–8 as the main east–west route. Highways 163, 52, and 94 act as connectors.

If you are going to drive around San Diego, study your maps before you hit the road. The freeways are convenient and fast most of the time, but if you miss your turnoff or get caught in commuter traffic, you'll experience a none-too-pleasurable hallmark of Southern California living—freeway madness. Southern California drivers rush around on a complex freeway system with the same fervor they use for jogging scores of marathons each year. They particularly enjoy speeding up at interchanges and entrance and exit ramps. Be sure you know where you're going before you join the freeway chase. Better yet, use public transportation or tour buses from your hotel and save your energy for walking in the sun.

Downtown and the Embarcadero

Numbers in the margin correspond to points of interest on the Central San Diego map.

Downtown San Diego, just 3 miles south of the international airport, is changing and growing rapidly, gaining status as a cultural and recreational center for the county's residents and visitors alike. This is the city that brought you the 1988 Super Bowl and the 1992 America's Cup Races. San Diego had 12.6 million overnight guests in 1990, with more than $3.36 billion spent by tourists, making tourism the city's third largest industry.

Downtown's natural attributes were easily evident to its original booster, Alonzo Horton, who arrived in San Diego in 1867. Horton looked at the bay and the acres of flatland surrounded by hills and canyons and knew he had found San Diego's center. Though Old Town, under the Spanish fort at the Presidio, had been settled for years, Horton knew it was too far away from the water to take hold as the commercial center of San Diego. He bought 960 acres along the bay at 27½¢ per acre and literally gave away the land to those who would develop it or build houses. Within months, he had sold or given away 226 city blocks of land; settlers camped on their land in tents as their houses and businesses rose. In 1868, Horton and other city fathers staked out 1,400 acres surrounding a mesa overlooking the harbor and created a permanent green belt overlooking downtown. That acreage officially became Balboa Park in 1911.

The transcontinental train arrived in 1885, and the grand land boom was on. The population soared from 5,000 to 35,000 in less than a decade—a foreshadowing of San Diego's future. In 1887, the tile-domed Santa Fe Depot was constructed at the foot of Broadway, two blocks from the water. Freighters chugged in and out of the harbor, and by the early 1900s, the navy had discovered this perfect West Coast command center. Today the navy has a strong presence in the harbor and on Point Loma as well as Coronado Island and is an integral part of the cityscape.

As downtown grew into San Diego's transportation and commercial hub, residential neighborhoods blossomed along the beaches and inland valleys. Downtown's business district gradually moved farther away from the original heart of downtown, at 5th Avenue and Market Street, past Broadway, up toward the park. Downtown's waterfront fell into bad times during World War I, when sailors, gamblers, prostitutes, and boozers were drawn like magnets to one another and the waterfront bars.

But Alonzo Horton's modern-day followers, city leaders intent on prospering while preserving San Diego's natural beauty, have reclaimed the waterfront. Replacing old shipyards and canneries are hotel towers and waterfront parks; the King Promenade project is slated to put 12½ acres of greenery along Harbor Drive from Seaport Village to the convention center and north to the Gaslamp Quarter by 1995. Nineteen ninety-two saw the completion of the part of the park near the $160 million, 760,000-square-foot San Diego Convention Center, which hosted its first events in early 1990. Since then downtown has been lively even when the offices and banks are closed. Hotels, restaurants, shopping centers, and housing developments are rising on every square inch of available space as downtown San Diego comes of age.

❶ Your first view of downtown, regardless of your mode of transportation, will probably include the **Embarcadero,** a waterfront walkway lined with restaurants, cruise ships, and tour boats along Harbor Drive. Your closest access to maps and brochures is the **Santa Fe Depot,** just two blocks away, at the corner of Broadway and Kettner Boulevard. A tourist information booth inside the station has bus schedules, maps, and a Traveler's Aid booth. The depot's unmistakable blue-and-yellow tiled dome has become dwarfed by One America Plaza, a massive 34-story office tower designed by renowned architect Helmut Jahn. The building includes a transit center linking the train, trolley, and bus systems; its signature crescent-shaped glass-and-steel canopy arches out over the trolley tracks. Tour buses to Mexico depart from here, and the Greyhound bus station is just a few blocks away at 120 West Broadway. The bright red San Diego Trolley that departs from One America Plaza runs through San Diego's south coastal communities—Chula Vista, National City, and Imperial Beach—to the Tijuana border. The fare for the 40-minute ride to the border is $1.50.

Begin your Embarcadero tour at the foot of Ash Street on Harbor Drive, where the harbor's collection of houseboats, ferries, cruise ships, naval destroyers, tour boats, and a fair share of seals and seagulls begins. The *Star of India*, a beautiful windjammer built in 1863, is docked at the foot of Grape Street on Harbor Drive, across from the Spanish-style San Diego County Administration Center. The *Star of India* is part of the ❸ **Maritime Museum,** a collection of three ships that have been restored and are open for tours. *The Maritime Museum headquarters is located in the* Berkeley *paddle wheeler by the B St. Pier, tel. 619/234–9153. Admission: $5 adults, $4 senior citizens and students 12–17, $1.25 children 6–12, $10 families. Ships open daily 9–8.*

A cement pathway runs from the *Star of India* along the water, past restaurants and fish markets to the docks for harbor tour boats and whale-watching trips (which are scheduled in January and February during the grand migration of the gray whales from the Pacific Northwest to southern Baja). This section of the Embarcadero, at Harbor Drive and the foot of Broadway, has become a tourists' gathering spot. A cluster of streetfront windows sell tickets for tours; those waiting for their boats grab a beer or ice cream at the diner-style Bay Cafe and sit on the upstairs patio or on benches along the busy pathway and watch the sailboats, paddle wheelers, and yachts vie for space.

❹ The pink-and-blue **B Street Pier** has become a central loading zone for catamaran trips to the island of Catalina, about three hours northeast, and cruise trips to Ensenada, Mexico's harborfront city about 80 land miles south of San Diego. Ships from major cruise lines use San Diego's pier as both a port of call and a departure point for cruises to Cabo San Lucas, Mazatlán, Puerto Vallerta, and Fort Lauderdale, Florida. The cavernous pier building has a cruise-information center and a small, cool bar and gift shop. There is a huge public parking lot ($5 a day) along the south side of the pier building. Since much of the parking along Harbor Drive is limited to two-hour meters, this lot is good if you're planning to tour the harbor for the day.

One of the most traditional, and delightful, boat trips to take from the pier is the **Bay Ferry** to Coronado Island.

Back along the Embarcadero are other traditional craft, some housing gift shops, some awaiting restoration. The navy's Eleventh Naval District has control of the next few waterfront blocks, and a series of destroyers, submarines, and carriers cruise in and out, some staying for weeks at a time. The navy occasionally offers tours of these floating cities.

A steady stream of joggers, bicyclists, and serious walkers pick up speed where the Embarcadero pathway passes the Tuna Harbor, where San Diego's tuna boats once gathered. The Fish Market Restaurant sits at the back of a large parking lot at the end of the pier, offering spectacular views of the harbor and downtown.

❺ **Seaport Village** (tel. 619/235–4013 for recorded information or 619/235–4014) is next. This stretch of prime waterfront, connecting the harbor with the hotel towers and convention center, is a privately developed and operated 14-acre shopping, dining, and recreational outdoor mall of sorts. The village's clapboard and stucco buildings house a seemingly unending series of specialty shops, snack bars, and restaurants—each with an independent theme. Seaport Village spreads from Harbor Drive to the waterfront, and is currently undergoing an expansion to include the old San Diego Police Department across the street. The **Broadway Flying Horses Carousel,** whose hand-carved animals rose and fell at Coney Island during the turn of the century, is surrounded by inexpensive ethnic cafés and takeouts and a video parlor for those who prefer their fun in the shade. Beside the wall is Seaport Village's official symbol, the 45-foot-high **Mulkilteo Lighthouse**, modeled after an 80-year-old lighthouse in Everett, Washington. The San Diego Pier

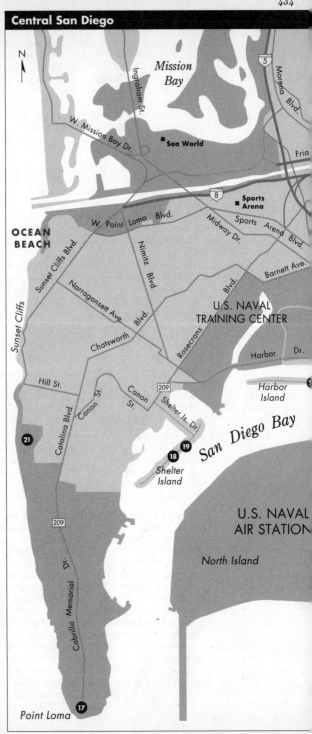

Central San Diego

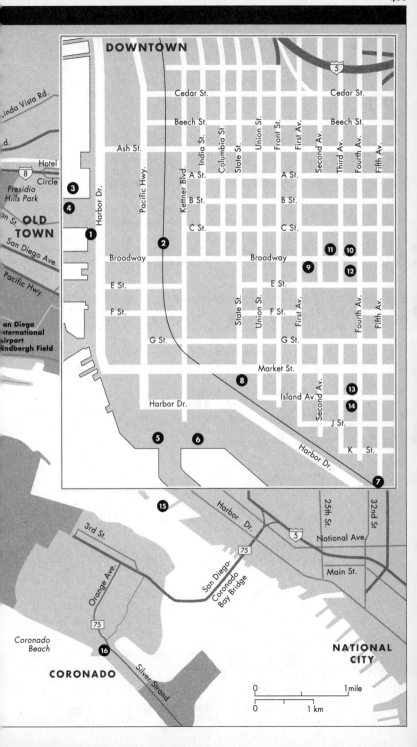

Cafe, an on-the-water seafood restaurant, occupies the light-house.

Seaport Village's center reaches out on a long grassy point into the harbor, where kite fliers, roller skaters, and picnickers hang out in the sun. Seasonal celebrations, replete with live music and fireworks, are held here throughout the year. Even when nothing special is planned, the village is filled with clowns, mimes, musicians, and magicians in a shopper's paradise.

6 The mirrored towers of the **San Diego Marriott Hotel and Marina** mark the end of Seaport Village. The waterfront walkway continues past the hotel's marina, where hotel guests moor their enormous, extravagant yachts. Just past the Marriott is **7** the **San Diego Convention Center,** designed by Arthur Erickson. The architecture is striking, especially against the blue sky and sea. The center often holds trade shows that are open to the public. Tours of the building are available.

To reach the heart of downtown, walk up Market Street from Seaport Village or up Broadway from the B Street Pier. The **8** **Olde Cracker Factory,** at Market and State streets, houses antiques and collectibles shops. Turn left here and go two blocks to G Street, where many of San Diego's new residential developments are clustered around the pretty **Pantoja Park.**

Walking up Broadway, you'll pass the Santa Fe Depot and several commercial high rises—including One America Plaza, the Koll Center, and the Emerald Shapery Center. A few blocks farther, at the corner of 1st Avenue and Broadway, is where **9** downtown comes alive. Here you'll pass the **Spreckels Theater,** a grand old stage that now presents pop concerts and touring plays.

10 The grand **U.S. Grant Hotel,** built in 1910, is across the street. Far more formal than most San Diego hotels, the U.S. Grant has massive marble lobbies, with gleaming chandeliers and hospitable doormen. The Grant Grill, closed for two years during the hotel's refurbishing, is the prime watering hole for San Diego's old guard, and the bar has become a popular after-work **11** gathering spot. One block away is the **Westgate Hotel,** another deluxe hostelry for visiting celebrities and royalty. The Westgate is French Provincial in style and has a nice piano bar on the main floor and an elegant French restaurant, Le Fontainebleau, at the top.

12 The theme of shopping in adventureland carries over from Seaport Village to downtown San Diego's centerpiece, **Horton Plaza.** Completed in August 1985, this shopping, dining, and entertainment mall fronts Broadway and G Street from 1st to 4th avenues and covers more than six city blocks. Designed by Jon Jerde, whose touch you might have seen in views from the 1984 Summer Olympics in Los Angeles, Horton Plaza is far from what one imagines a shopping center, or city center, to be. It rises in uneven, staggered levels to six floors and has great views of all downtown, from the harbor to Balboa Park and beyond. The 450-room Doubletree Hotel is connected to Horton Plaza and often hosts special events in conjunction with the plaza.

The **International Visitor Information Center** was opened in Horton Plaza by the San Diego Convention and Visitors Bureau in 1985, and it has become the traveler's best source for information on all San Diego. The staff members and volunteers who run the center speak an amazing array of languages and are well acquainted with the myriad needs and requests of tourists. They dispense information on hotels, restaurants, and tourist attractions, including Tijuana. Photos of San Diego's landmarks decorate the walls, and brochures and pamphlets in many languages are neatly arrayed by the counters. *11 Horton Plaza, street level at the corner of First Ave. and F St., tel. 619/236–1212. Open daily 8:30–5.*

Long before Horton Plaza became the bright star on downtown's redevelopment horizon, the **Gaslamp Quarter** was gaining attention and respect. A 16-block National Historic District, centered on 5th and 4th avenues, from Broadway to Market Street, the quarter contains most of San Diego's Victorian-style commercial buildings from the late 1800s, when Market Street was the center of early downtown. At the far- ● thest end of the redeveloped quarter, the **Gaslamp Quarter Association** is headquartered in the William Heath Davis house (410 Island Ave., tel. 619/233–5227), a restored 19th-century saltbox structure. Walking tours of the historic district leave from here on Saturdays at 10 and 1. A $2 donation is suggested. If you can't make the tour, stop by the house and pick up a brochure and map.

The William Heath Davis house is located in the heart of Alonzo Horton's New Town, so called to distinguish it from Old Town. In the late 1800s, businesses thrived in this area. But at the turn of the century, downtown's business district moved farther west, toward Broadway, and many of San Diego's first buildings fell into disrepair. During the early 1900s, the quarter became known as the Stingaree district, where hookers picked up sailors in lively taverns and dance halls. Crime flourished here, and the blocks between Market Street and the waterfront were considered to be seedy, dangerous, and best avoided. As the move for downtown redevelopment emerged, there was talk of destroying the buildings in the quarter, but in 1974, history buffs, developers, architects, and artists formed the Gaslamp Quarter Council. Bent on preserving the district, they gathered funds from the government and private benefactors and began the tedious, expensive task of cleaning up the quarter, restoring the finest old buildings, and attracting businesses and the public back to the heart of New Town.

Across the street from the Gaslamp Quarter Association's headquarters, at the corner of Island and 3rd avenues, is the ● 100-year-old **Horton Grand Hotel**, restored and operated in turn-of-the-century style. The hotel's central courtyard has become a popular wedding and party site. The 110 rooms are decorated with period furnishings, lace curtains, and gas fireplaces—some even have legendary ghosts. A small Chinese Museum serves as a tribute to the surrounding Chinatown district, which is nothing more than a collection of modest homes that once housed Chinese laborers and their families.

Many of the quarter's landmark buildings are located on 4th and Fifth avenues, between Island Avenue and Broadway. Among the nicest are the Backesto Building, the Keating Building, the Louis Bank of Commerce, and the Mercantile Building, all on 5th Avenue. Johnny M's 801, at the corner of 4th Avenue and F Street, is a magnificently restored turn-of-

the-century tavern with a 12-foot mahogany bar and a spectacular stained-glass domed ceiling.

Coronado

Coronado Island is a charming, peaceful community, essential-
ly left alone for decades to grow at its characteristically slow
pace. It is a city unto itself, ruled by its own municipal government. Longtime residents live in grand Victorian homes
handed down by their families for generations. North Island
Naval Air Station was established in 1911 on the island's north
end, across from Point Loma, and was the site of Charles Lindbergh's departure on his flight around the world. Today high-
tech air- and seacraft arrive and depart continually from North
Island, providing a real-life education in military armament.
Coronado's long relationship with the navy has made it an enclave of sorts for retired military personnel.

The streets are wide, quiet, and friendly, with lots of neighborhood parks where young families mingle with the island's many
senior citizens. Grand old homes face the waterfront and the
Coronado Municipal Golf Course, with its lovely setting under
the bridge, at the north end of Glorietta Bay, site of the annual
Fourth of July fireworks. Community celebrations and live-
band concerts take place in Spreckels' Park on Orange Avenue.
The Spaniards called the island "Los Coronados," or "the
Crowned Ones," in the late 1500s. The name stuck, and today's
island residents tend to consider their island to be a sort of royal encampment, safe from the hassles and hustle of San Diego
proper.

Coronado is visible from downtown and Point Loma and accessible via the arching blue 2.2-mile-long San Diego–Coronado
Bridge, a landmark just beyond downtown's skyline. There is a
$1 toll for crossing the bridge into Coronado, but cars carrying
two or more passengers may enter through the free car-pool
lane. The bridge handles more than 20,000 cars each day, and
rush hour tends to be slow, which is fine, since the view of the
harbor, downtown, and the island is breathtaking, day and
night. Until the bridge was completed in 1969, visitors and residents relied on the Coronado Ferry, which ran across the harbor from downtown. When the bridge was opened, the ferry
closed down, much to the chagrin of those who were fond of
traveling at a leisurely pace. In 1987, the ferry returned, and
with it came the island's most ambitious development in decades.

15 The Bay Ferry runs from the B Street Pier at downtown's Embarcadero to the **Old Ferry Landing,** which is actually a new
development on an old site. Its buildings resemble the gingerbread domes of the Hotel Del Coronado, long the island's main
attraction. The Old Ferry Landing is similar to Seaport Village, with small shops and restaurants and lots of benches facing the water. Nearby, the elegant Le Meridien Hotel
accommodates many wedding receptions and gala banquets.
The Bay Ferry is located at the B Street Pier, at Broadway and
Harbor Drive. Boats depart hourly from 9 AM to 10:30 PM. The
fare is $1.60 each way.

A trackless trolley runs from the landing down Orange Avenue,
the island's version of a downtown, to the Hotel Del Coronado.
Coronado's residents and commuting workers have quickly

adapted to this traditional mode of transportation, and the ferry has become quite popular with bicyclists who shuttle their bikes across the harbor and ride the island's wide, flat boulevards for hours.

⓰ The **Hotel Del Coronado** is the island's most prominent landmark. Selected as a National Historic Site in 1977, the Del (as natives say) celebrated its 100th anniversary in 1988. Celebrities, royalty, and politicians marked the anniversary with a weekend-long party that highlighted the hotel's colorful history. *1500 Orange Ave., tel. 619/435–6611. Guided tours ($10) from the lobby Thurs.–Sat. 10 and 11 AM.*

The hotel is integral to the island's history. In 1884, two wealthy financiers, Elisha Spurr Babcock, Jr., and H. L. Story, stopped hunting grouse and rabbits on the undeveloped island long enough to appreciate the long stretches of virgin beaches, the view of San Diego's emerging harbor, and the island's potential. They decided to build a luxurious resort hotel, formed the Babcock-Story Coronado Beach Company, and purchased the 4,100-acre parcel of land for $110,000 in 1885.

It took only one year to build the 400-room main hotel, though it was a mighty effort that employed hundreds of Chinese laborers racing against the clock. All materials and laborers had to be ferried to the island and transported up Orange Avenue on the Babcock-Story Railroad, which was capable of transporting private railroad cars popular with industrial tycoons. The hotel was completed in 1888, and Thomas Edison himself threw the switch as the Del became the world's first electrically lighted hotel. It has been a dazzler ever since.

The hotel's gingerbread architecture is recognized all over the world, for it has served as a set for many movies, political meetings, and extravagant social happenings. The Duke of Windsor met Wally Simpson here. Eight presidents have stayed here. The film *Some Like It Hot*, starring Marilyn Monroe, was filmed here. The hotel's underground corridors are lined with historic photos from the days when the hotel was first built. Of particular interest are the photos of the enormous tent city that was built during a major remodeling project in 1902. The tent city was so popular with guests that it was reerected every summer until 1939.

Coronado's other main attraction is its 86 historic homes and sites. Many of the homes are turn-of-the-century mansions. The **Glorietta Bay Inn**, across the street from the Del, was the home of John Spreckels, original owner of North Island and the property on which the Hotel Del Coronado now stands. Nearby is the **Boat House**, a small replica of the hotel that once served as the launching point for deep-sea fishing craft and now houses a Chart House restaurant. The Boat House is a great spot for watching the sails in the harbor and the sunset over downtown.

Point Loma, Shelter Island, and Harbor Island

Point Loma curves around the San Diego Bay west of downtown and the airport, protecting the center city from the Pacific's tides and waves. Though its main streets are cluttered with hotels, fast-food shacks, and military installations, Point Loma is an old and wealthy enclave of stately family homes for military officers, successful Portuguese fishermen, and political and professional leaders. Its bayside shores front huge estates, with sailboats and yachts packed tightly in private marinas.

17 **Cabrillo National Monument,** named after the Portuguese explorer Juan Rodríguez Cabrillo, sits at the very tip of Point Loma. Cabrillo was the first European to discover San Diego, which he called San Miguel, in 1542. In 1913 the monument grounds were set aside to commemorate his discovery. One of the most frequently visited of all National Park Service sites, Cabrillo National Monument simultaneously serves tourism and protects the 144-acre preserve's rugged cliffs and shores. Begin your tour at the Visitor Center, where films and lectures about the monument, the sea-level tidal pools, and the gray whales migrating offshore are presented frequently. Looking directly south across the bay from the Visitor Center, you see the North Island Naval Air Station on the west end of Coronado Island. Directly left on the shores of Point Loma is the Naval Ocean Systems Center and Ballast Point; nuclear-powered submarines are now docked where Cabrillo's small ships anchored in 1542. A new statue of Cabrillo overlooks downtown from the next windy promontory, where visitors gather to admire the stunning panorama over the bay, from the snowcapped San Bernardino mountains, some 200 miles northeast, to the hills surrounding Tijuana. Rest rooms and water fountains are plentiful along the paths that climb to the monument's various viewpoints, but there are no food facilities. Exploring the grounds consumes time and calories; bring a picnic and rest on a bench overlooking the sailboats headed to sea. *1800 Memorial Dr., tel. 619/557–5450. Admission: $1 per person or $3 per carload. Open daily 9–5:15.*

The oil lamp of the **Old Point Loma Lighthouse** was first lit in 1855. The light, sitting in a brass and iron housing above a painstakingly refurbished white wooden house, shone through a state-of-the-art lens from France and was visible from the sea for 25 miles. Unfortunately, it was too high above the cliffs to guide navigators trapped in Southern California's thick offshore fog and low clouds. In 1891 a new lighthouse was built on the small shore under the slowly eroding 400-foot cliffs. The old lighthouse is open to visitors, and the coast guard still uses the newer lighthouse and a mighty foghorn to guide boaters through the narrow channel leading into the bay.

18 **Shelter Island** sits in the narrow channel between Point Loma's eastern shore and the west coast of Coronado. In 1950 the port director thought there should be some use for the soil dredged to deepen the ship channel. Why not build an island?

His hunch paid off. Shelter Island's shores now support towering mature palms, a cluster of mid-range resorts, restaurants, and side-by-side marinas. It is the center of San Diego's yacht-building industry, and boats in every stage of construction are visible in the yacht yards. A long sidewalk runs from the land-**19** scaped lawns of the **San Diego Yacht Club** (tucked down Anchorage St. off Shelter Island Dr.), past boat brokerages to the hotels and marinas, which line the inner shore, facing Point Loma. On the bay side, fishermen launch their boats or simply stand onshore and cast. Families relax at picnic tables along the grass, where there are fire rings and permanent barbecue grills, while strollers wander to the huge Friendship Bell, given to San Diegans by the people of Yokohama in 1960.

❷⓪ Harbor Island, made from 3.5 million tons of rock and soil from the San Diego Bay, forms a peninsula adjacent to the airport. Again, hotels and restaurants line the inner shores, but here, the buildings are many stories high, and the views from the bayside rooms are spectacular. The bay shore has pathways, gardens, and picnic spots for sightseeing or working off the calories from the island restaurants' fine meals. On the west point, Tom Ham's Lighthouse restaurant has a coast guard–approved beacon shining from its tower.

❷① Sunset Cliffs Park is at the western side of Point Loma near Ocean Beach. The cliffs are aptly named, since their main attraction is their vantage point as a fine sunset-watching spot. The dramatic coastline here seems to have been carved out of ancient rock. Certainly the waves make their impact, and each year more sections of the cliffs sport caution signs. Don't climb around on the cliffs when you see these signs. It's easy to lose your footing and slip in the crumbling sandstone, and the surf can get very rough. Small coves and beaches dot the coastline and are popular with surfers drawn to the pounding waves and locals from the neighborhood who name and claim their special spots. The homes along Sunset Cliffs Boulevard are lovely examples of Southern California luxury, with pink stucco mansions beside shingle Cape Cod–style cottages. To reach the cliffs from Cabrillo Monument, take Catalina Boulevard to Hill Street. Turn left and drive straight to the cliffs. Sunset Cliffs Boulevard intersects Hill Street and runs through Ocean Beach to I–8.

Balboa Park

Numbers in the margin correspond to points of interest on the Balboa Park map.

If it were on the ocean, Balboa Park would encompass all that is wonderful about San Diego. But you can see the ocean, or the bay at least (Balboa Park straddles two mesas overlooking downtown), from many points in the park's 1,400 acres of cultural, recreational, and environmental delights. Many of the park's ornate Spanish-Moorish buildings were intended to be temporary structures housing exhibits for the Panama–California International Exposition of 1915. Fortunately, the city leaders realized the buildings' value and incorporated them into their plans for Balboa Park's development. The Spanish architectural theme was carved into the structures built for the California Pacific International Exposition of 1935–36. Most of San Diego's museums are located in the park, making it San Diego's cultural center. All the museums have free admission on a rotating basis on Tuesdays.

The Laurel Street Bridge, also known as Cabrillo Bridge, is the park's official gateway, leading over a vast canyon filled with downtown commuter traffic on Highway 163, to El Prado which, beyond the art museum, becomes the park's central pedestrian mall. At Christmas the bridge is lined with colored lights; bright pink blossoms on rows of peach trees herald the coming of spring. The 100-bell carillon in the California Tower tolls the hour. Figures of California's historic personages decorate the base of the 200-foot spire, and a magnificent blue-tiled dome shines in the sun.

❶ **The Museum of Man** sits under the California Tower and houses the extensive collection of archaeological and anthropological exhibits first assembled for the 1915 exposition. One of that fair's primary cultural highlights was the "Story of Man Through the Ages" display, with artifacts culled from expeditions throughout the world. Over the years the museum has amplified that original theme and is now one of the finest anthropological museums in the country. Exhibits focus on southwestern, Mexican, and South American cultures, and the museum sponsors expeditions and research in South America. *Tel. 619/239–2001. Admission: $3 adults, $1 children 13–18. Open daily 10–4:30.*

The **Simon Edison Center for the Performing Arts** (tel. 619/239–2255) sits beside the Museum of Man under the California Tower. It includes the Cassius Carter Centre Stage, the Lowell Davies Festival Theatre, and the Old Globe. Beside the center is the **Sculpture Garden,** an outdoor exhibit of traditional and modernistic sculptures. The Sculpture Garden Cafe, with tables set amid the art, is open for lunch.

❷ The **San Diego Museum of Art** faces the central parking lot, where an empty parking space is rarer than any painting. Traffic is diverted from the rest of El Prado here, with the roadway leading toward the park's southern circle of museums. Be sure to check out the Museum of Art's special shows, such as a recent exhibit of Fabergé eggs. *Tel. 619/232–7931. Admission: $5 adults, $4 senior citizens, $2 children 6–18. Open Tues.–Sun. 9–4:30.*

❸ The **Timken Art Gallery,** next to the museum, is a private gallery housing works of European masters and a collection of Russian icons. The Putnam Foundation operates the gallery, which is the only privately owned building in the park. *Tel. 619/239–5548. Admission free. Open Tues.–Sat. 10–4:30, Sun. 1:30–4:30. Closed Sept.*

Across the Prado, **The San Diego Art Institute** has occasional shows of students' works. *Tel. 619/234–5946. Admission free. Open Tues.–Sat. 10–5, Sun. 12:30–5.*

❹ The action gets lively in the next section of El Prado, where mimes, jugglers, and musicians perform on long lawns beside the Lily Pond, in front of the graceful **Botanical Building.** Built for the 1915 exposition, the latticed, open-air nursery houses more than 500 types of tropical and subtropical plants. The orchid collection is stunning, and there are benches beside cool, miniature waterfalls for resting away from the sun. The Lily Pond is filled with giant koi fish and blooming water lilies and is a popular spot for taking photographs. *Admission free. Open Tues.–Sun. 10–4:30.*

❺ The **Park Information Center** (tel. 619/239–0512), open daily 9:30–4, is located in the **House of Hospitality,** across El Prado from the pond. The office, staffed by volunteers, has maps and booklets on Balboa Park and sells the Passport to Balboa Park, which offers reduced-price coupons to the museums. Many of the city's cultural groups also have offices in this building, which surrounds a peaceful patio and Spanish fountain. Next door, the Cafe Del Rey Moro serves drinks, lunch, and dinner. The flowering grotto, hidden by eucalyptus trees behind the restaurant, is a favorite spot for weddings.

Balboa Park

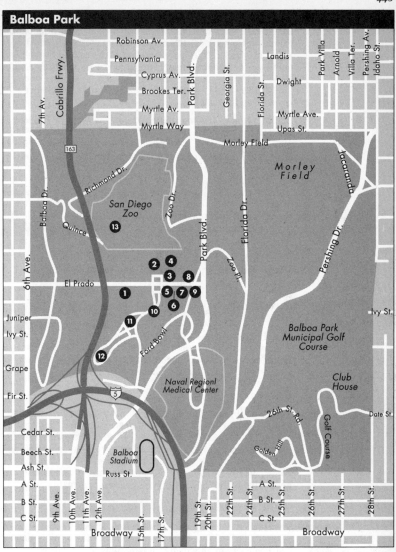

Botanical Building, **4**

House of Hospitality, **5**

House of Pacific Relations, **11**

Museum of Man, **1**

Museum of Photographic Arts, **7**

Natural History Museum, **8**

Organ Pavilion, **10**

Reuben H. Fleet Space Theater and Science Center, **9**

San Diego Aerospace Museum and International Aerospace Hall of Fame, **12**

San Diego Museum of Art, **2**

San Diego Sports Museum Hall of Champions, **6**

San Diego Zoo, **13**

Timken Art Gallery, **3**

6 Next in line, the **San Diego Sports Museum Hall of Champions** has a vast collection of memorabilia, paintings, and photographs honoring local athletes and sports history. San Diego, sometimes called the Sports Center of the United States, has nurtured the talents of many famous athletes, including Archie Moore, Dennis Conner, Bill Walton, and Maureen Connolly. *Tel. 619/234–2544. Admission: $3 adults, $1 children 6–17. Open daily 10–4:30.*

7 The **Museum of Photographic Arts,** in the **Casa de Balboa,** is one of the few museums in the country dedicated solely to photography. It will celebrate its 10th anniversary in 1993. MOPA exhibits the works of world-renowned as well as relatively obscure photographers. The museum has garnered a loyal following and a strong base of volunteers who lead tours through the changing exhibits. Within the next few years, the director hopes to open a downtown annex to MOPA that will concentrate on film and video as artistic media. *Tel. 619/239–5262. Admission: $2.50, children under 12 free. Open Mon.–Wed. and Fri.–Sun. 10–5, Thurs. 10–9.*

Below MOPA in the basement of the Casa de Balboa is the **San Diego Model Railroad Museum.** The room is filled with the sounds of chugging engines, screeching brakes, and shrill whistles when the six model-train exhibits are in operation. *Tel. 619/696–0199. Admission: $1.50 adults, children under 15 free. Open Wed.–Fri. 11–4, weekends 11–5.*

The **Museum of San Diego History** opened in 1990 in the Casa de Balboa under the auspices of the San Diego Historical Society. Rotating exhibits focus on local history after California became part of the United States. The society's research library is in the basement. *Tel. 619/232–6203. Donation requested. Open Wed.–Sun. 10–4:30.*

The short flight of steps leading to the park's main fountain is another gathering spot for talented street performers. On one **8** side of the fountain is the **Natural History Museum,** with displays on the plants and animals of Southern California and Mexico. Children seem particularly impressed by the dinosaur bones, while amateur gemologists admire the collection of gems, including beautiful rose-colored tourmaline crystals mined in San Diego County. *Tel. 619/232–3821. Admission: $3 adults, $1 children 6–18. Open daily 10–4:30.*

9 The **Reuben H. Fleet Space Theater and Science Center** is on the other side of the fountain. The Omnimax theater has a domed overhead screen on which fantastic films about nature, space, and life seem to lift the viewer into the action. The science center is like a giant laboratory playground, where clever interactive exhibits teach children and adults about basic and complex scientific principles. The Laserium has laser shows set to rock music at night. Shows change frequently, so call ahead if you have a particular one in mind. *Tel. 619/238–1168. Science Center admission: $2.25 adults, $1 children 5–15 or included with price of theater ticket. Theater tickets: $5.50 adults, $3 children 5–15; laser shows: $6 adults, $3.50 children 6–17. Open Sun.–Thurs. 9:30–9:30, Fri.–Sat. 9:30 AM–10:30 PM.*

El Prado ends in a bridge that crosses over Park Boulevard to a perfectly tended rose garden and a seemingly wild cactus grove. From here you can see across the canyon to even more parkland, with picnic groves, sports facilities, and acres of ranging chaparral. Back along El Prado, roads and pathways lead to more sights.

The main road off El Prado goes south from the parking lot by the Museum of Art. A long island of flowers divides the road **❿** that curves around the **Organ Pavilion** and the 5,000-pipe Spreckels Organ, believed to be the largest outdoor organ in the world. Much of the time it is locked up on a stage before rows of benches where wanderers rest and regroup. Concerts are sometimes given on Sunday afternoons and on summer evenings local military bands, gospel groups, and barbershop quartets give concerts in the pavilion. At Christmas the park's massive Christmas tree and life-size Nativity display turn the Organ Pavilion into a seasonal wonderland. A Japanese Friendship Garden will cover 11 acres east of the pavilion; currently there is a small garden and a Japanese teahouse. *Tel. 619/232–2171. Admission free. Open Fri.–Sun. 10 AM–4 PM.*

⓫ The **House of Pacific Relations,** across from the pavilion, is really a cluster of stucco cottages representing various foreign countries. The buildings are open on Sunday, and individual cottages often present celebrations on their country's holidays.

⓬ This southern road ends at the Pan American Plaza and the **San Diego Aerospace Museum and International Aerospace Hall of Fame.** The sleek, streamlined building, commissioned by the Ford Motor Company for the 1935 exposition, is unlike any other in the park. Round, with a line of blue neon outlining it at night, the structure looks like a landlocked UFO. Exhibits about aviation and aerospace pioneers line the rotunda, and a collection of real and replicated aircraft fill the center. *Tel. 619/234–8291. Admission: $4 adults, $1 children 6–17. Open daily 10–4:30.*

The **San Diego Automotive Museum** is housed in the building used as the Palace of Transportation for the 1935–36 Exposition. It maintains a large collection of classic cars and has an ongoing restoration program. *Tel. 619/234–8291. Admission: $4 adults, $1 children 6–17. Open daily 10–4:30.*

⓭ The **San Diego Zoo** is Balboa Park's most famous attraction. It ranges over 100 acres fronting Park Boulevard and is one of the finest zoos and tropical gardens in the world. More than 3,200 animals of 777 species roam in expertly crafted habitats that spread down into, around, and above the natural canyons. Equal attention has been paid to the flora and the fauna, and the zoo is an enormous botanical garden with one of the world's largest collections of subtropical plants. From the moment you walk through the entrance and face the swarm of bright pink flamingos and blue peacocks, you know you've entered a rare pocket of natural harmony. Exploring the zoo fully requires the stamina of a healthy hiker, but there are open-air trams running throughout the day on a 3-mile tour of 80% of the zoo's exhibits. The Skyfari ride soars 170 feet aboveground, giving a good overview of the zoo's layout and a marvelous panorama of the park, downtown San Diego, the bay, and the ocean, far past the Coronado Bridge. *Tel. 619/234–3153. Admission (including unlimited access to the Skyfari ride and the Children's Zoo): $12 adults, $4 children 3–15. Deluxe package (bus tour, Skyfari ride, and Children's Zoo): $15 adults, $6.50 children. Gates open daily 9–4; visitors may remain until 5 PM. Summer hours are 9–5; visitors may remain until 6.*

Old Town

Numbers in the margin correspond to points of interest on the Old Town San Diego map.

San Diego's Spanish and Mexican history and heritage are most evident in Old Town, just north of downtown at Juan Street, near the intersection of I–5 and I–8. It wasn't until 1968 that Old Town became a state historic park. Fortunately, private efforts kept the area's history alive until then, and many of San Diego's oldest structures remain in good shape.

Though Old Town is often credited as being the first European settlement in Southern California, the true beginnings took place overlooking Old Town from atop Presidio Park (*see* below). There, Father Junípero Serra established the first of California's missions, called San Diego de Alcalá, in 1769. San Diego's Indians, called the San Diegueños by the Spaniards, were forced to abandon their seminomadic lifestyle and live at the mission. In 1774 the hilltop was declared a Royal Presidio, or fortress, and the mission was moved to its current location along the San Diego River, 6 miles east of the original site. The Indians lost more of their traditional grounds and ranches as the mission grew along the riverbed. In 1775 the Indians attacked and burned the mission, destroying religious objects and killing Franciscan Padre Luis Jayme. Their later attack on the presidio was less successful, and their revolt was short-lived. By 1800, about 1,500 Indians were living on the mission's grounds, receiving religious instruction and adapting to the Spanish way of life.

The pioneers living within the presidio's walls were mostly Spanish soldiers, poor Mexicans, and mestizos of Spanish and Indian ancestry, all unaccustomed to farming San Diego's arid land. They existed marginally until 1821, when Mexico gained independence from Spain, claimed its lands in California, and flew the Mexican flag over the presidio. The Mexican government, centered some 2,000 miles away in Monterrey, stripped the Spanish missions of their landholdings, and an aristocracy of landholders began to emerge. At the same time, settlers were beginning to move down from the presidio to what is now called Old Town.

A rectangular plaza was laid out along today's San Diego Avenue to serve as the settlement's center. In 1846, during the war between Mexico and the United States, a detachment of marines raised the U.S. flag over the plaza on a pole said to have been a mainmast. The flag was torn down once or twice, but within six months, Mexico had surrendered California, and the U.S. flag remained. In 1850 San Diego became an incorporated city, with Old Town as its center.

❶ Old Town's historic buildings are clustered around the main plaza, called **Old Town Plaza,** with a view of the presidio from behind the cannon by the flagpole. Today the plaza serves much the same purpose it did when it was first laid out. It is a pleasant place for resting and regrouping as you plan your tour of Old Town and watch other visitors stroll by; art shows often fill the lawns around the plaza. San Diego Avenue is closed to traffic here, and the cars are diverted to Juan and Congress streets, both of which are lined with shops and restaurants. There are plenty of free parking lots on the outskirts of Old

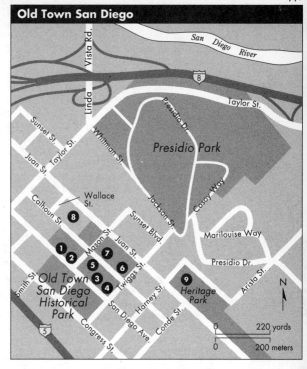

Old Town San Diego

Town, which is best explored on foot. Shopping and eating are essential for a true Old Town tour, so bring your wallet and an appetite.

The **Old Town State Historic Park** office is located in the ❷ **Robinson-Rose House,** on the south side of the plaza. Free guided tours of the park are available from here at 2 PM daily, and there is a good booklet for sale that provides a brief history and a self-guided tour map of the 12-acre park. The Robinson-Rose House was the original commercial center of old San Diego, housing railroad offices, law offices, and the first newspaper press; one room has been restored and outfitted with period furnishings. Park rangers now show films and distribute information from the living room. *4002 Wallace St., tel. 619/237–6770. Open daily 10–5. Free walking tour of the park weekends at 2 PM.*

The historic section of Old Town includes a collection of Mexi- ❸ can colonial–style adobe and log houses. **La Casa de Pedrorena,** a hacienda-style home built in 1869, is currently closed for ren- ❹ ovation. La Casa de Altamirano serves as the **San Diego Union Newspaper Historical Building.** A wood-frame structure prefabricated in Maine and shipped around Cape Horn in 1851, the building has been restored to replicate the newspaper's offices of 1868, when the first edition of the *San Diego Union* was printed.

❺ **La Casa de Estudillo,** across Mason Street from the plaza, is an original Old Town adobe built in 1827. The house has been restored to its former grandeur as the home of the prestigious ❻ Estudillo family, and it is now open for tours. The **Seeley Sta-**

bles became San Diego's stagecoach stop in 1867 and was the hub of Old Town until near the turn of the century, when the tracks of the Southern Pacific Railroad passing by the south side of the settlement became the favored route. The stables now house a collection of horse-drawn vehicles, western memorabilia, and Native American artifacts. There is a $1 admission fee to tour the stables, where a slide show on San Diego's history is presented three times a day.

7 **La Casa de Bandini,** next to the stables, is one of the loveliest haciendas in San Diego. Built in 1829 by a Peruvian, Juan Bandini, the house served as Old Town's social center during Mexican rule. In the 1850s, after Bandini's financial, political, and social standing fell as a result of various ill-fated political and business schemes, he lost the house. Albert Seeley, the stagecoach entrepreneur, purchased the home in 1869, built a second story, and turned it into the Cosmopolitan Hotel, a comfortable way station for travelers on the day-long trip south from Los Angeles. Casa Bandini's colorful gardens and main-floor dining rooms now house a good Mexican restaurant run by the owners of other highly successful Old Town businesses.

8 The unofficial center of Old Town is the **Bazaar del Mundo,** a shopping and dining enclave built to represent a colonial Mexican square. The central courtyard is always in blossom, with magenta bougainvillea, scarlet hibiscus and irises, poppies, and petunias in season. Ballet Folklorico and flamenco dancers perform in the outdoor gazebo on weekend afternoons, and the bazaar frequently holds arts-and-crafts exhibits and Mexican festivals in the courtyard.

9 **Heritage Park,** up the Juan Street hill east of the Seeley Stables, is the headquarters for SOHO, the Save Our Heritage Organization. The climb up to the park is a bit steep, but the view of the harbor is great. SOHO has moved several grand Victorian homes and a temple from other parts of San Diego to the park, where they have been restored. The homes are now used for offices, shops, and restaurants. The Heritage Park Bed & Breakfast Inn is housed in a particularly fine Queen Anne mansion and is a peaceful spot for a stay, away from traffic and noise.

Mission Bay and Sea World

Numbers in the margin correspond to points of interest on the Mission Bay Area map.

Mission Bay is San Diego's monument to sports and fitness. Action and leisure are the main themes of this 4,600-acre aquatic park, 75% of which is public land. Admission to its 27 miles of bayfront beaches and 17 miles of ocean frontage is free. All you need for a perfect day is a bathing suit, shorts, and the right selection of playthings.

When explorer Juan Rodríguez Cabrillo first spotted the bay in 1542, he called it "Baja Falso." The ocean-facing inlet led to acres of swampland, inhospitable to boats and inhabitants. In the 1960s the city planners decided to dredge the swamp and build a man-made bay with acres of beaches and lawns for play. Only 25% of the land would be used for commercial property, and now just a handful of resort hotels break up the natural landscape. Kite flying has become a fine art on the lawns facing

I–5, where the sky is flooded with the bright colors of huge, intricately made kites.

1 The **Visitor Information Center,** at the East Mission Bay Drive exit from I–5, is an excellent tourist resource for the bay and all of San Diego. Leaflets and brochures for most of the area's attractions are provided free, and information on transportation, reservations, and sightseeing is offered cheerfully. The center is a gathering spot for the runners, walkers, and exercisers who take part in group activities. *2688 E. Mission Bay Dr., tel. 619/276–8200. Open Mon.–Sat. 9–5:30, Sun. 9:30–5.*

A 5-mile-long pathway runs through this section of the bay from the trailer park and miniature golf course, south past the high-rise Hilton Hotel to Sea World Drive. Playgrounds and picnic areas abound on the beach and low grassy hills of the park. On weekday evenings, the path is filled with a steady stream of joggers, speed walkers, bikers, and skaters releasing the stress from a day at the office. The water is filled with anglers and boaters, some in single-man kayaks, others in crowded powerboats. The San Diego Crew Classic, which takes place in April, fills this section of the bay with crew teams from all over the country and college reunions complete with flying school colors and keg beer. Swimmers should note signs warning about water pollution; certain areas of the bay are chronically polluted, and bathing is strongly discouraged.

2 **Fiesta Island,** off Mission Bay Drive and Sea World Drive, is a smaller, man-made playground popular with jet- and water-skiers. In July the annual Over-the-Line Tournament, a local variety of softball, attracts thousands of players and oglers drawn by the teams' raunchy names and outrageous behavior.

3 Ingraham Street is another main drag through the bay, from the shores of Pacific Beach to Sea World Drive. **San Diego Princess Resort** on Vacation Isle is the focal point of this part of the bay, with its lushly landscaped grounds, model yacht pond, and bayfront restaurants. Ducks and cottontail bunnies are as common as tourists, and the village is a great family playground, though a bit noisy and often crowded.

4 West Mission Bay Drive runs from the ocean beyond Mission Boulevard to Sea World Drive. The pathways along the Mission Beach side of the bay are lined with vacation homes, many of which can be rented by the month. Those who are fortunate to live here year-round have the bay as their front yards, with wide sandy beaches, volleyball courts, and an endless stream of sightseers on the sidewalk. **Belmont Park,** once an abandoned amusement park at the corner of Mission Boulevard and West Mission Bay Drive, is now a shopping, dining, and recreation area between the bay and the Mission Beach boardwalk. Twinkling lights outline the old but recently refurbished Belmont Park roller coaster where screaming thrill-seekers can once again ride the coaster's curves. Nearby, younger riders enjoy the antique carousel, beside a stand selling fresh cotton candy. The Plunge, an indoor freshwater swimming pool, has also been renovated and is open to the public, making Belmont Park a focal point for the beach area.

5 **Sea World** is Mission Bay's grandest attraction, on the shore along Sea World Drive. The world's largest marine-life park, Sea World is an ocean-oriented amusement park set amid tropical landscaping along the bay. The Sky Tower's glass elevator

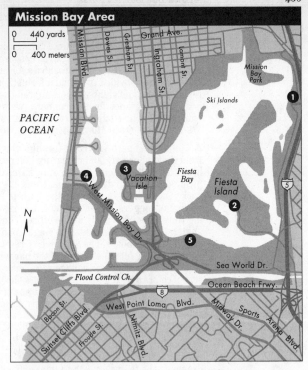

Mission Bay Area

PACIFIC OCEAN

takes you to the top, where the views of San Diego County from the ocean to the mountains are most pleasing in early morning and late evening. A gigantic Christmas tree of lights, stretching from the tower's peak to the ground, is a seasonal landmark.

The traditional favorite exhibit is the Shamu show, with giant killer whales performing in a newly constructed stadium. The Penguin Encounter has a moving sidewalk passing by a glass-enclosed arctic environment, where hundreds of emperor penguins slide over glaciers into icy waters. The shark exhibit, with fierce-looking sharks of a variety of species, is especially popular with imaginative youngsters.

Sea World spreads over 100 acres of bayfront land, where a cool breeze seems always to rise off the water. A sky tram travels between Sea World and the Atlantis Hotel across Mission Bay. In summer, a series of evening concerts as well as fireworks just after sunset attract many visitors. *Sea World is located on Sea World Dr. at the west end of I–8, tel. 619/226–3901, recorded information; 619/226–3815. Admission: $23.95 adults, $17.95 children 3–11. Gates open 9–dusk; extended hours during summer.*

La Jolla

Numbers in the margin correspond to points of interest on the La Jolla map.

La Jollans have long considered their village to be the Monte Carlo of California, and with good cause. Its coastline curves into natural coves backed by verdant hillsides and covered with lavish homes, now worth millions of dollars as housing values soar. Though La Jolla is considered part of San Diego, it has its own postal zone and a coveted sense of class. Movie stars and royalty frequent established hotels and private clubs, and the social scene is the stuff gossip columns are made of.

The Indians called it La Hoya, meaning "the cave," referring to the caves dotting the shoreline. The Spaniards changed the name to La Jolla, meaning "the jewel," and its residents have cherished the name and its allusions ever since. Though development and construction have radically altered the town's once-serene and private character, it remains a haven for the elite.

To reach La Jolla from I–5, take the Ardath Road exit if you're traveling north and drive slowly down this long hill so you can appreciate the breathtaking view. Traveling south, take the La Jolla Village Drive exit. If you enjoy meandering, the best way to reach La Jolla from the south is to drive through Mission and Pacific beaches on Mission Boulevard, past the crowds of roller skaters, bicyclists, and sunbathers headed to the beach. The clutter and congestion ease up as the street becomes La Jolla Boulevard, where quiet neighborhoods with winding streets lead down to some of the best surfing beaches in San Diego. The boulevard here is lined with expensive restaurants and cafés as well as a few takeout spots.

1 La Jolla's coastal attraction is **Ellen Browning Scripps Park** at the **La Jolla Cove.** Towering palms line the sidewalk along Coast Boulevard, where strollers in evening dress are as common as Frisbee throwers. The **Children's Pool,** at the south end of the park, is aptly named for its curving beach and shallow waters protected by a seawall from strong currents and waves.

2 The **La Jolla Caves** are at the far northern point of the cove, under the La Jolla Cave and Shell Shop. A trail leads down from the shop into the caves, with some 133 steps down to the largest, Sunny Jim Cave. For claustrophobic types, there are photos of the caves in the shop, along with a good selection of shells and coral jewelry. *1325 Coast Blvd., tel. 619/454–6080. Admission to caves: $1 adults, 50¢ children 3–11. Open Mon.–Sat. 10–5, Sun. 11–5.*

Prospect Street, La Jolla's main boulevard, overlooks the cove from one block up. The street is lined with excellent restaurants, expensive boutiques, and a recent proliferation of office buildings and two-story shopping complexes. Many of the restaurants on the west side of the street have great views of the cove. At the corner of Prospect and Girard streets sits the **3** charming pink Art Deco–style **La Valencia Hotel.** Its grand lobby with floor-to-ceiling windows overlooking the cove is a popular wedding spot, and its Whaling Bar is a regular hangout for La Jolla denizens. As Prospect Street grows ever more crowded, lines of Mercedeses and Jaguars crowd the valet stand at the hotel's entrance. Pretend you are visiting nobility and wander through the lobby to the outdoor balcony—the view is worth the deception.

Like Prospect Street, Girard Street is lined with expensive shops, where the wares are lovely to look at even if they are

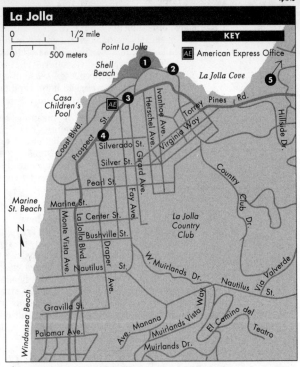

unaffordable. The shopping and dining district has spread to
Pearl and other side streets, with a steady parade of amblers
and sightseers strolling about, chatting in many languages.
Wall Street, a quiet tree-lined boulevard, was once the financial
heart of La Jolla, but banks and investment houses can now be
found throughout town. The nightlife scene is an active one
here, with jazz clubs, piano bars, and watering holes for the
elite younger set coming and going with the trends. Though the
village has lost some of its charm and its close-knit community
feeling, it has gained a cosmopolitan air that makes it a popular
vacation resort for the international set.

❹ The **San Diego Museum of Contemporary Art** is the village's cultural center, housed in a remodeled Irving Gill home, which is
being expanded and remodeled by architect Robert Venturi.
The museum has a permanent collection of post-1950 art and often exhibits shows of contemporary paintings and sculpture,
furnishings, and design. Film series and lectures are held frequently in Sherwood Hall. An excellent bookstore adjacent to
the museum has a varied collection of art books and magazines.
*700 Prospect St., tel. 619/454–3541. Admission: $4 adults, $2
children 12–18, $1 children under 12; free after 5 PM Wed. Open
Tues. and Thurs.–Sun. 10–5, Wed. 10–9.*

❺ North of the cove on La Jolla Shores Drive is the La Jolla Beach
and Tennis Club, host of many tennis tournaments. **La Jolla
Shores'** beaches are some of the finest in San Diego, with long
stretches allotted to surfers or swimmers. The **Scripps Institute
of Oceanography**, a longtime favorite with tourists and locals
alike, opened its **Stephen Birch Aquarium–Museum** in Septem-

ber 1992. Located next to the old facility, up the hill from the shore, the new aquarium has more than 30 huge tanks filled with colorful saltwater fish, as well as a spectacular 70,000-gallon tank that simulates a La Jolla kelp forest. Starfish, sea anemones, lobsters, crabs, and the myriad other sea creatures that inhabit the local shoreline swim in an outdoor tidal pool. "Exploring the Blue Planet," a comprehensive oceanographic exhibit, is the centerpiece of the new $1 million museum. An expanded bookstore offers a good selection of illustrated books and cards. Paths lead down from the institution's buildings to the beaches at La Jolla Shores; there's a natural tidal pool at the beach north of the Scripps Pier. *8602 La Jolla Shores Dr., tel. 619/534-6933. Suggested admission by donation: $3 adults, $2 children 12-18, $1 children 3-11. Open daily 9-5.*

San Diego for Free

San Diego's main attractions are its climate and natural beauty, which are accessible to all, free of charge. The 70 miles of beaches are free—no boardwalks with admission fees, no high-priced parking lots. All you need is a swimsuit and a towel. You can easily while away a week or two just visiting a different beach community each day, from the opulence of La Jolla to the laid-back hippie style of Ocean Beach. Nearly all San Diego's major attractions in our Exploring section are situated amid huge parks, gardens, and waterfronts, with plenty of natural wonders to keep you amused.

Mission Bay is a massive playground for all ages, with beaches for sunning and swimming, playgrounds and picnic tables, and fire rings for nighttime bonfires. **Balboa Park** is similarly entrancing, with its gorgeous gardens and recreational areas. **Seaport Village** hosts a variety of free seasonal events throughout the year, often with fireworks displays. Both the **Embarcadero Marina Park South** and **Sea World** have fireworks on summer evenings that are visible from downtown, Mission Bay, and Ocean Beach.

What to See and Do with Children

As if swimming, roller skating, biking, and hiking weren't enough, San Diego has plenty of additional activities to keep youngsters happy. The **San Diego Zoo** and **San Diego Wild Animal Park** both have children's petting zoos, where the animals are content to play nicely with curious children. The zoo's animal nursery is a lot of fun for the little ones, who can spot baby chimps and antelopes playing with the same brightly colored plastic toys that all children enjoy.

Many of **Balboa Park's** museums have special exhibits for children, who seem particularly entranced by the Museum of Man's "Lifestyles and Ceremonies" exhibit; teens delight in the small collection of mummies. The Natural History Museum's dinosaurs are always a hit. But best of all is the Science Center at the Reuben H. Fleet Space Theater, where the gadgets and hands-on experiments are fascinatingly clever and educational.

Sea World's Cap'n Kids' World is an imaginative, no-holds-barred playground that captivates youngsters and occupies their energy and time for hours on end. The playground is so popular that San Diegans often get yearly passes to Sea World so they can bring their children and have some time to sit peacefully in the sun while the youngsters play.

The **Children's Museum** in La Jolla Village Square has trunks filled with costumes for dress-up, plenty of arts-and-crafts supplies, and even a model dentist's chair where children can pretend to drill their parents' teeth. The Tide Pool at the **Stephen Birch Aquarium–Museum** gives children a chance to hold and pet starfish and sea anemones. **Mission Bay** and many of the beaches have large playgrounds by the water. The **Children's Pool** at La Jolla Cove is a shallow cove protected from the waves, safe enough to let the youngsters try snorkeling. In **Old Town,** Geppetto's toy store is a must-see for its inexpensive gadgets imported from Europe. The carousels at Balboa Park and the zoo are good for burning up some energy. **Belmont Park** in Mission Beach is a mini-amusement park by the sea, with a renovated 1925 roller coaster, a carousel, a photo booth where you can pose on a surfboard inside a plastic wave, and a life-size gyroscope ride.

Off the Beaten Track

Don't think you've finished seeing San Diego once you've hit all the main attractions. The real character of the place doesn't shine through until you've hit a few neighborhoods and mingled with the natives. Then you can say you've seen San Diego.

Mission Hills is an older neighborhood near downtown that has the charm and wealth of La Jolla and Point Loma, without the crowds. The prettiest streets are above Presidio Park and Old Town, where huge mansions with rolling lawns resemble eastern estates. Drive along Fort Stockton Drive up from the presidio, or Juan Street past Heritage Park in Old Town to Sunset Boulevard to see these homes. Washington Street runs up a steep hill from I–8 through the center of Mission Hills. Palmier's, at the corner of Washington Street and Goldfinch Street, is a French café and charcûterie with wonderful pâtés, pastries, and wines to eat there or to go. On Goldfinch, visit the Gathering, a neighborhood restaurant with great breakfasts and outdoor tables for reading the Sunday paper in the sun.

Hillcrest, farther up Washington Street beginning at 1st Avenue, is San Diego's Castro Street, the center for the gay community and artists of all types. University Avenue and 4th and 5th avenues are filled with cafés, boutiques, and excellent bookstores. The Corvette Diner, on 4th Avenue between University Avenue and Washington Street, is an outrageous '50s-diner sort of place, with burgers and shakes and campy waitresses. Quel Fromage, a coffeehouse on University Avenue between 4th and 6th avenues, has long been the place to go to discuss philosophical or romantic matters over espresso. Like most of San Diego, Hillcrest has been undergoing massive redevelopment. The largest project is the **Uptown District,** on University Avenue at 8th Avenue. This self-contained residential/commercial center was built to resemble an inner-city neighborhood, with shops and restaurants within easy walking distance of high-priced town houses. Washington Street eventually becomes Adams Avenue, San Diego's Antiques Row, with shops displaying an odd array of antiques and collectibles. Adams Avenue leads into Kensington and Talmadge, two lovely old neighborhoods overlooking Mission Valley. The Ken Cinema, at 4066 Adams Avenue, shows older cult movies and current art films.

Shopping

Most San Diego shops are open daily 10–6; department stores and shops within the larger malls stay open until 9 PM on week days. Almost every store will accept traveler's checks, with proper identification (driver's license, passport). Aside from their own credit cards, major department stores usually accept American Express, MasterCard, and Visa. Sales are advertised in the daily *San Diego Union* and San Diego edition of the *Los Angeles Times* and in the *Reader*, a free weekly that comes out on Thursday.

Shopping Districts San Diego's shopping areas are a mélange of self-contained megamalls, historic districts, quaint villages, funky neighborhoods, and chic suburbs.

Coronado. Across the bay, Coronado is accessible by car or ferry. **Orange Avenue,** in the center of town, has six blocks of ritzy boutiques and galleries. The elegant Hotel Del Coronado, also on Orange Avenue, houses exclusive (and costly) specialty shops. **Old Ferry Landing,** where the San Diego ferry docks, is a waterfront center similar to Seaport Village.

Downtown. Horton Plaza, in the heart of center city, is a shopper's Disneyland—visually exciting, multilevels of department stores, one-of-a-kind shops, fast-food counters, classy restaurants, a farmer's market, live theater, and cinemas. Surrounding Horton Plaza is the 16-block Gaslamp Quarter, a redevelopment area that features art galleries, antiques, and specialty shops housed in Victorian buildings and renovated ware houses.

Hotel Circle. The Hotel Circle area, northeast of downtown near I–8 and Freeway 163, has two major shopping centers. **Fashion Valley** and **Mission Valley Center** contain hundreds of shops, as well as restaurants, cinemas, and branches of almost every San Diego department store.

Kensington/Hillcrest. These are two of San Diego's older, established neighborhoods, situated several miles north and east of downtown. **Adams Avenue,** in Kensington, is Antiques Row. More than 20 dealers sell everything from postcards and kitchen utensils to cut glass and porcelain. **Park Boulevard,** in Hillcrest, is the city's center for nostalgia. Small shops, on either side of University Avenue, stock clothing, accessories, furnishings, and bric-a-brac of the 1920s–1960s. **Uptown District,** a shopping center on University Avenue, has the neighborhood's massive Ralph's grocery store, as well as several specialty shops.

La Jolla/Golden Triangle. La Jolla, about 15 miles northwest of downtown, on the coast, is an ultrachic, ultraexclusive resort community. High-end and trendy boutiques line Girard Avenue and Prospect Street. Coast Walk, nestled along the cliffside of Prospect Street, offers several levels of sophisticated shops, galleries, and restaurants, as well as a spectacular ocean view. The Golden Triangle area, several miles east of coastal La Jolla, is served by two malls. **La Jolla Village Square,** just west of I–5, is an indoor shopping complex; **University Towne Centre,** farther inland, between I–5 and Highway 805, is an open-air village. Both centers feature the usual range of department stores, specialty shops, sportswear chains, restaurants, and cinemas. **Costa Verde Centre,** on the corner of Genessee and La Jolla Village Drive, is an enormous strip mall of convenience stores and inexpensive eateries.

Old Town. North of downtown, off I–5, this popular historic district is reminiscent of a colorful Mexican marketplace. Adobe architecture, flower-filled plazas, fountains, and courtyards highlight the shopping areas of **Bazaar del Mundo, La Esplanade,** and **Old Town Mercado,** where you will find international goods, toys, souvenirs, and arts and crafts.

Seaport Village. On the waterfront, a few minutes from downtown, **Seaport Village** offers quaint theme shops, restaurants, arts-and-crafts galleries, and commanding views of Coronado, the bridge, and passing ships.

Participant Sports

At least one stereotype of San Diego is true—it is an active, outdoors-oriented community. People recreate more than spectate. It's hard not to, with such a wide variety of choices available.

Bicycling On any given summer day, Old Highway 101, from La Jolla to Oceanside, looks like a freeway for cyclists. Never straying more than a quarter-mile from the beach, it is easily the most popular and scenic bike route around. Although the roads are narrow and winding, experienced cyclists like to follow Lomas Santa Fe Drive in Solana Beach east into beautiful Rancho Santa Fe, perhaps even continuing east on Del Dios Highway, past Lake Hodges, to Escondido. For more leisurely rides, Mission Bay, San Diego Harbor, and the Mission Beach boardwalk are all flat and scenic. For those who like to race on a track, San Diego even has a velodrome in Balboa Park. Call the Velodrome Office at 619/296–3345 for more information.

Bikes can be rented at any number of bike stores, including **Alpine Rent A Bike** in Pacific Beach (tel. 619/273–0440), **Hamel's Action Sports Center** in Mission Beach (tel. 619/488–5050), and **California Bicycle** in La Jolla (tel. 619/454–0316). A free comprehensive map of all county bike paths is available from the local office of the **California Department of Transportation** (tel. 619/688–6699).

Diving Enthusiasts from all over the world flock to La Jolla to skin-dive and scuba dive in the areas off the La Jolla Cove that are rich in ocean creatures and flora. The area marks the south end of the **San Diego–La Jolla Underwater Park,** an ecological preserve. Farther north, off the south end of Black's Beach, **Scripps Canyon** lies in about 60 feet of water. Accessible by boat, the canyon plummets to more than 175 feet in some sections. Another popular diving spot is off Sunset Cliffs in Point Loma, where lobster and a wide variety of sea life are relatively close to shore, although the strong rip currents make it an area best enjoyed by experienced divers.

Diving equipment and boat trips can be arranged through **San Diego Divers** (tel. 619/224–3439), **Ocean Enterprises** (tel. 619/565–6054), or at the several **Diving Locker** locations throughout the area. It is illegal to take any wildlife from the ecological preserves in La Jolla or near Cabrillo Point. Spearfishing requires a license (available at most dive stores), and it is illegal to take out-of-season lobster and game fish out of the water. For general diving information, contact the San Diego City Lifeguards' Office at 619/221–8884).

Fishing Variety is the key. The Pacific Ocean is full of corbina, croaker, and halibut just itching to be your dinner. No license is required to fish from a public pier, such as the Ocean Beach pier. A fishing license from the state Department of Fish and Game (tel. 619/525–4215), available at most bait-and-tackle stores, is required for fishing from the shoreline, although children under 15 won't need one.

Several companies offer half-day, day, or multiday fishing expeditions in search of marlin, tuna, albacore, and other deepwater fish. **Fisherman's Landing** (tel. 619/221–8500), **H & M Landing** (tel. 619/222–1144), and **Seaforth Boat Rentals** (tel. 619/223–7584) are among the companies operating from San Diego. **Helgren's Sportfishing** (tel. 619/722–2133) offers trips from Oceanside Harbor.

Fitness Why let a gluttonous vacation or strenuous business trip interrupt your training schedule? Several hotels offer full health clubs, at least with weight machines, stationary bicycles, and spas, including, in the downtown area, the **Doubletree San Diego** (910 Broadway Circle, tel. 619/239–2200) and the **U.S. Grant Hotel** (326 Broadway, tel. 619/232–3121). Other hotels with health clubs include: the **Hotel Del Coronado** (1500 Orange Ave., Coronado, tel. 619/435–6611), **Sheraton Grand** (1580 Harbor Island Dr., Harbor Island, tel. 619/291–6400), **Le Meridien** (2000 2nd St., Coronado, tel. 619/435–3000), the **San Diego Hilton Beach and Tennis Resort** (1775 E. Mission Bay Dr., Mission Bay, tel. 619/276–4010), the **La Costa Hotel and Spa** (Costa del Mar Rd., Carlsbad, tel. 619/438–9111), and the **Olympic Resort Hotel** (6111 El Camino Real, Carlsbad, tel. 619/438–8330). Guests of the **Town and Country Hotel** (500 Hotel Circle, tel. 619/291–7131) and the **Hanalei Hotel** (2770 Hotel Circle, tel. 619/297–1101) have access to the tennis and racquetball courts, weight room, saunas, and other facilities of the nearby **Atlas Health Club** (901 Hotel Circle S., tel. 619/298–9321), in Mission Valley. The dozen **Family Fitness Centers** in the area (including centers in Mission Valley, tel. 619/281–5543; Sports Arena area, tel. 619/224–2902; and Golden Triangle, tel. 619/457–3930) allow nonmembers to use the facilities for a small fee. A company called **Sweat 'N Smile Inc.** (11494 Sorrento Valley Rd., tel. 619/259–5844) offers fitness and recreation programs, including classes, volleyball, and baseball, geared toward travelers.

Golf Listing the more than 70 golf courses in San Diego County requires more space than we have here. Suffice it to say that the following is merely a sampling of the variety available.

Balboa Park Municipal Golf Course (Golf Course Dr., San Diego, tel. 619/235–1184), with 18 holes, 5,900 yards, has a neighboring 9-hole course, driving range, equipment rentals, clubhouse, and restaurant.
Coronado Golf Course (2000 Visalia Row, Coronado, tel. 619/435–3121), with 18 holes, 6,700 yards, honors other memberships, and reservations are required; it has a driving range, equipment rentals, and a clubhouse.
Mission Bay Golf Course (2702 N. Mission Bay Dr., San Diego,

tel. 619/490–3370), with 18 holes, 3,175 yards, honors other memberships, and reservations are required; it has a driving range and equipment rentals.

Rancho Bernardo Inn and Country Club (17550 Bernardo Oaks Dr., tel. 800/487–0700) has 18 holes, 6,329 yards; reservations are required, and it offers a driving range, equipment rentals, and lodging.

Singing Hills Country Club (3007 Dehesa Rd., El Cajon, tel. 619/442–3425), with 54 holes, honors other memberships; reservations are required, and it offers a driving range, equipment rentals, and lodging.

Torrey Pines Municipal Golf Course (11480 N. Torrey Pines Rd., La Jolla, tel. 619/453–0380) has 36 holes; reservations are not required (but suggested), and it offers a driving range, equipment rentals, and lodging.

Whispering Palms Country Club (Via de la Valle, Rancho Santa Fe, tel. 619/756–2471), with 27 holes, honors other memberships; reservations are required, and lodging is available.

Horseback Riding Expensive insurance has severely cut the number of stables that offer horses for rent in San Diego County. The businesses that remain have a wide variety of organized excursions. **Holidays on Horseback** (tel. 619/445–3997) in the East County town of Descanso leads rides ranging from a few hours to a few days in the Cuyamaca Mountains. It rents special, easy-to-ride fox trotters to beginners. **Rancho San Diego Stables** (tel. 619/670–1861) is located near Spring Valley. South of Imperial Beach, near the Mexican border, **Hilltop Stables** (tel. 619/428–5441) and **Sandi's Rental Stables** (tel. 619/424–3124) lead rides through Border Field State Park.

Jogging There is no truth to the rumor that San Diego was created to be one big jogging track, but it often seems that way. From downtown, the most popular run is along the Embarcadero, which stretches around the bay. There are nice, uncongested sidewalks through most of the area. The alternative for downtown visitors is to head east to Balboa Park, where a labyrinth of trails snake through the canyons. Mission Bay, renowned for its wide sidewalks and basically flat landscape, may be the most popular jogging spot. Trails head west around Fiesta Island from Mission Bay, providing distance as well as a scenic route. The beaches, of course, are extremely popular with runners. But there is no reason to go where everyone else goes. Running is one of the best ways to explore San Diego, especially along the coast. There are organized runs almost every weekend. For more information, call *Competitor* magazine (tel. 619/259–7704) or **San Diego Track Club News** (tel. 792–6581). Some tips: Don't run in bike lanes, and check the local newspaper's tide charts before heading to the beach.

Surfing In San Diego, surfing is a year-round sport (thanks to wet suits in the winter) for people of all ages. Surprisingly, it's not hard to learn. Anyone can get on a board and paddle around. For the hard-core, some of the most popular surfing spots are the Ocean Beach pier, Tourmaline Surfing Park in La Jolla, Windansea Beach in La Jolla, South Cardiff State Beach, and Swami's (Sea Cliff Roadside Park) in Encinitas. Be aware that most public beaches have separate areas for surfers.

Many local surf shops rent boards, including **Star Surfing Company** (tel. 619/273–7827) in Pacific Beach and **La Jolla Surf Sys-**

tems (tel. 619/456–2777) and **Hansen's Sporting Goods** (tel. 619/753–6595) in Encinitas.

Tennis   Most of the more than 1,300 courts spread around the county are in private clubs, but there are a few public facilities. **Morley Field** (tel. 619/692–4919), in Balboa Park, has 25 courts, 12 of which are lighted. Nonmembers, however, cannot make reservations, so it's first come, first served. There is a nominal fee for the use of the courts. The **La Jolla Recreation Center** (tel. 619/552–1658) offers nine public courts near downtown La Jolla, five of them lighted. The use of the courts is free. There are 12 lighted courts at **Robb Field** (tel. 619/531–1563) in Ocean Beach, with a small day-use fee.

The list of hotel complexes with tennis facilities includes the **Bahia Resort Hotel** (tel. 619/488–0551), the **Hotel Del Coronado** (tel. 619/435–6611), the **Kona Kai Beach and Tennis Resort** (tel. 619/222–1191), **Hilton San Diego** (tel. 619/276–4010), the **La Costa Hotel and Spa** (tel. 619/438–9111), and the **Rancho Bernardo Inn and Country Club** (tel. 619/487–1611). Intense tennis instruction is available at **John Gardiner's Rancho Valencia Resort** (tel. 619/756–1123 or 800/548–3664) in Rancho Santa Fe. Some of the larger private clubs are **Atlas Health Club** (tel. 619/298–9321), **San Diego Country Estates** (tel. 619/789–3826), **San Diego Tennis and Racquet Club** (tel. 619/275–3270), and **Tennis La Jolla** (tel. 619/459–0869).

Waterskiing   Mission Bay is one of the most popular waterskiing areas in Southern California. It is best to get out early when the water is smooth and the crowds are thin. In Carlsbad, the **Snug Harbor Marina** (tel. 619/434–3089) is small but off the beaten path. Boats and equipment can be rented from **Seaforth Boat Rentals** (1641 Quivera Rd., near Mission Bay, tel. 619/223–7584). The private **San Diego and Mission Bay Boat and Ski Club** (2606 N. Mission Bay Dr., tel. 619/276–0830) operates a slalom course and ski jump in Mission Bay's Hidden Anchorage. Permission from the club or the Mission Bay Harbor Patrol (tel. 619/291–3900) must be obtained to use the course and jump.

One of the few lakes in the county that allow waterskiing is **Lake San Vicente** (tel. 619/562–1042), located north of Lakeside off I–8.

Spectator Sports

Ever since the Clippers left for Los Angles, San Diego hasn't had a professional basketball franchise. But it does have just about every other type of sporting team and event, including a few that are exclusive to the area. For information on tickets to any event, contact **Teleseat** (tel. 619/452–7328). **San Diego Jack Murphy Stadium** is located at the intersection of I–8 and I–805.

Baseball   From April through September, the **San Diego Padres** (tel. 619/283–4494) slug it out for bragging rights in the National League West. Match-ups with such rivals as the hated Los Angeles Dodgers and San Francisco Giants are usually the highlights of the home season at San Diego Jack Murphy Stadium. Tickets range from $5 to $11 and are usually readily available, unless the Padres are in the thick of the pennant race.

Basketball   There's no pro team, but the San Diego State University Aztecs (tel. 619/283–7378) are gaining national prominence. The Aztecs, competing in the Western Athletic Conference with such powers as the University of Texas at El Paso and Brigham Young University, play at the San Diego Sports Arena (tel. 619/224–4171) December through March.

Football The **San Diego Chargers** (tel. 619/280–2111) have been one of the National Football League's most exciting teams since the merger with the American Football League. The Chargers were one of the original AFL franchises, originally based in Los Angeles. They fill San Diego Jack Murphy Stadium August through December. Games with AFC West rivals Los Angeles Raiders and Denver Broncos are always particularly intense. Tailgating, partying in the parking lot before the game, is an accepted tradition.

Golf The La Costa Hotel and Spa (tel. 619/438–9111) hosts the prestigious **Tournament of Champions** in January, featuring the winners of the previous year's tournaments. The **Buick Invitational** brings the pros to the Torrey Pines Municipal Golf Course in February (tel. 619/281–4653). The Stoneridge Country Club (tel. 619/487–2117) hosts the **Ladies Professional Golf Association** in the spring.

Horse Racing Begun 50 years ago by Bing Crosby, Pat O'Brien, and their Hollywood cronies, the annual summer meeting of the **Del Mar Thoroughbred Club** (tel. 619/755–1141), located on the Del Mar Fairgrounds—"Where the Turf Meets the Surf" in Del Mar—attracts a horde of Beautiful People, along with the best horses and jockeys in the country. The meeting begins in July and continues through early September, every day except Tuesday. But that isn't the end of horse-racing action in Del Mar. The Del Mar Fairgrounds also serves as a satellite-wagering facility, with TV coverage of betting on races from tracks throughout California. Take I–5 north to the Via de la Valle Road exit (tel. 619/755–1161 for daily information).

Volleyball The U.S. men's and women's teams are based in San Diego. For information about competitions or practices, call 619/692–4162.

Beaches

Overnight camping is not allowed on any of the city beaches, but there are campgrounds at some state beaches. Lifeguards are stationed at city beaches (from Sunset Cliffs to Black's Beach) in the summertime, but coverage in winter is erratic. It should be noted that few beaches in San Diego are ideal for dogs, although exceptions are noted below and it is rarely a problem to bring your pet to unpatrolled, isolated beaches, especially during the winter. Glass is prohibited on all beaches, and fires are allowed only in fire rings or barbecues. Alcoholic beverages—including beer—are completely banned on some city beaches; others allow you to partake between 8 AM and 8 PM only. For more information on the beach-booze ban, call the San Diego Police Department Community Relations Storefront at 619/490–0920 or 619/531–1540. For a general beach and weather report, call 619/225–9494.

Beaches are listed from south to north. For information on Mission Bay, *see* Exploring, above.

Border Field State Beach. The southernmost San Diego beach is different from most California beaches. Located just north of the Mexican border, it is a marshy area with wide chaparrals and wildflowers, a favorite of horse riders and hikers. Fre-

quent sewage contamination from Tijuana makes the water unpleasant—if not downright dangerous—for swimming. There
is ample parking, and there are rest rooms and fire rings. *Exit
I–5 at Dairy Mart Rd. and head west along Monument Rd.*

South Beach. One of the few beaches where dogs are free to
romp, this is a good beach for long, isolated walks. The often-
contaminated water and rocky beach tend to discourage
crowds. The downside: There are few facilities, such as rest
rooms. *Located at the end of Seacoast Dr. Take I–5 to Coronado
Ave. and head west on Imperial Beach Ave. Turn left onto Seacoast Dr.*

Imperial Beach. This classic Southern California beach, where
surfers and swimmers congregate to enjoy the water and
waves, provides a pleasant backdrop for the Frisbee games of
the predominantly young crowd. Imperial Beach is also the site
of the U.S. Open Sand Castle Competition every July. There
are lifeguards on duty during the summer, parking lots, food
vendors nearby, and rest-room facilities. *Take Palm Ave. west
from I–5 until it hits water.*

Silver Strand State Beach. Farther north on the isthmus of Coronado (commonly mislabeled an island), Silver Strand was set
aside as a state beach in 1932. The name is derived from the tiny
silver seashells found in abundance near the water. The water
is relatively calm, making it ideal for families. Four parking lots
provide room for more than 1,500 cars. Parking costs $4 per
car. There is also an RV campground (cost: $14 per night) and a
wide array of facilities. Call for reservations. *Tel. 619/435–
5184. Take the Palm Ave. exit from I–5 west to State Hwy. 75;
turn right and follow the signs.*

Coronado Beach. With the famous Hotel Del Coronado as a
backdrop, this wide stretch of sandy beach is one of the largest
in the county. It is surprisingly uncrowded on most days, since
the locals go to the less touristy areas in the south or north. It's
a perfect beach for sunbathing or games of Frisbee and Smash
Ball (played with paddles and a small ball). Parking can be a little difficult on the busiest days, but there are plenty of rest
rooms and service facilities, as well as fire rings. The view
(even for a brief moment) as you drive over the Coronado
Bridge makes it a worthwhile excursion. *From the bridge, turn
left on Orange Ave. and follow the signs.*

Sunset Cliffs. Back on the mainland, beneath the jagged cliffs
on the west side of Point Loma peninsula, is one of the more secluded beaches in the area, popular primarily with surfers and
locals. The tide goes out each day to reveal tide pools teeming
with life at the south end of the peninsula, near Cabrillo Point.
Farther north, the waves attract surfers and the lonely coves
attract sunbathers. Stairs are available at the foot of Bermuda
and Santa Cruz avenues, but much of the access is limited to
treacherous cliff trails. Another negative: There are no available facilities. *Take I–8 west to Sunset Cliffs Blvd. and head
south.*

Ocean Beach. The north end of this beach, past the second jetty, is known as Dog Beach, the only beach within San Diego
city limits that allows dogs to romp around without a leash. The
south end of Ocean Beach, near the pier, is a hangout for surfers and transients. Much of the area, though, is a haven for local
volleyball players, sunbathers, and swimmers. Limited park-

ing, fire rings, and food vendors are available. *Reach Ocean Beach by taking I–8 west to Sunset Cliffs Blvd. and heading south. Turn right on Voltaire St., West Point Loma Blvd., or Newport Ave.*

Mission Beach. It's not Atlantic City, but the boardwalk stretching along Mission Beach is a popular spot for strollers, roller skaters, and bicyclists. The south end is a popular spot for surfers, swimmers, and volleyball players. It tends to get extremely crowded, especially on hot summer days. Toward the north end, near the Belmont Park roller coaster, the beach narrows and the water grows rougher—and the crowd gets even thicker. The newly refurbished Belmont Park is now a shopping and dining complex. Parking can be a challenge, but there are plenty of rest rooms and restaurants in the area. *Exit I–5 at Garnet Ave. and head west to Mission Blvd. Turn south and look for parking.*

Pacific Beach. The boardwalk turns into a sidewalk, but there are still bike paths and picnic tables running along the beachfront. The beach is a favorite of local teens, and the blare of rock music can be annoying. Parking, too, can be a problem, although there is a small lot at the foot of Ventura Place. *Same directions as for Mission Beach, except go north on Mission Blvd.*

Tourmaline Surfing Park and **Windansea Beach.** Immortalized in Tom Wolfe's 1965 book *The Pumphouse Gang*, these La Jolla beaches are two of the top surfing spots in the area. Tourmaline has the better parking area of the two. *Take Mission Blvd. north (it turns into La Jolla Blvd.) and turn west on Tourmaline St. (for the surfing park) or Nautilus St. (for Windansea Beach).*

Marine Street Beach. This is a classic stretch of sand for sunbathing and Frisbee games. *Accessible from Marine St. off La Jolla Blvd.*

Children's Pool. For the tykes, a shallow lagoon with small waves and no riptide provides a safe, if crowded, haven. *It can be reached by following La Jolla Blvd. north. When it forks, take the left, Coast Blvd.*

La Jolla Cove. Just north of the Children's Pool is La Jolla Cove, simply one of the prettiest spots in the world. A beautiful, palm-tree-lined park sits on top of cliffs formed by the incessant pounding of the waves. At low tide the tidal pools and cliff caves provide a goal for explorers. Seals sun themselves on the rocks. Divers explore the underwater delights of the San Diego–La Jolla Underwater Park, an ecological reserve. The cove is also a favorite of rough-water swimmers, for whom buoys mark distances. The beach below the cove is almost nonexistent at high tide, but the cove is still a must-see. *Follow Coast Blvd. north to the signs, or take the La Jolla Village Dr. exit from I–5, head west to Torrey Pines Rd., turn left and drive down the hill to Girard Ave. Turn right and follow the signs.*

La Jolla Shores. This is one of the most popular and overcrowded beaches in the county. On holidays such as Memorial Day, all access routes are usually closed. The lures are a wide sandy beach, relatively calm surf, and a concrete boardwalk paralleling the beach. There is also a wide variety of facilities, from posh restaurants to snack shops, within walking distance. Go early to get a parking spot. *From I–5 take La Jolla Village Dr. west and turn left onto La Jolla Shores Dr. Head west to Camino del Oro or Vallecitos St. Turn right and look for parking.*

Black's Beach. At one time this was the only legal nude beach in the country, before nudity was outlawed in the late 1970s. But that doesn't stop people from braving the treacherous cliff trails for a chance to take off their clothes. Above the beach, hang gliders and sail-plane enthusiasts launch from the Torrey Pines Glider Port. Because of the difficult access, the beach is always relatively uncrowded. The waves make it a favorite haunt of surfers. *Take Genessee Ave. west from I–5 and follow the signs to the glider port.*

Dining

Although San Diego claims one of the highest per capita ratios of dining places to population in the country–at last count there were some 4,000 food-service establishments in San Diego County–it still can't compete with such eating capitals as Los Angeles and New York, where the existence of top-rate restaurants is taken for granted.

But if the quality varies, almost any style of cooking can be found in town. More and more good restaurants open every year; moreover, a city that once stood solidly in the meat-and-potatoes camp now boasts Afghan, Thai, Vietnamese, and other exotic cuisines in addition to the more familiar French, Italian, and Chinese offerings. As one might expect in the city that hosts the Tijuana Trolley, there are hundreds of Mexican restaurants, but most serve up California-style fare, a distant cousin to the excellent south-of-the-border type. Still, good authentic Mexican places are here for the finding, and almost all are accessible, moderately priced, and informal. The city's gastronomic reputation rests primarily on its seafood, which is so popular that even modest restaurants offer several fish specials daily. But bear in mind the truism that better restaurants will serve better seafood. And here, as elsewhere, restaurants endowed with spectacular views—and there are many such in San Diego—often invest far more time and energy in washing the picture windows than in cooking.

Most restaurants in San Diego are open only for lunch and dinner; breakfast is largely the province of hotels and coffee shops. Reservations are generally accepted but rarely required, and, outside of the beach areas, waits are uncommon. Dress codes, by and large, do not exist beyond simple shirt and shoes requirements; a handful of top dining rooms require men to wear jackets. Restaurants are most crowded around 7:30 PM, when locals like to dine; few offer seating past 9:30 or 10 PM.

A good, cheap meal has become a rare commodity in San Diego. The best areas in which to find well-prepared, inexpensive meals are in off-the-beaten-track neighborhoods, such as the Convoy Street district in Kearny Mesa, which boasts virtually every kind of Oriental cuisine. The greatest concentration of restaurants is in the renovated downtown area; in historic Old Town, site of the first settlement and close to the downtown area; and in the beach neighborhoods, particularly exclusive La Jolla, a lovely resort town that slopes from the top of Mt. Soledad to the sea. Mission

Valley, with its myriad inexpensive motels and hotels, sprouts restaurants like weeds but is a virtual desert when it comes to high-quality cuisine. Similarly, the large, tourist-oriented eateries on Shelter and Harbor islands in effect rent out their enjoyable views and lively atmospheres by charging hefty prices for mediocre food.

Restaurants are grouped first by location and then by type of cuisine. Highly recommended restaurants are indicated by a star ★.

Category	Cost*
Very Expensive	over $35
Expensive	$25–$35
Moderate	$15–$25
Inexpensive	under $15

*per person, without tax (6.5%), service, or drinks

Beaches
American

Firehouse Beach Cafe. The great attractions here are the casual beach ambience, the sun deck that allows a leisurely meal in full view of the nearby Pacific, and an acceptably prepared menu of sandwiches, seafood, steaks, and other simple American fare. *722 Grand Ave., tel. 619/272–1999. No reservations. Wear anything that fits reasonably well. AE, D, MC, V. Inexpensive.*

Spice Rack. A longtime beach favorite for its hearty breakfasts and home-baked rolls and pastries, this restaurant offers a pleasant, if viewless, patio for lunching on San Diego's many sunny days. The lunch and dinner menus run to complicated sandwiches and formal beef, chicken, and fish entrées, but regard the Spice Rack as a good bet for omelets and other egg dishes at breakfast or lunch. *4315 Mission Blvd., tel. 619/483–7666. Reservations accepted for dinner. Dress: casual. AE, MC, V. Inexpensive.*

French
★

The Belgian Lion. A somewhat fusty, ugly duckling of a restaurant, The Belgian Lion serves one of the best roast ducklings to be found in the city, along with marvelous creamy soups, excellent braised sweetbreads, poached salmon in a delicious sorrel sauce, sauerkraut braised in champagne with smoked meats and sausages, and a rich cassoulet. The service and wine list are worthy of the menu, and although the decor lacks that certain *je ne sais quoi*, the place has a great deal of charm. *2265 Bacon St., tel. 619/223–2700. Reservations advised. Dress: casual. AE, D, DC, MC, V. Closed Sun. and Mon. Expensive.*

Seafood
★

McCormick and Schmick's. Since it opened in 1988, this excellent seafood house has posed a serious challenge to the city's older fish restaurants. The menu changes frequently and may include as many as 100 options, all uniformly well prepared and ranging from a lovely selection of fresh oysters to entire Dungeness crabs, a fine crab-and-salmon Newburg, grilled baby salmon, and just about everything else that swims, crawls, or ruminates under the waves. The service is good, the upstairs courtyard pleasant, and a few choice tables have ocean views. It's an especially good choice for a lazy, self-indulgent lunch. *4190 Mission Blvd., tel. 619/581–3938. Reservations advised. Dress: casual. AE, D, DC, MC, V. Moderate.*

Salmon House. As the name implies, this handsome waterfront restaurant specializes in salmon, grilled over alder wood in the style developed by the Indians of the Northwest. Offerings run to other fish, prime rib, and chicken, but the real drawing card is the salmon, which is hard to top. *1970 Quivera Rd., tel. 619/ 223–2234. Reservations accepted. Dress: casual. AE, DC, MC, V. Moderate.*

Red Sails Inn. Although this restaurant, on the San Diego Bay side of Point Loma, is not technically at the beach, it's a long-standing favorite of old salts and a natural for anyone in search of good, simple seafood at a waterfront location. The restaurant is surrounded by yacht basins and thus enjoys a large following among nautical types, who especially treasure its hearty, all-American breakfasts and late-night snacks. *2614 Shelter Island Dr., tel. 619/223–3030. Reservations required for large parties. Dress: casual. AE, DC, MC, V. Inexpensive.*

Steak and Seafood **Saska's.** Walk through the doors and you're in the genuine heart of Old Mission Beach, whose lazy pulse still throbs here when the conversation in the bar turns to sports, especially San Diego's peculiar form of baseball called over-the-line. The food is simple but first-rate; choices include shellfish cocktails, a fine crab chowder, the fresh fish offerings of the day (simply but beautifully grilled), and some of the best steaks in town. This is the only place that serves a full, quality menu until 3 AM nightly. *3768 Mission Blvd., tel. 619/488–7311. Reservations accepted. Waiters wear shorts, and you can, too. AE, D, MC, V. Moderate.*

Thai **Karinya.** Designed and operated by a Thai architect, Karinya is at once soothingly pretty and yet every bit as casual as the most beachy beach goer could desire (and in San Diego, that's pretty casual). Start with the spicy *larb* salad and the sweet *mee krob* noodles, then move along to the tart, savory *tom yum gai* soup. The entrée list gets hot and spicy with the curries (the beef *penang nuah*, and a fiery blend of shrimp and pineapple) and turns mild with myriad noodle dishes. Everything is quite, quite good, including the service. *4475 Mission Blvd., tel. 619/ 270–5050. Reservations accepted. Dress: jeans will suffice. AE, MC, V. Closed for lunch weekends and Mon. dinner. Inexpensive.*

Downtown **Dobson's.** Conspicuously and scrupulously San Franciscan in *American* style, Dobson's attracts San Diego's power brokers during the ★ day and well-heeled performing-arts types at night. The menu, which changes daily, is uniformly excellent, from the hallmark mussel bisque to the superb fish, veal, fowl, and beef entrées. The service and wine list are also superlative. *956 Broadway Circle, tel. 619/231–6771. Reservations advised. Dress: for success. AE, MC, V. Closed for lunch Sat., and Sun. Very Expensive.*

Chinese **Panda Inn.** This Horton Plaza restaurant, with its clean, grace- ★ ful lines and fine works of art, is a place to which you can take visiting Chinese friends with confidence. Thanks to superior kitchen and service staffs, this is not only the city's best Chinese restaurant but one of its best restaurants, period. Stop off after a day of shopping for "burnt" pork, sensational hot-and-pungent chicken and shrimp, succulent steamed dumplings, ridiculously delicious Szechuan-style green beans, and first-rate Peking duck. *506 Horton Plaza, tel. 619/233–7800. Reservations accepted. Dress: casual. AE, MC, V. Moderate.*

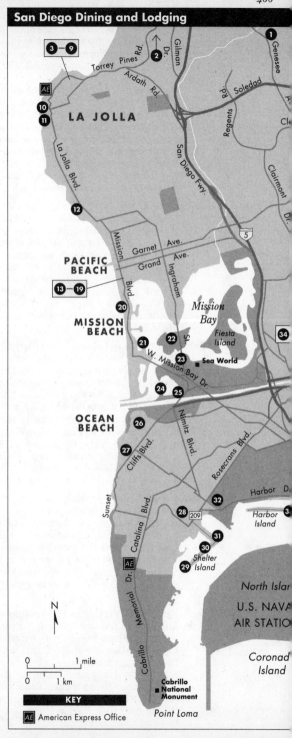

San Diego Dining and Lodging

467

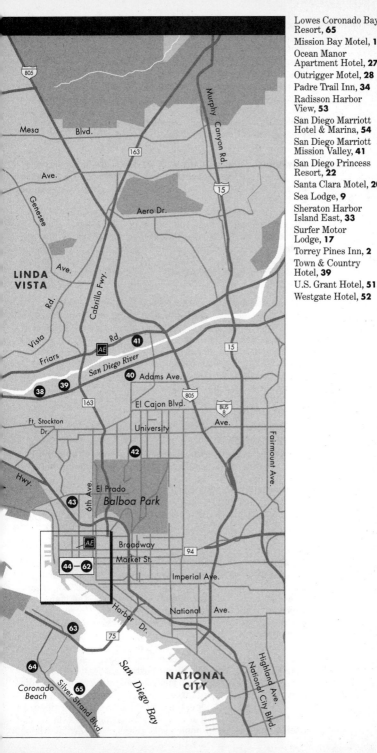

Continental **Croce's.** Thanks to its adjoining jazz cave, this rather funky Gaslamp Quarter bistro can be one of the liveliest spots in town. Run by the widow of late pop singer Jim Croce (the place is crammed with Croce memorabilia), this restaurant offers excellent pastas, good fish, and several fine Russian-Jewish dishes, including a knockout braised beef brisket with *tzimmes* (a casserole of carrots and sweet potatoes), and *kasha varnishkes* (buckwheat groats with bow-tie noodles). Blintzes and similar fare are a specialty at lunch. *802 5th Ave., tel. 619/233–4355. Reservations not necessary. Dress: casual. AE, D, DC, MC, V. Inexpensive.*

Italian **Salvatore's.** Situated in the posh Meridian tower, Salvatore's is
★ the place to go to for toney dining. The Roman-born owners present a typically Roman menu, which is to say pan-Italian, with regional specialties from the tip of the Italian boot to the creamy, buttery pastas of the northernmost provinces. Presentations are spectacular; for a dish of edible beauty, try the Caterina di Medici salad or the excellent grilled swordfish, garnished to look like a pineapple. The pastas are uniformly superior. *750 Front St., tel. 619/544–1865. Reservations ac cepted. Dress: for la dolce vita. AE, MC, V. No weekend lunch. Expensive.*

Mixed Menu **Old Columbia Brewery & Grill.** The first microbrewery in San Diego, Old Columbia can be forgiven for paying more attention to its house brews than to its menu. The draw here is the beer, tapped directly from tanks in the adjacent brewing room. Beer-battered fish-and-chips, hefty onion rings, and oversize hamburgers are good accompaniments to the Gaslamp Gold ale or the Downtown After Dark lager. Downtown mingles here when the sun sets, and the action runs late. *1157 Columbia St., tel. 619/234–2739. Reservations accepted. Dress: casual. MC, V. Inexpensive.*

Seafood **Anthony's Star of the Sea Room.** A perpetual favorite with longtime San Diegans and visitors alike, this formal, rather stodgy restaurant occupies a choice location on the Embarcadero, looking out across the water to the twinkling lights of Point Loma. For better or worse, the place specializes in cart service and turns in a good performance with its abalone dishes and the sole Admiral. The selection of fresh fish is admirable, but go with the simpler preparations. *1360 N. Harbor Dr., tel. 619/232–7408. Reservations advised. Jacket and tie required. AE, DC, MC, V. No lunch. Closed major holidays. Very Expensive.*

Harbor House. Although this deservedly popular place could coast on its location in jammed Seaport Village, it turns in a good-quality performance with its shellfish appetizers, creamy chowder, and a long list of daily fish specials, the majority of which are simply grilled over mesquite. *831 W. Harbor Dr., tel. 619/232–1141. Reservations accepted. Dress: casual. AE, MC, V. Moderate.*

The Fish Market. So close to the harbor that a decoy owl with flapping wings was installed on the copper roof to keep the seagulls at bay, this $10 million restaurant features an oyster bar, a sushi bar, a retail fish market, and a deck for outdoor dining; at "The Top of the Market," with its view of the entire bay and the Coronado Bridge, the atmosphere and the service are a touch more formal. All offer a wide assortment of Atlantic and Pacific seafood, good homemade pastas, New Zealand lamb, and Black Angus beef. This is the prime link in a growing California chain. *750 N. Harbor Dr., tel. 619/232–FISH. No reservations. Dress: casual. AE, DC. MC, V. Inexpensive–Moderate.*

Southwestern–
Nouvelle
Pacifica Grill. If you've never had *canarditas* (and you probably haven't), this is the place to go to for the juicy chunks of slowly cooked duck, garnished with any of a dozen spicy condiments and then rolled in fresh, hot, blue-corn tortillas. Since switching to the new southwestern style of cooking, this ever-trendy restaurant has seen its popularity soar almost as high as the atrium of its beautifully remodeled warehouse. The place also serves superior seafood and wildly imaginative pastas. *1202 Kettner Blvd., tel. 619/696–9226. Reservations accepted. Dress: to be noticed. AE, D, DC, MC, V. Closed for lunch weekends. Moderate.*

Spanish
La Gran Tapa. Carefully modeled on Madrid's fabled tapas bars, this noisy "in" spot prints up a daily menu of its classic Spanish snacks and appetizers; more substantial dishes and even an excellent hamburger are thrown in for traditionalists. If you're with a like-minded group, order two or three tapas per person and dive in. Choices include empanadas (spicy pies) filled with pork and olives, spinach and cheese, or whatever the chef has dreamed up; tiny fried squid; miniature shrimp croquettes; fresh, hot potato chips, and much more. This is a good spot for late-night dining. *611 B St., tel. 619/234–8272. Reservations advised. Dress: casual. AE, MC, V. Closed for lunch Sat. Closed Sun. Moderate.*

La Jolla
California
★
George's at the Cove. A lovely, art-filled dining room, excellent service, a good view of La Jolla Cove, and an imaginative, well-prepared menu make this one of the city's best restaurants. Pay special attention to the seafood, but the pasta, beef, and veal dishes, as well as the poultry specialties, are also uniformly excellent. Desserts are oversize, grandiose, and irresistible. *1250 Prospect St., tel. 619/454–4244. Reservations advised. Dress: as chicly as you can. AE, DC, MC, V. Expensive.*

French
St. James Bar. A new offering from leading San Diego restaurateur Paul Dobson, the St. James Bar is a magnet for the area's business folk at lunch and the glitterati at night. All are drawn by the creamy mussel bisque, the sweetbreads in truffle-juice sauce, the delicate poached Norwegian salmon in saffron sauce, and other beautifully executed offerings. One of the city's top-five eateries, St. James offers expert cuisine in a luxurious setting that includes marble floors, art from a top gallery, and an incongruous but handsome 100-year-old bar rescued from a Montana saloon. *4370 La Jolla Village Dr., tel. 619/453–6650. Reservations advised. Dress: casual. AE, MC, V. Closed for lunch Sat., and Sun. Very Expensive.*

★
Top O' the Cove. More or less synonymous with romance, Top O' the Cove has been the scene of thousands of marriage proposals in its 35-year history. Yet another place that boasts an extravagant view of La Jolla Cove, it also boasts a competent kitchen that turns out beautifully garnished, luxury fare dressed with creamy and well-seasoned sauces. The menu regularly hits all the bases—beef, veal, fowl, and seafood—but pay special attention to the nightly specials. The decor is lush, and the wine list, with more than 800 entries, has been the recipient of countless awards. *1216 Prospect St., tel. 619/454–7779. Reser-*

vations advised. Jacket and tie advised. AE, DC, MC, V. Very Expensive.

Indian   **Star of India.** Like many other chic, big-city neighborhoods, La Jolla hosts a good selection of upscale ethnic eateries. The Star of India is a case in point: Grander and more expensive than the city's other Indian houses, it also offers a better selection of dishes and a more talented kitchen staff. In addition to all the typical curries and kebabs, the menu offers several tandoori meats (baked in a special, superheated oven), quite a number of vegetarian dishes, and a superb selection of freshly prepared Indian breads. *1025 Prospect St., tel. 619/459-3355. Reservations accepted. Dress: casual. AE, D, DC, MC, V. Moderate.*

Italian   **Issimo.** La Jolla is blessed in its restaurants, and Issimo is third
★ in its trilogy of stars. Beautifully arranged plates are served in grand style in a small jewel box of a dining room. Start with a pasta or the incredible, homemade pâté de foie gras (yes, this is an Italian place, but the foie gras is fabulous), then move along to a dandy osso buco, a wonderful plate of baby lamb chops, a fine veal sauté, or a steak in a delicate sauce. This restaurant also speaks seafood fluently, and the desserts rival those made by the finest European pastry chefs. *5634 La Jolla Blvd., tel. 619/454-7004. Reservations advised. Jacket advised. MC, V. Closed Sun. Very Expensive.*

Avanti. For staid, old La Jolla, this starkly modern restaurant, with its mirrored ceiling and white-and-black and chrome interior design, comes as a refreshing surprise. Which explains why it is such a popular meeting place for trendy, successful natives looking for some sophisticated fun, with cuisine to match. An open-to-view kitchen allows you to watch chef John Cooke prepare such appetite-arousing dishes as tiny pasta rings mixed with ricotta and pistachios; scampi sautéed in olive oil, minced garlic, and white wine; beef fillet topped with a porcini mushroom sauce; and chicken breasts grilled with radicchio. Counting calories? There's a spa menu, too. *875 Prospect Ave., tel. 619/454-4288. Reservations advised. Dress: thoughtfully casual. AE, MC, V. Closed for lunch. Expensive.*

★ **Delicias.** Upon opening in 1990, this bright and cheerful trattoria was adopted by the natives of the tiny, pastoral village of Rancho Santa Fe (just east of La Jolla) as their local clubhouse. Wolfgang Puck acted as consultant in drawing up a Spagolike menu and training the chef, and the results include excellent pizza and calzone straight from a wood-burning oven, and, of course, a wide range of pastas and salads using fresh-daily ingredients from nearby vegetable farms. The service here benefits from being so far away from Los Angeles's moonlighting-actor pool. *6106 Paseo Delicias, Rancho Santa Fe, tel. 619/756-8000. Reservations advised. Dress: casual. AE, D, MC, V. Moderate.*

Piatti. Another recent link in this very popular minichain of trattorias that now extends from one end of California to the other, Piatti serves up good pizza, calzone, pasta, and an excellent selection of antipasto in a let's-have-fun setting. All in all, *molto simpatico. 2182 Avenida de La Playa. 619/454-1589. Reservations advised. Dress: casual. MC, V. Moderate.*

Mexican   **El Crab Catcher.** Although this spot is just one of many along San Diego's most fashionable restaurant row, its spectacular view of La Jolla Cove and casual Hawaiian atmosphere (yes, Hawaiian) make it a favorite. Specialties include numerous crab dishes, other shell- and fin-fish, and simple beef and chicken preparations. Get here in time for the sunset. *1298 Prospect St., tel. 619/454-9587. Reservations advised. Dress: casual. AE, D, MC, V. Moderate.*

Old Town **Cafe Pacifica.** The menu changes daily to reflect the market
Seafood availability of a globe-spanning selection of fish and shellfish, most of which are presumably very pleased to place themselves in Cafe Pacifica's competent hands. The approach is moderately nouvelle, which means that light, interesting sauces and imaginative garnishes are likely to be teamed with simply cooked fillets of salmon, sea bass, swordfish, and the like. Consider oysters and smoked fish as good opening courses, and don't miss the indulgent crème brûlée dessert. *2414 San Diego Ave., tel. 619/291-6666. Reservations accepted. Dress: thoughtfully informal. AE, D, DC, MC, V. Closed for lunch weekends. Moderate.*

Lodging

When choosing lodgings in San Diego, the first thing to consider is location. The city has many neighborhoods, each one possessing unique characteristics. Decide what type of atmosphere you prefer. Do you want to be in the middle of a bustling metropolitan setting, or would you rather have a serene beach bungalow? Second, take into account the hotel's proximity to attractions that you most want to see. And then, of course, consider the price.

Highly recommended hotels are indicated by a star ★.

Category	Cost*
Very Expensive	over $140
Expensive	$100–$140
Moderate	$60–$100
Inexpensive	under $60

for a double room

Coronado Coronado is a quiet, out-of-the-way place to stay, but if you plan to see many of San Diego's attractions, you'll probably spend a lot of time commuting across the bridge or riding the ferry.

Very Expensive **Hotel Del Coronado.** Built in 1888, the Del is a historic and social landmark (*see* Tour 2 in Chapter 3, Exploring San Diego, *for details*). The rooms and suites in the original Victorian-style building are charmingly quirky; some have baths larger than the sleeping areas, while others seem downright palatial. More standardized accommodations are available in the newer high rise. *1500 Orange Ave., 92118, tel. 619/435-6611 or 800/ 522-3088, fax 619/522-8238. 700 rooms. Facilities: pool, tennis courts, beach. AE, DC, MC, V.*

Loews Coronado Bay Resort. Coronado's newest resort hotel opened in late 1991 on a 15-acre peninsula on the Silver Strand. The property is surrounded by water on three sides, so all rooms and suites have spectacular views of the Coronado bridge, the downtown skyline, and the 90-slip marina. Water taxis ferry guests across the bay to San Diego's downtown.

4000 Coronado Bay Rd., 92118, tel. 619/424–4000, fax 619/424–4400. 450 rooms, 42 suites. Facilities: fitness center, marina, 5 tennis courts, private beach, 3 pools, 2 spas, bicycle, boat, Windsurfer and Jet-Ski rentals. AE, DC, MC, V.

Ski Expensive **Glorietta Bay Inn.** Adjacent to the Coronado harbor, the Del, and Coronado village, this property was built around the mansion of the Spreckels family, which once owned most of downtown San Diego,. Main building rooms are furnished with period antiques, while newer motel-style buildings offer more generic, contemporary rooms. Many fine restaurants and quaint shops are within walking distance. *1630 Glorietta Blvd., 92118, tel. 619/435–3101 or 800/283–9383, fax 619/435–6182. 100 rooms. Facilities: tennis, golf, pool. AE, MC, V.*

Downtown Downtown San Diego is presently in the midst of a decade-long redevelopment effort that has attracted many new hotels. There is much to be seen within walking distance of downtown accommodations—Seaport Village, the Embarcadero, the historic Gaslamp Quarter, a variety of theaters and night spots, and the spectacular Horton Plaza shopping center. The zoo and Balboa Park are also nearby. For nonstop shopping, nightlife, and entertainment, the downtown area can't be beat.

Very Expensive **Doubletree San Diego Hotel.** This high rise, completed in 1987, is lavishly decorated with marble, brass, and glass. The rooms are luxurious and modern. The lobby lounge is packed every night with local financiers and weary shoppers from the adjacent Horton Plaza. *910 Broadway Circle, 92101, tel. 619/239–2200 or 800/528–0444, fax 619/239–0509. 450 rooms. Facilities: 2 restaurants, disco, lounge, tennis courts, sauna, spa, pool, health club. AE, MC, V.*

San Diego Marriott Hotel and Marina. The two 25-story towers of this luxurious high rise, with a prime location between Seaport Village and the convention center, afford panoramic views of the bay and/or city. The North Tower offers balconies in all the rooms; in the South Tower, only the suites have them. *333 W. Harbor Dr., 92101, tel. 619/234–1500 or 800/228–9290, fax 619/234–8678. 1,355 rooms. Facilities: 3 restaurants, 2 lounges with piano music, boutiques, full-service salon, jogging path, health spa, tennis courts, sauna, 2 outdoor pools, charter boat. AE, DC, MC, V.*

★ **U.S. Grant Hotel.** Built in 1910 and reopened in 1985, this San Diego classic overlooks on Horton Plaza. Crystal chandeliers and marble floors in the lobby and mahogany furnishings in the rooms hark back to a more gracious era, as do ever-vigilant butlers and concierges. The hotel's Grant Grill is a longtime favorite of high-power business types. Guests have the use of an associated health club. *326 Broadway, 92101, tel. 619/232–3121; 800/237–5029; in CA, 800/334–6957; fax 619/232–3626. 280 rooms. AE, DC, MC, V.*

Westgate Hotel. It doesn't get much more opulent than this: The Westgate lobby is modeled after the anteroom at Versailles, replete with hand-cut Baccarat chandeliers, and rooms are furnished with antiques, including Italian marble counters, oversize bathtubs, and brass fixtures with 14-karat-gold overlay. Add breathtaking views of the harbor and the city (from the ninth floor up), high tea on weekday afternoons, and the award-winning cuisine and white-glove service of Le Fontaine-bleau in the evening. For a change of venue, the trolley can take you to Tijuana right from the hotel, and complimentary transportation is available within the downtown area. *1055 2nd Ave., 92101, tel. 619/238–1818; 800/221–3802; in CA, 800/522–1564. 223 rooms. Facilities: restaurant, lounge. AE, DC, MC, V.*

Expensive **Britt House.** Each of the charming rooms in this grand Victorian inn, located within walking distance of Balboa Park and the zoo, is individually furnished with antiques, and each has a sitting area in which guests can enjoy the fresh-baked goodies brought to them for breakfast. In keeping with Victorian tradition, every two rooms share a bath. Lovely gardens surround the building, and an elaborate high tea is served in the parlor every afternoon. Reservations are a must. *406 Maple St., 92101, tel. 619/234–2926. 10 rooms. AE, MC, V.*

Embassy Suites Downtown. It's a short walk to the convention center from one of downtown's most popular hotels. All rooms are suites, with their front doors facing the hotel's 12-story atrium. The contemporary-style decor is pleasant, and the views from rooms facing the harbor are spectacular. Business travelers will find it easy to set up shop here, and families can make good use of the in-room refrigerators and separate sleeping areas. *601 Pacific Hwy., 92101, tel. 619/239–2400 or 800/362–2779. 337 suites. Facilities: restaurant, bar, pool. AE, DC, MC, V.*

★ **Horton Grand Hotel.** San Diego's oldest hotel, built in 1886 in elegant European style and restored in 1986, the Horton Grand features delightfully retro rooms, individually furnished with period antiques, ceiling fans, and gas-burning fireplaces. In-room diaries give guests a sense of the past and allow them to put their mark on the future. The choicest rooms are those overlooking a garden courtyard, which twinkles with miniature lights each night. There's high tea in the afternoon and—a modern touch—jazz in the evening. *311 Island Ave., 92101, tel. 619/544–1886. 110 rooms. Facilities: restaurant, lounge, Chinatown museum. AE, DC, MC, V.*

Moderate– **Balboa Park Inn.** Directly across the street from Balboa Park,
Expensive this charming European-style bed-and-breakfast inn was built in 1915 and restored in 1982. Prices are reasonable for the one- and two-bedroom suites with kitchenettes housed in four two-story buildings connected by courtyards. Each suite has a different flavor—Italian, French, Spanish, or early Californian; some have fireplaces, wet bars, and whirlpool tubs. Continental breakfast and a newspaper are delivered to guests every morning. *3402 Park Blvd., 92103, tel. 619/298–0823. 25 suites with baths. Facilities: outdoor bar. AE, DC, MC, V.*

Moderate **Radisson Harbor View.** This high rise—at the foot of the I-5 entrance ramp to downtown at Front Street—is a good bet for business travelers. It's near the courthouse and legal offices, and offers a free shuttle to the convention center, 10 blocks away. The pastel-decorated rooms are sparkling clean, with small terraces with harbor views. Business services and a health club are available. *1646 Front St., 92101, tel. 619/239–6800 or 800/333–3333. 333 rooms. Facilities: rooftop pool, health club. AE, MC, V.*

Inexpensive **La Pensione.** At long last, a decent budget hotel downtown,
★ with daily, weekly, and monthly rates. Some rooms have harbor views, and all have kitchenettes. La Pensione is in a quiet neighborhood, and has a pretty central courtyard. *1546 2nd*

Ave., 92101, tel. 619/236–9292. 20 rooms. 606 W. Date St., tel. 619/236–8000. 80 rooms. Facilities: kitchenettes. MC, V.

Harbor Island/Shelter Island
Two man-made peninsulas located between downtown and the lovely community of Point Loma, Harbor Island and Shelter Island are both bordered by grassy parks, tree-lined paths, lavish hotels, and wonderful restaurants. Harbor Island is closest to the downtown area and less than five minutes from the airport, while Shelter Island is nearer to Point Loma. Both locations command breathtaking views of the bay and the downtown skyline. Not all the lodgings listed here are on the islands themselves, but all are in their vicinity.

Very Expensive
★ **Sheraton Harbor Island East.** Although less luxurious than the neighboring Sheraton Grand, this hotel has more character. Rooms above the eighth floor have the best views, especially those that look across the water to the lights of downtown. The restaurants and lounges here are popular for fine dining and dancing. *1380 Harbor Island Dr., 92101, tel. 619/291–2900 or 800/325–3535. 710 rooms. Facilities: tennis courts, sauna, spa, 3 pools, health club, jogging trails. AE, DC, MC, V.*

Expensive
★ **Humphrey's Half Moon Inn.** This sprawling South Seas–style resort has many grassy open areas with palm trees and tiki torches. The recently restored rooms are contemporary-generic but pleasant; some have views of the pool or the bay. Locals throng to Humphrey's, the hotel restaurant, for its good food and summer jazz concert series. *2303 Shelter Island Dr., 92106, tel. 619/224–3411 or 800/345–9995. 141 rooms. Facilities: putting green, pool, spa, bicycles. AE, DC, MC, V.*

Moderate
Best Western Posada Inn. One of the more upscale members of the Best Western chain, the Posada Inn is not on Harbor Island but is located on one of the neighboring thoroughfares adjacent to Point Loma. Many of the rooms, which are clean, comfortable, and nicely furnished, have wonderful views of the harbor. A number of excellent seafood restaurants are within walking distance. *5005 N. Harbor Dr., 92106, tel. 619/224–3254 or 800/528–1234. 112 rooms. Facilities: restaurant, lounge, pool, spa. AE, DC, MC, V.*
Kona Kai Beach and Tennis Resort. All the fine sports facilities of this hotel, which doubles as a prestigious members-only club for locals, are open to Kona Kai guests. The simple and tasteful rooms have a Hawaiian theme; those in the newer north wing are less expensive than the bayfront suites with lanais in the main building. *1551 Shelter Island Dr., 92106, tel. 619/222–1191, fax 619/226–7891. 89 rooms. Facilities: 2 restaurants, lounge, health club, tennis courts, racquetball courts, pool, spa, private beach. AE, DC, MC, V.*

Inexpensive
Outrigger Motel. This motel, adjacent to but not directly on the two resort peninsulas, is less expensive than its offshore counterparts. In a noisier but still picturesque setting, the Outrigger has fishing docks—as well as the famous Point Loma Seafoods Market and Restaurant—across the street. Guests can take a scenic walk along the bay to Harbor Island. *1370 Scott St., 92106, tel. 619/223–7105. 37 rooms with kitchens. Facilities: pool. AE, DC, MC, V.*

Hotel Circle/Mission Valley/Old Town
Lining both sides of the stretch of I–8 that lies between Old Town and Mission Valley are a number of moderately priced accommodations that constitute the so-called Hotel Circle. A car is an absolute necessity here, since the only nearby road is the

busiest freeway in San Diego. Although not particularly scenic or serene, this location is convenient to Balboa Park, the zoo, downtown, the beaches, the shops of Mission Valley, and Old Town. Old Town has a few picturesque lodgings and is developing a crop of modestly priced chain hotels along nearby I–5. It's not easy when you're in this area, but try to get a room that doesn't face the freeway.

Expensive
★ **Doubletree Hotel.** One of the best hotels in Mission Valley, this high rise offers three floors reserved for nonsmokers. The comfortable rooms are decorated in contemporary southwestern style. Children stay free and small pets are accepted. *901 Camino del Rio S., 92108, tel. 619/543–9000 or 800/528–0444. 350 rooms. Facilities: restaurant, lounge, spa, pool, fitness center. AE, DC, MC, V.*

Moderate–
Expensive
★ **Heritage Park Bed & Breakfast Inn.** In a quiet, picturesque area near Old Town, this romantic Queen Anne mansion built in 1889 has nine quaint guest rooms decorated with period antiques. Five of the rooms have private baths; the others share facilities. Breakfast and afternoon refreshments are included in the room rate. *2470 Heritage Park Row, 92110, tel. 619/295–7088. 9 rooms, 5 with bath. MC, V.*

★ **San Diego Marriott Mission Valley.** This high rise sits in the middle of the San Diego River valley, where the dry riverbed has been graded and transformed over the years into a commercial zone with sleek office towers and sprawling shopping malls. The hotel has become the valley's glamour spot, and the rooms are far more spacious and contemporary than those in nearby hotels. *8757 Rio San Diego Dr., 92108, tel. 619/692–3800 or 800/228–9290, fax 619/692–0769. 345 rooms. Facilities: pool, tennis court, health club. AE, DC, MC, V.*

Town and Country Hotel. Although the original part of this hotel was built in the 1950s, it has been refurbished many times and two high-rise sections were added in the 1970s. The rooms are somewhat incongruously—for Southern California—decorated in New England colonial style. Business travelers are the mainstay of this property, which has the largest convention facilities in Hotel Circle, but it is sufficiently resortlike to appeal to tourists as well. *500 Hotel Circle N, 92108, tel. 619/291–7131 or 800/854–2608, fax 619/291–3584. 1,000 rooms. Facilities: 5 restaurants, 5 lounges, 4 pools, golf, health club. AE, DC, MC, V.*

Moderate **Hacienda Hotel.** Because the white adobe buildings of this former shopping complex spread up a steep hillside, you'll have to do a bit of climbing if you stay here, but you'll be rewarded by a tranquil setting above the bustle of Old Town. Rooms at this all-suite property are decorated in tasteful southwestern style and equipped with microwaves, refrigerators, and VCRs. *4041 Harney St., 92110, tel. 619/298–4707 or 800/888–1991. 150 suites. Facilities: pool, free indoor parking. AE, MC, V.*

Hanalei Hotel. If it weren't for the view of I–8, you might be able to imagine you were in a tropical setting, what with the palm trees, waterfalls, koi ponds, and tiki torches that abound here. A two-story complex offers poolside rooms and a high-rise building surrounds a lovely Hawaiian-style garden. The rooms, also designed to evoke Honolulu, are clean and comfortable. *2270 Hotel Circle S, 92108, tel. 619/297–1101 or 800/542–6082. 425 rooms. Facilities: 2 restaurants, lounge, pool, spa. AE, DC, MC, V.*

Inexpensive **Padre Trail Inn.** This standard, family-style motel is located slightly southwest of Mission Valley. Historic Old Town, shopping, and dining are all within walking distance. *4200 Taylor St., 92110, tel. 619/297-3291. 100 rooms. Facilities: restaurant, lounge, pool. AE, DC, MC, V.*

La Jolla Million-dollar homes line the beaches and hillsides of La Jolla, one of the world's most beautiful, prestigious communities. The village—the heart of La Jolla—is chock-a-block with expensive boutiques, galleries, and restaurants. Don't despair, however, if you're not old money or even nouveau rich; this popular vacation spot has sufficient lodging choices for every pocket, even those on a budget.

Very Expensive **Sea Lodge.** This hidden gem faces the ocean between La Jolla Beach and Tennis Club and La Jolla Shores, one of the best beaches in the county. Three-story buildings with red-tile roofs form a low-lying compound on the beachfront, backed by the hills of La Jolla. The rooms have the sort of yellow, orange, and green decor popular in the '60s, and wooden balconies that look out on lush landscaping and the sea. Early reservations are a must here, and families will find plenty of room and distractions for both kids and parents. *8110 Camino del Oro, La Jolla 92037, tel. 619/459-8271 or 800/237-5211, fax 619/456-9346. 128 rooms, 19 with kitchenettes. Facilities: restaurant, lounge, heated pool, hot tub, beach, 2 tennis courts, pitch-and-putt golf course. AE, DC, MC, V.*

Expensive-
Very Expensive **La Valencia.** A La Jolla landmark, this pink-stucco, Art Deco
★ confection drew film stars down from Los Angeles in the '30s and '40s; the guests today tend to be less glamorous and somewhat older, but the lures are the same. The restaurants have excellent food, the Whaling Bar is a popular gathering spot, and the hotel is ideally located near the shops and restaurants of La Jolla village, as well as to what is arguably the prettiest beach in San Diego. *1132 Prospect St., La Jolla 92037, tel. 619/454-0771. 100 rooms. Facilities: 3 restaurants, lounge, pool. AE, MC, V.*

Expensive **Colonial Inn.** A tastefully restored Victorian-style building, this hotel offers turn-of-the-century elegance with such touches as fan windows and a mahogany-paneled elevator. Ocean views cost considerably more than village views. On one of La Jolla's main thoroughfares, the hotel is near boutiques, restaurants, and the cove. *910 Prospect St., La Jolla 92037, tel. 619/454-2181; 800/832-5525; in CA, 800/826-1278; fax 619/454-5679. 75 rooms. Facilities: restaurant, lounge, pool. AE, DC, MC, V.*

Moderate-
Expensive **La Jolla Cove Motel.** Offering studios and suites, some with spacious oceanfront balconies, this motel overlooks the famous
★ La Jolla Cove beach. *1155 S. Coast Blvd., La Jolla 92037, tel. 619/459-2621 or 800/248-COVE. 100 rooms. Facilities: kitchenettes, solarium, sun deck, freshwater pool, spa. AE, MC, V.*

Moderate **Torrey Pines Inn.** Located on a bluff between La Jolla and Del-Mar, this hotel commands a view of miles and miles of coastline. It's adjacent to the Torrey Pines Golf Course, site of the San Diego Open PGA golf tournament every January, and near scenic Torrey Pines State Beach; downtown La Jolla is a 10-minute drive away. This off-the-beaten path inn is a nice, reasonable place to stay. *11480 N. Torrey Pines Rd., La Jolla 92037, tel.*

619/453–4420, fax 619/453–0691. 74 rooms. Facilities: restaurant, lounge, golf course. AE, DC, MC, V.

Mission Bay and Beaches

Staying near the water is a priority for most people who visit San Diego. Mission and Pacific beaches have the highest concentration of small hotels and motels. Both these areas have a casual atmosphere and a busy coastal thoroughfare offering endless shopping, dining, and nightlife possibilities. Mission Bay Park, with its beaches, bike trails, boat-launching ramps, golf course, and grassy parks is also a hotel haven. You can't go wrong with any of these locations, as long as the frenzy of hundreds at play doesn't bother you.

Very Expensive

Hyatt Islandia. Located in one of San Diego's most beautiful seashore areas, Mission Bay Park, the Islandia has rooms in several low-level lanai-style units, as well as in a high-rise building. The landscaping is lush and tropical, and the tastefully modern accommodations have dramatic views of the bay area. This hotel is famous for its lavish Sunday buffet brunch. *1441 Quivira Rd., 92109, tel. 619/224–1234 or 800/233–1234. 423 rooms. Facilities: 2 restaurants, pool, spa. AE, DC, MC, V.*

★ **San Diego Princess Resort.** You'll feel as though you're staying in a self-sufficient village if you book one of the cottages in this resort, so beautifully landscaped that it's been the setting for a number of movies. The wide range of amenities includes access to a marina and beaches. Many of the accommodations have kitchens, and a number have bay views. With something for everyone, this hotel is favored by families, particularly during the summer. *1404 W. Vacation Rd., 92109, tel. 619/274–4630 or 800/344–2626, fax 619/581–5929. 450 cottages. Facilities: 3 restaurants, 8 tennis courts, 5 pools, bicycle and boat rentals, putting green, shuffleboard, volleyball courts, jogging path. AE, DC, MC, V.*

Moderate–Expensive

★ **Bahia Resort Hotel.** This huge complex on a 14-acre peninsula in Mission Bay Park has tastefully furnished studios and suites with kitchens. The price is reasonable for a place so well located—within walking distance of the ocean—and offering so many amenities. *998 W. Mission Bay Dr., 92109, tel. 619/488–0551; 800/228–0770; in Canada, 800/233–8172. 300 rooms. Facilities: tennis courts, water-sport rentals, spa, pool, evening bay cruises. AE, DC, MC, V.*

Dana Inn & Marina. This hotel, which has an adjoining marina, is a bargain in the Mission Bay area. The accommodations may not be as grand as those in the nearby hotels but they're more than adequate if you don't plan to stay cooped up in your room. *1710 W. Mission Bay Blvd., 92109, tel. 619/222–6440 or 800/445–3339, fax 619/222–5916. 196 rooms. Facilities: pool, spa, tackle shop. AE, DC, MC, V.*

Moderate

Surfer Motor Lodge. This high rise is located right on the beach and directly behind a shopping center with many restaurants and boutiques. Rooms are plain, but those on the upper floors have excellent views. *711 Pacific Beach Dr., 92109, tel. 619/483–7070. 52 rooms. Facilities: restaurant, cocktail lounge, pool. AE, DC, MC, V.*

Inexpensive–Moderate

★ **Ocean Manor Apartment Hotel.** Some guests have been returning for 20 years to this Ocean Beach hotel, which rents units by the day (with a 3-day minimum), week, or month; you'll need to reserve months in advance. Located right on Sunset Cliffs,

Ocean Manor offers lovely views, and beaches are within walking distance. The comfortable studios or one- or two-bedroom suites (with kitchens) are furnished plainly in 1950s style. There is no maid service but fresh towels are always provided. *1370 Sunset Cliffs Blvd., 92107, tel. 619/222–7901. 20 rooms. Facilities: pool. MC, V.*

Inexpensive **Mission Bay Motel.** Located one-half block from the beach, this motel offers centrally located, modest units. Great restaurants and nightlife are within walking distance, but you might find the area a bit noisy. *4221 Mission Blvd., 92109, tel. 619/483–6440. 50 rooms. Facilities: pool. MC, V.*

Santa Clara Motel. This small, no-frills motel is a block from the ocean and right in the middle of restaurant, nightlife, and shopping activity in Mission Beach. Some units have kitchens. Weekly rates are available. *839 Santa Clara Pl., 92109, tel. 619/488–1193. 17 rooms. AE, MC, V.*

The Arts

Top national touring companies perform regularly at the Civic Theatre, Golden Hall, Symphony Hall, and East County Performing Arts Center. San Diego State University, the University of California at San Diego, private universities, and community colleges present a wide variety of performing arts programs, from performances by well-known artists to student recitals. The daily *San Diego Union, Evening Tribune,* and the San Diego edition of the *Los Angeles Times* list current attractions and complete movie schedules. The *Reader,* a free weekly that comes out each Thursday, devotes an entire section to upcoming cultural events, as well as current theater and film reviews. *San Diego* magazine publishes a monthly "What's Doing" column that lists arts events throughout the county and reviews of current films, plays, and concerts.

It is best to book tickets well in advance, preferably at the same time you make hotel reservations. There are various outlets for last-minute tickets, though you risk either paying top rates or getting less-than-choice seats—or both. Half-price tickets to most theater, music, and dance events can be bought on the day of performance at the **TIMES ARTS TIX Ticket Center,** Horton Plaza, downtown (tel. 619/238–3810). Only cash is accepted. Advance full-price tickets may also be purchased through ARTS TIX.

Visa and MasterCard holders may buy tickets for many scheduled performances through **Ticketmaster** (tel. 619/238–3810 or 619/278–8497). Service charges vary according to the event, and most tickets are nonrefundable.

Theater **Coronado Playhouse** (1755 Strand Way, Coronado, tel. 619/435–4856). This cabaret-type theater, near the Hotel Del Coronado, stages regular dramatic and musical performances. Dinner packages are offered on Friday and Saturday.

La Jolla Playhouse (Mandell Weiss Center for the Performing Arts, University of California at San Diego, tel. 619/534–3960). Exciting and innovative presentations, early summer to fall, are under the artistic direction of Tony Award–winner Des McAnuff. Many Broadway productions, such as *A Walk in the Woods, Big River,* and works by Neil Simon, have previewed here before heading for the East Coast.

Lawrence Welk Village Theatre (8860 Lawrence Welk Dr.,

Escondido, tel. 619/749–3000 or 800/932–9355). About a 45-minute drive from downtown, this famed dinner theater puts on polished Broadway-style productions with a professional cast.

Lyceum Theatre (79 Horton Plaza, tel. 619/235–8025). Home to the San Diego Repertory Theatre, San Diego's first resident acting company performs contemporary works year-round on the 550-seat Lyceum stage and in a 225-seat theater that can be rearranged to suit the stage set.

Old Globe Theatre (Simon Edison Centre for the Performing Arts, Balboa Park, tel. 619/239–2255). The oldest professional theater in California performs classics, contemporary dramas, experimental works, and the famous summer Shakespeare Festival at the Old Globe and its sister theaters, the Cassius Carter Centre Stage and the Lowell Davies Festival Theatre.

San Diego Comic Opera (Casa del Prado Theatre, Balboa Park, tel. 619/231–5714). Four different productions of Gilbert and Sullivan and similar works are performed October–July.

Concerts **Open-Air Theatre** (San Diego State University, tel. 619/594–5200). Top-name rock, reggae, and popular artists pack in the crowds for summer concerts under the stars.

Organ Pavilion (Balboa Park, tel. 619/239–0512). Robert Plimpton performs on the giant 1914 pipe organ at 2 PM on most Sunday afternoons, and on most Monday evenings in summer. All concerts are free.

Sherwood Auditorium (700 Prospect St., La Jolla, tel. 619/454–3541). Many classical and jazz events are held in the 550-seat auditorium within San Diego Museum of Contemporary Art. La Jolla Chamber Music Society presents nine concerts, August–May, of internationally acclaimed chamber ensembles, orchestras, and soloists. San Diego Chamber Orchestra, a 35-member ensemble, performs once a month, October–April. Sherwood also hosts the wildly popular Festival of Animation January–March.

Sports Arena (2500 Sports Arena Blvd., tel. 619/224–4171). Big-name rock concerts play to more than 14,000 fans, using an end-stage configuration so that all seats face in one direction.

Opera **Civic Theatre** (202 C St., tel. 619/236–6510). The San Diego Opera draws such international stars as Luciano Pavarotti, Joan Sutherland, and Kiri Te Kanawa. The season of four operas runs January–April in the 3,000-seat, state-of-the-art auditorium. English translations of works sung in their original languages are projected on a large screen above the stage.

Dance **California Ballet** (tel. 619/560–5676). Four high-quality contemporary and traditional works, from story ballets to Balanchine, are performed September–May. The *Nutcracker* is staged annually at the Civic Theatre; other ballets take place at Symphony Hall, East County Performing Arts Center, and Nautilus Bowl at Sea World.

Issacs McCaleb & Dancers (tel. 619/296–9523). Interpretative dance presentations, incorporating live music, are staged at major theaters and concert halls around San Diego County.

Nightlife

The unbeatable variety of sun-and-surf recreational activities are the prime reason tourists come to San Diego, but most visitors are surprised and delighted by the new momentum the city gains after dark. The highly mercurial nightlife scene is constantly growing—the flavor of the month might be Top 40 or contemporary; reggae, pop-jazz, or strictly rock and roll. Live pop and fusion jazz have become especially popular—some say it's the ideal music for San Diego's typically laid-back lifestyle—and it can easily be found at a dozen or so venues throughout the county. Music at local rock clubs and nightclubs ranges from danceable contemporary Top 40 to original rock and new wave by San Diego's finest up-and-coming groups. Discothèques and bars in Mission Valley and at the beaches tend to be the most crowded spots in the county on the weekends, but don't let that discourage you from visiting these quintessential San Diego hangouts. And should your tastes run to softer music, there are plenty of piano bars in which to unfrazzle and unwind. Check the *Reader* for weekly band information or *San Diego* magazine's "Restaurant & Nightlife Guide" for the full range of nightlife possibilities.

California law prohibits the sale of alcoholic beverages after 2 AM. Bars and nightclubs usually stop serving at about 1:40 AM. You must be 21 to purchase and consume alcohol, and most places will insist on current identification. Be aware that California also has some of the most stringent drunken-driving laws; roadblocks are not an uncommon sight.

Bars and Nightclubs

Blarney Stone Pub. This cozy Dublin-style pub offers plenty of Irish brew and a wee bit of Irish folk music. *5617 Balboa Ave., Clairemont, tel. 619/279–2033. Open 10 AM–1:30 AM. No credit cards.*

The Jazz Note. Downstairs is a raucous disco, while upstairs the quieter, more sedate nightclub presents live jazz and jam sessions. This is a nonsmoking club. *860 Garnet Ave., Pacific Beach, tel. 619/272–1241. Open Thurs.–Sat. 8 PM–1 AM, Sun. 7 PM–midnight.*

La Bodega Lounge. Located in the renowned Rancho Bernardo Inn, this comfortable and elegant spot draws an older crowd with contemporary and big-band music. *17550 Bernardo Oaks Dr., Rancho Bernardo, tel. 619/277–2146. Open 10 AM–1:30 AM. Entertainment Tues.–Sat. 8:30 PM–1:30 AM. AE, MC, V.*

Megalopolis. This funky little club isn't nearly as large or as flashy as the name might suggest, but an eclectic roster of blues, rock, and folk bands is reason enough to visit. *4321 Fairmount Ave., University Heights, tel. 619/584–7900. Open Tues.–Sat. 9 PM–2 AM. No credit cards.*

Mick's P.B. In this spectacular club, rich with Honduran mahogany, chicly dressed singles from 25 to 45 dance to live contemporary rock and Top 40 hits played by bands predominantly from out of town. *4190 Mission Blvd., Pacific Beach, tel. 619/581–3938. Open 8 PM–1:30 AM. Entertainment Tues.–Sat. 9 PM–1:30 AM. AE, DC, MC, V.*

Jazz Clubs

Cargo Bar. The San Diego Hilton Hotel's nautical-theme bar has a can't-beat view of the bay and a don't-miss lineup of jazz and contemporary bands. *1775 E. Mission Bay Dr., Mission Bay, tel. 619/276–4010. Open 5 PM–1:30 AM. Entertainment 8:30 PM–1 AM. AE, DC, MC, V.*

Elario's. This club on the top floor of the Summer House Inn has a sumptuous ocean view and an incomparable lineup of internationally acclaimed jazz musicians every month. *7955 La Jolla Shores Dr., La Jolla, tel. 619/459–0541. Entertainment 8 PM–1 AM. AE, DC, MC, V.*

Humphrey's. This is the premier promoter of the city's best jazz, folk, and light-rock summer concert series held out on the grass. The rest of the year the music moves indoors for some first-rate jazz Saturday–Sunday. *2241 Shelter Island Dr., tel. 619/224–3577, taped concert information 619/523–1010. Entertainment 8 PM–midnight. AE, DC, MC, V.*

Rock Clubs **Belly Up Tavern.** Located in converted Quonset huts, this eclectic live-concert venue hosts critically acclaimed artists who play everything from reggae, rock, new wave, Motown, and folk to—well, you name it. *143 S. Cedros Ave., Solana Beach, tel. 619/481–9022. Open 11 AM–1:30 AM. Entertainment 9:30 PM–1:30 AM. MC, V.*

Bodie's. This Gaslamp Quarter bar hosts the best rock and blues bands in San Diego, as well as up-and-coming bands from out of town. *523 F St., tel. 619/236–8988. Open nightly 6 PM–2 AM.*

Casbah. This small club showcases rock, reggae, funk, and every other kind of band—except Top 40—every night of the week. *2812 Kettner Blvd., near downtown, tel. 619/294–9033. Live bands at 9:30 nightly. No credit cards.*

The Hype. One of San Diego's oldest bars keeps changing names, but the scene stays much the same—loud R & B, hip hop, funk, and '70s disco from the DJs, and, occasionally, performances by top local bands. *3595 Sports Arena Blvd., Loma Portal, tel. 619/223–5596. Open daily 6 PM–1:30 AM. MC, V.*

Old Bonita Store & Bonita Beach Club. This South Bay hangout attracts singles 25–35 and features locally produced rock acts. *4014 Bonita Rd., Bonita, tel. 619/479–3537. Entertainment Tues.–Sat. 9:15 PM–1:15 AM. AE, MC, V.*

Country/Western Clubs **Leo's Little Bit O' Country.** This is the largest country/western dance floor in the county—bar none. *680 W. San Marcos Blvd., San Marcos, tel. 619/744–4120. Open 4 PM–1 AM. Entertainment 8:30 PM–1 AM. Closed Mon. MC, V.*

Pomerado Club. The rustic dance hall, formerly a Pony Express station in the last century, now showcases the two-steppin' tunes of the house band, consisting of the owners. *12237 Pomerado Rd., Poway, tel. 619/748–1135. Entertainment Fri.–Sat. 9 PM–1:30 AM. No credit cards.*

Wrangler's Roost. This is a country/western haunt that appeals to both the longtime cowboy customer and the first-timer. *6608 Mission Gorge Rd., Santee, tel. 619/280–6263. Entertainment 9 PM–1:30 AM. MC, V.*

Comedy Clubs **Comedy Isle.** Located in the Bahia Resort Hotel, this club offers the latest in local and national talent. *998 W. Mission Bay Dr., Mission Bay, tel. 619/488–6872. Shows Tues.–Thurs. 8:30, Fri.–Sat. 8:30 and 10:30. AE, DC, MC, V.*

The Comedy Store. In the same tradition as the Comedy Store in West Hollywood, San Diego's version hosts some of the best national touring and local talent. *916 Pearl St., La Jolla, tel. 619/454–9176. Open Tues.–Thurs. 8–10:30 PM, Fri.–Sat. 8 PM–1 AM. Closed Sun.–Mon. AE, MC, V.*

The Improv. This is the superb Art Deco–style club with a distinct East Coast feel, where some of the big names in comedy present their routines. *832 Garnet Ave., Pacific Beach, tel. 619/483–4520. Open 6:30 PM–midnight. Entertainment 8 PM–midnight. AE, MC, V.*

Discos **Club Diego's.** This flashy discothèque and singles scene by the beach has excellent, nonstop dance music and friendly young

(25–35) dancers. *860 Garnet Ave., Pacific Beach, tel. 619/272–1241. Open 8 PM–1:30 AM. AE, MC, V.*

Club Mick's. Vintage rock and roll in the midst of the beach scene is the drawing card here. *4190 Mission Blvd., Mission Beach, tel. 619/581–3938. Open daily 5 PM–1:30 AM, Sat. 7 PM–1:30 AM. Closed Sun. No credit cards.*

Emerald City. Alternative dance music and an uninhibited clientele keep this beach-town spot unpredictable—which is just fine with everyone. *945 Garnet Ave., Pacific Beach, tel. 619/483–9920. Open 8:30 PM–2 AM. Closed Sun.–Mon. No credit cards.*

Full Moon. North County's favorite night spot is great for dancing to live and recorded music, with an ever-changing collection of acts, including occasional comedy and magic shows. *485 1st St., Encinitas, tel. 619/436–7397. Open daily 2 PM–2 AM. Entertainment Fri.–Sat. at 8. MC, V.*

Piano Bars **Top O' the Cove.** Show tunes and standards from the '40s to the '80s are the typical piano fare at this magnificent Continental restaurant in La Jolla. *1216 Prospect St., tel. 619/454–7779. Entertainment Wed.–Sun. 8 PM–midnight. AE, DC, MC, V.*

Westgate Hotel. One of the most elegant settings in San Diego offers piano music in the Plaza Bar. *1055 2nd Ave., downtown, tel. 619/238–1818. Open 11 AM–1 AM. Entertainment 8:30 PM–midnight. AE, DC, MC, V.*

Excursions to the North Coast

To say the north coast area of San Diego County is different from the city of San Diego is a vast understatement. From the northern tip of La Jolla to Oceanside, a half-dozen small communities each developed separately from urban San Diego. In fact, they developed separately from each other, and each has its own flavorful history. Del Mar, for example, exists primarily because of the lure its wide beaches and thoroughbred horse-racing facility extended to the rich and famous. Just a couple of miles away, agriculture, not paparazzi, played a major role in the development of Solana Beach and Encinitas. Up the coast, Carlsbad still reveals elements of its heritage, roots directly tied to the old Mexican rancheros and the entrepreneurial instinct of John Frazier, who told people the area's water could cure common ailments. In the late-19th century, not far from the current site of the posh La Costa Hotel and Spa, Frazier attempted to turn the area into a massive replica of a German mineral-springs resort.

Today, the north coast is a booming population center. An explosion of development throughout the 1980s turned the area into a northern extension of San Diego. The freeways started to take on the typically cluttered characteristics of most Southern California freeways.

Beyond the freeways, though, the communities have maintained their charm. Some of the finest restaurants, beaches, and attractions in San Diego County can be found in the area, a true slice of Southern California heritage. From the plush estates and rolling hills of Rancho Santa Fe and the beachfront restaurants of Cardiff to Mission San Luis Rey, a well-preserved remnant of California's first European settlers in Oceanside, the north coast is a distinctly different place.

Arriving and Departing

By Car I–5, the main freeway artery connecting San Diego to Los Angeles, follows the coastline. To the west, running parallel to it, is Old Highway 101, which never strays more than a quarter-mile from the ocean. Beginning north of La Jolla, where it is known as Torrey Pines Road, Old Highway 101 is a designated scenic route, providing access to the beauty of the coastline.

By Train **Amtrak** (tel. 619/239–9021 or 800/872–7245) operates trains daily between Los Angeles, Orange County, and San Diego. The last train leaves San Diego at approximately 9 PM each night; the last arrival is at 11:30 PM. There are stops in Oceanside and Del Mar.

By Bus **The San Diego Transit District** (tel. 619/722–6283) covers the city of San Diego up to Del Mar, where the **North County Transit District** takes over, blanketing the area with efficient, on-time bus service.

Greyhound/Trailways (tel. 619/239–9171) has regular routes connecting San Diego to points north, with stops in Del Mar, Solana Beach, Encinitas, and Oceanside.

By Taxi Several companies are based in the North County, including **Amigo Cab** (tel. 619/693–8681) and **Bill's Cab Co.** (tel. 619/755–6737).

By Plane **Palomar Airport** (tel. 619/758–6233), located in Carlsbad 2 miles east of I–5 on Palomar Airport Road, is a general aviation airport run by the county of San Diego and open to the public. Commuter airlines sometimes have flights from Palomar to Orange County and Los Angeles.

Guided Tours

Civic Helicopters (2192 Palomar Airport Rd., tel. 619/438–8424) offers whirlybird tours of the area from the air.

Exploring

Numbers in the margin correspond to points of interest on the San Diego North Coast map.

Any journey around the north-coast area naturally begins at the beach, and this one begins at **Torrey Pines State Beach,** just south of Del Mar. At the south end of the wide beach, perched ❶ on top of the cliffs, is the **Torrey Pines State Reserve,** one of only two places (the other place is Santa Rosa Island off the coast of Northern California) where the Torrey pine tree grows naturally. The park has a museum and an excellent set of hiking trails that snake through the 1,100-acre park, which is filled with exotic California shrubbery and features picturesque views from the cliffs. *Tel. 619/755–2063. Admission: $6 per car. Open daily dawn–sunset.*

❷ To the east of the state beach is **Los Penasquitos Lagoon,** one of the many natural estuaries that flow inland between Del Mar and Oceanside. Following Old Highway 101, the road leads into the small village of **Del Mar,** best-known for its volatile political

484

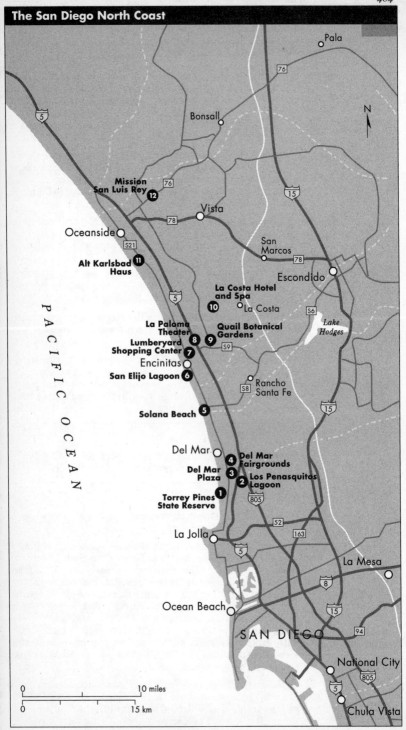

The San Diego North Coast

Pala

Bonsall

N

Mission San Luis Rey ⑫

76

Vista

Oceanside

S21

78

San Marcos

78

Escondido

Alt Karlsbad Haus ⑪

La Costa Hotel and Spa ⑩

La Costa

S6

Lake Hodges

La Paloma Theater ⑧ ⑨ Quail Botanical Gardens

Lumberyard Shopping Center ⑦

S9

Encinitas

San Elijo Lagoon ⑥

S8

Rancho Santa Fe

PACIFIC OCEAN

Solana Beach ⑤

Del Mar

Del Mar ④ Del Mar Fairgrounds

Del Mar Plaza ③

② Los Penasquitos Lagoon

Torrey Pines State Reserve ①

805

La Jolla

52

163

5

La Mesa

8

15

Ocean Beach

SAN DIEGO

94

National City

805

5

Chula Vista

0 _____ 10 miles

0 _____ 15 km

scene, celebrity visitors, and wide beaches. Years of spats be-
❸ tween developers and residents have resulted in the new **Del
Mar Plaza,** hidden by boulder walls and clever landscaping at
the corner of Old Highway 101 and 15th Street. The upper level
has a large deck and a view out to the ocean, and the restaurants and shops are excellent barometers of the latest in Southern California style. A left turn at 15th Street leads to
Seagrove Park, a small stretch of grass overlooking the ocean
where concerts are performed on summer evenings. A right
turn on Coast Boulevard provides access to Del Mar's beautiful
beaches, particularly popular with Frisbee and volleyball players.

Less than a half-mile north, Coast Boulevard merges with Old
❹ Highway 101. Across the road is the **Del Mar Fairgrounds,**
home to more than 100 different events a year, ranging from a
cat show to an auto race. *Via de la Valle Rd. exit west from I–5,
tel. 619/755–1161.*

The fairgrounds also host the annual summer meeting of the
Del Mar Thoroughbred Club (a.k.a "Where the Turf Meets the
Surf"). The track brings the top horses and jockeys to Del Mar,
along with a cross section of the rich and famous, eager to bet
on the ponies. Crooner Bing Crosby and his Hollywood bud-
dies, Pat O'Brien, Gary Cooper, and Oliver Hardy, among others, organized the track in the '30s, primarily because Crosby
thought it would be fun to have a track near his Rancho Santa
Fe home. Del Mar soon developed into a regular stop for the
stars of stage and screen.

During the off-season, horse players can still gamble at the
fairgrounds, thanks to a satellite wagering facility. Races from
other California tracks are televised, and people can bet as if
the races were being run right there. Times vary, depending on
which tracks in the state are operating. *Tel. 619/755–1141. Racing season: July–Sept., Wed.–Mon. Post time 2 PM.*

Next to the fairgrounds, on Jimmy Durante Boulevard, there is
a small exotic bird–training facility, **Freeflight,** which is open
to the public. Visitors are allowed to handle the birds—a guaranteed child pleaser. *2132 Jimmy Durante Blvd., tel. 619/481–
3148. Admission: $1. Open daily 9–5.*

Following Via de la Valle Road east from I–5 will take you to the
exclusive community of **Rancho Santa Fe,** one of the richest areas in the United States. Groves of huge, drooping eucalyptus
trees, first imported to the area by a railroad company in
search of trees to grow for railroad ties, cover the hills and valleys, hiding the posh estates. The little village of Rancho has
some elegant and quaint—and overpriced—shops and restaurants. But it is no accident that there is little else to see or do in
Rancho; the residents guard their privacy religiously. Even
the challenging Rancho Santa Fe Golf Course, the original site
of the Bing Crosby Pro-Am and considered one of the best
courses in Southern California, is still open only to members of
the Rancho Santa Fe community.

Back along the coast, along Old Highway 101 north of Del Mar,
❺ is the quiet little beach community of **Solana Beach.** A highlight
of Solana Beach is **Fletcher Cove,** located at the west end of Lomas Santa Fe Drive, and called Pill Box by the locals because of
a bunkerlike lifeguard station on the cliffs above the beach.
Early Solana settlers used dynamite to blast the cove out of the

cliffs. It is an easy-access beach, with a large parking lot complete with a small basketball court, a favorite of local pickup-game players.

North of Solana Beach, separating Solana Beach from Cardiff, **(6)** is the **San Elijo Lagoon,** home to many migrating birds. Trails wind around the entire area.

As you continue along Old Highway 101, past the cluster of hillside homes that make up Cardiff, past the campgrounds of the San Elijo State Beach, the palm trees of Sea Cliff Roadside Park (Swami's to the locals) and the golden domes of the Self-Realization Fellowship mark the entrance to downtown **Encinitas.** The Self-Realization Fellowship was built at the turn of the century and is a retreat and place of worship for the followers of an Indian religious sect. Its beautiful gardens are open to the public.

A new landmark of Encinitas (which was incorporated as a city in 1986, including the communities of Cardiff, Leucadia, and **(7)** Olivenhain) is the **Lumberyard Shopping Center,** a collection of small stores and restaurants that anchors the downtown shopping area. There is a huge selection of shopping centers inland at the intersection of Encinitas Boulevard and El Camino Real.

(8) An older landmark of Encinitas is the **La Paloma Theater** at the north end of town on Old Highway 101 (near the corner of Encinitas Blvd., tel. 619/436–7469). Built in the 1920s as a stop for traveling vaudeville troupes, it has served as a concert hall, movie theater, and meeting place for the area ever since. Plays are still being rehearsed and performed here.

Encinitas is best known as the "Flower Capital of the World," and although the flower industry is not as prevalent as it once was, the city is still home to Paul Ecke Poinsettias, the largest producer of the popular Christmas blossom. A sampling of the **(9)** area's dedication to horticulture can be found at the **Quail Botanical Gardens,** home to thousands of different varieties of plants. *Encinitas Blvd. east from I–5 and turn left on Quail Gardens Dr., tel. 619/436–3036. Parking $1. Open daily 8–5.*

Old Highway 101 continues north through Leucadia, a small community best-known for its small art galleries and stores. At the north end of Leucadia (which means "sheltered paradise" in Greek), La Costa Avenue meets Highway 101. Following La Costa Avenue east, past the Batiquitos Lagoon, you'll come to **(10)** the famous **La Costa Hotel and Spa** (tel. 619/438–9111), noted for its excellent golf and tennis facilities and restaurants.

La Costa is technically part of the city of Carlsbad, which is centered farther north, west of the Tamarack Avenue and Elm Avenue exits of I–5. In Carlsbad, Old Highway 101 is called Carlsbad Boulevard. Large rancheros owned by wealthy Mexicans were the first settlements inland, while the coastal area was developed by an entrepreneur, John Frazier, who lured people to the area with talk of the healing powers of mineral water bubbling from a coastal well. The water was found to have the same properties as water from the German mineral wells of Karlsbad, hence the name of the new community. Remnants **(11)** from the era, including the original well, are found at the **Alt Karlsbad Haus,** a small museum and gift shop. *2802A Carlsbad Blvd., tel. 619/729–6912. Admission free. Open Mon.–Sat. 10–5, Sun. 1–4:30.*

North of Carlsbad is **Oceanside,** home of Camp Pendleton, the country's largest marine base, as well as a beautiful natural harbor teeming with activity. Oceanside Harbor is the north-coast center for fishing, sailing, and all ocean-water sports. Oceanside Pier is a favorite hangout for fishermen. You can call for general harbor information (tel. 619/966–4570).

⑫ Oceanside is also home to **Mission San Luis Rey,** built by Franciscan friars in 1798 to help educate and convert local Indians. One of the best-preserved missions in the area, San Luis Rey was the 18th and largest of the California missions. Today there is a picnic area, gift shop, and museum on the grounds. Self-guided tours are available through the grounds, where retreats are held. *Tel. 619/757–3651. Take Mission Ave. east from I–5. Open Mon.–Sat. 10–4, Sun. 1–4.*

Dining

Given the north-coast reputation as a suburban area, there is a surprisingly large selection of top-quality restaurants. In fact, San Diegans often take the drive north to enjoy the variety of cuisines offered in the north county. Prices are for one person and do not include drinks, taxes, or tip.

**Expensive
($35–$50)
Del Mar** **The Bistro Garden.** This airy, French country–style restaurant in the elegant Inn L'Auberge offers patio dining. Creative nouvelle cuisine emphasizes fresh seafood specialties such as saffron lobster ravioli with caviar and crayfish. *1540 Camino del Mar, tel. 619/259–1515. Reservations advised. Jacket advised. AE, DC, MC, V.*

La Costa **Pisces.** Located near the La Costa Country Club, Pisces represents the upper crust of north-coast seafood restaurants. Traditional seafood, such as scallops and shrimp, is served in innovative and tasty dishes. *7640 El Camino Real, tel. 619/436–9362. Reservations accepted. Jackets required. AE, DC, MC, V.*

Rancho Santa Fe
★ **Mille Fleurs.** This gem of a French inn brightens a tiny village surrounded by country-gentlemen estates. Just a few miles from the county's famous vegetable farms, where the chef shops daily, this is a most romantic hideaway, with tempting cuisine to enhance the mood. *6009 Paseo Delicias, tel. 619/756–3085. Reservations advised. Jacket and tie advised. AE, DC, MC, V.*

Solana Beach **Frederick's.** This husband-and-wife-owned, friendly, relaxed bistro serves traditional French dishes with California-fresh overtones. Leave room for the freshly baked bread and one of the lush desserts. The menu changes weekly. *128 S. Acacia St., tel. 619/755–2432. Reservations advised. Dress: casual. DC, MC, V. Closed for lunch. Closed Mon.*

**Moderate
($20–$35)
Cardiff** **The Chart House.** The beach and the sunset above the Pacific are the chief attractions of this surfside dining spot. Entrées include fresh fish, seafood, and beef dishes; there's an exceptional salad bar. *2588 S. Hwy. 101, tel. 619/436–4044. Reservations advised. Dress: casual. AE, DC, MC, V.*

Del Mar **Il Fornaio.** Located within the Del Mar Plaza, this talk-of-the-town ristorante features northern Italian cuisine, such as fresh seafood, homemade pastas, and crispy pizzas. The outdoor piazza affords a splendid ocean view. *1555 Camino del Mar, tel. 619/755-8876. Reservations advised. Dress: casual. MC, V.*

Jake's. Another favorite of the racetrack crowd, Jake's is nestled on the shoreline, with the sort of view that turns one's thoughts to romance, not the Daily Double. There is a fresh-fish special each day, as well as a different pizza offering. Those who are foolish enough to eat and run will appreciate the quick snack-bar menu. *1660 Coast Blvd., tel. 619/755-2002. Reservations advised. Dress: casual. AE, MC, V. No Sat. lunch.*

Encinitas **Piret M.** This charming, sun-dappled French bistro looks as much like a sophisticated gourmet boutique (with delicacies for sale) as it does a countryside restaurant. The menu features hearty soups, quiches that will make a man of you, crisp fresh salads, a savory lamb ragout, large but elegant sandwiches, French omelets, and the sort of rich desserts that threaten the firmest of resolves. *897 First St., tel. 619/942-5152. Reservations advised. Dress: casual. AE, MC, V.*

Portofino's. This classy little restaurant attempts to re-create the atmosphere of the posh Riviera resort from which it gets its name. Homemade pasta and the seafood dishes are popular. *1108 First St., tel. 619/942-8442. Reservations accepted. Dress: casual. AE, DC, MC, V.*

Inexpensive **Los Olas.** Funky and inexpensive Los Olas, across the street
(under $20) from the beach in Cardiff, serves good food, especially the
Cardiff *chimichangas*—deep-fried flour tortillas stuffed with shredded stewed beef—and the tasty fried burritos with heaps of guacamole and sour cream. The beachside atmosphere is better suited for lunch than dinner, though. *2655 S. Hwy. 101, tel. 619/942-1860. Dress: casual. MC, V.*

Del Mar **Johnny Rockets.** This '50s-style malt-and-burger joint, on the Del Mar Plaza's lower level, dishes up juicy burgers, thick malts, and fries to die for. Booth and counter seating come complete with nickel-a-tune jukeboxes. *1555 Camino del Mar, tel. 619/755-1954. Dress: casual. No credit cards.*

Solana Beach **Chung King Loh.** One of the better Chinese restaurants along the coast, Chung King Loh offers an excellent variety of Mandarin and Szechuan dishes. *552 Stevens Ave., tel. 619/481-0184. Dress: casual. AE, DC, MC, V. Closed for lunch Sun.*

Fidel's. Rich in North County tradition, both Fidel's restaurants serve a wide variety of well-prepared dishes in a low-key, pleasant atmosphere. The original restaurant in Solana Beach, a two-story building with an outdoor patio area, is particularly nice. *607 Valley Ave., tel. 619/755-5292; 3003 Carlsbad Blvd., Carlsbad, tel. 619/729-0903. Dress: casual. AE, MC, V.*

Lodging

The prices below reflect the cost of a room for two people. Many hotels offer discount rates from October to May.

Very Expensive **The Inn L'Auberge.** Now managed by the prestigious Bel Air
(over $120) Hotel Company, the Inn sits across the street from the Del Mar
Carlsbad Plaza and one block from the ocean. Modeled on the Tudor-style Hotel Del Mar, playground for Hollywood's elite in the early 1900s, the Inn is filled with dark-wood antiques, fireplaces, and lavish floral arrangements—though its refined style is somewhat out of keeping with the sun-drenched Southern California scene just outside its doors. The grounds are

gorgeous, with stone paths winding throughout 5.2 acres, and leading to gazebos and pools; the spa specializes in European herbal wraps and treatments. *1540 Camino del Mar, Del Mar 92014, tel. 619/259–1515 or 800/553–1336. 120 rooms. Facilities: restaurant, 2 tennis courts, 2 pools, Jacuzzi, European-style spa. AE, MC, V.*

La Costa Hotel and Spa. This famous resort recently received a $100 million renovation, and the style is now mildly southwestern. Contemporary rooms are decorated in neutral tones, or rose and turquoise. You'll find all amenities, including supervised children's activities and a movie theater. *Costa del Mar Rd., 92009, tel. 619/438–9111 or 800/854–5000. 478 rooms. Facilities: 5 restaurants, pool, exercise room, golf, tennis, theater. AE, DC, MC, V.*

Expensive (over $75) *Carlsbad* **Carlsbad Inn Beach and Tennis Resort.** This hotel and time-share resort near the beach features modern amenities and rooms with an Old World feel. *3075 Carlsbad Blvd., 92008, tel. 619/434–7020. 200 rooms. Facilities: 2 restaurants, pool, health club, Jacuzzis, video room. AE, MC, V.*

Rancho Santa Fe **Rancho Valencia.** This resort is so luxurious that several high-style magazines have chosen it for fashion backdrops, and have named it the most romantic hideaway in the United States. The suites are in red-tile-roofed casitas with fireplaces and private terraces. Tennis is the other draw here, with 18 courts and a resident pro. *5921 Valencia Circle, tel. 619/756–1123 or 800/548–3664. 43 suites. Facilities: restaurant, 18 tennis courts, pool, 2 Jacuzzis, sauna. AE, MC, V.*

Moderate ($55–$75) *Carlsbad* **Best Western Beach View Lodge.** Reservations are essential at this reasonably priced hotel at the beach. Some rooms have kitchenettes; others have fireplaces. Families tend to settle in for a week or more. *3180 Carlsbad Blvd., 92008, tel. 619/729–1151. 41 rooms. Facilities: Jacuzzi, sauna, swimming pool. AE, DC, MC, V.*

Del Mar **Stratford Inn.** The inn offers a pleasant atmosphere just outside the center of town and three blocks from the ocean. Rooms are clean and well maintained; some have ocean views. Suites are available. Note: Not all rooms are air-conditioned, so be sure to ask before you reserve. *710 Camino del Mar, 92014, tel. 619/755–1501. 110 rooms. Facilities: 2 pools, Jacuzzi. AE, DC, MC, V.*

Encinitas **Moonlight Beach Hotel.** This folksy, laid-back motel is a favorite of those who enjoy the area's post-hippie aura and don't mind the traffic just outside their doors. All rooms have kitchens, and the beach is a few blocks away. *233 2nd St., 92024, tel. 619/753–0623. 24 rooms. AE, MC, V.*

Radisson Inn Encinitas. Formerly called the Sanderling, this hotel on the east side of Old Highway 101 sits on a slight hill near the freeway. The rooms—some with an ocean view—are efficiently designed and unobtrusively decorated. *85 Encinitas Blvd., 92024, tel. 619/942–7455 or 800/333–3333. 92 rooms. Facilities: restaurant, pool, whirlpool, putting green. AE, DC, MC, V.*

Inexpensive (under $55) *Carlsbad* **Carlsbad Lodge.** The lodge is more than an easy walk from the beach, but there is a lovely park nearby. The rooms are clean and pleasant. *3570 Pio Pico Dr., 92008, tel. 619/729–2383. 66 rooms. Facilities: Jacuzzi, sauna, swimming pool. AE, DC, MC, V.*

Encinitas **Budget Motels of America.** This motel is adjacent to the freeway and within a block of the beach. Some rooms have VCRs and in-room movies—a good deal. *133 Encinitas Blvd., 92024, tel. 619/944–0260. 124 rooms. AE, DC, MC, V.*

Leucadia **Pacific Surf Motel.** It will never be compared with The Ritz, but it is clean, comfortable, and near all the shops and restaurants of Encinitas. *1076 N. Hwy. 101, 92024, tel. 619/436–8763. 30 rooms. AE, MC, V.*

Oceanside **Oceanside TraveLodge.** It's near the beach and centrally located. *1401 N. Hill St., 92054, tel. 619/722–1244. 30 rooms. AE, DC, MC, V.*

Excursions to Anza-Borrego Desert State Park

Every spring, the stark desert landscape east of the Cuyamaca mountains explodes with color. It's the annual blooming of the wildflowers in the Anza-Borrego Desert State Park, less than a two-hour drive from central San Diego. The beauty of this annual spectacle, as well as the natural quiet and blazing climate, lures tourists and natives to the area.

The area features a desert and not much more, but it is one of the favorite parks of those Californians who travel widely in their state. People seeking bright lights and glitter should look elsewhere. The excitement in this area stems from watching a coyote scamper across a barren ridge or a brightly colored bird resting on a nearby cactus, or from a waitress delivering another cocktail to a poolside chaise longue. For hundreds of years, the only humans to linger in the area were Indians from the San Dieguito, Kamia, and Cahuilla tribes, but the extreme temperature eventually forced the tribes to leave, too. It wasn't until 1774, when Mexican explorer Captain Juan Bautista de Anza first blazed a trail through the area as a shortcut from Sonora to San Francisco, that modern civilization had its first glimpse of the oddly beautiful wasteland.

Today more than 500,000 acres of desert are included in the Anza-Borrego Desert State Park, making it the largest state park in the United States. It is also one of the few parks in the country where people can camp anywhere. No campsite is necessary; just follow the trails and pitch a tent wherever you like.

Following the trails is an important point, since vehicles are prohibited from driving off the road in most areas of the park. However, 14,000 acres have been set aside in the eastern part of the desert near Ocotillo Wells for off-road enthusiasts. General George S. Patton conducted field training in the Ocotillo area to prepare for the World War II invasion of North Africa, and the area hasn't been the same since.

The little town of Borrego Springs acts as an oasis in this natural playground. Not exactly like Palm Springs—it lacks the wild crowds and preponderance of insanely wealthy residents —Borrego is basically a small retirement community, with the average age of residents about 50. For visitors who are uninterested in communing with the desert without a shower and pool nearby, Borrego provides several pleasant hotels and restaurants.

We recommend visiting this desert between October and May because of the extreme summer temperatures. Winter temperatures are comfortable, but nights (and sometimes days) are cold, so bring a warm jacket.

Arriving and Departing

By Car Take I–8 east to Highway 79 north. Turn east on Highway 78.

By Bus The **Northeast Rural Bus System** (NERBS) (tel. 619/765–0145) connects Julian, Borrego Springs, Oak Grove, Ocotillo Wells, Agua Caliente, Ramona, and many of the other small communities that dot the landscape with El Cajon, 15 miles east of downtown San Diego, and the East County line of the San Diego trolley, with stops at Grossmont shopping center and North County Fair.

By Plane Borrego Springs Airport (tel. 619/767–5548) has the nearest runway.

Important Addresses and Numbers

For general information about the Borrego and desert areas, contact the **Borrego Chamber of Commerce** (tel. 619/767–5555). For information on the state park, contact the Visitor Center, **Anza-Borrego Desert State Park** (Box 299, Borrego Springs 92004, tel. 619/767–5311). You can call the Visitor Center for information on when the wildflowers will be in bloom, or you can send a self-addressed postcard and it will be returned to you with the information. For campsite information, call **MISTIX** (tel. 800/444–7275).

Exploring

The **Anza-Borrego Desert State Park** is too vast to even consider exploring in its entirety. Most people stay in the hills surrounding Borrego Springs. An excellent underground **Visitor Information Center** (tel. 619/767–5311) and museum are reachable by taking the Palm Canyon Drive spur west from the traffic circle in the center of town. The rangers are helpful and always willing to suggest areas for camping or hiking. There is also a short slide show about the desert, shown throughout the day. A short, very easy trail from the Visitor Center to the campground will take you past many of the cacti illustrated in Visitor Center displays.

One of the most popular camping and hiking areas is **Palm Canyon,** just a few minutes west of the Visitor Information Center. A 1½-mile trail leads to a small oasis with a waterfall and palm trees. If you find palm trees lining city streets in San Diego and Los Angeles amusing, seeing this grove of native palms around a pool in a narrow desert valley may give you a new vision of the dignity of this tree. The Borrego Palm Canyon campground (on the desert floor a mile or so below the palm oasis) is one of only two developed campgrounds with flush toilets and showers in the park. (The other is Tamarisk Grove Campground at the intersection of Hwy. 78 and Yaqui Pass Rd.)

Other points of interest include **Split Mountain** (take Split
Mountain Rd. south from Hwy. 78 at Ocotillo Wells), a narrow
gorge with 600-foot perpendicular walls. You can drive the mile
from the end of the paved road to the gorge in a passenger car if
you are careful (don't get stuck in the sand). Don't attempt the
drive in bad weather, when the gorge can quickly fill with a tor-
rent of water.

On the way to Split Mountain (while you are still on the paved
road), you'll pass a grove of the park's unusual **elephant trees**
(10 ft. tall, with swollen branches and small leaves). There is a
self-guided nature trail; pick up a brochure at the parking lot.

You can get a good view of the Borrego Badlands from **Font's
Point,** off Borrego–Salton Seaway (S22). The badlands are a
maze of steep ravines that are almost devoid of vegetation.
Park rangers sometimes give guided tours of the region above
the badlands. You drive your own car in a caravan behind the
ranger, stopping for closer looks and detailed information.

In **Borrego Springs** itself, there is little to do besides lie in the
sun, the shade, or take advantage of the hot days and recreate
in the sun. The challenging 18-hole Rams Hill Country Club
course is open to the public (tel. 619/767–5000), as is the
Borrego Roadrunner Club (tel. 619/767–5374), but you'll have
to know a member to play the private 18 holes of the De Anza
Country Club located in the north end of the valley (tel. 619/
767–5105).

For tennis fans, the Borrego Tennis Club (tel. 619/767–9725)
has four lighted courts that are open to the public. One of the
best and most appreciated deals in town is the Borrego Springs
High School pool, located at the intersection of Saddle and
Cahuilla roads; it is open to the public during the summer.

Most people prefer to explore the desert in a motorized vehicle.
While it is illegal to ride two- or four-wheel vehicles off the
trails in the state park, the **Ocotillo Wells State Vehicular Recreation Area** (tel. 619/767–5391), reached by following Highway 78 east from Borrego, is a popular haven for off-road
enthusiasts. The sand dunes and rock formations are challenging as well as fun. Camping is permitted throughout the area,
but water is not available. The only facilities are in the small
town (or, perhaps, it should be called no more than a corner) of
Ocotillo Wells.

To the east of Anza-Borrego is the Salton Sink, a basin that (although not as low as Death Valley) consists of more dry land below sea level than anywhere else in this hemisphere. The Salton
Sea is the most recent of a series of lakes here, divided from the
Gulf of California by the delta of the Colorado River. The current lake was created in 1905–7 when the Colorado flooded
north through canals meant to irrigate the Imperial Valley.
The water is extremely salty, even saltier than the Pacific
Ocean, and it is primarily a draw for fishermen seeking corbina, croaker, and tilapia. Some boaters and swimmers also use
the lake. The state runs a pleasant park, with sites for day
camping, recreational vehicles, and primitive camping. *Take
Hwy. 78 east to Hwy. 111 north, tel. 619/393–3052.*

Bird-watchers particularly will love the **Salton Sea National
Wildlife Refuge.** A hiking trail and observation tower make it
easy to spot the dozens of varieties of migratory birds stopping

at Salton Sea. *At the south end of Salton Sea, off Hwy. 111, tel. 619/348–5278.*

For hunters, the **Wister Wildlife Area** (tel. 619/348–0577), off Highway 111 on the east side of Salton Sea, controls the hunting of waterfowl in the area. There are campsites available.

Dining

Quality, not quantity, is the operable truism of dining in the Borrego area. Restaurants are scarce and hard to find, but the best are truly top quality. Prices are based on the cost of a complete meal for one, not including beverage, tax, or tip.

Moderate **La Casa del Zorro.** This restaurant offers an elegant Continen-
($10–$20) tal dining experience. It also serves Sunday brunch. *3845 Yaqui Pass Rd., tel. 619/767–5323. Reservations accepted. No shorts or jeans. AE, DC, MC, V.*

Rams Hill Country Club. This is another top-notch Continental restaurant in the middle of the desert, also offering Sunday brunch. *1881 Rams Hill Rd., tel. 619/767–5006. Reservations accepted. Dress: casual, but jacket required Sat. AE, MC, V. Closed for dinner Mon.–Wed. July–Oct. 1.*

Inexpensive **Chefs for You.** This deli is located in the largest shopping center
(under $10) in Borrego. *561 The Mall, tel. 619/767–3522.*

Lodging

If camping isn't your thing, there are two very nice resorts near Borrego Springs that offer fine amenities minus the overdevelopment of Palm Springs. Prices are based on the cost of a room for two. In the summer months, rates drop by as much as 50%.

Expensive **Ram's Hill Country Club.** This relatively new hacienda-style
(over $70) country club is right in the middle of the desert. Patio units are on the golf course. *Box 664, Borrego Springs 92004, tel. 619/767–5028. 20 units. Facilities: tennis courts, whirlpool. AE, MC, V.*

La Casa del Zorro. This is a small, low-key resort complex in the heart of the desert. You need walk only a few hundred yards to be alone under the sky, and you may well see roadrunners crossing the highway. The accommodations are in comfortable one- to three-bedroom ranch-style houses complete with living rooms and kitchens. *3845 Yaqui Pass Rd., 92004, tel. 619/767–5323 or 800/325–8274. 77 suites, 94 rooms, 19 casitas. Facilities: tennis courts, golf course, horseback riding, bicycles. AE, DC, MC, V.*

Palm Canyon Resort. This is one of the largest facilities in the area, with a hotel, an RV park, a restaurant, and recreational facilities. *221 Palm Canyon Dr., 92004, tel. 619/767–5342; in CA, 800/242–0044. 44 rooms. Facilities: restaurant, 138 RV spaces, 2 pools, 2 whirlpools, general store, laundromat.*

15 Palm Springs

What do you get when you start with dramatic scenery, add endless sunshine, mix in deluxe resorts, and spice things up with a liberal dash of celebrities? Palm Springs, a magnet for socialites, sun worshipers, and stargazers.

This fashionable desert resort community, nestled beneath 10,831-foot Mt. San Jacinto, has more than 80 golf courses in a 20-mile radius, more than 600 tennis courts, 35 miles of bicycle trails, horseback riding, 10,000 or so swimming pools, and even cross-country skiing. Those inclined to less strenuous activities are drawn indoors by such names as Gucci, I. Magnin, and Saks Fifth Avenue. The "in crowd" gathers at exclusive country clubs and openings at the city's numerous art galleries. It's been said that socializing is the top industry in Palm Springs; after a few days here, you'll probably agree.

Year-round, Palm Springs is both a vacation retreat and a residence for celebrities and famous politicians. Bob Hope is the city's honorary mayor, and Gene Autry, Frank Sinatra, Gerald Ford, and other luminaries can be spotted at charity events and restaurants and on the golf course. Carrie Fisher and Bette Midler have done stints at the Palms spa, while Donna Mills, Goldie Hawn, and Kurt Russell have been poolside stars at the Ingleside Inn. Palm Springs resorts are not new territory to celebrity visitors: Esther Williams once practiced her strokes at the El Mirador pool, Spencer Tracy played chess at the Racquet Club, and Joan Bennett pedaled her bicycle down Palm Canyon Drive.

Palm Springs became a haven for the stars in 1930, after the arrival of noted silent-film pros Charlie Farrell and Ralph Bellamy. For $30 an acre, the two actors bought 200 acres. This was the beginning of the Palm Springs Racquet Club, which soon listed Ginger Rogers, Humphrey Bogart, and Clark Gable among its members. Today you can take a tour that points out the homes of the celebrities of yesterday and today.

The desert's stunning natural beauty is a major contributor to the area's magnetism. Nature dominates the area: City buildings are restricted to a height of 30 feet; flashing, moving, and neon signs are prohibited, preserving an intimate village feeling; and 50% of the land consists of open spaces with palm trees and desert vegetation.

This beauty is particularly evident in the canyons surrounding Palm Springs. Lush Tahquitz Canyon, one of the five canyons that line the San Jacinto mountains, was the setting for Shangri-La in an early movie version of *Lost Horizon*. The original inhabitants of these rock canyons were the Cahuilla Indians. Their descendants came to be known as Agua Caliente—"hot water"—Indians, named after the hot mineral springs that flowed through their reservation. The Agua Caliente still own about 32,000 acres of Palm Springs desert, 6,700 of which lie within the city limits of Palm Springs.

Despite the building restrictions, Palm Springs has a suitable array of sophisticated spots, from the outstanding Desert Museum and Annenberg Theatre to the chic shops and galleries along the palm tree–lined Palm Canyon Drive. The trendy El Paseo Drive, 10 miles south of Palm Springs in neighboring Palm Desert, is often compared to Rodeo Drive in Beverly Hills.

One brief comment on the weather: While daytime temperatures average a pleasantly warm 88° Fahrenheit, you are still in the desert. And that means during the middle of the day in the summer it is going to be very hot—sometimes uncomfortably so. You'll be told that "it is a dry heat." And it is. But it is still desert hot: Plan activities in the morning and late afternoon, and wear a hat and plenty of sunscreen if you're out for a midday stroll.

Arriving and Departing

By Plane Major airlines serving Palm Springs Regional Airport include **Alaska Airlines, American Airlines, American Eagle, America West, Skywest/Delta Connection, Trans World Airlines, United Airlines,** and **United Express.** The airport is about 2 miles east of the city's main downtown intersection; most hotels provide service to and from the airport. Bermuda Dunes Airport in Palm Desert is served by **Pacific Coast Airlines** (tel. 800/456–5400).

By Train **Amtrak** passenger trains service the Indio area, 20 miles east of Palm Springs. For information and reservations call 800/USA–RAIL. From Indio, **Greyhound/Trailways** bus service is available to Palm Springs.

By Bus **Greyhound/Trailways** Bus Lines (311 N. Indian Canyon Dr., tel. 619/325–2053).

By Car Palm Springs is about a two-hour drive east of Los Angeles and a three-hour drive northeast of San Diego. Highway 111 brings you right onto Palm Canyon Drive, the main thoroughfare in Palm Springs. From Los Angeles take the San Bernardino Freeway (I–10E) to Highway 111. From San Diego, I–15N connects with the Pomona Freeway (I–60E), leading to the San Bernardino Freeway (I–10E). If you're coming from the Riverside area, you might want to try the scenic Palms-to-Pines Highway (Hwy. 74). This 130-mile route begins in Hemet and connects directly with Highway 111; the trek from snowcapped peaks to open desert valley is breathtaking.

Getting Around

Downtown Palm Springs is distinctly walkable. Beyond that, you will find that having a car is the easiest way to get around and take in nearby attractions like the Aerial Tramway and El Paseo Drive in Palm Desert.

By Bus **SunBus** serves the entire Coachella Valley from Desert Hot Springs to Coachella with regular routes. Call 619/343–3451 for route and schedule information.

By Taxi **Desert Cab** (tel. 619/325–2868) and **Caravan Yellow Cab** (tel. 619/346–2981).

By Car If you're not driving into Palm Springs, you might do well to check with one of the many rental agencies, all of which offer fairly competitive rates. Agencies include **Avis** (tel. 619/778–6300), **Aztec** (tel. 619/325–2294), **Budget** (tel. 619/327–1404), **Dollar** (tel. 619/325–7334), **Enterprise** (tel. 619/328–9393), **Hertz** (tel. 619/778–5120), and **National** (tel. 619/327–4100).

Important Addresses and Numbers

Tourist Information **Desert Resorts Bureau** (tel. 619/770–9000) is located at 69–930 Highway 111, Suite 201, Rancho Mirage 92270.
Palm Springs Visitor Information Center (2781 N. Palm Canyon Dr., Palm Springs 92262, tel. 800/347–7746) provides tourist information.

Emergencies Dial 911 for **police** and **ambulance** in an emergency.

Doctors **Desert Hospital** (tel. 619/323–6511).

Dentists Dental emergency service is available from R. Turnage, D.D.S. (tel. 619/327–8448) 24 hours a day.

Guided Tours

Orientation Tours **Gray Line Tours** (tel. 619/325–0974) offers several good general bus tours, from the hour-long Palm Springs Special highlight tour to the tour through Palm Springs, Cathedral City, Rancho Mirage, and Palm Desert, including a stop at a date shop. Prices are $14.25 for adults, $8.25 for children. Most departures are in the morning; call for reservations. Pickup and drop-off service are available to most hotels. For a different perspective of the desert, try floating over the valley in a balloon. Trip lengths and prices vary; call **Fantasy Balloon Flights** (tel. 619/568–0997) or **Sunrise Balloons** (tel. 800/548–9912) for information.

Special-Interest Tours In Palm Springs, special-interest tours mean one thing: celebrity homes. **Gray Line** and **Palm Springs Celebrity Tours** (tel. 619/325–2682) both cover this turf well. Prices range from $10 to $14 for adults. **Desert Off Road Adventures** (tel. 619/324–3378) takes to the wilds with Jeep tours of Indian Canyons, off-road in the Santa Rosa mountains and into a mystery canyon. Customized helicopter tours are also available from **Sunrise Balloons. Covered Wagon Tours** (tel. 619/347–2161) will take you on an old-time two-hour exploration of the desert with a cookout at the end of the journey.

Exploring

Numbers in the margin correspond to points of interest on the Palm Springs map.

Physically, Palm Springs proper is easy to understand. Palm Canyon Drive runs north–south through the heart of downtown; the intersection with Tahquitz–McCallum is pretty much the center of the main drag. Heading south, Palm Canyon Drive splits: South Palm Canyon Drive leads you to the Indian Canyons and East Palm Canyon takes you through the growing satellite resort areas of Cathedral City, Rancho Mirage, and Palm Desert. The Aerial Tramway is at the northern limits of Palm Springs. Joshua Tree National Monument is about an hour's drive north.

Most Palm Springs attractions can be seen in anywhere from an hour or two to an entire day, depending upon your interests. Do you want to take the tram up Mt. San Jacinto, see the view, and come right back down, or spend the day hiking? Would you rather linger for a picnic lunch in one of the Indian Canyons, or double back for a snack and people-watching at Hyatt's sidewalk café? Your best bet is to think of the list of sights and activities as if it were an à la carte menu and pick and choose according to your appetite. To help you organize your outings, we will start in the north and work our way south and southeast. A separate tour of Joshua Trees follows.

Palm Springs and Environs ❶ Take the **Palm Springs Aerial Tramway** to get a stunning overview of the desert. The 2½-mile ascent brings you to an elevation of 8,516 feet in less than 20 minutes. On clear days, which are common, the view stretches some 75 miles from the peak of Mt. San Gorgonio to the north and the Salton Sea in the southeast. At the top you'll find several diversions. Mountain Station has an Alpine buffet restaurant, cocktail lounge, apparel and gift shops, and picnic facilities. Mt. San Jacinto State Park offers 54 miles of hiking trails and camping and picnic areas; during winter the Nordic Ski Center has cross-country ski equipment for rent. *Tram cars depart at least every 30 min from 10 AM weekdays and 8 AM weekends. Cost: $14.95 adults, $9.95 children 3–12. Closed for 2–4 wks after Labor Day for maintenance. Call 619/325–1391 for information; 619/325–4227 for ski and weather conditions.*

Strolling down **Palm Canyon Drive,** Palm Springs' version of Main Street, should satisfy even the most avid shopper; everything from Saks Fifth Avenue to T-shirt and yogurt shops line the street. With a good pair of comfortable walking shoes you should be able to walk from one end of the drive to the other in a couple of hours.

Downtown **horse-drawn carriages** promenade the city streets to the narrative of their guide/drivers. Their "Star House Tour" is especially fun. *Carriage Trade LTD, tel. 619/327–3214. $60 for 1 to 4 people. Rides start at the corner of Tahquitz Way and Palm Canyon Dr.*

❷ For all its up-to-the-minute chicness, downtown Palm Springs is not without its historical treasures. The **Village Green Heritage Center** illustrates pioneer life in Palm Springs in three museums. McCallum Adobe, dating back to 1885, displays the collections of the Palm Springs Historical Society and McCallum family memorabilia. Miss Cornelia White's House, dating back to 1894, exhibits this pioneer family's memorabilia, including an extensive collection of Bibles, clothing, tools, books, paintings, even the first telephone in Palm Springs. Roddy's General Store Museum dates from a later pioneer era, the 1930s and 1940s, and displays signs, packages, and products of the period. *221 and 223 S. Palm Canyon Dr. Nominal admission. House open Wed. and Sun. noon–3, Thurs.–Sat. 10–4; store open Thurs.–Sun 10–4; summer hours flexible.*

❸ If further evidence is needed to prove that the desert is no barren wasteland, there is the **Desert Museum.** Art exhibits here tend to have a Western flavor, from California Contemporary to shows like "Art and Treasures of the Old West" from the Buffalo Bill Historical Center. *101 Museum Dr., just north of Tahquitz Way (on the south side of the Desert Fashion Plaza), tel. 619/325–7186. Admission: $4 adults, $2 children under 17. (Admission free the first Tues. of every month.) Open Tues.– Fri. 10–4, weekends until 5. Closed Mon. and June–mid-Sept.*

❹ A short drive or distinctly long walk farther south on Palm Canyon is the **Moorten Botanical Garden.** More than 2,000 plant varieties cover the 4-acre site in settings that simulate the

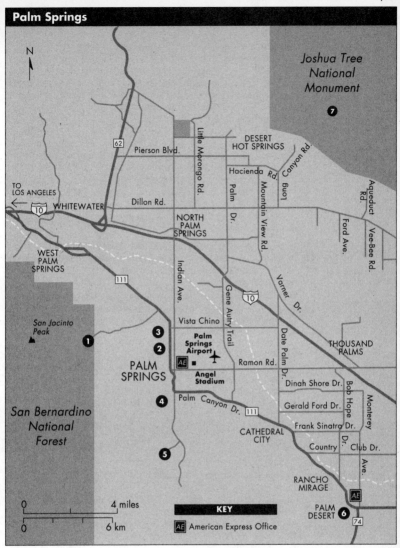

Palm Springs

Desert Museum, **3**
Indian Canyons, **5**
Joshua Tree National Monument, **7**
Living Desert Reserve, **6**

Moorten Botanical Garden, **4**
Palm Springs Aerial Tramway, **1**
Village Green Heritage Center, **2**

plants' original environments. Indian artifacts and rock, crystal, and wood forms are exhibited. *1701 S. Palm Canyon Dr.*

❺ The **Indian Canyons,** 5 miles south of downtown Palm Springs, are the ancestral home of the Agua Caliente Band of Indians. The Indians selected these canyons for their lush oases, abundant water, and wildlife. Even now visitors can see remnants of this life: rock art, house pits and foundations, irrigation ditches, bedrock mortars, pictographs, and stone houses and shelters built atop high cliff walls. Four canyons are open to visitors: Palm Canyon, noted for its lush stand of Washingtonia palms, the largest such stand in the world; Tahquitz, noted for waterfalls and pools; Murray, home of Peninsula bighorn sheep and a herd of wild ponies; and Andreas, where a stand of fan palms contrasts with sharp rock formations. A Trading Post in Palm Canyon has hiking maps, refreshments, Indian art, jewelry, and weavings. *End of S. Palm Canyon Dr., tel. 619/325–5673. Admission: $3.50 adults, $1 children. Open Sept.–June daily 8–5.*

❻ Bighorn sheep, coyotes, eagles, and other desert wildlife roam in naturalistic settings at the **Living Desert Reserve,** in Palm Desert. There is a 6-mile nature walk, a walk through an aviary, a coyote grotto, a desert reptile exhibit, and regularly scheduled animal shows. This is a particularly enjoyable learning experience for children. *47-900 Portola Ave., less than 2 mi south of Hwy. 111, tel. 619/346–5694. Admission: $6 adults, $3 children 3–15. Open daily 9–5, closed mid-June–Aug.*

Time Out The Agua Caliente people got relaxation and relief in the hot springs that flow here. The world-famous **Palm Springs Spa Hotel and Mineral Springs** in town is located on an ancient hot spring. You can sample the spa experience for an hour or longer; visit the inhalation room with its soothing menthol vapors, the steam room, the natural hot mineral spring and cooling room. Facials and massage are also available. *100 N. Indian Canyon Dr., Palm Springs, tel. 619–778–1772. Prices begin at $25. Open daily 8:30–6.*

Joshua Tree National Monument **❼** **Joshua Tree National Monument** is about a one-hour drive from Palm Springs, whether you take I–10 north to Highway 62 to the Oasis Visitor Center or I–10 south to the Cottonwood Visitor Center. The northern part of the park is in the Mojave (or high) Desert and has the Joshua trees. The southern part is Colorado (or low) Desert; in spring this is one of the desert's best wildflower-viewing areas, covered with carpets of white, yellow, purple, and red flowers stretching as far as the eye can see on the hillsides east of I-10. It's possible to take a loop drive through the monument in a single long day; enter the monument by way of the Visitor Center at Twentynine Palms on the east side or at Cottonwood, just east of I–10 south of Indio. Whichever route you select, pack a picnic and water, as facilities are limited in the area.

On the northern route to the national monument, you may want to consider stopping at the **Big Morongo Wildlife Reserve.** Once an Indian village, then a cattle ranch, and now a regional park, the reserve is a serene natural oasis supporting a wide variety of plants, birds, and animals. There is a shaded meadow for picnics and choice hiking trails. *From I–10 or Indian Ave., take Hwy. 62 east to East Dr. Admission free. Open 7:30–sunset.*

The monument itself is immense, complex, and ruggedly beautiful. Its mountains of jagged rock, lush oases shaded by tall, elegant fan palms, and natural cactus gardens mark the meeting place of the Mojave and Colorado deserts. This is prime hiking and exploring country, where you can expect to see such wildlife as coyotes and desert pack rats, and exotic plants such as the red-tipped ocotillo, sharp-barbed cholla cactus, smoke trees, and creamy white yucca. Extensive stands of Joshua trees give the monument its name. The trees were named by early white settlers who thought their unusual forms resembled the Biblical Joshua raising his arms toward heaven. The **Oasis Visitor Center,** outside Twentynine Palms at the eastern edge of the monument, is probably the best place to start. The center has an excellent selection of free and low-cost brochures, books, posters, and maps as well as several educational exhibits. Rangers are on hand to answer questions and offer advice. *Hwy. 62 to the town of Twentynine Palms, follow the signs a short distance south to the Visitor Center. There is a $5-per-vehicle entry fee to the monument.*

Right at the Visitor Center is the **Oasis of Mara.** Inhabited first by Indians and later by prospectors and homesteaders, the oasis now provides a home for birds, small mammals, and other wildlife. Once inside the monument, you will find nine campgrounds with tables, fireplaces, and primitive rest rooms and several picnic areas for day use. Sights in the monument range from the Hidden Valley, a legendary cattle rustlers' hideout reached by a trail winding through massive boulders; and the Lost Horse Mine, a remnant of the gold-mining days; to Keys View, an outstanding scenic point commanding a superb sweep of valley, mountain, and desert. Sunrise and sunset are magic times to be at the monument, when the light throws rocks and trees into high relief before (or after) bathing the hills in brilliant shades of red, orange, and gold. The National Parks Service map available at the Visitor Center tells you where to find these and other impressive sights within the monument.

Palm Springs for Free

Palm Springs Gallery Association (215 N. Palm Canyon Dr.) publishes a walking guide to 22 art and antiques galleries in town, and schedules occasional art walks.

There are two dozen or so municipal and school **tennis courts** scattered throughout Palm Springs that are absolutely free. Check the "Courts and Courses" listing in *Desert Guide*, available at most hotels and at the Convention and Visitors Bureau.

What to See and Do with Children

Children's Museum of the Desert offers hands-on fun in an art-recycling workshop, bakery, garden/science lab, dentist's office, and radio station. *42-501 Rancho Mirage La., Rancho Mirage, tel. 619/346-2900. Open Thurs. 3–7, Fri.–Sat. 9–3. Admission: $2.*

The Dinosaur Gardens are a must-see. Claude Bell designed and built the 150-foot-long brontosaurus and matching Tyrannosaurus rex right off the main highway. The dinosaurs starred in the movie *Pee-wee's Big Adventure. 5800 Seminole*

Dr., Cabazon, just off I–10, just before Hwy. 111, 18 mi north-west of Palm Springs, no phone. Open Wed.–Mon. 9–5.

At the **Palm Springs Swim Center,** an Olympic-size pool has a separate children-only section. Swimming instruction is available for all ages. *405 S. Pavilion, adjacent to the corner of Sunrise Way and Ramon Rd., tel. 619/323–8278. Hours and admission vary by season.*

Children can also make a splash at the **Oasis Water Resort.** Tubing, water slides, "Squirt City," and other watery delights will entertain a wide range of age groups. *1500 Gene Autry Trail, between Hwy. 111 and Ramon Rd., tel. 619/325–7873. Hours and admission vary by season.*

California Angels spring-training baseball games—and the requisite autograph hunt—can make for a fun afternoon *(see* Spectator Sports, below, for more information).

Aerial Tramway *(see* Exploring, above).

The Living Desert *(see* Exploring, above).

Indian Canyons. Hiking and picnic areas, Indian cultural remains *(see* Exploring, above).

Off the Beaten Track

Dogsled races in Palm Springs? Why not . . . ? Snow conditions permitting, the **Moosehead Championship Sled Dog Races** are held in January atop Mt. San Jacinto. Take the Aerial Tramway up. Call 619/325–1449 for more information.

The Eldorado Polo Club (50-950 Madison Blvd., Indio, tel. 619/342–2223), known as the "Winter Polo Capital of the West," is home of world-class polo events including the 1993 U.S. Open Polo Championships, scheduled for October. You can pack a picnic and watch practice matches free during the week; there's a $6 per person charge on weekends.

Hadley's Fruit Orchards (I-10 at Apache Trail, Cabazon) contains a vast selection of dried California fruit, plus nuts, date shakes, and wines. Taste samples before you buy.

Shopping

The Palm Springs area is full of tony boutiques and lively art galleries. The resort community also has several large air-conditioned indoor malls with major department stores and chic shops. El Paseo in nearby Palm Desert is the desert's other shopping mecca, with its own collection of upscale and elegant galleries and shops. Most stores are open 10–5 or 6, Monday–Saturday, and a fair number are open on Sunday, typically noon–5.

Shopping Districts **Palm Canyon Drive** is Palm Springs' main shopping destination. What began as a dusty two-way dirt road is now a one-way, three-lane thoroughfare with parking on both sides. Its shopping core extends from Alejo Road on the north to Ramon Road on the south. Expect to find everything your heart desires—though your wallet may have a tough time keeping up. Furs, jewelry, sportswear, home furnishings, books, shoes, and crafts will tempt you on this busy street. Anchoring the center of the drive is the Desert Fashion Plaza, which features such big names as Saks Fifth Avenue, I. Magnin, Gucci, La Mariposa, and Sabina Children's Fashions.

The Courtyard (777 E. Tahquitz Canyon Way, tel. 619/320–9772) at the Bank of Palm Springs Center brings Paris to Palm Springs. Expect to be dazzled by the high fashion of Rodier and Yves St. Laurent. There's also a six-screen movie theater.

El Paseo Village is touted as a true shopping experience rather than just another shopping center. The complex's architecture has a Spanish motif, and the shops are clustered among flower-lined paths and fountained courtyards along a 2-mile elegant avenue. There's a fine selection of apparel and specialty stores, investment-quality art dealers, and home-furnishing shops. Don't miss Polo/Ralph Lauren (73-111 El Paseo, tel. 619/340–1414), featuring classic fashions and accessories for men and women, and Cabale Cachet (73-111 El Paseo, tel. 619/346–5805), for a collection of European haute couture.

The Palm Desert Town Center is an enclosed mall anchored by five major department stores, including Bullocks and The May Co. There are 140 shops, seven movie theaters, an Ice Capades Chalet, and a child-care center.

Rancho las Palmas, at Highway 111 and Bob Hope Drive, Rancho Mirage, is an open-air center containing 15 home-furnishing stores, interior-design studios, and restaurants.

Department Stores The exclusive **Saks Fifth Avenue** (201 N. Palm Canyon Dr., tel. 619/327–4126) is a department store with class, so you should expect cutting-edge fashions but no bargain prices. Other major department stores can be found in the various malls listed above.

Specialty Shops Although Palm Springs is known for glamour and high prices, *Discount* the city does offer bargains if you know where to look. Several outlets can be found in the **Loehmann's Shopping Center** (2500 North Palm Canyon Dr.), including **Fieldcrest-Cannon** (tel. 619/322–3229), **Dansk** (tel. 619/320–3304), and **Loehmann's** (tel. 619/322–0388). **Desert Hills Factory Stores** (48650 Seminole Rd., Cabazon, tel. 714/849–6641) is an outlet center with about 50 name fashion shops selling at a discount.

Golf Equipment **John Riley Golf** (72-060 Hwy. 111 in El Paseo in Palm Desert, tel. 619/341–6994) offers personally fitted golf clubs.
Nevada Bob's Discount Golf & Tennis (4721 E. Palm Canyon Dr., Palm Springs, tel. 619/324–0196) offers a large selection of golf and tennis equipment, clothing, and accessories.

Participant Sports

The "Desert Guide" from *Palm Springs Life*, available at most hotels and the Convention and Visitors Bureau, lists "Courts and Courses." The Convention and Visitors Bureau also publishes a handy "Desert Golf Guide" describing courses open to the public, private/reciprocal courses, and annual tournaments; a map will help with locations.

Bicycling There are more than 35 miles of bike trails, with six mapped-out city tours. Trail maps are available at the **Palm Springs Recreation Department** (401 S. Pavilion, tel. 619/323–8276) and bike-rental shops. You can rent a bike at **Mac's Native Cyclery** (70-155 Hwy. 111, Rancho Mirage, tel. 619/327–5721) and **Burnett's Bicycle Barn** (429 S. Sunrise Way, tel. 619/325–7844).

Golf Palm Springs is known as the "Winter Golf Capital of the World." The area has more than 70 golf courses, a number of which are open to the public. Among these are the **Palm Springs Municipal Golf Course** (1885 Golf Club Dr., tel. 619/328–1005); **Fairchilds Bel-Aire Greens Country Club** (1001 S. El Cielo Rd.; Palm Springs, tel. 619/327–0332); and **Desert Dunes Golf Course** (19300 Palm Dr., North Palm Springs, tel. 619/329–2941), a Robert Trent Jones course nominated as one of the best new courses in the country. Don't be surprised to spot well-known politicians and Hollywood stars on the greens.

Hiking Nature trails abound in the Indian Canyons, Mt. San Jacinto State Park and Wilderness, and Living Desert Reserve (*see* Exploring, above).

Physical Fitness The **Clark Hatch Physical Fitness Center** (Hyatt Regency Suites Hotel, 285 N. Palm Canyon Dr., tel. 619/322–2778) is the latest in a worldwide chain of Hatch health clubs. The facilities are high-quality and low-key. Fees are $10 daily, $65 monthly.

Tennis Of the 350 or so tennis courts in the area, the following are open to the public: the **Palm Springs Tennis Center** (1300 Baristo Rd., tel. 619/320–0020), nine lighted courts; **Ruth Hardy Park** (Tamarisk and Caballeros, no phone), eight lighted courts, with no court fee; and **Demuth Park** (4375 Mesquite Ave., tel. 619/325–8265), four lighted courts.

Spectator Sports

Baseball The **California Angels** hold their annual spring training and play several exhibition games in Palm Springs during March and early April. Games typically begin at 1 PM at California Angels Stadium, located on Baristo Road between Sunrise Way and Farrell. Reserved and general admission seats are available. Call 619/327–1266 for more information.

Golf More than 100 golf tournaments are presented in Palm Springs; the two most popular are the **Bob Hope Desert Classic** (Jan.) and the **Dinah Shore Championship** (Mar. or Apr.). Call the Convention and Visitors Bureau (*see* above) for exact dates and places.

Tennis The *Newsweek* **Champions Cup** tournament (Feb. or Mar.), held at Hyatt Grand Champions Resort in Indian Wells, attracts the likes of Boris Becker and Yannick Noah. For tickets, tel. 619/341–2757.

Dining

So many L.A. residents have second homes or condos "down in the Springs" that local restaurateurs try to outdo themselves to match the Big City's standards—and more and more are succeeding. Most of the restaurants listed below are on or near Highway 111 running from Palm Springs to Palm Desert.

Category	Cost*
Expensive	over $35
Moderate	$15–$30
Inexpensive	under $15

* *per person, without tax (8.25%), service, or drinks*

Palm Springs
Expensive
Melvyn's Restaurant. "Lifestyles of the Rich and Famous" calls this Old World–style spot "one of the 10 best." It isn't, but the French-Continental cooking is above average. Snugly nestled in the gardens of the Ingleside Inn, weekend brunch here is a Palm Springs tradition. There is also a piano bar. *200 W. Ramon Rd., tel. 619/325–2323. Reservations advised. Jacket required. MC, V.*

Le Vallauris. Formerly a private club, this stylish, rather romantic restaurant's cuisine ranges from classic French to nouvelle desert. *385 W. Tahquitz–McCallum Way, tel. 619/325–5059. Reservations advised. Jacket advised. Valet parking. AE, DC, MC, V.*

Moderate–Expensive
Lyon's English Grille. When was the last time you had real hon-est-to-goodness roast beef and Yorkshire pudding as only the Brits can make it? Lyon's has it, and other old-country favorites. Good value and good food make this a popular stop for the locals. *233 E. Palm Canyon Dr., tel. 619/327–1551. Reservations suggested. Dress: casual. AE, DC, MC, V. Closed for lunch and in summer.*

Moderate
Bono. Palm Springs' former mayor, Sonny Bono, serves the southern Italian dishes like those his mother used to make. It's a favorite feeding station for show-biz folk and the curious, and a good place for pasta, chicken, veal, and scampi dishes. Outdoor dining is available. *1700 N. Indian Ave., tel. 619/322–6200. Reservations advised. Dress: casual. Valet parking. AE, D, DC, MC, V. Closed for lunch weekends.*

Brussels Cafe. The best spot in town for people-watching is this sidewalk café in the heart of Palm Canyon Drive. Try the Belgian waffles or homemade pâté. Beers from around the world are featured, and there's entertainment nightly. *109 S. Palm Canyon Dr., tel. 619/320–4177. Reservations required. Dress: casual. AE, D, MC, V.*

Cafe St. James. From the plant-filled balcony you can watch the passing parade below, and dine on Mediterranean-Italian cuisine. *254 N. Palm Canyon Dr., tel. 619/320–8041. Reservations advised. Dress: casual. AE, DC, MC, V. Closed for lunch and Mon.*

Las Casuelas Original. A longtime favorite of residents and visitors alike, this restaurant offers great (in size and taste) margaritas and average Mexican dishes: crab enchilada, carne asada, lobster Ensenada. It gets very, very crowded during the winter months. *368 N. Palm Canyon Dr., tel. 619/325–3213. Reservations advised. Dress: casual. AE, MC, V.*

Flower Drum. Related to the highly popular New York Flower Drum, this health-conscious Chinese restaurant features Hunan, Peking, Shanghai, Canton, and Szechuan cuisines in a setting meant to resemble a Chinese village. *424 S. Indian Ave., tel. 619/323–3020. Reservations advised. Dress: casual. AE, MC, V.*

Riccio's. Tony Riccio, formerly of the Marquis and Martoni's, in Hollywood, serves the old-fashioned Italian food that comforts his steady patrons: fettuccine Alfredo, veal piccata, chicken Vesuvio, and a luscious Italian cheesecake. *2155 N. Palm Canyon Dr., tel. 619/325–2369. Reservations advised. Jacket required. Closed for lunch weekends.*

Inexpensive
Di Amico's Steak House. Hearty eaters will enjoy this early California-style restaurant. Prime eastern corn-fed beef, liver steak vaquero, and Son-of-a-Gun stew are featured. *500 E.*

Palm Canyon Dr., tel. 619/325–9191. Reservations advised. Dress: casual. MC, V. Closed for lunch Sun.

Elmer's Pancake and Steak House. Forget about Aunt Jemima. Elmer's offers 25 varieties of pancakes and waffles. There are steaks, chicken, and seafood on the dinner menu. A children's menu is also available. *1030 E. Palm Canyon Dr., tel. 619/327–8419. Dress: casual. AE, D, DC, MC, V.*

Louise's Pantry. A local landmark, in the center of downtown Palm Springs for almost 40 years, the 1940s-style down-home cooking at Louise's features chicken and dumplings and short ribs of beef. You can get soup, salad, entrée, beverage, and dessert for under $15. There's usually a line to get in. *124 S. Palm Canyon Dr., tel. 619/325–5124. Dress: casual. No credit cards.*

Cathedral City, Rancho Mirage, Palm Desert
Expensive

Dominick's. An old favorite of Frank Sinatra's and what's left of his "rat pack," the steaks, pasta, and veal dishes here are the order of the day. *70-030 Hwy. 111, tel. 619/324–1711. Reservations advised. Dress: casual. AE, DC, MC, V. Closed for lunch, and Mon. and Tues.*

Mama Gina's. Generally considered the best Italian food in the Palm Springs area, this attractive, simply furnished trattoria was opened by the son of the original Mama Gina in Florence, Italy. There is an open kitchen where you can watch the chef from Tuscany prepare such specialties as deep-fried artichokes, fettuccine with porcini mushrooms, and prawns with artichoke and zucchini. The soups are robust. *73- 705 El Paseo, tel. 619/568–9898. Reservations required. Dress: casual. AE, DC, MC, V.*

Wally's Desert Turtle. If price is no object, and you like plush, gilded decor, then this is where to come. You'll be surrounded by the golden names of Palm Springs and Hollywood society, and served old-fashioned French cooking: rack of lamb, imported Dover sole, braised sea bass, veal Oscar, chicken Normande, and dessert soufflés. *71-775 Hwy. 111, tel. 619/568–9321. Reservations required. Jacket required. Valet parking. AE, MC, V. Closed for lunch Sat.–Thurs.*

Moderate

The Rusty Pelican. A seafood restaurant in the desert? Why not? This restaurant has fresh seafood flown in from both coasts, then serves it up in a nautical atmosphere. The Oyster Bar shucks to order. There's live entertainment and dancing. *72-191 Hwy. 111, Palm Desert, tel. 619/346–8065. Dress: casual. Reservations suggested. AE, DC, MC, V. Closed for lunch.*

The Wilde Goose. The award-winning restaurant is popular with celebrities for its beef and lamb Wellington, and five varieties of duck. A specialty of the house is duck with apricot and Triple Sec sauce. The food and the service here are dependable. *67-938 Hwy. 111, Cathedral City, tel. 619/328–5775. Reservations recommended. Dress: casual. AE, D, DC, MC, V. Closed for lunch.*

Inexpensive

Stuft Pizza. What would any listing be without at least one pizza parlor? This one is popular for its thick, Chicago-style crusts and generous heaps of fresh toppings. *67-555 Hwy. 111, Cathedral City, tel. 619/321–2583. MC, V.*

Indian Wells
Expensive
★

Sirocco. This restaurant in the Stouffer Esmeralda Hotel features dishes of the Mediterranean shores: a splendid Spanish paella, roast lamb encrusted with herbs and peppercorns, seafood pastas. This is probably the best hotel restaurant in Palm Springs, both for its food and its gracious, impeccable service. *44400 Indian Wells La., tel. 619/773–4444. Reservations rec-*

ommended. Jacket required. AE, D, DC, MC, V. Closed for lunch.

La Quinta
Expensive
★

Dolly Cunard's. This restaurant in a converted country-style home features a Franco-Italian menu. The warm atmosphere and inventive cuisine, such as charred chili with four cheeses, cannelloni di casa, and salmon in parchment with crème fraîche and fresh herbs, have made it the area's biggest hit. *73-045 Calle Cadiz, tel. 619/564-4443. Reservations advised. Jacket and tie requested. AE, MC, V. Closed for lunch, and June–Sept.*

Lodging

One of the reasons Palm Springs attracts so many celebrities, entertainment-industry honchos, and other notables is its stock of luxurious hotels. There is a full array of resorts, inns, clubs, spas, lodges, and condos, from small and private to big and bustling. Room rates cover an enormous range—from $40 to $1,600 a night—and also vary widely from summer to winter. It is not unusual for a hotel to drop its rates from 50% to 60% during the summer (June through early Sept.). For a growing number of off-season travelers, the chance to stay in a $180 room for $60 is an offer they just can't refuse.

Don't even think of visiting here during winter and spring holiday seasons without advance reservations. The Palm Springs Chamber of Commerce (tel. 619/325–1577), Desert Resorts Bureau (tel. 619/770–9000), and Palm Springs Tourism (tel. 800/347–7746) can help you with hotel reservations and information. For a more comprehensive hotel guide complete with prices, pick up a copy of the *Convention and Visitors Bureau Accommodations Guide* (tel. 800/347–7746).

The most highly recommended lodgings are indicated by a star★.

Category	Cost*
Very Expensive	over $150
Expensive	$100–$150
Moderate	$70–$100
Inexpensive	under $70

**double occupancy*

Rentals. Condos, apartments, and even individual houses may be rented by the day, week, month, or for longer periods. Rates start at about $400 a week for a one-bedroom condo, $750–$1,000 a week for two bedrooms, and $3,200 for a three-bedroom house for a month. Contact **The Rental Connection** (Box 8567, Palm Springs 92263, tel. 619/320–7336; in the U.S., 800/468–3776; in CA, 800/232–3776; in Canada, 800/458–3776).

Palm Springs
Very Expensive

Autry Resort Hotel. This venerable resort has recently undergone a complete renovation. Rooms are in two buildings and bungalows on 13 landscaped acres. The place is decked out for a number of activities, including tennis instruction at the Reed Anderson Tennis School, and dining and entertainment are offered nightly. *4200 E. Palm Canyon Dr., 92262, tel. 619/328–1171 or 800/443-6328. 187 units. Facilities: restaurant, 3 pools,*

Jacuzzis, 6 lighted tennis courts, fitness center with sauna and massage services. AE, DC, MC, V.

Hyatt Regency Suites. Located adjacent to the downtown Desert Fashion Plaza, this hotel's striking six-story asymmetrical lobby houses two restaurants, including the popular outdoor Cafe 285. *285 N. Palm Canyon Dr., 92262, tel. 619/322–9000 or 800/233–1234. 194 suites. Facilities: 2 restaurants, pool, health club. AE, DC, MC, V.*

La Mancha Private Pool Villas and Court Club. Only four blocks from downtown Palm Springs, this Hollywood-style retreat blocks out the rest of the world with plenty of panache. Villas are oversize and opulent; one is equipped with a screening room and private pool. *444 N. Avenida Caballeros, tel. 619/323–1773. 54 rooms. Facilities: tennis courts, paddle tennis courts, pool, croquet lawns. AE, DC, MC, V.*

Palm Springs Hilton Resort and Racquet Club. The cool, white marble elegance of this plant-filled resort hotel, just off Palm Canyon Drive, and its two superb restaurants make it a popular choice for visitors to the city. *400 E. Tahquitz Way, 92262, tel. 619/320–6868 or 800/522–6900. 260 rooms. Facilities: 2 restaurants, pool, tennis, spa, Jacuzzi. AE, DC, MC, V.*

The Palm Springs Marquis. Posh, desert-modern style with pastel color schemes, marble, and greenery mark this centrally located hotel. *150 S. Indian Canyon Dr., 92262, tel. 619/322–2121 or 800/223–1050. 264 rooms. Facilities: restaurant, cafe, 2 pools, tennis, fitness center, Jacuzzi, meeting and convention facilities. AE, DC, MC, V.*

★ **Spa Hotel and Mineral Springs.** Like the name says, the therapeutic mineral springs and the wide variety of water, sports, and fitness activities are the attractions here. *100 N. Indian Canyon Dr., 92262, tel. 619/325–1461. 230 rooms. Facilities: restaurant, cocktail lounge, mineral springs, pool, 35 whirlpool tubs, fitness center, tennis. AE, DC, MC, V.*

Sundance Villas. Beautifully decorated, spacious villas include fireplace, wet bar, kitchen, and private patio for dining or sunning. Each villa has a private pool and Jacuzzi. This is not a place for the weak of pocketbook. *303 Cabrillo Rd., Palm Springs 92262, tel. 619/325–3888. 19 villas. Facilities: tennis, Jacuzzi, pool. AE, MC, V.*

Expensive **Ingleside Inn.** This hacienda-style inn has individually deco-
★ rated rooms that are furnished with antiques. Each room is equipped with a steam shower and whirlpool. The gardens on the grounds are lush and lovely. *200 W. Ramon Rd., 92262, tel. 619/325–0046. 29 rooms. Facilities: pool, Jacuzzi. AE, MC, V.*

Racquet Club of Palm Springs. Built by Charlie Farrell and Ralph Bellamy in 1933, the Racquet Club marked the beginning of Palm Spring's glamour era. The grounds cover 25 acres, and it is said that Marilyn Monroe was "discovered" on the tennis courts here. *2743 N. Indian Canyon Dr., 92262, tel. 619/325–1281. 124 units. Facilities: lounge, 4 pools, Jacuzzi, fitness center, 12 tennis courts. AE, DC, MC, V.*

Moderate **Courtyard by Marriott.** This property represents part of the Marriott chain's effort to expand into comfortable, smaller hotels offering a good value. The concept works nicely. *1300 Tahquitz Canyon Way, tel. 619/322–6100. 149 rooms. Facilities: restaurant, pool, fitness center, Jacuzzi, tennis. AE, DC, MC, V.*

Mira Loma Hotel. The small scale and friendly atmosphere makes this hotel popular with European guests. Rooms and suites have eclectic decor, some Oriental, some 1940s Hollywood style; and all have refrigerators, patios, and fireplaces. Marilyn Monroe slept here. Really. *1420 N. Indian Canyon Dr., 92262, tel. 619/320–1178. 12 rooms. Facilities: pool. AE, MC, V.*

Tuscany Manor Apartment-Hotel. The lovely one- and two-bedroom apartments in this hotel are furnished simply, but with taste. Esther Williams shot her first movie here. *350 Chino Canyon Rd., 92262, tel. 619/325–2349. 24 units. Facilities: pool, theraputic pool. D, MC, V.*

Villa Royale. In this charming bed-and-breakfast, each room is individually decorated with a European theme. Some rooms have private Jacuzzis, fireplaces, kitchens. The grounds feature lush gardens. *1620 Indian Trail, 92264, tel. 619/327–2314. 34 rooms. Facilities: pool. AE, MC, V.*

Inexpensive **Monte Vista Hotel.** Boasting a prime Palm Canyon Drive location, this hotel has comfortable accommodations. *414 N. Palm Canyon Dr., 92262, tel. 619/325–5641. 32 rooms. Facilities: pool, Jacuzzi, shuffleboard. AE, MC, V.*

Mt. View Inn. A friendly atmosphere and convenient location make this small inn a great favorite of people staying in town for more than a couple of days. The rooms have kitchens and patios. *200 S. Cahuilla Rd., 92262, tel. 619/325–5281. 12 rooms. Facilities: 2 pools, Jacuzzi. Pets allowed. No credit cards.*

Westward Ho Seven Seas Hotel. A swimming pool, therapy pool, and cocktail lounge grace this modest property. *701 E. Palm Canyon Dr., 92262, tel. 619/320–2700. 207 rooms. Facilities: lounge, pool, therapy pool. AE, MC, V.*

Outside **Doubletree Resort at Desert Princess.** This luxury resort hotel
Palm Springs has a full slate of amenities. *67–967 Vista Chino, Cathedral*
Very Expensive *City 92234, tel. 619/322–7000. 277 rooms, 12 suites. Facilities: 3 restaurants, golf course, pool, Jacuzzi, tennis and racquetball courts. AE, DC, MC, V.*

Hyatt Grand Champions Resort. This elegant resort takes its fun seriously with two 18-hole golf courses, tennis courts featuring three court surfaces, the largest tennis stadium in the West, and a health club with a full complement of workout equipment and pampering treatments. There are three restaurants: Trattoria, mixing California and Italian cusines; Charlies, featuring southwestern specialities; and Austin's, for steak and seafood. *44-600 Indian Wells La., Indian Wells 92210, tel. 619/341–1000. 336 rooms. AE, DC, MC, V.*

Marriott's Desert Springs Resort and Spa. The most luxurious spa facilities in the desert, two 18-hole golf courses, and a complex of waterways with boat transport around the resort let you know this is no run-of-the-mill resort. There are 16 tennis courts, a 25-yard lap pool, Jacuzzis, exercise lawn, five restaurants, and a European spa with Turkish steam room and Finnish sauna. *74855 Country Club Dr., Palm Desert 92260, tel. 619/341–2211. 891 rooms. AE, DC, MC, V.*

★ **The Ritz Carlton Rancho Mirage.** The poshest gem in the desert collection is located on a 650-foot-high plateau in the foothills of the Santa Rosas, adjacent to a reserve for bighorn sheep. Needless to say, it has all the amenities you would expect from one of the world's classiest hotel chains: restaurants, entertainment, pools, bar, 10-court tennis center, 9-hole putting green. *68-900 Frank Sinatra Dr., Rancho Mirage 92270, tel. 619/321–8282. 240 rooms including 19 suites. AE, DC, MC, V.*

Stouffer Esmeralda Resort. This is a luxurious Mediterranean-style resort with all the amenities a Sybarite could desire. An eight-story atrium lobby contains original art, lush greenery, fountains, lakes, and waterways. Spacious, well-appointed guest rooms have sitting areas, balconies, and refreshment centers. There are two 18-hole golf courses, seven tennis courts, fitness center with sauna and steam room, Jacuzzis, three swimming pools including one with a sandy beach and another with a 10-foot wall of water. There are restaurants, bars, and cocktail lounges. *44-400 Indian Wells La., Indian Wells 92210-9971, tel. 619/773-4444 or 800/552-4386. 560 rooms and suites. AE, DC, MC, V.*

Westin Mission Hills Resort. This is a luxurious 360-acre resort with two 8-hole golf courses, seven nightlighted tennis courts, three swimming pools, a 60-foot water slide, Jacuzzis, fitness center, and children's activities. There are two restaurants, plus lounges, snack bars, and a pool bar. *71333 Dinah Shore Dr., Rancho Mirage 92270, tel. 619/328-5955. 512 rooms. AE, DC, MC, V.*

Expensive **Two Bunch Palms.** Reputedly built by Al Capone as an escape from the pressures of gangsterdom in 1920s Chicago, this collection of white-walled villas on 250 acres is still something of a secret hideaway. Antiques recapture the flavor of the pre-World War II years. There are palm-shaded mineral pools, tennis courts, and a restaurant. *67-425 Two Bunch Palms Trail, Desert Hot Springs 92240, tel. 619/329-8791 or 800/472-4334. 44 villas. AE, MC, V.*

The Arts

For complete listings of upcoming events, pick up a copy of *Palm Springs Life* magazine or *Palm Springs Life's Desert Guide*, a free monthly publication found in any hotel.

The McCallum Theatre (73-000 Fred Waring Dr., Palm Desert, tel. 619/340-2787), in the Bob Hope Cultural Center, is probably the desert's premier venue for the performing arts. The theater hosts touring productions of plays and musicals, and performers such as the Canadian Brass, Michael Feinstein, and Vicki Carr.

The Annenberg Theatre (101 Museum Dr., just north of Tahquitz Way, on the south side of the Desert Fashion Plaza, tel. 619/325-7186 or 619/325-4490) of the Palm Springs Desert Museum is the area's other major arts center. Featured performers have ranged from the Second City improv troupe to Liza Minnelli, Frank Sinatra, and a slew of international musicians in its Sunday Afternoon Concerts series.

Concerts **The College of the Desert** (43-500 Monterey Ave., Palm Desert, tel. 619/346-8041) is where the annual Joanna Hodges Piano Conference and Competition is held.

Theater **VPG Theatre** (225 S. El Cielo Rd., tel. 619/320-9898) is the home of the Valley Players Guild, and offers a lively mix of theatrical events.

Nightlife

Two good sources for finding current nightlife attractions are the *Desert Sun* (the local newspaper) and *Guide* magazine, a monthly publication distributed free at most downtown merchants' counters.

Live entertainment, ranging from soft dinner music to song-and-dance numbers, is frequently found in the city's hotels and restaurants. The piano bars at **Rennick's** and **Melvyn's Ingleside Inn** are popular.

Jazz **Hank's Fish House** (in the Holiday Inn, 155 S. Belardo, Palm Springs, tel. 619/778–7171) is a cool place for light jazz every evening, followed by more serious jamming mixed with dancing after 9 PM. For refreshments, look to Hank's oyster bar.

Discos Between the flashing lights of its Top 40 disco and the retro-memorabilia in its new '50s–'60s room, **Cecil's** (1775 E. Palm Canyon Dr., tel. 619/320–4202) is bound to keep you dancing. There's dancing to live country music at the **Cactus Corral** (67–501 E. Palm Canyon Dr., Cathedral City, tel. 619/321–8558).

Pompeii (67–399 Hwy. 111, Palm Springs, tel. 619/328–5800) is a large disco playing Top 40 music. You'll know you've found this lively joint when you see the fiery torches out front. **Zelda's** (169 N. Indian Canyon Dr., Palm Springs, tel. 619/325–2375) is another active spot featuring talent and fashion shows, hot-body competitions, and limbo contests.

Comedy Clubs **The Comedy Haven.** Stand-up comics and improv groups are dished up here with American/Italian fare. *Desert Fashion Plaza (enter parking lot from Tahquitz Way), tel. 619/320–7855.*

16 The Mojave Desert and Death Valley

By Aaron
Sugarman

When most people put together their "must-see" list of California attractions, the desert isn't often among the top contenders. What with the heat and the vast, seemingly empty tracts of land, the desert is certainly no Disneyland. But then, that's precisely why it deserves a closer look. The desert is truly one of the last frontiers. It offers an overwhelming richness of natural beauty: rolling waves of sand dunes, black cinder cones thrusting up hundreds of feet into the air from a blistered desert floor, riotous sheets of wildflowers, the bizarre shape of the Joshua tree basking in an orange glow at sunset, unspoiled valleys surrounded by rings of mountains, and an abundant silence that is both dramatic and startling.

Unlike cities, which regularly tear down and build over their history, the progress of man is preserved with striking clarity in the desert. An archaeological site in Calico was determined to be approximately 200,000 years old; stone tools and other artifacts uncovered there are believed to be the oldest evidence of human activity in the Americas. Petroglyphs—prehistoric rock art—are scattered throughout the California deserts. There is a bewildering array of images, deer and mountain sheep, human figures, spears and shields, and seemingly abstract geometric patterns, carved from 2,000 to 10,000 years ago. The more recent, and much romanticized, past is on display, too. Ghost towns, mills, old rail stations, and other pieces of the Old West dot the countryside.

What is probably most surprising about the desert is its accessibility. The days of the 20-mule-team wagons and the railroad, which brought prosperity to the towns it reached in the late 1800s and early 1900s, are long gone. A surprisingly large portion of the desert can be seen from the comfort of an air-conditioned car. And don't despair if you are without air-conditioning—just avoid the middle of the day and the middle of the summer, good advice for all desert travel. Believe everything you've ever heard about desert heat; it can be brutal. A temperature of 134° was once recorded at Furnace Creek in Death Valley, the hottest place on the planet. But during mornings and evenings, particularly in the spring and fall, the temperature ranges from cool and crisp to pleasantly warm and dry: perfect for hiking and driving. And while the air at Death Valley can certainly be quite still, much of the desert is breezy, if not downright windy.

The Mojave Desert begins just north of the San Bernardino mountains along the northern edge of Los Angeles, and extends north 150 miles into the Eureka Valley and east 200 miles to the Colorado River. Death Valley lies north and east of the Mojave, bordering Nevada. Mojave, with elevations ranging from 3,000 to 5,000 feet above sea level, is known as the High Desert; Death Valley, with points at almost 300 feet below sea level, is the lowest spot in the United States.

Due to the vast size of California's deserts, an area about as big as Ohio, and the weather, careful planning is essential for an enjoyable desert adventure. Conveniences, facilities, trails, gas stations, and supermarkets do not lurk just around the corner from many desert sights. Different pieces of the desert can be easily handled in day trips, more extensive exploring will require overnight stays; it's a good idea to know in advance which approach you will be taking. Reliable maps are a must, as signage is limited, and, in some places, nonexistent. The Automobile Club of America (AAA) is probably the best source for maps. Other important accessories include: a compass, extra food and water, sunglasses, extra clothes (for wind or cool nights), a hat (if you're going to do any walking around in the sun), and plenty of sunscreen. Other than that, a pair of binoculars can come in handy, and don't forget your camera: You're likely to see things you've never seen before.

Getting Around

By Car   The Mojave is shaped like a giant *L*, with one leg north and the other east. To travel north through the Mojave, take I–10 east out of Los Angeles to I–15 north. Just through the Cajon Pass, pick up U.S. 395, which runs north through Victor Valley, Boron, the Rand Mining District, and China Lake. To travel east, continue on I–15 to Barstow. From Barstow there are two routes: I–40, which passes through the mountainous areas of San Bernardino County, whisks by the Providence mountains and enters Arizona at Needles (noted for being the hometown of Snoopy's brother Spike in the "Peanuts" cartoons); or the more northerly I–15, which passes south of Calico, near Devil's Playground and the Kelso Sand Dunes, and then veers northeast toward Las Vegas.

Death Valley National Monument can be entered from the southeast or the west. Exit U.S. 395 at either State Highway 190 or 178 to enter from the west. From the southeast: Take Highway 127 north from I–15 and then link up with either Highway 178, which travels west into the valley and then cuts north past Funeral Peak, Badwater, Dante's View, and Zabriskie Point before meeting up with Highway 190 at Furnace Creek, or continue on Highway 127 north for 28 miles and then take Highway 190 west straight into the middle of Death Valley.

Guided Tours

The following organizations regularly sponsor hikes, tours, and outings in the California deserts. Call or write them for more information.

Audubon Society (Western Division, 555 Audubon Pl., Sacramento, CA 95825, tel. 916/481–5332).
California Native Plant Society (909 12th St., Suite 116, Sacramento, CA 95814, tel. 916/447–CNPS).
Nature Conservancy (785 Market St., San Francisco, CA 94103, tel. 415/777–0487).
Sierra Club (730 Polk St., San Francisco, CA 94109, tel. 415/776–2211).

Important Addresses and Numbers

Tourist Information   **Bureau of Land Management** (BLM) (California Desert District Office, 6221 Box Springs Blvd., Riverside 92507, tel. 619/375–7125) can also provide information on BLM campgrounds.

Emergencies   **BLM Rangers** (tel. 714/383–5652). **Police:** *San Bernardino County Sheriff* (tel. 619/256–1796). **Hospital:** *Community Hospital* (Barstow, tel. 619/256–1761).

Exploring

Numbers in the margin correspond to points of interest on the Mojave Desert map.

Although the Mojave Desert is a sprawling space, many of its visitable attractions are conveniently on a north–south axis along U.S. 395 and Highway 178, and an east–west axis that runs between I–15 and I–40. We'll describe tours stretching roughly 120 miles along each axis, and a third tour that winds its way through Death Valley, which is between the two routes. Keep in mind that there is a very limited number of hotels in the desert, so if you plan to spend the night somewhere, make sure your tour leaves you time to get to places like Furnace Creek in Death Valley, or Barstow, where there are rooms to be found.

The Western Mojave

① On I–15, just before you reach U.S. 395 on the northbound tour, you cross Cajon Pass, riding over the infamous **San Andreas Fault**—an apocalyptic way to start a desert trip.

② About 70 miles later you enter the **Rand Mining District,** consisting of the towns of Randsburg, Red Mountain, and Johannesburg. Randsburg is one of the few authentic gold-mining communities that hasn't become a ghost town. The town first boomed with the discovery of gold in the Rand Mountains in 1895, and along with the neighboring settlements grew to support the successful Yellow Aster Mine. Rich tungsten ore was discovered during World War I and silver in 1919. All told, the money brought in by these precious metals is estimated at more than $35 million. Randsburg still sports its authentic Old West heritage. The picturesque town has some original Gold Rush buildings, plus a few antiques shops, a general store, and the **Randsburg Desert Museum,** which is crammed with mining and frontier-life memorabilia. *U.S. 395 to Johannesburg, then follow the signs 1 mi southwest to Randsburg. The museum, tel. 619/374–2111, is open weekends and holidays, 10–5.*

③ Just to the northwest of the Rand Mining District is **Red Rock Canyon State Park.** The canyon is a feast for the eyes with its layers of pink, white, red, rust, and brown rocks. Entering the park from the south, you pass through a narrow, steep-walled gorge and enter a wide bowl tinted pink by what was once hot volcanic ash. The human history of this area goes back some 20,000 years to the ancient canyon dwellers known only as the Old People. Mojave Indians roamed the land for several hundred years until Gold Rush fever hit the region in the mid- to late 1800s; remains of mining operations dot the countryside. The canyon was later invaded by filmmakers, and has starred in numerous westerns. The state park can be found on either side of Highway 14 about 10 miles south of where it meets U.S. 395. The ranger station is northwest on Abbott Drive from Highway 14.

④ The nearby **Petroglyph Canyons** provide one of the desert's most amazing spectacles. The two canyons, commonly called Big and Little Petroglyph, contain what is probably the greatest concentration of rock art in the country. Scratched or pecked into the shiny desert varnish (oxidized minerals) that coats the canyon's dark basaltic rocks are thousands of images. Some are figures of animals and people, some seemingly abstract—maybe just the doodles of ancient man, and all are exceptionally preserved and protected. The feeling of living

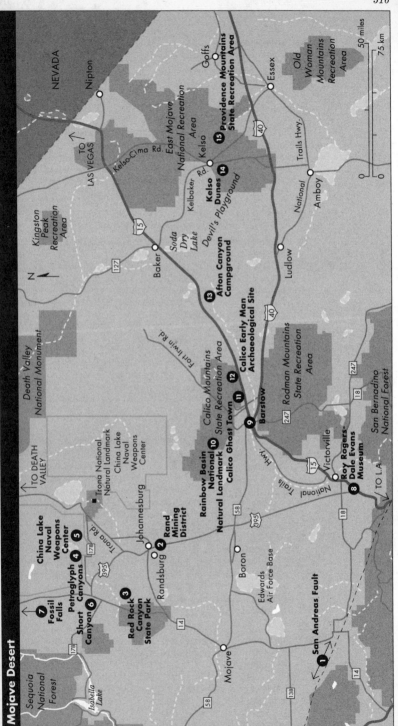

Mojave Desert

NEVADA

Niplon

Kingston Peak Recreation Area

Death Valley National Monument

TO DEATH VALLEY

TO LAS VEGAS

Kelso-Cima Rd.

East Mojave National Recreation Area

Goffs

15 Providence Mountains State Recreation Area

Essex

Old Woman Mountains Recreation Area

50 miles

75 km

Kelbaker Rd.

Kelso

14 Kelso Dunes

Devil's Playground

127

Soda Dry Lake

15

Baker

Trails Hwy.

Amboy

National Trails Hwy.

Ludlow

40

13 Afton Canyon Campground

Calico Early Man Archaeological Site

N

Fort Irwin Rd.

Calico Mountains State Recreation Area

12

11

Rodman Mountains State Recreation Area

247

18

Trona National Natural Landmark

China Lake Naval Weapons Center

9 Barstow

247

San Bernardino National Forest

Victorville

8 Roy Rogers-Dale Evans Museum

10 Rainbow Basin National Natural Landmark

Calico Ghost Town

15

National Trails Hwy.

China Lake Naval Weapons Center 5

4

Petroglyph Canyons

Johannesburg

2 Rand Mining District

58

Randsburg

395

TO L.A.

18

7 Fossil Falls

Trona Rd.

178

395

6 Short Canyons

3 Red Rock Canyon State Park

14

Boron

Edwards Air Force Base

138

58

Mojave

14

Sequoia National Forest

178

Isabella Lake

San Andreas Fault

1

⑤ history is incredible. The canyons are in the **U.S. Naval Weapons Center at China Lake,** and access is limited. Weekend tours must be arranged in advance through the **Maturango Museum** (China Lake Blvd. and Las Flores Ave., Ridgecrest, tel. 619/ 375–6900), which will also provide you with background on what you will see. *Admission: $17, children under 6 not admitted.*

⑥ Heading northwest, you will find **Short Canyon** about ½ mile from the intersection of Highway 14 and U.S. 395. Sierra snows and natural springs feed the stream that flows down the rocky canyon, spills over a falls, and then sinks into the sand. In good years, there are large beds of wildflowers, and, even in very dry years, there are still some splashes of color. In the spring, a ½-mile hike along the stream brings you to a 20-foot waterfall. Head west on the canyon road you'll find just south of Brady's Cafe on U.S. 395, but only after checking on current road conditions with the BLM (tel. 619/375–7125) or High Desert District California State Parks (tel. 805/942–0662).

⑦ **Fossil Falls** is 20 miles up U.S. 395. On the way you'll pass Little Lake, a good place to see migrating waterfowl in the spring and fall, including several varieties of ducks and geese and probably pelicans as well. The area just north of the lake is often covered with wildflowers. As you pass the lake, **Red Hill** comes into view ahead of you. The hill is a small volcano that was active in the neighborhood of 20,000 years ago. Approaching the falls you cross a large volcanic field; the falls themselves drop an impressive distance along the channel cut by the Owens River through the hardened lava flows. Mammoth bones and human tools dating back 10,000 to 20,000 years ago have been found in this area. *The falls are about 20 mi north of the intersection of Hwy. 14 and U.S. 395, then ½ mi east on Cinder Cone Rd. A dirt road leads south to a parking area. There are usually BLM signs directing the way.*

The Eastern Mojave We'll start the eastward tour in **Victorville,** less than 20 miles from Cajon Pass. The bit of water flowing along the eastern side of the freeway, near Mojave Narrows Regional Park, is one of the few places where the Mojave River runs aboveground. For the most part, the 150-mile-long river flows from the San Bernardino mountains north and east underneath the desert floor. The park itself offers boat rentals, an equestrian center, **⑧** fishing, and camping. Then there is the **Roy Rogers–Dale Evans Museum,** exhibiting the personal and professional memorabilia of the famous western stars. Yes, Roy's faithful horse Trigger is here. *Mojave Narrows Park, 18000 Yates Rd., tel. 619/245–2226, is open daily 7 AM–dusk; there is a $4 per-vehicle entry fee. Camping is $9 a night, or $10 with two fishing passes. Roy Rogers-Dale Evans Museum, 15650 Seneca Rd., tel. 619/243–4547, is open daily 9–5; admission: $3 adults, $2 children ages 13–16 and senior citizens, $1 children ages 6–12. Closed Thanksgiving and Christmas.*

⑨ Continue along I–15 to **Barstow,** established in 1886 when a subsidiary of the Atchison, Topeka and Santa Fe Railroad began construction of a depot and hotel at this junction of its tracks and the 35th-parallel transcontinental lines. The **Desert Information Center** (831 Barstow Rd., tel. 619/256–8313) contains exhibits about desert ecology, wildflowers, wildlife, and other features of the desert environment; a helpful and knowledgeable staff is on hand to answer questions.

There is an impulse to describe many areas of the desert as
⑩ seemingly belonging to another planet. **Rainbow Basin,** 8 miles
north of Barstow, looks as if it could be on Mars, perhaps because so many sci-fi movies depicting the red planet have been
filmed here. There is a tremendous sense of upheaval; huge
slabs of red, orange, white, and green stone tilt at crazy angles
like ships about to capsize. At points along the spectacularly
scenic 6-mile drive it is easy to imagine you are alone in the
world, hidden among the colorful badlands that give the basin
its name. Hike the many washes and you are likely to see the
fossilized remains of creatures that roamed the basin 12 million
to 16 million years ago: mastodons, large and small camels, rhi-
nos, dog-bears, birds, and insects. Do leave any fossils you find
where they are—they are protected by Federal law. *Take Fort
Irwin Rd. about 5 mi north to Fossil Bed Rd., a graded dirt
road, and head west 3 mi. Call the Desert Information Center
in Barstow (tel. 619/256–8313) for more information.*

After a 10-mile drive northeast from Barstow, you can slip into
⑪ the more recent past at **Calico Ghost Town.** Calico became a
wild—and rich—mining town after a rich deposit of silver was
found around 1881. In 1886, after more than $85 million worth
of silver, gold, and other precious metals were harvested from
the multicolored "calico" hills, the price of silver fell and the
town slipped into decline. "Borax" Smith helped revive the
town in 1889 when he started mining the unglamorous but profitable mineral borax there, but that boom busted by the turn of
the century. The effort to restore the ghost town was started
by Walter Knott of Knott's Berry Farm fame in 1960. Knott
handed the land over to San Bernardino County in 1966 and it
became a regional park. Today, the 1880s come back to life as
you stroll the wooden sidewalks of Main Street, browse
through several western shops, roam the tunnels of Maggie's
Mine, and take a ride on the Calico–Odessa Railroad. Special
festivals in March, May, October, and November add to Calico's Old West flavor. *Ghost Town Rd., 3 mi north of I–15, tel.
619/254–2122. There is a $4 per vehicle entry fee. The town is
open 9–5 daily.*

⑫ If you're at all curious about life 200,000 years ago, the **Calico
Early Man Archeological Site** is a must-see. Nearly 12,000
tools—scrapers, cutting tools, choppers, hand picks, stone
saws, and the like—have been excavated from the site since
1964. Prior to finding the site, many archaeologists believed
the first humans came to North America "only" 10,000 to
20,000 years ago. Dr. Louis Leakey, the noted archaeologist,
was so impressed with the findings that he became the Calico
Project director from 1963 to his death in 1972; his old camp is
now a visitors center and museum. The Calico excavations provide a rare opportunity to see artifacts, buried in the walls and
floors of the excavated pits, fashioned by the earliest known
Americans. *15 mi northeast of Barstow via I–15; take Minneo-
la Rd. north for 3 mi. The site is open Wed.–Sun. 8–4:30, closed
Mon. and Tues. Guided tours of the dig are offered Thurs.–
Sun. at 9:30, 11:30, 1:30, and 3:30. Trail maps are available for
self-guided tours.*

⑬ Because of its colorful, steep walls, **Afton Canyon** is often called
the Grand Canyon of the Mojave. The canyon was carved out
over many thousands of years by the rushing waters of the Mojave River, which makes another of its rare aboveground ap-

pearances here. And where you find water in the desert, you'll find trees, grasses, and wildlife. The canyon has been a popular spot for a long time; Indians and later white settlers following the Mojave Trail from the Colorado River to the Pacific coast often set up camp here, near the welcomed presence of water. *About 38 mi from Barstow on I–15; take the Afton turnoff and follow a good dirt road about 3 mi southwest.*

Although there is a broad range of terrain that qualifies, nothing says "desert" quite like graceful, wind-blown sand dunes. **⑭** And the white-sand **Kelso Dunes**, located about 40 miles southeast of Baker, are perfect, pristine desert dunes. They cover 70 square miles, often at heights of 500–600 feet, and can be reached in an easy ½-mile walk from where you have to leave your car. When you reach the top of one of the dunes, kick a little bit of sand down the lee side and find out why they say the sand "sings." In Kelso, there is a Mission Revival depot dating from 1925, one of the very few of its kind still standing. *I–15 to Baker, then take Kelbaker Rd. south for 35 mi to the town of Kelso. The dunes are an additional 7 mi ahead.*

⑮ Our last stops in the Eastern Mojave are the **Providence Mountains State Recreation Area** and the **Mitchell Caverns Natural Preserve.** The recreation area's visitor center, at an elevation of 4,300 feet, offers spectacular views of mountain peaks, dunes, buttes, rocky crags, and desert valleys. The caves, known as El Pakiva and Tecopa, offer a rare opportunity to see all three types of cave formations—dripstone, flowstone, and erratics—in one place. The year-round 65° temperature is also a nice break from the heat. *Take I–40 east from Barstow 100 mi to Essex Rd., then head northwest for 16 mi to the state recreation area. If you have a 4-wheel-drive vehicle, you can continue south from Kelso on Kelbaker Rd. about 3 mi to the poleline road; bear left and drive about 12 mi over Foshay Pass to Essex Rd. Admission free. Guided tours of the caves are offered Sept.–June, weekdays at 1:30 PM, weekends and holidays at 1:30 and 3; weekends only during the summer. Tours gather at the visitor center.*

Death Valley *Numbers in the margin correspond to points of interest on the Death Valley map.*

The topography of Death Valley National Monument is a minilesson in geology. Two hundred million years ago seas covered the area, depositing layers of sediment and fossils. Between 5 million and 35 million years ago, faults in the earth's crust and volcanic activity pushed and folded the ground, causing mountain ranges to rise and the valley floor to drop. The valley was then filled periodically by lakes, which eroded the surrounding rocks into fantastic formations and deposited the salts that now cover the floor of the basin. Today, the area sports an astounding variety of physical features: 14 square miles of sand dunes, 200 square miles of crusty salt flats, 11,000-foot mountains, hills and canyons of many colors. There are more than 1,000 species of plants and trees—21 of which are unique to the valley, like the yellow Panamint Daisy, and the blue-flowered Death Valley sage.

❶ Starting from the northernmost tip of the monument, **Scotty's Castle** is an odd apparition rising out of a canyon. This $2.5-million Moorish mansion, begun in 1924 and never completed, takes its name from Walter Scott, better known as Death Valley

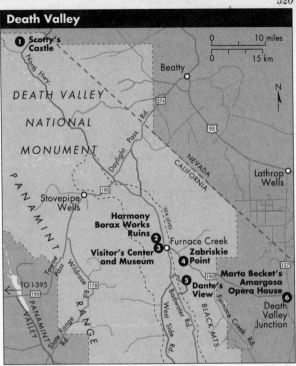

Death Valley

Scotty. An ex-cowboy, prospector, and performer in Buffalo Bill's Wild West Show, Scotty always told people the castle was his, financed by gold from a secret mine. That secret mine was, in fact, a Chicago millionaire named Albert Johnson, who was advised by doctors to spend time in a warm, dry climate. The house sports works of art, imported carpets, handmade European furniture, and a tremendous pipe organ. While it would probably all look perfectly normal in Beverly Hills, in Death Valley it is the wildest of mirages. *Located on the North Hwy. 190N, tel. 619/786–2392. Admission: $6 adults, $3 children 6–11. Grounds open daily 7 AM–6 PM; tours 9–5.*

➋ Following Highway 190 south, you'll come to the remains of the famed **Harmony Borax Works,** from which the renowned 20-mule teams hauled borax to the railroad town of Mojave. Those teams were a sight to behold: 20 mules hitched up to a single massive wagon, carrying a load of 10 tons of borax to a town 165 miles away through burning desert. The teams plied the route between 1884 and 1907, when the railroad finally arrived in Zabriskie. You can visit the ruins of the Harmony Borax Works. The Borax Museum, 2 miles farther south, houses original mining machinery and historical displays in a building that used to serve as a boardinghouse for miners; the adjacent structure is the original mule-team barn. *Look for the Harmony Borax Works Rd. on Hwy. 190, about 50 mi south of Scotty's Castle; take the road west a short distance to the ruins.*

➌ Between the ruins and the museum you will see a sign for the **Visitor's Center** at Furnace Creek. The center provides guided walks, exhibits, publications, and helpful rangers. *Open 8–8. Call the National Park Service in Death Valley (tel. 619/786–2331) for more information on visitors center services.*

4 **Zabriskie Point,** about 4 miles south of the visitor's center, is one of the monument's most scenic spots. Not particularly high—only about 710 feet—it overlooks a striking badlands panorama with wrinkled, cinammon-color hills. You may recognize it—or at least its name—from the film *Zabriskie Point* by the Italian director Michaelangelo Antonioni. When Highway 178 splits off from Highway 190, follow it south about 13 **5** miles to **Dante's View.** This viewpoint is more than 5,000 feet up in the Black Mountains. In the dry desert air, you can see most of the 110 miles the valley is stretched across. The oasis of Furnace Creek is a green spot to the north. The view up and down is equally astounding: The tiny blackish patch far below you is Badwater, the lowest point in the country at 280 feet below sea level; on the western horizon is Mt. Whitney, the highest spot in the continental United States at 14,495 feet. Those of you in great shape may want to try the 14-mile hike up to Telescope Peak. The view, not surprisingly, is breathtaking—as is the 3,000-foot elevation gain of the hike. The best time to visit any of these viewpoints is early morning or late afternoon when the colors and shapes of the surrounding desert are highlighted.

Just outside the monument, at Death Valley Junction, is an un-**6** expected pleasure to rival Scotty's Castle—**Marta Becket's Amargosa Opera House.** Marta Becket is an artist and dancer from New York who first saw the town of Amargosa while on tour in 1964. Three years later she came back, had a flat tire in the same place, and on impulse decided to buy a boarded-up theater amid a complex of run-down Spanish colonial buildings. Today, the population of the town is still two people and about a dozen cats, but three nights a week, cars, motor homes, and buses roll in to catch the show she has been presenting for more than 20 years. To compensate for the sparse crowds her show attracted in the early days, Becket painted herself an audience, making the theater a masterpiece of trompe l'oeil painting. Now she often performs her blend of classical ballet, mime, and 19th-century melodrama to sell-out crowds. After the show, you can meet her in the adjacent art gallery, where she sells her paintings and autographs her posters and books. *Amargosa Opera House, Box 8, Death Valley Junction, CA 92328, tel. 619/ 852–4316. Call ahead for reservations. Performances Nov.–Apr., Fri., Sat., and Mon. at 8:15 PM; May and Dec., shows Sat. only. The opera house is closed during the summer. Admission: $8 adults, $5 children.*

What to See and Do with Children

Many of the desert's attractions should delight children. The following are of particular interest; for more information, *see* the Exploring section, above.

Rand Mining District
Roy Rogers–Dale Evans Museum, Victorville
Calico Ghost Town
Mitchell Caverns
Marta Becket's Amargosa Opera House

Off the Beaten Track

The desert is not a particularly well-beaten track to begin with, but some spots are a bit farther out of the way, or more difficult to reach. **Trona Pinnacles National Natural Landmark,** just west of the China Lake Naval Weapons Center, is not easy to get to. There are several dirt roads leading to the tufa area—where towering spires of calcium carbonate reach heights of up to 140 feet. Unfortunately, the best road to the area changes depending on the weather; you either have to be lucky enough to follow someone who knows the best way, or keep trying until you get there. And forget about it if the roads are wet. Still, the pinnacles are considered the best examples of tufa towers in the country, and the area is a great place in which to dream up a science-fiction flick. *Take Hwy. 178 north from U.S. 395 for 29 mi. There you will find a dirt intersection; turn southeast and go ½ mi to a fork. Continue south via the right fork, cross some railroad tracks, and continue about 5 mi to the pinnacles.*

Lodging

Barstow **Best Western Desert Villa.** This is a slightly above-average AAA-approved motel with a pool and whirlpool. Rooms start at $52. *1984 E. Main St., tel. 619/256–1781. 79 units. AE, DC, MC, V.*

Death Valley **Furnace Creek Inn.** The rambling stone structure tumbling down the side of a hill is something of a desert oasis. There are pleasantly cool dining rooms, a heated pool, tennis courts, golf, horseback riding, and a cocktail lounge with entertainment. Doubles range from $175 to $350, including breakfast and dinner. *Box 1, Death Valley 92328, tel. 619/786–2345. 67 rooms and suites. AE, DC, MC, V. Closed mid-May–mid-Oct.*

Furnace Creek Ranch. An annex of the inn, about 1 mile away on the valley floor, this was originally crew headquarters for a borax company. The newer section has very good rooms. The ranch also features a coffee shop, steak house, cocktail lounge, and a general store. Double rooms with TV and telephone start at $95. *Box 1, Death Valley 92328, tel. 619/786–2345. 225 rooms. AE, DC, MC, V.*

Stove Pipe Wells Village. A landing strip for light aircraft is an unusual touch for a motel, as is a heated mineral pool, but the rest is pretty basic. The property includes a dining room, grocery store, pool, and cocktail lounge. Rooms start at $50. *Hwy. 190, tel. 619/786–2387. 82 rooms. MC, V.*

Camping

The Mojave Desert and Death Valley have about two dozen campgrounds in a variety of desert settings. Listed below is a sampling of what is available. For further information the following booklets are useful: *High Desert Recreation Resource Guide,* from the Mojave Chamber of Commerce (15836 Sierra Hwy., Mojave, CA 93591); *San Bernardino County Regional Parks,* from the Regional Parks Department (825 E. 3rd St., San Bernardino, CA 92415); and *California Desert Camping,* from the Bureau of Land Management (California Desert District Office, 6221 Box Springs Blvd., Riverside, CA 92507).

Death Valley **Mahogany Flat** (east of Hwy. 178). Ten well-shaded tent spaces in a forest of juniper and piñon pine. Tables, pit toilets; no water. Open Apr.–Nov.

Mesquite Springs (Hwy. 190 near Scotty's Castle). Sixty tent or RV spaces, some shaded, with stoves or fireplaces, tables, flush toilets, water.

Wildrose (west of Hwy. 178). Thirty-nine tent or RV sites, some shaded, in a canyon. Stoves or fireplaces, tables, water, pit toilets.

Mojave Desert **Mid-Hills Campground** (123 mi east of Barstow via I–40). Hiking, horseback riding, in a wooded setting. Thirty campsites, pit toilets, water.

Mojave Narrows (I–15). Eighty-seven camping units, hot showers. Secluded picnic areas and two lakes surrounded by cottonwoods and cattails. Fishing, rowboat rentals, bait shop, specially designed trail for the handicapped.

Owl Canyon Campground (12 mi north of Barstow and 1 mi east of Rainbow Basin). Thirty-one camping units, cooking grills, vault toilets, water.

WHEREVER YOU TRAVEL, *H*ELP IS NEVER FAR AWAY.

From planning your trip to replacing lost Cards, American Express® Travel Service Offices* are always there to help.

LONG BEACH
301 E. Ocean Blvd.
310-432-2029

LOS ANGELES
327 No. Beverly Dr.
Beverly Hills
310-274-8277

The Hilton Center
901 W. 7th St.
213-627-4800

8493 W. 3rd St.
at La Cienega Blvd.
310-659-1682

251 South Lake Ave
Pasadena
818-449-2281

ORANGE COUNTY
Main Place Mall
2800 N. Main St.
Santa Ana
714-541-3318

SACRAMENTO
515 "L" Street
916-441-1780

SAN DIEGO
1020 Prospect St., La Jolla
619-459-4161

Mission Valley Center
1640 Camino Del Rio, N.
619-297-8101

258 Broadway
619-234-4455

SAN FRANCISCO
237 Post St.
415-981-5533

455 Market St,
415-512-8250

295 California St.
415-788-4367

Sheraton, Fisherman's Wharf
415-788-3025

500 E. 12th St., Suite 115, Oakland
510-834-2833

393 Stanford Shopping Center, Palo Alto
415-327-3711

American Express Travel Service Offices are found in central locations throughout California.

Index

Personal Itinerary

Departure *Date*

Time

Transportation

Arrival *Date*   *Time*

Departure *Date*   *Time*

Transportation

Accommodations

Arrival *Date*   *Time*

Departure *Date*   *Time*

Transportation

Accommodations

Arrival *Date*   *Time*

Departure *Date*   *Time*

Transportation

Accommodations

Personal Itinerary

Arrival *Date*   *Time*

Departure *Date*   *Time*

Transportation

Accommodations

Arrival *Date*   *Time*

Departure *Date*   *Time*

Transportation

Accommodations

Arrival *Date*   *Time*

Departure *Date*   *Time*

Transportation

Accommodations

Arrival *Date*   *Time*

Departure *Date*   *Time*

Transportation

Accommodations

Personal Itinerary

Arrival *Date* *Time*

Departure *Date* *Time*

Transportation

Accommodations

Arrival *Date* *Time*

Departure *Date* *Time*

Transportation

Accommodations

Arrival *Date* *Time*

Departure *Date* *Time*

Transportation

Accommodations

Arrival *Date* *Time*

Departure *Date* *Time*

Transportation

Accommodations

Personal Itinerary

Arrival *Date*   *Time*

Departure *Date*   *Time*

Transportation

Accommodations

Arrival *Date*   *Time*

Departure *Date*   *Time*

Transportation

Accommodations

Arrival *Date*   *Time*

Departure *Date*   *Time*

Transportation

Accommodations

Arrival *Date*   *Time*

Departure *Date*   *Time*

Transportation

Accommodations

Addresses

Name	*Name*
Address	*Address*
Telephone	*Telephone*
Name	*Name*
Address	*Address*
Telephone	*Telephone*
Name	*Name*
Address	*Address*
Telephone	*Telephone*
Name	*Name*
Address	*Address*
Telephone	*Telephone*
Name	*Name*
Address	*Address*
Telephone	*Telephone*
Name	*Name*
Address	*Address*
Telephone	*Telephone*
Name	*Name*
Address	*Address*
Telephone	*Telephone*
Name	*Name*
Address	*Address*
Telephone	*Telephone*

Addresses

Name

Address

Telephone

Name

Address

Telephone

Name

Address

Telephone

Name

Address

Telephone

Name

Address

Telephone

Name

Address

Telephone

Name

Address

Telephone

Name

Address

Telephone

Name

Address

Telephone

Name

Address

Telephone

Name

Address

Telephone

Name

Address

Telephone

Name

Address

Telephone

Name

Address

Telephone

Name

Address

Telephone

Name

Address

Telephone

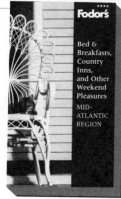

Fodor's Travel Guides

U.S. Guides

Alaska

Arizona

Boston

California

Cape Cod, Martha's
Vineyard, Nantucket

The Carolinas & the
Georgia Coast

Chicago

Disney World & the
Orlando Area

Florida

Hawaii

Las Vegas, Reno,
Tahoe

Los Angeles

Maine, Vermont,
New Hampshire

Maui

Miami & the Keys

New England

New Orleans

New York City

Pacific North Coast

Philadelphia & the
Pennsylvania Dutch
Country

San Diego

San Francisco

Santa Fe, Taos,
Albuquerque

Seattle & Vancouver

The South

The U.S. & British
Virgin Islands

The Upper Great
Lakes Region

USA

Vacations in New York
State

Vacations on the
Jersey Shore

Virginia & Maryland

Waikiki

Washington, D.C.

Foreign Guides

Acapulco, Ixtapa,
Zihuatanejo

Australia & New
Zealand

Austria

The Bahamas

Baja & Mexico's
Pacific Coast Resorts

Barbados

Berlin

Bermuda

Brazil

Budapest

Budget Europe

Canada

Cancun, Cozumel,
Yucatan Penisula

Caribbean

Central America

China

Costa Rica, Belize,
Guatemala

Czechoslovakia

Eastern Europe

Egypt

Euro Disney

Europe

Europe's Great Cities

France

Germany

Great Britain

Greece

The Himalayan
Countries

Hong Kong

India

Ireland

Israel

Italy

Italy's Great Cities

Japan

Kenya & Tanzania

Korea

London

Madrid & Barcelona

Mexico

Montreal &
Quebec City

Morocco

The Netherlands
Belgium &
Luxembourg

New Zealand

Norway

Nova Scotia, Prince
Edward Island &
New Brunswick

Paris

Portugal

Rome

Russia & the Baltic
Countries

Scandinavia

Scotland

Singapore

South America

Southeast Asia

South Pacific

Spain

Sweden

Switzerland

Thailand

Tokyo

Toronto

Turkey

Vienna & the Danube
Valley

Yugoslavia

Fodor's Travel Guides

Special Series

Fodor's Affordables

Affordable Europe

Affordable France

Affordable Germany

Affordable Great Britain

Affordable Italy

Fodor's Bed & Breakfast and Country Inns Guides

California

Mid-Atlantic Region

New England

The Pacific Northwest

The South

The West Coast

The Upper Great Lakes Region

Canada's Great Country Inns

Cottages, B&Bs and Country Inns of England and Wales

The Berkeley Guides

On the Loose in California

On the Loose in Eastern Europe

On the Loose in Mexico

On the Loose in the Pacific Northwest & Alaska

Fodor's Exploring Guides

Exploring California

Exploring Florida

Exploring France

Exploring Germany

Exploring Paris

Exploring Rome

Exploring Spain

Exploring Thailand

Fodor's Flashmaps

New York

Washington, D.C.

Fodor's Pocket Guides

Pocket Bahamas

Pocket Jamaica

Pocket London

Pocket New York City

Pocket Paris

Pocket Puerto Rico

Pocket San Francisco

Pocket Washington, D.C.

Fodor's Sports

Cycling

Hiking

Running

Sailing

The Insider's Guide to the Best Canadian Skiing

Fodor's Three-In-Ones (guidebook, language cassette, and phrase book)

France

Germany

Italy

Mexico

Spain

Fodor's Special-Interest Guides

Cruises and Ports of Call

Disney World & the Orlando Area

Euro Disney

Healthy Escapes

London Companion

Skiing in the USA & Canada

Sunday in New York

Fodor's Touring Guides

Touring Europe

Touring USA: Eastern Edition

Touring USA: Western Edition

Fodor's Vacation Planners

Great American Vacations

National Parks of the West

The Wall Street Journal Guides to Business Travel

Europe

International Cities

Pacific Rim

USA & Canada

CNN TRAVEL GUIDE

PASSPORT TO THE WORLD

Join host Valerie Voss for an entertaining and informative program that takes you to the four corners of the earth. With expert advice from Michael Spring, Fodor's Editorial Director, *CNN Travel Guide* is the perfect companion for anyone planning a trip or just interested in travel.

Drawing on CNN's vast network of international correspondents, you'll discover an exciting variety of new destinations from the most exotic locales to some well-kept secrets just a short trip away. You'll also find helpful tips on everything from hotels and restaurants to packing and planning. So tune in to *CNN Travel Guide*. And make it your first stop on any trip.

SUNDAY 1:00AM ET   SUNDAY 8:30AM ET